Marketing

second canadian edition
an introduction

Gary Armstrong
University of North
Carolina

Philip Kotler
Northwestern
University

Peggy Cunningham
Queen's
University

Peter Mitchell
British Columbia
Institute of Technology

Lilly Anne Buchwitz
Brock
University

with contributions from

Louise Ripley
York University

Corien Kershey
Algonquin College

Cyri Jones
Capilano College

IN-CLASS EDITION

PEARSON

Prentice
Hall

Toronto

Library and Archives Canada Cataloguing in Publication

Marketing: an introduction / Gary Armstrong ... [et al.]. — 2nd Canadian ed.

Includes bibliographical references and index.
ISBN 0-13-185720-7

1. Marketing—Textbooks.
HF5415.M295 2006   658.8   C2005-907643-7

ISBN 0-13-185720-7

Vice-President, Editorial Director: Michael J. Young
Editor-in-Chief: Gary Bennett
Acquisitions Editor: Laura Paterson Forbes
Marketing Manager: Eileen Lasswell
Developmental Editor: Rema Celio
Production Editor: Cheryl Jackson
Copy Editor: Karen Alliston
Proofreader: Ann McInnis
Production Coordinator: Patricia Ciardullo
Page Layout: Jansom
Permissions and Photo Researcher: Lisa Brant
Art Director: Julia Hall
Cover and Interior Design: Anthony Leung

2 3 4 5 6   11 10 09 08 07

Printed and bound in United States of America

BRIEF CONTENTS

CONTENTS

PART 2   UNDERSTANDING THE MARKETPLACE AND CUSTOMERS   124

PART 3   Designing a Customer-Driven Marketing Strategy and Marketing Mix   246

ABOUT THE AUTHORS

Gary Armstrong is Crist W. Blackwell Distinguished Professor of Undergraduate Education in the Kenan-Flagler Business School at the University of North Carolina at Chapel Hill. He holds undergraduate and masters degrees in business from Wayne State University in Detroit, and he received his Ph.D. in marketing from Northwestern University. Dr. Armstrong has contributed numerous articles to leading business journals. As a consultant and researcher, he has worked with many companies on marketing research, sales management, and marketing strategy. But Professor Armstrong's first love is teaching. His Blackwell Distinguished Professorship is the only permanent endowed professorship for distinguished undergraduate teaching at the University of North Carolina at Chapel Hill. He has been very active in the teaching and administration of Kenan-Flagler's undergraduate program. His recent administrative posts include Chair of the Marketing Faculty, Associate Director of the Undergraduate Business Program, Director of the Business Honors Program, and others. He works closely with business student groups and has received several campus-wide and business school teaching awards. He is the only repeat recipient of the school's highly regarded Award for Excellence in Undergraduate Teaching, which he won three times. In 2004, Professor Armstrong received the UNC Board of Governors Award for Excellence in Teaching, the highest teaching honour bestowed at the University of North Carolina at Chapel Hill.

Philip Kotler is the S. C. Johnson & Son Distinguished Professor of International Marketing at the Kellogg Graduate School of Management, Northwestern University. He received his master's degree at the University of Chicago and his Ph.D. at M.I.T., both in economics. Dr. Kotler is author of *Marketing Management: Analysis, Planning, Implementation, and Control* (Prentice Hall), now in its eleventh edition and the most widely used marketing textbook in graduate schools of business. He has authored several successful books and has written over 100 articles for leading journals. He is the only three-time winner of the coveted Alpha Kappa Psi award for the best annual article in the *Journal of Marketing*. Dr. Kotler's numerous major honours include the Paul D. Converse Award given by the American Marketing Association to honour "outstanding contributions to science in marketing" and the Stuart Henderson Britt Award as Marketer of the Year. He was named the first recipient of two major awards: the Distinguished Marketing Educator of the Year Award given by the American Marketing Association and the Philip Kotler Award for Excellence in Health Care Marketing presented by the Academy for Health Care

Services Marketing. He has also received the Charles Coolidge Parlin Award which each year honours an outstanding leader in the field of marketing. In 1995, he received the Marketing Educator of the Year Award from Sales and Marketing Executives International. Dr. Kotler has served as chairman of the College on Marketing of the Institute of Management Sciences (TIMS) and a director of the American Marketing Association. He has received honourary doctorate degrees from DePaul University, the University of Zurich, and the Athens University of Economics and Business. He has consulted with many major U.S. and foreign companies on marketing strategy.

Peggy Cunningham is the Marie Shantz Teaching Associate Professor of Marketing at Queen's School of Business. She received her undergraduate degree from Queen's University, her MBA from the University of Calgary, and her Ph.D. from Texas A&M University. She was the founding Director of the Accelerated MBA program for business graduates (2001–2004). She previously was the Co-Chair of the E-Commerce Research Program (1998–2001), and she is currently one of the founding members of the Global Responsible Leadership Initiative (2004–present). She has considerable international experience and has been a visiting professor at universities and government training programs in France, Germany, China, the U.K., and the U.S. Her experience in industry and consulting helps her bring the perspective of the practitioner to the study of marketing. Her research interests centre on two related themes: marketing ethics and marketing partnerships (international strategic alliances and partnerships between for-profit and not-for-profit organizations). While these may seem like totally divergent areas of study, they are linked by their focus on the concepts of trust, integrity, and commitment which are the core elements to both ethical behaviour and successful partnership behaviour. She has received a number of awards for this work including the ANBAR citation award for her Strategic Alliances article written with Rajan Varadarajan, and a nomination for the 2006 Accenture Award for her work in Social Alliances with Ida Berger and Meme Drumwright. Her research is published in a number of journals including the *Journal of the Academy of Marketing Science*, the *California Management Review*, and the *Journal of International Marketing*. She is a devoted teacher who tries to inspire her students to realize their full and unique potential. She currently teaches courses in marketing management and strategy, marketing ethics, and branding in the B.Comm., M.Sc., Ph.D., and Executive training programs. She is one of Queen's University's most acclaimed and awarded teaching professors. In 2004, she received the PriceWaterhouseCoopers Leaders in Management Education award. She was named the Academy of Marketing Science's Outstanding Teacher in 2001. She has been nominated twice for the Frank Knox Award for Teaching Excellence, one of the most prestigious awards given at Queen's for undergraduate teaching. She won this award in 1993. Dr. Cunningham also does a considerable amount of research and writing to further educational practice. She has written over 40 cases that have been used in case competitions and have been published in a number of leading North American marketing textbooks.

Peter Mitchell is an instructor in Marketing Management faculty, The School of Business at the British Columbia Institute of Technology (BCIT), in Burnaby, B.C. He has an Honours Degree in Business Administration, an Advanced Diploma in Management, and a Master's Degree in Education with an online specialization. Before embarking on his academic career, he spent 30 years in senior marketing and management roles with major international organizations, such as Nabisco Brands, Pepsi, and Southam. Immediately prior to joining the faculty at BCIT, he was president and part-owner of a specialized business-to-business distribution company in Vancouver, B.C. He has previously co-authored a text on professional selling, as well as the first edition of this text. Mitchell's teaching career includes 15 years of adult education and training in BCIT's part-time studies programs. He moved to full-time teaching in 1998.

Lilly Anne Buchwitz is an Instructor in the Faculty of Business at Brock University in St. Catharines, Ontario. An academic only since 2001, for 10 years she held senior management positions in marketing communications and online marketing at several Internet and high tech companies in Canada and the United States. As marketing manager for the Open Text Index, the first full-text (and only Canadian) Internet search engine, she pioneered search engine advertising. In 1996 she helped launch About.com in New York and, three years later, Chapters.ca in Toronto. During those years she became, and remains, a popular speaker at trade conferences where she gives presentations on topics such as marketing your small business on the Internet, search engine marketing, and trends in online advertising. She holds undergraduate degrees in English Literature and Education from McGill University, an MBA from Wilfrid Laurier University, and is preparing to defend her PhD thesis titled, A Postmodern History of Internet Advertising. She has taught undergraduate and MBA courses in Internet marketing, e-commerce, and marketing communications in China and in Canada, and currently teaches introductory marketing and marketing communications at Brock University.

PREFACE

Most marketing students, whether majors or non-majors, want a complete picture of basic marketing principles and practices. However, they don't want to drown in a sea of details or be overwhelmed by marketing's complexities. They want a text that is complete, yet easy to manage and master. The goal for the second Canadian edition of *Marketing: An Introduction* is to create the most effective text from which to learn about and teach marketing in Canada.

Marketing: An Introduction strikes a careful balance between depth of coverage and ease of learning. This edition presents the latest marketing thinking, building upon a marketing framework that positions marketing simply as the art and science of creating value *for* customers in order to capture value *from* customers in return. Marketing is discussed in collaboration with other company departments—such as accounting, information technology, finance, operations, and human resources—and with marketing partners outside the company to jointly bring value to customers. *Marketing: An Introduction* applies concepts through examples in which well-known and lesser-known companies assess and solve marketing challenges.

As part of Pearson Education Canada's commitment to providing students with value, choice, and the tools for educational success, the second Canadian edition of *Marketing: An Introduction* has been designed as an In-Class Edition. This innovative new presentation is designed to focus on student learning and self-study. Questions are posed at the beginning of each chapter to stimulate student interest in the chapter material, in-class notes are matched to instructor PowerPoint® slides with space for students to make their own notes, an embedded study guide is included at the end of each chapter, and a laminated study card is bound into the back of the text, giving students another great tool for study.

IN-CLASS EDITION: LEARNING MADE EASY

As an in-class edition, the second Canadian edition of *Marketing: An Introduction* is specially designed to help students succeed. This innovative presentation includes the following features:

☐ **Test Yourself.** Questions are provided at the beginning of each chapter, immediately following the chapter-opening vignette. These questions challenge students to think about the issues that will be addressed in the chapter.

☐ **In-Class Notes.** Selected in-class notes (correlated to instructor's PowerPoint slides) that cover key concepts are reproduced directly in the text, with space for students to make notes while in class or while reading. This encourages active reading and participation, and students can refer back to the notes in the original context when reviewing material for tests or exams.

☐ **Embedded Study Guide.** As a further strategy to encourage practice and mastery, study guide questions – multiple-choice, true/false, and concept check – are inserted at the end of each chapter, with answers at the back of the text.

☐ **Marketing Study Charts for Students.** Bound in at the back of the text, a handy laminated card outlines key concepts and terminology in note form.

WHAT'S NEW: CUSTOMER VALUE IS THE KEY

Marketing: An Introduction has been thoroughly revised to reflect the major trends and forces that are changing marketing in this new age of customer relationships. Important revisions made to the second Canadian edition include:

1. A "customer-relationships/customer-equity" framework.

Marketing: An Introduction presents an innovative framework for understanding and learning about marketing. Today's marketing managers understand that marketing is all about building profitable customer relationships. And that process begins with understanding the needs and wants of the customer—whether that customer is a business, a not-for-profit organization, or an individual consumer. Marketing managers must then decide which market segments the organization can best serve and develop a compelling value proposition to attract, keep, and grow those customers. If the organization does these things well, it will reap the rewards in terms of market share, profits, and customer equity. Simply put, marketing is the art and science of creating value *for* customers in order to capture value *from* customers in return. From beginning to end, *Marketing: An Introduction* presents and develops this customer-relationships/customer-equity framework.

☐ *The customer relationship management/customer equity framework* is established from the start of the text, in the completely revised Chapter 1, *Marketing: Managing Profitable Customer Relationships*, and carried forward throughout the text.

☐ The framework is presented in a five-step model of the marketing process, a model that details how marketing creates customer value and captures value in return. This model can be found in simplified form on page 7 and expanded form on page 36.

☐ The opening chapter includes an important new section on *Building Customer Relationships,* which covers customer relationship management, the changing nature of customer relationships, and partner relationship management. The chapter also features a new section on *Capturing Value from Customers,* which addresses topics such as building customer loyalty and retention, growing "share of customer," identifying customer relationship groups, and managing customer equity.

☐ The managing-customer-relationships theme continues in Chapter 2, *Strategic Planning and the Marketing Process.* This chapter places profitable customer relationships at the centre of marketing strategy and the marketing mix. It also extends the corollary concept of *partner relationship* management, working closely with marketing partners inside and outside the company to build strong customer relationships.

2. Brand strategy and managing brand equity.

☐ Chapter 7, *Segmentation, Targeting, and Positioning: Building the Right Relationships with the Right Customers,* presents new discussions on developing brand positioning statements and brand positioning maps.

☐ Chapter 8, *Product and Branding Strategy,* now includes a separate and expanded section—*Branding Strategy: Building Strong Brands.* The new section includes new material on brand equity and brand value, brand positioning, managing brands, and re-branding.

3. Marketing using technology and marketing in a socially responsible way around the globe.

☐ *Marketing and technology.* Technological advances continue to have a dramatic impact on consumer and business buyer behaviour, marketing channels, new product development, and marketing communications. Each chapter considers the impact of new technologies on marketing. In addition, Chapter 13, *Marketing and the Internet,* explores the exciting strategies and tactics that marketers are developing on this newest communications technology.

☐ *Marketing ethics, environmentalism, and social responsibility.* Chapter 3 focuses on *Marketing and Society: Social Responsibility and Marketing Ethics* and new coverage is integrated chapter-by-chapter.

☐ *Global marketing.* Coverage is integrated chapter-by-chapter.

- Marketing at Work 1.1: NASCAR: Creating Customer Experiences 11
- Rapid Globalization 30
- The Boston Consulting Group Approach 56
- Deciding Whether to Go International 60
- Partnering with Others in the Marketing System 63
- Environmental Sustainability 101–103, 106
- Marketing at Work 3.3: The Grey Zone: International Marketing Ethics 112
- The Global Marketing Environment 150
- International Marketing Research 188
- Consumer Behaviour Across International Borders 226
- Segmenting International Markets 260
- Deciding on the Global Marketing Program 269
- International Product and Services Marketing 326
- International Pricing 400
- Designing International Distribution Channels 444
- International Advertising Decisions 483
- Marketing at Work 13: The World Is the Customer's Oyster: The Ins and Outs of Global E-commerce 524

4. Consolidated coverage.

☐ *Marketing Channels.* Rather than devoting an entire chapter to retailing and wholesaling, these two topics have been integrated into Chapter 11, *Marketing Channels and Supply Chain Management.*

☐ *Integrated Marketing Communications.* All five elements of integrated marketing communications—advertising, sales promotion, direct marketing, public relations, and personal selling—are now covered in Chapter 12, *Integrated Marketing Communications.*

MARKETING IN THE REAL WORLD

Marketing: An Introduction tells the stories of real marketers in real situations, and highlights many Canadian marketing successes:

☐ how WestJet Airlines flies high on the wings of its classic "less-for-much-less" value proposition

☐ how Canadian Tire became a world leader in online retail

☐ how NASCAR creates avidly loyal fans by selling not just stock car racing but a high-octane, totally involving experience

☐ how Dove's latest branding campaign is attempting to redefine our culture's concept of beauty

Many in-text elements help link the classroom to the real-world of marketing in Canada:

☐ ***Chapter-Opening Vignettes.*** Each chapter starts with an exciting, real-world marketing story that introduces the chapter material.

☐ ***Marketing at Work Boxes.*** Additional examples demonstrating marketing in action are highlighted in Marketing at Work boxes throughout the text.

☐ ***Comprehensive Case.*** From our eye-catching cover to the comprehensive case in the text, students are introduced to Cake Beauty, the small Canadian company that made it *big*. The comprehensive case examines the development of the company and looks at how the combination of high-quality products, strategic pricing and distribution, and creative marketing communications resulted in success. Students then are invited to read Cake Beauty's marketing plan, which serves as a model and teaching tool. The Cake story has it all—a clear vision and strong branding, partnerships with well-established manufacturers and retailers, a global presence, and socially responsible marketing.

KEYS TO SUCCESS: OUR LEARNING APPROACH

Additional learning aids are located throughout each chapter to help students review, link, and apply marketing concepts:

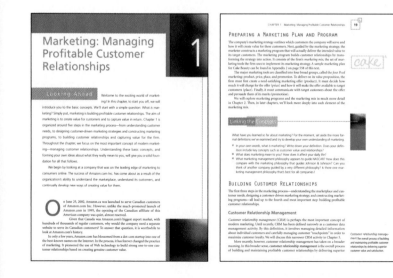

Looking Ahead. A section at the beginning of each chapter briefly previews chapter concepts, links them with previous chapter concepts, outlines chapter learning objectives, and introduces the chapter-opening vignette.

Linking the Concepts. "Concept checks" are inserted at key points in each chapter to help students be certain they are grasping and applying key concepts and links. Each Linking the Concepts box consists of a brief statement and a few concept and application questions.

Looking Back. A brief summary of key concepts at the end of each chapter.

Reviewing the Concepts. A summary of each of the chapter learning objectives.

Key Terms. A list of the chapter's key terms. Definitions of the key terms can be found in the margin of the page where the term is first defined and in the glossary at the end of the book.

Discussing the Issues. Discussion questions to help students keep track of and apply what they've studied in the chapter.

Marketing Applications. Interesting case histories, real-life situations, and timely descriptions of business situations put students in the place of a marketing manager so they can make real marketing decisions.

Video Cases. Every chapter is supplemented with a video case that can be accessed on our Video Central website (www.pearsoned.ca/highered/videocentral).

Cases. Every chapter ends with a case that challenges students to apply marketing principles to companies in real situations.

Glossary and Indexes. At the end of the book, an extensive glossary provides quick reference to the key terms found in the book. Subject, company, and author indexes reference all information and examples in the book.

ADDITIONAL RESOURCES FOR THE STUDENT

Companion Website (www.pearsoned.ca/armstrong). Part of this text's integrated study package is a Companion Website, including Practice Quizzes and Internet Exercises. Students can also find a PowerPoint presentation for each chapter (a valuable starting point for lecture notes) and a Virtual Library to make research quick and efficient. Students can review the videos that accompany the text and the video cases simply by clicking on the Video Central link on the splash page. This Companion Website offers a valuable starting point for study and assignments, so bookmark it right away!

VangoNotes. Study on the go with **VangoNotes**—chapter reviews from your text in downloadable mp3 format. Now wherever you are—whatever you're doing—you can study by listening to the following for each chapter of your textbook:

☐ Big Ideas: Your "need to know" for each chapter

☐ Practice Test: A gut check for the Big Ideas—tells you if you need to keep studying

☐ Key Terms: Audio "flashcards" to help you review key concepts and terms

☐ Rapid Review: A quick drill session—use it right before your test

VangoNotes are **flexible**; download all the material directly to your player, or only the chapters you need. And they're **efficient**. Use them in your car, at the gym, walking to class—wherever. So get yours today. And get studying.

VangoNotes.com

TEACHING AND LEARNING SUPPORT

A successful marketing course requires more than a well-written book. Today's classroom requires a dedicated teacher and a fully integrated teaching package. A total package of teaching and learning supplements extends this edition's emphasis on effective teaching and learning. The following aids support *Marketing: An Introduction*:

Instructor's Resource CD-ROM (ISBN 0-13-204328-9). This is the one-stop-shop for all your supplement needs. The CD-ROM contains the entire Instructor's Resource Manual, TestGen, PowerPoint Presentations, and Image Library.

Instructor's Resource Manual and Video Guide (ISBN 0-13-204327-0). This invaluable resource not only includes chapter-by-chapter teaching strategies, it also features notes about the PowerPoint slides and the video cases.

Pearson TestGen (ISBN 0-13-204326-2). This computerized test bank includes up to 110 multiple choice and true/false questions, plus essay and short answer questions. All questions include the correct answer, page reference, and are linked to a learning objective from the chapter.

PowerPoint Presentations: Extended! (ISBN 0-13-204320-3) and **PowerPoint Presentations: Express** (ISBN 0-13-204325-4). Two sets of PowerPoint slides are available with this edition. Each set contains a minimum of 25 slides per chapter. PowerPoint Extended! includes live weblinks and video clips embedded into key slides. The Basic version is shorter, and is aimed at instructors who prefer to customize the slides. Both versions can be accessed on the Instructor's Resource CD-ROM or through the Companion Website.

Image Library (ISBN 0-13-204324-6). Includes figures, tables, and photos from the text.

Companion Website (0-13-204321-1). This web resource provides instructors with a complete array of teaching material including downloadable versions of the Instructor's Resource Manual and PowerPoint Presentations, and a Syllabus Builder to help plan your course. Also included are an interactive and exciting online study guide, plus great resources such as current events and Internet exercises.

VangoNotes for complete text (ISBN 0-13-204833-7) and **VangoNotes for individual chapters** (ISBN 0-13-204832-9) The VangoNotes Live Audible Study Guides are designed to meet the growing needs students have for on-the-go study resources that can easily be downloaded to portable music devices. These audible study guides provide students with a powerful way to review their textbooks and prepare for upcoming tests. Written by content experts following script guidelines, the VangoNotes are read by professional voice talents and recorded into downloadable audio files. VangoNotes are offered as complete audiobooks or on a per-chapter basis to best suit student's needs.

ACKNOWLEDGMENTS

The revision of a textbook is a lengthy process requiring the time, knowledge, and dedication of many individuals. On behalf of Gary Armstrong, Philip Kotler, Peggy Cunningham, and Peter Mitchell, I would like to thank the following people for their contributions: Cyri Jones (Capilano College) for revising several chapters; Louise Ripley (York University) for revising chapters and for her work on the Study Card; and Corien Kershey (Algonquin College) for creating the In-Class Edition material.

We could not have provided such a detailed comprehensive case and marketing plan without the considerable contributions of Heather Reier, founder of Cake Beauty, and

Lauren Baswick, Marketing and Communications Manager at Cake Beauty. They provided us with all of the information we needed and were wonderful to work with.

Four years ago Pam Voves at Pearson gave me my first opportunity to contribute to a marketing textbook, and though she was not directly involved with this one, I want to thank her for that. Without her, I would never have had the opportunity to meet, and work with, such a fine group of editors as these: Cheryl Jackson, Production Editor, who, even as I write this is working on the final proofs of this book; Karen Alliston, Copyeditor, whose painstakingly thorough copyediting makes my writing sound better than I'd ever imagined was possible; Gary Bennett, Editor-in-Chief, for believing in me; Anthony Leung, Designer, for making the book look beautiful; Eileen Lasswell, Marketing Manager, for taking the book to the market; and Angela Kurmey, Developmental Editor, who spent untold hours patiently waiting for me to get back to her with work I'd promised days earlier, and somehow always managed to improve upon it.

Many reviewers at colleges and universities across Canada provided valuable comments and suggestions for this edition. Reviewers for the second Canadian edition included:

Denton Anthony, St. Francis Xavier University

Debra Basil, University of Lethbridge

Peter Burgess, George Brown College

Rita Cossa, McMaster University

Paul Cubbon, Capilano College

Webb Dussome, University of Alberta

Morai Forer, SIAST

E. Stephen Grant, University of New Brunswick

Albert Mastromartino, Sir Sandford Fleming College

Allen Richert, Confederation College

Charles Royce, McGill University

Murray Sang, Concordia University

Diana Serafini, Dawson College

Robert Soroka, Dawson College

On a personal note, I would like to thank David Weinberger, author of *Small Pieces Loosely Joined*, for his contribution to the Marketing on the Internet chapter and for his many years of encouragement; Craig Fleisher at the University of Windsor, for introducing me to Pearson, and for giving me my first university teaching job; Brad Davis at Wilfrid Laurier University, for teaching me how to teach marketing communications; Carman Cullen and Martin Kusy, for allowing me the privilege of teaching at Brock University; Dr. Peter Tingling, at Simon Fraser University, for blazing the PhD trail for me; and Tim Bray, creator of the Open Text Index, for introducing me to the possibilities of Internet marketing, and for allowing me to make mistakes.

—Lilly Anne Buchwitz

A Great Way to Learn and Instruct Online

The Pearson Education Canada Companion Website is easy to navigate and is organized to correspond to the chapters in this textbook. Whether you are a student in the classroom or a distance learner you will discover helpful resources for in-depth study and research that empower you in your quest for greater knowledge and maximize your potential for success in the course.

Companion
Website

[www.pearsoned.ca/armstrong]

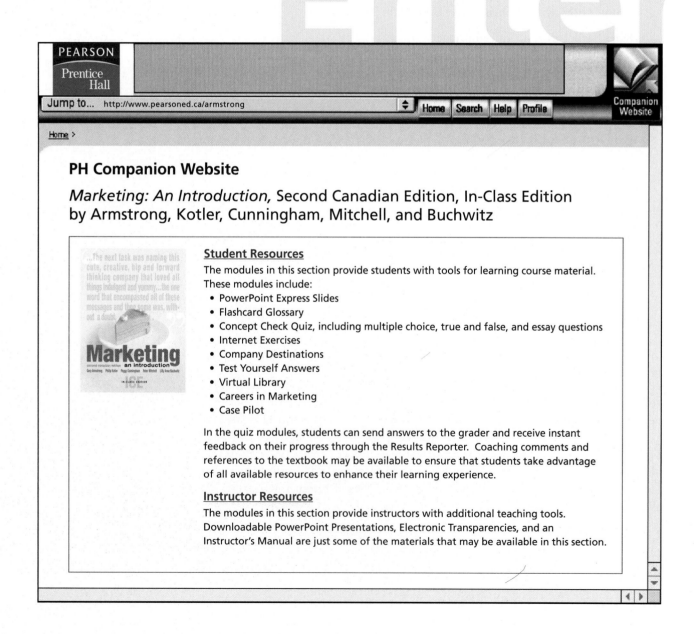

PEARSON
Prentice
Hall

Jump to... http://www.pearsoned.ca/armstrong   Home | Search | Help | Profile

Companion
Website

Home >

PH Companion Website

Marketing: An Introduction, Second Canadian Edition, In-Class Edition
by Armstrong, Kotler, Cunningham, Mitchell, and Buchwitz

Student Resources

The modules in this section provide students with tools for learning course material. These modules include:

- PowerPoint Express Slides
- Flashcard Glossary
- Concept Check Quiz, including multiple choice, true and false, and essay questions
- Internet Exercises
- Company Destinations
- Test Yourself Answers
- Virtual Library
- Careers in Marketing
- Case Pilot

In the quiz modules, students can send answers to the grader and receive instant feedback on their progress through the Results Reporter. Coaching comments and references to the textbook may be available to ensure that students take advantage of all available resources to enhance their learning experience.

Instructor Resources

The modules in this section provide instructors with additional teaching tools. Downloadable PowerPoint Presentations, Electronic Transparencies, and an Instructor's Manual are just some of the materials that may be available in this section.

Part 1 DEFINING MARKETING AND
THE MARKETING PROCESS

After reading this chapter, you should be able to

1. define marketing and outline the steps in the marketing process

2. explain the importance of understanding customers and the marketplace, and identify the five core marketplace concepts

3. identify the key elements of a customer-driven marketing strategy, and discuss the marketing management orientations that guide marketing strategy

4. discuss customer relationship management, and identify strategies for creating value *for* customers and capturing value *from* customers in return

5. describe the major trends and forces that are changing the marketing landscape in this new age of relationships

Marketing: Managing Profitable Customer Relationships

1

Looking Ahead

Welcome to the exciting world of marketing! In this chapter, to start you off, we will introduce you to the basic concepts. We'll start with a simple question: What *is* marketing? Simply put, marketing is building profitable customer relationships. The aim of marketing is to create value for customers and to capture value in return. Chapter 1 is organized around five steps in the marketing process—from understanding customer needs, to designing customer-driven marketing strategies and constructing marketing programs, to building customer relationships and capturing value for the firm. Throughout the chapter, we focus on the most important concept of modern marketing—managing customer relationships. Understanding these basic concepts, and forming your own ideas about what they really mean to you, will give you a solid foundation for all that follows.

We begin by looking at a company that was on the leading edge of marketing to consumers online. The success of Amazon.com Inc. has come about as a result of the organization's ability to understand the marketplace, understand its customers, and continually develop new ways of creating value for them.

On June 25, 2002, Amazon.ca was launched to serve Canadian customers of Amazon.com Inc. However, unlike the much-promoted launch of Amazon.com in 1995, the opening of the Canadian affiliate of this American company was quiet, almost reserved.

Given that Canada was Amazon.com's biggest export market, with hundreds of thousands of regular customers, why would the company need a separate website to serve its Canadian customers? To answer that question, it is worthwhile to look at Amazon.com's history.

In only a few years, Amazon.com has blossomed from a dot-com startup into one of the best-known names on the Internet. In the process, it has forever changed the practice of marketing. It pioneered the use of Web technology to build strong one-to-one customer relationships based on creating genuine customer value.

Amazon.com first opened its virtual doors in mid-July 1995, operating out of founder Jeff Bezos's garage in suburban Seattle. It still sells books—by the millions. But it now sells goods and services in a dozen other categories as well: from music, videos, consumer electronics, and computers to tools and hardware, kitchen and housewares, apparel, and toys and baby products. The company's slogan changed from "Earth's Biggest Bookstore" to "Earth's Biggest Selection."

To its core, the company is relentlessly customer driven. "The thing that drives everything is creating genuine value for customers," says Bezos. "Nothing happens without that." A few years back, when asked when Amazon.com would start putting profits first rather than growth, Bezos replied, "Customers come first. If you focus on what customers want and build a relationship, they will allow you to make money."

The relationship with customers is the key to the company's future. Anyone at Amazon.com will tell you that the company wants to do much more than just sell books or DVDs or digital cameras. It wants to deliver a special *experience* to every customer. "The customer experience really matters," says Bezos. "We've focused on just having a better store, where it's easier to shop, where you can learn more about the products, where you have a bigger selection, and where you have the lowest prices. You combine all of that stuff together and people say, 'Hey, these guys really get it.'"

In addition to the ability to develop personalized relationships with millions of customers, selling on the Internet gives Amazon.com some real advantages over brick-and-mortar rivals. By selling only online, the company reaps significant cost advantages. It avoids the huge costs of building and operating stores and carrying large inventories. And whereas traditional retailers must continually build new stores to increase revenues, Amazon.com grows by adding new product lines, developing new partnerships, and expanding—virtually—into new markets.

Amazon.com obsesses over making each customer's experience uniquely personal. For example, the site's "Personal Recommendations" feature prepares personalized product recommendations, and its "New for You" feature links customers through to their own personalized home pages. Amazon.com was the first to use "collaborative filtering" technology, which sifts through each customer's past purchases and the purchasing patterns of customers with similar profiles to come up with personalized site content. "We want Amazon.com to be the right store for you as an individual," says Bezos. "If we have 35 million customers, we should have 35 million stores."

Amazon.com's special attention to the needs of its customers may offer a clue to why the company launched Amazon.ca. Visitors to the Canadian website receive a unique blend of benefits: The site is bilingual, offers a huge selection, good value, convenience, and what Amazon.ca vice president Jason Kilar calls "discovery." In books alone, for example, Amazon.ca offers an easily searchable virtual selection of more than 1.5 million titles, seven and a half times more than any physical bookstore. Good value comes in the form of reasonable prices, with everyday discounts off suggested retail. And to be totally consistent with the U.S. site, it's irresistibly convenient to buy. With Amazon.ca's one-click checkout feature, you can log on, find what you want, and order with a single mouse click, all in less time than it takes to find a parking space at the local mall. Canadians no longer get the unpleasant surprises they did when they ordered from the American site. Many Canadian consumers were upset and refused to re-order when they discovered that customs charges and the cost of shipping were sometimes more than the price of the order.

Bezos characterized the new bilingual Canadian site as a benefit for Canadian publishers and consumers, as well as a champion for Canadian culture as a whole. "Anyone who is a proponent of Canadian culture should be ecstatic," Bezos stated in an interview. "We are going to make it available to the world." As evidence of this commitment, you simply have to look for the Canadian Essentials section on the website. This section promotes the 50 best-selling Canadian books in addition to "essential" music and DVD products.

Amazon's sites have become so good at managing online relationships that many traditional brick-and-mortar retailers are turning to Amazon for help in adding more clicks to their bricks. For example, Amazon.com now partners with well-known retailers such as Target, Toys "R" Us, Circuit City, and Borders to help them run their Web interfaces. The brick-and-mortar partners handle purchasing and inventory; Amazon.com oversees the customer experience—maintaining the website, attracting customers, and managing customer service. Amazon.com has also formed alliances with dozens, even hundreds, of retailers who sell their wares through the Amazon.com site. For example, Amazon.com's "apparel store" is more of a mall, featuring clothing, shoes, and accessories from partners such as Gap, Old Navy, Eddie Bauer, Spiegel, Foot Locker, Nordstrom, and Sears-owned Lands' End. The Canadian site has yet to form these types of retail partnerships, but as demand for the services the site offers grows, the addition of toys and apparel in partnership with leading retailers becomes possible within a business expansion strategy.

As a further "customer connection" feature, and as a competitive tactic to offset possible defections to Internet-based auction services such as eBay, Amazon.com has developed a "Sell Your Stuff" service whereby customers can buy and sell new, used, and collectible items. It's fast and simple, and listings for resale articles are seen by the customers who shop on the site every day. Amazon.com even collects the payment after sale and sends the seller the profits.

Whatever its fate, Amazon.com has forever changed the face of marketing. "No matter what becomes of Amazon," says one analyst, "it has taught us something new."[1]

TEST YOURSELF

Answers to these questions can be found on our website at www.pearsoned.ca/armstrong.

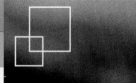

1. Amazon.com offers a wide array of products beyond books, including clothing, cooking gadgets, and toys. But Amazon.ca, unlike its parent Amazon.com, is not yet offering products beyond books, CDs, DVDs, games, and software. Why would Amazon.ca take this approach?
   a) Because consumers don't want to buy products like clothing and toys online
   b) Because it makes it easier to keep track of inventory
   c) Because Amazon.ca wants to build strong relationships with its customers on a small scale before expanding
   d) Because Amazon.ca wants to focus on cultural products, such as books, that make a positive contribution to society
   e) Because it keeps shipping costs low

2. Amazon.ca has built partnerships with predominantly brick-and-mortar retailers such as HMV. Why is it necessary for Amazon.ca to build these kinds of partnerships?
   a) Because these retailers help Amazon expand its offerings to customers while also giving these retailers a low-risk, low-cost way to enter the e-commerce arena
   b) Because Amazon needs more products to keep their customers
   c) Because Amazon is afraid of competition from these retailers
   d) Because the more products Amazon can offer, the lower they can keep their book prices
   e) Because these retailers have enough power to close Amazon down if Amazon does not sell their merchandise

3. The Web is global, of course, and with the simple click of a mouse Canadians were easily able to access Amazon.com. So the decision to put major investment into an Amazon.ca site is an excellent example of the value and importance of
   a) Patriotic marketing
   b) Segmenting and targeting
   c) Cross-border custom regulations
   d) Customer profiling
   e) Product marketing

4. Amazon is a "click-only" company in that it markets, sells, and communicates with its customers only through the Web and email. The special advantages of the Internet have allowed Amazon to provide unique marketing offers for each individual customer. Why is it important for Amazon.ca to provide these individualized offers?
   a) Because Amazon's competitors started doing so earlier
   b) Because individualized offers allow Amazon to charge higher prices
   c) Because Amazon collects individualized customer information and sells it to other Internet-based companies
   d) Because individualized offers are common and expected on e-commerce sites
   e) Because anticipating customer wants delivers exceptional value and grows long-term relationships

5. Amazon's ability to provide superior value to each individual customer, deliver high customer satisfaction, and maintain profitable customer relationships is the result of what key marketing philosophy:
   a) Profit concept
   b) Marketing concept
   c) Customer concept
   d) Product concept
   e) Promotion concept

Today's successful companies at all levels have one thing in common: Like Amazon's various sites, they are strongly customer focused and heavily committed to marketing. These companies share a passion for understanding and satisfying customer needs in well-defined target markets. They motivate everyone in the organization to help build lasting customer relationships through superior customer value and satisfaction. As co-founder Bernie Marcus of Home Depot asserted, "All of our people understand what the Holy Grail is. It's not the bottom line. It's an almost blind, passionate commitment to taking care of customers."

WHAT IS MARKETING?

Marketing, more than any other business function, deals with customers. Building customer relationships based on customer value and satisfaction is at the very heart of modern marketing. Although we will soon explore more-detailed definitions of marketing, perhaps the simplest definition is this one: Marketing is managing profitable customer relationships. The twofold goal of marketing is to attract new customers by promising superior value and to keep and grow current customers by delivering satisfaction.

Wal-Mart has become the world's largest retailer by delivering on its promise, "Always low prices. Always!" Ritz-Carlton promises—and delivers—truly "memorable experiences" for its hotel guests. At Disney theme parks, "imagineers" work wonders in their quest to "make a dream come true today." Dell Computer leads the personal computer industry by consistently making good on its promise to "be direct." Dell makes it easy for customers to custom-design their own computers and have them delivered quickly to their doorsteps or desktops. These and other highly successful companies know that if they take care of their customers, market share and profits will follow.

Sound marketing is critical to the success of every organization—large or small, for-profit or not-for-profit, domestic or global. Large for-profit firms such as Procter & Gamble, Microsoft, Sony, Wal-Mart, IBM, and Marriott use marketing. But so do not-for-profit organizations such as colleges and universities, hospitals, museums, symphony orchestras, and even churches. Moreover, marketing is practised not only in North America but also in the rest of the world.

You already know a lot about marketing—it's all around you. You see the results of marketing in the abundance of products in your nearby shopping mall. You see marketing in the advertisements that fill your TV screen, spice up your magazines, stuff your mailbox, or enliven your webpages. At home, at school, where you work, and where you play, you see marketing in almost everything you do. Yet there is much more to marketing than meets the consumer's casual eye. Behind it all is a massive network of people and activities competing for your attention and purchases.

This book will give you a more complete and formal introduction to the basic concepts and practices of today's marketing. In this chapter, we begin by defining marketing and the marketing process.

Marketing Defined

What does the term *marketing* mean? Many people think of marketing only as selling and advertising. And no wonder—every day we are bombarded with television commercials, newspaper ads, direct-mail offers, sales calls, and Internet pitches. However, selling and advertising are only the tip of the marketing iceberg.

Today, marketing must be understood not in the old sense of making a sale—"telling and selling"—but in the new sense of satisfying customer needs. If the marketer does a good job of understanding who its customers are; develops products that provide superior value; and prices, distributes, and promotes them effectively, these products will sell very easily. Thus, selling and advertising are only part of a larger "marketing mix"—a set of marketing tools that work together to affect the marketplace.

We define **marketing** as a social and managerial process by which individuals and groups obtain what they need and want through creating and exchanging value with others.[2] In a business setting, marketing involves building and managing profitable exchange relationships with customers.

Marketing A social and managerial process by which individuals and groups obtain what they need and want through creating and exchanging value with others.

The Marketing Process

Figure 1.1 presents a simple five-step model of the marketing process. In the first four steps, companies work to understand customers, create customer value, and

Figure 1.1   **A Simple Model of the Marketing Process**

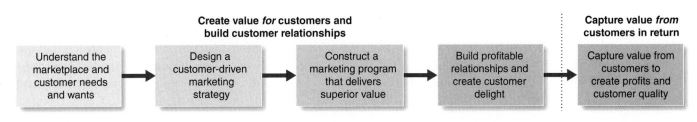

Create value *for* customers and build customer relationships				Capture value *from* customers in return
Understand the marketplace and customer needs and wants	Design a customer-driven marketing strategy	Construct a marketing program that delivers superior value	Build profitable relationships and create customer delight	Capture value from customers to create profits and customer quality

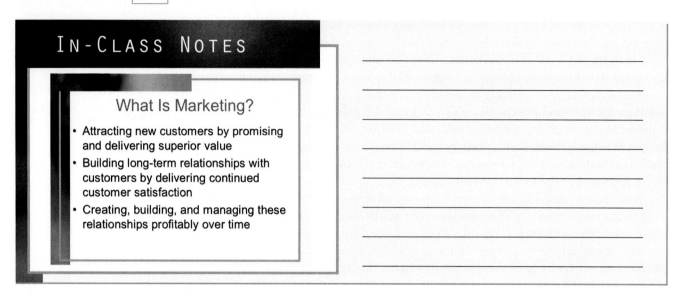

IN-CLASS NOTES

What Is Marketing?

- Attracting new customers by promising and delivering superior value
- Building long-term relationships with customers by delivering continued customer satisfaction
- Creating, building, and managing these relationships profitably over time

build strong customer relationships. In the final step, companies reap the rewards of creating superior customer value. By creating value *for* their customers, they in turn capture value *from* those customers in the form of sales, profits, and long-term customer equity.[3]

In this and the next chapter, we will examine the steps of this simple model of marketing. In this chapter, we'll review each step but focus more on the customer relationship steps—understanding customers, building customer relationships, and capturing value from customers. In Chapter 2 we'll look more deeply into the second and third steps—designing marketing strategies and constructing marketing programs.

UNDERSTANDING THE MARKETPLACE AND CUSTOMER NEEDS

The marketing process begins, continues, and ends with customers. As a first step, marketers need to understand customer needs and wants and the marketplace within which they operate. We now examine five core marketplace concepts: needs, wants, and demands; marketing offers (goods, services, and experiences); value and satisfaction; exchanges, transactions, and relationships; and markets.

Needs, Wants, and Demands

Needs States of felt deprivation.

The most basic concept underlying marketing is that of human needs. Human **needs** are states of felt deprivation. They include basic *physical* needs for food, clothing, warmth, and safety; *social* needs for belonging and affection; and *individual* needs for knowledge and self-expression. These needs were not created by marketers; they are a basic part of the human makeup.

Wants The form human needs take as shaped by culture and individual personality.

Wants are the form human needs take as they are shaped by culture and individual personality. In Canada, we *need* food but we *want* a Big Mac, french fries, and a soft drink. A person in Mauritius *needs* food but *wants* a mango, rice, lentils, and beans. Wants are shaped by one's society and are described in terms of objects that will satisfy needs. When backed by buying power, wants become **demands**. Given their wants and resources, people demand products with benefits that add up to the most value and satisfaction.

Demands Human wants that are backed by buying power.

Outstanding marketing companies go to great lengths to learn about and understand their customers' needs, wants, and demands. They conduct consumer research and analyze mountains of customer data. Their people at all levels—including top management—stay close to customers. For example, top executives from Wal-Mart spend two days each week visiting stores and mingling with customers. At Disney World, at least once in his or her career, each manager spends a day touring the park in a Mickey, Minnie, Goofy, or other character costume.

At consumer products giant Procter & Gamble, top executives even visit with ordinary consumers in their homes and on shopping trips. "We read the data and look at the charts," says one P&G executive, "but to shop [with consumers] and see how the woman is changing retailers to save 10 cents on a loaf of bread [so she can] spend it on things that are more important—that's important for us to keep front and center."[4]

Marketing Offers—Products, Services, and Experiences

Customers' needs and wants are fulfilled through a **marketing offer**—some combination of goods, services, information, or experiences offered to a market to satisfy a need or want. These marketing offers are usually referred to as products, but are not limited to physical goods. A product may be a tangible good, such as a car or an item of clothing, but services such as mortgages, airline tickets, and manicures are also products offered to a market. Marketing offers may include any combination of tangible goods, intangible services, activities, or benefits offered for sale. Examples of services include banking, airline, hotel, tax preparation, and home repair services. Service businesses now account for the greater part of the Canadian economy (69 percent) and the sector has been growing faster than the manufacturing sector.[5] More broadly, marketing offers also include other entities, such as persons, places, organizations, information, and ideas.

Many sellers make the mistake of paying more attention to the specific products they offer than to the benefits and experiences produced by these products. These sellers suffer from "*marketing myopia.*" They are so taken with their products that they focus only on existing wants and lose sight of underlying customer needs.[6] They forget that a product is only a tool to solve a problem. A manufacturer of quarter-inch drill bits may think that the customer needs a drill bit. But what the customer *really* needs is a quarter-inch hole. These sellers will have trouble if a new product comes along that serves the customer's need better or less expensively. The customer with the same *need* will *want* the new product.

Smart marketers look beyond the attributes of the products and services they sell. They create brand meaning and brand experiences for consumers. For example, Coca-Cola means much more to consumers than just something to drink—it has become a global icon with a rich tradition and meaning. And Nike is more than just shoes; it's what the shoes do for you and where they take you.

By carefully combining goods, services, and other benefits, companies can create, stage, and market brand experiences. A visit to Disney World is an experience; so is a ride on a Harley-Davidson motorcycle. You can buy a book and a cup of coffee at an Indigo bookstore, but Indigo also creates an inviting experience for consumers through its design and decor. A visit to Amazon.ca presents a variety of marketing offers, from products for sale to

Most children aren't shy about showing affection. Which makes them excellent spreaders of the flu.

Products do not have to be physical objects. Here the product is an idea.

free services such as searching inside the book and benefits such as personalized recommendations. And you don't just watch a NASCAR race, you immerse yourself in the NASCAR experience (see Marketing at Work 1.1). In fact, experiences have emerged for many firms as the next step in differentiating the company's offer. "What consumers really want [are offers] that dazzle their senses, touch their hearts, and stimulate their minds," declares one expert. "They want [offers] that deliver an experience."[7]

Value and Satisfaction

Whenever people make purchasing decisions, they are faced with many different options that might satisfy a given need. How do they choose among these many marketing offers? People make choices based on their perceptions of the value and satisfaction that various products deliver. They form expectations about the value of various marketing offers and buy accordingly. Satisfied customers buy again and tell others about their good experiences. Dissatisfied customers often switch to competitors and disparage the product to others.

Marketers must be careful to set the right level of expectations. If they set expectations too low, they may satisfy those who buy but fail to attract enough buyers. If they raise expectations too high, buyers will be disappointed. Customer value and customer satisfaction are key building blocks for developing and managing customer relationships. We will revisit these core concepts later in the chapter.

Exchange, Transactions, and Relationships

Exchange The act of obtaining a desired object from someone by offering something in return.

Transaction A trade of values between two parties.

Marketing occurs when people decide to satisfy needs and wants through exchange. **Exchange** is the act of obtaining a desired object from someone by offering something in return. Whereas exchange is the core concept of marketing, a transaction, in turn, is marketing's unit of measurement. A **transaction** consists of a trade of values between two parties: One party gives X to another party and gets Y in return. For example, you pay Future Shop $350 and receive a television set.

In the broadest sense, the marketer tries to bring about a response to some marketing offer. The response may be more than simply buying or trading goods and services. A political candidate, for instance, wants votes, a church wants membership, and a social action group wants idea acceptance. Marketing consists of actions taken to build and maintain desirable *exchange relationships* with target audiences involving a good, service, idea, or other object. Beyond simply attracting new customers and creating transactions, the goal is to retain customers and grow their business with the company. Marketers want to build strong economic and social relationships by consistently delivering superior value. We will expand on the important concept of customer relationship management later in the chapter.

Markets

Market The set of all actual and potential buyers of a product or service.

The concepts of exchange and relationships lead to the concept of a *market*. A **market** is the set of actual and potential buyers of a product. These buyers share a particular need or want that can be satisfied through exchange relationships. The size of a market depends on the number of people who exhibit the need, have resources to engage in exchange, and are willing to exchange these resources for what they want.

Marketers are keenly interested in markets. Marketing means managing markets to bring about profitable exchange relationships. However, creating exchange relationships

Marketing at Work | 1.1

NASCAR: Creating Customer Experiences

NASCAR (the National Association for Stock Car Auto Racing) is one great marketing organization. And for fans, NASCAR is a lot more than a stock car race. It's a high-octane, totally involving experience.

NASCAR is now the second-highest-rated regular season sport on TV. NASCAR fans are 75 million strong—4 of every 10 people in the United States regularly watch or attend NASCAR events. An estimated 30 000 Canadians travel across the border to watch NASCAR races in Michigan, and TSN's NASCAR coverage consistently draws more viewers than open-wheel racing. An ardent NASCAR fan experiences almost nine hours of NASCAR media coverage per week and spends nearly $833 a year on NASCAR-related clothing, collectibles, and other items.

NASCAR races attract the largest crowds of any U.S. sporting event. To get fans even closer to the action, in addition to grandstands and skyboxes, track facilities include RV parks next to and right inside the racing oval. Rather than fleecing fans with overpriced food and beer, NASCAR tracks encourage fans to bring their own. Marvels one sponsor, "[In] what other sport can you drive your beat-up RV or camper into the stadium and sit on it to watch the race? . . . How many NFL stadiums go so far as to print the allowable cooler dimensions on the back of the ticket?" Such actions mean that NASCAR might lose a sale today, but it will keep the customer tomorrow.

To further the experience, NASCAR makes the sport a wholesome family affair. Tracks feature professionally landscaped grounds, with manicured flower beds, no litter, and ample restrooms. The environment is safe for kids—uniformed security guards patrol the track to keep things in line.

And, unlike the aloof and often distant athletes in other sports, NASCAR drivers are approachable, friendly, and readily available to mingle with fans and sign autographs.

Can't make it to the track? No problem. NASCAR TV coverage reaches 20 million viewers weekly. Well-orchestrated coverage and in-car cameras put fans in the middle of the action, giving them vicarious thrills that keep them glued to the screen. NASCAR.com serves up a glut of news and entertainment to more than 2 million fans each month.

Ultimately, all of this fan enthusiasm translates into financial success for NASCAR, and for its sponsors. Television networks pay some $2.4 billion per year for the rights to broadcast NASCAR events. And the sport is third in licensed merchandise sales,

behind only the NFL and the NCAA. It rings up more than $1.3 billion in sales of NASCAR-branded retail merchandise every year.

Sources: Quotes and other information from Mark Woods, "Readers Try to Explain Why Racin' Rocks," *The Florida Times Union*, February 16, 2003, p. C1; Tina Grady, "NASCAR Fan Base More Than Just Blue Collar," *Aftermarket Business*, May 2002, p. 11; George Pyne, "In His Own Words: NASCAR Sharpens Winning Strategy," *Advertising Age*, October 28, 2002, p. S6; Peter Spiegel, "Heir Gordon," *Forbes,* December 14, 1998, pp. 42–46; Tony Kontzer, "Backseat Drivers—NASCAR Puts You in the Race," *InformationWeek*, March 25, 2002, p. 83; Lisa Matte, "The Race Is On: Marketing Partnerships with Racing Teams Increase Awareness of, Loyalty to Hotel Brands," *Hotel & Motel Management*, August 2002, p. 127; Matthew Futterman, "What Fuels NASCAR," *The Star-Ledger,* February 16, 2003, p. 1; www.NASCAR.com, July 2003; Dan Hamilton, "Canada, NASCAR'S Field of Opportunity," www.insiderracingnews.com, accessed October 24, 2004.

NASCAR's incredible success results from creating memorable experiences that translate into lasting customer relationships. The resulting fan loyalty attracts hundreds of marketers, who pay to sponsor cars and get their corporate logos emblazoned on team uniforms and on the hoods or side panels of cars.

takes work. Sellers must search for buyers, identify their needs, design good marketing offers, set prices for them, promote them, and store and deliver them. Activities such as product development, research, communication, distribution, pricing, and service are core marketing activities.

Figure 1.2 shows the main elements in a modern marketing system. In the usual situation, marketing involves serving a group of customers and potential customers—a target market—in the face of competitors. The company and the competitors send their respective offers and messages to the market, either directly or through marketing intermediaries. All the factors in the system are affected by major environmental forces (demographic, economic, physical, technological, political/legal, social/cultural).

Figure 1.2   Elements of a Modern Marketing System

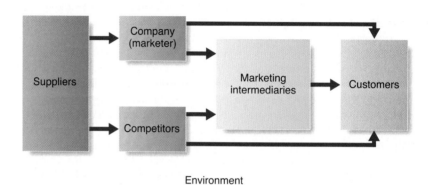

Each party in the system adds value for the next level. Thus, a company's success at building profitable relationships depends not only on its own actions but also on how well the entire system serves the needs of its customers. Wal-Mart cannot fulfill its promise of low prices unless its suppliers provide merchandise at low costs. And Ford cannot deliver high quality to car buyers unless its dealers provide outstanding service.

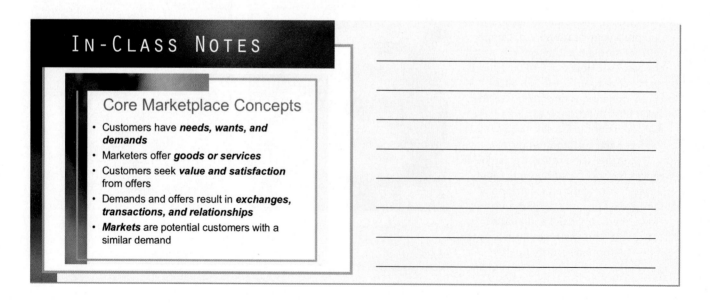

IN-CLASS NOTES

Core Marketplace Concepts

- Customers have **needs, wants, and demands**
- Marketers offer **goods or services**
- Customers seek **value and satisfaction** from offers
- Demands and offers result in **exchanges, transactions, and relationships**
- **Markets** are potential customers with a similar demand

DESIGNING A CUSTOMER-DRIVEN MARKETING STRATEGY

Once it fully understands the marketplace, marketing management can design a customer-driven marketing strategy. We define **marketing management** as the art and science of choosing target markets, presenting a marketing offer to them, acquiring customers, and building profitable relationships with them. The marketing manager's aim is to get, keep, and grow customers by creating, delivering, and communicating superior customer value. To design a winning marketing strategy, the marketing manager must answer two important questions: Which individuals or organizations will we serve (what's our target market?) and how can we serve these customers best (what's our value proposition?). We will discuss these marketing strategy concepts briefly here, then look at them in more detail in the next chapter.

Marketing management The art and science of choosing target markets, presenting a marketing offer to them, acquiring customers, and building profitable relationships with them.

Selecting Customers to Serve

The company must first decide *who* it will serve. It does this by dividing the market into segments of customers (*market segmentation*) and selecting which segments it will cultivate (*target marketing*). A company may present its marketing offers to groups of people (called consumers) or to groups of companies or other organizations, or to both. For example, Canadian high-tech company RIM, which markets the popular line of communications devices called the BlackBerry, markets products to consumers for their individual use as well as to small and large businesses that buy BlackBerries for their employees or for departmental use. Many of RIM's products are marketed with associated services such as telephone and Internet connections. Some people think of marketing management as finding as many customers as possible and increasing demand. But marketing managers know that they cannot serve all customers in every way. Trying to serve all customers usually results in not serving any customers well. Instead, the company wants to select customers that it can serve well and profitably. For example, Porsche profitably targets affluent professionals; Hyundai profitably targets families with more modest means.

Some marketers may seek *fewer* customers and reduced demand. For example, Banff National Park is badly overcrowded in the summer. And power and water companies sometimes have trouble meeting demand during peak usage periods. In these and other cases of excess demand, **demarketing** may be required to reduce the number of customers or to shift their demand temporarily or permanently. For instance, to reduce demand for power consumption, BC Hydro has developed the Power Smart program of ideas and incentives to reduce electricity usage. The details about promotions for both residential and business users are available on the BC Hydro website.[8]

Demarketing Marketing to reduce demand temporarily or permanently; the aim is not to destroy demand but only to reduce or shift it.

Service providers such as BC Hydro demarket by providing customers with practical ways to reduce the amount of electricity they use.

Thus, marketing managers must decide which customers they want to target, and on the level, timing, and nature of their demand. Simply put, marketing management is *customer management* and *demand management*.

Deciding on a Value Proposition

The company must also decide *how* it will serve targeted customers—how it will *differentiate* and *position* itself in the marketplace. A company's *value proposition* is the set of

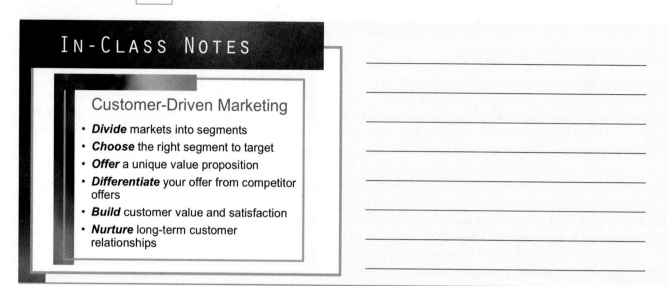

benefits or values it promises to deliver to its target markets to satisfy their needs. Porsche promises driving performance and excitement: "What a dog feels when the leash breaks." Tide laundry detergent promises powerful, all-purpose cleaning, whereas Gain "cleans and freshens like sunshine." Altoids positions itself as "the curiously strong mint."

Such value propositions differentiate one brand from another. They answer the customer's question "Why should I buy your brand rather than a competitor's?" Companies must design strong value propositions that give them the greatest advantage in their target markets.

MARKETING MANAGEMENT ORIENTATIONS

Marketing management wants to design strategies that will result in profitable relationships with the organization's customers. But what *philosophy* should guide these marketing strategies? What weight should be given to the interests of customers, the organization, and society? Very often these interests conflict.

There are five alternative concepts under which organizations design and carry out their marketing strategies: the production, product, selling, marketing, and societal marketing concepts.

The Production Concept

Production concept The idea that buyers will favour products that are widely available and highly affordable.

The **production concept** holds that buyers will favour products that are widely available and highly affordable. Therefore, management should focus on improving production and distribution efficiency. This concept is one of the oldest orientations that guide companies.

The production concept is still a useful philosophy in two types of situations. The first occurs when the demand for a product exceeds the supply. Here, management should look for ways to increase production. The second situation occurs when the product's cost is too high and improved productivity is needed to bring it down. For example, Henry Ford's philosophy was to perfect the production of the Model T so that its cost could be reduced and more people could afford it. He is credited with inventing the assembly line.

Although useful in some situations, the production concept can lead to marketing myopia. Companies adopting this orientation run the risk of focusing too narrowly on their own operations and losing sight of the real objective—building customer relationships by satisfying customers' needs.

The Product Concept

The **product concept** holds that buyers will favour products that offer the most in quality, performance, and innovative features. Under this concept, marketing strategy should focus on making continuous product improvements. Some manufacturers believe that if they can build a better mousetrap, the world will beat a path to their door.[9] But they are often rudely shocked. Buyers may well be looking for a better solution to a mouse problem but not necessarily for a better mousetrap. The solution might be a chemical spray, an exterminating service, or something that works better than a mousetrap. Furthermore, a better mousetrap will not sell unless the manufacturer designs, packages, and prices it attractively; places it in convenient distribution channels; brings it to the attention of people who need it; and convinces buyers that it is a better product.

Thus, the product concept also can lead to the unfortunate situation where marketers are too narrow in their focus, and fail to see the bigger picture. For instance, railroad management once thought that users wanted *trains* rather than *transportation* and overlooked the growing challenge of airlines, buses, trucks, and automobiles. Kodak assumed that consumers wanted photographic film rather than a way to capture and share memories and at first overlooked the challenge of digital cameras. Although it now leads the digital camera market in sales, it has yet to make significant profits from this business.[10]

Product concept The idea that buyers will favour products that offer the most in quality, performance, and innovative features.

The Selling Concept

Many companies follow the **selling concept**, which holds that the market will not buy enough of the firm's products unless it undertakes a large-scale selling effort. The concept is typically practised with unsought goods—those that buyers do not normally think of buying, such as insurance or blood donations. These industries must be good at tracking down prospects and selling them on product benefits.

Most firms practise the selling concept when they face overcapacity. Their aim is to sell what they make rather than make what the market wants. Such a marketing strategy carries high risks. It focuses on creating sales transactions rather than on building long-term, profitable customer relationships. It assumes that customers who are coaxed into buying the product will like it. Or, if they don't like it, they will possibly forget their disappointment and buy it again later. These are usually poor assumptions. Most studies show that dissatisfied customers do not buy again. Worse yet, whereas the average satisfied customer may tell four or five others about good experiences, the average dissatisfied customer tells twice as many others about his or her bad experiences.[11]

Selling concept The idea that the market will not buy enough of the firm's products unless it undertakes a large-scale selling effort.

The Marketing Concept

The **marketing concept** holds that achieving organizational goals depends on knowing the needs and wants of target markets and delivering the desired satisfactions better than competitors do. Under the marketing concept, customer focus and value are the *paths* to sales and profits.

Instead of a product-centred "make and sell" philosophy, the marketing concept is a customer-centred "sense and respond" philosophy. It views marketing not as "hunting,"

Marketing concept The marketing management philosophy that holds that achieving organizational goals depends on knowing the needs and wants of target markets and delivering the desired satisfactions better than competitors do.

but as "gardening." The job is not to find the right customers for your product, but the right products for your customers. As stated by famed direct marketer Lester Wunderman, "The chant of the Industrial Revolution was that of the manufacturer who said, 'This is what I make, won't you please buy it.' The call of the Information Age is the market asking, 'This is what I want, won't you please make it.'"[12]

Figure 1.3 contrasts the selling concept and the marketing concept. The selling concept takes an *inside-out* perspective. It starts with the factory, focuses on the company's existing products, and calls for heavy selling and promotion to obtain profitable sales. It focuses primarily on customer conquest—getting short-term sales with little concern about who buys or why.

Figure 1.3   The Selling and Marketing Concepts Contrasted

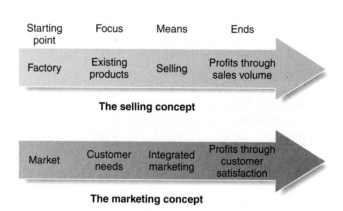

In contrast, the marketing concept takes an *outside-in* perspective. In the words of a Ford executive, "If we're not customer driven, our cars won't be either." The marketing concept starts with a well-defined market, focuses on customer needs, and integrates all the marketing activities that affect customers. In turn, it yields profits by creating long-term customer relationships with the right customers based on customer value and satisfaction. Many successful and well-known companies have adopted the marketing concept. Procter & Gamble, Disney, Wal-Mart, Roots, the Royal Bank, Dell Computer, and WestJet Airlines follow it faithfully.

Implementing the marketing concept often means more than simply responding to customers' stated desires and obvious needs. *Customer-driven* companies research current customers deeply to learn about their desires, gather new product and service ideas, and test proposed product improvements. Such customer-driven marketing usually works well when a clear need exists and when customers know what they want.

In many cases, however, customers *don't* know what they want or even what is possible. For example, 20 years ago, how many people would have thought to ask for cell phones, home copiers, 24-hour Internet brokerage accounts, DVD players, handheld global satellite positioning systems, or wearable PCs? Such situations call for customer-driven marketing—understanding customer needs even better than customers themselves do and products that will meet existing and latent needs, now and in the future.

As Sony's visionary leader, the late Akio Morita, put it: "Our plan is to lead the public with new products rather than ask them what kinds of products they want. The public does not know what is possible, but we do." And according to an executive at 3M, "Our goal is to lead customers where they want to go before *they* know where they want to go."[13]

The Societal Marketing Concept

The *societal marketing* concept questions whether the pure marketing concept overlooks possible conflicts between the short-term needs and wants of individuals and the long-run welfare of society. Is a firm that senses, serves, and satisfies immediate needs, wants, and interests of the market always doing what's best for society in the long run? The **societal marketing concept** holds that marketing strategy should deliver value to the organization's customers in a way that not only maintains or improves the organization's relationship with those customers, but that also maintains or improves the well-being of society.

Consider the fast-food industry. You may see today's giant fast-food chains as offering tasty and convenient food at reasonable prices. Yet many consumer and environmental groups have voiced concerns. Critics point out that hamburgers, fried chicken, french fries, and most other foods sold by fast-food restaurants are high in fat and salt. Meals are now "super-sized," leading consumers to overeat and contributing to the obesity problem. The foods are wrapped in convenient packaging, but this leads to waste and pollution. Thus, in satisfying short-term wants, the highly successful fast-food chains may be harming people's health and causing environmental problems in the long run.[14]

As Figure 1.4 shows, the societal marketing concept calls on marketers to balance three considerations in setting their marketing strategies: company profits, individual wants and needs, *and* society's interests. Originally, most companies based their marketing decisions largely on short-run company profit. Eventually, they recognized the importance of satisfying both short- and long-term wants and needs, and the societal marketing concept emerged. Now most companies consider society's interests when making their marketing decisions.

The iPod Nano, released in late 2005, is as thin as a pencil and not much bigger than a credit card, yet it stores and plays approximately 1000 songs.

Societal marketing concept A principle of enlightened marketing that holds that marketing strategy should deliver value to the organization's customers in a way that maintains or improves the well-being of society.

Figure 1.4   Three Considerations Underlying the Societal Marketing Concept

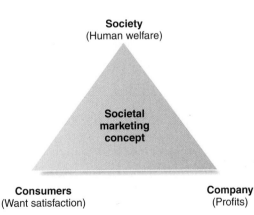

Society
(Human welfare)

Societal marketing concept

Consumers
(Want satisfaction)

Company
(Profits)

Our Credo

We believe our first responsibility is to the doctors, nurses and patients,
to mothers and fathers and all others who use our products and services.
In meeting their needs everything we do must be of high quality.
We must constantly strive to reduce our costs
in order to maintain reasonable prices.
Customers' orders must be serviced promptly and accurately.
Our suppliers and distributors must have an opportunity
to make a fair profit.

We are responsible to our employees,
the men and women who work with us throughout the world.
Everyone must be considered as an individual.
We must respect their dignity and recognize their merit.
They must have a sense of security in their jobs.
Compensation must be fair and adequate,
and working conditions clean, orderly and safe.
We must be mindful of ways to help our employees fulfill
their family responsibilities.
Employees must feel free to make suggestions and complaints.
There must be equal opportunity for employment, development
and advancement for those qualified.
We must provide competent management,
and their actions must be just and ethical.

We are responsible to the communities in which we live and work
and to the world community as well.
We must be good citizens — support good works and charities
and bear our fair share of taxes.
We must encourage civic improvements and better health and education.
We must maintain in good order
the property we are privileged to use,
protecting the environment and natural resources.

Our final responsibility is to our stockholders.
Business must make a sound profit.
We must experiment with new ideas.
Research must be carried on, innovative programs developed
and mistakes paid for.
New equipment must be purchased, new facilities provided
and new products launched.
Reserves must be created to provide for adverse times.
When we operate according to these principles,
the stockholders should realize a fair return.

Johnson & Johnson

Johnson & Johnson's concern for society is summarized in its credo and in the company's actions over the years.

One such company is Johnson & Johnson, which has been rated each year in a *Fortune* magazine poll as one of America's most admired companies. Johnson & Johnson's concern for societal interests is summarized in a company document called "Our Credo," which stresses honesty, integrity, and putting people before profits. Under this credo, Johnson & Johnson would rather take a big loss than ship a bad batch of one of its products. Consider the tragic tampering case in which eight people died from swallowing cyanide-laced capsules of Tylenol, a Johnson & Johnson brand. Although Johnson & Johnson believed that the pills had been altered in only a few stores, not in the factory, it quickly recalled all of the product. The recall cost the company $240 million in earnings. In the long run, however, the company's swift recall of Tylenol strengthened consumer confidence and loyalty, and Tylenol remains one of the nation's leading brands of pain reliever.

In this and other cases, Johnson & Johnson management has found that doing what's right benefits not only the company, but the company's customers and the general public as well.

Says Johnson & Johnson's chief executive, "The Credo should not be viewed as some kind of social welfare program . . . it's just plain good business. If we keep trying to do what's right, at the end of the day we believe the marketplace will reward us." Thus, over the years, Johnson & Johnson's dedication to the consuming public and community service has made it one of North America's most-admired companies *and* one of the most profitable.[15]

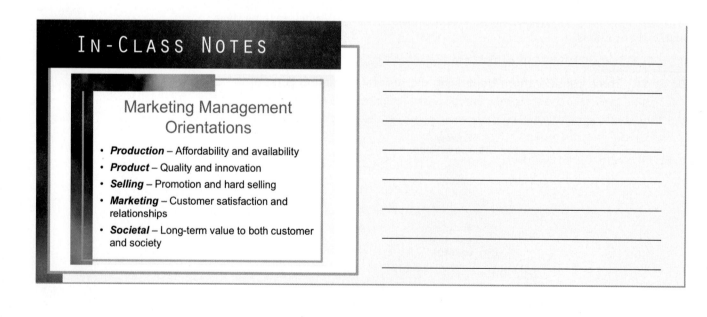

IN-CLASS NOTES

Marketing Management Orientations

- **Production** – Affordability and availability
- **Product** – Quality and innovation
- **Selling** – Promotion and hard selling
- **Marketing** – Customer satisfaction and relationships
- **Societal** – Long-term value to both customer and society

PREPARING A MARKETING PLAN AND PROGRAM

The company's marketing strategy outlines which customers the company will serve and how it will create value for these customers. Next, guided by the marketing strategy, the marketer constructs a marketing program that will actually deliver the intended value to its target customers. The marketing program builds customer relationships by transforming the strategy into action. It consists of the firm's *marketing mix*, the set of marketing tools the firm uses to implement its marketing strategy. A sample marketing plan for Cake Beauty can be found in Appendix 2 on page 558 of this text.

The major marketing tools are classified into four broad groups, called the *four Ps* of marketing: product, price, place, and promotion. To deliver on its value proposition, the firm must first create a need-satisfying marketing offer (product). It must decide how much it will charge for the offer (price) and how it will make the offer available to target customers (place). Finally, it must communicate with target customers about the offer and persuade them of its merits (promotion).

We will explore marketing programs and the marketing mix in much more detail in Chapter 2. Then, in later chapters, we'll look more deeply into each element of the marketing mix.

Linking the Concepts

What have you learned so far about marketing? For the moment, set aside the more formal definitions we've examined and try to develop your own understanding of marketing.

- In *your own words*, what *is* marketing? Write down *your* definition. Does your definition include key concepts such as customer value and relationships?
- What does marketing *mean* to you? How does it affect your daily life?
- What marketing management philosophy appears to guide NASCAR? How does this compare with the marketing philosophy that guides Johnson & Johnson? Can you think of another company guided by a very different philosophy? Is there one marketing management philosophy that's best for all companies?

BUILDING CUSTOMER RELATIONSHIPS

The first three steps in the marketing process—understanding the marketplace and customer needs, designing a customer-driven marketing strategy, and constructing marketing programs—all lead up to the fourth and most important step: building profitable customer relationships.

Customer Relationship Management

Customer relationship management (CRM) is perhaps the most important concept of modern marketing. Until recently, CRM has been defined narrowly as a customer data management activity. By this definition, it involves managing detailed information about individual customers and carefully managing customer "touchpoints" in order to maximize customer loyalty. We will discuss this narrower CRM activity in Chapter 5.

More recently, however, customer relationship management has taken on a broader meaning. In this broader sense, **customer relationship management** is the overall process of building and maintaining profitable customer relationships by delivering superior

Customer relationship management The overall process of building and maintaining profitable customer relationships by delivering superior customer value and satisfaction.

customer value and satisfaction. Today's companies are going beyond designing strategies to *attract* new customers and create *transactions* with them. They are using customer relationship management to *retain* current customers and build profitable, long-term *relationships* with them. The new view is that marketing is the science and art of finding, retaining, *and* growing profitable customers. For example, today's consumers are finding, and in many cases preferring, self-service at retail outlets. Self-serve gas stations are now the norm, and gone are the days when shoppers were accosted in department stores with offers of assistance from sales staff. Some retailers, however, are discovering that there is a segment of the market that prefers higher levels of service, and are catering to it. Holt Renfrew, for example, offers personal shoppers to assist its customers.[16]

Why the new emphasis on retaining and growing customers? In the past, many companies took their customers for granted. Facing an expanding economy and rapidly growing markets, companies could practise a "leaky bucket" approach to marketing. Growing markets meant a plentiful supply of new customers. Companies could keep filling the marketing bucket with new customers without worrying about losing old customers through holes in the bottom of the bucket.

However, companies today face some new marketing realities. Changing demographics, more sophisticated competitors, and overcapacity in many industries mean that there are fewer customers to go around. Many companies are now fighting for shares of flat or fading markets. As a result, the costs of attracting new customers are rising. In fact, on average, it costs 5 to 10 times as much to attract a new customer as it does to keep a current customer satisfied. Sears even found that it costs them 12 times more to attract a customer than to keep an existing one.[17] Given these new realities, companies now go all out to keep their profitable customers.

Relationship Building Blocks: Customer Value and Satisfaction The key to building lasting customer relationships is to create superior customer value and satisfaction. Satisfied customers are more likely to be loyal customers and to give the company a larger share of their business.

Customer Value. Attracting and retaining customers can be a difficult task. Customers often face a bewildering array of marketing offers from which to choose. A customer buys from the firm that offers the highest **customer perceived value**—the customer's evaluation of the difference between all the benefits and all the costs of a marketing offer relative to those of competing offers.

> **Customer perceived value** The customer's evaluation of the difference between all the benefits and all the costs of a marketing offer relative to those of competing offers.

For example, Purolator Courier customers gain a number of benefits. The most obvious is fast and reliable package delivery. However, by using Purolator, customers also may receive some status and image values. The Purolator brand itself adds value because it usually makes both the package sender and the receiver feel more important. When deciding whether to send a package via Purolator, customers will weigh these and other perceived values against the money, effort, and psychological costs of using the service. Moreover, they will compare the value of using Purolator against the value of using other shippers—UPS, FedEx, DHL, Canada Post. They will select the service that gives them the greatest perceived value.

Customers often do not judge product values and costs accurately or objectively. They act on *perceived* value. For example, does Purolator really provide service to the most destinations in Canada? If so, is this better service worth a higher price? Canada Post argues that its express service is comparable, and its prices are much lower. However, judging by market share, most Purolator customers perceive otherwise. Each week, they entrust Purolator, Canada's largest courier, with 5.5 million packages.[18]

> **Customer satisfaction** The extent to which a product's perceived performance matches a buyer's expectations.

Customer Satisfaction. Customer satisfaction depends on the product's perceived performance relative to a buyer's expectations. If the product's performance falls short of expectations, the customer is dissatisfied. If performance matches expectations, the cus-

Customers often do not judge product values and costs accurately or objectively. They act on *perceived* value. Does Purolator really provide service to the most destinations in Canada? If so, is this better service worth a higher price?

tomer is satisfied. If performance exceeds expectations, the customer is highly satisfied or delighted.

Outstanding organizations go out of their way to keep important customers satisfied. Highly satisfied customers make repeat purchases and tell others about their good experiences with the product. The key is to match customer expectations with company performance. Smart companies aim to *delight* customers by promising only what they can deliver, then delivering *more* than they promise (see Marketing at Work 1.2).[19]

Marketing at Work | 1.2

Customer Relationships: Keeping Customers Satisfied

At some companies, exceptional value and customer service are more than a set of policies or actions—they are a companywide attitude.

Some companies go to extremes to satisfy their customers. Consider the following examples:

- Lexus Canada went to great lengths to get a car key to a driver who had lost his keys while fishing on Lake Kenogami, north of Regina. Not only did the local dealer replace the key, but it also booked a charter flight for the driver, since he had missed the once-a-week plane because of the mishap.
- An American Express cardholder fails to pay more than $5000 of his

September bill. He explains that during the summer he had purchased expensive rugs in Turkey. When he got home, appraisals showed that the rugs were worth half of what he'd paid. Rather than ask questions or demand payment, the American Express representative notes the dispute, asks for a letter summarizing the appraisers' estimates, and offers to help solve the problem. Until the conflict is resolved, American Express doesn't ask for payment.
- A frustrated homeowner faces a difficult and potentially costly home plumbing repair. He visits the nearby Home Depot store and picks up an armful of parts and supplies—worth $67—that

he thinks he'll need to do the job. Before he gets to the checkout, a Home Depot salesperson convinces the do-it-yourselfer that there's a simpler solution to his repair problem. The cost: $5.99 and a lot less trouble.

Keeping customers satisfied involves more than simply opening a complaints department, smiling a lot, and being nice. Companies that do the best job of taking care of customers set high customer service standards and often make seemingly outlandish efforts to achieve them.

American Express loves to tell stories about how its people have rescued customers from disasters ranging from civil wars to earthquakes, no matter

(continued)

The Lexus philosophy: Delight a customer and continue to delight that customer, and you will have a customer for life.

approval from management, Dyment hopped on a plane and returned the briefcase. The company named Dyment Employee of the Year. There's no simple formula for taking care of customers, but neither is the process a mystery. According to the president of L.L. Bean, "A lot of people have fancy things to say about customer service . . . but it's just a day-in, day-out, ongoing, never-ending, unremitting, persevering, compassionate type of activity." For the companies that do it well, it's also very rewarding.

Sources: Bill Kelley, "Five Companies That Do It Right—and Make It Pay," *Sales and Marketing Management,* April 1988, pp. 57–64; Patricia Sellers, "Companies That Serve You Best," *Fortune,* 31 May 1993, pp. 74–88; Rahul Jacob, "Why Some Customers Are More Equal Than Others," *Fortune,* 19 September 1994, pp. 215–224; Brian Silverman, "Shopping for Loyal Customers," *Sales and Marketing Management,* March 1995, pp. 96–97; Howard E. Butz, Jr., and Leonard Goodstein, "Measuring Customer Value: Gaining the Strategic Advantage," *Organizational Dynamics,* Winter 1996, pp. 63–77.

what the cost. The company gives cash rewards of up to $1000 to "Great Performers." Four Seasons Hotels, long known for its outstanding service, tells its employees the story of Ron Dyment, a doorman in Toronto who forgot to load a departing guest's briefcase into his taxi. The doorman called the guest, a lawyer in Washington, DC, and learned that he desperately needed the briefcase for a meeting the following morning. Without asking for

The American Customer Satisfaction Index, which tracks customer satisfaction in more than two dozen U.S. manufacturing and service industries, shows that overall customer satisfaction has been declining slightly in recent years.[20] While we don't have an equivalent Canadian service or data, it is reasonable to assume that Canadians perceive a similar general decline in overall customer satisfaction. It is unclear whether this has resulted from a decrease in product and service quality or from an increase in customer expectations. In either case, it presents an opportunity for companies that can consistently deliver superior customer value and satisfaction.

However, although the customer-centred firm seeks to deliver high customer satisfaction compared with its competitors, it does not attempt to *maximize* customer satisfaction. A company can always increase customer satisfaction by lowering its price or increasing its services. But this may result in lower profits. Thus, the purpose of marketing is to generate customer value profitably. This requires a very delicate balance: The marketer must continue to generate more customer value and satisfaction but not as a risk to long-term profitability.

Customer Relationship Levels and Tools Companies can build customer relationships at many levels, depending on the nature of the target market. At one extreme, a company with many low-margin customers may seek to develop *basic relationships* with them. For example, Procter & Gamble does not phone or call on all of its Tide customers to get to know them personally. Instead, P&G creates relationships through brand-building advertising, sales promotions, a 1–800 customer response number, and its Tide Fabric Care Network website.

At the other extreme, in markets with few customers and high margins, sellers want to create *full partnerships* with key customers. For example, P&G customer teams work closely with Wal-Mart, Loblaws, and other large retailers. And Boeing partners with WestJet and other airlines in designing airplanes that fully satisfy their requirements. In between these two extreme situations, other levels of customer relationships are appropriate.

Today, most leading companies are developing customer loyalty and retention programs. Beyond offering consistently high value and satisfaction, marketers can use specific marketing tools to develop stronger bonds with their customers.[21] First, a company might build value and satisfaction by adding financial benefits to the customer relationship. For example, many companies now offer frequency marketing programs that reward customers who buy frequently or in large amounts. Air Canada's Aeroplan program and Shoppers Drug Mart's Optimum Card are examples of what marketers call "loyalty programs."

A second approach is to add *social benefits* as well as financial benefits. Many companies sponsor *club marketing programs* that offer members special discounts and create member communities. Harley-Davidson is one example:

> Harley-Davidson sponsors the Harley Owners Group (H.O.G.), which gives Harley riders "an organized way to share their passion and show their pride." H.O.G. membership benefits include two magazines (*Hog Tales* and *Enthusiast*), a *H.O.G. Touring Handbook,* a roadside assistance program, a specially designed insurance program, theft reward service, a travel center, and a "Fly & Ride" program that enables members to rent Harleys while on vacation. The company also maintains an extensive H.O.G. Web site, which offers information on H.O.G. chapters, rallies, events, and benefits. The worldwide club now numbers more than 1,300 local chapters and 700,000 members.[22]

A third approach to building customer relationships is to add *structural ties* as well as financial and social benefits. For example, a business marketer might supply customers with special equipment or websites that help them manage their orders, payroll, or inventory. McKesson Corporation, a leading pharmaceutical wholesaler, has invested millions of dollars in such linkages. It has set up direct computer links with drug manufacters and an online system to help small pharmacies manage their inventories, their order entry, and their shelf space. Purolator offers Web links to its customers to keep them from defecting to competitors such as UPS. Customers can use the website to arrange shipments and track the status of their packages anywhere in the system.

Building customer relationships: Harley-Davidson sponsors the Harley Owners Group (H.O.G.), which gives Harley owners "an organized way to share their passion and show their pride." The worldwide club now numbers more than 1300 local chapters and 700 000 members.

Partner Relationship Marketing

When it comes to creating customer value and building strong customer relationships, today's marketers know that they can't go it alone. They must work closely with a variety of marketing partners. In addition to being good at *customer relationship management*, marketers must also be good at **partner relationship management**. Major changes are occurring in how marketers partner with others inside and outside the company to jointly bring more value to customers.

> **Partner relationship management** Working closely with partners in other company departments and outside the company to jointly bring greater value to customers.

Partners Inside the Company Traditionally, marketers have been charged with understanding customers and representing customer needs to different company departments. The old thinking was that marketing is done only by marketing, sales, and customer support people. However, in today's more connected world, marketing no longer has sole ownership of customer interactions. Every functional area can interact with customers, especially electronically. The new thinking is that every employee must be customer focused. David Packard, co-founder of Hewlett-Packard, wisely said, "Marketing is far too important to be left only to the marketing department."[23]

Today, rather than letting each department go its own way, firms are linking all departments in the cause of creating customer value. Rather than assigning only sales and marketing people to customers, they are forming cross-functional customer teams. For example, Procter & Gamble assigns "customer development teams" to each of its major retailer accounts. These teams—consisting of sales and marketing people, operations specialists, market and financial analysts, and others—coordinate the efforts of many P&G departments toward helping the retailer be more successful.

Marketing Partners Outside the Firm Changes are also occurring in how marketers connect with their suppliers, channel partners, and even competitors. Most companies today are networked companies, relying heavily on partnerships with other firms.

Marketing channels consist of distributors, retailers, and others who connect the company to its buyers. The *supply chain* describes a longer channel, stretching from raw materials to components to final goods that are carried to final buyers. For example, the supply chain for personal computers consists of suppliers of computer chips and other components, the computer manufacturer, and the distributors, retailers, and websites that sell the computers.

Through *supply chain management*, many companies today are strengthening their connections with partners all along the supply chain. They know that their fortunes rest not just on how well they perform. Success at building customer relationships also rests on how well their entire supply chain performs compared with competitors' supply chains. These companies don't treat suppliers just as vendors and distributors just as customers. They treat both as partners in delivering customer value. On the one hand, for example, Lexus works closely with carefully selected suppliers to improve quality and operations efficiency. On the other hand, it works with its franchise dealers to provide top-grade sales and service support that will bring customers in the door and keep them coming back.

Beyond managing the supply chain, today's companies are also discovering that they need *strategic* partners if they hope to be effective. In the new, more competitive global environment, going it alone is going out of style. *Strategic alliances* are booming across almost all industries and services. For example, Dell Computer ran advertisements telling how it partners with Microsoft and Intel to provide customized e-business solutions. The ads ask: "Why do many corporations choose Windows running on Dell PowerEdge servers with Intel Pentium processors to power their e-business solutions?" The answer: "At Dell, Microsoft, and Intel, we specialize in solving the impossible." As Jim Kelly, former CEO at UPS, puts it, "The old adage 'If you can't beat 'em, join 'em,' is being replaced by 'Join 'em and you can't be beat.'"[24]

CAPTURING VALUE FROM CUSTOMERS

The first four steps in the marketing process involve building customer relationships by creating and delivering superior customer value. The final step involves capturing value in return, in the form of current and future sales, market share, and profits. By creating superior customer value, the firm creates highly satisfied customers who stay loyal and buy more. This, in turn, means greater long-term returns for the firm. Here, we discuss the outcomes of creating customer value: customer loyalty and retention, share of market and share of customer, and customer equity.

Creating Customer Loyalty and Retention

Good customer relationship management creates customer delight. In turn, delighted customers remain loyal and talk favourably to others about the company and its products. Studies show big differences in the loyalty of customers who are less satisfied, somewhat satisfied, and completely satisfied. Even a slight drop from complete satisfaction can create an enormous drop in loyalty. Thus, the aim of customer relationship management is to create not just customer satisfaction, but customer delight.[25]

Companies are realizing that losing a customer means losing more than a single sale. It means losing the **customer lifetime value**; that is, the entire stream of purchases that the customer would make over a lifetime of patronage. Here is a dramatic illustration:

> Stew Leonard, who operates a highly profitable three-store supermarket chain, says that he sees $50,000 flying out of his store every time he sees a sulking customer. Why? Because his average customer spends about $100 a week, shops 50 weeks a year, and remains in the area for about 10 years. If this customer has an unhappy experience and switches to another supermarket, Stew Leonard's has lost $50,000 in revenue. The loss can be much greater if the disappointed customer shares the bad experience with other customers and causes them to defect. To keep customers coming back, Stew Leonard's has created what the *New York Times* has dubbed the "Disneyland of Dairy Stores," complete with costumed characters, scheduled entertainment, a petting zoo, and animatronics throughout the store. From its humble beginnings as a small dairy store in 1969, Stew Leonard's has grown at an amazing pace. It has built 29 additions onto the original store, which now serves more than 250,000 customers each week. This legion of loyal shoppers is largely a result of the store's passionate approach to customer service. Rule #1 at Stew Leonard's—The customer is always right. Rule #2—If the customer is ever wrong, reread rule #1.[26]

Stew Leonard is not alone in assessing customer lifetime value. Lexus estimates that a single satisfied and loyal customer is worth $600 000 in lifetime sales. The customer lifetime value of a Taco Bell customer exceeds $12 000.[27] Thus, working to retain and grow customers makes good economic sense. In fact, a company can lose money on a specific transaction but still benefit greatly from a long-term relationship.

This means that companies must aim high in building customer relationships. Customer delight creates an emotional relationship with a product or service, not just a rational preference. Hanging on to customers is "so basic, it's scary," claims one marketing executive. "We find out what our customers' needs and wants are, and then we overdeliver."[28]

Growing Share of Customer

Beyond simply retaining good customers to capture customer lifetime value, good customer relationship management can help marketers to increase their **share of**

Customer lifetime value The value of the entire stream of purchases that the customer would make over a lifetime of patronage.

Share of customer The portion of the customer's purchasing in its product categories that a company gets.

customer—the portion they get of the customer's purchasing in their product categories. Many marketers are now spending less time figuring out how to increase share of market and more time trying to grow share of customer. Thus, banks want to increase "share of wallet." Supermarkets and restaurants want to get a greater "share of stomach." Car companies want to increase "share of garage" and airlines want greater "share of travel."

To increase share of customer, firms can leverage customer relationships by offering greater variety to their current customers, thus encouraging those customers to purchase more from the firm. Or they can train employees to cross-sell and up-sell in order to sell more to existing customers. For example, Unilever, which for many years marketed a line of soap products under the Dove brand, recently began marketing brand extensions. These include shampoo, conditioner, deodorant, and cosmetics such as anti-aging cream and firming lotions. For every consumer who has been a loyal purchaser of Dove soap and is now able to choose the Dove brand in other product categories, Dove's share of customer has increased.

Building Customer Equity

We can now see the importance of not just acquiring customers, but of keeping and growing them as well. Customer relationship management is oriented toward the long term. Today's smart companies not only want to create profitable customers, they want to "own" them for life, capture their customer lifetime value, and earn a greater share of their purchases.

Customer equity The total combined customer lifetime values of all of the company's customers.

What Is Customer Equity? The ultimate aim of customer relationship management is to produce high *customer equity*.[29] **Customer equity** is the total combined customer lifetime values of all of the company's customers. Clearly, the more loyal the firm's profitable customers, the higher the firm's customer equity. Customer equity may be a better measure of a firm's performance than current sales or market share. Whereas sales and market share reflect the past, customer equity suggests the future. Consider Cadillac:

> In the 1970s and 1980s, Cadillac had some of the most loyal customers in the industry. To an entire generation of car buyers, the name "Cadillac" defined North American luxury. Cadillac's share of the luxury car market reached a whopping 51 percent in 1976. Based on market share and sales, the brand's future looked rosy. However, measures of customer equity would have painted a bleaker picture. Cadillac customers were getting older (average age, 60), and average customer lifetime value was falling. Many Cadillac buyers were on their last car. Thus, although Cadillac's market share was good, its customer equity was not. Compare this with BMW. Its more youthful and vigorous image didn't win BMW the early market share war. However, it did win BMW younger customers with higher customer lifetime values. The result: Cadillac now captures only about a 15 percent market share, lower than BMW's. And BMW's customer equity remains much higher—it has more customers with a higher average customer lifetime value. Thus, market share is not the answer. We should care not just about current sales but also about future sales. Customer lifetime value and customer equity are the name of the game.[30]

Building the Right Relationships with the Right Customers Few firms today still practise true mass marketing—selling in a standardized way to any customer who comes along. Today, most marketers realize that they don't want relationships with every customer. Instead, companies are now targeting fewer, more profitable customers.

Many companies now use customer profitability analysis to weed out losing customers and target winning ones for pampering. Once they identify profitable customers, firms can create attractive offers and special handling to capture these customers and earn their loyalty.

Companies should manage customer equity carefully. They should view customers as assets that need to be managed and maximized. But not all customers, not even all loyal ones, are good investments. Surprisingly, some loyal customers can be unprofitable, and some disloyal customers can be profitable. Which customers should the company acquire and retain? "Up to a point, the choice is obvious: Keep the consistent big spenders and lose the erratic small spenders," says one expert. "But, what about the erratic big spenders and the consistent small spenders? It's often unclear whether they should be acquired or retained, and at what cost."[31]

The company can classify customers according to their potential profitability and manage its relationships with them accordingly. Figure 1.5 classifies customers into one of four relationship groups, according to their profitability and projected loyalty.[32] Each group requires a different relationship management strategy. "Strangers" show low profitability and little projected loyalty. There is little fit between the company's offerings and their needs. The relationship management strategy for these customers is simple: Don't invest anything in them.

Figure 1.5 Customer Relationship Groups

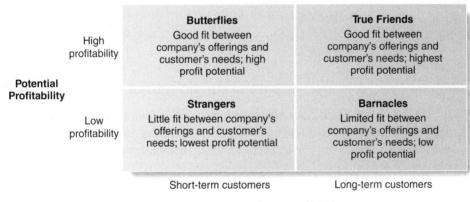

Source: Reprinted by permission of *Harvard Business Review.* Adapted from "The Mismanagement of Customer Loyalty" by Werner Reinartz and V. Kumar, July 2002, p. 93. Copyright © by the president and fellows of Harvard College; all rights reserved.

"Butterflies" are profitable but not loyal. There is a good fit between the company's offerings and their needs. However, like real butterflies, we can enjoy them for only a short while and then they're gone. An example is stock market investors who trade shares often and in large amounts, but who enjoy hunting out the best deals without building a regular relationship with any single brokerage company. Efforts to convert butterflies into loyal customers are rarely successful. Instead, the company should enjoy the butterflies for the moment. It should use promotional blitzes to attract them, create satisfying and profitable transactions with them, and then cease investing in them until the next time around.

"True friends" are both profitable and loyal. There is a strong fit between their needs and the company's offerings. The firm wants to make continuous relationship investments to delight these customers and nurture, retain, and grow them. It wants to turn true friends into "true believers," who come back regularly and tell others about their good experiences with the company.

"Barnacles" are highly loyal but not very profitable. There is a limited fit between their needs and the company's offerings. An example is smaller bank customers who bank regularly but do not generate enough returns to cover the costs of maintaining their accounts. Like barnacles on the hull of a ship, they create drag. Barnacles are per-

IN-CLASS NOTES

The Customer's Experience

- **Customer Perceived Value**
  - Customer's subjective view of the offer's value compared to competitive offers
- **Customer Satisfaction**
  - Customer's subjective view of the value received in return for the purchase price
- **Customer Delight**
  - Customer's subjective view of the increased value received above the purchase price

Linking the Concepts

Take some time to develop *your own* thoughts about marketing.

- In *your own words*, what *is* marketing and what does it seek to accomplish?
- How well does Lexus manage its relationships with customers? What customer relationship management strategy does it use? What relationship management strategy does Wal-Mart use?
- Think of a company for which you are a "true friend." What strategy does this company use to manage its relationship with you?

haps the most problematic customers. The company might be able to improve their profitability by selling them more, raising their fees, or reducing service to them. However, if they cannot be made profitable, they should be "fired."

The point here is an important one: Different types of customers require different relationship management strategies. The goal is to build the *right relationships* with the *right customers*.

THE NEW MARKETING LANDSCAPE

As the world spins through the first decade of the twenty-first century, dramatic changes are occurring in the marketing arena. Richard Love of Hewlett-Packard observes, "The pace of change is so rapid that the ability to change has now become a competitive advantage." Technological advances, rapid globalization, and continuing social and economic shifts—all are causing profound changes in the marketplace. As the marketplace changes, so must those who serve it.

In this section, we examine the major trends and forces that are changing the marketing landscape and challenging marketing strategy. We look at five major developments: new technologies, rapid globalization, the call for more ethics and social responsibility, the growth in not-for-profit marketing, and the new world of marketing relationships.

New Technologies

The explosive growth in computer, telecommunications, information, transportation, and other technologies has had a major impact on the ways companies bring value to their customers. Now, more than ever before, we are all connected to each other and to things near and far in the world around us. Moreover, we are relating in new and different ways. Where it once took weeks or months to travel across Canada, we can now travel around the globe in only hours or days. Where it once took days or weeks to receive news about important world events, we now see them as they are occurring through live satellite broadcasts. Where it once took weeks to correspond with others in distant places, they are now only moments away by phone or the Internet.

Technology has created exciting new ways to learn about and track customers, and to create product offerings that are tailored to individual customer needs. Technology is also helping companies to distribute products more efficiently and effectively. And it's helping them to communicate with customers in large groups or one-to-one. For example, through videoconferencing, marketing researchers at a company's headquarters in Vancouver can look in on focus groups in London or Hong Kong without ever stepping onto a plane. With only a few clicks of a mouse button, a marketer can access an online database and organize a direct mail campaign.

Using today's vastly more powerful computers, marketers create detailed databases and use them to target individual customers with offers designed to meet their specific needs and buying patterns. Technology has also brought a new wave of communication and advertising tools—cell phones, personal communications devices such as the BlackBerry and the iPod, email, and the Web. Marketers can use these tools to more accurately target and reach appropriate market segments with appropriate messages. Through websites, consumers and businesses alike can easily learn about, design, and often order and pay for goods and services online. From virtual reality displays that test new products to online retailers that sell them, the technology boom is affecting every aspect of marketing.

Internet penetration in Canada now tops 64 percent, with some 7.9 million people accessing the Web regularly.[33] Most experts believe that it won't be long before researching shopping purchases and shopping online is as commonplace a consumer phenomenon as watching television. For marketers, this brings opportunities in the form of access to new markets and access to existing markets through new channels. It also brings challenges in the form of understanding and serving a changing market nature.

Today, customer data is collected through electronic cash registers and stored in central databases; banking transactions are recorded electronically and stored indefinitely; airlines and drugstores alike offer member cards and record member transactions; and websites offer benefits to registered visitors who willingly give their contact information in exchange for those benefits. And all that data can be transmitted and accessed with lightning speed, from anywhere in the world, thanks to the Internet. As a result, marketers risk being overwhelmed with data. They face enormous challenges in managing and organizing customer information—and balancing the use of that information with the necessity of protecting customer privacy.

New technologies have had a major impact on the ways marketers connect with and bring value to their customers.

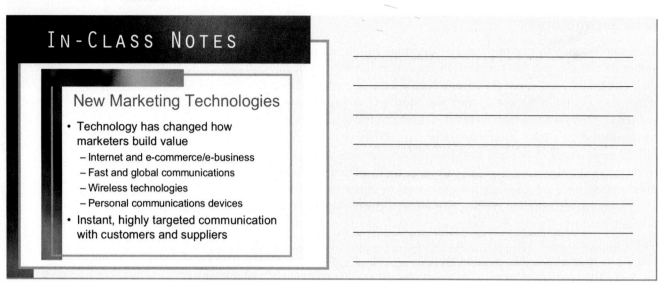

IN-CLASS NOTES

New Marketing Technologies

- Technology has changed how marketers build value
  - Internet and e-commerce/e-business
  - Fast and global communications
  - Wireless technologies
  - Personal communications devices
- Instant, highly targeted communication with customers and suppliers

Technology such as wireless internet, websites, and email makes it easier for marketers to serve customers directly, and to personalize that service. Some marketers envision a day when all buying and selling will involve direct connections between companies and their customers. Others see it as just one more way to approach the marketplace. We will explore the impact of Internet technologies on marketing in more detail in Chapter 13.

Rapid Globalization

As they are redefining their relationships with customers and partners, marketers are also taking a fresh look at the ways in which they connect with the broader world around them. In an increasingly smaller world, many marketers are now connected *globally* with their customers and marketing partners.

The world economy has undergone radical change during the past two decades. Geographical and cultural distances have shrunk with the advent of jet planes, fax machines, world satellite television broadcasts, global Internet hookups, and other technical advances. This has allowed companies to greatly expand their geographical market coverage, purchasing, and manufacturing. The result is a vastly more complex marketing environment for both companies and consumers.

International trade is booming. Since 1969, the number of multinational corporations in the world's 14 richest countries has more than tripled, from 7000 to 24 000. Experts predict that, by 2005, world exports of goods and services will have reached 28 percent of world gross domestic product, up from only 9 percent 20 years ago. With $412 billion in exports of goods and services in 1999, Canada is one of the world's leading trading nations and the most export-oriented of the G–8 industrialized economies. In fact, one in three jobs in Canada is tied to trade. We export more, proportionally, than the United States or Japan. More than 43 percent of Canada's GDP is linked to trade. With the projected increase in exports, soon half of Canada's output will be sent overseas. Compare these figures with those of the United States, where international trade now accounts for a quarter of GDP. Although Canadian companies have long been criticized for depending excessively on the easily accessible U.S. market, more firms are broadening their trade horizons. Companies exporting to both the U.S. *and* other countries increased by 53 percent in 2000.[34]

Today, almost every company, large or small, is touched in some way by global competition. A neighbourhood florist buys its flowers from Mexican nurseries, while a large

Canadian electronics manufacturer competes in its home markets with giant Japanese rivals. A fledgling Internet retailer finds itself receiving orders from all over the world at the same time that a Canadian consumer-goods producer introduces new products into emerging markets abroad.

Canadian firms have been challenged at home by the skillful marketing of European and Asian multinationals. Companies such as Toyota, Siemens, Nestlé, Sony, and Samsung have often outperformed their competitors in domestic markets. Similarly, Canadian companies in a wide range of industries have found new opportunities abroad. McCain's Foods, Bombardier, IBM, General Electric, SNC Lavalin, Alcan, Magna International, and dozens of other Canadian companies have developed truly global operations, making and selling their products worldwide. Coca-Cola offers a mind-boggling 300 different brands in more than 200 countries.

Today, companies are not only trying to sell more of their locally produced goods in international markets, but are also buying more supplies and components abroad. For example, Denis Gagnon, one of Canada's top fashion designers, may choose leather and cloth from different parts of the world. He will design a pair of pants and jacket and then email the drawings to a Hong Kong agent, who will place the order with a Chinese factory. Finished collections will be air-freighted to Toronto, where they will be shown on Canadian fashion runways, eventually manufactured, and finally distributed to specialty stores around the country.

The longer companies delay taking steps toward internationalizing, the more they risk being shut out of growing markets in Western Europe, Eastern Europe, the Pacific Rim, and elsewhere. All companies first have to answer some basic questions: What market position should we try to establish in our country, in our economic region, and globally? Who will our global competitors be and what are their strategies and resources? Where should we produce or source our products? What strategic alliances should we form with other firms around the world?

Many American companies have developed truly global operations. Coca-Cola offers more than 300 different brands in more than 200 countries including BPM Energy drink in Ireland, Mare Rosso Bitter in Spain, Sprite Ice Cube in Belgium, Fanta in Chile, and NaturAqua in Hungary.

Although the need for companies to go abroad is great, so are the risks. Companies that go global confront several major problems. High debt, inflation, and unemployment in many countries have resulted in highly unstable governments and currencies, which limits trade and exposes global firms to many risks. For example, in 1998 Russia created a global economic crisis when it devalued the ruble, effectively defaulting on its global debts. A more widespread Asian economic downturn had a far-reaching impact on Western firms with significant markets or investments there.

Governments are placing more regulations on foreign firms, such as requiring joint ownership with domestic partners, mandating the hiring of nationals, and limiting profits that can be taken from the country. Moreover, foreign governments often impose high tariffs or trade barriers to protect their own industries. Finally, corruption is an increasing problem: Officials in several countries often award business not to the best bidder but to the highest briber.

Global industry An industry in which the strategic positions of competitors in given geographic or national markets are affected by their overall global positions.

Global firm A firm that, by operating in more than one country, gains R&D, production, marketing, and financial advantages that are not available to purely domestic competitors.

Still, companies selling in global industries have no choice but to internationalize their operations. A **global industry** is one in which the competitive positions of firms in given local or national markets are affected by their global positions. A **global firm** is one that, by operating in more than one country, gains marketing, production, R&D, and financial advantages that are not available to purely domestic competitors. The global company sees the world as one market. It minimizes the importance of national boundaries and raises capital, obtains materials and components, and manufactures and markets its goods wherever it can do the best job. Global firms gain advantages by planning, operating, and coordinating their activities worldwide. For example, Ford's "world truck" sports a cab made in Europe and a chassis built in Canada; it is assembled in Brazil and imported to the United States for sale. Otis Elevator gets its elevator-door systems from France, small geared parts from Spain, electronics from Germany, and special motor drives from Japan. It uses the United States only for systems integration.

Because firms around the world are going global at a rapid rate, domestic firms in global industries must act quickly before the window closes. This does not mean that small and medium-sized firms must operate in a dozen countries to succeed; these firms can practise global niching. In fact, companies marketing on the Internet may find themselves going global whether they intend it or not. But the world is shrinking, and every company operating in a global industry, whether large or small, must assess and establish its place in world markets.

Thus, managers in countries around the world are increasingly taking a global, not just local, view of the company's industry, competitors, and opportunities. They are asking: What is global marketing? How does it differ from domestic marketing? How do global competitors and forces affect our business? To what extent should we "go global"? Many companies are forming strategic alliances with foreign companies, even competitors, who serve as suppliers or marketing partners. Winning companies in the next century may well be those that have built the best global networks. We will discuss the global marketplace in various chapters throughout the book.

The Call for More Ethics and Social Responsibility

Marketers are re-examining their relationships with social values and responsibilities and with the very earth that sustains us. As the worldwide consumerism and environmentalism movements mature, today's marketers are being called upon to take greater responsibility for the social and environmental impacts of their actions. Corporate ethics and social responsibility have become hot topics for almost every business. And few companies can ignore the renewed and very demanding environmental movement.

The social-responsibility and environmental movements will place even stricter demands on companies in the future. Some companies resist these movements, budg-

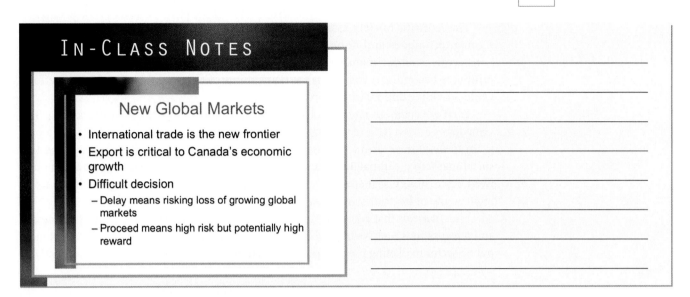

IN-CLASS NOTES

New Global Markets

- International trade is the new frontier
- Export is critical to Canada's economic growth
- Difficult decision
  - Delay means risking loss of growing global markets
  - Proceed means high risk but potentially high reward

ing only when forced to by legislation or organized consumer outcries. More forward-looking companies, however, readily accept their responsibilities to the world around them. They view socially responsible actions as an opportunity to do well by doing good. They seek ways to profit by serving the best long-run interests of their customers and communities.

Some companies—such as Vancity Credit Union, John Fluevog, Saturn, Wal-Mart, Telus, the Royal Bank, and others—are practising "caring capitalism" and distinguishing themselves by being more civic-minded and caring. They are following the societal marketing concept by building social responsibility and action into their company value and mission statements. For example, consider Vancity Credit Union in Vancouver, named by a *Maclean's* magazine survey as "Best Employer in Canada" in 2004. Its mission statement makes clear its commitment to linking strong business performance to community health: "To be a democratic, ethical, and innovative provider of financial services to our members. Through strong financial performance, we serve as a catalyst for the self-reliance and economic well-being of our membership and community." [35] We will revisit the relationship between marketing and social responsibility in greater detail in Chapter 3.

The Growth of Not-for-Profit Marketing

In the past, marketing has been most widely applied in the for-profit business sector. In recent years, however, marketing has also become a major part of the strategies of many not-for-profit organizations. Many different kinds of organizations, such as colleges and universities, hospitals, museums, symphony orchestras, and even churches, are using marketing to connect with customers and other important constituencies.

In 2003, according to the Canadian Centre for Philanthropy (now known as Imagine Canada), Canada had 161 000 incorporated and registered charities and nonprofit organizations. [36] These range from small community-based organizations such as the Brockville Volunteer Firefighters Association to large national charities such as the United Way and the Heart and Stroke Foundation. With cutbacks in government funding, competition for donors is intensifying and nonprofit organizations are adopting more marketing practices. Some are building alliances. Witness the birth in 1998 of the Girl Child Network, a joint initiative funded by World Vision Canada, Foster Parents Plan of Canada, Christian Children's Fund of Canada, and Save the Children. The four organizations shared costs on a mass-market advertising campaign to address global issues that specifically affect young girls: child prostitution, child labour, and female genital mutilation.

The Arthritis Society, Care Canada, and other charities are turning to the data-mining techniques and donor lifetime value analysis used by for-profit firms. Kelly Ducharme, database manager at Care Canada's Ottawa headquarters, notes that data mining is becoming a trend since it helps nonprofits target their fundraising efforts while providing donors with more accountability.

Even government agencies are showing an increased interest in marketing. The Canadian Forces have a marketing plan to attract recruits; Transport Canada has a program to discourage drunk driving; and Health and Welfare Canada has long-standing social marketing campaigns to discourage smoking, excessive drinking, and drug use. Even once-stodgy Canada Post has developed innovative marketing programs to increase use of its priority mail services.

Thus, it seems that every type of organization can connect with the people, businesses, and organizations it serves through marketing. And the continued growth of nonprofit and public-sector marketing presents new and exciting challenges for marketing managers.

The New World of Marketing Relationships

As our discussion of the marketing process suggests, the major new developments in marketing can be summed up in a single word: *relationships*. Today, smart marketers of all kinds are taking advantage of new opportunities for building relationships with their customers, their marketing partners, and the world around them. Table 1.1 compares the old marketing thinking with the new. The old marketing thinking saw marketing as little more than selling or advertising. It viewed marketing as customer acquisition rather than customer care. It emphasized trying to make a profit on each sale rather than trying to profit by managing long-term customer equity. And it concerned itself with trying to sell products rather than trying to understand, create, communicate, and deliver real value to customers.

Fortunately, this old marketing thinking is now giving way to newer ways of thinking. Modern organizations are improving their customer knowledge and customer relationships. They are targeting profitable customers, then finding innovative ways to capture and keep these customers. They are forming more-direct connections with customers and building lasting customer relationships. Using more-targeted media and integrating their marketing communications, they are delivering meaningful and consistent messages through every customer contact. They are employing more technologies such as videoconferencing, sales automation software, CRM systems, and the Internet. They view their suppliers and distributors as partners, not adversaries. In sum, today's companies are connecting in new ways to deliver superior value to and build relationships with their customers.

SO, WHAT IS MARKETING? PULLING IT ALL TOGETHER

At the start of this chapter, Figure 1.1 presented a simple model of the marketing process. Now that we've discussed all of the steps in the model, Figure 1.6 presents an expanded model that will help you pull it all together. What is marketing? Simply put, marketing is the process of building profitable customer relationships by creating value for customers and capturing value in return.

The first four steps of the marketing process focus on creating value for customers. The company starts by researching the needs and wants of the target market, and managing marketing information to gain a full understanding of the marketplace. It then designs a customer-driven marketing strategy based on the answers to two simple questions. The first question is "What market segments will we serve?" (market segmentation and targeting). Good marketers know that they cannot serve all segments of the market

Table 1.1   Marketing Relationships in Transition

	The Old Marketing Thinking	The New Marketing Thinking
Relationships with Customers	Be sales and product centred	Be market and customer centred
	Practise mass marketing	Target selected market segments or individuals
	Focus on products and sales	Focus on customer satisfaction and value
	Make sales to customers	Develop customer relationships
	Get new customers	Keep old customers
	Grow share of market	Grow share of customer
	Serve any customer	Serve profitable customers, "fire" losing ones
	Communicate through mass media	Connect with customers directly
	Make standardized products	Develop customized products
Relationships with Marketing Partners	Leave customer satisfaction and value to sales and marketing	Enlist all departments in the cause of customer satisfaction and value
	Go it alone	Partner with other firms
Relationships with the World Around Us	Market locally	Market locally *and* globally
	Assume profit responsibility	Assume social and environmental responsibility
	Market for profits	Market for nonprofits
	Conduct commerce in market*places*	Conduct e-commerce in market*spaces*

in every way. They need to focus their resources on those segments they can serve best and most profitably. The second marketing strategy question is "How can we serve our target market segments better than our competitors?" (differentiation and positioning). Here, the marketer outlines a value proposition that spells out what benefits and values the company will deliver in order to win customers.

With its marketing strategy decided, the company now constructs a marketing program—consisting of the four marketing mix elements, or the four Ps—that transforms the marketing strategy into real value for customers. The company develops product offers and creates strong brand identities for them. It prices these offers to create real customer value and distributes the offers to make them available to the market. Finally, the company develops promotion programs that communicate the value proposition to the target market segments and persuade them to act on the marketing offer.

Perhaps the most important step in the marketing process involves building value-laden, profitable relationships with target customers. Throughout the process, marketers practise customer relationship management to create customer satisfaction and delight. In creating customer value and relationships, however, today's outstanding companies know that they cannot go it alone. They must work closely with marketing partners inside the company and throughout the marketing system. Thus, in addition to practising good customer relationship management, firms must also practise good partner relationship management.

The first four steps in the marketing process create value *for* customers. In the final step, the company reaps the rewards of the strong customer relationships by capturing value *from* customers. Delivering superior customer value creates highly satisfied cus-

Figure 1.6   An Expanded Model of the Marketing Process

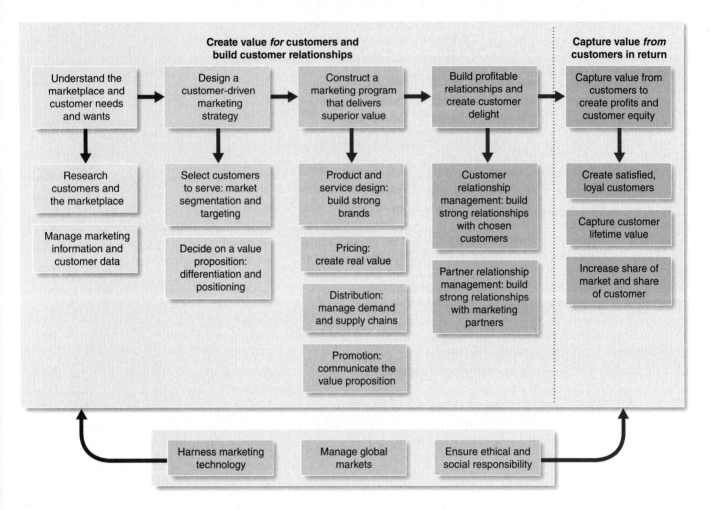

tomers who will buy more and will buy again. This helps the company to capture customer lifetime value and a greater share of customer. The result is increased long-term customer equity for the firm.

Finally, in the face of today's changing marketing landscape, companies must take into account three additional factors. In building customer and partner relationships, they must harness technology, take advantage of global opportunities, and ensure that they act in an ethical and socially responsible way.

Figure 1.6 provides a good roadmap to future chapters of the text. Chapters 1 and 2 introduce the marketing process, with a focus on perhaps the most important steps—building customer relationships and capturing value from customers. These steps result from and provide a guiding framework for the earlier steps. Chapter 3 examines marketing ethics and social responsibility. Chapters 4, 5, and 6 address the first step of the marketing process—understanding the marketing environment, managing marketing information, and understanding buyer behaviour. In Chapter 7, we look more deeply into the two major marketing strategy decisions: selecting which markets to serve (segmentation and targeting) and deciding on a value proposition (differentiation and positioning). Chapters 8 through 12 discuss the marketing mix variables, one by one. Finally, Chapter 13 examines marketing and the Internet. So, here we go, down the road to learning marketing.

LOOKING BACK

Today's successful companies—whether large or small, for-profit or not-for-profit, domestic or global—share a strong customer focus and a heavy commitment to marketing. The goal of marketing is to build and manage profitable customer relationships. Marketing seeks to attract new customers by promising superior value and to keep and grow current customers by delivering satisfaction. Marketing operates within a dynamic environment, which can quickly make yesterday's winning strategies obsolete. To be successful, companies will have to be strongly customer focused.

REVIEWING THE CONCEPTS

1. Define marketing and outline the steps in the marketing process.

Marketing is a social and managerial process whereby individuals and groups obtain what they need and want through creating and exchanging products and value with others. More simply, it's managing profitable customer relationships.

The marketing process involves five steps. The first four steps create value *for* customers. First, marketers need to understand the marketplace and customer needs and wants. Next, marketers design a customer-driven marketing strategy with the goal of getting, keeping, and growing target customers. In the third step, marketers construct a marketing program that actually delivers superior value. All of these steps form the basis for the fourth step, building profitable customer relationships and creating customer delight. In the final step, the company reaps the rewards of the strong customer relationships by capturing value *from* customers.

2. Explain the importance of understanding customers and the marketplace, and identify the five core marketplace concepts.

Outstanding marketing companies go to great lengths to learn about and understand their customers' needs, wants, and demands. This understanding helps them design want-satisfying marketing offers and build value-laden customer relationships by which they can capture customer lifetime value and greater share of customer. The result is increased long-term customer equity for the firm.

The core marketplace concepts are *needs, wants,* and *demands; marketing offers (goods, services, and experi-*

ences); value and *satisfaction; exchange, transactions,* and *relationships;* and *markets. Wants* are the form taken by human needs when shaped by culture and individual personality. When backed by buying power, wants become *demands.* Companies address needs by putting forth a *value proposition,* a set of benefits that they promise. The value proposition is fulfilled through a *marketing offer,* which delivers customer value and satisfaction, resulting in long-term exchange relationships with customers.

3. Identify the key elements of a customer-driven marketing strategy, and discuss the marketing management orientations that guide marketing strategy.

To design a winning marketing strategy, the company must first decide *who* it will serve. It does this by dividing the market into segments of customers (*market segmentation*) and selecting which segments it will cultivate (*target marketing*). Next, the company must decide *how* it will serve targeted customers (how it will *differentiate and position* itself in the marketplace).

Marketing management can adopt one of five competing market orientations. The *production concept* holds that management's task is to improve production efficiency and bring down prices. The *product concept* holds that buyers favour products that offer the most in quality, performance, and innovative features; thus, little promotional effort is required. The *selling concept* holds that buyers will not buy enough of the organization's products unless it undertakes a large-scale selling and promotion effort. The *marketing concept* holds that achieving organizational goals depends on determining the needs and wants of target markets and delivering the desired satisfactions more effectively and efficiently than competitors do. The *societal marketing concept* holds that generating customer satisfaction *and* long-run societal well-being are the keys to both achieving the company's goals and fulfilling its responsibilities.

4. Discuss customer relationship management, and identify strategies for creating value *for* customers and capturing value *from* customers in return.

Broadly defined, customer relationship management is the overall process of building and maintaining profitable customer relationships by delivering superior customer value and satisfaction. The aim of customer relationship management is to produce high customer equity, the total combined customer lifetime values of all of the company's customers.

The key to building lasting relationships is the creation of superior *customer value* and *satisfaction*, and companies need to understand the determinants of these important elements. *Customer perceived value* is the difference between total customer value and total customer cost. Customers will usually choose the offer that maximizes their perceived value. *Customer satisfaction* results when a company's performance has fulfilled a buyer's expectations. Customers are dissatisfied if performance is below expectations, satisfied if performance equals expectations, and delighted if performance exceeds expectations. Highly satisfied customers buy more, are less price sensitive, talk favourably about the company, and remain loyal longer.

Companies want not only to acquire profitable customers, but to build relationships that will keep them and grow "share of customer." Companies must decide the level at which they want to build relationships with different market segments and individual customers, ranging from basic relationships to full partnerships. Today's marketers use a number of specific marketing tools to develop stronger bonds with customers by adding *financial* and *social benefits* or *structural ties*. Different types of customers require different customer relationship management strategies. The marketer's aim is to build the *right relationships* with the *right customers*. In return for creating value *for* targeted customers, the company captures value *from* customers in the form of profits and customer equity.

In building customer relationships, good marketers realize that they cannot go it alone. They must work closely with marketing partners inside and outside the company. In addition to being good at customer relationship management, they must also be good at *partner relationship management*.

5. Describe the major trends and forces that are changing the marketing landscape in this new age of relationships.

The explosive growth in computer, telecommunications, information, transportation, and other technologies has had a major impact on marketing. The technology boom has created exciting new ways to learn about and track customers, and to create goods and services tailored to individual customer needs.

In an increasingly smaller world, many marketers are now connected *globally* with their customers and marketing partners. Today, almost every company, large or small, is touched in some way by global competition. Thus, managers in countries around the world are increasingly taking a global, not just local, view of the company's industry, competitors, and opportunities.

Today's marketers are also re-examining their social values and societal responsibilities. As the world-wide consumerism and environmentalism movements mature, marketers are being called upon to take greater responsibility for the social and environmental impacts of their actions. Corporate ethics and social responsibility have become hot topics for almost every business. And few companies can ignore the renewed and very demanding environmental movement.

In the past, marketing has been most widely applied in the for-profit business sector. In recent years, however, marketing also has become a major part of the strategies of many not-for-profit organizations, such as colleges, hospitals, museums, symphony orchestras, and even churches. Finally, as discussed throughout the chapter, the major new developments in marketing can be summed up in a single word: *relationships*. Today, smart marketers of all kinds are taking advantage of new opportunities for building relationships with their customers, their marketing partners, and the world around them.

KEY TERMS

customer equity *26*
customer lifetime value *25*
customer perceived value *20*
customer relationship
  management *19*
customer satisfaction *20*
demands *8*
demarketing *13*
exchange *10*

global firm *32*
global industry *32*
market *10*
marketing *7*
marketing concept *15*
marketing management *13*
marketing offer *9*
needs *8*

partner relationship
  management *24*
product concept *15*
production concept *14*
selling concept *15*
share of customer *25*
societal marketing concept *17*
transaction *10*
wants *8*

STUDY GUIDE

After completing this self-test, check your answers against the Answer Key at the back of the book.

MULTIPLE CHOICE

1. A recent TV commercial features a group of oil industry executives questioning the wisdom of their CEO in purchasing a large tract of corn-growing land when their business is refining crude oil. The CEO points out that they are in the energy business, not the carbon-based oil business, and that corn-based fuels are the future. His executive team was making what marketing error?
   a. Marketing myopia
   b. Production concept marketing
   c. Latent marketing
   d. Customer disenfranchisement
   e. Short-range value delivery

2. McDonald's has always done a good job of delivering the product that its consumers want—fast, inexpensive, tasty food—even if what the consumers want isn't very good for their health. McDonald's has now modified its marketing approach by creating new offerings that are lighter and healthier. Increasingly, McDonald's is moving toward
   a. Customer fulfillment
   b. Long-range value delivery
   c. Societal marketing
   d. Non-profit-driven marketing
   e. Positioning

3. Lester Wunderman, one of the gurus of direct marketing, noted that "The chant of the Industrial Revolution was that of the manufacturer who said 'This is what I make, won't you buy it.' The call of the Information Age is the consumer asking, 'This is what I want, won't you please make it.'" Wunderman's observation can be best related to the contrasting ideas of
   a. Factory manufacturing vs. customized manufacturing
   b. Profit-driven marketing vs. altruistic marketing
   c. Inventory vs. just-in-time delivery
   d. Inside-out marketing vs. outside-in marketing
   e. Undifferentiated vs. differentiated marketing

4. As a product, the experience of a visit to Disney World is compelling and of real value. Ticket packages are flexible and affordable for most families. Ticket packages are easily purchased by phone or online, and regular flights and easy airport shuttles make the location easily accessible. Consistent advertising and sales promotions help generate interest in trips to Disney World. Disney World has skillfully used _____ to create a compelling position.
   a. The marketing mix
   b. Departmental planning
   c. The product-market expansion grid
   d. Customer relationship management
   e. Niche marketing

5. The leaky bucket approach to marketing holds that a company can keep attracting new customers constantly in a growing market and therefore does not have to worry about losing unhappy customers. This approach no longer works largely because
   a. There are too many companies in each market competing for the same customers
   b. Changing demographics have created more differentiated segments
   c. Competitors are increasingly more sophisticated
   d. Markets are flat or shrinking
   e. All of the above

6. Marketing concept-oriented companies strive for high customer value and satisfaction. However, despite this strong emphasis on customer experience, most companies steer clear of _____ in order to ensure ongoing profitability.
   a. Delivering customer delight
   b. Maximizing customer satisfaction
   c. Investing in customer relationship management systems
   d. Value-based pricing
   e. Warranties

7. International trade is critical to a country's economic growth. Canada is the most export-oriented of the G8 countries, with international trade comprising 43 percent of Canada's GDP and accounting for 30 percent of all jobs. For Canadian companies, the major drawback to delaying the decision to market and sell globally is
   a. The risk of being shut out of growing global markets
   b. The inability to take advantage of lucrative tax concessions
   c. The inability to pay globally competitive wages and salaries
   d. Unavailability of raw materials
   e. Higher import costs

8. Technology has had a huge impact on how marketing is practised and how companies build and nurture relationships with customers. Brick-and-mortar companies are increasingly becoming click and mortar, combining traditional methods of distribution with Internet-based selling. Of particular note, the Internet has caused a major resurgence of what type of promotional marketing technique?
   a. Mass marketing
   b. Loss leader pricing
   c. No-return exchange policies
   d. Direct marketing/direct mail
   e. Undifferentiated marketing

9. Newly graduated health professionals often receive financial aid in buying equipment for their offices from companies that make the kind of products these professionals would regularly recommend or prescribe. The practitioner can either repay the financial aid in straight monies or through prescriptions, purchases etc. This latter route is typical of creating a long-term customer/supplier relationship through
   a. Coercion
   b. Debt restructuring
   c. Structural ties
   d. Supplication
   e. None of the above

10. Very successful companies take marketing concept approach a step further by striving to deliver new, innovative products to customers before customers ask. As one corporate leader observed, his company "leads customers to where they want to go before they know where they want to go." This type of marketing approach is known as
    a. Customer-driven marketing
    b. Personal marketing
    c. Formulated marketing
    d. New product marketing
    e. Co-founded marketing

TRUE/FALSE

T F 1. Companies who band with their competitors to take advantage of customers through price fixing and collusion are guilty of demarketing.

T F 2. There are no circumstances in modern marketing in which companies would or should choose to practise production, product, or selling concept marketing.

T F 3. While a customer-driven approach to marketing can be highly successful, it could be said that in some cases this approach creates false wants that unfairly target susceptible customers.

T F 4. Partnerships between the various departments of an organization are no longer as important in building strong customer relationships. In recent years, more and more responsibility for customer satisfaction and value has moved to marketing and sales departments.

T F 5. Some companies today rid themselves of low-spending customers because the lifetime value of those customers is less than the total cost of servicing them.

CONCEPT CHECK

1. _____ is a social and managerial process whereby individuals and groups obtain what they need and want through creating and exchanging products and value with others.

2. Today, marketing must be understood not in the old sense of making a sale—"telling and selling"—but in the new sense of _____.

3. The concept of _____ is not limited to physical objects—anything capable of satisfying a need can be called a _____.

4. _____ is the difference between the benefits the customer gains from owning and using a product and the costs of obtaining the product.

5. Smart companies aim to _____ customers by promising only what they can deliver and delivering more than they promise.

6. The goal of _____ is to deliver long-term value to customers, and the measures of success are long-term customer satisfaction and retention.

7. A _____ is the set of actual and potential buyers of a product.

8. There are five alternative concepts under which organizations conduct their marketing activities: they are the _____, _____, _____, _____, and _____ concepts.

9. "We make it happen for you," "To fly, to serve," "We're not satisfied until you are," and "Let us exceed your expectations" are all colourful illustrations of the _____ concept.

10. The major force behind the new connectedness in the "connected" world is _____.

STUDENT MATERIALS

Visit our website at www.pearsoned.ca/armstrong for online quizzes, Internet exercises, and more!

DISCUSSING THE ISSUES

1. Why is understanding customer wants so critical for marketers? How are the concepts of value and satisfaction related to each other? Explain the difference between transactions and relationships.

2. Why is target-market selection important for a customer-driven marketing strategy? Discuss some of the negative consequences a company might incur from not paying enough attention to selecting its target market.

3. Discuss the differences between the production, product, selling, marketing, and societal marketing concepts. Identify circumstances where each one may be appropriate.

4. What are the advantages for a company in building relationships with its customers? What are some ways in which a company can build customer relationships?

5. Discuss the potential for technological advances and globalization to change the manner in which companies interact with their customers and business partners.

6. Think of a company in your town or neighbourhood with which you have a relationship. What value do you get from that relationship and how does that company capture value from you in return?

MARKETING APPLICATIONS

One of the most loyal but hard-to-reach markets is the skateboarder segment. Of all the clothing and tennis shoe manufacturers, only California-based Vans, Inc. has really been successful in reaching the mostly male children and teens who constitute this market segment. Vans noticed that skateboarding has come a long way from the days when kids made a board by nailing a pair of roller-skates to the bottom of a wooden plank. By pioneering thick-soled, slip-on sneakers that can absorb the shock of 1-m to 1.5-m leaps, Vans has remained cool with the skateboard crowd. The problem is, how can Vans grow its market when the target customers are part of an outlaw culture that has been banned from most modern malls, shopping centres, city streets, and most public places? Vans believes that branching out into elaborate skateboard parks (eight have opened at the very malls that have banned skateboarders), designing clothing lines, and manufacturing snowboard boots and boots for various riding activities will be the strategies that will serve them well in the next decade. Using its own branded 140 retail stores as well as a number of independents, Vans has carved out a 1 percent to 2 percent share of the giant sneakers market in the United States.

In Canada, Vans has targeted independent retailers that cater to their youthful and adventurous target market, such as Antisocial, Comor Sports, Pacific Snowboarder,

and Snowcovers in Vancouver; Mike E's Skateboard Shop, Sporting Life, and Olly Shoes in Toronto; and Spin, Diz, Street and Snow, and Underworld Skate Shop in Montreal.

Though not exactly a Nike (which owns more than 50 percent of this lucrative market), Vans is betting its future on a plan that will position them in the growing number of "extreme" sports. However, one area that Vans is avoiding is inline skating, since most Vans loyalists and skateboard enthusiasts consider this a sport for "wimps." Therefore, it appears that the main guiding principle for Vans' strategic positioning in the future will be to remain authentic and loyal to their roots.

THINKING LIKE A MARKETING MANAGER

1. What elements of the marketing concept does Vans appear to be applying with their strategies?

2. Go to a retail outlet that carries Vans shoes, or go online to www.vans.com, and review their product lines. What seem to be the advantages and the disadvantages of products they sell? After considering Vans' target market and its outlaw image, what do you think would be the best way to reach this market in Canada? Is Vans on the right track in using a highly focused distribution strategy with independent retailers or should it consider the U.S. concept of Vans branded retail outlets?

3. It has been reported that Vans is now attempting to reach the female market with its clothing line. Present three relationship- or value-oriented strategies that you believe might help it to accomplish this goal.

4. Keeping in mind the marketing concept, relationship marketing, and customer value, design a strategy to help Vans enter the snowboard market with a line of snowboard boots. How will industry leader Burton Snowboards (www.burton.com) likely react to Vans' entry and strategy? How would you deal with this reaction? Present your strategy and ideas to the class.

VIDEO CASE

Go to Pearson Canada's Video Central site (www.pearsoned.ca/highered/videocentral) to view the video and accompanying case for this chapter.

CASE 1   THE SELF-SERVE SOCIETY

It is now possible to buy an airline ticket online from your home in Toronto, then check in at an automated kiosk at Pearson International and fly to Vancouver. For your return flight, you can check in at the Fairmont Vancouver Airport Hotel using the self-serve kiosk and fly back to Toronto—all without ever having to speak to another human being. Is this an unusual situation? There was a time not many years ago when this kind of technology was only in the realm of science fiction.

For better or worse, self-service technology is here. The irony of the foregoing example is obvious—the travel and hospitality industry, traditionally based on high levels of personal customer service, is now indicating that they'd rather have customers fend for themselves. From an overall marketing perspective, how far can we go with the technology and at what cost to relationship building?

One of the major enablers of the technology is *Interac*. This organization was created in the mid 1980s as a cooperative venture among five Canadian financial institutions: Royal Bank, CIBC, Scotiabank, TD Bank, and La Confédération des caisses Desjardins du Québec. It is the network that allows Canadians to access funds (called Shared Cash Dispensing, or SCD) from automated bank machines (ABMs) across the country. By 1986, the association had grown to 10 members, including the Bank of Montreal and Credit Union Central. Based on the success of the initial service, the association then launched *Interac* Direct Payment (IDP), Canada's national debit card service. IDP has surpassed cash as the preferred payment method for Canadians. A report by the Strategic Council for the *Interac* Association showed that 85 percent of Canadians use a bank card to make automated transactions. In 2002, Canadians used the Interac service 2.4 billion times at 40 000 ABMs and other self-serve locations. And at 54.3 transactions per capita (compared with only 27.5 per capita in the U.S.), Canada leads the world in the use of debit payments and automated bank machines.

Who would have guessed that ABMs would be so pervasive? And today, banks aren't the only ones offering self-service. The technology is now available at gas stations, movie theatres, and libraries. In Ontario, citizens can even use self-serve kiosks to buy various licences from the provincial government.

Famous Players Theatres uses 1000 self-serve ticket dispensers across Canada in their theatres. According to Andrew Sherbin, manager of corporate affairs for Famous Players Theatres, "Guests appreciate the convenience." One-third of the theatre chain's customers use the self-serve kiosks, which in some cases look like aliens, a distinguished character from the Ming Dynasty, or an Egyptian mummy.

Much of the enabling technology behind these electronic "line busters" is available from The Kiosk Factory in Toronto. The company is an innovative designer and builder of high-quality kiosks and interactive POP displays. It specializes in solving problems associated with customer service, customer access, and information presentation. The products and technology offered range from heavy-duty kiosks for demanding public environments such as theatres and malls to high-visibility, interactive point of sale displays for retailers.

The company's success, and the growth of the self-serve society, are based on a simple fact: "People don't like lines," states Robert Machen, vice-president of Customer-facing Technology at Hilton Hotels. And pilot projects of automated check-in services at hotels in New York and Chicago have also helped reduced lineup times.

Other applications of the company's technology are available in Ontario's electric power plants, where the company has installed shop-floor database access kiosks. Other installations include health education kiosks in public health centres, student access kiosks for Canadian and U.S. universities, library book checkout machines for Canadian and U.S. libraries, and historical exhibits in Toronto's Fort York. In the spring of 2004 the company unveiled a custom simulator housing for the new Air and Space Museum in Washington, D.C.

What are the future possibilities for this technology? Could fast food providers such as McDonald's ever go self-serve? The concept could be as simple as turning the cash register around. By reducing the number of items available to the customer and reorganizing the cash register facade, anyone could order their own Happy Meal. Could Starbuck's or Second Cup be candidates for self-serve? Julian Bowron of the Kiosk Factory thinks so. "By our estimates, the vast majority—75 percent—of people would settle for a narrower range of menu options in exchange for speed." So, an automated self-serve line could be the next new thing at your favourite coffee shop.

How about the grocery store? At selected Loblaws stores, self-serve checkout lanes are available. You simply pass your packages over the bar-code scanner, which reads the codes on your packages. You can even check out fresh produce by weighing the items and using a keypad on the self-service screen to identify the type of produce. The machine then calculates the cost of your purchases and communicates it to you. Your final step is to swipe your credit/debit card or insert cash in the checkout machine, and then you're away in less time than it would take to use the typical checkout service.

To suggest we have some confusing and conflicting social trends is understating the obvious. On the one hand is the self-serve revolution where consumers are willing to make sacrifices for quicker service, and on the other hand are consumers seeking to be pampered in indulgent, time-consuming experiences—for example, witness the growth of spas in the last five years.

Many experts agree that the self-serve society will expand much further in the coming years: not because of the technology, but because it provides a level of independence for the consumer.

Questions

1. Does the marketing concept apply to organizations that rely on self-service for a high proportion of transactions?

2. Is it possible for self-serve based organizations to create customer value? If so, what value(s) can be created?

3. How do companies with significant levels of self-service exemplify a new model of connecting with customers, as explained in this chapter?

4. Take the position of a company such as the Kiosk Factory. What would be an industry that you would target for integrating self-serve technology?

Sources: S. Agrell, "Farewell to Full Serve," *National Post,* October 23, 2004, pp. RB1–RB4; "Kissimmee Counts on Kiosks to Extend Online Capabilities," *Government Procurement,* October 2004, p. 35; www.thekioskffactory.com/news.html, accessed November 2004; Ian Limbach, "At Your Self-Service," *Total Telecom Magazine,* October 2004, p. 38; R. Machen, *The Windsor Star,* October 2, 2004, p. F.1; G. Lamb, "The Big Picture," *Telegram,* St. John's, September 5, 2004, p. A.11.

1. explain companywide strategic planning and its four steps

2. discuss how to design business portfolios and develop strategies for growth and downsizing

3. explain marketing's role in strategic planning and how marketing works with its partners to create and deliver customer value

4. describe the elements of a customer-driven marketing strategy and marketing mix, and the forces that influence them

5. list the functions of marketing management

Strategic Planning and the Marketing Process

2

Looking Ahead

In the first chapter, you learned the core concepts and philosophies of marketing and how organizations, whether they are goods manufacturers, service companies, or not-for-profit organizations, offer value to their customers in order to capture value in return. Next, you'll investigate the marketing process with specific emphasis on steps two and three—designing customer-driven marketing strategies and constructing marketing programs that deliver superior value. But first we'll examine marketing's role in the broader organization. We start with the strategic planning process. Marketing contributes to and is guided by the organization's overall strategic plan. First, marketing urges a whole-company philosophy that puts customers at the centre. Then, marketers work with other company functions to design strategies for delivering value to carefully targeted customers and to develop marketing mixes—comprising product, price, distribution, and promotion tactics—to carry out these strategies profitably. The first two chapters will fully introduce you to the basics of marketing, the decisions marketing managers make, and where marketing fits into an organization. After that, we'll look at the environments in which marketing operates.

The Canadian airline industry can be best described as turbulent. Can a well-defined corporate strategy, consistently well executed, provide a buffer to ride out the ups and downs of the market and provide for long-term survival and success?

The current market for air travel is an often frustrating one for travellers and airline marketers alike. And entering this market as a new air travel provider is, to say the very least, a challenge. Yet Calgary-based discount air carrier WestJet did just that in 1995.

WestJet is the underdog: a small fish in a pond dominated by one major player. In Canada, when we think of airlines, most of us think first of Air Canada—the country's largest air carrier and the tenth largest air carrier in the world. But although it's top of mind among consumers, it is not always top of the list in their

preferences. In a poll conducted in 2004 among readers of *Canadian Business* and *Marketing* magazines, 46 percent of respondents identified Air Canada as the "worst managed brand" out of 157 alternative organizations.

Add to this the less than encouraging figures being reported by the industry as a whole. In 2003 the Canadian airline industry market value for passengers fell 5.5 percent from 2002, the third straight year of declining industry revenues and a full 17.7 percent drop from a 2000 high. And only a modest growth rate of 2 percent is forecast through 2008. These revenue declines are a result of declining passenger traffic, which has in turn resulted from a number of causes. Joe Chidley, writing in *Canadian Business* magazine, may be expressing an emerging issue confronting all airlines when he observes, "Jet travel used to be cachet—sophistication, speed and luxury all in one expensive experience. These days, it's barely a notch up from taking the bus. Most people will fly on whatever's cheapest, and who can blame them?"

Yet into this turbulence flies the upstart new airline, WestJet. Though the company is only 10 years old it has done what other giant airlines thought impossible—it remains consistently profitable and it doesn't have a mountain of debt. How has it managed these rare feats? By constantly and unrelentingly following a strategy of cost leadership that allows it to offer the lowest prices in the Canadian skies.

Before starting their airline, WestJet's founders did their homework. They analyzed hundreds of other airlines and the dynamics of the airline industry. Their analysis of the Canadian marketplace revealed that the needs of a significant portion of the Canadian market were not being met. At the time of its launch, all Canadian competitors were look-alikes. WestJet decided to offer no-frills service, and based on the company's financial results, consumers can clearly see the difference.

WestJet flies one type of aircraft, the Boeing 737. Having only one type of aircraft lowers the costs of training and maintenance and allows for bulk-purchase efficiencies. WestJet also keeps a grip on its marketing costs. It uses a ticketless software system for its bookings, and low-cost media such as newspapers, radio, and outdoor advertisements to carry its message of friendly, low-cost service. It has only recently moved into TV advertising.

In addition to its low-cost strategy, WestJet selected markets and competitors carefully. Rather than attacking its major competitors head on and relying on business travellers to ensure profitability, WestJet began by specializing in serving what it calls "VFR customers" in western Canada (people who are visiting friends and relatives). It saw its main competitor as the family car and realized that if it could offer low airfares, people would choose to fly rather than drive to visit friends and family.

Another key to WestJet's success is its corporate culture. Founder Clive Beddoe regards his employees as his partners. To reinforce the airline's low-cost strategy, his own office is simply furnished and the entrance to the executive suite bears the self-deprecating sign "Big Shots." WestJet's unconventional culture and laid-back attitude are further demonstrated by employees. Gate attendants have been known to offer first boarding only to those travellers wearing brown socks. In-flight crew tell jokes that can be corny ("plane bad humour") and their antics range from wearing full cowboy outfits during the Calgary stampede to organizing in-flight toilet-paper-rolling contests. A group of employees calling themselves the WestJesters have even written a manual for boarding and in-flight humour.

In May 2002 the airline made a major competitive move and began flying into Toronto's Pearson Airport, Air Canada's power base. This was followed by adding WestJet service to London, Ontario. Not to be outdone, Air Canada countered by launching a new no-frills airline, Zip, and establishing operations on WestJet's western doorstep. However, the strategy further confused consumers. In September of 2004, Zip operations ceased and Air Canada now offers low-priced seats using its Tango fares to better compete with the discount carriers.

WestJet's strategy and success haven't gone unnoticed. The company has received numerous awards, including the Ernst & Young Entrepreneur of the Year Award (2000), an International Entrepreneurship award for Outstanding Teamwork (2001), and the "Most Respected Corporation" title for Innovative Practices (2003). In both 2003 and 2004 it was ranked among the top five firms in the list of Canada's Most Respected Corporations compiled by Ipsos-Reid and was recognized as the top firm in terms of its customer service.

WestJet's record of profitability is especially amazing when you consider the turbulence that characterizes the airline industry in Canada and worldwide. Rising fuel prices and a slowing economy are making profitability a challenge for all high flyers. Price wars are rampant and deregulation has shaken up the industry. Since 2000, numerous airlines, including Royal Airlines, Canada 3000, Roots Air, and JetsGo have tried and failed to prosper in the Canadian skies.

That's not to say that WestJet hasn't had its own obstacles to overcome. By April 2004, Air Canada, which had seen its share of domestic air travel fall from 85 percent to 66 percent, launched a well-publicized lawsuit against WestJet. The airline is claiming $220 million in damages related to corporate espionage allegations that certain executives at WestJet gained access to a confidential website containing information on Air Canada flight loading, which could have been used to identify Air Canada's most profitable routes. Predictably, WestJet has retaliated with a countersuit, claiming that Air Canada is abusing the court system and using illegal means to interfere with WestJet's business.

Despite these distractions, WestJet remains profitable and sticks to its strategy of low-cost airfares and excellent customer service. All of the airline's new Boeing 737–700 aircraft have been equipped with leather seats and more leg room for more passenger comfort. It has begun using TV advertising to attract even more travellers. In addition, WestJet continues to carry out its expansion plans to the United States, with flights to Los Angeles, San Francisco, San Diego, Phoenix, Fort Lauderdale, Tampa Bay, Orlando, Palm Springs, and New York.

Declining markets, increasing cost pressures, service expansion costs and risks, and multi-million dollar lawsuits large enough to bankrupt the company have not deterred WestJet from consistently following through on its corporate strategy. The company continues to be an example of the importance of strategic development, strategic planning, and excellent execution of that strategy.[1]

TEST YOURSELF

Answers to these questions can be found on our website at www.pearsoned.ca/armstrong.

1. Doing the right research and asking the right questions up front even before strategic planning begins is often critical for success. Why did WestJet's founders put so much effort into their research?
   a) Because they were new to the airline business and needed to learn it
   b) Because they were not able to obtain the information as secondary data from Air Canada or other sources
   c) Because they wanted to select the right target segment and to identify their real competition from the start
   d) Because they had already made several mistakes and didn't want to repeat them
   e) Because the founders initially disagreed on what strategic direction to take

2. In order to maintain a cost leadership strategy, WestJet has had to be strict on what other front and why?
   a) Control costs in order to offer the lowest price and yet stay profitable
   b) Create a fun and unusual corporate culture that attracts customers
   c) Use corporate espionage aggressively to stay competitive
   d) Maximize customer delight and operate unprofitably for the first several years
   e) Control debt in order to ensure that they can repay their corporate loans over the appropriate period of time

3. WestJet made a number of strategic decisions from the start and has been successful as a result. What has been the main success factor in the execution of those decisions?
   a) The founders are down to earth, and so the employees have been motivated to produce
   b) The company has never deviated from its strategy and is always consistent
   c) WestJet was able to win early investment and could execute without debt
   d) The founders developed an excellent mission statement that provided guidance to internal stakeholders
   e) WestJet was flexible, shifting its strategic direction quickly in order to react to changing market conditions

4. Founded in 1995, WestJet began to compete more aggressively in 2002. Why did WestJet choose that time to take Air Canada on more directly?
   a) Because WestJet was entering a period of financial difficulty and needed to increase revenues
   b) Because deregulation in the airline industry allowed WestJet to make strategic changes
   c) Because September 11, 2001, created so much upheaval in the airline industry
   d) Because Air Canada's woes culminated in 2001 with bankruptcy protection, opening up potential new markets for WestJet
   e) Because U.S. routes became available to WestJet

5. Compared to WestJet, Air Canada does poorly both financially and in terms of brand reputation and perceived value. What does Air Canada do differently from WestJet to create this poor business performance?
   a) Air Canada tries to service many different target segments
   b) Air Canada does a poor job of controlling costs and therefore cannot offer competitive pricing
   c) Air Canada tries to compete with WestJet instead of differentiating itself from WestJet
   d) Air Canada has no clearly stated strategy and changes direction often
   e) All of the above

Marketing strategies and programs operate within the context of broader, company-wide strategic plans. Thus, to understand the role of marketing within an organization, we must first understand the organization's overall strategic planning process. Like WestJet, all companies must look ahead and develop long-term strategies to meet the changing conditions in their industries and ensure long-term survival.

In this chapter, we look first at the organization's overall strategic planning. Next, we discuss how marketers, guided by the strategic plan, work closely with others inside and outside the organization to service customers. Finally, we examine marketing strategy and planning—how marketers choose target markets, position their marketing offers, and develop marketing mixes in support of programs.

COMPANYWIDE STRATEGIC PLANNING: DEFINING MARKETING'S ROLE

The hard task of developing an overall company strategy for long-term survival and growth is called strategic planning. Each company must develop a game plan that makes the most sense given its specific situation, opportunities, objectives, and resources. This is the focus of **strategic planning**—the process of developing and maintaining a strategic fit between an organization's goals and capabilities and changing marketing opportunities. As is often said, "If you fail to plan, you are planning to fail."[2]

Strategic planning sets the stage for the rest of the planning in the firm. Companies usually prepare annual plans, long-range plans, and strategic plans. The annual and long-range plans deal with the company's current businesses and how to keep them going. In contrast, the strategic plan involves adapting the firm to take advantage of opportunities in its constantly changing environment.

At the corporate level, the company starts the strategic planning process by defining its overall purpose and mission (see Figure 2.1). This mission is then turned into detailed supporting objectives that guide the entire company. Next, senior managers decide what portfolio of business activities and products is best for the company and how much support to give each one. In turn, each business unit and product group develops detailed plans for their department. All these plans, including the marketing plan, must support the organization's strategic plan. Thus, marketing planning occurs at the business-unit, product, and market levels. It supports company strategic planning with more detailed plans for specific marketing opportunities.[3]

> **Strategic planning** The process of developing and maintaining a strategic fit between the organization's goals and capabilities and its changing marketing opportunities.

Figure 2.1   Steps in Strategic Planning

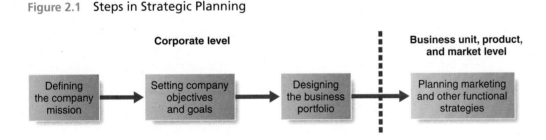

Defining a Market-Oriented Mission

All organizations exist to market something—a good, a service, a brand, an idea—to a group of customers. All organizations also start out with a clear purpose or mission, but over time, that mission may change as the organization grows, adds new products and markets, or faces new conditions in the environment. Senior managers at all organizations must periodically revisit the questions: What is our business? Who is our customer? What do our customers value? What should our business be? These simple-sounding questions are among the most difficult the organization will ever have to answer. Successful companies continually raise these questions and answer them carefully and completely.

Many organizations develop a formal mission statement that answers these questions. A **mission statement** is a statement of the organization's purpose—what it wants to accomplish in the larger environment. A clear mission statement acts as an "invisible hand" that guides people in the organization and should include the following three components:

1. Core values to which the firm is committed

2. Core purpose of the firm

3. Visionary goals the firm will pursue to fulfill its mission.[4]

> **Mission statement** A statement of the organization's purpose—what it wants to accomplish in the larger environment.

Some companies define their missions in terms of their products ("We manufacture furniture") or in technological terms ("We are a chemical-processing firm"). But mission statements should be *market oriented* (see Marketing at Work 2.1). Products and technologies eventually become outdated, but basic market needs can last forever.

The following historical mission statements for some of the world's most recognized organizations indicate management's belief in the long-term potential of their companies at the time.

"Become a $125 billion company by the year 2000" (Wal-Mart, 1990)

"Become the company most known for changing the worldwide poor-quality image of Japanese products" (Sony, mid–1950s)

Marketing at Work   2.1

Norco: Performance Is Their Mission

Norco, a British Columbia–based manufacturer and marketer of performance bikes with an international reputation, has developed an extensive expression of company mission and values that includes customers, employees, and stakeholders.

Our Mission
We are dedicated to building rewarding, long-term relationships with our Customers, our Employees, and our Suppliers. We are driven by our customers to supply innovative cycle products and outstanding service and marketing support that will promote their growth and success.

Our Values Respect and Integrity
Dealing fairly, openly and honestly with our Customers, our Employees, and our Suppliers.

Quality
Continually bettering our standards for performance and safety.

Dedication to Service
Building a strong team to do what it takes to meet internal and external Customer needs.

Innovation
Developing new products and new ways of doing business.

Fiscal Responsibility
Managing our resources wisely, with a vision committed to long term growth and stability.

Our Customers
We will be the number one supplier to our customers, partnering with them in the adventure of cycling.

Our Products
We will be an industry leader in developing and delivering innovative performance products.

Our Profitability
We will maintain the financial stability of the company and ensure an adequate return on investment for our shareholders.

Our People
People are our greatest asset. We will provide a rewarding and challenging environment where our employees and the company can grow together on a progressive basis.

Source: Norco's company profile, www.norco.com, accessed August 3, 2005.

Norco supplies "innovative cycle products and outstanding service and marketing support that will promote their growth and success."

"Become the dominant player in commercial aircraft and bring the world into the jet age" (Boeing, 1950)

"Ford will democratize the automobile" (early 1900s)[5]

A market-oriented mission statement defines the business in terms of satisfying basic customer needs. Bell doesn't merely provide traditional landline and cellular services; it is in the communications business. Part of Bell's strategy is "to deliver unrivalled integrated communications to customers across Canada."[6] Likewise, 3M does more than just make adhesives, scientific equipment, health care, and communications products. It solves people's problems by putting innovation to work for them. Table 2.1 provides several other examples of product-oriented versus market-oriented business definitions.

Management should avoid making its mission too narrow or too broad. A pencil manufacturer that says it is in the communication equipment business is stating its mission too broadly. A mission should be *realistic*. WestJet would be deluding itself if it adopted the mission to become the world's largest airline. A mission should also be *specific*. Many mission statements are written for public relations purposes and lack specific, workable guidelines. Too often, companies develop mission statements that look much like this tongue-and-cheek version:

> We are committed to serving the quality of life of cultures and communities everywhere, regardless of sex, age, sexual preference, religion, or disability, whether they be customers, suppliers, employees, or shareholders—we serve the planet—to the highest ethical standards of integrity, best practice, and sustainability, through policies of openness and transparency vetted by our participation in the International Quality Business Global Audit forum, to ensure measurable outcomes worldwide. . . ."[7]

Such generic statements sound good but provide little real guidance or inspiration. In contrast, Celestial Seasonings' mission statement is very specific:

Company mission: 3M does more than just make adhesives, scientific equipment, and health care and communications products. It solves people's problems by putting innovation to work for them.

Table 2.1 **Market-Oriented Business Definitions**		
Company	**Product-Oriented Definition**	**Market-Oriented Definition**
M·A·C Cosmetics	We make cosmetics.	We sell lifestyle and self-expression; tolerance of diversity, and a platform for the outrageous.
Zellers	We run discount stores.	We offer products and services that deliver superior value to Canadians.
Canadian Tire	We sell tools and home improvement items	We provide advice and solutions that transform people into do-it-yourselfers.

To create and sell healthful, naturally oriented products that nurture people's bodies and uplift their souls. Our products must be:

☐   superior in quality

☐   of good value

☐   beautifully artistic

☐   philosophically inspiring[8]

Missions should fit the *market environment*. The Girl Guides would not recruit successfully in today's environment with its former mission: "to prepare young girls for motherhood and wifely duties." Today, its mission is to be "a Movement of girls and women that challenges Members in their personal development and empowers them to be responsible citizens."[9] The organization should base its mission on its *distinctive competencies*. McDonald's could probably enter the solar energy business, but that would not take advantage of its core competence—providing low-cost food and fast service to large groups of customers.

Finally, mission statements should be *motivating*. A company's mission should not be stated as the desire to increase sales or profits—profits are only a reward for undertaking a useful activity. A company's employees need to feel that their work is significant and that it contributes to people's lives. One study found that "visionary companies" set a purpose beyond making money. Hummingbird Ltd., a Canadian-based global leader in enterprise content management (ECM) solutions, articulates their mission through a customer-focused business strategy statement: "Our principal business strategy is to develop and market an integrated suite of software applications that empower organizations to leverage the full range of enterprise business content. Hummingbird is dedicated to delivering enterprise content management solutions designed to generate rapid return on investment to our network of customers and partners worldwide."[10]

Setting Company Objectives and Goals

The company's mission needs to be turned into detailed supporting objectives for each level of management. Each manager should have objectives and be responsible for reaching them. For example, the mission statement of Telus Mobility, a major force in Canadian wireless communications, is to "efficiently develop future friendly wireless solutions that are easy to sell, buy and use and that deliver clear value to our clients,

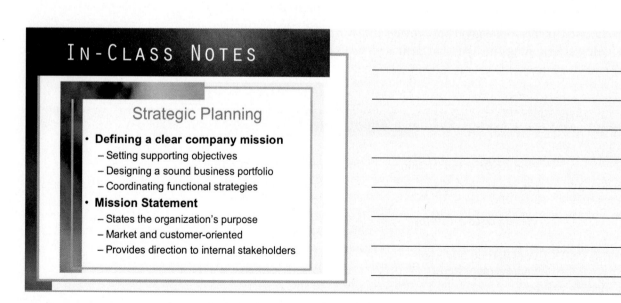

IN-CLASS NOTES

Strategic Planning

• **Defining a clear company mission**
 – Setting supporting objectives
 – Designing a sound business portfolio
 – Coordinating functional strategies
• **Mission Statement**
 – States the organization's purpose
 – Market and customer-oriented
 – Provides direction to internal stakeholders

channels, employees and shareholders." This mission leads to a hierarchy of objectives, including business objectives and marketing objectives.

Telus Mobility has consistently been recognized as a leader in wireless telecommunications in Canada. It stands to reason, then, that one of the company's primary overall objectives is to maintain that leadership position. Telus's top ranking is due in part to its high subscriber and revenue growth, so increasing that growth becomes another major Telus objective. It can attract new subscribers by offering more and better services than other wireless companies. In this way it does not have to cut its prices to attract new customers, and so it increases its revenue with each new subscriber. High levels of customer satisfaction are also a factor in Telus Mobility's top ranking, so keeping customers happy is another major objective.

Marketing strategies and programs must be developed to support these marketing objectives. To make sure that Telus offers better services than its competitors, the company focuses on expanding its distribution of such leading-edge goods as phones with colour screens, built-in cameras, and MP3 players, and such services as their MIKE™ brand Direct Connect two-way radio service and wireless Web access. To maintain high levels of customer satisfaction, Telus has call centres in B.C., Alberta, Ontario, and Quebec that are staffed with 5000 customer service representatives.[11] These are its broad marketing strategies. Each broad marketing strategy must then be defined in greater detail. For example, providing leading-edge products may require additional investment in research and development; if so, this will have to be spelled out. In this way, the firm's mission is translated into a set of objectives for the current period.

Designing the Business Portfolio

Guided by the company's mission statement and objectives, management now must plan its **business portfolio**—the collection of businesses and products that compose the company. The best business portfolio is the one that best fits the company's strengths and weaknesses to opportunities in the environment. The company must analyze its *current* business portfolio and decide which businesses should receive more, less, or no investment. Second, it must shape the future portfolio by developing strategies for growth or downsizing.

Analyzing the Current Business Portfolio The major activity in strategic planning is business **portfolio analysis**, whereby management identifies and evaluates the products and businesses making up the company. The company will want to put strong resources into its more profitable businesses and phase down or drop its weaker ones.

Management's first step is to identify the key businesses making up the company. Many organizations have only one business, but larger companies such as Nortel, Loblaws, and Pfizer typically organize themselves into business units, sometimes called **strategic business units**, or SBUs. An SBU is a unit of the company that has its own mission and objectives and that can be planned independently from other company businesses. An SBU can be a company division, a group of similar products or customers, or sometimes a single product or brand.

For example, the pharmaceutical company Pfizer organizes itself into three "business segments" by product category: health care (prescription medications), consumer health care (over-the-counter medicinal products such as Listerine), and animal health (veterinary medicines and other animal care products). RBC Financial Group, on the other hand, organizes its businesses by broad customer group: personal banking (for consumers), small business, and corporate (for large businesses).

The next step in business portfolio analysis calls for management to assess the attractiveness of its various SBUs and decide how much support each deserves. In some

Business portfolio The collection of businesses and products that compose the company.

Portfolio analysis A tool management uses to identify and evaluate the businesses that compose the company.

Strategic business unit (SBU) A unit of the company that has its own mission and objectives and that can be planned independently from other company businesses.

companies, this is done informally. Management looks at the company's collection of businesses or products and judges how much each SBU should contribute and what resources it should receive. It is usually a good idea for companies to focus on products and businesses that fit closely with the firm's core philosophy and competencies.

The purpose of strategic planning is to find ways that the company can best use its strengths to take advantage of attractive opportunities. Most standard portfolio-analysis methods evaluate SBUs on two important dimensions: the attractiveness of the SBU's market or industry and the strength of the SBU's position in that market or industry. The best-known portfolio-planning method was developed by the Boston Consulting Group, a leading management consulting firm.

The Boston Consulting Group Approach. Using the Boston Consulting Group approach, a company classifies all of its SBUs according to the **growth-share matrix**, which evaluates a company's SBUs in terms of their market growth rate and relative market share, classifying the SBUs as "stars," "cash cows," "question marks," or "dogs." An example is shown in Figure 2.2. On the vertical axis, *market growth rate* provides a measure of market attractiveness. On the horizontal axis, *relative market share* serves as a measure of company strength in the market. By dividing the growth-share matrix as indicated, the four types of SBUs can be distinguished:

> **Growth-share matrix** A portfolio-planning method that evaluates a company's SBUs in terms of their market growth rate and relative market share. SBUs are classified as stars, cash cows, question marks, or dogs.

☐ *Stars.* Stars are high-growth, high-share businesses or products. They often need heavy investment to finance their rapid growth. Eventually their growth will slow down, and they will turn into cash cows.

☐ *Cash cows.* Cash cows are low-growth, high-share businesses or products. These established and successful SBUs need less investment to hold their market share. Thus, they produce a lot of cash that the company uses to pay its bills and to support other SBUs that need investment.

☐ *Question marks.* Question marks are low-share business units in high-growth markets. They require a lot of cash to hold their share, let alone increase it. Management has to think hard about which question marks it should try to build into stars and which it should phase out.

☐ *Dogs.* Dogs are low-growth, low-share businesses and products. They may generate enough cash to maintain themselves but do not promise to be large sources of cash.

The 10 circles in the growth-share matrix represent a company's 10 current SBUs. The company has two stars, two cash cows, three question marks, and three dogs. The

Figure 2.2   The Boston Consulting Group's Growth-Share Matrix

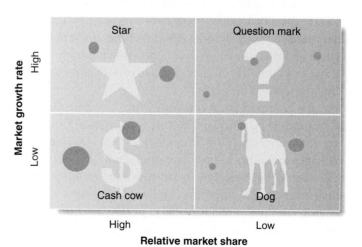

areas of the circles are proportional to the SBU's dollar sales. This company is in fair shape, although not in good shape. It wants to invest in the more promising question marks to make them stars and to maintain the stars so that they will become cash cows as their markets mature. Fortunately, it has two good-sized cash cows whose income helps finance the company's question marks, stars, and dogs. The company should take some decisive action concerning its dogs and its question marks. The picture would be worse if the company had no stars, if it had too many dogs, or if it had only one weak cash cow.

Once it has classified its SBUs, the company must determine what role each will play in the future. One of four strategies can be pursued for each SBU. The company can invest more in the business unit to *build* its share. Or it can invest just enough to *hold* the SBU's share at the current level. It can *harvest* the SBU, milking its short-term cash flow regardless of the long-term effect. Finally, the company can *divest* the SBU by selling it or phasing it out and using the resources elsewhere.

As time passes, SBUs change their positions in the growth-share matrix. Each SBU has a life cycle. Many SBUs start out as question marks and move into the star category if they succeed. They later become cash cows as market growth falls, then finally die off or turn into dogs toward the end of their life cycle. The company needs to add new products and units continually so that some of them will become stars and, eventually, cash cows that will help finance other SBUs.

Problems with Matrix Approaches. The BCG method and other formal methods revolutionized strategic planning. However, such approaches have limitations. They can be difficult, time consuming, and costly to implement. Management may find it difficult to define SBUs and measure market share and growth. In addition, these approaches focus on classifying *current* businesses but provide little advice for *future* planning. Management must still rely on its own judgment to set the business objectives for each SBU, to determine what resources each will be given, and to figure out which new businesses should be added.

Formal planning approaches can also place too much emphasis on market-share growth or growth through entry into attractive new markets. Using these approaches, many companies plunged into unrelated and new high-growth businesses that were beyond their ability to manage—with very bad results. At the same time, these companies were too quick to abandon, sell, or milk to death their healthy mature businesses. As a result many companies that diversified too broadly in the past are now narrowing their focus and getting back to the basics of serving one or a few industries that they know best.

Because of such problems, many companies have dropped formal matrix methods in favour of more customized approaches that are better suited to their situations. Unlike former strategic planning efforts, which rested mostly in the hands of senior managers in a company's headquarters, today's strategic planning has been decentralized. Increasingly, companies are placing responsibility for strategic planning in the hands of cross-functional teams who are close to their markets. Some teams even include customers and suppliers in their strategic-planning processes.[12]

Developing Strategies for Growth and Downsizing Beyond evaluating current businesses, designing the business portfolio involves finding businesses and products the company should consider in the future. Companies need growth if they are to compete more effectively, satisfy their stakeholders, and attract top talent. "Growth is pure oxygen," states one executive. "It creates a vital, enthusiastic corporation where people see genuine opportunity. . . . In that way, growth is more than our single most important financial driver; it's an essential part of our corporate culture." At the same time, a firm must be careful not to make growth itself an objective. The company's objective must be "profitable growth."

Marketing has the main responsibility for achieving profitable growth for the company. Marketing must identify, evaluate, and select market opportunities and lay down

Product–market expansion grid
A portfolio-planning tool for identifying company growth opportunities through market penetration, market development, product development, or diversification.

strategies for capturing them (see Marketing at Work 2.2). One useful device for identifying growth opportunities is the **product–market expansion grid** shown in Figure 2.3.[13] This grid is a portfolio-planning tool for identifying company growth opportunities through market penetration, market development, product development, or diversification. We apply it here to Cake Beauty, a Canadian cosmetics company.

Figure 2.3   The Product–Market Expansion Grid

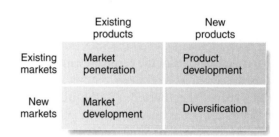

Market penetration A strategy for entering the market with a new product, then focusing efforts on increasing the sales of that product in order to capture market share.

Product development A strategy for company growth by offering modified or new products to current market segments.

Market development A strategy for company growth by identifying and developing new market segments for current company products.

Cake Beauty's strategy begins with **market penetration**—entering the market with a new product, then focusing efforts on increasing the sales of that product in order to capture market share. Cake relies on carefully targeted promotions and media coverage to attract new customers within their target market and to entice current customers to buy more Cake products.

Second, Cake focuses on **product development**—offering modified or new products to the market. In 2005 Cake introduced such new products as Satin Sugar Hair and Body Refreshing Powder and Milk Made Smoothing Hand Buffer, as well as new scents of existing products.

Third, the company explores possibilities for **market development**—identifying and developing new markets segments for its current products. Cake Beauty has entered the global market, with plans to expand further in Australia, Asia, and Europe.

Marketing at Work   2.2

Tim Hortons: Where Things Are Really Perking

Canadians, it appears, *always have time for Tim Hortons*. Generations of competitors have come and gone, but none has managed to defeat Tim Hortons. In 2003 the company ranked number 1 in market share at breakfast and afternoon/early evening snack time and number 2 at lunch. Although owned by Wendy's International since 1995, the company is still headquartered in Oakville, Ontario, employing about 760 people. In fact, it has become a Canadian icon.

One has to wonder how Tim Hortons has achieved this status, since

it offers such standard items as coffee and baked goods. The company's strategy is deceptively simple. First, it has followed one consistent product and positioning strategy throughout its history. Its promise of "Always Fresh" is never broken. Next, it builds outlets in focal areas until they reach a large enough critical mass to justify advertising.

Tim Hortons spends about $3 million a year on advertising, which has been important to its growth strategy. Throughout much of the 1990s, the chain's ads focused on its new food

offerings—bagels, sandwiches, and soup—to get consumers to see Tim Hortons as more than a doughnut shop. New products also increased revenues for both the corporation and its franchisees. Advertising served to build the brand message that Tim Hortons is "relaxed, caring, friendly, and honest."

To further strengthen the equity of the brand, "feel-good advertising" followed the more traditional product advertising. The True Stories campaign (by Toronto agency Enterprise Advertising), launched in 1997, has worked to build an emotional connec-

(continued)

Tim Hortons doesn't advertise until it has enough outlets in a region to justify the expense. It knows advertising has more impact when people can see its outlets in their daily travels.

tion between Tim Hortons and its customers. One ad featured the crew of the HMCS *Toronto* and described how much they missed Tim's coffee while they were stationed in the Persian Gulf. Another ad featured a four-legged customer, Sammi, a golden retriever who picks up her owner's coffee from the drive-through. In 2004 Tim Hortons aired 17 English TV ads, a mix of monthly promotional spots and ads that convey the brand character. In addition to the True Stories campaign, it launched its "Change the rules" kids' hockey campaign. The four 30-second

TV spots and one 60-second spot feature some very cute kids learning how to play the game. All the ads work to make Tim Hortons appear unpretentious and an integral part of the Canadian culture.

Given Tim Hortons' track record, it's hard to imagine how it could expand any further. There seems to be an outlet on the corner of every major intersection. This is not surprising, given that the chain boasts more than 2350 Canadian outlets. Yet even an institution needs to be willing to change and grow. And change is

exactly what Tim Hortons has done in recent years. In a bid to broaden its appeal and attract more women and young people, the chain has branched out into new product lines, such as iced cappuccino and steeped tea. It also retooled its lunchtime offerings, offering the Tim's Own brand of soups and sandwiches.

The firm isn't about to stop there. Tim Hortons plans to continue to open new locations across Canada. It is also using the clout of its partner-owner, Wendy's, to tap into the U.S. market. Tim Hortons sees tremendous opportunity south of the border, where "no one else is really doing everyday morning coffee and baked goods very well." According to a company spokesperson, "In the U.S., they don't have high expectations for morning destinations. . . . People will grab a coffee from a gas station in the morning, [but] we're promising that consistent experience."

Sources: Lesley Daw, "More Than Just a Doughnut Shop," *Marketing* (Online edition), August 21, 2000; Craig Saunders, "Tim Horton's Issues Wakeup Call," *Strategy*, February 14, 2000, p. 25; Sinclair Stewart, "Top Client, Retail–Restaurants: Tim Horton's Brews up Fresh Ideas"; John Gray, "King of the Cruller," *Canadian Business*, June 7, 2004, pp. 45, 46; www.wendys-invest.com/fin/annual/2003, accessed September 12, 2004; www.timhortons.com/en/news/news_releases.html, accessed December 12, 2004.

Fourth, Cake might consider **diversification**, starting up or buying businesses outside of its current products and markets. For example, it could develop a line of home decor products. Diversification must be approached with caution. Companies that diversify too broadly into unfamiliar products or industries can lose their market focus. Tim Hortons president has been quoted as saying "We could probably sell Tim Hortons screwdrivers if we wanted, but we never will; that's not our business."[14]

Companies must not only develop strategies for growing their business portfolios but also strategies for **downsizing** them, that is, reducing the business portfolio by eliminating products or businesses that are not profitable or that no longer fit the company's overall strategy. There are many reasons why a firm would want to exit some of their existing businesses. The market environment might change, reducing sales and profits of the company's products. This could be the result of an economic downturn, or the actions of a stronger competitor. One of the biggest reasons, however, is that some products or business units simply age and die.

When a firm finds products or businesses that no longer fit its overall strategy, it must carefully prune, harvest, or divest them. Weak businesses usually require a disproportionate amount of management attention. Managers should focus on promising growth opportunities, not waste resources trying to salvage fading ones.

Diversification A strategy for company growth by starting up or acquiring businesses outside the company's current products and markets.

Downsizing Reducing the business portfolio by eliminating products or businesses that are not profitable or that no longer fit the company's overall strategy.

IN-CLASS NOTES

Analyze Opportunities

- Product–Market Expansion Grid identifies four potential growth areas

	Existing Products	New Products
Existing Markets	Market Penetration	Product Development
New Markets	Market Development	Diversification

DECIDING WHETHER TO GO INTERNATIONAL

Although many firms view themselves as local businesses serving their immediate communities, they must become aware of the globalization of competition even if they never plan to go overseas themselves. Too many companies have recognized the dangers too late and have gone out of business when faced with new competitors. Companies that operate in global industries, where their strategic positions in specific markets are affected strongly by their overall global positions, have no choice but to think and act globally. Thus, Nortel must organize globally if it is to gain purchasing, manufacturing, financial, and marketing advantages. Firms in a global industry must be able to compete worldwide if they are to succeed.

Several factors may draw a company into the international arena. Global competitors may attack the company's domestic market by offering better products or lower prices. The company may want to counterattack these competitors in their home markets to tie up their resources. Or it may discover foreign markets that present higher profit opportunities than the domestic market does. The company's domestic market may be shrinking, or the company may need a larger customer base to achieve economies of scale. Or it may want to reduce its dependence on any one market to reduce its risk. Finally, the company's customers may be expanding abroad and require international servicing.

Before going abroad, the company must weigh the risks and assess its ability to operate globally. Can the company learn to understand the preferences and buyer behaviour of customers in other countries? Can it offer competitively attractive products? Will it be able to adapt to other countries' business cultures and deal effectively with foreign nationals? Do the company's managers have the necessary international experience? Has management considered the impact of regulations and the political environments of other countries?

Because of the risks and difficulties of entering international markets, most companies do not act until some situation or event thrusts them into the global arena. Someone—a domestic exporter, a foreign importer, a foreign government—may ask the company to sell abroad. Or the company may be saddled with overcapacity and must find additional markets for its goods.

Deciding Which Markets to Enter

Before going abroad, the company must set its international *marketing objectives and policies.* First, it must decide what *volume* of foreign sales it wants. Most companies start small when they go abroad. Some plan to stay small, seeing international sales as a small part of their business. Other companies have bigger plans, seeing international business as equal to or even more important than their domestic business.

The company must choose *how many* countries it wants to market in. Generally, it makes sense to operate in fewer countries with deeper commitment and penetration in each. The Bulova Watch Company decided to operate in many international markets and expanded into more than 100 countries; unfortunately, it had spread itself too thin, made profits in only two countries, and lost around $55 million.

Next, the company must decide on the *types* of countries to enter. A country's attractiveness depends on the product, geographical factors, income and population, political climate, and other factors. The seller may prefer certain country groups or parts of the world. In recent years, many major markets have emerged, offering both substantial opportunities and daunting challenges.

After listing possible international markets, the company must screen and rank each one. Consider this example:

> Many mass marketers dream of selling to China's more than 1.3 billion people. For example, Colgate is waging a pitched battle in China, seeking control of the world's largest toothpaste market. This country of infrequent brushers offers great potential. Only 20 percent of China's rural dwellers brush daily, so Colgate and its competitors are aggressively pursuing promotional and educational programs, from massive ad campaigns to visits to local schools to sponsoring oral care research. Through such efforts, in this $350 million market dominated by local brands, Colgate has expanded its market share from 7 percent in 1995 to 24 percent today.[15]

Colgate's decision to enter the Chinese market seems straightforward: China is a huge market without established competition. Given the low rate of brushing, this already huge market can grow even larger. Yet we still can question whether market size *alone* is reason enough for selecting China. Colgate must also consider other factors. Will the Chinese government remain stable and supportive? Does China provide for the production and distribution technologies needed to produce and market Colgate's products profitably? Will Colgate be able to overcome cultural barriers and convince Chinese consumers to brush their teeth regularly? Can Colgate compete effectively with dozens of local competitors? Colgate's current success in China suggests that it could answer yes to all of these questions. Still, the company's future in China is filled with uncertainties.

A company should rank possible global markets on several factors, including market size, market growth, cost of doing business, competitive advantage, and risk level to determine the potential of each market, and then decide which ones offer the greatest long-run return on investment.

PLANNING MARKETING: PARTNERING TO BUILD CUSTOMER RELATIONSHIPS

The company's strategic plan establishes what kinds of businesses the company will be in and its objectives for each. Then, within each business unit, more detailed planning must take place. The major functional departments in each unit—marketing, finance, accounting, purchasing, manufacturing, information systems, human resources, and others—must work together to accomplish strategic objectives.

Marketing plays a key role in the company's strategic planning in several ways. First, marketing provides a guiding *philosophy*—the marketing concept—that suggests company strategy should revolve around serving the needs of customers and prospective customers. Second, marketing provides *inputs* to strategic planners by helping to identify attractive market opportunities and by assessing the firm's potential to take advantage of them. Finally, within individual business units, marketing designs *strategies* for reaching the unit's objectives. Once the unit's objectives are set, marketing's task is to carry them out profitably.

Customer value and satisfaction are important ingredients in the marketer's formula for success. However, as we noted in Chapter 1, marketing alone cannot produce superior value for customers. Although marketing plays a leading role, it can only be a partner in attracting, keeping, and growing customers. In addition to *customer relationship management*, marketers must also practise *partner relationship management*. They must work closely with partners in other functional areas of the company to form an effective *value chain* that serves the customer. Moreover, marketers must partner with other companies in the marketing system—suppliers, distribution channel members—to form a competitively superior *value delivery-network*.

Partnering with Other Company Departments

Value chain The series of departments that carry out value-creating activities to design, produce, market, deliver, and support a firm's products.

Each company department can be thought of as a link in the company's **value chain**.[16] That is, each department carries out value-creating activities to design, produce, market, deliver, and support the firm's products. The firm's success depends not only on how well each department performs its work but also on how well the activities of various departments are coordinated.

For example, Wal-Mart's goal is to create customer value and satisfaction by providing shoppers with the merchandise they want at the lowest possible prices. Marketers at Wal-Mart play an important role. They learn what consumers need and want and stock the store's shelves with it—usually at prices below those of their competitors. They prepare advertising and merchandising programs and assist shoppers with customer service. Through these and other activities, Wal-Mart's marketers help deliver value to customers. However, the marketing department needs help from the company's other departments. For example, Wal-Mart's ability to offer the right products at low prices depends on the purchasing department's skill in tracking down the needed suppliers and buying from them at low cost. Similarly, Wal-Mart's information systems department must provide fast and accurate information about which products are selling in each store. And its operations people must provide effective, low-cost merchandise handling.

Indeed, an important part of Wal-Mart's overall business strategy is the efficient movement of inventory, which is necessary to keep retail prices down. As skids of mer-

The value chain: Wal-Mart's ability to offer the right products at low prices depends on the contributions from people in all of the company's departments—marketing, purchasing, information systems, and operations.

chandise are moved from the manufacturer to each Wal-Mart store, if they pass through a warehouse for handling they are processed by "cross docking," meaning the skids are moved from one truck to another without spending time on the warehouse floor. Each skid is also encoded by the manufacturer with a RFID (radio frequency identification) chip so that its contents can be quickly identified with a scanner. These procedures greatly reduce the amount of time Wal-Mart's inventory sits still—and the faster goods move physically the more costs can be kept down, resulting in lower prices for consumers.

A company's value chain is only as strong as its weakest link. Thus, success depends on how well each department performs its work of adding value for customers and on how well the activities of various departments are coordinated. At Wal-Mart, if purchasing can't wring the lowest prices from suppliers or if operations can't distribute merchandise at the lowest costs, then marketing can't deliver on its promise of lowest prices.

Ideally, then, a company's different functions should work in harmony to create value for customers. But, in practice, departmental relations are full of conflicts and misunderstandings. The marketing department takes the customer's point of view. But when marketing tries to develop customer satisfaction it can unwittingly cause other departments to do a poor job *in their terms*. Marketing department actions can increase purchasing costs, disrupt production schedules, increase inventories, and create budget overruns. Thus, the other departments may resist the marketing department's efforts.

Yet marketers must find a way to get all departments to "think customer" and to develop a smoothly functioning value chain. Marketing management can best gain support for its goal of customer satisfaction by working to understand the company's other departments. Marketing managers need to work closely with managers of other functions to develop a system of plans under which the different departments can work together to accomplish the company's overall objectives.

Partnering with Others in the Marketing System

In its quest to create customer value, the firm needs to look beyond its own value chain and create a **value delivery network**, made up of the company, suppliers, distributors, and ultimately customers who partner with one another to improve the performance of the entire system.

Value delivery network The network made up of the company, suppliers, distributors, and ultimately customers who partner with one another to improve the performance of the entire system.

For example, Canadian auto parts giant Magna International provides many of the components of the Ford Explorer SUV. Seats, metal underbody stampings and assemblies, front and rear door panels, fuel filter, door latches, radiator assemblies, and various engine components are designed, manufactured, and delivered according to Ford's (the customer) requirements. This is one way to create customer value—by actually partnering with customers. A company can also partner with its other divisions or subsidiaries.

Linking the Concepts

Apply what you've read in the first part of this chapter.

- Why are we talking about companywide strategic planning so early in a marketing text? What *does* strategic planning have to do with marketing?
- What are Norco's mission and strategy? What role does marketing play in helping Norco accomplish this mission and strategy?
- What roles do other functional departments play, and how can Norco marketers work more effectively with these other functions to maximize overall customer value?

Magna Steyr, one of Magna's European Divisions, contracts with organizations to perform complete niche vehicle assembly. Magna Steyr recently partnered with BMW to develop and manufacture the new BMW X3 Sports Activity Vehicle. Engineers from the BMW Group worked out the detailed vehicle concept and forwarded it to Magna Steyr Engineering for series development. Magna Steyr Fahrzeugtechnik in Graz, Austria, then took over production.

MARKETING STRATEGY AND THE MARKETING MIX

The strategic plan defines the company's overall mission and objectives. Within each business unit, marketing plays a role in helping to accomplish the overall strategic objectives. Marketing's role and activities in the organization are shown in Figure 2.4, which summarizes marketing strategy and the marketing mix.

Figure 2.4   Managing Marketing Strategy and the Marketing Mix

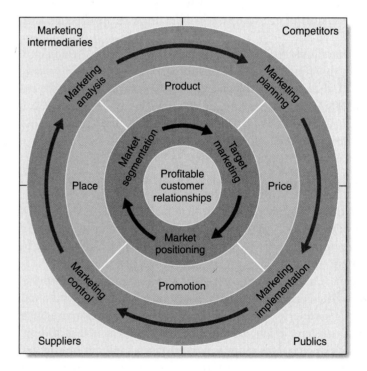

Customers stand in the centre. The goal is to build strong and profitable customer relationships. Next is **marketing strategy**—the marketing logic by which the company hopes to achieve these profitable customer relationships. Through market segmentation, targeting, and positioning, the company decides which customers to serve and how. It identifies the total market, then divides it into smaller segments, selects the most promising segments and focuses on serving and satisfying these segments.

Guided by marketing strategy, the company designs a marketing mix made up of factors under its control—product, price, place, and promotion. To find the best marketing mix and put it into action, the company engages in marketing analysis, planning, implementation, and control. Through these activities, the company watches and adapts to the actors and forces in the marketing environment. We will now look briefly at each element in the marketing process. In later chapters, we will discuss each element in more depth.

Marketing strategy The marketing logic by which the company hopes to achieve strong and profitable customer relationships.

Customer-Centred Marketing Strategy

As we emphasized in Chapter 1, to succeed in today's competitive marketplace, all organizations must be customer centred. They must win customers from competitors, then keep and grow them by delivering greater value.

But before it can satisfy its customers, a company or organization must first understand their needs and wants. Thus, sound marketing requires a careful analysis of all the potential customers in the market. Companies know that they cannot connect profitably with all the potential customers (businesses or consumers) in a given market—at least not all customers in the same way. There are too many different kinds of customers with too many different kinds of needs. Some companies are in a better position to serve certain segments of the market. Thus, each company must divide up the total market, choose the appropriate segments, and design strategies for profitably serving those chosen segments better than its competitors do. This process involves three steps: *market segmentation, target marketing,* and *market positioning.*

Market Segmentation The market consists of many types of customers, products, and needs, and the marketer has to determine which segments offer the best opportunity for achieving company objectives. Potential customers, whether they are businesses or individuals, can be grouped and served in various ways based on geographic, demographic, psychographic, and behavioural factors. The process of dividing a market into distinct groups of buyers with different needs, characteristics, or behaviour who might need separate products or marketing mixes is called **market segmentation.**

Every market has segments, but not all ways of segmenting a market are equally useful. For example, Tylenol would gain little by distinguishing between male and female consumers of pain relievers if both respond the same way to marketing efforts. A **market segment** consists of a group of potential customers who respond in a similar way to a given set of marketing efforts. In the automobile market, for example, people who choose the biggest, most comfortable car regardless of price make up one market segment. Another segment is families who need a multiple-use vehicle, and who care about price and operating economy. It would be difficult to make one model of car that was the first choice of every person. Companies are wise to focus their efforts on meeting the distinct needs of each market segment they decide to serve.

When segmenting markets, caution and sound ethics must be used. In 2005 considerable controversy arose when such companies as Walt Disney aggressively began targeting young children with an array of cartoonish phones featuring the images of Barbie and Mickey Mouse. Bell Canada had its own version, the Kittyphone, a bright yellow device that was shaped a little like a cat and that could be pre-programmed with five telephone numbers children could call if they needed help. While critics recognized the desire of parents to keep their children safe, they condemned marketers for not making the potential health risks to children arising from cell phone use better known.[17]

Target Marketing After a company has defined a set of market segments, it can decide to enter one or more than one of those segments. **Target marketing** is the process of evaluating each market segment's attractiveness and selecting the most appropriate ones to enter. A company should choose its target market segments based on an analysis of which ones it feels will profitably generate the greatest customer value and sustain it over time.

Sometimes, organizations choose to serve relatively small market segments, called *niches.* Rolex, for example, serves a niche market in the very large market for wristwatches. Other luxury brands such as Lamborghini serve a very small, though lucrative market. But niche markets aren't only high-end markets: A company called Ostriches Online claims to be, and very likely is, the world's largest international ostrich products

Market segmentation Dividing a market into distinct groups with distinct needs, characteristics, or behaviour that might need separate products or marketing mixes.

Market segment A group of potential customers who respond in a similar way to a given set of marketing efforts.

Target marketing The process of evaluating each market segment's attractiveness and selecting the most appropriate ones to enter.

company—they sell merchandise such as carnival masks and boas made from ostrich feathers, products made from ostrich leather, and ostrich novelty products.

Most companies enter a new market by serving a single segment, and if this proves successful, they expand to serve additional segments. Very large organizations sometimes strive to serve the entire market of potential customers. General Motors, for example, says that it makes a car for every "person, purse, and personality."

Market Positioning After a company has decided which market segments to enter, it must decide what position it wants to occupy in each segment. A product's *position* is the place the product occupies in the mind of the potential customer, and relative to competitors. If a product is perceived to be exactly like another product on the market, buyers have no reason to choose it.

Market positioning Arranging for a product to occupy a clear, distinctive, and desirable place relative to competing products in the mind of the buyer.

Market positioning is arranging for a product to occupy a clear, distinctive, and desirable place relative to competing products in the mind of the buyer. Thus, marketers plan positions that distinguish their products from competing brands and give them the greatest strategic advantage in their target markets. It's important to appreciate that although marketers strive to "create" positioning, it exists in the mind of the individual. In other words, it derives from what that individual thinks about the product, or company, or brand—which is not always the same as what the marketers want them to think. The marketers at automobile companies work very hard to position their brand, and each of their models, in the minds of consumers. The new Toyota Prius, for example, is positioned as the "alternative" car for people concerned about the environment.

Another way to understand positioning is to arrange a set of familiar brands in your mind, relative to each other. For example, consider the following hotel brands: Marriott, Comfort Inn, Hilton, Intercontinental, Fairmont, Days Inn, and Motel 6. Now, think about where you position Marriott in relation to Days Inn. As a consumer you need not necessarily have stayed in all of these hotels in order to assign them a "position" in your mind, relative to their competitors.

In positioning a product, the marketer first identifies possible competitive advantages on which to build the position. To gain competitive advantage, the company must offer greater value to its target segments, either by charging lower prices than competitors do or by offering more benefits. But if marketing positions the product as *offering* greater value, it must then *deliver* that greater value. Thus, effective positioning begins with actually *differentiating* the company's marketing offer so that it gives customers more value than they are offered by the competition. Once the company has chosen a position, it must take strong steps to deliver and communicate that position to its target markets. The marketing program must then support the positioning strategy. For example, Cake Beauty sets itself apart from the competition by positioning its products on two main dimensions. Not only are they indulgent, trendy, and fun; they are also made with nourishing ingredients. These two attributes set the firm apart from its competition.

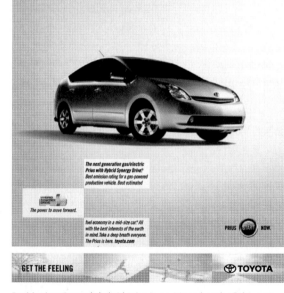

Lifetime supply of fresh air with every purchase.

The next generation gas/electric Prius with Hybrid Synergy Drive. Best emission rating for a gas-powered production vehicle. Best estimated

The power to move forward.

fuel economy in a mid-size car. All with the best interests of the earth in mind. Take a deep breath everyone. The Prius is here. toyota.com

PRIUS START NOW.

GET THE FEELING

TOYOTA

Positioning: Toyota's hybrid Prius is positioned as the "alternative car for people concerned about the environment."

Developing the Marketing Mix

Once the organization's marketing strategy has been developed, its target market segments chosen, and its positioning decided, the next step is to begin planning the details of the marketing mix, one of the major concepts in modern marketing. The

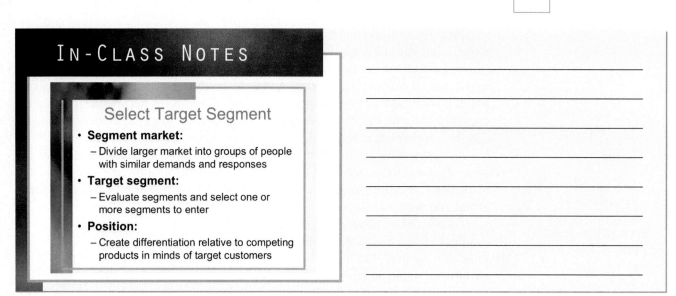

Select Target Segment

- **Segment market:**
  - Divide larger market into groups of people with similar demands and responses
- **Target segment:**
  - Evaluate segments and select one or more segments to enter
- **Position:**
  - Create differentiation relative to competing products in minds of target customers

marketing mix is the set of controllable, tactical marketing tools that the firm blends to produce the response it wants in the target market. The marketing mix consists of everything the firm can do to influence the demand for its product. The many possibilities are collected into four groups of variables known as the "four Ps": *product, price, place,* and *promotion.* Figure 2.5 shows the particular marketing tools under each P.[18]

Marketing mix The set of controllable tactical marketing tools—product, price, place, and promotion—that the firm blends to produce the response it wants in the target market.

Figure 2.5   The Four *P*s of the Marketing Mix

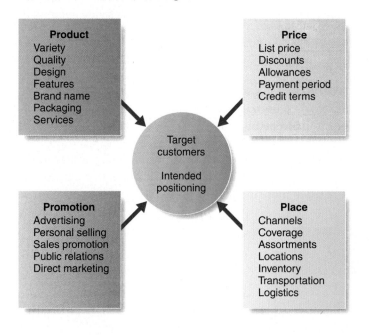

Product means the goods-and-services combination the company offers to the target market. For example, a Toyota Prius is a good that may be augmented by a service agreement, warranty, or other services, all of which are part of the product "package."

Price is the amount of money customers have to pay to obtain the product. The retail price of a consumer product may be suggested by the manufacturer, but retailers are free to set any price they wish for items sold in their stores. In business-to-business sales, the price of a product is usually negotiated.

Place or distribution refers to the locations where the product is available to the customer. Most consumer products are available at retail outlets—grocery stores, drug stores, department stores, convenience stores—but the choice of which retailers, in which cities, is a marketing decision. And every product, whether it is a consumer or a business product, must begin somewhere, and must, somehow, get into the hands of the customer. The path that the product takes, from point of origin to point of sale, is the distribution channel, an important part of the marketing mix.

Promotion is the set of activities that communicates the merits of the product and persuades prospective customers to buy it. These activities include everything related to marketing communications: advertising, sales promotion, public relations, direct marketing, and personal selling.

An effective marketing program blends all elements of the marketing mix into a coordinated plan designed to achieve the company's marketing objectives by delivering value to customers. The marketing mix constitutes the company's tactical tool kit for establishing strong positioning in target markets.

Some critics feel that the four Ps may omit or underemphasize some important activities. For example, they ask, "Where are services?" Just because they don't start with a P doesn't justify omitting them. The answer is that services, such as banking, buying an airline ticket, having your car serviced, or staying in a hotel, are products too. In fact, as we'll learn in Chapter 8, a product can be a physical good, a service, an idea, a person, even a country. As Figure 2.5 suggests, many marketing activities that might appear to be left out of the marketing mix are subsumed under one of the four Ps. The issue is not whether there should be four, six, or ten Ps but what framework is most helpful in designing marketing programs.

Another concern, however, is valid. It holds that the four Ps concept takes the seller's view of the market, not the buyer's view. From the buyer's viewpoint, in this age of connectedness, the four Ps might be better described as the four Cs:[19]

Four Ps	Four Cs
Product	Customer solution
Price	Customer cost
Place	Convenience
Promotion	Communication

Thus, while marketers see themselves as promoting products to a target market, customers see themselves as buying value or solutions to their problems. And customers are interested in more than just the price; they are interested in the total costs of

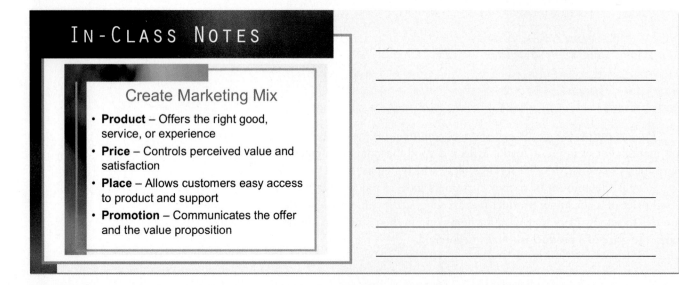

In-Class Notes

Create Marketing Mix

- **Product** – Offers the right good, service, or experience
- **Price** – Controls perceived value and satisfaction
- **Place** – Allows customers easy access to product and support
- **Promotion** – Communicates the offer and the value proposition

obtaining, using, and disposing of a product. Customers want the goods and services they purchase to be as conveniently available as possible. Finally, they want two-way communication. Marketers would do well to first think through the four Cs and then build the four Ps on that platform.

MANAGING THE MARKETING EFFORT

In addition to being good at the marketing in marketing management, companies need to pay attention to the management in marketing management. Managing the marketing process requires the four marketing management functions shown in Figure 2.6—*analysis, planning, implementation,* and *control.* Marketing analysis provides the information and evaluations needed to develop companywide strategic plans. These plans are then translated into marketing and other plans for each division, product, and brand. Through implementation, the company turns the plans into actions. Control consists of measuring and evaluating the results of marketing activities and taking corrective action where needed.

Figure 2.6 Marketing Analysis, Planning, Implementation, and Control

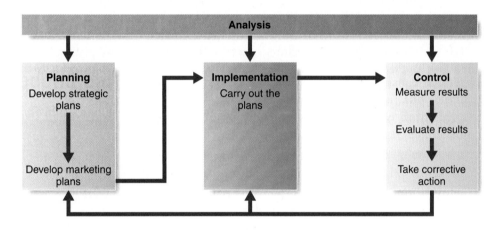

Marketing Analysis

Managing the marketing function begins with a complete analysis of the company's situation. The company must analyze its markets and marketing environment to find attractive opportunities and to avoid environmental threats. It must analyze company strengths and weaknesses, as well as current and possible marketing actions, to determine which opportunities it can best pursue. Marketing analysis provides input to each of the other marketing management functions. We discuss marketing analysis more fully in Chapter 5.

Marketing plan A detailed plan for a business, product, or brand that assesses the current marketing situation and outlines marketing objectives, a marketing strategy, action programs, budgets, and controls.

Marketing Planning

Through strategic planning, the company decides what it wants to do with each business unit. Marketing planning involves deciding on marketing strategies that will help the company reach its overall strategic objectives. A **marketing plan**—a detailed plan that assesses the current marketing

Marketers must continually plan their analysis, implementation, and control of activities.

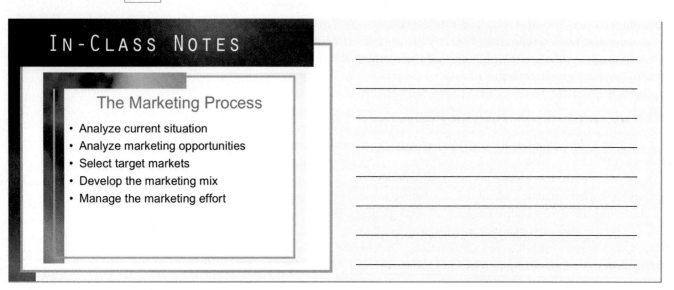

IN-CLASS NOTES

The Marketing Process

- Analyze current situation
- Analyze marketing opportunities
- Select target markets
- Develop the marketing mix
- Manage the marketing effort

situation and outlines marketing objectives, a marketing strategy, action programs, budgets, and controls—is needed for each business, product, or brand. What does a marketing plan look like? Our discussion focuses on product or brand plans.

Table 2.2 outlines the major sections of a typical product or brand plan. The plan begins with an executive summary, which quickly overviews major assessments, goals, and recommendations. The main section of the plan presents a detailed analysis of the current marketing situation as well as potential threats and opportunities. It next states major objectives for the brand and outlines the specifics of a marketing strategy for achieving them.

A *marketing strategy* consists of specific strategies for target markets, positioning, the marketing mix, and marketing expenditure levels. In this section, the planner explains how each strategy responds to the threats, opportunities, and critical issues spelled out earlier in the plan. Additional sections of the marketing plan lay out an action program for implementing the marketing strategy, along with the details of a supporting *marketing budget*. The last section outlines the controls that will be used to monitor progress and take corrective action.

A sample marketing plan for Cake Beauty, the Canadian cosmetics company, is included in Appendix II.

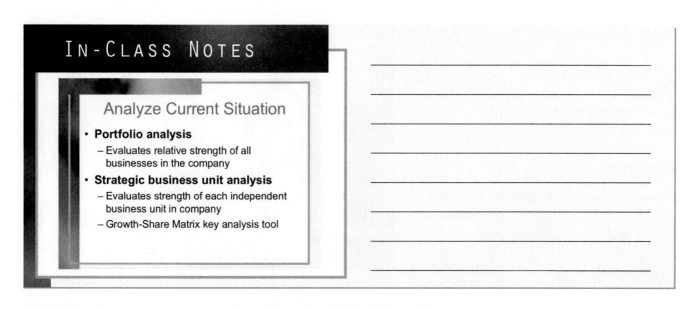

IN-CLASS NOTES

Analyze Current Situation

- **Portfolio analysis**
  - Evaluates relative strength of all businesses in the company
- **Strategic business unit analysis**
  - Evaluates strength of each independent business unit in company
  - Growth-Share Matrix key analysis tool

Table 2.2   Contents of a Marketing Plan

Section	Purpose
Executive summary	Presents a brief summary of the main goals and recommendations of the plan for management review, helping top management to find the plan's major points quickly. A table of contents should follow the executive summary.
Current marketing situation	Describes the target market and the company's position in it, including information about the market, product performance, competition, and distribution. This section includes • A *market description* that defines the market and major segments, reviews customer needs, and outlines factors in the marketing environment that may affect customer purchasing. • A *product review* that shows sales, prices, and gross margins of the major products in the product line. • A review of *competition* that identifies major competitors and assesses their market positions and strategies for product quality, pricing, distribution, and promotion. • A review of *distribution* that evaluates recent sales trends and other developments in major distribution channels.
SWOT analysis	Assesses major strengths and weaknesses as well as threats and opportunities that the product may face, helping management to anticipate important positive or negative developments that may affect the firm and its strategies.
Objectives and issues	States the marketing objectives that the company would like to attain during the plan's term and discusses key issues that will affect their attainment. For example, if the goal is to achieve a 15 percent market share, the key issue is how market share can be increased.
Marketing strategy	Outlines the broad marketing logic by which the business unit hopes to achieve its marketing objectives and the specifics of target markets, positioning, and marketing expenditure levels. It outlines specific strategies for each marketing mix element and explains how each responds to the threats, opportunities, and critical issues spelled out earlier in the plan.
Action program	Indicates how marketing strategies will be turned into specific action programs that answer the following questions: *What* will be done? *When* will it be done? *Who* is responsible for doing it? *How much* will it cost?
Budgets	Details a supporting marketing budget that is essentially a projected profit-and-loss statement. It shows expected revenues (forecast number of units sold and the average net price) and expected costs (of production, distribution, and marketing). The difference is the projected profit. Once approved by higher management, the budget is the basis for materials buying, production scheduling, personnel planning, and marketing operations.
Controls	Outlines the controls that will be used to monitor progress and allow higher management to review implementation results and spot products that are not meeting their goals.

Marketing Implementation

Planning good strategies is only part of successful marketing. A brilliant marketing strategy counts for little if the company fails to implement it properly. **Marketing implementation** is the process that turns marketing *plans* into marketing *actions* to accomplish strategic marketing objectives. Implementation involves daily and monthly activities that effectively put the marketing plan to work. Whereas marketing planning addresses the *what* and *why* of marketing activities, implementation addresses the *who*, *where*, *when*, and *how*.

Marketing implementation The process that turns marketing plans into marketing actions to accomplish strategic marketing objectives.

Many managers think that "doing things right" (implementation) is as important as, or even more important than "doing the right things" (strategy). The fact is that both are critical to success, and companies can gain competitive advantages through effective implementation.[20] One firm can have essentially the same strategy as another, yet win in the marketplace through faster or better execution. Still, implementation is difficult—it is often easier to create good marketing strategies than it is to carry them out.

In an increasingly connected world, people at all levels of the marketing system must work together to implement marketing plans and strategies. At Black & Decker, for example, marketing implementation for the company's power tools requires daily decisions and actions by thousands of people both inside and outside the organization. Marketing managers make decisions about target segments (Black & Decker brand for the do-it-yourself or home segment and DeWalt Tools for the professional segment), branding, packaging, pricing, promoting, and distributing. They connect with people elsewhere in the company to get support for their products and programs. They talk with engineering about product design, with manufacturing about production and inventory levels, and with finance about funding and cash flows. They also connect with outside people, such as advertising agencies to plan ad campaigns and the media to obtain publicity support. The sales force urges Home Hardware, Canadian Tire, RONA, Home Depot, Wal-Mart, and other retailers to promote Black & Decker products in-store, provide ample shelf space, and use company displays.

Successful marketing implementation depends on how well the company blends its people, organizational structure, decision and reward systems, and company culture into a cohesive action program that supports its strategies. At all levels, employees must have the needed skills, motivation, and personal characteristics. The company's formal organizational structure plays an important role in implementing marketing strategy; so do its decision and reward systems. For example, if a company's compensation system rewards managers for short-run profit results, they will have little incentive to work toward long-run market-building objectives.

Finally, to be successfully implemented, the firm's marketing strategies must fit with its company culture, the system of values and beliefs shared by people in the organization. A study of the most successful companies found that these companies have almost cultlike cultures built around strong, market-oriented missions. At companies such as Tim Hortons, Wal-Mart, Microsoft, Roots, Procter & Gamble, Walt Disney, and Hewlett-Packard, "employees share such a strong vision that they know in their hearts what's right for their company."[21]

Marketing Department Organization

The company must design a marketing department that can carry out marketing strategies and plans. If the company is very small, one person might do all the marketing work—research, selling, advertising, customer service, and other activities. As the company expands, a marketing department organization emerges to plan and carry out marketing activities. In large companies, this department contains many specialists. Thus, General Electric and Microsoft have product and market managers, sales managers and salespeople, market researchers, advertising experts, and other specialists.

Modern marketing departments can be arranged in several ways. The most common form of marketing organization is the *functional organization* in which different marketing activities are headed by a functional specialist—a sales manager, advertising manager, marketing research manager, customer service manager, new-product manager. A company that sells across the country or internationally often uses a *geographic organization* in which its sales and marketing people are assigned to specific countries, regions, and districts. Geographic organization allows salespeople to settle into a territory, get to know their customers, and work with a minimum of travel time and cost.

Companies with many very different products or brands often create a *product management organization.* Using this approach, a product manager develops and implements a complete strategy and marketing program for a specific product or brand. Product management first appeared at Procter & Gamble in 1929. A new company soap, Camay, was not doing well, and a young P&G executive was assigned to give his exclusive attention to developing and promoting this brand. He was successful, and the company soon added other product managers.[22] Since then, many firms, especially consumer products companies, have set up product management organizations.

For companies that sell one product line to many different types of markets and customers that have different needs and preferences, a *market* or *customer management organization* might be best. A market management organization is similar to the product management organization. Market managers are responsible for developing marketing strategies and plans for their specific markets or customers. This system's main advantage is that the company is organized around the needs of specific customer segments.

Large companies that produce many different products flowing into many different geographic and customer markets usually employ some *combination* of the functional, geographic, product, and market organization forms. This ensures that each function, product, and market receives its share of management attention. However, it can also add costly layers of management and reduce organizational flexibility. Still, the benefits of organizational specialization usually outweigh the drawbacks.

Marketing organization has become an increasingly important issue in recent years. As we discussed in Chapter 1, many companies are finding that today's marketing environment calls for less focus on products, brands, and territories and more focus on *customer relationship management.* They are moving away from managing just a product or brand profitability and toward managing customer profitability and customer equity.[23] And many companies such as Procter & Gamble and Black & Decker have large teams, or even whole divisions, set up to serve their large customers like Shoppers Drug Mart and Canadian Tire.

Marketing Control

Because many surprises occur during the implementation of marketing plans, the marketing department must practise constant marketing control. **Marketing control** is the process of measuring and evaluating the results of marketing strategies and plans and taking corrective action to ensure that objectives are attained.

Figure 2.7 shows that four steps are involved in marketing control. Management first sets specific marketing goals. It then measures its performance in the marketplace and evaluates the causes of any differences between expected and actual performance. Finally, management takes corrective action to close the gaps between its

Marketing control The process of measuring and evaluating the results of marketing strategies and plans and taking corrective action to ensure that objectives are achieved.

Figure 2.7   **The Marketing Control Process**

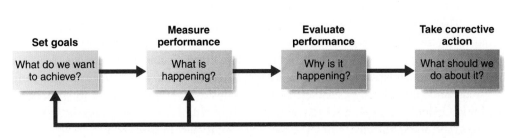

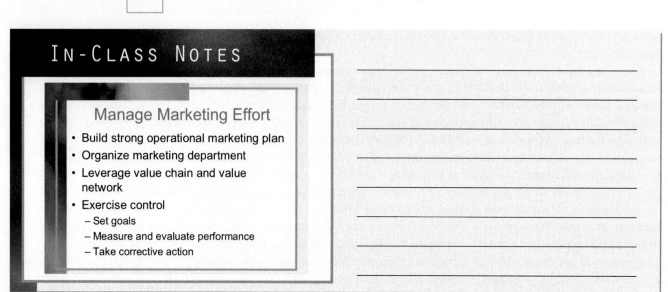

Manage Marketing Effort

- Build strong operational marketing plan
- Organize marketing department
- Leverage value chain and value network
- Exercise control
  - Set goals
  - Measure and evaluate performance
  - Take corrective action

Marketing audit A comprehensive, systematic, independent, and periodic examination of a company's environment, objectives, strategies, and activities to determine problem areas and opportunities and to recommend a plan of action to improve the company's marketing performance.

goals and its performance. This step may require changing the action programs or even changing the goals.

Operating control involves checking ongoing performance against the annual plan and taking corrective action when necessary. Its purpose is to ensure that the company achieves the sales, profits, and other goals set out in its annual plan. It also involves determining the profitability of different products, territories, markets, and channels.

Strategic control involves looking at whether the company's basic strategies are well matched to its opportunities. Marketing strategies and programs can quickly become outdated, and each company should periodically reassess its overall approach to the marketplace. A major tool for such strategic control is a *marketing audit*. The **marketing audit** is a comprehensive, systematic, independent, and periodic examination of a company's environment, objectives, strategies, and activities to determine problem areas and opportunities and to recommend a plan of action to improve the company's marketing performance.

The marketing audit covers all major marketing areas of a business, not just a few trouble spots. It assesses the marketing environment, marketing strategy, marketing organization, marketing systems, marketing mix, and marketing productivity and profitability. The audit is normally conducted by an objective and experienced outside party. The findings may come as a surprise—and sometimes as a shock—to management. Management then decides which actions make sense and how and when to implement them.

THE MARKETING ENVIRONMENT

Managing the marketing function would be hard enough if the marketer had to deal only with the controllable marketing mix variables. But the company operates in a complex marketing environment, consisting of uncontrollable forces to which the company must adapt. The environment produces both threats and opportunities. The company must carefully analyze its environment so that it can avoid the threats and take advantage of the opportunities.

The company's marketing environment includes forces close to the company that affect its ability to serve its customers, such as other company departments, channel members, suppliers, competitors, and the public. It also includes broader demographic and economic forces, political and legal forces, technological and ecological forces, and social and cultural forces. Marketers need to consider all these forces in the process of building and maintaining profitable relationships with customers and marketing partners. The marketing environment is discussed more fully in Chapter 4.

LOOKING BACK

What have you learned so far? In Chapter 1, we defined marketing and outlined the steps in the marketing process. We learned that the aim of marketing is to create value for customers in order to capture value in return. In this chapter, we examined companywide strategic planning and marketing's role in the organization. Then, we looked more deeply into marketing strategy and the marketing mix, and reviewed the major marketing management functions. So you've had a pretty good overview of the fundamentals of modern marketing. In future chapters, we'll expand on these fundamentals.

REVIEWING THE CONCEPTS

1. Explain companywide strategic planning and its four steps.

Strategic planning sets the stage for the rest of the company's planning. Marketing contributes to strategic planning, and the overall plan defines marketing's role in the company. Although formal planning offers a variety of benefits to companies, not all companies use it or use it well. Although many discussions of strategic planning focus on large corporations, small business also can benefit greatly from sound strategic planning.

Strategic planning involves developing a strategy for long-term survival and growth. It consists of four steps: defining the company's mission, setting objectives and goals, designing a business portfolio, and developing functional plans. *Defining a clear company mission* begins with drafting a formal mission statement, which should be market oriented, realistic, specific, motivating, and consistent with the market environment. The mission is then transformed into detailed *supporting goals and objectives* to guide the entire company. Based on those goals and objectives, headquarters designs a *business portfolio*, deciding which businesses and products should receive more or fewer resources. In turn, each business and product unit must develop *detailed marketing plans* in line with the companywide plan. Comprehensive and sound marketing plans support company strategic planning by detailing specific opportunities.

2. Discuss how to design business portfolios and develop strategies for growth and downsizing.

Guided by the company's mission statement and objectives, management plans its *business portfolio*, or the collection of businesses and products that make up the company. The firm wants to produce a business portfolio that best fits its strengths and weaknesses to opportunities in the environment. To do this, it must analyze and adjust its *current* business portfolio and develop growth and downsizing strategies for adjusting the *future* portfolio. The company might use a formal portfolio-planning method. But many companies are now designing more-customized portfolio-planning approaches that better suit their unique situations. The *product/market expansion grid* suggests four possible growth paths: market penetration, market development, product development, and diversification.

3. Explain marketing's role in strategic planning and how marketing works with its partners to create and deliver customer value.

Under the strategic plan, the major functional departments—marketing, finance, accounting, purchasing, operations, information systems, human resources, and others—must work together to accomplish strategic objectives. Marketing plays a key role in the company's strategic planning by providing a *marketing-concept philosophy* and *inputs* regarding attractive market opportunities. Within individual business units, marketing designs *strategies* for reaching the unit's objectives and helps to carry them out profitably.

Marketers alone cannot produce superior value for customers. They can be only a partner in attracting, keeping, and growing customers. A company's success depends on how well each department performs its customer value-adding activities and how well the departments work together to serve the customer. Thus, marketers must practise *partner relationship management*. They must work closely with partners in other company departments to form an effective *value chain* that serves the customer. And they must partner effectively with other companies in the marketing system to form a competitively superior *value-delivery network*.

4. Describe the elements of a customer-driven marketing strategy and marketing mix, and the forces that influence them.

Customer relationships are at the centre of marketing strategy and programs. Through market segmentation, target marketing, and market positioning, the company divides the total market into smaller segments, selects the segments it can best serve, and decides how it wants to bring value to target customers. It then designs a *marketing mix* to produce the response it wants in the target market. The marketing mix consists of product, price, place, and promotion decisions.

5. List the functions of marketing management.

To find the best strategy and mix and to put them into action, the company engages in marketing analysis, planning, implementation, and control. The main components of a *marketing plan* are the executive summary, current marketing situation, threats and opportunities, objectives and issues, marketing strategies, action programs, budgets, and controls. To plan good strategies is often easier than to carry them out. To be successful, companies must also be effective at *implementation*—turning marketing strategies into marketing actions.

Much of the responsibility for implementation goes to the company's marketing department. Modern marketing departments can be organized in one or a combination of ways: *functional marketing organization, geographic organization, product management organization,* or *market management organization.* In this age of customer relationships, more and more companies are now changing their organizational focus from product or territory management to customer relationship management. Marketing organizations carry out *marketing control,* both operating control and strategic control. They use *marketing audits* to determine marketing opportunities and problems and to recommend short-run and long-run actions to improve overall marketing performance. Through these activities, the company watches and adapts to the marketing environment.

Key Terms

STUDY GUIDE

After completing this self-test, check your answers against the Answer Key at the back of the book.

Multiple Choice

1. When a company wishes to provide guidance about its business to its employees and other internal stakeholders, the first tool it should use is
   a. Employee handbook
   b. Strategic plan
   c. The mission statement
   d. Positioning statement
   e. Annual report

2. Milax Industries has implemented the BCG matrix in its planning. The company has two self-funding dogs, one strong cash cow, no stars, and a costly question mark. The most reasonable action that Milax can take is

   a. Hold the dogs, hold and harvest the cow, invest in the question mark, and strive to build the question mark into a star
   b. Divest the dogs, harvest the cow aggressively, and build the question mark aggressively
   c. Divest the dogs and the question mark and hold the cow, building cash reserves while undergoing research to enter into a new high-growth market
   d. Hold the dogs, divest the question mark, and invest back into the cow to ensure its longevity.
   e. Any of the above depending on the company's strategic objectives and risk tolerance.

3. Rogers Communications started as a single radio station and now has business units offering Canadians cable television, wireless communications, Internet access, and value-priced long-distance phone services. The expansion philosophy that most closely matches that practised by Rogers is
   a. Diversification
   b. Market expansion
   c. Customer-driven expansion
   d. Brand continuity
   e. Product expansion

4. When Labatt announced that it was divesting all its business units except its beer-brewing business, the company embarked on a strategic path of
   a. Downsizing
   b. Revenue rationalization
   c. Market regression
   d. Product pullback
   e. Divestification

5. Marketing is too important to be left to the marketing department alone. In truth, however, many companies suffer from misalignment of marketing goals and actions with those of other departments. This misalignment generally results in
   a. The need to constantly replace marketing managers
   b. The need for the CEO to find points of compromise to keep things moving
   c. Additional planning sessions to find a strategy that everyone can live with
   d. Conflict in the value chain and thus disruption in delivering value to customers
   e. The need to outsource all marketing to an outside, objective company or agency

6. Originally released as a pain and fever reliever for colds and flu, Aspirin now brings value to three distinctive customer groups, each with a specific need: (a) families or individuals as an all-purpose pain reliever; (b) individuals with long-term inflammatory joint conditions such as arthritis; and (c) seniors as a blood thinner for preventing heart attacks. These specific groups of customers represent Aspirin's
   a. Product expansion groups
   b. Cash cows
   c. Target segments
   d. Niches
   e. Differentiated mass markets

7. A key part of creating a compelling marketing offering to a market segment is to differentiate the offering from those of competitors. For example, Oil of Olay is a premium soap that makes mature skin look younger, Ivory is "pure and gentle" for babies, while No-name provides basic cleansing at a low, low cost. In each case, the soap is carefully _____ for its target segment.

   a. Positioned
   b. Branded
   c. Productized
   d. Promoted
   e. Distributed

8. Procter & Gamble makes a number of different brands of shampoos and conditioners, each one carefully positioned for its target segments. In order to bring their product to market in a way that strengthens its positioning, each brand manager must carefully balance the elements of
   a. Brand identity
   b. The marketing mix
   c. Promotional techniques
   d. Profit and loss
   e. Market expansion

9. Companies often make adjustments to promotional campaigns based on results and how closely they match objectives. This type of activity is critical to the marketing management function, specifically
   a. Goal setting
   b. Matrix management
   c. Cost control
   d. Marketing control
   e. Expectation management

10. The best strategic and operational plans can come to grief because the organization is not able to
    a. Effectively communicate and put the plan into practice across the company
    b. Calculate the cost of doing the activities
    c. Keep changing the plans to reflect shifting market conditions
    d. Convince their partners that it's a plan for success
    e. Extend the plans out to international markets

TRUE/FALSE

T F 1. If a company has solid operational and long-range plans, strategic planning is generally not needed.

T F 2. In order to succeed, companies with a clear mission should nevertheless be prepared to deviate from that mission if market conditions change.

T F 3. Companies undertaking strategic planning for future business should always rely on the BCG Growth-Share Matrix.

T F 4. A single-line-of-business company should nevertheless go through a business unit analysis, whether formally or informally.

T F 5. A small company servicing a local market generally has no need to consider global business and competition.

CONCEPT CHECK

1. _____ is the process of developing and maintaining a strategic fit between the organization's goals and capabilities and its changing marketing opportunities.

2. A _____ is a statement of the organization's purpose—what it wants to accomplish in the larger environment.

3. Management should avoid making its mission too narrow or too broad. According to this section of the text, missions should be _____, _____, fit the _____, and be _____.

4. A business portfolio is the collection of businesses and products that make up the company. The best business portfolio is the one that _____ _____.

5. A company can classify all its SBUs according to a growth-share matrix. Four types of SBUs can usually be identified. The _____ are low-growth, high-share businesses or products. They produce a lot of cash that is used to support other SBUs.

6. Once a company has classified its SBUs, the company must determine what role each will play in the future. The company may choose one of four strategies. These strategies are to _____, _____, _____, or _____ the SBU.

7. When the marketing manager considers growth strategies, _____ would be chosen if the goal of the company wants to make more sales to current customers without changing products.

8. When each department within a firm carries out value-creating activities to design, produce, market, deliver, and support the firm's products, the department can be thought of as a link in the company's _____.

9. _____ is the process of dividing a market into distinct groups of buyers with different needs, characteristics, or behaviour who might require separate products or marketing mixes.

10. The four Ps of the marketing mix are _____, _____, _____, and _____.

11. The four marketing management functions are _____, _____, _____, and _____.

12. A _____ is the marketing logic whereby the company hopes to achieve its marketing objectives.

STUDENT MATERIALS

Visit our website at www.pearsoned.ca/armstrong for online quizzes, Internet exercises, and more!

NOTES

_____

_____

_____

_____

_____

_____

_____

_____

_____

_____

_____

_____

_____

_____

_____

_____

_____

_____

_____

_____

_____

_____

DISCUSSING THE ISSUES

1. Define strategic planning. List and briefly describe the four steps of the strategic-planning process.

2. In a series of job interviews, you ask three recruiters to describe the missions of their companies. One says, "to make profits." Another says, "to create customers." The third says, "to fight world hunger." Analyze and discuss what these mission statements tell you about each company. Which appears to be more *market oriented?* Explain and justify.

3. An electronics manufacturer obtains the semiconductors it uses in production from a company-owned subsidiary that also sells to other manufacturers. The subsidiary is smaller and less profitable than competing producers, and its growth rate has been below the industry average during the past five years. Define which cell of the BCG growth-share matrix this strategic business unit would fall into. Explain your choice. What should the parent company do with this SBU?

4. Beyond evaluating current businesses, designing the business portfolio involves finding businesses and products the company should consider in the future. Using the product–market expansion grid, illustrate the process that a company can use to evaluate a portfolio. Pick an example for your demonstration that is different from the one used in the text. Be sure your example covers all cells.

5. To succeed in today's marketplace, companies must be customer centred. Explain how (a) Rogers Wireless, (b) the Toronto Blue Jays, and (c) Mountain Equipment Co-op can use the processes of market segmentation, marketing targeting, and marketing positioning to become more customer centred. Suggest a "new" position for each organization and explain and justify the position you have suggested.

MARKETING APPLICATIONS

Sony has found the right approach for surrounding its customers with electronic wizardry and entertainment. From PlayStation to online games, from movies to TV, DVD, and music, Sony is tops in entertainment. But rivals are on the horizon. With hungry competitors such as Disney, Panasonic, and a host of others, Sony must constantly adjust its strategic plans and look for new opportunities. For more general information on Sony and its offerings, see www.sony.com.

THINKING LIKE A MARKETING MANAGER

1. After considering Sony's approach to the world of electronics and entertainment, identify new and promising product opportunities for Sony.
2. Choose one of the product opportunities you identified. What makes it distinctive and promising?
3. What target market would you pursue for this product opportunity?
4. What marketing mix would be appropriate?

VIDEO CASE

Go to Pearson Canada's Video Central site (www.pearsoned.ca/highered/videocentral) to view the video and accompanying case for this chapter.

CASE 2 DUELLING MARKETING STRATEGIES: MICROSOFT VS. APPLE

Marketing strategy is about more than just developing new products and promoting them to the marketplace. Long-term thinking, a careful eye on the competition, the ability to anticipate and plan for best and worst case market situations, are skills today's marketing manager must have.

Take the iPod, the wildly popular portable music storage and playing device. Or is it? The marketers at Apple Computer Inc., the makers of the iPod, are more likely to think of their product as a stepping stone in the longer term development of personal content devices. Apple's longtime rival in the personal computer software business, Microsoft, is also thinking long term. "The battle is really about who controls the next generation of home entertainment; how content is received, stored, viewed, manipulated and distributed," says one technology journalist.

The global market for recorded music is valued at an estimated $35 billion U.S. Today, Apple estimates that one in three portable music players owned by consumers is an iPod. At Microsoft headquarters in Redmond, Washington, the penetration rate is even higher: Eight out of ten employees who carry a personal music playing device carry an iPod. The success of Apple's iPod has caused arch-rival Microsoft to sit up and take notice, but it's not the first time that Microsoft's strategy has changed direction as a result of a move by the competition.

Netscape developed their popular, user-friendly Web browser in 1994, and it wasn't until two years later that Microsoft followed with Internet Explorer. No one, not even Microsoft, claimed that Internet Explorer was a superior product, so how did Microsoft manage to take over nearly 100 percent of the browser market within a year and hold onto it for almost ten? They had a brilliant strategy: Link the Internet Explorer software to the Windows operating system. Since the release of Windows 98, everyone who buys a Windows-based computer has an icon for the Internet Explorer Web browser built into their desktop. Microsoft's strategy was to control the distribution, to make it easy, almost automatic, for users to use their product rather than Netscape's. Microsoft's strategy was so successful it eventually resulted in Netscape going out of business.

In May 2004 Apple created a separate business unit for the iPod, so that marketers and others responsible for the development, positioning, targeting, distribution, and selling of the iPod could work together, setting their own goals and developing their own strategy. This strategic decision to reorganize the company shows that Apple is planning for changes in the nature of the market. According to Michael Gartenberg, vice president and research director at Jupiter Research, "Apple recognizes that their market goes beyond the Mac now, [and that] consumers want all their digital entertainment in one place."

The iPod is a star product at Apple. The company reported that the product accounted for approximately one-third of total revenues for the second quarter of 2005. Not bad for a product that's only four years old. Unfortunately for Microsoft, Apple's star is casting a shadow on Microsoft's cash cow—its Windows operating system and Windows-based desktop software products such as Word and Excel. These products generated US$22.3 billion in revenue for the company in 2004. That's 60 percent of the company's total revenue for that year. The problem? Computer users who choose the iPod for their music are becoming loyal Apple customers, and many are switching from PCs to Macs. That's a turn of events that could eventually spell disaster for Microsoft. A new strategy was needed.

Microsoft's mission is to "help people and businesses throughout the world realize their full potential." Rival Apple's mission statement is similar: "Apple Computer is committed to protecting the environment, health and safety of our employees, customers and the global communities where we operate." Each company's mission guides its strategy, and though consumers have only recently seen the tangible results of the strategy, Microsoft has undoubtedly spent years analyzing the market and carefully developing and planning its strategy for entering the market for personal devices.

And for Microsoft, helping people realize their full potential means giving them options, so Microsoft recently struck back at Apple by introducing a new product called the Portable Media Center, or PMC, a Windows-based personal music storage and playing device. It's not enough to provide only the hardware device to consumers, though; the music lover must have something to play on it. So Apple introduced iTunes and Microsoft followed with its MSN Music, one of the largest digital libraries in the world.

"Music, like other digital media, is only a spoke; for Microsoft's strategy, it all comes back to the hub," says the technology journalist. The "hub" he's referring to is the Windows operating system, meaning that Microsoft's PMC strategy supports those of its other divisions. The PMC can store and play back recorded TV shows, downloaded videos, home movies, music, and photos. It works with Microsoft's Windows Media Player, the software needed to play back music and video. And that software is free; it comes with the Windows operating system purchased for the computer. And since music files recorded in Windows Media Player format aren't compatible with files recorded with Apple's Quicktime software, consumers are forced to choose between Microsoft and Apple, not only for their hardware device but for everything associated with it. For the consumer, it's a long-term commitment. For the two companies, it's a clever strategy designed to lock in their market segment.

It's also a strategy developed in response to the changing market. Ten years ago a personal computer was something to write documents and balance your chequebook with. Today it's a window to the Internet, a movie player, a place to store and organize photo albums, and a device for storing and playing back recorded music. The iPod and the PMC were developed to take advantage of these changes, and so far, it looks like the strategy is working. But both companies will need to monitor the marketplace and be ready to adapt their strategy to new technologies, changing consumer behaviour, and, of course, to what the other company does.

Questions

1. Visit Apple's website and read about the company. How many business divisions or SBUs does the company have? How are they organized? Now, visit Microsoft's website and examine how their business divisions are organized. Are the two companies similar, or different, in their company organization?

2. Imagine you are a marketer responsible for the iPod marketing strategy. How would you classify the iPod as a product? How would you segment the market for the iPod? Describe the target market for the iPod.

3. Describe the positioning of Apple's iPod versus the positioning of Microsoft's PMC. What other personal music playing devices are available on the market? How does their positioning differ from the iPod and the PMC? Which device would you choose, as a consumer? Why?

Sources: Simon Avery, "Software Giant Plays Catch-up," *Globe and Mail*, April 16, 2005; Blane Warrene, "Apple Carves Out New iPod Division," MacNewsWorld.com, May 20, 2004.

1. *1.* understand marketing's multiple responsibilities, and identify the major social and ethical criticisms of marketing

2. *2.* define *consumerism* and *environmentalism* and explain how they affect marketing strategies

3. *3.* describe the principles of socially responsible marketing

4. *4.* explain the role of ethics in marketing

Marketing and Society: Social Responsibility and Marketing Ethics

3

Looking Ahead   In this chapter, we'll focus on marketing as a social institution. First, we'll look at some common criticisms of marketing as it impacts individual consumers, other businesses, and society as a whole. Then, we'll examine consumerism and consumer-based legislation, environmentalism, and other citizen and public actions that keep marketing in check. Finally, we'll see how companies themselves can benefit from proactively pursuing socially responsible and ethical practices. You'll see that social responsibility and ethical actions are more than just the right thing to do; they're also good for business.

When was the last time you considered the societal implications of the cup of coffee you were drinking? If you're like most people, the answer to that question is never. As consumers, we rarely think consciously about what went into the production and marketing of the product we are purchasing. As consumers, our role is to consume the product—ingest it, wear it, drive it, or use it until it no longer suits our purpose, at which time we discard it and purchase a replacement.

The role of the producer of those products, on the other hand, is to manufacture, or grow, or somehow provide, and then to promote—in other words, to *market*—the product to us. While many companies do the work of production quietly, preferring that we, as consumers, not know the details about how and where the product is being produced, other companies, those with a "social conscience," take great pride in the ethical and social considerations that go into the production of their product— and they want consumers to know about them.

The Ethical Bean Company of Vancouver is one such organization. The company was founded by Lloyd Bernhardt and Kim Schachte, two coffee lovers who say they feel a "deep, personal connection with Latin America." Ethical Bean sells only 100 percent certified fair trade coffee. What is "fair trade" coffee, you ask?

Fair trade is a movement among businesses who import, distribute, and market products that originate in third world countries. Coffee is the world's second-largest commodity (oil is the largest), and most of it is produced in countries whose citizens have a much lower standard of living than we do as Canadians. Marketers and business owners who believe in the principles of fair trade vow to deal only with farmers and producers who are able to earn a decent living for their efforts—and they work to ensure that this happens. Organizations that deal in fair trade coffee work to set a guaranteed minimum price for the coffee, and strive to eliminate intermediaries wherever possible in an attempt to allow farmers to reap the direct benefits of their production.

Communities in Latin America benefit from the ethical marketing principles of companies such as Ethical Bean, not only because their farmers earn a better wage but because social programs instituted by fair trade organizations bring better education, training, and health care to these countries. Ethical Bean is just one Canadian business that believes it has a responsibility to be a good global citizen. "Ethical Bean understands that the decisions we make can change lives and build futures," boasts the company's website.

The socially responsible business decisions made by Ethical Bean are not limited to their supplier relationships, however. Each December Ethical Bean organizes a promotion through which a portion of their revenues goes toward aiding children in Guatemala. The company challenges other Vancouver businesses to match its donations. Together, Ethical Bean and other local companies have helped raise funds for Child Aid, a nonprofit organization that helps underprivileged children in Latin America.

Ethical Bean believes in environmental sustainability. The company roasts and sells only coffee that is grown under environmentally friendly conditions; that is, organic, shade grown, and "bird friendly." It deals only with coffee bean suppliers who strive, in their operations, to preserve their surrounding environment.

The coffee roasted and sold by Ethical Bean is 100 percent organically grown. This is important to the company, because it believes that as coffee consumers we should be aware of, and sensitive to, the long-term repercussions of producing a farmed commodity such as coffee. Refraining from using chemical fertilizers and pesticides promotes the long-term health and viability of the soil, water, and air that surround the coffee farms. In order to be certified organic a coffee farmer must prove that no chemicals have been used in the growing and processing of the coffee for three years.

Environmentally friendly coffee is grown in the shade. Coffee grows naturally in the forest, but modern mass production encouraged farmers to grow coffee in an open field. Doing so increases production but has devastating effects on the soil and destroys the forests to create the plantations. Furthermore, removing the coffee plants from their natural habitat forces farmers to use chemical fertilizers to replace the organic forest material that naturally fertilizes the plants. Finally, preserving the forest canopy while growing coffee protects the habitats of birds and other small animals; it is in this way that Ethical Bean considers its coffee to be bird friendly.

Educating the consumer is another important part of Ethical Bean's business. The company's website (www.ethicalbean.com) encourages coffee drinkers to exercise choice, to consider environmental issues, and to activate their power as a coffee consumer. The site provides links to the websites of organizations such as TransFair Canada, which certifies fair trade products in Canada, and Coffee Kids, a nonprofit that works with non-government organizations in Latin America to develop education, health care, and training programs for coffee farmers and their families.

Socially responsible marketing requires a socially responsible consumer. So if it's important to you to deal with companies that are concerned about society and the environment, then, as Ethical Bean suggests, exercise your power as a consumer. The next time you buy a cup of coffee, or ground coffee, or beans to take home, ask whether that coffee is fair trade certified.[1]

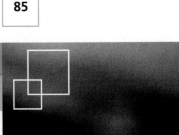

TEST YOURSELF

Answers to these questions can be found on our website at
www.pearsoned.ca/armstrong.

1. Socially responsible marketers strive to deal fairly with all customers, even disadvantaged consumers. The Ethical Bean Company (EB) has a different take on this issue, feeling that it is equally important to deal fairly with
   a) Aggressive competitors
   b) Other fair trade companies
   c) Disadvantaged suppliers
   d) Environmental sustainability
   e) Latin American governments

2. Why does EB put so much of its profits back into the children of the countries from where its coffee comes?
   a) Because those children will grow into farmers loyal to EB
   b) Because it can advertise this fact and thus sell more coffee
   c) Because the farmers consider the education of their children part of the wholesale price of their coffee beans
   d) Because EB believes that it has a responsibility to create social good
   e) Because social programs is a required part of being a "fair trade" company

3. The survival of fair trade companies like EB depends largely on the support of
   a) Government trade laws
   b) Coffee farmers
   c) Multinational coffee corporations
   d) Ethically concerned coffee consumers
   e) Strong distribution networks

4. If EB is so concerned about the welfare of small coffee farmers, then why doesn't it encourage these farmers to expand their farms through clear cutting and chemical use?
   a) Because a critical part of EB's fair trade mandate is to support environmentally sustainable farming practices
   b) Because these smaller farmers cannot afford to use mass production farming techniques
   c) Because it would then be competing directly with multinational companies
   d) Because it compromises the quality of the coffee beans
   e) Because it raises farming costs and thus reduces EB's profits

5. Why does EB go to such lengths to provide educational information on its website, particularly information that is not directly related to its coffee products?
   a) Because educating consumers about the social and environmental implications of their buying choices is important to changing their buying behaviours
   b) Because consumers want to know how the money they spend with EB is being used to further EB's social and environmental beliefs
   c) Because without informed consumers making ethical choices, EB would struggle to survive
   d) Because providing this information allows EB's customers to directly support the organizations that EB supports
   e) All of the above

A majority of Canadians believe that social responsibility should be one of the highest priorities of large companies. According to GlobeScan's 2005 Corporate Social Responsibility Monitor, a whopping 92 percent of Canadians said they are more likely to purchase the products of a company that has shown itself to be socially and environmentally responsible, and 93 percent of Canadians felt that social responsibility should be as important to companies as profit and shareholder value. And it's not just as consumers that we express these feelings: 91 percent said they would prefer to work for such a company.

On the other hand, 50 percent of those surveyed feel that Canadian companies are "just average" in their social responsibility, and 40 percent said they would not purchase from a company they felt was not acting in a socially responsible manner. Canadians, it seems, have high expectations of their companies. In fact, when it comes to demanding that companies act responsibly in their treatment of consumers, employees, and the environment, Canadians are among the most demanding in the world. We are the most likely to reward a socially responsible company with our business, and the most likely to punish one by withholding it.[2]

Such trends are important to responsible marketers, who constantly strive to discover what consumers want and respond with marketing offers that give satisfaction and value to buyers and profit to the producer. They adhere to the *marketing concept,* which was defined in Chapter 1 as a philosophy of creating customer value while making a profit. Socially responsible marketers take this a step further and adhere to the societal marketing concept, providing value to customers in a way that maintains or improves both the customer's and society's well being.

Suncor, a Calgary-based integrated energy company employing over 3400 people, is a good example of a company that remains profitable while fulfilling a values-led mission. Its website proclaims,

> Today, we see social responsibility as encompassing every area of our business. It's reflected in the kind of workplace opportunities we provide and in how healthy and safe we make that workplace for our employees, our contractors and all others who may be affected by our operations. It comes to life in the way we communicate and interact with stakeholders and in our recognition of the economic and special needs of neighbouring communities. It is made visible by the encouragement we provide to community growth and involvement—whether that means supporting an employee in volunteer efforts, or providing financial help to a community project through the Suncor Energy Foundation.[3]

HP Canada is another company that takes the views of Canadians into consideration. Concerned because the ink and toner cartridges for its printers have the potential to clog landfills and pollute the environment, HP Canada actively encourages recycling through its Envelope in the Box program. Used toner cartridges can be placed in the postage-paid envelope that comes in the box with a new cartridge, and mailed back to the company for recycling.

Sometimes quietly adhering to the societal marketing concept is not enough—some companies, after having been criticized for social or environmental irresponsibility, need to take steps to show the public that they've changed. For example, Shell's image was severely damaged in 1995 when it made the decision to sink an abandoned and contaminated oil platform, the Brent Spar, in the North Atlantic. Greenpeace staged a protest over the decision, after which Shell's sales in Germany dropped 30 percent. Employees left the company in droves, and new recruits were difficult to find. The entire Shell brand was in trouble as a result of its corporate activities and the judgments made upon them by the general public.

Shell's solution was an advertising and public relations campaign. Full-page ads explaining the company's position were published in newspapers, including the *Globe and Mail.* In Canada, Shell held open-house meetings with First Nations communities in Alberta, and a series of academic roundtables at the University of Alberta, University of Toronto, Dalhousie, University of British Columbia, and Queen's.[4]

Not all marketers follow the societal marketing concept, however, and certainly there are companies that use questionable marketing practices. Moreover, some marketing actions that seem innocent in themselves nevertheless affect society. Consider alcoholic beverages, for example. The sale of these products to consumers, while controlled, is perfectly legal in Canada; however, misuse of the product can affect society.

Pregnant women are discouraged by their doctors from consuming alcohol, lest it adversely affect the health of their babies. Drinking and driving is against the law, and in the last 20 years the punishments for breaking that law have become more severe. Consuming alcohol while taking medication can lead to health problems. In all these cases, people other than the individual consumer of the product are affected.

Socially responsible marketers of alcoholic beverages, such as Molson and Labatt, include the message "Please consume responsibly" on their advertising; run their own campaigns with the message "Don't drink and drive"; and put their money where their mouth is by sponsoring taxi programs to help those who have been drinking get home safely.

SOCIAL CRITICISMS OF MARKETING

Marketing is often criticized in the press and by the general public. Some of the criticism is justified; much is not. It cannot be denied, however, that marketers must understand the ethical and social issues associated with their profession and work to resolve these issues. There are ethical issues associated with each and every aspect of marketing practice.

Consumer Concerns

Consumers have many concerns about how well the marketing efforts of commercial organizations serve their interests. Surveys usually show that consumers hold mixed or even slightly unfavourable attitudes toward marketing and advertising. Consumers, consumer advocate groups, government agencies, and other critics have accused some businesses of harming consumers through high prices, high-pressure selling, and outright deceptive marketing practices. Consumers are also concerned about unsafe products, planned obsolescence, and discriminatory pricing.

High Prices Consumers complain that unreasonably high prices result from "unnecessary" and expensive advertising. In 2004 Air Canada was roundly criticized in the press when, after having filed for bankruptcy protection and then forcing its labour unions to accept pay cuts, the company turned around and spent millions on a new branding campaign that included lavishly produced television commercials, the repainting of all its planes, new uniforms for all its staff, and a private party at which Céline Dion performed.

Consumers also complain that high retail prices are a result of too many intermediaries, sometimes portrayed as "greedy middlemen" who add nothing to the value chain yet mark up the price of goods as they pass through their hands. How do marketers answer these charges? They argue that intermediaries do work that would otherwise have to be done by manufacturers or consumers. Markups reflect services that consumers themselves want—more convenience, larger stores, greater variety, longer store hours, and return privileges. Regardless of how many distributors or wholesalers are working behind the scenes, the costs involved in operating a retail store are not inconsequential. In fact, retailers point out, retail competition is so intense that margins are actually quite low. For example, after taxes, supermarket chains are typically left with anywhere from a bare 1 percent

Air Canada was criticized for spending millions on a new branding campaign shortly after having filed for bankruptcy protection.

to 10 percent gross margin on their sales, depending on the product category. And if some retailers try to charge too much relative to the value they add, others will step in with lower prices. Stores that compete on the basis of low price, such as Zellers and Wal-Mart, pressure their competitors to operate efficiently and keep their prices down.

The modern marketing phenomenon of brand name vs. "no name" or generic products draws criticism when consumers ask why Tylenol, for example, costs so much more than the Shoppers Drug Mart's store brand acetaminophen, or why Tide is more expensive than other, less expensively promoted brands of laundry detergent. Marketers respond that though it's true that consumers can usually buy functional versions of products at lower prices, many consumers *want* and are willing to pay more for national brands. Recognized brands provide consumers with psychological benefits—they make them feel wealthy, attractive, or special. Brand-name products may cost more, but branding gives buyers assurances of consistent quality. Advertising these brand-name products may be part of the reason why the brand costs more than the no-name version, but advertising also informs consumers of the availability and merits of that brand. If consumers want to know what is available on the market, they must expect that marketers will have to spend money on advertising.

Another consumer complaint is the apparent outrageousness of the markups on some consumer products. Though most consumers understand that a pill that costs a few pennies to manufacture sells for much more than that because of the research that went into developing it, they have a more difficult time comprehending why a blank CD costs $1, a music CD $15 to $25, and a CD containing the latest version of Microsoft Windows, $150. A CD is a CD, isn't it? It's just a piece of plastic, after all. But when we think about it we realize that it's not the plastic we're paying for, but what's on the CD and the expertise that went into producing it.

Modern marketers are keenly aware of consumer concerns about high prices, and realize that their task is to provide *value* to the customer. For example, Cake Beauty grew out of Heather Reier's passion for beauty products. A consumer of many popular brands herself, Reier observed that there was a hole in the market. Consumers had to choices: expensive apothecary-style products or mass-produced products that were well-packaged but made of cheap ingredients. There were no sassy products with decadent ingredients and sophisticated packaging. Marketing, as was described in Chapter 1, is the exchange of value between a business and a customer. At one level, this exchange is simply one of money for goods, but value comprises more than just that. Ask yourself why you purchased the last item you purchased, and why you bought it from that particular location. Was it solely because of price, or were there other factors—perhaps convenience of location, or brand name? Perhaps you became aware of your choice through an advertisement. Marketers must understand the value of the product they are marketing—but so must consumers. When you buy a prescription medicine at the drug store you are paying for the value of getting well, not for the couple of millilitres of powder and gelatin. When you pay to have your car serviced you are paying for the mechanic's expertise, not for his physical movements around your car. And when you choose a sweater or a bicycle or a bedspread in a retail store, part of the value you are paying for is the selection; that is, the ability to choose from many sweaters, bicycles, and bedspreads.

High-Pressure Selling The high-pressure sales associate, usually working on commission, is a marketer that most consumers have complained about at one time or another. Automobile retailers have been vilified for years because their sales representatives are perceived by consumers as trying as hard as they can to get the highest possible price for the car. Of course, that is exactly what they are doing, but now that consumers have become empowered by the Internet, those who are in the market for a new car are no longer woefully uninformed. Today it is rare that a car shopper enters a car dealership without printouts from automobile websites comparing features and prices. For consumers, information is power.

When the consumer doesn't have access to information, however, it can be part of the value exchange of the product being marketed. For example, if you are shopping in an electronics store for a new television, you might very well appreciate the helpful, informed assistance of a sales associate. On the other hand you likely would not appreciate a pushy sales rep who tries to persuade you, against your will, to purchase a more expensive television than what you had in mind. It's a fine line for marketers to walk. Some stores, such as Home Depot and Business Depot, have highly trained employees who have specialized knowledge in their departments, whether it be paint, lumber, or computers. These employees are paid well for their expertise, pride themselves in their knowledge, and can be of great assistance—and hence value—to the consumer.

In Canada, consumers are protected from high-pressure selling tactics and other potentially unfair or fraudulent marketing practices by the federal *Consumer Protection Act,* which was revised in July 2005 to include even stronger protections. The new laws were praised by the Consumers Council of Canada, and described by Government Services Minister Gerry Phillips as protecting consumers and promoting a fair marketplace.[5] Under the new Act, the final cost of a home renovation or other repair cannot be more than 10 percent higher than the original estimate, or the difference must be paid by the contractor, not the consumer. So-called negative option billing is also prohibited under the Act. Consumers may refuse to pay for products that are not delivered within 30 days of when they were promised. The Act also stipulates "cooling off periods"; that is, the number of days during which a consumer may change his or her mind about a high-priced purchase such as a home or a car. There's even a 10-day cooling off period for purchasing gym memberships! And under the Act consumers have exactly the same rights when purchasing products online as they do for any other form of purchase. In fact, it is the marketing reality of the Internet that required the Act to be updated—it was last revised in the 1970s.

Deceptive Practices Marketers are sometimes accused of deceptive practices that lead consumers to believe that they will get more value than they actually do. It is important to point out that such practices as deceptive pricing, untrue statements in advertisements, false promotions, and deceptive packaging are all illegal in Canada, and are regulated by the *Competition Act* and the Competition Bureau. They are also closely monitored by consumer advocate groups and trade associations. Most organizations, whether they are small or large businesses, service organizations, or not-for-profit organizations, are staffed with professional marketers who are aware of the laws that regulate marketing practices and who work within the boundaries of those laws.

The legal definition of deceptive pricing is a price that is falsely advertised as having been reduced from the "regular" price when in fact the product was never offered for sale at that price. The Competition Bureau will take action against marketers who engage in deceptive pricing. In 2005, for example, Sears Canada Inc. was ordered to pay a total of $487 000 under the *Competition Act*'s Deceptive Marketing Practices provisions. The Competition Tribunal decided that Sears breached the Act when it ran ads that misled consumers about how much they would save on certain tires. Not all cases end in fines, however. Sometimes a firm acts immediately to address the concern, as in the 2005 case of GoodLife Fitness Clubs Inc., which owns and operates 90 fitness clubs across Canada. The Bureau was concerned about the way the Clubs advertised their prices, particularly the fact that it failed to disclose additional mandatory fees in its advertising of membership offers. Goodlife quickly amended its advertising to comply with the law.[6]

It is illegal in Canada to advertise, for example in a newspaper flyer, a particular product for sale at a particular price, and then tell consumers who come to the store that the product is not available. This tactic is sometimes used even by reputable retailers, often when their sales staff works on commission. Legally the sales associate may *try* to persuade you to buy a different, higher priced item; however, if you insist that what you want is the advertised item at the advertised price, the retailer is legally obliged to sell it to you.

In Canada there are also strict regulations about the information that must be included on labels and packaging. Marketers who lie about or exaggerate this information will find themselves in serious trouble, and may find their companies going out of business.

Telemarketing fraud is a problem in Canada, and one of the most pervasive forms of white-collar crime. As consumers, we need to be aware of the differences between legitimate telemarketing efforts (an industry that generates $500 billion in revenue in Canada by selling everything from online banking to carpet cleaning services) and the fraudulent scams operated by criminals posing as "marketers." According to PhoneBusters, the RCMP-run national reporting centre for telemarketing fraud, deceptive telemarketing and lottery schemes have bilked Canadians out of more than $40 million since 1995.[7] Criminals use telecommunications to prey on innocent victims, especially those most vulnerable, such as senior citizens.

Since deceptive practices hurt the reputation of reputable professional marketers, Advertising Standards Canada has published several guidelines forbidding these practices. As well, the Canadian Marketing Association (CMA) works to develop codes of ethics and standards of good practice so that the industry can regulate itself better. The CMA also works with policymakers to strengthen the *Competition Act*. The toughest problem is defining what is "deceptive." In the case of telemarketing fraud, the CMA launched a public education campaign designed to help consumers avoid becoming victims of such scams. The "Stop Phone Fraud, It's a Trap!" campaign consists of posters, pamphlets, public service announcements, an upgraded website for PhoneBusters, and educational materials to help consumers learn how to tell the difference between an honest telemarketer and a scam artist. Training videos are also made available to volunteer groups that work with seniors.[8]

The media is often quick to report deceptive practices. Canadian-produced shows, like CBC's *Marketplace,* keep an eye out for products or marketing practices that may harm consumers. And, as consumers, it is our responsibility to report deceptive marketing and advertising practices to the appropriate authorities—after all, the GlobeScan survey tells us we are among

Telemarketing fraud hurts consumers and the marketing profession. Members of the Deceptive Telemarketing Prevention Forum developed a campaign to educate consumers about phone scams.

the toughest consumers in the world. If you notice a retailer engaging in deceptive pricing, report it to the Competition Bureau. Its website (www.competitionbureau.gc.ca) includes tips to protect yourself against deceptive practices, warnings about fraudulent telemarketing schemes that may be operating in your city, and names and contact information for your complaints.

Unsafe Products Consumers also complain about product safety. Unsafe or shoddy products can result from manufacturer indifference, increased production complexity, poorly trained labour, or poor quality control. For years, Consumers Union, the not-for-profit organization that publishes *Consumer Reports* magazine, has reported hazards in products it has tested: electrical dangers in appliances, carbon monoxide poisoning from poorly ventilated devices, injury risks from lawn mowers, and faulty automobile design. The organization's testing and other activities have helped consumers make better buying decisions, and have encouraged businesses to eliminate product flaws (see Marketing at Work 3.1).

Most manufacturers *want* to produce quality goods. They operate not only within the bounds of what is legal, but within the ethical boundaries of their company and their trade. The way a company deals with product quality and safety problems can damage or help its reputation. Companies selling poor-quality or unsafe products risk damaging conflicts with consumer groups and regulators. More fundamentally, unsafe products can result in product liability suits and large awards for damages. Moreover, consumers who are unhappy with a firm's products may avoid future purchases and talk other consumers into doing the same.

Consider what happened to Merck. This company's blockbuster arthritis drug Vioxx was pulled from the market worldwide in 2004 because new research data showed that it could increase the risk of heart attacks and strokes. And not only did the firm have to bear the cost of the recall; shares of pharmaceutical giant lost more than a quarter of their value the day after the recall was announced. The firm also lost a number of lawsuits launched by people who were injured by the drug or by spouses of people who died as a result of taking it.[9]

Thus, quality missteps can have severe consequences. Today's marketers know that customer-driven quality results in customer satisfaction, which in turn creates profitable customer relationships.

Planned Obsolescence There are consumers and critics who feel that marketers who follow a program of planned obsolescence are unethical. It's said that the technology exists to build a lightbulb that will last for 100 years—so why can't we buy one in our local hardware store? Marketers are accused of holding back features, then introducing them later to make older models obsolete: Critics claim that this occurs in the consumer electronics and computer industries. For example, Intel and Microsoft have been accused in recent years of holding back their next-generation computer chips and software until demand is exhausted for the current generation. Still other producers are accused of using materials and components that will break, wear, rust, or rot sooner than they should. One writer put it this way: "The marvels of modern technology include the development of a soda can which, when discarded, will last forever—and a . . . car, which, when properly cared for, will rust out in two or three years."[10]

Marketers respond that consumers *like* style changes. They get tired of the old goods and want a new look in fashion or a new design in cars. No one has to buy the new look and if too few people like it, it will simply fail. Companies that withhold new features run the risk that a competitor will introduce the new feature and steal the market.

For example, consider personal computers. Some consumers grumble that the consumer electronics industry's constant push to produce "faster, smaller, cheaper" models means that they must continually buy new machines just to keep up. Their old computers

Marketing at Work   3.1

When *Consumer Reports* Talks, Buyers Listen

Founded in 1936, *Consumer Reports* has given buyers the lowdown on everything from sports cars to luggage to lawn sprinklers. Published by Consumers Union, a nonprofit product-testing organization, the magazine's mission can be summed up by CU's motto: "Test, Inform, Protect." With more than 4 million subscribers, *Consumer Reports* is one of North America's most read magazines. Its companion website, Consumer Reports Online, established in 1997, is the Web's largest paid-subscriber site, with 350 000 users.

The Consumers Union has had a huge impact. It was one of the first to investigate the effectiveness of seat belts and the harm caused by smoking. Since 1988, it has investigated vehicle rollover problems. When it rated Suzuki's topple-prone Samurai as "not acceptable" in 1988 (meaning don't even take one as a gift), sales plunged by 70 percent the following month. More recently, when it raved about Saucony's Jazz 3000 sneakers, sales doubled.

Although some may view *Consumer Reports* as a dull shoppers' guide to major household appliances, the magazine does a lot more than rate cars and refrigerators. It has looked at almost anything consumable—from mutual funds, mortgages, and public health policies to retirement communities and prostate surgery.

When a recent Consumers Union study found that less than one-third of consumers trust e-commerce websites, the organization launched Consumer WebWatch (www.consumerwebwatch.org). The project's mission is "to investigate, inform, and improve the credibility of information published on the World Wide Web." The site gives ratings on everything from the disclosure of transaction fees and business partnerships to the publication of privacy policies and the labelling of pop-up ads.

To avoid even the appearance of bias, CU has a strict no-ads, no-freebies policy. It buys all its product samples on the open market anonymously. And this steadfast editorial independence has made *Consumer Reports* the bible of consumerism.

"We're very single-minded about who we serve," says Rhoda Karpatkin, CU's recently retired president. "We serve the consumer."

To the business community, *Consumer Reports* was at first viewed as a clear threat to business. But through the years, only 13 companies have filed suit against CU challenging findings unfavourable to their products. To this day Consumers Union has never lost or settled a libel suit.

Sources: "To Buy or Not to Buy, That Is the Question at *Consumer Reports*," *Smithsonian,* September 1993, pp. 34–43; Robin Finn, "Still Top Dog, Consumers' Pitt Bull to Retire," *New York Times,* October 5, 2000, p. B2; Barbara Quint, "Consumers Union Launches Consumer WebWatch," *Information Today,* June 2002, p. 48; www.consumersunion.org; www.consumerreports.org, accessed August 2002.

Consumers Union carries out its testing mission: Suitcases bang into one another inside the huge "Mechanical Gorilla," and a staffer coats the interior of self-cleaning ovens with a crusty concoction called "Monster Mash."

then enter landfills and present a major disposal problem. Others, however, can hardly wait for the latest model to arrive.

There was a time not so long ago when planned obsolescence was a troubling ghost in the machine. That was then. In today's topsy-turvy world of personal computers, obsolescence is not only planned, it is extolled by marketers as a principal virtue. Moreover, there has been hardly a peep from consumers, who dutifully line up to buy each new generation of faster, more powerful machines, eager to embrace the promise of simpler, happier, and more productive lives. Today's computer chips are no longer designed to wear out; in fact, they will last for decades or longer. Even so, hapless consumers now rush back to the store ever more quickly, not to replace broken parts but to purchase new computers that will allow them to talk longer, see more vivid colours, or play cooler games.[11]

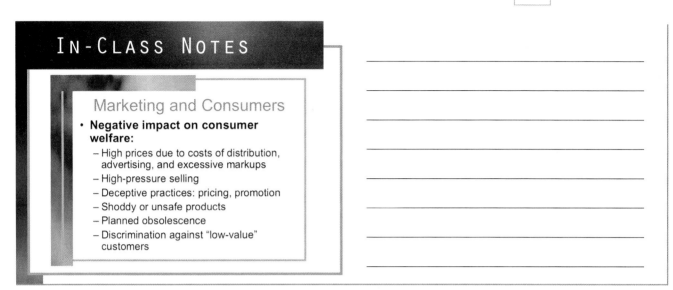

IN-CLASS NOTES

Marketing and Consumers

- **Negative impact on consumer welfare:**
  - High prices due to costs of distribution, advertising, and excessive markups
  - High-pressure selling
  - Deceptive practices: pricing, promotion
  - Shoddy or unsafe products
  - Planned obsolescence
  - Discrimination against "low-value" customers

Thus, companies do not design their products to break down earlier because they do not want to lose customers to other brands; instead, they seek constant improvement to ensure that products will consistently meet or exceed customer expectations. Much of so-called planned obsolescence is the working of the competitive and technological forces in a free society—forces that lead to ever-improving goods and services.

Weblining   In the days before computers, businesses such as banks and retailers sometimes discriminated against groups of customers based on the neighbourhoods they lived in. This practice was called *redlining*, and it is obsolete in the information age. The proliferation of computer databases and the ease with which they can be managed, updated, and accessed means that today, marketers can "discriminate" their customers into groups based on purchase behaviour, loyalty status, and amount spent. Banks, for example, assign their customers, whether they are consumers or businesses, a status based on credit history, history with the bank, and number of products (banking "products" are chequing accounts, savings accounts, mortgages, etc.).

Modern marketers, therefore, recognize the necessity of scrutinizing their customers, and identifying those that are high value from those that are money losers. On the Internet, businesses that discriminate in this manner against "low value" customers

Linking the Concepts

Few marketers *want* to abuse or anger consumers—it's simply not good business. Instead, as you know well by now, most marketers work to build long-term, profitable relationships with customers based on a meaningful exchange of values for both parties.

- Think about your experiences as a consumer in the past few months: all the advertising you've seen or read, the retail stores you've entered, and the purchases you've made. What complaints or concerns do you have about the marketing activities you've been exposed to?

- Have you seen, or experienced as a customer, an example of deceptive marketing practices? Describe the deceptive practice. Then, browse the Government of Canada websites that offer consumer information, and determine to which organization it would be the most appropriate to express a complaint about this marketer.

have been accused of *weblining*. With the oceans of information available on the internet, plus ever faster computers and software, companies can maintain the equivalent of profit-and-loss statements on every customer. They can sort people into more categories and, in some cases, predict how they will behave.

"This idea about 'whatever the customer wants' is gone," says a software developer who works on banking systems. "Now it's whatever companies can afford to offer, based on each customer's worth. Not all customers are created equal."

While marketers consider the power of customer information a benefit, giving them the ability to "micro-segment" customers into groups and serve each group according to its needs, some critics aren't so sure. An analyst at Forrester Research comments, "Left to evolve, this technology could lead to a commercial culture in which high value customers are bought and sold like derivative securities."[12]

Marketing's Impact on Society as a Whole

The marketing system has been accused of adding to several "evils" in society at large. Advertising has been a special target.

False Wants and Too Much Materialism Critics, led by Professor Rick Pollay of the University of British Columbia and organizations like AdBusters, have charged that the marketing system in general, and advertising in particular, urge too much interest in material possessions. While Pollay recognized that many of the consequences of advertising were unintended, he damned advertising for undermining family values, reinforcing negative stereotypes, and creating a class of perpetually dissatisfied consumers.[13] Advertising encourages people to judge themselves and others by what they *own* rather than by who they *are*. To be considered successful, some people believe they must own a large home, two cars, and the latest high-tech gadgets.

Today, even though many social scientists have noted a reaction against the opulence and waste of previous decades and a return to more basic values and social commitment, our infatuation with material things continues. While the Professional Marketing Research Association of Canada has done studies that indicate that Canadians are less materialistic than our American neighbours, it's hard to escape the notion that what all North Americans really value is stuff. We build more shopping malls than high schools. We save less and spend more. Nearly two-thirds of adults agree that wearing "only the best designer clothing" conveys status. Even more feel this way about owning expensive jewellery. Big homes are back in vogue, which means North Americans have more space in which to fulfill their acquisitive fantasies, from master bathrooms doubling as spas and gyms to fully wired home entertainment centres.[14]

Marketing critics do not view this interest in material things as a natural state of mind but rather as a matter of false wants created by marketing. Businesses hire advertisers to stimulate people's desires for goods, and advertisers use the mass media to create materialistic models of the good life. People work harder to earn the necessary money to purchase these items. Their purchases increase the output of North American industry, and industry in turn uses advertisers to stimulate more desire for the industrial output. Thus, marketing is seen as creating false wants that benefit industry more than they benefit consumers.

These criticisms overstate the power of business to create needs, however. People have strong defences against advertising and other marketing tools. Marketers are most effective when they appeal to existing wants rather than when they attempt to create new ones. Furthermore, people seek information when making important purchases and often do not rely on single sources. Even minor purchases that can be affected by advertising messages lead to repeat purchases only if the product performs as promised. Finally, the high failure rate of new products shows that companies are not able to control demand.

On a deeper level, our wants and values are influenced not only by marketers, but also by family, peer groups, religion, ethnic background, and education. If North Americans are highly materialistic, these values arose out of basic socialization processes that go much deeper than business and mass media alone could produce. Moreover, some social critics even see materialism as a positive and rewarding force.

Too Few Social Goods Business has been accused of overselling private goods at the expense of public goods. As private goods increase, they require more public services that are usually not forthcoming. For example, an increase in automobile ownership (private good) requires more highways, traffic controls, parking spaces, and police services (public goods). The overselling of private goods results in "social costs." For cars, the social costs include traffic congestion, air pollution, and deaths and injuries from car accidents.

A way must be found to restore a balance between private and public goods. One option is to make producers bear the full social costs of their operations. For example, the federal government requires automobile manufacturers to build cars with very strict safety and pollution-control systems. These changes, however, result in auto makers having to raise their prices to cover the cost of these improvements. But if buyers find the price of some cars too high, the demand would move to those producers that could support the sum of the private and social costs.

A second option is to make consumers pay the social costs. Some Canadians have demanded that people who get lost in backcountry areas while pursuing extreme sports experiences should pay for the cost of rescues, or that smokers should pay a premium for health care. A number of highway authorities around the world are starting to charge "congestion tolls" in an effort to reduce traffic congestion.

Cultural Pollution Critics charge the marketing system with creating *cultural pollution*. Our senses are being assaulted constantly by advertising. Commercials interrupt our television and radio programs; movies, which once were sacrosanct, now include commercials *before* the trailers, and even *on* the DVDs; nearly every printed page in a magazine or newspaper includes an advertisement; billboards mar beautiful scenery; video screens now talk to us from on top of the gas pump and above the baggage carousel at airports. It's been posited that the average urban Canadian comes into contact with approximately 3000 promotional messages on an average day.

Cultural pollution: Our senses are sometimes assaulted by commercial messages.

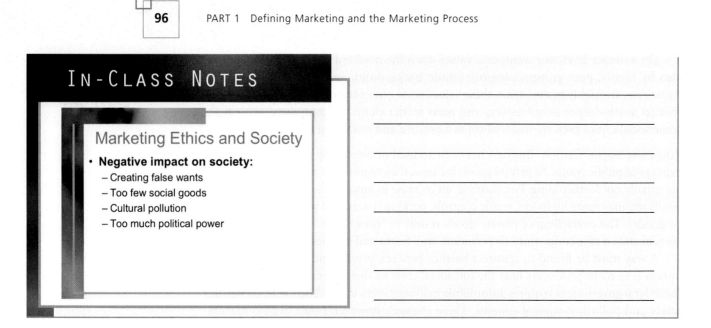

Unfortunately, the problem of cultural pollution is a vicious circle. The more advertisements there are in the cluttered landscape of traditional media, the more advertisers must strive to make their commercial messages stand out from their competitors'. The more they try to do so, the more they come up with novel forms of advertising, such as stickers on the tops of pool tables, postcards in bars and restaurants, ads in public bathrooms, and swinging hubcap ads on taxis. And in September 1995, when Microsoft launched its newest operating system, Windows 95, an enormous banner was even hung on the side of the CN Tower in Toronto, obscuring the tourists' view from the glass-enclosed elevator shaft.

Too Much Political Power   Another criticism is that business wields too much political power. Oil, tobacco, automobile, and pharmaceutical firms lobby governments to promote their interests against the public interest. Advertisers are accused of holding too much power over the mass media, limiting their freedom to report independently and objectively. One critic has asked: "How can [most magazines] afford to tell the truth about the scandalously low nutritional value of most packaged foods . . . when these magazines are being subsidized by such advertisers as General Foods, Kellogg's, Nabisco, and General Mills? . . . The answer is *they cannot and do not.*"[15]

Canadian industries promote and protect their interests. They have a right to representation in Parliament and the mass media, although their influence can become too great. Fortunately, many powerful business interests once thought to be untouchable have been tamed in the public interest. For example, Petro-Canada was formed to give Canadians greater control over the oil industry. Amendments to the *Tobacco Products Control Act* made it necessary for cigarette manufacturers to place stronger warnings on their packages about the dangers of smoking.

Marketing's Impact on Other Businesses   Critics charge that a company's marketing practices can harm other companies and reduce competition. Three problems are involved: acquisitions of competitors, marketing practices that create barriers to entry, and unfair competitive marketing practices.

Critics claim that firms are harmed and competition reduced when companies expand by acquiring competitors rather than by developing their own new products. The large number of acquisitions and rapid pace of industry consolidation over the past several decades have caused concern that vigorous young competitors will be absorbed and that competition will be reduced. In virtually every major industry—retailing, entertainment,

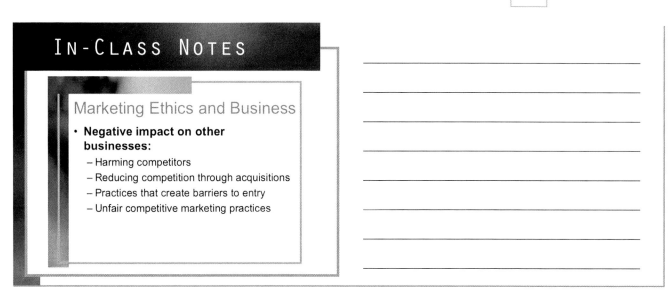

Marketing Ethics and Business

- **Negative impact on other businesses:**
  - – Harming competitors
  - – Reducing competition through acquisitions
  - – Practices that create barriers to entry
  - – Unfair competitive marketing practices

financial services, utilities, transportation, automobiles, telecommunications—the number of major competitors is shrinking. The *Globe and Mail* newspaper merged with CTV under the umbrella of Bell Globemedia, and its only major competitor is the equally powerful *National Post*/Global TV partnership. Food giant Sobeys acquired Oshawa Foods, and, just recently, Quebec grocery chain Metro bought A&P's Canadian stores for $1.78 billion.

Acquisition is a complex subject. Acquisitions can sometimes be good for society. The acquiring company may gain economies of scale that lead to lower costs and lower prices. A well-managed company may take over a poorly managed company and improve its efficiency. An industry that was not very competitive may become more competitive after the acquisition. Even people opposed to mergers among Canada's banks recognize that there are economic advantages of doing global business on a large scale. But acquisitions can also be harmful and, therefore, are regulated by the government.

Critics have charged that marketing practices bar new companies from entering an industry. Large companies can use patents and heavy promotional spending, and can tie up suppliers or dealers to keep out or drive out competitors. Some barriers that limit competition could be challenged by existing and new laws. For example, some critics have proposed a progressive tax on advertising spending to reduce the role of selling costs as a major barrier to entry.

Finally, some firms have used unfair competitive marketing practices with the intention of hurting or destroying other firms. They may set their prices below costs, threaten to cut off business with suppliers, or discourage the buying of a competitor's products. Various laws work to prevent such predatory competition. It is difficult, however, to prove that the intent or action was really predatory. In recent years, Wal-Mart, Intel, and Microsoft have all been accused of predatory practices. Since 2000, Air Canada has faced a number of charges of predatory pricing as it has attempted to halt the erosion of its market share by discount airlines such as WestJet and CanJet.[16]

CITIZEN AND PUBLIC ACTIONS TO REGULATE MARKETING

Because some people view business as the cause of many economic and social ills, grass-roots movements have arisen from time to time to keep business in line. The two major movements are *consumerism* and *environmentalism*.

Consumerism

The first consumer movements took place in the early 1900s and in the mid–1930s. Both were sparked by an upturn in consumer prices. Another movement began in the 1960s. Consumers had become better educated, products had become more complex and hazardous, and people were questioning the status quo. Many accused big business of wasteful and unethical practices. Since then, many consumer groups have been organized and several consumer laws have been passed. The consumer movement has spread beyond North America and has become global in nature. Protestors, fearing negative outcomes on consumers and manufacturers alike, have disrupted conferences held by the World Trade Organization (WTO). While the demonstrations were peaceful at the 2002 talks held in Kananaskis outside of Calgary, they have degraded to violence in other areas.[17]

Consumerism An organized movement of citizens and government agencies to improve the rights and power of buyers in relation to sellers.

But what is the consumer movement? **Consumerism** is an organized movement of citizens and government agencies to improve the rights and power of buyers in relation to sellers. It must be remembered that both parties have rights. Traditional *sellers' rights* include:

☐ The right to introduce any product in any size and style, provided it is not hazardous to personal health or safety; or, if it is, to include proper warnings and controls.

☐ The right to charge any price for the product, provided no discrimination exists among similar kinds of buyers.

☐ The right to spend any amount to promote the product, provided it is not defined as unfair competition.

☐ The right to use any product message, provided it is not misleading or dishonest in content or execution.

☐ The right to use any buying incentive schemes, provided they are not unfair or misleading.

The Consumers' Association of Canada (CAC) has acted as a consumer advocate and has provided information to Canadian consumers for over 50 years. This volunteer-based, non-governmental organization was founded in 1947. With offices in every province, the association lobbies government to secure consumer rights in areas of food, health care, environment, consumer goods and services, regulated industries (phone, electricity, telecommunications, cable), financial institutions, taxation, trade, and any other issue of concern to Canadians facing complex buying decisions. The association establishes annual priorities. Recent issues include health-care reform, privacy protection, electrical utilities deregulation, consumer education, purchasing literacy, GST reform, price visibility, package downsizing, and environmental rights and responsibilities. The association has also outlined a number of fundamental consumer rights, including[18]

☐ *The right to safety.* Consumers have the right to be protected against the marketing of goods that are hazardous to health or life.

☐ *The right to be informed.* Consumers must be protected against fraudulent, deceitful, or grossly misleading information, advertising, labelling, or other practices. They are to be given the facts needed to make an informed choice.

☐ *The right to choose.* Consumers have the right to choose, wherever possible, among a variety of goods and services at competitive prices. In industries where competition is not workable and government regulation is substituted, consumers must be assured of satisfactory quality and service at fair prices.

☐ *The right to be heard.* It is important that consumers' voices be heard. Thus, they must receive full and sympathetic consideration in the formulation of government policy, and fair and expeditious treatment in its administrative tribunals.

☐ *The right to redress against damage.* Consumers have the right to seek redress from a supplier of goods and services for any loss or damage suffered because of bad infor-

Consumer desire for more information led to putting ingredients and nutrition and dating information on product labels.

mation, or faulty products or performance, and shall have easy and inexpensive access to settlement of small claims.

☐ *The right to consumer education.* Canadian consumers have the right to be educated as school children so that they will be able to act as informed consumers through their lives. Adults also have the right to consumer education.

Each proposed right has led to more specific proposals by consumerists. The right to be informed, for example, includes the right to know the true interest on a loan (truth in lending), the true cost per unit of a brand (unit pricing), the ingredients in a product (ingredient labelling), the nutrition in foods (nutritional labelling), product freshness (open dating), and the true benefits of a product (truth in advertising).

In addition to the CAC and the Competition Bureau, the Better Business Bureau offer tips to consumers to protect themselves from fraud or shady business practices. Consumers have not only the *right* but also the *responsibility* to protect themselves instead of leaving this function to someone else. Consumers who believe they got a bad deal have several remedies available, including writing to the company president or to the media; contacting federal, provincial, or local agencies; and going to small claims court.

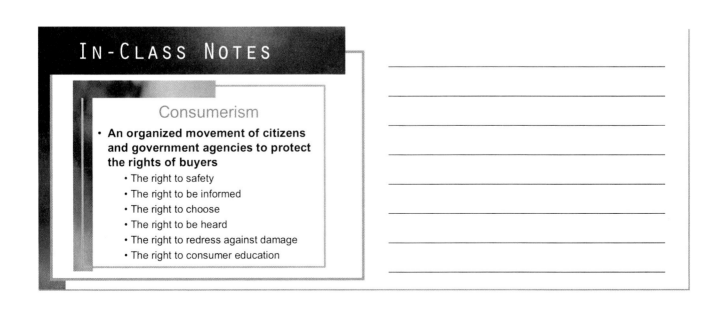

Environmentalism

Whereas consumerists consider whether the marketing system is efficiently serving consumer wants, environmentalists are concerned with marketing's effects on the natural environment and with the costs of serving consumer needs and wants. **Environmentalism** is an organized movement of concerned citizens, businesses, and government agencies working to protect and improve the natural environment. Environmentalists are not against marketing and consumption; they simply want people and organizations to operate with more care for the environment. The marketing system's goal, they assert, should not be to maximize consumption, consumer choice, or consumer satisfaction, but rather to maximize life quality. And "life quality" means not only the quantity and quality of consumer goods and services, but also the quality of the environment. Environmentalists want environmental costs included in both producer and consumer decision making.

The first wave of modern environmentalism in North America was driven by environmental groups and concerned consumers in the 1960s and 1970s. They were concerned with damage to the ecosystem and loss of natural areas caused by stripmining, forest depletion, acid rain, loss of the atmosphere's ozone layer, toxic wastes, and litter. The second environmentalism wave was driven by government, which passed laws and regulations during the 1970s and 1980s governing industrial practices impacting the environment. This wave hit some industries hard. Steel companies and utilities, for example, had to invest billions of dollars in pollution control equipment and costlier fuels.

Buying behaviour has changed as sensitivity to this issue has grown. The late 1980s saw the birth of a new product attribute—environmentally friendly or "green." A recent survey conducted by the Grocery Product Manufacturers of Canada found that 80 percent of respondents said they would be willing to pay more for green products. Companies began to respond to these changes in demand. Retailers in both Canada and the United States are demanding more environmentally sensitive products: Wal-Mart has asked its suppliers to provide more of these types of products, while Loblaws has developed an entire product line under its G.R.E.E.N. President's Choice label.

In response to the concerns of environmentalists, the Canadian government has undertaken a number of initiatives to improve the environment. It froze production levels of chlorofluorocarbons (CFCs), the major cause of ozone layer depletion, and Canada's environment ministers established a voluntary program intended to reduce excessive packaging. Despite a heated debate, the Kyoto Accord was endorsed in 2002, and to be aligned with the protocol, industrialized countries must cut their greenhouse gas emissions to below 1990 levels within 10 years.[19]

Marketers cannot ignore the urgency of environmental issues or be blind to the fact that governments are increasingly willing to take action and pass regulations restricting marketing practices. All parts of the marketing mix are affected. Advertisers are accused of adding to the solid waste problem when they use direct mail or newspaper inserts. Manufacturers are criticized for making goods that incorporate materials that increase pollution or cannot be recycled.[20] Distribution systems have been cited for adding to air pollution as trucks move goods from the factory to the store. Critics claim that even when environmentally friendly products are available, they are priced too high for many consumers to afford.

The first two environmentalism waves are now merging into a third and stronger wave in which companies are accepting responsibility for doing no harm to the environment. They are shifting from protest to prevention, and from regulation to responsibility. More and more companies are adopting policies of **environmental sustainability**— developing strategies that both sustain the environment and produce profits for the

Environmentalism An organized movement of concerned citizens, businesses, and government agencies working to protect and improve the natural environment.

Environmental sustainability A management approach that involves developing strategies that both sustain the environment and produce profits for the company.

company. According to one strategist, "The challenge is to develop a *sustainable global economy:* an economy that the planet is capable of supporting indefinitely. . . . [It's] an enormous challenge—and an enormous opportunity."[21]

Figure 3.1 shows a grid that companies can use to gauge their progress toward environmental sustainability. At the most basic level a company can practise pollution prevention. This involves more than just pollution control—cleaning up waste after it is created. The emphasis shifts to prevention: eliminating or minimizing waste before it is created.

Figure 3.1   The Environmental Sustainability Grid

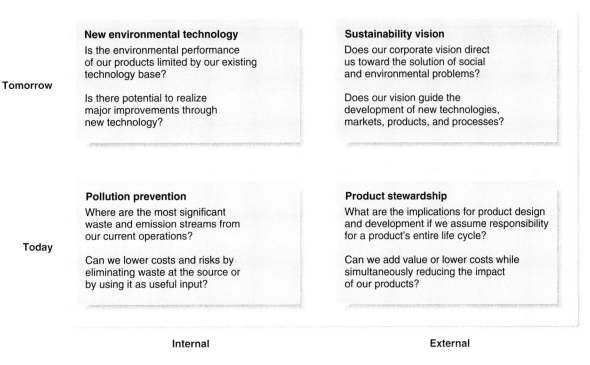

Tomorrow

New environmental technology

Is the environmental performance of our products limited by our existing technology base?

Is there potential to realize major improvements through new technology?

Sustainability vision

Does our corporate vision direct us toward the solution of social and environmental problems?

Does our vision guide the development of new technologies, markets, products, and processes?

Today

Pollution prevention

Where are the most significant waste and emission streams from our current operations?

Can we lower costs and risks by eliminating waste at the source or by using it as useful input?

Product stewardship

What are the implications for product design and development if we assume responsibility for a product's entire life cycle?

Can we add value or lower costs while simultaneously reducing the impact of our products?

Internal   **External**

Sustainability is a crucial but difficult goal. John Browne, chairman of British oil gaint BP, asked this question: "Is genuine progress still possible? Is development sustainable? Or is one strand of progress—industrialization—now doing such damage to the environment that the next generation won't have a world worth living in?"[22] Browne sees the situation as an opportunity, and as a result BP broke ranks with the oil industry on environmental issues. "There are good commercial reasons to do right by the environment," says Browne. Under his leadership, BP has become active in public forums on global climate issues and has worked to reduce emissions in exploration and production. It has begun marketing cleaner fuels and invested significantly in exploring alternative energy sources, such as photovoltaic power and hydrogen. In 2002, BP opened "the world's most environmentally friendly service station" near London:

> The new BP Connect service station features an array of innovative green initiatives that show BP's commitment to environmental responsibility. The station runs entirely on renewable energy and generates up to half of its own power, using solar panels installed on the roofs and three wind turbines. More than 60 percent of the water needed for the restrooms comes from rainwater collected on the shop roof, and water for hand washing is heated by solar panels. The site's vapour recovery systems collect and recycle even the fuel vapour released from customers' tanks as they pump gas. BP has planted landscaping around the site

Environmental sustainability: BP recently opened "the world's most environmentally friendly service station" near London, featuring an array of innovative green initiatives.

with indigenous plant species. And, to promote biodiversity awareness, the company has undertaken several initiatives to attract local wildlife to the area, such as dragonflies and insect-feeding birds. The wildflower turf under the wind farm will even provide a habitat for bumble bees.[23]

Environmentalism creates some special challenges for global marketers. As international trade barriers come down and global markets expand, environmental issues are having a growing impact on international trade. Countries in North America, Western Europe, and other developed regions are developing stringent environmental standards. A side accord to the North American Free Trade Agreement (NAFTA) set up a commission for resolving environmental matters.[24]

Environmental policies vary widely from country to country, and uniform worldwide standards are not expected for many years. Although countries such as Canada, Denmark, Germany, Japan, and the United States have fully developed environmental policies and high public expectations, other major countries such as China, India, Brazil, and Russia are only in the early stages of developing such policies. Moreover, environmental factors that motivate consumers in one country may have no impact on con-

IN-CLASS NOTES

Environmentalism

- **An organized movement of citizens, businesses, and government agencies**
  - Protect and improve the living environment
  - Maximize life quality, rather than consumption, choice, or satisfaction
  - Strive for environmental sustainability
  - Enact government regulation to support these goals

sumers in another. For example, PVC soft-drink bottles cannot be used in Switzerland or Germany. However, they are preferred in France, which has an extensive recycling process for them. Thus, international companies are finding it difficult to develop standard environmental practices that work around the world. Instead, they are creating general policies and then translating these into tailored programs to meet local regulations and expectations.

Business Actions Toward Socially Responsible Marketing

Today, most marketers understand and acknowledge that consumers have rights, and that as marketers they need to take those rights into consideration. Companies may oppose certain pieces of legislation as inappropriate ways to solve certain consumer problems, but they recognize the consumer's right to information and protection. Many of these companies have responded positively to the demands of consumer groups and environmentalism in order to serve consumer needs better. Figure 3.2 provides an overview of the numerous decisions that can affect marketing managers.

Enlightened Marketing

The philosophy of **enlightened marketing** holds that a company's marketing should support the best long-run performance of the marketing system. Enlightened marketing consists of five principles: *customer-oriented marketing, innovative marketing, value marketing, sense-of-mission marketing,* and *societal marketing.*

Enlightened marketing A marketing philosophy holding that a company's marketing should support the best long-run performance of the marketing system.

Figure 3.2   Legal Issues Facing Marketing Management

Selling decisions
Bribing?
Stealing trade secrets?
Disparaging customers?
Misrepresenting?
Disclosure of customer rights?
Unfair discrimination?

Advertising decisions
False advertising?
Deceptive advertising?
Bait-and-switch advertising?
Promotional allowances and services?

Channel decisions
Exclusive dealing?
Exclusive territorial distributorships?
Tying agreements?
Dealer's rights?

Product decisions
Product additions and deletions?
Patent protection?
Product quality and safety?
Product warranty?

Packaging decisions
Fair packaging and labelling?
Excessive cost?
Scarce resources?
Pollution?

Price decisions
Price-fixing?
Predatory pricing?
Price discrimination?
Minimum pricing?
Price increases?
Deceptive pricing?

Competitive relations decisions
Anticompetitive acquisition?
Barriers to entry?
Predatory competition?

Customer-oriented marketing
A philosophy of enlightened marketing that holds that the company should view and organize its marketing activities from the customer's point of view.

Customer-Oriented Marketing **Customer-oriented marketing** means that the company should view and organize its marketing activities from the customer's point of view. It should work hard to sense, serve, and satisfy the needs of a defined group of customers. Consider this example:

> Montreal-based Walsh Integrated Environmental Systems Inc. was founded by David Walsh, right after he graduated from business school. After conducting a 12-week waste audit at Montreal's Royal Victoria Hospital, he realized what a huge waste-management problem hospitals faced. Disposing of biohazardous waste costs 20 times as much as getting rid of regular waste and can result in bills of over $450 000 per year. Yet Walsh also saw that other materials, from pop cans to newspapers, were thrown in the biohazardous containers the hospital was using. In fact, about 65 percent of the material in the garbage could go into the regular waste stream. Walsh's new business developed a system called the Waste Tracker that allows hospital staff to track the waste from each department, identify how much is biohazardous, and uncover who is misusing the system. Today his company serves over 300 Canadian and U.S. hospitals and he has expanded his services to include a quality support system that helps hospitals monitor the cleanliness of their rooms and labs as well as control their waste.[25]

Every successful company that we discuss in this text has this in common: an all-consuming passion for delivering superior value to carefully chosen customers. Only by seeing the world through its customers' eyes can the company build lasting and profitable customer relationships.

Innovative marketing A principle of enlightened marketing that requires a company to continuously seek real product and marketing improvements.

Innovative Marketing The principle of **innovative marketing** requires that the company continuously seek real product and marketing improvements. The company that overlooks new and better ways to do things will eventually lose customers to another company that has found a better way. An excellent example of an innovative marketer is Colgate-Palmolive:

> Colgate-Palmolive has become somewhat of a new-product machine in recent years. Worldwide, new products contribute 35 percent of Colgate's revenues, and the company has received the New Product Marketer of the Year award from the American Marketing Association. Colgate took the honours by launching an abundance of innovative and highly successful new consumer products, including Colgate Total toothpaste, which holds a substantial 35 percent market share compared with Procter & Gamble's 25 percent.
>
> In 2002 Colgate launched a related product, its battery-powered full-motion toothbrush. In its creative marketing campaign, Colgate held free dental clinics at Toronto's Union Station during rush-hour periods, offering advice from a George Brown College dental hygiene student. Participants were given a coupon for $2 off a brush and all transit passengers were offered a Colgate Total toothpaste sample in exchange for a donation to the United Way. As senior product manager James Masterson noted, "The grassroots initiatives provide an opportunity to interact directly with consumers to effectively communicate the benefits of proper oral hygiene in a fun and engaging way."[26]

Value marketing A principle of enlightened marketing that holds that a company should put most of its resources into value-building marketing investments.

Value Marketing According to the principle of **value marketing**, the company should put most of its resources into value-building marketing investments. Many things marketers do—one-shot sales promotions, minor packaging changes, advertising puffery—may raise sales in the short run but add less *value* than would actual improvements in the product's quality, features, or convenience. Enlightened marketing calls for building long-term customer loyalty by continually improving the value customers receive from the firm's marketing offer.

Sense-of-Mission Marketing **Sense-of-mission marketing** means that the company should define its mission in broad *social* terms rather than narrow *product* terms. When a company defines a social mission, employees feel better about their work and have a clearer sense of direction. For example, defined in narrow product terms, Mountain Equipment Co-op sells high-quality outdoor gear. However, the organization states its mission more broadly as one of "striving for social and environmental leadership."[27] Reshaping the basic task of selling consumer products into the larger mission of serving the interests of consumers, employees, the environment, and others in the organization's various "communities" gives MEC a vital sense of purpose. Like MEC, many companies today are undertaking socially responsible actions or even building social responsibility into their underlying missions (see Marketing at Work 3.2).

Sense-of-mission marketing
A principle of enlightened marketing that holds that a company should define its mission in broad social terms rather than narrow product terms.

Societal Marketing Following the principle of **societal marketing**, an enlightened company makes marketing decisions by considering market wants and needs, the company's requirements, and society's long-run interests. The company is aware that neglecting societal long-run interests is a disservice to consumers and society. Alert companies and organizations view societal problems as opportunities. This is just what Hockey Canada did.

Societal marketing A principle of enlightened marketing that holds that a company should make marketing decisions by considering consumers' wants, the company's requirements, and society's long-run interests.

> Canadians have a reputation for being polite, reserved, and well mannered—unless of course they are watching their children wobbling around a hockey rink. In towns and cities across Canada, parents seem to have gone mad. They scream at their kids, hurl insults at rival teams, and beat refs to within an inch of their lives. For many kids, such behaviour was destroying Canada's best-loved game, so Hockey Canada decided to call a penalty shot. In a series of funny but provocative ads, it reverses the roles of parent and kid. One spot shows a man pulled over for a traffic violation. As the officer is writing up the ticket, the man's 10-year-old son is losing it in the back seat, furious because his spineless dad won't stand up to the cop. In another, a girl berates her father in front of his golf buddies as he tries to

Marketing at Work 3.2

Mission: Social Responsibility

In a recent poll, 88 percent of Canadians agreed that business should do more than simply make a profit, create jobs, and obey laws. And a poll conducted in the United States suggested that more than three-quarters of its respondents would switch brands and retailers when price and quality are equal for a product associated with a good cause. It's not surprising, therefore, that cause-related marketing by companies has increased more than 500 percent during the past decade.

Today, acts of good corporate citizenship abound. For example, on Camp Day, Tim Hortons store owners donate coffee sales and collect public donations to send kids to camp. Maxwell House, a division of Kraft Foods, created a partnership with Habitat for Humanity to build 100 homes in as many days. Bell Canada is the long-time sponsor of the Kids Help Phone. Alarm company ADT gives away personal security systems to battered women. Avon, CIBC, Ford Canada, Kitchen Aid, and Cake Beauty all contribute to the fight against breast cancer. And Nissan Canada partners with Meals on Wheels to deliver hot lunches to the elderly and shut-ins.

Beyond aligning with good causes, socially responsible companies care about and serve the communities in which they operate. Take Saturn, a company that has always claimed to focus more on its employees, customers, and communities than on revenues and bottom lines. Saturn's CEO notes that "a part of Saturn's business philosophy is to meet the needs of our neighbours." Saturn Playgrounds, for example, provides young children with a safe, fun environment during non-school hours as an alternative to gangs, drugs, and crime. Backed by Saturn retailers, local Saturn employees and customers join with community members to build a community playground in a single day. So far,

(continued)

Saturn and its customers have built over 223 playgrounds in towns across Canada.

But playgrounds aren't the only things needed by communities. Saturn retailers are the eyes and ears of the company, and when a community need arises, Saturn tries to respond. Saturn planted trees in areas hard hit by the 1997 ice storm. In North Bay, it provided funds for a new heart-monitoring unit.

Social responsibility is no longer viewed as the enemy of good business. Instead, it's at the forefront of sound business practice. Moreover, doing what's good for a company's communities can also be good for the company. A recent study shows that, on average, companies that make the list of best corporate citizens score 10 percent higher on *Business Week*'s rankings of financial performance than the remaining companies in the S&P 500. "This may be the most concrete evidence now available that good citizenship really does pay off on the bottom line."

Backed by Saturn retail facility dollars, local Saturn employees and customers join with community members to build a community playground in a single day.

Sources: Paul Welsh, "From Trademarks to Trustmarks," *Strategy,* February 24, 2003, p. 17; "Saturn Dealers Build Six New Playgrounds in One Weekend," *PR Newswire,* June 4, 1997; and Saturn Corporation, "Community: Saturn Playgrounds," www.saturnbp.com/mysaturn/mycommunity, accessed September 2002; information also provided by Chuck Novak, Brand Manager Saturn Canada, in an interview with Peggy Cunningham on July 21, 1999; Sinclair Steward, "Putting the Customer First," *Strategy,* November 9, 1998, p. 21; Tom Klusmann, "The 100 Best Corporate Citizens in 2000," *Business Ethics,* March–April 2000; Philip Johansson, "The 100 Best Corporate Citizens for 2001," *Business Ethics,* March–April 2001; Cynthia Wagner, "Economics: Evaluating Good Corporate Citizenship," *The Futurist,* July–August 2001, p. 16; "The 100 Best Corporate Citizens for 2002," *Business Ethics,* April 2002.

sink a putt. The breakthrough campaign has made us all aware of the problem and caused us to take a fresh look at our behaviour.[28]

A societally oriented marketer wants to design products that are not only pleasing but also beneficial. Examples of products that create immediate customer satisfaction as well as long-term social benefits abound. Philips Lighting's Earth Light compact fluorescent lightbulb provides good lighting at the same time that it gives long life and energy savings. Toyota's gas-electric hybrid Prius gives both a quiet ride and fuel efficiency. Maytag's front-loading Neptune washer provides superior cleaning along with water savings and energy efficiency. President's Choice "Too Good to Be True" soup mixes, developed for people with special dietary needs, have been welcomed by consumers who want good-tasting, high-fibre, low-fat, easy-to-prepare, healthful food. Another example is Herman Miller's office chairs, which are not only attractive and functional but are also environmentally responsible:

Herman Miller, one of the world's largest office furniture makers, has received numerous awards for environmentally responsible products and business practices. More than a decade ago, the company formed a Design for the Environment team responsible for infusing the company's design process with its environmental values. The team carries out a "cradle-to-cradle" life cycle analysis on the company's products, including everything from how much of a furniture item can be made from recycled materials to how much of it can be recycled at the end of its useful life. For example, the team redesigned the company's chairs for the lowest possible ecological impact and high recyclability. Herman Miller's

Herman Miller's Design for the Environment team is responsible for infusing the company's design process with its environmental values. For example, its new Mirra chair is made from 42 percent recycled materials and is 96 percent recyclable.

Aeron chair is constructed of 66 percent recycled materials (from pop bottles and recycled aluminum) and is 90 percent recyclable. The frames need no paint or other finish. No ozone-depleting materials are used. Chairs are shipped partially assembled, thus reducing the packaging and energy needed to ship them. Finally, materials schematics are imbedded in the bottoms of chair seats to help recycle chairs at the end of their lives. Herman Miller chairs are truly desirable—they've won awards for design and function *and* for environmental responsibility. Most recently, Herman Miller introduced the Mirra chair, which is made from 42 percent recycled materials and is 96 percent recyclable.[29]

Companies should try to turn everything they manufacture and market into such desirable, environmentally friendly products. They should avoid the temptation to sell products that may end up hurting the consumer and the environment. The environmentally responsible marketing opportunity, therefore, is to add long-run benefits without reducing the product's pleasing qualities.

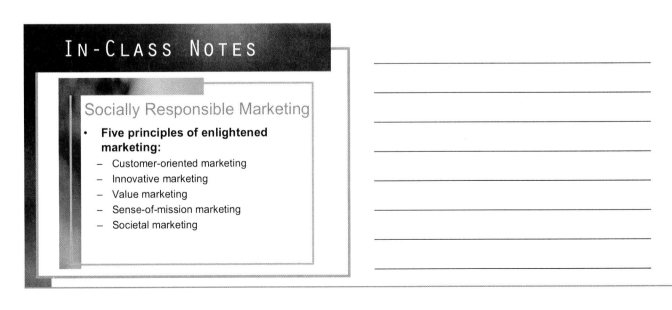

IN-CLASS NOTES

Socially Responsible Marketing

- **Five principles of enlightened marketing:**
  - Customer-oriented marketing
  - Innovative marketing
  - Value marketing
  - Sense-of-mission marketing
  - Societal marketing

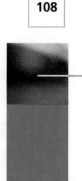

Linking the Concepts

Take another look at the Societal Marketing Concept section in Chapter 1.

- How does Figure 1.4 apply to the Enlightened Marketing section in this chapter?
- Use the five principles of enlightened marketing to assess the actions of a company that you believe exemplifies socially responsible marketing. (If you can't think of one, use one of the companies discussed in this chapter.)
- Use the principles to assess the actions of a company that you believe falls short of socially responsible marketing.

Marketing Ethics

Conscientious marketers face many moral dilemmas. Each area of marketing practice has ethical issues associated with it. Table 3.1 outlines just a few of the ethical issues marketers may face when fulfilling their roles. When facing these dilemmas, the best thing to do is often unclear. Because not all managers have fine moral sensitivity, companies need to develop *corporate marketing ethics policies*—broad guidelines that everyone in the organization must follow. These policies should cover distributor relations, advertising standards, customer service, pricing, and product development, as well as general ethical standards.

The finest guidelines cannot resolve all the difficult ethical situations the marketer faces. Table 3.2 lists some difficult ethical situations that marketers could face during their careers. If marketers choose immediate sales-producing actions in all these cases, their marketing behaviour may well be described as immoral or even amoral. If they refuse to go along with *any* of the actions, they may be ineffective as marketing managers and unhappy because of the constant moral tension. Managers need a set of principles that will help them determine the moral importance of each situation and decide how far they can go in good conscience.

But *what* principle should guide companies and marketing managers on issues of ethics and social responsibility? One philosophy is that such issues are decided by the free market and legal system. Under this principle, companies and their managers are not responsible for making moral judgments. Companies can in good conscience do whatever the system legally allows.

A second philosophy puts responsibility not in the system but in the hands of individual companies and managers. This more enlightened philosophy suggests that a company should have a "social conscience." Companies and managers should apply high standards of ethics and morality when making corporate decisions, regardless of "what the system allows." History provides an endless list of examples of company actions that were legal and allowed but were highly irresponsible. Consider this example:

> Prior to the [United States] *Pure Food and Drug Act,* the advertising for a diet pill promised that a person taking this pill could eat virtually anything at any time and still lose weight. Too good to be true? Actually the claim was quite true; the product lived up to its billing with frightening efficiency. It seems that the primary active ingredient in this "diet pill" was tapeworm larvae. These larvae would develop in the intestinal tract and, of course, be well fed; the pill taker would in time, quite literally, starve to death.[30]

Each company and marketing manager must work out a philosophy of socially responsible and ethical behaviour. Under the social marketing concept, companies and

Table 3.1 Ethical Issues Associated with Marketing Practice

Marketing Element	Examples of Ethical Issues
Marketing Research	Invalid and/or unreliable research studies (agencies conducting research studies using inappropriate methods or measures)
	Invasion of privacy
	Disguising sales as research
	Failure to ensure voluntary and informed participation (pressuring consumers to comply through high-pressure tactics or high-value incentives)
	Failure to respect the confidentiality of respondents (revealing respondents' individual identities)
	Competitive intelligence gathering using unethical tactics (hiring competitors' employees, dumpster diving, spying)
Segmentation and Target Marketing	Redlining: discriminating against poor or disadvantaged consumers
	Targeting inappropriate products to vulnerable audiences (diet pills to anorexic women, violent video games to children)
Positioning	Making socially undesirable products desirable (promoting use of disposable cleaning devices that add to landfill crisis versus reuseable ones)
	Positioning on questionable benefits (relating increased sexual attractiveness to alcohol consumption)
Product	Failure to market products that are safe for the intended use (lead in children's toys)
	Product testing (animal testing, failure to test sufficiently to reveal safety concerns)
	Marketing socially controversial products (cigarettes, firearms)
Packaging and Labelling	Actual size vs. apparent size (using design elements to make packages look larger than they are)
	Inadequate efforts with regard to product recalls
	Nutritional information (is information displayed in a fashion that can and will be processed?)
	Unclear or misleading labelling (terms such as "lite," "healthy," etc. are ambiguous and may imply benefits not actually associated with the product)
	Excess or environmentally unfriendly packaging (use of double and triple packaging that does little to protect the product but adds to waste stream, use of harmful dyes, failure to use recycled materials)
Pricing	Price collusion: the illegal practice of forming price agreements with competitors
	Negative option billing: sending unrequested goods and billing consumers for them
	Prejudice in negotiated prices: research has demonstrated that women and racial minorities pay more in negotiated price situations such as car buying
	Price discrimination: charging different segments different prices that are not based on cost (e.g., charging high prices in low-income neighbourhoods)
Advertising	Sex-role stereotyping in advertising (always showing women in domestic roles, not using women's voices in voice-overs in advertising)
	Dehumanizing images and portraying people as products: showing body parts versus the whole human being
	Bait-and-switch advertising: enticing consumers into retail establishments with offers of low-priced goods and then switching them to higher-priced alternatives
Sales and Channel Management	High-pressure sales tactics
	Unfairly disparaging competitors' goods
	Channel loading: pressuring channel members to take unneeded inventory at the end of a sales period to make the firm's sales numbers look better for reporting purposes

Table 3.2   Some Morally Difficult Situations in Marketing

1. You work for a toy company that has a very thorough quality control and testing procedure that ensures that every toy is as safe as it can possibly be for children. The company's newest product has a hinge that, if moved the wrong way, could possibly cause minor injuries to a child. The company's engineers have estimated the risk at one in ten thousand children. The vice president feels this is acceptable. You do not. What do you do?

2. Your R&D department has changed one of your products slightly. It is not really "new and improved," but you know that putting this statement on the package and in advertising will increase sales. What do you do?

3. You have been asked to add a stripped-down model to your line that could be advertised to attract customers to the store. The product won't be very good, but salespeople will be able to switch buyers up to higher-priced units. You are asked to give the green light for this stripped-down version. What do you do?

4. You are considering hiring a product manager who just left a competitor's company. She would be more than happy to tell you all the competitor's plans for the coming year. What do you do?

5. One of your top dealers in an important territory has recently had family troubles, and his sales have slipped. It looks like it will take him some time to straighten out his family trouble. Meanwhile, you are losing many sales. Legally, you can terminate the dealer's franchise and replace him. What do you do?

6. You have a chance to win a big account that will mean a lot to you and your company. The purchasing agent hints that a "gift" would influence the decision. Your assistant recommends sending an iPod to the buyer's home. What do you do?

7. You have heard that a competitor has a new product feature that will make a big difference in sales. The competitor will demonstrate the feature in a private dealer meeting at the annual trade show. You can easily send a "spy" to this meeting to learn about the new feature. What do you do?

8. You have to choose between three ad campaigns outlined by your agency. "A" is a soft-sell, honest information campaign. "B" uses sex-loaded emotional appeals and exaggerates the product's benefits. "C" involves a noisy, irritating commercial that is sure to gain audience attention. Pretests show that the campaigns are effective in the following order: C, B, and A. What do you do?

9. You are interviewing a capable woman applicant for a job as a salesperson. She is better qualified than the men just interviewed. Nevertheless, you know that some of your important customers prefer dealing with men, and you will lose some sales if you hire her. What do you do?

10. You are a sales manager at a duct-cleaning company. Your competitor's salespeople are getting into homes by pretending to take a research survey. After they finish the survey, they switch to their sales pitch. This technique seems to be very effective. What do you do?

managers must look beyond what is legal and allowed and develop standards based on personal integrity, corporate conscience, and long-term consumer welfare. A clear and responsible philosophy will help the company deal with knotty issues such as the one faced a few years ago by 3M:

In late 1997, a powerful new research technique for scanning blood kept turning up the same odd result: Tiny amounts of a chemical 3M had made for nearly 40 years were showing up in blood drawn from people living all across North America. If the results held up, it meant that virtually all North Americans may be carrying some minuscule amount of the chemical, called perfluorooctane sulfonate (PFOS), in their systems.

Even though they had yet to come up with definitive answers—and they insisted that there was no evidence of danger to humans—the company reached a drastic decision. In mid–2000, although under no mandate to act, 3M decided to phase out products containing PFOS and related chemicals, including its popular Scotchgard fabric protector. This was no easy decision. Since there was as yet no replacement chemical, it meant a potential loss of US$500 million in annual sales.

3M's voluntary actions drew praise from regulators. "3M deserves great credit for identifying the problem and coming forward," says an Environmental

Protection Agency administrator. "It took guts," comments another government scientist. "The fact is that most companies . . . go into anger, denial, and the rest of that stuff. [We're used to seeing] decades-long arguments about whether a chemical is really toxic." For 3M, however, it shouldn't have been all that difficult a decision—it was simply the right thing to do.[31]

As with environmentalism, the issue of ethics provides special challenges for international marketers (see Marketing at Work 3.3). Business standards and laws vary widely from one country to the next. For example, whereas bribes and kickbacks are illegal for North American firms, they are standard business practice in many South American countries. One recent study found that companies from some nations were much more likely to use bribes when seeking contracts in emerging-market nations. The most flagrant bribe-paying firms were from Russia and China, with Taiwan and South Korea close behind. The least corrupt were companies from Australia, Sweden, Switzerland, Austria, and Canada.[32] The question arises as to whether a company must lower its ethical standards to compete effectively in countries with lower standards. In one study, two researchers posed this question to chief executives of large international companies and got a unanimous response: No.[33]

When firms give a covert payment to a government official to obtain a concession, they are no longer just committing an unethical act, they are committing an illegal one, violating Canada's *Corruption of Foreign Public Officials Act* (1998).

Professional Marketing Ethics

All professions have their professional associations and professional ethics, and marketers are no different. Canadian marketing practitioners, whether they are CMOs (Chief Marketing Officers), vice presidents, marketing managers, or junior marketing associates, may become members of the Canadian Marketing Association, the professional association for marketing practitioners and marketing academics in Canada.

The CMA has composed a Code of Ethics that all members of the association promise to uphold (see Table 3.3).

In addition to the professional code of ethics of marketers, companies may create their own internal code of ethics. PricewaterhouseCoopers (PwC) is a good example. In 1996, PwC established an ethics office and comprehensive ethics program headed by a high-level chief ethics officer. The ethics program begins with a code of conduct called "The Way We Do Business." In a comprehensive ethics training program called "Navigating the Grey," PwC employees learn about the code and about how to handle thorny ethics issues. The program also includes an ethics help line and continuous communications at all levels. "Ethics is in everything we say and do," says PwC's CEO, Samuel DiPiazza. Last year alone, the PwC training program involved 40 000 employees, and the help line received over 1000 calls from people asking for guidance in working through difficult ethics dilemmas.

Still, written codes and ethics programs do not ensure ethical behaviour. Ethics and social responsibility require a total corporate commitment. They must be a component of the overall corporate culture. According to PwC's DiPiazza, "I see ethics as a mission-critical issue . . . deeply imbedded in who we are and what we do. It's just as important as our product development cycle or our distribution system. . . . It's about creating a culture based on integrity and respect, not a culture based on dealing with the crisis of the day. . . . We ask ourselves every day, 'Are we doing the right things?'"[34]

Canada's 74 000 charities and nonprofit organizations are not immune to questions of ethics. While few question the importance of these worthy causes, there has been growing criticism about some of the fundraising methods they use. Two major concerns have surfaced. More charities are using lotteries to raise funds. These not only add to the

Marketing at Work 3.3

The Grey Zone: International Marketing Ethics

Decisions that marketers must make are often fraught with conflicts of values—and these conflicts can become even more fraught in the arena of international businesses, where people from different cultures, political systems, economies, value systems, and ethical standards must interact. For example, in some countries, giving and receiving gifts is customary at the close of business transactions. However, for many Canadian firms, acceptance of gifts, other than mere tokens of appreciation such as chocolates or flowers, is viewed as unethical and may even be illegal.

Ethical issues can arise in market-entry decisions, bribery and gift giving, contract negotiations, human resource issues, crisis management situations, product policy, advertising practices, pricing and transfer pricing, information systems management and privacy, grey markets, environmental concerns, accounting, finance and taxation, and production. Many of these areas are of specific concern to marketers. International advertising, for example, often raises ethical concerns. Although many European countries use nudity and sexual innuendo in their advertising, some Americans find this offensive. In Canada, we are more likely to find violence offensive. In some countries, such as India, even showing people kissing is objectionable.

Offering certain products for sale in some countries has also raised ethical criticism. American companies have been criticized for marketing harmful chemicals overseas, chemicals that are banned from use in their home markets. Avon has been criticized for selling cosmetics to people in countries where many people cannot afford enough food. And even though a product itself may not be inherently harmful, some companies haven't taken measures to prevent harm arising to consumers who incorrectly used products (like baby formula, drugs, or pesticides) because of high rates of illiteracy and inability to understand instructions. Even packaging can be a concern. In some countries, such as Germany, manufacturers must recycle all packaging. In others, because of a lack of disposal facilities, packaging adds to pollution problems.

Pricing raises yet another set of ethical concerns. Higher prices may have to be charged as a result of higher costs in marketing overseas, but sometimes overly high prices are levied just because a firm has a monopoly in a foreign country. Firms have also been criticized for their refusal to send female sales representatives or managers into countries with adverse gender stereotypes even though this hampers women's chances for advancement or higher earnings.

And although bribery is viewed as a "normal" way of doing business in some countries, in most it's an illegal practice. Some North American businesspeople hold the stereotypical belief that bribes are expected overseas, and make the mistake of offering such a payment when they perceive the slightest hesitation in signing a business deal. Not only is the offering of a bribe illegal, it will often terminate the relationship.

We've all read reports of companies being blocked from doing business in South America because of rigged bidding systems, or losing sales in China or Korea because firms cannot legally pay the bribes necessary to get the business. But some countries may have higher moral standards than North Americans do. For example, one survey showed that fewer Japanese executives will cheat on their expense sheets than will a comparable group of North American executives. Other surveys of Canadian businesspeople have shown that most ethical problems arise not in doing business in exotic locales, but rather in dealing with our closest neighbour, the United States. Although this may be because we do more business with the United States than with any other country, problems such as industrial espionage, product safety concerns, sales practices, and hiring practices have been areas of growing ethical concern.

As a minimum, marketers working for Canadian companies must abide by the laws of the countries in which they operate. However, being an ethical marketer often means going beyond the mere provisions of a legal system. Marketers also must consider what is right or wrong. Such considerations involve respecting the human rights of people, no matter what country they reside in. It involves avoiding the exploitation of individuals or their environment.

Planning for ethical behaviour must begin at the same time as the rest of the strategic international market planning effort. Ethics cannot be an afterthought. This type of planning includes deciding which international markets to enter. Does the firm want to enter markets dominated by totalitarian and military regimes, or those known for their record of human rights violations or ongoing environmental damage? Other questions include what types of products to market. The marketing of pesticides, tobacco, liquor, and pharmaceuticals, for example, all have unique ethical questions associated with them.

So while international marketing can be one of the most exciting and rewarding areas of the profession, be aware that it also presents some of the most difficult ethical problems and issues.

Source: Peggy Cunningham, "Managing Marketing Ethics in International Business: Literature Review and Directions for Future Research," Proceedings of the ASAC Conference, Windsor, June 1995.

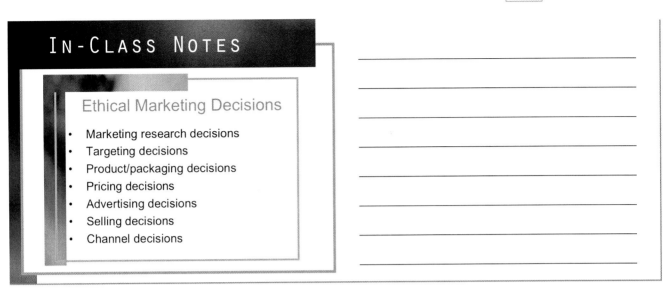

IN-CLASS NOTES

Ethical Marketing Decisions

- Marketing research decisions
- Targeting decisions
- Product/packaging decisions
- Pricing decisions
- Advertising decisions
- Selling decisions
- Channel decisions

Table 3.3 Excerpts from the Canadian Marketing Association's Code of Ethics and Standards of Practice

A1. Purpose of Code of Ethics and Standards of Practice

Preamble: Marketers acknowledge that the establishment and maintenance of high standards of practice are a fundamental responsibility to the public, essential to winning and holding public confidence, and the foundation of a successful and independent information-based marketing industry in Canada.

A2. Application and Governing Legislation

A2.2 Members of the Canadian Marketing Association recognize an obligation—to the public, to the integrity of the discipline in which they operate and to each other—to practice to the highest standards of honesty, truth, accuracy and fairness.

A2.4 No marketer shall participate in any campaign involving the disparagement of any person or group on the grounds of race, colour, religion, national origin, gender, sexual orientation, marital status.

B. Accuracy of Representation

B1 *Accuracy:* Offers must be clear and truthful and shall not misrepresent a product, service, solicitation or program and shall not mislead by statement, or technique of demonstration or comparison.

B5 *Disguise:* No person shall make offers or solicitations in the guise of research or a survey when the real intent is to sell products, services, or to raise funds.

C. Constituent Elements and Characteristics of the Offer

C1 *Disclosure:* The offer shall contain clear and conspicuous disclosure of the following terms:

☐ The exact nature of what is offered;

☐ The price;

☐ The terms of payment, including any additional charges, such as shipping and handling; and

☐ The consumer's commitment and any ongoing obligation in placing an order.

C2 *Comparisons:* Comparisons included in offers must be factual, verifiable and not misleading.

E. Media-Specific Standards of Practice

E1.2 *Broadcast—Misrepresentation:* Marketers shall not employ presentations likely to mislead reasonable consumers that the presentation is news, information, public service or entertainment programming.

E2.2 *Printed Media—Description:* All printed materials shall accurately and fairly describe the product or service offered. Type size, colour, contrast, style, placement or other treatment shall not be used to reduce the legibility or clarity of the offer, exceptions to the offer, or terms and conditions.

E3.2 *Telephone—Identification:* Marketers shall identify themselves and the business or organization represented promptly at the beginning of each outbound telemarketing call.

(continued)

Table 3.3   continued

E3.3   *Telephone—Privacy:* No marketer shall knowingly call any person who has an unlisted or unpublished telephone number, except where the telephone number was furnished by the customer to that marketer. In addition:

☐ Marketers will promptly remove from their lists the telephone numbers of consumers who request them to do so, or non-customers who have registered with the CMA's Do Not Call Service.

F.   Product Safety

F1   *Introduction:* Products offered by marketers shall be safe in normal use and, where applicable, shall conform to product safety regulations established by Health and Welfare Canada and by the Canadian Standards Association and/or other recognized Canadian authorities.

G.   Special Considerations in Marketing to Children

G1   *Age:* For purposes of this Code of Ethics and Standards of Practice, the term *child* refers to someone who has not reached his or her 13th birthday. In addition:

☐ Marketers are expected to use discretion and sensitivity in marketing to persons between 13 years and the age of majority, to address the age, knowledge, sophistication and maturity of this audience.

G2   *Responsibility:* Marketing to children imposes a special responsibility on marketers. Marketers shall recognize that children are not adults and that not all marketing techniques are appropriate for children.

H.   Protection of the Environment

H1   *Environmental Responsibility:* Marketers recognize and acknowledge a continuing responsibility to manage their businesses to minimize environmental impact.

H2   *Three Rs:* Marketers shall incorporate the "Three *R*s" of environmental responsibility in the operation of their businesses. More specifically, to:

☐ Reduce material use;

☐ Reuse materials; and,

☐ Recycle materials.

I.   Protection of Personal Privacy

Privacy: All marketers shall recognize and abide by the six principles of personal privacy adopted by the Canadian Marketing Association:

Principle #1: Giving Consumers Control of How Information About Them Is Used

Principle #2: Providing Consumers with the Stage of Access to Information

Principle #3: Enabling Consumers to Reduce the Amount of Mail They Receive

Principle #4: Controlling the Use of Information by Third Parties

Principle #5: Safely Storing Information About Consumers

Principle #6: Respecting Confidential and Sensitive Information

J.   Enforcement Procedures for the Standards of Practice

J1   Upon receipt of information that would indicate a violation of the criminal laws of Canada, the Association will promptly forward such information to the appropriate authorities and the organization concerned.

Source: Canadian Marketing Association, "Code of Ethics and Standards of Practice," www.the-cma.org/consumer/ethics.cfm.

pressures on people to gamble; they may also jeopardize the welfare of the nonprofit. Use of professional telemarketers is another source of ethical concern. They raise funds on the part of nonprofit organizations, but the charity may see only a small portion of the money raised. In the face of growing public scrutiny, nonprofits have to be as ethically aware and socially responsible as their for-profit counterparts.

The future holds many challenges and opportunities for marketing managers as they move through the new millennium. Technological advances in every area, from

Ethics programs:
PricewaterhouseCoopers established
a comprehensive ethics program that
begins with a code of conduct called
"The Way We Do Business." Says
PwC's CEO, "Ethics is in everything
we say and do."

telecommunications, information technology, and the Internet to health care and entertainment, provide abundant marketing opportunities. However, forces in the socioeconomic, cultural, and natural environments increase the limits under which marketing can be carried out. Companies that are able to create new values in a socially
responsible way will have a world to conquer.

LOOKING BACK

In this chapter, we've covered many important concepts involving marketing's sweeping impact on consumers, other businesses,
and society as a whole. You learned that responsible marketers discover what consumers want and respond with
the right products, priced to give good value to buyers
and profit to the producer. A marketing system should
sense, serve, and satisfy consumer needs and improve the
quality of consumers' lives. In working to meet consumer
needs, marketers may take some actions that are not to
everyone's liking or benefit. Marketing managers should
be aware of the main criticisms of marketing.

REVIEWING THE CONCEPTS

1. Understand marketing's multiple responsibilities, and identify the major social and ethical
criticisms of marketing.

Marketing's *impact on individual consumer welfare* has
been criticized for its high prices, deceptive practices,
high-pressure selling, shoddy or unsafe products,
planned obsolescence, and poor service to disadvantaged consumers. Marketing's *impact on society* has been
criticized for creating false wants and too much materialism, too few social goods, cultural pollution, and too

much political power. Critics have also criticized marketing's *impact on other businesses* for harming competitors and reducing competition through acquisitions, practices that create barriers to entry, and unfair competitive marketing practices.

2. Define *consumerism* and *environmentalism* and explain how they affect marketing strategies.

Concerns about the marketing system have led to *consumer action movements*. *Consumerism,* or *consumer activism,* is an organized social movement intended to strengthen the rights and power of consumers relative to sellers. Alert marketers view it as an opportunity to serve consumers better by providing more consumer information, education, and protection. *Environmentalism* is an organized social movement seeking to minimize the harm done to the environment and quality of life by marketing practices. The first wave of modern environmentalism was driven by environmental groups and concerned consumers; the second wave was driven by government, which passed laws and regulations governing industrial practices affecting the environment. Today, the first two environmentalism waves are merging into a third and stronger wave in which companies are accepting responsibility for doing no environmental harm. Companies now are adopting policies of *environmental sustainability*—developing strategies that both sustain the environment and produce profits for the company.

3. Describe the principles of socially responsible marketing.

Many companies originally opposed these social movements and laws, but most of them now recognize a need for positive consumer information, education, and protection. Some companies have followed a policy of *enlightened marketing,* which holds that a company's marketing should support the best long-run performance of the marketing system. Enlightened marketing consists of five principles: *consumer-oriented marketing, innovative marketing, value marketing, sense-of-mission marketing,* and *societal marketing.*

4. Explain the role of ethics in marketing.

Increasingly, companies are responding to the need to provide company policies and guidelines to help their managers deal with questions of *marketing ethics.* Of course, even the best guidelines cannot resolve all the difficult ethical decisions that individuals and firms must make. But there are some principles among which marketers can choose. One principle states that such issues should be decided by the free market and legal system. A second and more enlightened principle puts responsibility not in the system but in the hands of individual companies and managers. Each firm and marketing manager must develop a philosophy of socially responsible and ethical behaviour. Under the societal marketing concept, managers must look beyond what is legal and allowable and develop standards based on personal integrity, corporate conscience, and long-term consumer welfare.

Because business standards and practices vary among countries, the issue of ethics poses special challenges for international marketers. The growing consensus among today's marketers is that it is important to make a commitment to a common set of shared standards worldwide.

KEY TERMS

consumerism *98*
customer-oriented marketing *104*
enlightened marketing *103*

environmental sustainability *100*
environmentalism *100*
innovative marketing *104*

sense-of-mission marketing *105*
societal marketing *105*
value marketing *104*

STUDY GUIDE

After completing this self-test, check your answers against the Answer Key at the back of the book.

MULTIPLE CHOICE

1. A bottle of Asacol, a drug for controlling intestinal inflammation, is more expensive than a bottle of the same drug as a generic product. Consumers accuse pharmaceutical manufacturers of unfair markups when the brand price is compared to the lower price of the generic product. In these cases, brand drug marketers answer this charge by pointing out that
   a. As long as they are the only ones providing the drug, there is nothing unethical about charging the highest possible price
   b. Delivering value to customers includes the expertise that went into the design and development
   c. Generic drug makers are practising predatory pricing
   d. The Canadian government subsidizes all generic drugs
   e. Generic drugs are of inferior quality

2. Recently, consumers have been exposed to advertising for products that claim to whiten teeth within weeks. Critics of marketing have accused marketers of these and similar products of creating
   a. False wants
   b. Predetermined needs
   c. Planned obsolescence
   d. Socialized marketing
   e. Self-actualized needs

3. In the mid-20th century, planned obsolescence meant building products that would break down within a certain time frame, ensuring a viable market for manufacturers as consumers replaced worn out items. That practice, however, has changed since manufacturers now fear that products that wear out predictably and quickly will prompt
   a. Consumer apathy
   b. Lower prices
   c. Customer disloyalty
   d. More competition
   e. Less innovation

4. As the demand for convenient, secure, and attractive product packaging satisfies consumers, it also creates significant social problems by congesting landfills and wasting natural resources. The balance that must be achieved in satisfying both consumer want and social responsibility is best described as

   a. Product concept vs. societal marketing concept
   b. Social need vs. consumer demand
   c. Personal want vs. social want
   d. Consumerism vs. environmentalism
   e. Private good vs. public good

5. The ethics of alcohol and tobacco advertising have long been debated. A powerful argument against the advertising of these products is that such advertising directly contravenes the *Consumer Protection Act* by violating the consumer's right to
   a. Safety
   b. Make informed decisions
   c. Exercise free will
   d. Know about all available products
   e. Satisfy basic needs

6. In some European countries, companies are legally responsible for disposing of the garbage that their product packaging creates. This type of legal requirement is a sign of a dominant _____ movement.
   a. Social consumption
   b. Consumerism
   c. Environmentalism
   d. Sense-of-mission
   e. Municipal

7. In late summer 2005, China's government adamantly stated that it will not set any national targets for the reduction of greenhouse gases. This refusal has placed into jeopardy the success of the
   a. Environmental Sustainability Agreement
   b. United National Pollution Treaty
   c. NAFTA Pollution Reduction System
   d. Kyoto Accord
   e. Berlin Environment Testament

8. Ballard is a company that makes fuel cells for powering vehicles. The cells use hydrogen as the fuel source and the only exhaust emission it creates is water. Ballard is seen as a key player in commercializing clean alternative energy while making a profit doing so, a sign that _____ is achievable.
   a. Environmental sustainability
   b. Real societal marketing
   c. Responsible consumption
   d. Social mission marketing
   e. Environmental consumerism

9. Customer-oriented marketing and the marketing concept are very similar: They both strive to deliver real value to a target segment and build profitable, ongoing customer relationships. There is, however, one key difference that separates them: The customer-oriented marketing organization
   a. Provides only environmentally friendly products
   b. Targets a small, countable, individually selected and knowable group of customers
   c. Uses CRM systems to capture information on large numbers of customers
   d. Uses Web technologies to personalize a customer's website experience
   e. Conducts only personal interview research

10. There are a number of marketing practices that, while not illegal, are considered unethical. Which of the following is an example of an unethical but technically legal marketing activity?
    a. Advertising a sale price that is actually the usual price
    b. Selling lists of customer names without their permission
    c. Obtaining documents from a competitor by searching through discarded garbage
    d. Paying a bribe to a foreign government in exchange for contracts or concessions
    e. Paying a competitor's employees to provide information

TRUE/FALSE

T   F   1. Low-price retailers are often seen as unethical marketers by consumer groups because they create too much pressure on competitors.

T   F   2. In Canada, it is legal for a grocery store to entice customers to the store by selling milk for one week at a price lower than the milk cost the grocery store.

T   F   3. Customers who buy via the Internet and e-commerce do so at their own risk and are not shielded by the *Consumer Protection Act*.

T   F   4. Sense-of-mission marketing and societal marketing are interchangeable terms for the same marketing approach.

T   F   5. Marketers could defend weblining by pointing out that it is nothing more than identifying and serving only the most profitable customers and customer segments, a common and well-founded marketing practice.

CONCEPT CHECK

1. Consumers, consumer advocates, government agencies, and other critics have accused marketing of harming consumers through high prices, deceptive practices, _____, _____, _____, and poor service to disadvantaged consumers.

2. Many critics charge that the North American marketing system causes prices to be higher than they would be under more "sensible" systems. Three factors contribute to the high price perception: _____, _____, and _____.

3. The _____ is a piece of legislation that protects Canadian consumers from high-pressure selling tactics and other potentially unfair or fraudulent marketing practices.

4. Critics have charged that some producers follow a program of _____, causing their products to become obsolete before they actually should need replacement.

5. Common criticisms against modern advertising practice include indictments that advertising has, creates, or contributes to _____, _____, _____, and too much political power.

6. _____ is an organized movement of citizens and government agencies to improve the rights and power of buyers in relation to sellers.

7. Traditional *buyer's rights* include the right to not buy a product that is offered for sale; the right to expect _____; and the right to expect _____.

8. _____ is an organized movement of concerned citizens, businesses, and government agencies to protect and improve people's living environment.

9. The environmental sustainability grid consists of four cells: new environmental technology, _____, _____, and _____.

10. Enlightened marketing consists of five principles: consumer-oriented marketing, _____, _____, _____, and societal marketing.

11. _____ marketing means that the company should define its mission in broad social terms rather than narrow product terms.

STUDENT MATERIALS

Visit our website at www.pearsoned.ca/armstrong for online quizzes, Internet exercises, and more!

DISCUSSING THE ISSUES

1. Discuss the claim that the high cost of distribution, high cost of advertising and promotion, and excessive markups lead to higher than necessary costs for Canadian consumers. Do you agree or disagree with this position?

2. What is the difference between consumerism and environmentalism? How are they alike and different? Give an example of a cause that would be championed by each movement.

3. Distinguish between the five principles of enlightened marketing: consumer-oriented marketing, innovative marketing, value marketing, sense-of-mission marketing, and societal marketing.

4. Write a corporate marketing ethics policy for a company selling mortgage services online. How would such a policy influence ethical decision making among employees in this company?

5. Search through news reports to find a story about a company that is acting in a socially responsible manner. Would this information influence your buying decision if you were in the market to buy the type of product this firm sells? What impact do you think the socially responsible action reported in the news story has on the employees of the organization?

MARKETING APPLICATIONS

A forest full of trees has been spared thanks to a new paperless wine list being used at Aureole restaurants in Las Vegas and New York. The wine selection boasts an awe-inspiring 4000 different wine labels that would be impractical to print onto paper in the form of a manageable wine list. Instead of a paper wine list, customers are presented with a lightweight, wireless computer tablet. Pages are turned and selections are made by the customer using either a stylus or their finger. Aside from the positive environmental impact, there are other marketing applications for the electronic wine list. For example, the tablet can be used to display brief wine reviews and narratives about the winery, customers are allowed to bookmark favourite wine selections, and it has the ability to let

customers request that wine selection information and special offers be emailed to them at home.

THINKING LIKE A MARKETING MANAGER

1. Consider other opportunities that electronic tablets have for replacing material that is traditionally printed on paper (e.g., textbooks, novels).

2. What sort of resistance do you think consumers may have to accessing printed material in an electronic format? How could such resistance be overcome?

3. What do you see as the environmental benefits of such a system?

VIDEO CASE

Go to Pearson Canada's Video Central site (www.pearsoned.ca/highered/videocentral) to view the video and accompanying case for this chapter.

CASE 3 "DO WELL BY DOING GOOD"

zations like Share our Strength, a hunger-fighting charity, Skills USA, which promotes excellence for students in vocational trades, and the Student Conservation Association, which provides conservation services in national parks, forests, refuges, and urban areas. Its partnership with this last group has led to the company's active involvement in Earth Day each year. Timberland employees are given 40 hours per year of paid time for community service. And in 2001 the company implemented a "service sabbatical," enabling up to four employees annually to spend three to six months working at nonprofits that support civic issues. Today, as a $1.8 billion company, Timberland has transformed itself and the communities it serves.

According to *Maclean's* 2004 annual Top 100 Employers issue, an organization that has recognized the importance of social values from its inception is also the best place to work in Canada. And that place is Vancouver Savings Credit Union (VanCity). Founded in 1945, it's Canada's largest credit union, with $9.0 billion in assets, 305 000 members, and 41 branches throughout Greater Vancouver, the Fraser Valley, and Victoria. VanCity owns Citizens Bank of Canada, serving members across the country by telephone, ATM, and the Internet. Both VanCity and Citizens Bank are guided by a commitment to *corporate social responsibility*, and to improve the quality of life in the communities where the company "lives and works." VanCity believes further that this commitment gives it an advantage over the competition.

One of the ways VanCity supports communities is its providing low-income members access to products and services. In the past year over $25 million in loans were granted to businesses that did not have enough collateral to satisfy the traditional banks' lending criteria. VanCity has also acquired Real Assets, a full-service portfolio management company that focuses solely on socially responsible investments. Finally, VanCity has created the VanCity Award, a $1 million grant aimed at supporting innovative schemes in the community.

Do you have to be big to do good? While organizational wealth has its advantages, there are companies in Canada that get involved in the betterment of society simply by offering products and services that are socially responsible. One of them is Winnipeg's Humboldt's Legacy (named after 19th-century scientist and ecologist Baron von Humboldt, one of the first true naturalists). The store, located on a quiet Winnipeg street, is a sanctuary for green consumers. It sells household products that support the consumer shift to an alternative, sustainable economy. Customers can find recycled paper, shampoos and detergents in refillable containers, bedding made from organic cotton, and books and magazines on "green" subjects. All the products offered are environmentally and socially responsible alternatives to those purchased every day by consumers. Willi Kurtz, who with his wife, Chris, owns the store, truly believes they can change the world.

By becoming socially responsible and supporting sustainability initiatives, companies large and small may actually change the world by doing good.

Questions

1. Research local companies and determine if any of them are involved in supporting socially responsible charities or community projects.

2. Research your local government, such as the municipality where your home or school is located, to determine what services are offered to the community. You can also research community organizations and service groups (such as Kiwanis) or nonprofit agencies or charities that are active in your community.

3. Based on this research, determine whether there is a potential for local companies to get involved in supporting social causes in the community through partnership with either local governments or service groups.

4. What problems can you foresee developing as a company becomes more socially focused?

5. What are the costs of increasing a company's role in supporting the community? What are the payoffs?

Sources: www.conference-board.org/publications/describe.cfm?id=456, accessed November 2004, www.macleans.ca/topstories/polls/article.jsp?content=20031218_150312_2984, accessed November 2004, www.timberland.com/timberlandserve/timberlandserve_index.jsp, accessed November 2004, www.vancity.com/Community/AboutUs/MediaCentre/MediaReleases2004/August17:BCnon-profitscompetefor$1-Milliongrant, accessed November 2004, www.mori.com/polls/1999/millpoll.shtml.

c4rb

w.dove.ca/c4rb/ ⌄ Q▾ Google

dCh...! – Content   WeightWatche...s Stories –   Leap Frog – ... of All Ages   Making the B... Futurosity   BCSC–Health Facts   Pomanders   Rum Pot – Rumtopf   Funny Flash ...du

Dove.

Dove on Beauty   Dove Products   Dove Promotions

Campaign for Real Beauty   Dove Self-Esteem Fund   Articles

Campaign for Real Beauty

For Women of Every Shape, Size, Age and Culture

Dove invites you to participate in the Campaign for Real
Beauty, a global initiative that's giving women around the
world a chance to challenge stereotypes, shake up
perceptions and explore how genuinely stunning real beauty
can be.

☐ fat?

☐ fab?

Visit the official website where you can:

- Share your thoughts on beauty
- Participate in online discussions, polls and debates
- Read about the latest beauty research and events

**The following link will take you from Dove.ca to a Campaign
for Real Beauty website:**

Campaign for Real Beauty

Français   Privacy Policy   Terms of Use   Disclaimer   Contact Dove   Campaign for Real Beauty

...ding this chapter, you should be able to

1. describe the environmental forces that affect the company's ability to serve its customers

2. explain how changes in the demographic and economic environments affect marketing decisions

3. identify the major trends in the firm's natural and technological environments

4. explain the key changes in the political and cultural environments

5. discuss how companies can react to the marketing environment

The Marketing Environment

In Part 1 (Chapters 1, 2, and 3), you learned about the basic concepts of marketing; the steps in the marketing process for building profitable relationships with targeted groups of customers; and the relationship of marketing to society as a whole.

In Part 2, we'll look more deeply into the first step of the marketing process—understanding the marketplace and customer needs and wants. In this chapter, you'll discover that marketing does not operate in a vacuum, but rather in a complex and changing marketplace environment. Other forces in this environment—suppliers, intermediaries, customers, competitors, publics, and others—may work with or against the company. Major environmental forces—demographic, economic, natural, technological, political, and cultural—shape marketing opportunities, pose threats, and affect the organization's ability to serve its customers and develop valuable relationships with them. To understand marketing, and to develop effective marketing strategies, you must first understand the context in which marketing operates.

In Chapter 3 we learned how companies like Ethical Bean are able to blend social activism and a concern for the environment into their marketing strategies and programs. Now let's look at how the marketing environment can influence a company's approach to the marketing of its products. While most savvy marketers today are aware of the environment that surrounds and influences their marketing activities, there are few who are brave enough to attempt to *change* that environment.

A recent survey of 3200 women in 10 countries around the world, including Canada, revealed that most women do not think of themselves as beautiful. If you were a marketer of women's beauty products, how would you respond to these findings? The marketers of Dove brand cosmetics took a radical approach: They set out to redefine our culture's concept of beauty.

n our celebrity-obsessed culture, images of beauty as portrayed in Hollywood movies, fashion magazines, television programs, and beauty and talent contests such as Miss Universe and *American Idol* are rarely anything but "perfect." This cultural view has affected the marketing of most consumer goods, from clothing to food to shampoo. The customary approach taken by most companies in advertising cosmetics and personal care products to women is to promise that Hollywood perfection—shiny hair, white teeth, flawless skin, and thin bodies—and to dictate those standards of perfection by using only beautiful models in their product and advertising images.

Dove's "Campaign for Real Beauty," which began in 2004 in the U.K., the United States, and Canada, turns our culture's idea of beauty on its head, and instead advocates the idea that "normal" women are beautiful—whether they are overweight, old, or covered in freckles. In a way, says *Advertising Age* magazine, the campaign "undermines the basic proposition of decades of beauty-care advertising [because it tells] women—and young girls—they're beautiful just the way they are."

By commissioning the study, then basing a major marketing campaign on its findings, the Dove marketing team dared to challenge our culture's stereotypes, and, even more boldly, attempted to change them.

The international Campaign for Real Beauty was created by Ogilvy & Mather in Chicago and Toronto. The campaign ran first in the U.K., where it focused on a new Dove product, a body firming lotion, which at that time was not yet available in Canada or the United States. The advertisements in the U.K. featured "real" women recruited off the streets, who posed in their underwear under copy that celebrated their "real" thighs. In the United States, print ads and billboards featured a photo of plus-sized Tabatha Roman, an account executive at Ogilvy & Mather, that asked, "Oversized? or Outstanding?" In Canada the copy was changed to read "Fat? or Fab?"

The Dove campaign challenged the norms on every level, including media vehicles. The outdoor campaign was interactive—an unusual move for any marketer—and sought to involve the public in answering the question of what is the definition of beauty. The Fat?/Fab? creative execution, which ran in magazines in Canada and the United States, also took the form of an interactive billboard in Toronto in the fall of 2004. The single billboard, located alongside the highly trafficked Gardiner Expressway, included a toll-free number and featured a digital display that was updated in real time as people called in their votes.

Online marketing was also an important component of the campaign. A special website was created for each country at campaignforrealbeauty.com, .ca, and .co.uk. A public relations initiative, the Dove Self-Esteem Fund, raised money through the websites and at points of purchase, and worked with local agencies to provide funding for programs that, in some way, work to increase the self-esteem of girls and young women. In Canada the Dove Self-Esteem Fund worked with the National Eating Disorder Information Centre, while in the U.S. it aided an organization called Uniquely Me!, a self-esteem program for Girl Scout troops in disadvantaged communities.

In fact, an important goal of the campaign was to foster self-esteem in young girls. In Canada the campaign included cinema and television ads featuring Canadian girls saying what they don't like about themselves while Cyndi Lauper's "True Colors" plays in the background. The girls were not models or actors; they were real girls who were asked to speak on camera about their thoughts and feelings. When these beautiful little girls tell us they think they're fat, or ugly, or they wish they were blonde, it is, as the company's website says, "a wake up call to all of us, highlighting the need to pay more attention to the issue of self-esteem."

Can Dove's campaign really change our cultural environment? Will it start a new trend, one that sees more advertisements featuring real women instead of perfect models? Not everyone thinks so. One trend expert believes that while Dove's campaign is novel and may work as a gimmick, it's not likely to change our society's notion of ideal beauty: "We are so driven to worship perfection, which at the moment happens to be in the guise of celebrities."

The final tally of votes on the Toronto billboard's Fat?/Fab? question was a nearly even split, with approximately 50 percent of people saying Tabatha Roman was fat, 50 percent believing she was fab. It seems that companies like Dove still have a long way to go before they can truly change our cultural environment— but they do seem to be having an influence.[1]

TEST YOURSELF

Answers to these questions can be found on our website at www.pearsoned.ca/armstrong.

1. Why did Dove include young girls who are not users of Dove in their Real Beauty campaign?
   a) Because it is cheaper to market to young girls
   b) Because young girls when they grow up will become Dove's target segment, and Dove wants to establish positive self-esteem and positive brand identity with them early
   c) Because young girls are more suggestible and vulnerable than adult women
   d) Because Dove is trying to change its product line from products for adult women to skin care and cosmetics for girls 11 to 16 years old
   e) Because Dove is made by Procter & Gamble, which also makes products for teenagers

2. How could Dove later use the information they collected during their survey and interactive billboard campaign?
   a) Develop specific advertising campaigns and messages that address women's different views of beauty and culture
   b) Sell the information to makers of diet aids and weight loss plans
   c) Provide the information to the governments of the three countries to augment census information
   d) Lobby the government to change laws about what are acceptable images depicting female beauty
   e) All of the above

3. What is the major reason that a marketer of beauty products like Dove would conduct a survey on self-concepts about beauty and then run a campaign to convince women that they are already beautiful?
   a) Because they want to establish self-esteem in Dove customers and build closer relationships with those customers
   b) Because Dove products, like most cosmetic products, cannot deliver on all the hype
   c) Because they want to raise the price of Dove products
   d) Because Procter & Gamble wants to start selling these customers higher-end, more expensive beauty products under a different brand
   e) Because such a campaign is less expensive than a worldwide product advertising campaign

4. Why would Dove have set up different campaign styles and use different websites and wording for Canada, the U.S., and the U.K.?
   a) Because legally each country is its own trade area and Dove has to sell to them separately
   b) Because retailers of Dove in Canada and the U.K. would not tolerate any risk of customers buying for U.S. online sellers
   c) Because the survey data revealed that these three countries contained the majority of Dove's customers
   d) Because the survey data revealed that each country has different views on beauty as well as different standards regarding language, expression, and advertising
   e) Because women from these three countries were the only respondents willing to answer the survey questions

5. The Dove survey and campaign extend beyond Dove's current customers to include all women. Why would Dove, which is clearly positioned as a skin beauty product for young women, launch a campaign that extends beyond their target segment and positioning?
   a) Because Dove wants to expand its product line with products for every age group
   b) Because Dove did not think through this campaign clearly and spent money that it won't be able to recover through increased sales
   c) Because Dove wants to build its reputation and brand recognition with the general public as part of a strategy to build positive public relations
   d) Because Procter & Gamble was hoping to reuse the survey information to develop campaigns for all its skin beauty brands
   e) Because Dove wants to expand further internationally and therefore used the survey more as an exploratory tool to judge cultural definitions of beauty

---

Marketing environment The forces outside marketing that affect marketing management's ability to build and maintain successful relationships with target customers.

As noted in previous chapters, marketers need to be good at building relationships with customers, others in the company, and external partners. To do this effectively, marketers must understand the major environmental forces that surround all of these relationships. A company's **marketing environment** consists of the forces outside marketing that affect marketing management's ability to build and maintain successful relationships with target customers. The marketing environment offers both opportunities and threats. Successful companies know the vital importance of continually watching and adapting to the changing environment.

Today, both consumers and marketers wonder what the future will bring. The environment continues to change rapidly. More than any other group in the company, marketers must be the trend trackers and the opportunity seekers. Although every manager in an organization needs to observe the outside environment, marketers are fortunate enough to have tools designed specifically for that purpose: market research and marketing intelligence, the collecting, organizing, and "mining" of data about customers and their purchase behaviour. Marketers also typically spend more time in the customer and competitor environments. By carefully studying the environment, marketers can adapt their strategy, plans, and programs to meet new marketplace challenges and opportunities.

Microenvironment The forces close to the company that affect its ability to serve its customers—the company, suppliers, marketing intermediaries, customer markets, competitors, and publics.

Macroenvironment The larger societal forces that affect the organization's marketing activities—demographic, economic, natural, technological, political, and cultural forces.

The marketing environment is made up of a *microenvironment* and a *macroenvironment*. The **microenvironment** consists of the forces close to the company that affect its ability to serve its customers—the company, suppliers, marketing intermediaries, customer markets, competitors, and publics. The **macroenvironment** consists of the larger societal forces that can affect the organization's marketing activities—demographic, economic, natural, technological, political, and cultural forces. We look first at the company's microenvironment.

IN-CLASS NOTES

Marketing Environment Defined

The factors and forces outside marketing's direct control that affect marketing management's ability to develop and maintain successful relationships with customers.

THE MARKETING MICROENVIRONMENT

Marketing management's job is to build relationships with customers by creating customer value and satisfaction. However, marketing managers cannot do this alone. Figure 4.1 shows the major forces that affect the marketer's microenvironment. Marketing success will require building relationships with other company departments, suppliers, marketing intermediaries, customers, competitors, and various publics, which combine to make up the company's value delivery network.

Figure 4.1   Major Forces in the Marketing Microenvironment

The Company

In designing marketing plans, marketing management takes other company groups into account—groups such as top management, finance, research and development (R&D), purchasing, operations, and accounting. All these interrelated groups form the internal environment. Top management sets the company's mission, objectives, broad strategies, and policies. Marketing managers make decisions within the strategies and plans made by top management.

Marketing managers must also work closely with other company departments. Finance is concerned with finding and using funds to carry out the marketing plan. The R&D department focuses on designing safe and attractive products. Purchasing worries about getting supplies and materials, whereas operations is responsible for producing and distributing the desired quality and quantity of goods. Accounting has to measure revenues and costs to help marketing know how well it is achieving its objectives. Together, all of these departments have an impact on the marketing department's plans and actions. Under the marketing concept, all of these functions must "think customer." They should work in harmony to provide superior customer value and satisfaction.

Suppliers

Suppliers form an important link in the company's overall customer value delivery system. They provide the resources needed by the company to produce its goods and services. Supplier problems can seriously affect marketing. Marketing managers must watch supply availability—supply shortages or delays, labour strikes, and other events can cost sales in the short run and damage customer satisfaction in the long run. For example, as a result of a labour dispute at the Vancouver Port Authority, in 2005 millions of dollars' worth of wine shipped to Canada through Vancouver were in danger of spoiling in the heat before it could be delivered to retailers across the country. Marketing managers also monitor the price trends of their key inputs. Rising supply costs may force price increases that can harm the company's sales volume.

Most marketers today treat their suppliers as partners in creating and delivering customer value. Wal-Mart goes to great lengths to work with its suppliers. For example, it helps them to test new products in its stores. And its Supplier Development Department publishes a Supplier Proposal Guide and maintains a supplier website, both of which help suppliers to navigate the complex Wal-Mart buying process. It knows that good partnership relationship management results in success for Wal-Mart, suppliers, and, ultimately, its customers.

Marketing Intermediaries

Marketing intermediaries Firms that help the company to promote, sell, and distribute its goods to its customers.

Marketing intermediaries help the company to promote, sell, and distribute its goods to its customers. They include *retailers, wholesalers, distributors, brokers, marketing services agencies,* and *financial intermediaries. Retailers* buy merchandise from manufacturers, wholesalers, and distributors and resell them, usually in stores, to consumers. Loblaws, Shoppers Drug Mart, and The Bay are all retailers, but so are car dealerships and gas stations. *Wholesalers* buy merchandise from various manufacturers, organize it, and sell it to retailers.

Distributors physically stock and move goods from their points of origin to their destinations, usually from the manufacturer to the wholesaler or directly to the retailer. *Brokers* are another type of marketing intermediary. Brokers arrange for the movement of goods from their point of origin to the retailer or wholesaler, but never physically touch or take possession of the merchandise. The value they add to the distribution chain is the knowledge of, and relationship with, the producers of the goods. For example, a broker in the seafood business may travel to Asia and establish relationships with 20 or 30 shrimp farms; then, back home at the office, the broker deals with retailers such as Sobeys, Loblaws, and A&P. *Marketing services agencies* are the marketing research firms, advertising agencies, media firms, and marketing consulting firms that help the company target and promote its products to the right markets. When the company decides to use one of these agencies, it must choose carefully because these firms vary in creativity, quality, service, and price. *Financial intermediaries* include banks, credit companies, insurance companies, and other businesses that help finance transactions or insure against the risks associated with the buying and selling of goods. Most firms and customers depend on financial intermediaries to finance their transactions.

Like suppliers, marketing intermediaries form an important component of the company's value delivery system. In its quest to create satisfying customer relationships, the company must do more than just optimize its own performance. It must partner effectively with marketing intermediaries to optimize the performance of the entire system.

Customers

There are three broad types of customers that an organization may serve. Some organizations may serve more than one type of customer, but every organization, whether it is IBM, The Bay, the Canadian Cancer Society, your local veterinarian, or a junior hockey team, is *itself* a customer to other businesses. *Consumers* are individuals who buy goods and services for their own use or "consumption"—hence the term consumer. Consumers typically buy items one at a time, do not negotiate prices, and buy from retailers. *Business buyers* fall into one or more subcategories: There are business buyers who purchase goods and services for use in their production process; for example, car manufacturers must buy thousands of parts with which to build their cars—and they buy them in very large quantities. Business buyers also include resellers such as retailers and wholesalers, who buy goods from manufacturers or producers to resell at a profit. And every business, no matter how large or small, must buy supplies such as pens and paper, computers, and telephone services. Finally, g*overnment buyers* purchase goods and services to produce public services or transfer the goods and services to others who need them.

Competitors

The marketing concept states that to be successful, a company must provide greater customer value and satisfaction than its competitors do. Thus, marketers must do more than simply adapt to the needs of their customers. They also must gain strategic advantage by positioning their offerings strongly against their competitors' offerings in the minds of those customers.

No single competitive marketing strategy is best for all companies. Each firm should consider its own size and industry position compared with those of its competitors. Large firms with dominant positions in an industry can use certain strategies that smaller firms cannot afford. But being large is not enough. There are winning strategies for large firms, but there are also losing ones. And small firms can develop strategies that give them better rates of return than large firms enjoy.

Publics

The company's marketing environment also includes various publics. A **public** is any group of people that has an actual or potential interest in or impact on an organization's ability to achieve its objectives. We can identify seven types of publics.

Public Any group that has an actual or potential interest in or impact on an organization's ability to achieve its objectives.

- *Financial publics* influence the company's ability to obtain funds. Banks, investment houses, and stockholders are the major financial publics.
- *Media publics* carry news, features, and editorial opinion. They include newspapers, magazines, and radio and television stations.
- *Government publics.* Management must take government developments into account. Marketers must often consult the company's lawyers on issues of product safety, truth in advertising, and other matters.
- *Citizen-action publics.* A company's marketing decisions may be questioned by consumer organizations, environmental groups, minority groups, and others. Its public relations department can help it stay in touch with consumer and citizen groups.

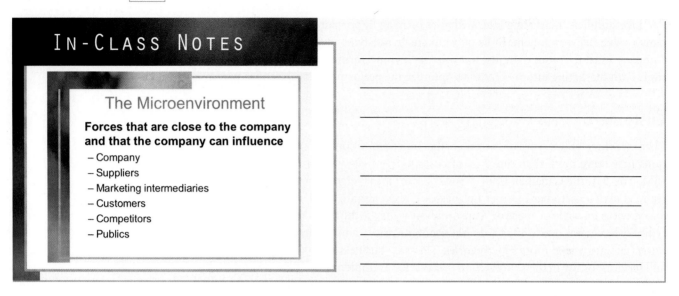

☐ *Local publics* include neighbourhood residents and community organizations. Large companies usually appoint a community relations officer to deal with the community, attend meetings, answer questions, and contribute to worthwhile causes.

☐ *General public.* A company needs to be concerned about the general public's attitude toward its products and activities. For example, Martha Stewart's highly publicized legal troubles, which culminated in her 2004 prison sentence, resulted in the general public forming an opinion about her and, by extension, her company, Martha Stewart Omnimedia—regardless of whether those members of the general public were Martha Stewart customers.

☐ *Internal publics* include workers, managers, volunteers, and the board of directors. Large companies use newsletters and other means to inform and motivate their internal publics. When employees feel good about their company, this positive attitude spills over to external publics.

A company can prepare marketing plans for its publics as well as for its target markets. Public relations is the area of marketing that is responsible for communicating messages about the organization to its publics. We'll look more closely at public relations in Chapter 12, Intergrated Marketing Communications.

THE MARKETING MACROENVIRONMENT

Every organization, along with the elements of its microenvironment just described, operates in a larger macroenvironment of forces that can shape opportunities or pose threats to the company. Figure 4.2 shows the six major forces in the marketing macroenvironment. In the remaining sections of this chapter, we examine these forces and show how they affect marketing plans.

Demographic Environment

Demography The study of human populations in terms of size, density, location, age, gender, race, occupation, and other statistics.

Demography is the study of human populations in terms of size, density, location, age, gender, race, occupation, and other statistics. The demographic environment is of major interest to marketers because it involves people, and people make up markets.

Statistics Canada data indicate that Canada's population increased only 0.9 percent between 2003 and 2004, reaching 31 946 316 in 2004. Since 2001, Canada's population has increased only 3 percent. This trend is expected to continue, with the total popula-

Figure 4.2   Major Forces in the Marketing Macroenvironment

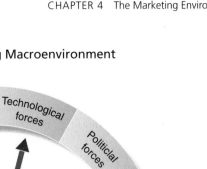

tion in 2011 estimated to be 33 361 700. There are a number of reasons for the slow growth in population. One such factor is the total fertility rate (TFR), which fell to the lowest rate ever recorded in Canada of 1.55 children per woman in 1997. This low rate, combined with a decrease in immigration levels and longer life expectancies, could accelerate the aging of the Canadian population.[2]

Although Canada's population growth rate remains low, the world's population is growing at an explosive rate and will total 7.9 billion by the year 2025.[3] This population explosion has been of major concern to governments and various groups around the world, since the earth's finite resources can support a limited number of people, particularly at the living standards to which many countries aspire (see Marketing at Work 4.1).

People who study demographics assume that people do certain things and purchase certain things at certain ages. For example, people in their thirties tend to have begun their families and thus are the major purchasers of baby products. Although demographic information can be useful when it comes to predicting macro trends and purchases within a product category, marketers should use the information with some caution. According to veteran Canadian pollster Allan Gregg, demographics "can be wildly simplistic."[4] Complex factors—everything from the marketing itself to an individual's values and attitudes—influence why a person buys a particular brand within a product category. Moreover, despite the best demographic predictions, people don't always follow predictable patterns. Given an aging North American population, many predicted that people would follow a healthier lifestyle and diet. But a recent report suggests that, "when it comes to food, Canadians are tired of worrying about what's good for them."[5] Unlike with many Europeans, vegetarianism isn't a lifestyle choice for many Canadians; in fact, only 4 percent of Canadians follow this type of diet.

The world's large and highly diverse population presents both opportunities and challenges. Therefore, marketers must keep close track of demographic trends and developments in their markets, both at home and abroad—changing age and family structures, geographic population shifts, educational characteristics, and population diversity. Statistics Canada offers a wealth of information for marketers interested in demographic trends. Here, we discuss the most important demographic trends in Canada.

Changing Age Structure of the Canadian Population Canada's population is getting *older*. The median age of the Canadian population—the point at which half of the population is younger and half is older—is now 38. Just 30 years ago, the median age was 25.[6]

During the **baby boom** that followed World War II and lasted until the early 1960s, the annual birth rate reached an all-time high. The baby boom created a huge "bulge" in age distribution—the nine million baby boomers account for almost one-third of

baby boom The major increase in the annual birth rate following World War II and lasting until the early 1960s. The baby boomers, now moving into middle age, are a prime target for marketers.

Marketing at Work 4.1

If the World Were a Village . . .

If we reduced the world to a village of 1000 people representative of the world's population, this would be our reality:

- ☐ Our village would have 520 females and 480 males including 330 children and 60 people over age 65, 10 college graduates, and 335 illiterate adults.
- ☐ We'd have 52 North Americans, 55 Russians, 84 Latin Americans, 95 Europeans, 124 Africans, and 584 Asians.
- ☐ Communication would be difficult: 165 of us would speak Mandarin, 85 English, 83 Hindi, 64 Spanish, 58 Russian, and 37 Arabic. The other half of us would speak one of more than 5000 other languages.
- ☐ Among us we'd have 329 Christians, 178 Muslims, 32 Hindus, 60 Buddhists, 3 Jews, 167 nonreligious, 45 atheists, and 86 others.
- ☐ About one-third of our people would have access to clean, safe drinking water. About half of our children would be immunized against infections.
- ☐ The woodlands in our village would be decreasing rapidly and wasteland would be growing. Forty percent of the village's cropland, nourished by 83 percent of our fertilizer, would produce 72 percent of the food to feed its 270 well-fed owners. The remaining 60 percent of the land and 17 percent of the fertilizer would produce 28 percent of the food to feed the other 730 people. Five hundred people in the village would suffer from malnutrition.

- ☐ Only 200 of the 1000 people would control 75 percent of our village's wealth. Another 200 would receive only 2 percent of the wealth. Seventy people would own cars. One would have a computer, and that computer probably would not be connected to the Internet.

Source: www.questconnect.org/global_citizen.htm, accessed August 2003.

The world population is growing at an explosive rate, presenting both opportunities and challenges for marketers. Think for a few minutes about the world and your place in it.

Canada's population and as the baby-boom generation ages, the nation's average age increases. Because of its sheer size, many major demographic and socioeconomic changes in Canada and the United States are tied to the baby-boom generation.

The baby boom was followed by a "birth dearth," and by the mid-1970s the birth rate had fallen sharply. This decrease was caused by smaller family sizes, the result of the desire to improve personal living standards, the increasing number of women working outside the home, and improved birth control. Although family sizes are expected to remain smaller, the birth rate has climbed again as the baby boom generation moves through the childbearing years and creates a second but smaller "baby boomlet." Following this boomlet, however, the birth rate will again decline as we move further into the 21st century.[7]

Figure 4.3 shows the changing age distribution of the Canadian population through 2041. The differing growth rates for various age groups will strongly affect marketers' targeting strategies. For example, the upper end of the "tween" market, the 9- to 14-year-old offspring of the baby boom generation, is 2.5 million strong. They are grabbing marketers' attention not only because of the size of this market, but also because of its spending power. New products are being developed just for them—from shampoos and snack products to portable music products and downloadable ring tones for their cell phones. They're wired and media savvy, and marketers are rushing to build brand loyalty among them or to create new brands they might regard as "cool." (See Marketing at Work 4.2.)

Figure 4.3   Age Projection for Canada, Provinces and Territories, 1993–2041

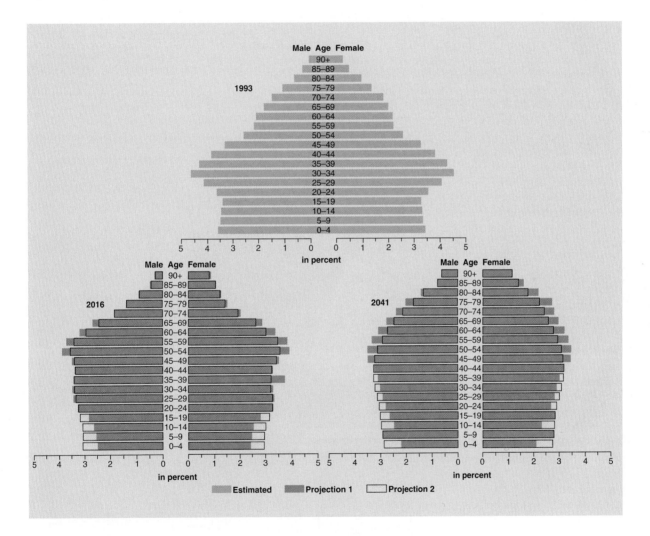

Source: Statistics Canada, Catalogue 91520 occasional, December 1994.

At the other end of the spectrum, almost 13 percent of Canadians were over age 65 in 2004, with the percentage projected to increase to 25 percent by 2031. As this group grows, so will the demand for retirement communities, quieter forms of recreation, single-portion food packaging, life care and health care services, and leisure travel.[8]

Changing Canadian Households When the term *household* is used, a stereotype of the typical family living in the suburbs with its two children comes to mind. However, this stereotype is far from accurate. The 2001 Census data from Statistics

Marketing at Work   4.2

The Teen Market: Youth Will Be Served

Gone are the days when kids saved up their pennies for candy and ice cream. Today's teens are big spenders. According to Canada's *Marketing* magazine, the average disposable income of a Canadian teenage girl is $131 a week. Teens make 54 mall visits a year and they intend to buy something about 50 percent of the time. With so much cash to spend, teens represent a lucrative market for companies willing to cater to their often fickle, trend-driven tastes.

To tap into this vast market of potential customers, companies are targeting teens with new or modified products. Some of these products are naturals for the teen market, such as action movies, acne creams, teen magazines, and cell phones. Since teens are heavy users of text messaging and wireless phones, advertisers are itching to forge agreements with wireless phone companies like Bell Mobility, Telus Mobility, and Rogers AT&T Wireless. Roman Bodnarchuk, founder of N5R, a Toronto-based consulting firm that specializes in loyalty marketing, explains why teens and young adults have been attracted to this technology. "BlackBerries are cool, but very expensive. And wireless laptops are not that portable. And besides, email is too slow for these kids; they want instant response. Text messaging is portable, it's silent—making communication possible during science class—and cheap." He also notes that marketers have to be teen savvy if they are going to be successful. Teens have come up with a language to fit the space limitations of the tiny phone screens. For example, POS means "parents over shoulder"; TOY is "thinking of you."

Software Company Wildseed has spent years conducting research to develop cell phones and intelligent faceplates for teens. For the last two years, the company has regularly summoned teenagers to focus groups, paying them $20 to lounge around, eat pizza, play Xbox video games, and give their thumbs-up or thumbs-down on various proposals. What teens want from a cell phone ranges from the concrete (music, messaging, and games) to the abstract (style, personality, and individuality). As a result, Wildseed-inspired phones will have "Smart Skins™"—replaceable intelligent faceplates with computer chips that allow teens to individualize the phone's functions and appearance to match their personalities.

Sources: Susan Henrich, "R u redi 4 Text Marketing?" *National Post,* March 17, 2003, www.nationalpost.com; Frank Washington, "Aim Young; No, Younger," *Advertising Age,* April 9, 2001; Nancy Keates, "Family Travel: Catering to Kids," *Wall Street Journal,* May 3, 2002, p. W-1; Jennifer Lee, "Youth Will Be Served, Wirelessly," *New York Times,* May 30, 2002, p. G1; and Brian Steinberg, "Pop-In Pasta Aims to Lure Teenagers to Drop the Chips," *Wall Street Journal,* April 8, 2002, p. A.21.

Marketing to teens: Based on focus group research, Wildseed developed cell phones with "smart skins"—replaceable faceplates with computer chips that let teens individualize the phone's functions and appearance to match their personalities.

Canada shows that common-law and lone-parent families together make up almost 30 percent of all families in Canada, compared with 26 percent in 1996.

The 2001 Census was the first to provide data on same-sex partnerships. A total of 34 000 couples identified themselves as same-sex common-law couples; they constituted only 0.5 percent of the total. Female same-sex partnerships were more likely to have children, with 15 percent of female same-sex couples living with children versus only 3 percent for male same-sex partnerships.

The total number of families (with or without children) in Canada increased to 8 194 000 in 2000, an increase of 9.1 percent over 1991. An increase in smaller families contributed to the rise. From 1981 to 2001 the average Canadian household reduced in size from 3.3 persons to 3.0.[9] And the latest data now show that the size of the average Canadian household has decreased to the point where there are as many households of one as there are of four.

The employment rate of women with children has grown particularly sharply in the past two decades, especially for those with preschool-aged children. One result is the growth of child-care services.

Responsibility for household tasks and the care of children is also changing. Approximately 60 percent of women aged 15 and older had jobs in 2001 compared with only 42 percent in 1976. Women in the Canadian labour force continue to grow in importance. Growth in female employment increased 8.7 percent since 1997, while male employment increased only 5.9 percent.[10]

Marriage continues to appear to be a fragile bond. Divorces continue to increase, with the number of divorced Canadians 13.5 percent higher in 2004 than in 2001.

Population and Growth Shifts The total population of Canada increased by 925 000 between 2001 and 2004, a total growth rate of only 3 percent. As Table 4.1 shows, however, growth rates across all provinces are not uniform: The populations of Newfoundland and Saskatchewan decreased from 2001 to 2004, while the populations of other provinces either stabilized or grew.[11]

Canadians are a mobile people. For more than a century, Canadians have been moving from rural to urban areas. The urban areas have a faster pace of living, higher incomes, and greater variety of goods and services than can be found in the small towns and rural areas that dot Canada. But Canada's cities are changing as well. Canadian cities are often surrounded by large suburban areas. Statistics Canada calls these combinations of urban and suburban populations "census metropolitan areas" (CMAs). Over one-third of Canada's population lives in Canada's three major CMAs (Toronto, Montreal, and Vancouver) and approximately 50 percent lives in the top 25 CMAs. Information about CMAs is useful for marketers trying to decide which geographical segments represent the most lucrative markets for their products and which areas are most critical in terms of buying media time. Marketers also track the relative growth of these markets to see which areas are expanding and which ones are contracting.

The shift in where people live has also caused a shift in where they work. For example, the migration toward metropolitan and suburban areas has resulted in a rapid increase in the number of people who "telecommute"—work at home or in a remote office and conduct their business by phone, fax, modem, or the Internet. This trend, in turn, has created a booming SOHO (small office/home office) market. Fifteen percent of Canadian households report that they have a home office. In addition to commuters, it

Table 4.1 Canada's Population Trends		
	2001 (thousands)	**2004 (thousands)**
Canada	**31021.3**	**31946.3**
Newfoundland and Labrador	522.0	517.0
Prince Edward Island	136.7	137.9
Nova Scotia	932.4	937.0
New Brunswick	749.9	751.4
Quebec	7397.0	7542.8
Ontario	11897.6	12392.7
Manitoba	1151.3	1170.3
Saskatchewan	1000.1	995.4
Alberta	3056.7	3210.9
British Columbia	4078.4	4196.4
Yukon	30.1	31.2
Northwest Territories	40.8	42.8
Nunavut	28.1	29.6

Sources: Adapted from Statistics Canada, "Population, Provinces and Territories," www.statcan.ca/english/Pgdb/ demo02.htm, accessed May 14, 2003; "Demographic Statistics," *The Daily*, September 24, 2004, accessed November 6, 2004.

estimated that there were 618 000 home-based businesses in Canada. Typically, home-based business operators are male (60.3 percent) and between the ages of 25 and 54 (76.4 percent). Many (31 percent) are highly educated. The top five industries for home-based businesses are professional, scientific, and technical services (17.8 percent); agriculture (12.1 percent); trade (10.2 percent); health care and social assistance (9.2 percent); and construction (8.3 percent).[12]

Increasing Diversity Countries vary in their ethnic and racial composition. At one extreme are homogeneous countries like Japan, where almost everyone is of Japanese descent. At the other are such countries as Canada and the United States whose populations are "salad bowls" of mixed races. Anyone who has walked the streets of Vancouver, Montreal, or Toronto will immediately understand that visible minorities in Canada are a large group. The United Nations reported that Toronto is the world's most multicultural city, and the Canadian Advertising Foundation recently predicted that the combined purchasing power of ethnic markets will soon exceed $300 billion. Many ethnic markets are growing in size. For example, the Italian and German markets in Canada each have populations of more than 400 000. In total, there are almost 4 million people living in Canada who report that they are members of visible minorities. Over 1 million people with Chinese background now live in Canada, along with another 900 000 people with South Asian origins. There are 662 000 black Canadians, almost 200 000 of Arabic descent, and 100 000 with Korean ancestors.[13]

Marketers must avoid negative stereotypes when it comes to serving ethnic markets. Seventeen percent of immigrants hold university degrees, compared with only 11 percent of people born in Canada. Immigrants are also more likely to hold managerial or professional jobs and have more stable family lives than people born in Canada.

Targeting ethnic markets involves far more than mere tokenism, many ethnic marketing specialists warn. Merely placing a person from a visible minority in an advertisement is not sufficient evidence that one is an ethnic marketer. Communicating in the consumer's native language is often mandatory, but marketers must also face the challenge of not alienating sophisticated second-generation individuals. The TD Bank recently demonstrated the power of providing information in potential customers' native language. The bank launched a Chinese Green Info Line to target potential Chinese investors. More than 300 callers per month take advantage of the service, which has generated considerable investments.

Diversity goes beyond ethnic heritage. For example, many major companies have recently begun to target gay and lesbian consumers explicitly. A Simmons Research study of readers of the National Gay Newspaper Guild's 12 publications found that, compared with the average American, respondents are 12 times more likely to be in professional jobs, almost twice as likely to own a vacation home, 8 times more likely to own a notebook computer, and twice as likely to own individual stocks. They are twice as likely as the general population to have a household income between $60 000 and $250 000. More than two-thirds have graduated from college, and 20 percent hold a master's degree. In addition, gays and lesbians tend to be early adopters, with word-of-mouth clout in their communities, making them a very attractive market segment. Accordingly, the Canadian Tourism Commission has launched a $300 000 campaign to try to attract gay tourists from the United States. Ontario is also reaching out to American homosexuals, with a link to "Gay & Lesbian Travel" on the Ontario Travel website.

Diversity can also include people with disabilities. Almost 18 percent of Canadians have some form of disability. People with mobility challenges are an ideal target market for companies such as Grocery Gateway, which offers online grocery shopping and home delivery. They also represent a growing market for travel, sports, and other leisure-oriented goods and services. Consider the following example:

> Volkswagen targets people with disabilities who want to travel. For example, it recently launched a special marketing campaign for its EuroVan. The campaign touted the EuroVan's extra-wide doors, high ceilings, and overall roominess as features that accommodate most wheelchair lifts and make driving more fun for those traditionally ignored by mainstream automakers. To make the EuroVan even more accessible, Volkswagen offers its Mobility Access Program. Drivers with disabilities who purchase or lease any VW can take advantage of $1,500 in purchase

Anyone who has walked the streets of Vancouver, Montreal, Calgary, or Toronto will immediately understand that visible minorities in Canada are a large group. Many firms, such as Air Canada, are recognizing racial diversity in their advertising.

Volkswagen targets people with disabilities who want to travel. It offers a Mobility Access Program and has even modified its catchy "Drivers Wanted" tag line to appeal to motorists with disabilities: "All Drivers Wanted."

We build cars for people who love to drive. Some of them happen to use

wheelchairs. For these drivers, and for families who transport someone

in a wheelchair, we present the Volkswagen Mobility Access Program.

This is our way of lending a hand to anyone who needs to make a new

Volkswagen° more accessible. If you need to add hand controls, we'll

refund up to $500! If you need to add a lift, we'll refund up to $1000!

After all, when we say "Drivers wanted," we mean every one of them.

Linking the Concepts

For a moment, think about how deep an impact these demographic factors have on all of us and, as a result, on marketers' strategies.

- Apply these demographic developments to your own life. Think of some specific examples of how the changing demographic factors affect you and your buying behaviour.
- Identify a specific company that has done a good job of reacting to the shifting demographic environment—generational segments, the changing Canadian family, and increased diversity. Compare this company with one that's done a poor job.

assistance for modifications such as hand controls and wheelchair lifts. Volkswagen even modified its catchy tag line "Drivers Wanted" to appeal to motorists with disabilities, coining the new slogan "All Drivers Wanted." The VW Web site sums up, "We build cars for people who love to drive. Some just happen to use wheelchairs."[14]

As the Canadian population grows more diverse, successful marketers will continue to diversify their marketing programs to take advantage of opportunities in fast-growing segments. Says one expert, "Diversity will be more than a buzzword—diversity will be the key to economic survival."[15]

Economic Environment

Marketers require that the customers in the market segments they serve have buying power sufficient to purchase the goods and services that the company is marketing. Changing economic conditions can have wide-reaching effects on the marketing of products in certain categories. For example, pharmaceutical products such as insulin and syringes for diabetics are necessities for consumers in that market segment, and whether the economy is "good" or "bad," it doesn't affect the diabetic consumer's need for those products, and therefore will have little effect on the sales of the company marketing them. On the other hand, luxury products are not necessities, and in times of economic downturn the sales of such products will suffer. Marketers must be aware of, and monitor, the economic environment and, furthermore, must be aware of how "necessary" their products are to their target customers.

The **economic environment** consists of factors that affect consumer purchasing power and spending patterns. Nations vary greatly in their levels and distribution of income. Some countries have *subsistence economies*—they consume most of their own agricultural and industrial output. These countries offer few market opportunities. At the other extreme are *industrial economies*, which constitute rich markets for many different kinds of goods. Marketers must pay close attention to major trends and consumer spending patterns both across and within their world markets. Following are some of the major economic trends in Canada.

Economic environment Factors that affect consumer purchasing power and spending patterns.

Changes in Income During the 1980s, the economy entered its longest peacetime boom. Consumers fell into a consumption frenzy, fuelled by income growth, federal tax reductions, rapid increases in housing values, and a boom in borrowing. They bought and bought, seemingly without caution, amassing record levels of debt. "It was fashionable to describe yourself as 'born to shop. '. . . In the 1980s, many . . . became literally addicted to personal consumption."[16]

Free spending and high expectations were dashed by the economic slowdowns in the early 1990s. Consumers sobered up, pulled back, and adjusted to leaner times. *Value marketing* became the watchword for many marketers.

The late 1990s and early 2000s saw a turnaround in the economy. Despite a downturn in the U.S. economy and growing uncertainty arising from 9/11 and the war in Iraq, Canada's economy continued to grow. For example, in the first quarter of 2003, the unemployment rate continued to drop and real personal disposable income increased by more than 2 percent to reach an average per capita that was 13 percent higher than the low reached in 1996. Consumer expenditures continued to grow by more than 4 percent, but savings rates fell. Despite continued spending, consumer confidence has declined slightly.[17] Thus, marketers may need to look for ways to offer today's more financially cautious buyers greater value—just the right combination of quality and good service at a fair price.

Marketers should pay attention to *income distribution* as well as average income. Income distribution in Canada is still very skewed. At the top are *upper-class* consumers, whose spending patterns are not affected by current economic events and who are a major market for luxury goods. There is also a comfortable *middle class,* which is somewhat careful about its spending but can still afford the good life some of the time. The *working class* must stick close to the basics of food, clothing, and shelter, and must try hard to save. Finally, the *underclass* (persons on welfare and some retirees) must count their pennies even when making the most basic purchases.

The growing income divide has sent marketers in opposite directions. On one hand, they have responded with a ceaseless array of pricey, upscale products aimed at satisfying the appetites of the wealthier classes. On the other hand, deep discount stores like dollar stores are proliferating across Canada. Some manufacturers even produce different versions of their products to serve these polarized market segments. Levi's jeans, for example, can be purchased in upscale department stores like The Bay as well as in downscale department stores like Zellers, though the price will be much lower at Zellers. The jeans at Zellers, though they may be the same style and have the same label, are manufactured with a lower-quality fabric and thread, and therefore can be produced less expensively and sold at a lower price.

Changing Consumer Spending Patterns Although food, housing, and transportation continue to use up a large percentage of household income, consumer spending patterns have changed considerably in the past 50 years. In 1947, spending on the basics (food, clothing, housing, fuel) accounted for 69 cents out of every dollar. What expenditures account for the money no longer spent on the basics? Canadians are spending more on two categories—what Statistics Canada refers to as personal goods and services; and recreation, entertainment, education, and cultural services.[18] However, consumers at different income levels have different spending patterns. Some of these differences were noted over a century ago by Ernst Engel, who studied how people shifted their spending as their income rose. He found that as family income rises, the percentage spent on food declines, the percentage spent on housing remains constant (except for utilities such as gas, electricity, and public services, which decrease), and both the percentage spent on other categories and that devoted to savings increase. **Engel's laws** have been generally supported by later studies.

Engel's laws Differences noted over a century ago by Ernst Engel in how people shift their spending across food, housing, transportation, health care, and other goods and services categories as family income rises.

Changes in major economic variables such as income, cost of living, interest rates, and savings and borrowing patterns have a large impact on the marketplace. Companies watch these variables by using economic forecasting. Businesses do not have to be wiped out by an economic downturn or caught short in a boom. With adequate warning, they can take advantage of changes in the economic environment.

Natural Environment

Natural environment Natural resources that are needed as inputs by marketers or that are affected by marketing activities.

The **natural environment** involves the natural resources that are needed as inputs by marketers or that are affected by marketing activities. Environmental concerns have grown steadily during the past three decades. In many cities around the world, air and water pollution have reached dangerous levels. World concern continues to mount about the possibilities of global warming, and many environmentalists fear that we soon will be buried in our own trash.

Marketers should be aware of several trends in the natural environment. The first involves growing *shortages of raw materials*. Air and water may seem to be infinite resources, but some groups see long-run dangers. Air pollution chokes many of the world's large cities, and water shortages are already a big problem in some parts of the world, including California. Renewable resources, such as forests and food, also have to be used wisely. The limited quantities of nonrenewable resources, such as oil, coal, and various minerals, pose a serious problem. Firms producing goods that require these scarce resources can find their marketing plans subject to the whims of nature. After Hurricane Katrina devastated the U.S. Gulf Coast in 2005, for example, gas prices spiked and sales of SUVs fell dramatically.

Environmental responsibility: Loblaws has made a substantial commitment to the so-called "green movement."

A second environmental trend is *increased pollution.* Industry will almost always damage the quality of the natural environment. Consider the disposal of chemical and nuclear wastes; the dangerous mercury levels in the ocean; the quantity of chemical pollutants in the soil and food supply; and the littering of the environment with non-biodegradable bottles, plastics, and other packaging materials.

A third trend is *increased government intervention* in natural resource management. The governments of different countries vary in their concern and efforts to promote a clean environment. Some, like the German government, vigorously pursue environmental quality. But when then Prime Minister Jean Chrétien announced at the September 2002 Earth Summit that Parliament would vote on ratifying the Kyoto agreement by the end of the year, cries of protest were heard from Alberta politicians and the oil patch. Other governments, especially many poorer nations, do little about pollution, largely because they lack the needed funds or political will.

Concern for the natural environment has spawned the "green movement." Today, enlightened companies go beyond what government regulations dictate. They are developing environmentally sustainable strategies and practices in an effort to create a world economy that the planet can support indefinitely. They are responding to consumer demands with ecologically safer products, recyclable or biodegradable packaging, better pollution controls, and more energy-efficient operations. For example, Loblaws began its G.R.E.E.N. program in 1989, and today it is one of the most successful environmentally friendly product lines in the world. More than 100 new products have been launched since the program's inception, while manufacturing changes have helped make dozens of other products environmentally friendly. Increasingly, then, companies are recognizing the link between a healthy economy and a healthy ecology.[19]

Technological Environment

The **technological environment** consists of forces that create new technologies, which in turn create new product and market opportunities. Technology is perhaps the most dramatic force now shaping our destiny. It has enabled the creation of such wonders as antibiotics, organ transplants, notebook computers, and the Internet. It also has released such horrors as nuclear missiles, chemical weapons, and assault rifles. It has contributed to the invention of such mixed blessings as the automobile, television, and credit cards. Our attitude toward technology depends on whether we are more impressed with its wonders or its blunders. For example, what would you think about having tiny little transmitters implanted in all the goods you buy that would allow tracking these goods from their point of production though use and disposal? On the one hand, it would provide many advantages. On the other hand, it could be a bit scary. Either way, it probably won't be long before it happens, as discussed in Marketing at Work 4.3.

New technologies create new markets and new opportunities, and marketers must be aware of new technology developments in order to take advantage of them and not be driven out of business by them. Transistors hurt the vacuum-tube industry, xerography hurt the carbon-paper business, the automobile hurt the railroads, and compact disks hurt cassette tapes. When old industries fought or ignored new technologies, their businesses declined. Thus, marketers should watch the technological environment closely. Companies that do not keep up with technological change soon will find their products outdated. And they will miss new product and market opportunities.

Scientists today are researching a wide range of promising new products. In recent years, these research projects have focused on products ranging from practical solar energy, electric cars, and cancer cures to voice-controlled computers and genetically engineered food crops. Today's research is usually carried out by research teams rather than by lone inventors. Many companies are adding marketing people to R&D teams to

Technological environment
Forces that create new technologies, creating new product and market opportunities.

Marketing at Work   4.3

Tiny Transmitters in Every Product: Is This Great Technology, or What?

Envision a world in which every product contains a tiny transmitter, loaded with information. Imagine a time when we could track every item electronically—anywhere in the world, at any time. Producers could track the precise flow of goods up and down the supply chain, ensuring timely deliveries and lowering inventory and distribution costs. Retailers could track real-time merchandise movements in their stores, helping them manage inventories, keep shelves full, and automatically reorder goods.

Seem far-fetched? Not according to the Auto-ID Center. Founded in 1999, the Center formed a unique partnership among almost 100 global companies and five of the world's leading research universities. The Auto-ID Center's aim was "to change the world . . . to give companies something that, until now, they have only dreamed of: near-perfect supply chain visibility." This seems like a lofty mission. But it might soon become a reality with the backing of such marketing heavyweights as Wal-Mart, Home Depot, Target, Best Buy, Procter & Gamble, Coca-Cola, IBM, and Gillette.

The Auto-ID Center developed tiny, affordable radio-frequency identification (RFID) transmitters—or smart chips—that can be embedded in all the goods you buy. The transmitters can be packed with coded information and can be read and rewritten at any point in the supply chain. Auto-ID technology provides producers and retailers with amazing new ways to track inventories, trends, and sales. The smart chips make today's bar code systems seem badly outmoded. Whereas bar codes must be visible to be read, embedded RFID chips can be read in any location. Bar codes identify only a product's manufacturer. In contrast, the chips can identify each individual product item and can carry codes that, when paired with a database containing the details, reveal an almost endless supply of information. Thus, beyond identifying an item as a gallon of Dairyland 2% skim milk, an embedded smart chip can identify that *specific* gallon of milk—its manufacture date, expiration date, location in the supply chain, and a storehouse of other product-specific information.

RFID technology is already in use at companies like Wal-Mart and Gillette. Gillette uses embedded transmitters to track goods from the factory to grocery store shelves. They hope the technology will not only improve service to its retail customers but also reduce its inventories by 5 to 25 percent. Gillette has also installed readers on shelves in selected Wal-Mart and Tesco stores. It claims that retailers lose more than $30 billion a year in sales because shelves aren't fully stocked. The shelf readers track Gillette's razors as they come and go, and prompt store staff to restock when quantities dwindle. "We'll have a world where shelves are always full," says Gillette's vice president for global business management. The readers also alert staff when unusually large quantities of razors leave a shelf in a short time, helping to reduce theft.

Smaller retailers are also putting smart chips to work. Fashion retailer Prada recently installed the chips in its store in New York City. Based on scans of items in customers' hands, video screens show personalized product demonstrations and designer sketches. In dressing rooms, readers identify each item of clothing a customer tries on and offer additional size, colour, and design information through interactive touch screens.

With innovations like these, you'd think most consumers would welcome the tiny transmitters. But some consumers and many consumer advocates worry about invasion-of-privacy issues. If companies can link products to specific consumers and track consumer buying and usage, they fear, marketers would gain access to too much personal information. To counter these concerns, Auto-ID technology proponents point out that the transmitters have limited range, most under six and a half metres (20 feet). So reading chips inside consumers' homes or tracking them on the move would be nearly impossible. According to an Auto-ID consultant, the basic mission is not to spy on consumers. It's to serve them better. "It's not Orwellian. That is absolutely, positively not the vision of Auto-ID," she says. "The vision is for . . . brand manufacturers and retailers to be able to have right-time, right-promotion, real-time eye-to-eye [contact] with the consumer."

Sources: Jack Neff, "A Chip over Your Shoulder?" *Advertising Age,* April 22, 2002, p. 4; Kimberly Hill, "Prada Uses Smart Tags to Personalize Shopping," April 24, 2002, accessed online at www.crmdaily.com; "Business: The Best Thing Since the Bar-Code: The IT Revolution," *The Economist,* February 8, 2003, pp. 57–58; "Gillette, Michelin Begin RFID Pilots," *Frontline Solutions,* March 2003, p. 8; "RFID Benefits Apparent," *Chain Store Age,* March 2003, p. 63; Faith Keenan, "If Supermarket Shelves Could Talk," *Business Week,* March 31, 2003, pp. 66–67; information accessed online at www.autoidcenter.org, July 2003, and at www.autoidlabs.org, November 2003.

Technological environment: Technology is perhaps the most dramatic force shaping the marketing environment. Here, a herder makes a call on his cell phone.

try to obtain a stronger marketing orientation so that breakthroughs are not only technically feasible but also commercially viable.

As products and technology become more complex, the public needs to know that they are safe. Canada has a complex web of departments and regulations devoted to issues associated with product safety. For example, Agriculture Canada and the Canadian Food Inspection Agency monitor the safety of food products. The Department of Justice oversees the *Consumer Packaging and Labelling Act,* the *Food and Drug Act,* and the *Hazardous Products Act.* Health and Welfare Canada also has a food safety and product safety division. The Department of Transport governs vehicle recalls.

Political Environment

Marketing decisions are strongly affected by developments in the political environment. The **political environment** consists of laws, government agencies, and pressure groups that influence or limit various organizations and individuals in a given society.

Even the most liberal advocates of free-market economies agree that the system works best with at least some regulation. Well-conceived regulation can encourage competition and ensure fair markets for goods and services. Thus, governments develop *public policy* to guide commerce, by enacting laws and regulations that limit business for the good of society as a whole. Almost every marketing activity is subject to a wide range of laws and regulations.

The marketing of Cake Beauty products is one example. These products are made in Canada, and are therefore subject to certain laws and regulations here, but because they are also marketed in the United States, the company must consider American market regulations. For example, all of Cake Beauty's packaging must be bilingual in order to comply with Canadian regulations. Product volume must be expressed in metric units, such as Cake's It's a Slice Supremely Rich Bath and Shower Froth, which comes in a 250 ml bottle. But because the products must also appeal to Americans, the volume also appears on the package as 8.5 fl. oz.

Legislation affecting business around the world has increased steadily over the years. Canada has many laws covering such issues as competition, fair trade practices, environmental protection, product safety, truth in advertising, packaging and labelling, pricing,

Political environment Laws, government agencies, and pressure groups that influence and limit various organizations and individuals in a given society.

cake ®

and other important areas (see Table 4.2). The European commission has been active in establishing a new framework of laws covering competitive behaviour, product standards, product liability, and commercial transactions for the nations of the European Union.

Some countries have especially strong consumer protection legislation. For example, Norway bans several forms of sales promotion—trading stamps, contests, premiums—as being inappropriate or unfair ways of promoting products. Thailand requires food processors selling national brands to market low-price brands also, so that low-income consumers can find economy brands on the shelves. In India, food companies must obtain special approval to launch brands that duplicate those already existing on the market, such as additional soft drinks or new brands of rice.

Understanding the public policy implications of a particular marketing activity is not a simple matter. For example, in Canada, many laws are created at the federal, provincial, and municipal levels, and these regulations often overlap. Moreover, regulations are constantly changing—what was allowed last year may now be prohibited, and what was prohibited may now be allowed. The North American Free Trade Agreement (NAFTA) replaced the Free Trade Agreement in August 1992. It governs free trade among Canada, the United States, and Mexico. As trade among the three countries expands, the provisions of NAFTA will continue to be updated and amended. Marketers must work hard to keep up with changes in regulations and their interpretations.

Business legislation has been enacted for various reasons. The first is to *protect companies* from each other. Although business executives may praise competition, they sometimes try to neutralize it when it threatens them. So laws are passed to define and prevent unfair competition.

Table 4.2 Major Federal Legislation Affecting Marketing

The *Competition Act* is a major legislative act affecting the marketing activities of companies in Canada. Specific sections and the relevant areas are as follows:

☐ Section 34: Pricing—Forbids suppliers from charging different prices to competitors purchasing like quantities of goods (price discrimination). Forbids price-cutting that lessens competition (predatory pricing).

☐ Section 36: Pricing and Advertising—Forbids advertising prices that misrepresent the "usual" selling price (misleading price advertising).

☐ Section 38: Pricing—Forbids suppliers from requiring subsequent resellers to offer products at a stipulated price (resale price maintenance).

☐ Section 33: Mergers—Forbids mergers by which competition is, or is likely to be, lessened to the detriment of the interests of the public.

Other selected Acts that have an impact on marketing activities are as follows:

☐ *National Trade Mark and True Labelling Act*—Established the term Canada Standard, or CS, as a national trademark; requires certain commodities to be properly labelled or described in advertising for the purpose of indicating material content or quality.

☐ *Consumer Packaging and Labelling Act*—A statute that specifies the rules that must be followed by manufacturers and marketers in the packaging, labelling, sale, importation, and advertising of prepackaged products. The purpose of the Act is to help consumers make informed purchase decisions.

☐ *Motor Vehicle Safety Act*—Regulates the manufacture and importation of cars, trucks, buses, motorcycles, and other motorized vehicles as well as motor vehicle parts such as tires.

☐ *Food and Drug Act*—Prohibits the advertisement and sale of adulterated or misbranded foods, cosmetics, and drugs.

☐ *Personal Information Protection and Electronic Documents Act*—Establishes rules to govern the collection, use, and disclosure of personal information that recognize the right of privacy of individuals. The law recognizes the needs of organizations to collect, use, and disclose personal information for appropriate purposes.

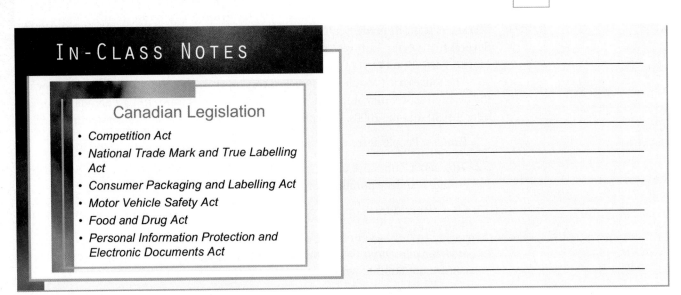

IN-CLASS NOTES

Canadian Legislation

- *Competition Act*
- *National Trade Mark and True Labelling Act*
- *Consumer Packaging and Labelling Act*
- *Motor Vehicle Safety Act*
- *Food and Drug Act*
- *Personal Information Protection and Electronic Documents Act*

The second purpose of government regulation is to *protect consumers* from unfair business practices. Some firms, if left alone, would make shoddy goods, lie in their advertising, and deceive consumers through their packaging and pricing. Various agencies have defined unfair business practices and enforce their regulation.

The third purpose of government regulation is to *protect the interests of society* against unrestrained business behaviour. Profitable business activity does not always create a better quality of life. Regulation arises to ensure that firms take responsibility for the social costs of their production or products.

Business executives must watch these developments of new laws and their enforcement when planning their products and marketing programs. Marketers need to know about the major laws protecting competition, consumers, and society at the municipal, provincial, federal, and international levels.

Cultural Environment

The **cultural environment** is composed of institutions and other forces that affect a society's basic values, perceptions, preferences, and behaviours. People grow up in a particular society that shapes their basic beliefs and values. They absorb a world view that defines their relationships with others. The following cultural characteristics can affect marketing decision making.

Cultural environment Institutions and other forces that affect society's basic values, perceptions, preferences, and behaviours.

Persistence of Cultural Values People in a given society hold many beliefs and values. Their core beliefs and values have a high degree of persistence. For example, most Canadians believe in working, getting married, giving to charity, and being honest. These beliefs shape more specific attitudes and behaviours found in everyday life. *Core* beliefs and values are passed on from parents to children and are reinforced by schools, churches, businesses, and government.

Secondary beliefs and values are more open to change. Believing in marriage is a core belief; believing that people should get married early in life is a secondary belief. Marketers have some chance of changing secondary values but little chance of changing core values. For example, family-planning marketers could argue more effectively that people should get married later than that they should not get married at all.

Shifts in Secondary Cultural Values Although core values are fairly persistent, cultural swings do take place. Consider the impact of popular music groups, movie personalities, and other celebrities on young people's hairstyles, clothing, and sexual norms.

Marketers want to predict cultural shifts in order to spot new opportunities or threats. Several firms offer "futures" forecasts in this area, such as the Yankelovich Monitor, Market Facts' BrainWaves Group, and the Trends Research Institute.

The Yankelovich Monitor has tracked consumer value trends for years. At the dawn of the twenty-first century, it looked back to capture lessons from the past decade that might offer insight into the 2000s. It identified the following eight major consumer themes:[20]

1. *Paradox:* People agree that "life is getting better and worse at the same time."

2. *Trust not:* Confidence in doctors, public schools, TV news, newspapers, federal government, and corporations drops sharply.

3. *Go it alone:* More people agree with the statement "I rely more on my own instincts than on experts."

4. *Smarts really count:* For example, fewer people agree with "It's risky to buy a brand you are not familiar with."

5. *No sacrifices:* For example, many people claim that looks are important but not at any price, that keeping house for show instead of comfort is over, and that giving up taste for nutrition is no longer acceptable.

6. *Stress hard to beat:* For example, more people claim that they are "concerned about getting enough rest."

7. *Reciprocity is the way to go:* More people agree that "Everybody should feel free to do his or her own thing."

8. *Me 2:* For example, people express the need to live in a world that is built by "me," not by you.

The major cultural values of a society are expressed in people's views of themselves and others, as well as in their views of organizations, society, nature, and the universe.

People's Views of Themselves. People vary in their emphasis on serving themselves versus serving others. Some people seek personal pleasure, wanting fun, change, and escape. Others seek self-realization through religion, recreation, or the avid pursuit of careers or other life goals. People use goods, brands, and services as a means of self-expression, and they buy products that match their views of themselves.

In the 1980s, personal ambition and materialism increased dramatically, with significant marketing implications. In a "me society," people buy their "dream cars" and take their "dream vacations." They tend to spend to the limit on self-indulgent goods and services. Today, in contrast, people are adopting more conservative behaviours and ambitions. In this new millennium, materialism, flashy spending, and self-indulgence have been replaced by more sensible spending, saving, family concerns, and helping others. The maturing baby boomers are limiting their spending to goods and services that improve their lives instead of boosting their images. This suggests a bright future for goods and services that serve basic needs and provide real value rather than those relying on glitz and hype.

People's Views of Others. Recently, observers have noted a shift from a "me society" to a "we society" in which more people want to be with and serve others. Notes one trend tracker, "People want to get out, especially those . . . people working out of their home and feeling a little cooped up [and] all those shut-ins who feel unfulfilled by the cyber-stuff that was supposed to make them feel like never leaving home." This trend suggests a greater demand for "social support" goods and services that improve direct communication between people, such as health clubs and family vacations.[21]

People's Views of Organizations. People vary in their attitudes toward corporations, government agencies, trade unions, universities, and other organizations. By and large, people are willing to work for major organizations and expect them, in turn, to carry out society's work. In recent years, there has been an overall decline in organizational loyalty. Waves of company downsizings have bred cynicism and distrust. Corporate scandals at Enron, WorldCom, and Nortel resulted in a further loss of confidence in big business. Many people today see work not as a source of satisfaction but as a required chore to earn money to enjoy their non-work hours. Canadians increasingly desire greater autonomy and personal freedom in the workplace. If they can't control their work, many are turning to self-employment as a means of achieving the autonomy desired.[22] This trend suggests that organizations need to find new ways to win consumer and employee confidence.

People's Views of Society. People vary in their attitudes toward their society; patriots defend it, reformers want to change it, malcontents want to leave it. People's orientation to their society influences their consumption patterns, levels of savings, and attitudes toward the marketplace. For example, more and more Canadians have a sense of national pride. Some companies, such as Zellers, responded with "made-in-Canada" themes and promotions. Others, such as Clearly Canadian, Molson Canadian, and Upper Canada Brewing Company, made national identity part of their branding strategy.

People's Views of Nature. People vary in their attitudes toward the natural world. Some feel ruled by it, others feel in harmony with it, and still others seek to master it. A long-term trend has been people's growing mastery over nature through technology and the belief that nature is bountiful. More recently, however, people have recognized that nature is finite and fragile, that it can be destroyed or spoiled by human activities.

Love of nature is leading to more camping, hiking, fishing, bird-watching, and other outdoor activities. Business has responded by offering more goods and services catering to these interests. Tour operators are offering more wilderness adventures, and retailers are offering more fitness gear and apparel. Marketing communicators are using appealing natural backgrounds in advertising their products. And food producers have found growing markets for natural and organic foods. Natural and organic food products are now a $3 billion industry, growing at a rate of 20 percent annually. Niche marketers, such as Whole Foods Markets and Capers, have sprung up to serve this market, and traditional food chains such as Safeway and Loblaws have added separate natural and organic food sections to their stores.[23]

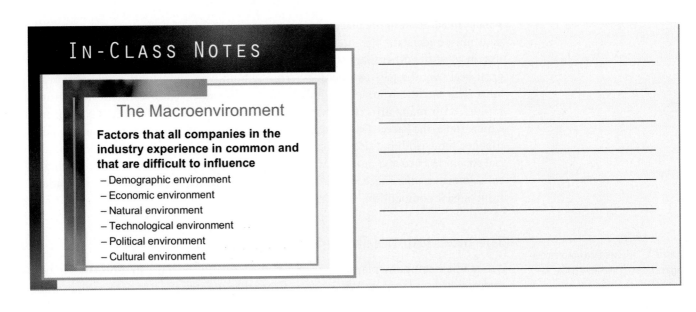

IN-CLASS NOTES

The Macroenvironment

Factors that all companies in the industry experience in common and that are difficult to influence
- Demographic environment
- Economic environment
- Natural environment
- Technological environment
- Political environment
- Cultural environment

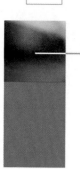

Linking the Concepts

You've now read about the forces in the microenvironment and the macroenvironment that affect marketers and the decisions they must make. How are all of these environments *linked* with each other and with company marketing strategy?

- How are major demographic forces linked with economic changes and with major cultural trends? How are the natural and technological environments linked? Think of an example of a company that has recognized one of these links and turned it into a marketing opportunity.
- Is the marketing environment uncontrollable—something that the company can only prepare for and react to? Or can companies be proactive in changing environmental factors? Think of a good example that makes your point, then read on.

People's Views of the Universe. People vary in their beliefs about the origin of the universe and their place in it. Although many Canadians have religious beliefs, attendance at religious services has been dropping off gradually over the years. The 2001 Census shows Canadians continuing to slide out the doors of the country's churches, temples, and synagogues. In 1946, 67 percent of adult Canadians regularly attended religious services, but by 2001, the figure had dropped to 20 percent. Yann Martel, Canadian author of the acclaimed *Life of Pi,* noted in an interview that Canadians and Americans are going in opposite directions with regard to religion. "America is a very religious, almost puritanical country. In Canada, secularism is triumphant, and to talk noncynically, nonironically about religion is strange," he says. Only 30 percent of Canadians report that religion is very important to them, compared with 59 percent of Americans. (The statistics would be even more skewed were it not for the growing number of devout Muslim, Sikh, and Hindu immigrants now living in Canada.) Therefore, Canadian marketers have to use caution when picking up lifestyle ads from the United States. Although showing people in religious settings may draw attention from American consumers, they may strike Canadians as inappropriate.[24]

THE GLOBAL MARKETING ENVIRONMENT

Finally, in addition to the macro and micro environments that affect marketing, a company must understand the international marketing environment if it intends to do business in countries other than its home. The global marketing environment has changed a great deal over the past two decades, creating both new opportunities and new problems. The world economy has globalized. World trade and investment have grown rapidly, with many attractive markets opening up in Western and Eastern Europe, China, India, the Pacific Rim, Russia, and elsewhere. Global brands have grown in automobiles, food, clothing, electronics, and many other categories. The international financial system has become more complex and fragile, and Canadian companies wishing to enter foreign markets face increasing trade barriers erected to protect domestic markets from outside competition.

The International Trade System

A Canadian company planning to enter a foreign market must first understand the international *trade system.* When selling to another country, the firm faces various trade restrictions. The most common is the **tariff**, which is a tax levied by a foreign govern-

Tariff A tax levied by a government against certain imported goods to either raise revenue or protect domestic firms.

ment against certain imported goods. The tariff may be designed either to raise revenue or to protect domestic firms. The exporter also may face a **quota**, which sets limits on the amount of goods the importing country will accept in certain product categories. The purpose of the quota is to conserve on foreign exchange and to protect local industry and employment. An **embargo**, or boycott, bans an import.

Firms may face **exchange controls**, which limit the amount of foreign exchange and the exchange rate against other currencies. They also may encounter **nontariff trade barriers**, such as biases against bids or restrictive product standards that go against North American product features. The Japanese have found a clever way to keep foreign manufacturers out of their domestic market: They plead "uniqueness."

> Japanese skin is different, the government argues, so foreign cosmetics companies must test their products in Japan before selling there. The Japanese say their stomachs are small and have room for only the *mikan*, the local tangerine, so imports of U.S. oranges are limited. Now the Japanese have come up with what may be the flakiest argument yet: Their snow is different, so ski equipment should be too.[25]

At the same time, certain forces *help* trade between nations. Examples are the General Agreement on Tariffs and Trade and various regional free trade agreements.

The World Trade Organization The World Trade Organization (WTO) is a global organization that deals with the rules of trade between nations. It exists to help producers, manufacturers, and marketers conduct their business in foreign markets. The WTO has 148 member countries. Canada has been a member since 1995, the year the WTO was established. Detailed information about each member country, including population, trade to GDP ratio, rankings in world trade, and trade policies, can be found on the WTO's website.

The WTO grew out of GATT, the General Agreement on Tariffs and Trade, which was first signed in 1947 to provide an international forum for encouraging free trade between member countries, and to provide a common mechanism for resolving trade disputes.

Economic Communities Some countries have formed *free trade zones* or **economic communities**—groups of nations organized to work toward common goals in the regulation of international trade. One such free trade zone is the European Union (EU), whose purpose is to create a single European market by reducing barriers to the free flow of goods, services, finances, and labour among member countries and developing policies on trade with nonmember nations. As of 2005 there were 25 member countries in the EU.

The United States, Canada, and Mexico agreed in 1989 to phase out trade barriers between their countries. In January 1994, the North American Free Trade Agreement (NAFTA) established a free trade zone among the United States, Mexico, and Canada. How effective has the trade agreement been a decade after its birth? The answer will depend on whom you ask, since the agreement has been controversial from its inception.

In 2004, 10 years after its initiation, trilateral trade among the three countries has doubled to $US620 billion yearly. And Canada now enjoys an unprecedented $139 billion annual trade surplus with the U.S., our largest trade partner. Our exports to Mexico have tripled since the agreement's launch, and Canada is now Mexico's second-biggest export market while Mexico is our sixth. The Canadian government reports that since the agreement came into force the economy has grown by an average of 3.8 percent annually, generating 2.1 million jobs.

The Canadian Labour Congress, however, doesn't share the government's enthusiasm. It estimates that total employment in manufacturing is now 10 percent below the pre-NAFTA levels. Another critic, the Canadian Auto Workers union, claims that 7000 auto assembly jobs have shifted to Mexico from Canada. Despite these criticisms and some trade disputes, however, most agree that the agreement has had many positive outcomes.[26]

Quota A limit on the amount of goods that an importing country will accept in certain product categories to conserve on foreign exchange and to protect local industry and employment.

Embargo A ban on the import of certain goods.

Exchange controls Government limits on the amount of its foreign exchange with other countries and on its exchange rate against other currencies.

Nontariff trade barriers Nonmonetary barriers to foreign products, such as biases against a foreign company's bids or product standards that go against a foreign company's product features.

Economic community A group of nations organized to work toward common goals in the regulation of international trade.

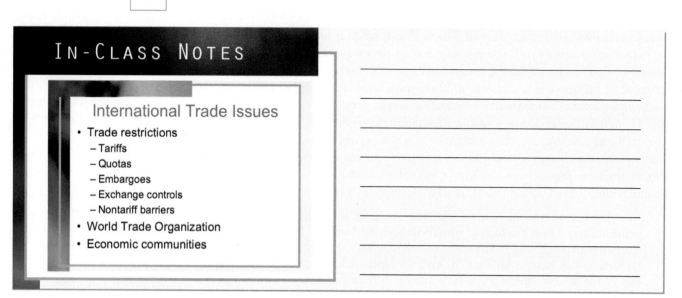

Canada is also a member of APEC—the Asia-Pacific Economic Cooperation. APEC was formed in 1989 and has 21 members, which together account for one-third of the world's population, 60 percent of the world's GDP, and 47 percent of world trade. And there are other free trade zones and economic communities. MERCOSUR, for example, is a free trade agreement between Bolivia, Chile, Colombia, Ecuador, Mexico, Peru, and Venezuela.

Whether conducting business in North America or venturing further afield, Canadian businesspeople must realize that each nation has unique features that must be understood. A nation's readiness for different goods and services and its attractiveness as a market to foreign firms depend on its economic, politico-legal, ethical, and cultural environments—in other words, on its macro and microenvironments.

RESPONDING TO THE MARKETING ENVIRONMENT

Someone once observed, "There are three kinds of companies: those who make things happen, those who watch things happen, and those who wonder what's happened."[27] Many companies view the marketing environment as an uncontrollable element to

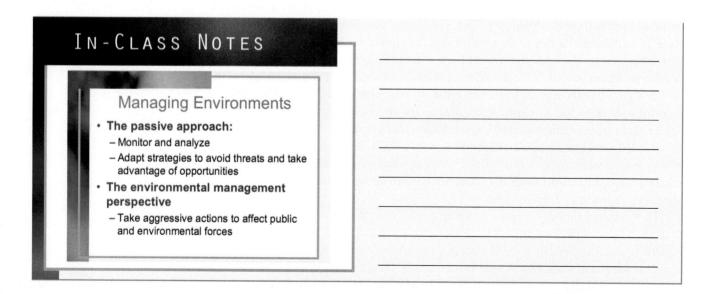

which they must adapt. They passively accept the marketing environment and do not try to change it. They analyze the environmental forces and design strategies that will help the company avoid the threats and take advantage of the opportunities the environment provides.

Other companies take an **environmental management perspective**.[28] Rather than simply watching and reacting, these firms take aggressive actions to affect the various publics and forces in their marketing environment. Such companies hire lobbyists to influence legislation affecting their industries and stage media events to gain favourable press coverage. They run advertorials (ads expressing editorial points of view) to shape public opinion. They press lawsuits and file complaints with regulators to keep competitors in line, and they form contractual agreements to better control their distribution channels.

Marketing management cannot always control environmental forces. In many cases, it must settle for simply watching and reacting to the environment. For example, a company would have little success trying to influence geographic population shifts, the economic environment, or major cultural values. But whenever possible, smart marketing managers will take a *proactive* rather than *reactive* approach to the marketing environment.

Environmental management perspective A management perspective in which the firm takes aggressive actions to affect the publics and forces in its marketing environment rather than simply watching and reacting to them.

LOOKING BACK

In this chapter, you learned about the environments of marketing and how companies analyze these environments to discover marketplace opportunities and create effective marketing strategies. Companies must constantly watch and adapt to the marketing environment in order to seek opportunities and ward off threats. The marketing environment comprises all the actors and forces influencing the company's ability to transact business effectively with its target market.

REVIEWING THE CONCEPTS

1. Describe the environmental forces that affect the company's ability to serve its customers.

The company's *microenvironment* consists of forces close to the company that combine to form the company's value delivery network or that affect its ability to serve its customers. It includes the company's other departments and management levels, as they influence marketing decision making. *Marketing-channel firms*— suppliers and marketing intermediaries, including retailers, wholesalers, distributors, brokers, marketing services agencies, and financial intermediaries—cooperate to create customer value. Three types of customer *markets* include consumer, business, and government markets. *Competitors* vie with the company in an effort to serve customers better. Finally, various *publics* have an actual or potential interest in or impact on the company's ability to meet its objectives.

The *macroenvironment* consists of larger societal forces that affect the entire microenvironment. The six forces making up the company's macroenvironment include demographic, economic, natural, technological, political, and cultural forces. These forces shape opportunities and pose threats to the company.

2. Explain how changes in the demographic and economic environments affect marketing decisions.

Demography is the study of the characteristics of human populations. Today's *demographic environment* shows a changing age structure, shifting family profiles, geographic population shifts, a better-educated and more white-collar population, and increasing diversity. The *economic environment* consists of factors that affect buying power and patterns. The economic environment is characterized by more consumer concern for value and shifting consumer spending patterns. Today's squeezed consumers are seeking greater value—just the right combination of good quality and service at a fair price. The distribution of income also is shifting. The rich have grown richer, the middle class has shrunk, and the poor have remained poor, leading to a two-tiered market. Many companies now tailor their marketing offers to two different markets—the affluent and the less affluent.

3. Identify the major trends in the firm's natural and technological environments.

The *natural environment* shows three major trends: shortages of certain raw materials, higher pollution levels, and more government intervention in natural resource management. Environmental concerns create marketing opportunities for alert companies. The marketer should watch for trends in the *technological environment*. Marketers must be aware of new technology developments in order to take advantage of them and not be driven out of business by them. Companies that fail to keep up with technological change will miss out on new product and marketing opportunities.

4. Explain the key changes in the political and cultural environments.

The *political environment* consists of laws, agencies, and groups that influence or limit marketing actions.

Increasing legislation regulating business affects the ways that products can be marketed. The *cultural environment* is made up of institutions and forces that affect a society's values, perceptions, preferences, and behaviours. The environment shows long-term trends toward a "we society," a lessening trust of institutions, increasing patriotism, and greater appreciation for nature.

5. Discuss how companies can react to the marketing environment.

Companies can passively accept the marketing environment as an uncontrollable element to which they must adapt, avoiding threats and taking advantage of opportunities as they arise. Or they can take an *environmental management perspective*, proactively working to change the environment rather than simply reacting to it. Whenever possible, companies should try to be proactive rather than reactive.

KEY TERMS

baby boom   *133*
cultural environment   *147*
demography   *132*
embargo   *151*
economic environment   *141*
economic community   *151*
Engel's laws   *142*

environmental management
    perspective   *153*
exchange controls   *151*
macroenvironment   *128*
marketing environment   *128*
marketing intermediaries   *130*
microenvironment   *128*

natural environment   *142*
nontariff trade barriers   *151*
political environment   *145*
public   *131*
quota   *151*
tariff   *150*
technological environment   *143*

STUDY GUIDE

After completing this self-test, check your answers against the Answer Key at the back of the book.

MULTIPLE CHOICE

1. In the last several years stock markets have witnessed some significant increases in the value of companies that provide funeral services and extended nursing care, respectively. This increase in value is partly a result of
   a. A demographic shift as baby boomers begin to enter their senior years
   b. An increase in the discretionary income of the adult children of baby boomers
   c. An increase in cancer rates over the past 10 years
   d. Government cutbacks in funding programs for seniors
   e. Stock market speculation in which day traders have been buying and selling these stocks on margin

2. Most cities in Canada have seen major increases in the construction of luxury suburban houses even though population growth is considerably slower. This increase in luxury house starts is in line with
   a. Our cultural ideal that a luxury house is something to aspire to
   b. Engel's law that as income increases, spending on housing as a percentage of total income remains the same
   c. The poor quality of most rental housing
   d. A massive and continuing influx of wealthy immigrants into Canada
   e. Hard-sell promotions of these new luxury subdivisions

3. Many companies enjoy rapid growth due to the alignment of positive conditions in a number of macroenvironments. Likewise, negative conditions can cause these companies to fail. The rise and fall of Napster, for example, can be directly attributed to what environments, respectively?
   a. Demographic and economic
   b. Public and cultural
   c. Technological and political
   d. Technological and legal
   e. Cultural and economic

4. Consumerism is an active movement that affects most consumer-product companies. In order to keep tabs on future trends in consumerism, marketers must closely monitor
   a. Citizen action publics and political forces
   b. Public relations
   c. Competitors and customers
   d. Consumer legislations
   e. The general public and cultural forces

5. In 2004 tobacco companies began a collective campaign encouraging smokers to express themselves and assert their right to smoke. In this way the tobacco companies were attempting to change anti-smoking sentiment in the general public as well as public policy, an example of
   a. Cultural trend management
   b. Demarketing techniques
   c. Aggressive environmental management
   d. Anti-societal marketing
   e. Consumer lobbying

6. Many marketers have argued that competitors should not be considered as part of the microenvironment but rather of the macroenvironment. This argument is largely based on the idea that
   a. Companies have relatively little control over their competitors
   b. Competition is really an economic issue
   c. Competitors are not part of the value delivery network
   d. Competitors often share the same customers sometimes so they should not be in the same environment
   e. Competition rules are often legislated and are therefore part of the political force

7. While packaged-goods companies must be constantly aware of all environmental factors, they put far more time, skill, and money into researching and understanding _____ than most other forces and factors.
   a. Legislation and political issues

b. Customers
c. Employee morale and satisfaction
d. Competitors
e. Suppliers

8. When Volkswagen first entered the North American market after World War II, the little car had a difficult time winning acceptability. The makers of Volkswagen faced what negative macroenvironmental force when introducing the Beetle?
   a. Economic slowdown combined with a high price tag
   b. An abundance of gasoline
   c. Strong opposition from North American car makers
   d. Cultural negativism about Germany
   e. Laws preventing the import of European automobiles

9. Magna International is a leading maker of car parts, reselling their products to the world's major car makers. In order to develop meaningful and actionable strategic plans, Magna International must be sure to include _____ in the strategic planning process from the very beginning.
   a. Shareholders
   b. Employee groups
   c. International trade officers
   d. Raw material suppliers
   e. Their customers

10. Several years ago Black and Decker attempted to sell their tools directly to consumers via their own website. Their major retail partners balked at this attempt and gave the manufacturer an ultimatum: Stop or lose us as retailers for your products. Black and Decker made what error?
    a. They had not researched their marketing intermediaries sufficiently to understand their own role in the distribution process
    b. They had not sufficiently researched and understood the power of their own branded website to undermine the sales of their distribution partners
    c. They had not understood the value that these retailers provided as partners relative to the value to be gained from some selling direct
    d. They had not understood the value that each member of the distribution process brings to the end consumer
    e. All of the above

TRUE/FALSE

T   F   1. All microenvironments affect all industries in the same way and to the same degree.

T F 2. Publics belong in the microenvironment because companies can directly manage their relationships with them.

T F 3. Demographic data is often more powerful, revealing, and usable when combined with economic data.

T F 4. Understanding the marketing environment is critical only for those companies that practise the marketing and societal marketing philosophies.

T F 5. As companies look to expand into international markets, they generally do not need to reassess their microenvironments.

Concept Check

1. A company's _____ consists of the forces outside marketing that affect marketing management's ability to develop and maintain successful relationships with target customers.

2. The _____ consists of the forces close to the company that affect its ability to serve its customers—the company, marketing channel firms, customer markets, competitors, and publics.

3. _____ (such as retailers, wholesalers, distributors, brokers, marketing services agencies, and financial intermediaries) help the company to promote, sell, and distribute its goods to final buyers.

4. The company's marketing environment includes various publics. If a company's marketing decisions were questioned by residents of a neighbourhood or a community organization, then the company would need to develop strategies to respond to these _____ publics.

5. One of _____ laws is that as family income rises, the percentage spent on food declines.

6. Marketers should be aware of several trends in the natural environment. Chief among these are the
_____, _____, and _____.

7. Business legislation has been enacted for a number of reasons. Chief among these are to protect _____ _____, to protect _____ _____, and to protect _____.

8. The major cultural values of a society are expressed in people's views of themselves and others. Recent studies suggest that consumers are interested in getting out more, in family concerns, and in helping others. This is evidence that our society is moving more toward a "_____-society."

9. Companies that take an _____ _____ take aggressive actions to affect the publics and forces in their marketing environment rather than simply watching and reacting to them.

Student Materials

Visit our website at www.pearsoned.ca/armstrong for online quizzes, Internet exercises, and more!

Notes

_____

_____

_____

_____

_____

_____

_____

_____

_____

_____

_____

_____

_____

_____

DISCUSSING THE ISSUES

1. The microenvironment includes a variety of publics that have an interest in the company or can have an impact on its operations. Discuss how the goals of some of these publics may be opposed to one another. How would opposing goals among a company's relevant publics have an impact on its strategy?

2. The changing structure of the Canadian family was identified as an important demographic force shaping the opportunities and threats to the company. Explain how a grocery store could change its positioning to appeal to each of the following segments: married couples with children, single parents, and adults living alone.

3. Value marketing—the right combination of quality and good service at a fair price—has increased in popularity. Pick an industry and identify two competing companies, one that is good at value marketing and one that is poor at value marketing. For the company that is poor at value marketing, discuss why consumers purchase from that company. What need is it fulfilling better than the firm that is good at value marketing?

4. An environmental management perspective advocates taking a proactive, rather than reactive, approach to dealing with the marketing environment. Identify a company you feel characterizes this approach. What specific actions do they take to proactively influence their environment?

MARKETING APPLICATIONS

Customer loyalty for online travel companies is low, with the average consumer checking three travel websites for the best prices on airlines, hotels, and rental cars. Today, approximately 15 percent of all travel is purchased online, with airline ticket sales accounting for about half of that amount. Three online travel companies, Expedia (36 percent of the market), Travelocity (24 percent), and Orbitz (13 percent) account for the majority of online travel sales in the U.S. While consumers have been focused on where to get the best deals, many online travel companies have been investing in new technology that will allow them to differentiate themselves with regard to the services they provide rather than the prices they offer.

THINKING LIKE A MARKETING MANAGER

1. What macroenvironmental forces do you feel will have the largest positive and largest negative impact on online travel companies? Why?

2. Discuss how online travel companies should address these negative impacts.

3. What do you think is the long-run future of the online travel industry?

4. What do you feel are the most significant environmental issues facing the online travel industry in the next five years?

VIDEO CASE

Go to Pearson Canada's Video Central site (www.pearsoned.ca/highered/videocentral) to view the video and accompanying case for this chapter.

CASE 4   AN APPLE A DAY KEEPS THE MP3S IN PLAY

MP3 players are a new product category based on a new technology. The foundation of today's portable music players, however, dates back 50 years to the invention of the transistor by Bell Labs. It also dates back to Akio Morita, the founder of the Sony Corporation, and Masaru Ibuka, the engineering and product-design force behind Sony's inventions. One of Sony's first products was a small pocket-sized transistor radio launched in 1957, creating a new market for "portable music" in the bargain.

Fast-forward to 1979, when Sony's Morita observed his children and their friends playing music from morning until night. He noticed people listening to music in their cars and carrying large stereos to the beach and the park. Despite resistance from Sony's engineering department, who were opposed to the concept of a tape player without a recording function (it would be added later), Morita would not be denied. He insisted on a product that sounded like a high-quality car stereo yet was portable and allowed the user to listen while doing something else—thus the product and the name Walkman. This was followed by development and commercialization of even more advanced technology, with products such as portable CD players and cell phones with music capability.

Fast-forward again to 1987 and an unlikely start to the current state of the portable music market. A German company called Moving Picture Experts Group (mpeg), working in concert with a subdivision of the International Standards Organization (ISO), developed a technology that compressed video signals. They called it mpeg-1. This was followed by mpeg-2, which became the standard for DVD audio and video compression. Finally, mpeg-layer III, an audio-only compression technology, was commercialized in 1998 and is better known today as mp3: the beginning of truly digital audio.

The first company to incorporate the new technology was RIO, a wholly owned subsidiary of D&M Holdings—a company better known for its home audio and video expertise with brands such as Denon, Marantz, and McIntosh Laboratory. Then, in 1999, Reigncom Ltd. introduced the iRiver Brand. And Singapore-based Creative Labs—the originator of the Sound Blaster, a multi-media personal computer application—launched its MP3 player that same year.

In December 2001 Apple introduced the iPod, weighing in at 6.5 ounces and capable of holding about 1000 songs. And as the iPod's technology continued to develop, the market saw the addition of the iPod Mini, the iPod Photo, and the iPod U2 Special Edition.

While the technology behind the digital music industry, and specifically Apple's iPod, is impressive, it's backed up by an integrated business model. That is, one of the advantages of the iPod relates to another service offered by Apple. The iTunes Music Store, launched in April 2003, has revolutionized the way people legally buy music online. This service was originally available only for those with Mac computers. Then, in October 2003, Apple launched the iTunes for Windows digital jukebox software. Over a million songs were purchased and downloaded by Windows iTunes users in the first three and a half days of the launch. Today, the iTunes Music Store offers both Windows and Mac users the same 99 cents-per-song pricing.

There are now more than 200 iPod accessories, ranging from $25 pink plastic cases to $375 portable stereos from Bose. Even BMW has jumped on the iPod bandwagon. In 2004 it sold 12 000 adapters that allow the iPod to be integrated with the car's sound system—and dealerships now have long waiting lists for the accessory.

As further evidence of consumer interest in the portable/digital music market, sales of hard-drive-based MP3 players like the iPod were projected to reach 10.4 million units in 2004—a five-fold sales increase over 2003. Within this market, Apple's various iPod entries have captured an 82 percent share. The brand, in short order, has achieved virtual cult status. A survey among teenagers done by Piper Jaffray & Co., a large U.S.-based financial advisor, determined that clothes, money, a car, and an iPod were on the "most wanted list" for the Christmas season in 2004. The fact that the iPod was ranked fourth was surprising to the researchers, since it wasn't even suggested on the questionnaires administered to the survey respondents—the response was written in!

Advancing technology is fuelling more competition in an already crowded market. There are literally dozens of MP3 brands and hundreds of product variations. In 2004, Dell and Virgin launched their own versions of the MP3 player. And Puretracks, a Canadian music download provider, began operations even before iTunes was available in Canada.

"Can Apple Keep Leading the Band?" This *Business Week* headline asks the tough question. Despite Apple's current technological lead, history is not on Apple's side. Many a technological leader has seen its market share dominance fall. Apple is a classic failed example in the PC market. Others, like Palm in Personal Digital Assistants and Nintendo in games consoles, are also glaring examples of market dominance waning. Within the MP3 player category, as in most consumer-driven markets, price may eventually be a product differentiator for certain consumer segments. The iPod and other brands such as Dell's and Sony's entries are hard-drive-based, allowing for high storage capacity but higher prices. And because they have moving parts (like a computer's hard drive), they are subject to skipping. Flash-based players, on the other hand, rely on flash memory, and although their capacity is constrained, they have no moving parts, are less costly, and can be used in more active environments such as jogging.

What will portable music playing devices look like five years from now? How will new developments and new technologies affect the market? Will Apple continue to lead, or will it be overtaken by some upstart company not yet in existence? No one knows, but smart marketers are monitoring their environment for signs.

Questions

1. Though the technological environment had the greatest influence on the development of products such as the iPod, it's never just one element of the macro environment that influences the creation of a new product. Which other elements of the macroenvironment contributed to the development of MP3 players? Explain.

2. Imagine you are a musician, singer, or member of a band. How does the technological environment affect your ability, as a marketer of music, to market your product? Have inventions such as MP3 players and downloadable music helped or harmed musicians?

3. The marketing environment affects the development of new products, but in turn, the development of new products can affect the marketing environment. How has the marketing environment changed as a result of the popularity of MP3 players? Consider the political, cultural, and competitive environments, and describe how each has been affected.

Sources: www.mp3.com/tech/players_inex.php, accessed November/December 2004; http://digitalmusic. weblogsinc.com/entry/123000077022009, accessed December 2004; www.businessweek.com/ print/magazine/content/04_45/b3907064_mz011.htm, accessed December 2004; www.emarketer.com/ Article.aspx?1003096, accessed December 2004; www.marketingmag.ca/shared/print.jsp?content= 20040809_62899_62899, accessed December 2004; www.bloomberg.com/apps/news?pid=71000001& refer=us&sid=a58iozj_2jXM, accessed December 2004; www.macnn.com/news/27021, accessed December 2004; www.apple.com/ipod, accessed December 2004; www.sony.com, accessed December 2004; www.dell.com, accessed December 2004; www.ecommercetimes.com/story/36850.html, accessed December 2004.

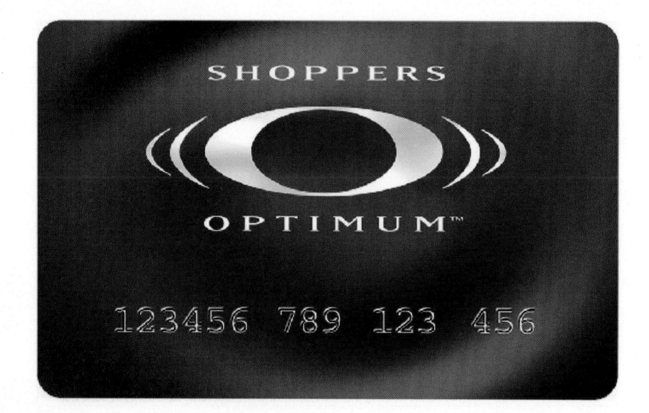

After reading this chapter, you should be able to

1. explain the importance of information to the company

2. define the marketing information system and discuss its parts

3. outline the steps in the marketing research process

4. explain how companies analyze and distribute marketing information

5. discuss the special issues some marketing researchers face, including public policy and ethics issues

Managing Marketing Information

5

Looking Ahead   In the last chapter, you learned about the complex and changing marketing environment. In this chapter, we'll look at how companies develop and manage information about important elements of the environment—about their customers, competitors, products, and marketing programs. We'll examine marketing information systems designed to give managers the right information, in the right form, at the right time to help them make better marketing decisions. We'll also take a close look at the marketing research process and at some special marketing research considerations. To succeed in today's marketplace, companies must know how to manage mountains of marketing information effectively.

What's the difference between data and information? This is a question that a good marketing manager must always be considering. For example, what data should be collected about our customers, and how can we transform that data into information so that we can better serve our customers? There's lots of data that might be gathered: not only customers' name, address, phone number, and email address, but also such factors as their colour, style, and size preferences and their frequency of purchases. But what information about their customers do marketers really need, and to what use do they put it?

Customer data by itself is of little use to marketers. It is only when data about a large number of customers can be collected, statistically analyzed, and organized that marketers can turn that data into information, or marketing intelligence, and begin to *understand* something about their customer market.

It's a delicate balance, however. Most consumers are unwilling to give marketers any information about themselves, unless there's something in it for them. Wise marketers understand this, and never ask for data unless they can demonstrate the value that having it will provide you, the customer.

For example, many retailers today might ask you to provide them with some basic information, such as name, address, and phone number, so that they can build a customer profile and personalize their service to you. Black's photo stores ask for your phone number when you drop a film off to be developed. The next time you go into the store, simply by giving your phone number the sales clerk can call up your preferences—matte or glossy finish, border or no border, CD or paper, and whether you usually choose a double set of prints—along with your name, and quickly and easily print your receipt. When your favourite retailers are able to know and remember you this way, they are able to improve their services, making things more convenient for you. Other retailers, such as The Source and Winners, ask for your phone number so that they can understand which neighbourhoods their customers are coming from. This type of marketing data also allows the retailers to better serve their customer market—and you, as a consumer.

Loyalty programs such as Air Canada's Aeroplan and the Shoppers Optimum Program™ are another way for marketers to collect data about their customers, and for customers to benefit from the perks of being a loyal customer. Loyalty programs are popular with Canadians—a recent survey found that 76 percent of us belong to at least one. And if you have a Shoppers Optimum Card™, you already know its benefits. Special offers are mailed to card holders, and each purchase you make at a Shoppers earns you points that can be redeemed at a later date for merchandise. But have you ever wondered what the stores get out of it?

There's no fee to join the Shoppers Optimum Program. Members get a Shoppers Optimum Card, which they hand to the cashier, who swipes the card's magnetic strip through a reader. When you sign up for the card, Shoppers Drug Mart® collects your name, birth date, address, and the ages of your children, if you chose to fill out that information. Every time you use the card you collect points, and Shoppers collects data about the purchases you made that day and adds that information to your customer record. Once the company knows a little about you, they can begin marketing more effectively to you.

For example, if you are a 19-year-old unmarried female university student, with no children, you might appreciate getting special offers for cosmetics and hair care products but would have no use for coupons for diapers and other baby products. A 35-year-old woman with two small children, on the other hand, might appreciate getting both. When Gillette launches its latest men's shaving products, Shoppers might promote them to male Shoppers Optimum Card holders between the ages of 18 and 50, but not to its female members. Likewise, products such as arthritis medication and denture care products would be promoted only to adults over 50.

The Shoppers Optimum Program provides the marketers at Shoppers Drug Mart with raw data that they can turn into marketing information using data mining techniques. For example, there's the "raw" data given by the consumer to Shoppers in exchange for becoming a member: name, address, etc. From this, Shoppers knows that a consumer is a 19-year-old female. Then there's the data collected at the point of purchase every time the consumer shops at Shoppers. Every time that 19-year-old shops, her purchases are recorded. Into the database goes the data about what hair care products she chooses, and how frequently she buys them. Let's say that she's bought shampoo and conditioner specifically designed for blonde hair. Maybe she's also purchased a home highlighting kit for blondes. An analysis of this customer data, using data mining techniques, would identify this customer as a blonde, and flag her as a good candidate to send special offers and new product information about new hair products for blondes.

In Canada the collection of personal data is strictly legislated, and so in their privacy statement Shoppers declares that they do not rent, sell, or provide to others the personal information of Shoppers Optimum members. Not only is that politically correct, but it's smart marketing as well. Shoppers is in the business of providing consumers with a retail assortment of personal care items. They strive to do this better than their competitors. The more they can understand about their customers, and their customers' behaviours and preferences, the better they can provide those services—and, in theory, the happier you will be as a customer when shopping there. The last thing in the world that a smart marketer wants to do is let its competitors know the secrets of its success. After all, if Shoppers doesn't carefully guard its data—if it were to be foolish enough to

TEST YOURSELF

Answers to these questions can be found on our website at www.pearsoned.ca/armstrong.

1. Air Canada and Shoppers Drug Mart provide discounts in exchange for customer data. Why are these companies willing to take less money from customers in exchange for this data?
   a) Because they can prevent their competitors from obtaining the information as well
   b) Because information about both the collective and individual wants of customers allows these companies to build better and closer long-term customer relationships
   c) Because they can sell the information to related but non-competitive retailers and consumer-products companies
   d) Because customers expect loyalty programs and go elsewhere if stores don't offer them
   e) Because they want to identify and stop servicing customers who don't spend enough

2. Shoppers Drug Mart and other store chains often share the aggregated customer-buying data generated by loyalty programs with the manufacturers of the consumer goods that they sell. Why do these chains do this?
   a) Because makers of consumer goods want to know how well they sell in relation to competitors
   b) Because store chains want more price discounts from the manufacturers they buy from, and sharing data is one way to get these discounts
   c) Because makers of consumer goods want to know which stores sell more of their products, and then reward those stores
   d) Because makers of consumer goods pay for this information and it adds to the revenues of the store chain
   e) Because makers of consumer goods can create winning new products and add more value to existing products if they can better understand the customer's wants and buying habits

3. Shoppers Drug Mart may suffer from a common problem: too much data. Why in our information-driven age is too much data a problem for most companies?
   a) Because the cost of data storage is very high and companies spend a lot of money managing these databases
   b) Because the right software tools are not yet available to sort through data and turn it into information
   c) Because data in itself is meaningless until it's analyzed and turned into actionable information
   d) Because data is vulnerable to electronic theft, and the more data a company has the more risk it runs of competitors accessing it
   e) Because most data is redundant, and so is mostly useless

4. Companies like Black's and The Source now ask for your postal code when you make a purchase. As well, when you access Zellers' online weekly flyers, you are asked to enter your postal code. Why do companies do this?
   a) Because research has indicated that buying preferences, family types, and income levels are different in different neighbourhoods, and so these companies create special offerings for each area
   b) Because they want to understand how far they would need to ship product to you and how much it would cost
   c) Because they can sell that information to other non-competitive stores in the area
   d) Because Canada Post wants to know which postal code areas are most affluent
   e) Because the federal government collects this information as part of their Census data gathering

5. Companies like Shoppers Drug Mart not only gather information on their customers but also do considerable ongoing research on their suppliers, channel partners, competitors, and other groups. Why do they need extensive information on these as well?
   a) Because customer data has value only in relation to other kinds of data
   b) Because this kind of data is gathered just in the course of doing business: These companies do not actively seek to gather this information
   c) Because companies are legally required to maintain financial and other types of information on partners and competitors
   d) Because the value of each company's market offerings is relative to that of the competition and depends on the total effect of the company and its outside partners
   e) Because all competitors and most partners are disloyal by nature

Information overload: "In this oh-so-overwhelming Information Age, it's all too easy to be buried, burdened, and burned out by data overload."

sell it—the first organization that would line up to buy it would be PharmaPlus.[1]

In order to produce superior value and satisfaction for customers, companies need information at almost every turn. Good products and marketing programs begin with a thorough understanding of customer needs and wants. Companies also need an abundance of information on their competitors, marketing channels partners, and other actors and forces in the marketplace.

Increasingly, marketers are viewing information not only as an input for making better decisions but as an important strategic asset and marketing tool. A company's information may prove to be its chief competitive advantage. Competitors can copy each other's equipment, products, and procedures, but they cannot duplicate the company's information and intellectual capital. Several companies have recently recognized this by appointing vice presidents of knowledge, learning, or intellectual capital.[2]

In today's more rapidly changing environments, managers need up-to-date information to make timely, high-quality decisions. In turn, with the recent explosion of information technologies, companies can now generate information in great quantities. In fact, today's managers often receive too much information. One study found that with all the compa-

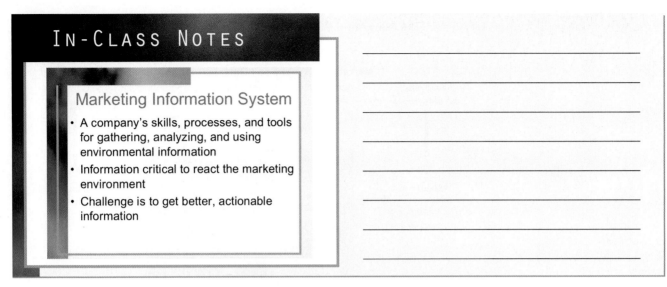

Marketing Information System

- A company's skills, processes, and tools for gathering, analyzing, and using environmental information
- Information critical to react the marketing environment
- Challenge is to get better, actionable information

nies offering data, and with all the information now available through supermarket scanners, a packaged-goods brand manager is bombarded with one million to one *billion* new numbers each week. Another study found that, on average, North American office workers spend 60 percent of their time processing information; a typical manager reads about a million words a week. Thus, running out of information is not a problem, but seeing through the "data smog" is. "In this oh so overwhelming Information Age," comments one observer, "it's all too easy to be buried, burdened, and burned out by data overload."[3]

Despite this data glut, marketers frequently complain that they lack enough information of the *right* kind. A recent survey of managers found that although half the respondents said they couldn't cope with the volume of information coming at them, two-thirds wanted even more. The researcher concluded that, "Despite the volume, they're still not getting what they want."[4] Thus, most marketing managers don't need *more* information, they need *better* information. Companies must design effective marketing information systems that give managers the right information, in the right form, and at the right time to help them make better marketing decisions.

A **marketing information system** consists of people, equipment, and procedures to gather, sort, analyze, evaluate, and distribute needed, timely, and accurate information to marketing decision makers. Figure 5.1 shows that the information system begins and ends with information users—marketing managers, internal and external partners, and others who need marketing information. First, it interacts with these information users to assess *information needs*. Next, it *develops needed information* from internal company databases, marketing intelligence activities, and marketing research. Then it helps users to analyze information to put it in the right form for making marketing decisions and managing customer relationships. Finally, the information system *distributes* the marketing information and helps managers *use* it in their decision making.

Marketing information system
The people, equipment, and procedures to gather, sort, analyze, evaluate, and distribute needed, timely, and accurate information to marketing decision makers.

ASSESSING MARKETING INFORMATION NEEDS

The marketing information system primarily serves the company's marketing and other managers. However, it may also provide information to external partners, such as suppliers or marketing services agencies. For example, Wal-Mart might give Procter & Gamble and other key suppliers access to information on customer buying patterns and inventory levels. In addition, important customers may be given limited access to the information system. Dell Computer allows its business customers access to special areas of its website, where they can find out about new products, track their order status, and

Figure 5.1   The Marketing Information System

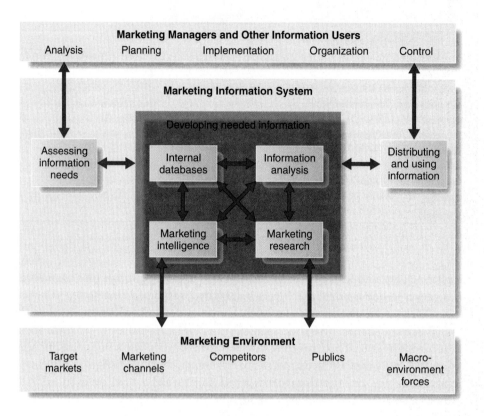

get product support and service information. Purolator lets customers into its information system to schedule and track shipments. In designing an information system, then, the company must consider the needs of all these users.

A good marketing information system balances the information users would *like* to have against what they really *need* and what is *feasible* to offer. The company begins by interviewing managers to find out what information they would like. Some managers will ask for whatever information they can get without thinking carefully about what they really need. Too much information can be as harmful as too little. Other managers may omit things they ought to know, or they may not know to ask for some types of information they should have. For example, managers might need to know that a competitor plans to introduce a new product during the coming year. Because they do not know about the new product, they do not think to ask about it. The marketing information system must monitor the marketing environment and provide decision makers with information they should have to make key marketing decisions.

Sometimes the company cannot provide the needed information, either because it is not available or because of information systems limitations. For example, a brand manager might want to know how competitors will change their advertising budgets next year and how these changes will affect industry market shares—but those competitors are not likely to make that information available to them. Though it is nearly impossible for marketers to get customer data from their competitors, they can, of course, study the competitors' products and keep detailed data about them in their own information system. The most valuable information a company has, however, is the information it collects and manages about its own customers: what products they have purchased, when they purchased them, and how many they purchased.

Finally, the costs of obtaining, processing, storing, and delivering information can mount quickly. The company must decide whether the benefits of having additional information are worth the costs of providing it, and both value and cost are often hard to assess. By itself, data has no worth; its value comes from the use a marketing manager puts it to; how it is translated into actionable *information*. In many cases, additional data will do little to change or improve a manager's decision, or the costs of the data may exceed the returns from the improved decision. Marketers should not assume that additional data will always be worth obtaining. Rather, they should weigh carefully the costs of additional data against the benefits resulting from it.

DEVELOPING MARKETING INFORMATION

Marketers can obtain the needed information from *internal data, marketing intelligence,* and *marketing research.*

Internal Data

Many companies build extensive **internal databases**, electronic collections of data obtained from sources within the company. Marketing managers can readily access and work with these databases to identify marketing opportunities and problems, plan programs, and evaluate performance.

Internal databases Electronic collections of data obtained from sources within the company.

Information in the database comes from many sources. The accounting department prepares financial statements and keeps detailed records of sales, costs, and cash flows. Manufacturing reports on production schedules, shipments, and inventories. The sales force reports on reseller transactions and competitor activities. The marketing department furnishes information on customer demographics, psychographics, and buying behaviour, and the customer service department keeps records of customer satisfaction and service problems. Research studies done for one department may provide useful information for several others.

Canon Canada provides an example of how companies use their internal databases to make better marketing decisions. The company "recently introduced a 24-hour toll-free help line to help the company better understand the home-office market. Since customer service and repair capabilities are key features of Canon's large-business marketing efforts, it uses this help line to assess the effectiveness of these efforts for the relatively undeveloped home-office market."[5]

Internal databases usually can be accessed more quickly and cheaply than other information sources, but they also present some problems. Because internal information was collected for other purposes, it may be incomplete or in the wrong form for making marketing decisions. For example, sales and cost data used by the accounting department for preparing financial statements must be adapted for use in evaluating product, sales force, or channel performance. Data ages quickly; keeping the database current requires a major effort. In addition, a large company produces mountains of information, and keeping track of it all is difficult. The organization's databases must be well integrated and readily accessible through user-friendly interfaces so that managers can find the data they need easily, and use it effectively.

Marketing Intelligence

Competitive intelligence is the practice of collecting and analyzing publicly available information about competitors and their products. Competitive-intelligence specialists collect and analyze data, then write reports for senior management explaining their findings and suggesting the uses the information could be put to. Their job is to turn the raw data into *actionable* intelligence for senior management.

Marketing intelligence is a specific branch of competitive intelligence. It is the systematic collection and analysis of publicly available information about competitors and developments in the marketing environment. The goal of marketing intelligence is to improve strategic decision making, assess and track competitors' actions, and provide early warning of opportunities and threats.

Much intelligence can be collected from people inside the company—executives, engineers and scientists, purchasing agents, and the sales force. Consider this example:

> While talking with a Kodak copier salesperson, a Xerox technician learned that the salesperson was being trained to service Xerox products. The Xerox employee reported back to his boss, who in turn passed the news to Xerox's intelligence unit. Using such clues as a classified ad Kodak placed seeking new people with Xerox product experience, Xerox verified Kodak's plan—code-named Ulysses—to service Xerox copiers. To protect its profitable service business, Xerox designed a Total Satisfaction Guarantee, which allowed copier returns for any reason as long as *Xerox* did the servicing. By the time Kodak launched Ulysses, *Xerox* had been promoting its new program for three months.[6]

The company can also obtain important intelligence information from suppliers, resellers, and key customers. Or it can get good information by observing competitors. It can buy and analyze competitors' products, monitor their sales, check for new patents, and examine various types of physical evidence. For example, one company regularly checks out competitors' parking lots—full lots might indicate plenty of work and prosperity; half-full lots might suggest hard times.[7]

Competitors may reveal intelligence information through their annual reports, business publications, trade show exhibits, press releases, advertisements, and webpages. The Internet is proving to be a vast new source of competitor-supplied information. Most companies now place volumes of information on their websites, providing details to attract customers, partners, suppliers, or franchisees. For example, Mail Boxes Etc., a chain of mailing services, provides data on its average franchise, including floor area, number of employees, operating hours, and more—all valuable insights for a competitor.

For a fee, companies can also obtain information by subscribing to any of more than 3000 online databases and information search services such as Dialog, DataStar, Lexis-Nexis, Dow Jones News Retrieval, UMI ProQuest, and Dun & Bradstreet's Online Access. Scott Hogan, a strategic market analyst at Nortel Networks and former chairman of the Eastern Ontario chapter of the Society of Competitive Intelligence Professionals, has a mantra that guides his every move. He follows Frederick the Great, who said, "It is pardonable to be defeated but never to be surprised."

Professionals such as Hogan see competitive intelligence (CI) as a systematic and ethical program of gathering and analyzing information. They turn data into actionable intelligence that managers from sales, manufacturing, R&D, marketing, and product management can use in real time to make better decisions. Actionable intelligence is information that arrives at the desk of decision makers in time for them to act on it.

CI is also value-added information analysis. For example, Hogan knows it isn't enough to report on the contents of a competitor's press release. His group must interpret what the press release means for the group's competitive strategy. Hogan stresses that CI is not a crystal ball or a compilation of rumours flying around the Internet. Moreover, CI is *not* industrial espionage. Espionage is the use of illegal means to gather information. Hogan emphasizes that Nortel follows strict ethics codes, including its own *Code of Business Conduct* and the *SCIP Code of Ethics.*[8]

Marketing intelligence A systematic collection and analysis of publicly available information about competitors and developments in the marketing environment.

CI is an early-warning tool to alert management to both threats and opportunities. For example, CI can help a company determine whether it wants to continue its own product development if competitors have taken the lead. CI is an ongoing process used as a means of seeing outside the organization. CI is especially important in high-tech environments, since the timeline for product change is very short compared with other industries. The cycle time from product definition to product shipping is approximately 18 months, and this cycle is constantly getting shorter. Furthermore, a cloud of competitors potentially lurks on every front—customers, suppliers, and partners. Since some companies have customers in more than 100 countries, they have to be aware of competitors from diverse geographies. If the scope of competition is wide, CI may have to cover a wide market segment and the deployment of internal as well as external information resources.

The growing use of marketing intelligence raises some ethical issues. Although most of the preceding techniques are legal, and some are considered shrewdly competitive, some may involve questionable ethics. Clearly, companies should take advantage of publicly available information; however, they should not stoop to spying. With all the legitimate intelligence sources now available, a company does not have to break the law or accepted codes of ethics to get good intelligence.[9]

Marketing Research

In addition to information about competitor and environmental happenings, marketers often need formal studies of specific situations. For example, Toshiba wants to know how many and what kinds of people or companies will buy its new notebook computer. In such situations, marketing intelligence will not provide the detailed information needed. Managers will need marketing research.

Marketing research is the systematic design, collection, analysis, and reporting of data relevant to a specific marketing situation facing an organization. Companies use marketing research in a wide variety of situations. For example, marketing research can help marketers assess market potential and market share; understand customer satisfaction and purchase behaviour; and measure the effectiveness of pricing, product, distribution, and promotion activities.

Some large companies have their own research departments that work with marketing managers on marketing research projects. This is how large consumer products

Marketing research The systematic design, collection, analysis, and reporting of data relevant to a specific marketing situation facing an organization.

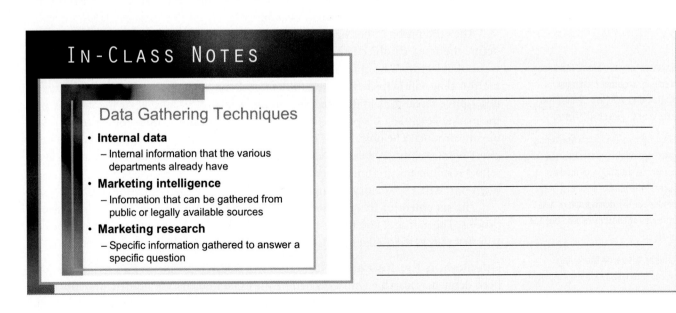

IN-CLASS NOTES

Data Gathering Techniques

- **Internal data**
  - Internal information that the various departments already have
- **Marketing intelligence**
  - Information that can be gathered from public or legally available sources
- **Marketing research**
  - Specific information gathered to answer a specific question

companies like Kraft and Procter & Gamble, telecommunications companies, and financial services organizations like banks and insurance companies handle marketing research. In addition, these companies—like their smaller counterparts—frequently hire outside research specialists to consult with management on specific marketing problems and to conduct marketing research studies. Sometimes firms simply purchase data collected by outside firms to aid in their decision making.

The marketing research process has four steps (see Figure 5.2):

1. defining the problem and the research objectives

2. developing the research plan

3. implementing the research plan

4. interpreting and reporting the findings

Figure 5.2   The Marketing Research Process

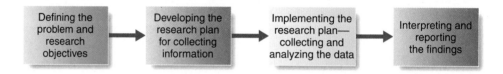

Defining the Problem and the Research Objectives Marketing managers and researchers must work closely to define the problem and agree on the research objectives. The manager best understands the decision for which information is needed; the researcher best understands marketing research and how to obtain the information.

Defining the problem and the research objectives is often the hardest step in the research process. The manager may know that something is wrong, without knowing the specific causes. For example, managers of a large discount retail store chain hastily decided that falling sales were caused by poor advertising, and they ordered research to test the company's advertising. When this research showed that current advertising was reaching the right people with the right message, the managers were puzzled. It turned out that the real problem was that the chain was not delivering the prices, products, and service promised in the advertising. Careful problem definition would have avoided the cost and delay of doing advertising research.

After the problem has been defined carefully, the manager and researcher must define the research objectives. A marketing research project might have one of three types of objectives. The objective of **exploratory research** is to gather preliminary information that will help define the problem and suggest hypotheses. The objective of **descriptive research** is to describe marketing problems, situations, or markets, such as the market potential for a product or the demographics and attitudes of consumers who buy the product. The objective of **causal research** is to test hypotheses about cause-and-effect relationships. For example, would a 10 percent decrease in tuition at a private school result in an enrollment increase sufficient to offset the reduced tuition? Managers often start with exploratory research and later follow with descriptive or causal research.

The statement of the problem and research objectives guides the entire research process. The manager and the researcher should put the statement in writing to be certain that they agree on the purpose and expected results of the research.

Developing the Research Plan Once the research problems and objectives have been defined, researchers must determine the exact information needed, develop a plan for gathering it efficiently, and present the plan to management. The research plan out-

Exploratory research Marketing research to gather preliminary information that will help define problems and suggest hypotheses.

Descriptive research Marketing research to better describe marketing problems, situations, or markets, such as the market potential for a product or the demographics and attitudes of consumers who buy the product.

Causal research Marketing research to test hypotheses about cause-and-effect relationships.

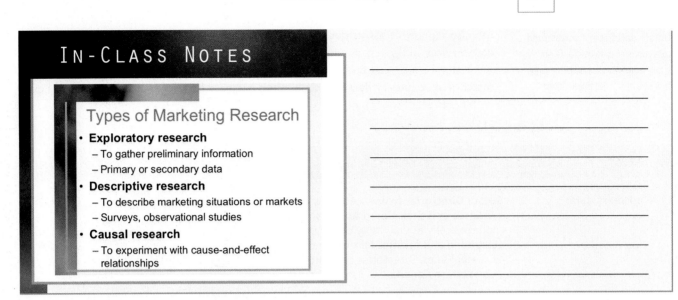

lines sources of existing data and spells out the specific research approaches, contact methods, sampling plans, and instruments that researchers will use to gather new data.

Research objectives must be translated into specific information needs. For example, suppose Campbell decides to conduct research on how consumers of its soup would react to the introduction of the bowl-shaped plastic containers that it has used successfully for several of its other products. The containers would cost more but would allow consumers to heat the soup in a microwave oven without adding water or milk and to eat it without using dishes. This research might call for the following specific information:

☐ The demographic, economic, and lifestyle characteristics of current soup users (busy working couples might find the convenience of the new packaging worth the price; families with children might want to pay less and wash the pan and bowls)

☐ Consumer-usage patterns for soup: how much soup they eat, where, and when (the new packaging might be ideal for adults eating lunch on the go but less convenient for parents feeding lunch to several children)

☐ Retailer reactions to the new packaging (failure to get retailer support could hurt sales of the new package)

☐ Consumer attitudes toward the new packaging (the red-and-white Campbell can has become an institution—will consumers accept the new packaging?)

☐ Forecasts of sales of both new and current packages (will the new packaging increase Campbell's profits?)

Campbell managers will need these and many other types of information to decide whether to introduce the new packaging.

The research plan should be presented in a *written proposal*. A written proposal is especially important when the research project is large and complex or when an outside firm carries it out. The proposal should cover the management problems addressed and the research objectives, the information to be obtained, and the way the results will help management decision making. The proposal should also include research costs.

To meet the manager's information needs, the research plan can call for gathering primary data, secondary data, or both. **Primary data** consist of information collected for the specific purpose at hand. **Secondary data** consist of information that already exists somewhere, having been collected for another purpose.

Gathering Secondary Data Researchers usually start by gathering secondary data. The company's internal database provides a good starting point. However, the company

Primary data Information collected for the specific purpose at hand.

Secondary data Information that already exists somewhere, having been collected for another purpose.

Online databases Computerized collections of data available online, either from closed, subscriber-only services, or via the public Internet.

can also tap a wide assortment of external information sources, including commercial data services and government sources (see Table 5.1).

Using commercial **online databases**, marketing researchers can conduct their own searches of secondary data sources. Online database services such as Dialog and Lexis-

---

Table 5.1   Sources of Secondary Data

For business data:

Scott's Directories (www.scottsinfo.com) lists, on an annual basis, manufacturers, their products, and their North American Industry Classification (NAICS) codes, alphabetically as well as by city and region. The directory also provides the names and telephone and fax numbers of chief executives, as well as corporate information such as annual sales. Directories come in four volumes: Ontario, Quebec, Atlantic Canada, and Western Canada.

Canadian Trade Index (www.ctidirectory.com) **and Fraser's Canadian Trade Directory** (www.frasers.ca) provide information on manufacturers of different product categories, manufacturing equipment, and supplies.

AC Nielsen Canada (www.acnielsen.ca) and **Nielsen Media Research Canada** (www.nielsenmedia.ca) provide supermarket scanner data on sales, market share, and retail prices; data on household purchasing; and data on television audiences.

Information Resources, Inc. (www.infores.com) provides supermarket scanner data for tracking grocery product movement and new product purchasing data.

Arbitron (www.arbitron.com) provides local-market and Internet radio audience and advertising expenditure information, among other media and ad spending data.

Simmons Market Research Bureau (www.smrb.com) provides detailed analysis of consumer patterns in 400 product categories in selected American markets.

Dun & Bradstreet (www.dnb.com) maintains a database containing information on more than 50 million companies around the globe.

Dialog (www.dialog.com), one of the first online information services, in business since 1966, operates in 27 countries providing information to businesses, science, engineering, finance, and law.

LEXIS-NEXIS (www.lexis-nexis.com) features articles from business, consumer, and marketing publications plus tracking of firms, industries, trends, and promotion techniques.

Dow Jones (www.dowjones.com) specializes in in-depth financial, historical, and operational information on public and private companies.

Hoovers Online (www.hoovers.com) provides business descriptions, financial overviews, and news about major companies around the world.

American Demographics (www.americandemographics.com) reports on demographic trends and their significance for businesses.

Marketing journals include the *Canadian Journal of Marketing Research, Journal of Marketing, Journal of Marketing Research, Journal of Consumer Research*, and *Journal of the Academy of Marketing Science*.

Useful trade magazines include *Strategy* (www.strategymag.com), *Marketing* (www.marketingmag.ca), *Advertising Age, Chain Store Age, Progressive Grocer, Sales & Marketing Management*, and *Stores*.

Useful general business magazines include *Canadian Business, The Globe and Mail Report on Business, Business Week, Fortune, Forbes*, and *Harvard Business Review*.

(continued)

Table 5.1	**Continued**
	The Interactive Advertising Bureau of Canada (www.iabcanada.com) is an industry association for Internet marketers, and also provides research about Internet marketing in Canada. Other good sources of information about Internet marketing are the ClickZ Network (www.clickz.com) and Internet.com.
	comScore Networks (www.comscore.com, formerly Media Metrix) does Internet audience measurement and custom survey research.
	Jupiter Research (www.jupiterresearch.com) provides industry research to help companies develop strategies for integrating the Internet into their business practices.
	The Gartner Group (www.gartner.com) and **Forrester Research** (www.forrester.com) have hundreds of experts and consultants who prepare comprehensive research reports for the information technology sector. Companies can buy data reports from outside suppliers.[10] For example, NPD Canada maintains the country's longest-running national diary panel, the *Consumer Panel of Canada*. It also has an *OnLine Panel* that companies can use to get insights about Canada's Web-savvy population as well as specialized reports such as the *Canadian Apparel Market Monitor* and *National Eating Trends,* which reports on in-home and out-of-home consumption behaviour.
For government data:	**Statistics Canada** (www.statcan.ca) provides summary data on demographic, economic, social, and other aspects of the Canadian economy and society.
	Industry Canada's Strategis website (www.strategis.ic.gc.ca) provides resources for Canadian businesses.
	SEDAR (www.sedar.com) provides financial filings of Canadian public companies.
	Securities and Exchange Commission Edgar database (www.sec.gov) provides financial data on U.S. public corporations.
	Small Business: many provincial governments post sites aimed at helping small business (for example, see www.ontariobusinesscentral.ca and www.smallbusinessbc.ca). There are also a number of commercial sites tailored to small business owners (for example, see sbinfocanada.about.com). *Small Business Canada* magazine (www.sbcmag.com/) and *Profit* magazine (www.profitguide.com/index.jsp) are other useful resources.
	Canadian Census (www12.statcan.ca/english/census01/home/index.cfm) provides detailed statistics and trends relating to the Canadian population.
	Stat-USA (www.stat.usa.gov), a U.S. Department of Commerce site, highlights statistics on U.S. business and international trade.

Nexis put an incredible wealth of information at the keyboards of marketing decision makers. Beyond commercial websites offering information for a fee, almost every industry association, government agency, business publication, and news medium offers at least some free information. University and public libraries offer a variety of searchable databases, such as ABI/Inform, where marketing researchers can access articles from thousands of industry, trade, technical, and scholarly journals. In the modern information age, marketers can find just about anything they need online.

Secondary data can usually be obtained faster and at a lower cost than primary data. For example, an Internet search might provide all the information Campbell's needs on soup usage, quickly and inexpensively. A study to collect primary information might take weeks or months and cost thousands of dollars. Secondary sources can sometimes provide data that an individual company cannot collect on its own—information that either is not directly available or would be too expensive to collect. For example, it would be too expensive for Campbell's to conduct a continuing retail store audit to find out about the market shares, prices, and displays of competitors' brands. But it can buy

INFORMATION TO
change
the
world

Dial•g

Pharmaceutical, chemical and medical journals. Company financials. Patents and trademarks. Newspapers, newswires, trade publications and scholarly sources. Domain names. Engineering literature. Market research and brokerage reports.

One Company.　　　One Interface.　　　One Relationship.

www.dialog.com

THOMSON
DIALOG

Online database services such as Dialog put an incredible wealth of information at the keyboards of marketing decision makers. Dialog puts "information to change the world, or your corner of it," at your fingertips.

Observational research The gathering of primary data by observing relevant people, actions, and situations.

much of this information from AC Nielsen Canada, which has a huge database that was formed by tracking the point-of-sale activity of many brands sold across Canada.

Secondary data can also present problems. The needed information may not exist—researchers can rarely obtain all the data they need from secondary sources. For example, Campbell's will not find existing information about consumer reactions to new packaging that it has not yet placed on the market. Even when data can be found, they might not be very usable. The researcher must evaluate secondary information carefully to make certain it is *relevant* (fits research project needs), *accurate* (reliably collected and reported), *current* (up to date enough for current decisions), and *impartial* (objectively collected and reported).

Primary Data Collection Secondary data provide a good starting point for research and often help to define problems and research objectives. In most cases, however, the company must also collect primary data. Just as researchers must carefully evaluate the quality of secondary information, they also must take great care when collecting primary data to ensure that it will be relevant, accurate, current, and unbiased. Table 5.2 shows that designing a plan for primary data collection calls for decisions on *research approaches, contact methods, sampling plan,* and *research instruments.*

Research Approaches. Research approaches for gathering primary data include observation, surveys, and experiments. **Observational research** involves gathering primary data by observing relevant people, actions, and situations. For example, a consumer packaged-goods marketer might visit supermarkets and observe shoppers as they browse the store, pick up products and examine packages, and make actual buying decisions. Or a bank might evaluate possible new branch locations by checking traffic patterns, neighbourhood conditions, and the location of competing branches. Fisher-Price even set up an observation lab in which it could observe the reactions of little tots to new toys:

> The Fisher-Price Play Lab is a sunny, toy-strewn space where, since 1961, lucky kids have tested Fisher-Price prototypes. Today three boys and three girls, all four-year-olds, speed through the front door. Two boys tug quietly, but firmly, for the wheel of a new radio-controlled race set—a brand-new offering. The girls skid to a stop near a small subdevelopment of dollhouses. And from behind the one-way glass, toy designers study the action intently, occasionally stepping out to join the play. At the Play Lab, creation and (attempted) destruction happily coexist.

Table 5.2 **Planning Primary Data Collection**

Research Approaches	Contact Methods	Sampling Plan	Research Instruments
Observation	Mail	Sampling unit	Questionnaire
Survey	Telephone	Sample size	Mechanical instruments
Experiment	Personal	Sampling procedure	

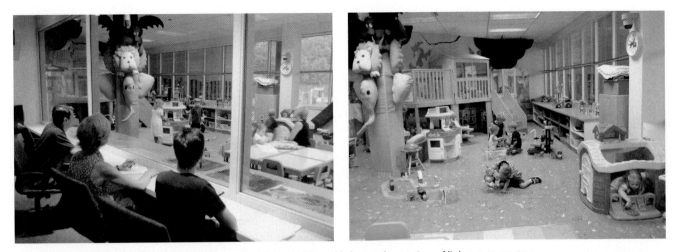

Observational research: Fisher-Price set up an observation lab in which it could observe the reactions of little tots to new toys.

Over an eight week session with these kids, designers will test dozens of toy concepts, sending out crude models, then increasingly sophisticated revisions, to figure out what gets kids worked up into a new-toy frenzy.[11]

Many companies collect data through *mechanical* observation via machine or computer. For example, Nielsen Media Research attaches *meters* to television sets in selected homes to record who watches which programs. BBM Canada recruits volunteers to fill out a one-week diary of their radio listening, then compiles that data to produce information for advertisers planning radio campaigns. Other companies use *checkout scanners* to record shoppers' purchases so that manufacturers and retailers can assess product sales and store performance.

Observational research can obtain information that people are unwilling or unable to provide. In some cases, observation may be the only way to obtain the needed information. In contrast, some things simply cannot be observed, such as feelings, attitudes and motives, or private behaviour. Long-term or infrequent behaviour is also difficult to observe. Because of these limitations, researchers often use observation along with other data collection methods. Ethnographic research, involving intense observation, is discussed in Marketing at Work 5.1.

Survey research, the most widely used method for primary data collection, is the approach best suited for gathering *descriptive* information. **Survey research** is the gathering of primary data by asking people questions about their knowledge, attitudes, preferences, and buying behaviour.

Some firms provide marketers with a more comprehensive look at buying patterns through **single-source data systems**. These systems combine surveys of huge consumer panels—carefully selected groups of consumers who agree to participate in ongoing research—and electronic monitoring of respondents' purchases and exposure to various marketing activities in an effort to better understand the link among consumer characteristics, attitudes, and purchase behaviour.

The major advantage of survey research is its flexibility—it can be used to obtain many different kinds of information in many different situations. However, survey research also presents some problems. Sometimes people are unable to answer survey questions because they cannot remember or have never thought about what they do and why. People may be unwilling to respond to unknown interviewers or about subjects that they consider private. Respondents may answer survey questions even when they do not know the answer in order to appear smarter or more informed. Or they may try to help the interviewer by giving pleasing answers. Finally, busy people may not take the time, or they might resent the intrusion into their privacy.

Survey research The gathering of primary data by asking people questions about their knowledge, attitudes, preferences, and buying behaviour.

Single-source data systems Systems that combine surveys of huge consumer panels and electronic monitoring of respondents' purchases and exposure to various marketing activities in an effort to better understand the link among consumer characteristics, attitudes, and purchase behaviour.

Marketing at Work 5.1

Ethnographic Research: Keeping a Close Eye on Consumers

What do customers really think about your product? How do they really use it? Will they tell you? These are difficult questions for most marketers. And too often, traditional research simply can't provide accurate answers. To get better insights, many companies are now turning to an increasingly popular research approach: ethnographic or observational research.

Ethnographic research combines intense observation with customer interviews to get an up-close and personal view of how people actually live with products—how they buy and use them in their everyday lives.

Four years ago, Sunbeam wanted to extend its Coleman brand—known for its distinctive forest green encased lanterns and its red coolers—into gas barbecue grills. But company execs couldn't decide how to design and position the new line. Even after hours of focus groups and reams of quantitative data, the outdoor cooking team felt like it had a whole lot of information but little insight. "We were hearing a lot of passion about grilling, particularly among men," says a Sunbeam marketer, "but they couldn't really describe *why* they had the passion." Sunbeam execs turned

to ethnography for help. Researchers hoisted video cameras onto shoulders and headed to their consumers' native habitat: the backyard. By hanging out with the guys around the grill and listening in on the gab, the team eventually gathered a key insight: A gas grill isn't really a tool that cooks hamburgers and hot dogs. Rather, it's the centrepiece of warm family moments worthy of a summer highlights reel. So, rather than create and promote the new Coleman Grill in terms of BTUs, rotisserie options, and cooking square inches, Sunbeam designed the grill to evoke nostalgia for the camping experience with friends and family. The company positioned the product and grilling experience as "a relaxing ritual where the grilling area is the stage," an event that takes place in a "backyard oasis." The result: The Coleman Grill did a scorching $50 million in sales in its first year, making the product line one of the most successful launches in Sunbeam history.

Montreal-based Bugle Boy found that traditional focus groups fail miserably in getting the scoop on teens. These often-cynical young people are

skeptical of sales pitches and just won't speak up in a conference room with two-way mirrors. So, Bugle Boy turned to ethnographic research. It chose four young men at random, handed each of them a camcorder, and told them to document their lives. The young amateurs were given only broad categories to work with: school, home, closet, and shopping. Bugle Boy then used the videos to prompt discussions of product and lifestyle issues in free-form focus groups held in unconventional locations, such as restaurants. Says one Bugle Boy ad manager, "I think this really helped us to get a handle on what these kids do. It let us see what their lives are all about, their awareness of the Bugle Boy brand, and how they perceive the brand."

Increasingly, marketers are keeping a close eye on consumers. "Knowing the individual consumer on an intimate basis has become a necessity," says a research industry consultant, "and ethnography is the intimate connection to the consumer."

Sources: Excerpts from Kendra Parker, "How Do You Like Your Beef?" *American Demographics*, January 2000, pp. 35–37; Gerry Khermouch, "Consumers in the Mist," *Business Week*, 26 February 2001, pp. 92–94; and Alison Stein Wellner, "Watch Me Now," *American Demographics*, October 2002, p. S1–S4.

Experimental research The gathering of primary data by selecting matched groups of subjects, giving them different treatments, controlling unrelated factors, and checking for differences in group responses.

Whereas observation is best suited for exploratory research and surveys for descriptive research, **experimental research** is best suited for gathering *causal* information. Experiments involve selecting matched groups of subjects, giving them different treatments, controlling unrelated factors, and checking for differences in group responses. Thus, experimental research tries to explain cause-and-effect relationships.

For example, before adding a new sandwich to its menu, McDonald's might use experiments to test the effects on sales of two different prices it might charge. It could introduce the new sandwich at one price in one city and at another price in another city. If the cities are similar, and if all other marketing efforts for the sandwich are the same, then differences in sales in the two cities could be related to the price charged.

Contact Methods. Information can be collected by mail, telephone, personal interview, or online. Table 5.3 shows the strengths and weaknesses of each of these contact methods.

Table 5.3   Strengths and Weaknesses of the Four Contact Methods

	Mail	Telephone	Personal	Online
Flexibility	Poor	Good	Excellent	Good
Quantity of data that can be collected	Good	Fair	Excellent	Good
Control of interviewer effects	Excellent	Fair	Poor	Fair
Control of sample	Fair	Excellent	Fair	Poor
Speed of data collection	Poor	Excellent	Good	Excellent
Response rate	Fair	Good	Good	Good
Cost	Good	Fair	Poor	Excellent

Source: Adapted with permission of Macmillan Publishing Company from Donald S. Tull and Del I. Hawkins, *Marketing Research: Measurement and Method,* 7th ed., Macmillan Publishing Company, 1993.

Mail questionnaires can be used to collect large amounts of information at a low cost per respondent. Respondents may give more honest answers to more personal questions on a mail questionnaire than to an unknown interviewer in person or over the phone. Since no interviewer is involved, one form of bias is eliminated. However, mail questionnaires are not very flexible—all respondents answer the same questions in a fixed order. Mail surveys usually take longer to complete, and the response rate—the number of people returning completed questionnaires—is often very low. Finally, the researcher often has little control over the mail questionnaire sample. Even with a good mailing list, it is hard to control *who* at the mailing address fills out the questionnaire.

Telephone interviewing is the one of the best methods for gathering information quickly, and it provides greater flexibility than mail questionnaires. Interviewers can explain difficult questions and, depending on the answers they receive, skip some questions or probe on others. Response rates tend to be higher than with mail questionnaires, and interviewers can ask to speak to respondents with the desired characteristics or even by name.

However, with telephone interviewing, the cost per respondent is higher than with mail questionnaires. Also, people may not want to discuss personal questions with an interviewer. The method also introduces interviewer bias—the way interviewers talk, how they ask questions, and other differences may affect respondents' answers. Finally, different interviewers may interpret and record responses differently, and under time pressures some interviewers might even cheat by recording answers without asking questions. Government privacy legislation also has a bearing on the use of the telephone for research purposes. In the fall of 2004, the federal government introduced "Do Not Call" legislation, similar to a system in the U.S where anyone can have their name placed on a list to stop unauthorized sources from calling, with heavy fines for the company doing the phoning. The issue here is whether this will so reduce the available respondent pool that the telephone survey will be rendered obsolete.

Personal interviewing takes two forms—individual and group interviewing. Individual interviewing involves talking with people in their homes or offices, on the street, or in shopping malls. Such interviewing is flexible. Trained interviewers can guide interviews, explain difficult questions, and explore issues as the situation requires. They can show subjects actual products, advertisements, or packages and observe reactions and behaviour. However, individual personal interviews may cost three to four times as much as telephone interviews.

Focus groups are a market research tool designed to collect qualitative data from a small group of people, chosen as representatives of the target market. A **focus group** is a

Focus group A moderated, small-group discussion, typically conducted by marketers during the new product development process.

moderated, small-group discussion, typically conducted by marketers during the new product development process. Participants, who are normally paid a small sum for attending, are led in an informal discussion by the moderator while the marketers watch from behind a one-way glass partition.

Focus groups are an important marketing research tool for gaining insight into consumer thoughts and feelings. However, focus group studies usually employ small sample sizes to keep time and costs low, and it may be hard to generalize from the results. And because interviewers have more freedom in personal interviews, the problem of interviewer bias is greater.

Today, modern communications technology is changing the way that focus groups are conducted:

> Videoconferencing links, television monitors, remote-control cameras, and digital transmission are boosting the amount of focus group research done over long-distance lines. [In a typical videoconferencing system], two cameras focused on the group are controlled by clients who hold a remote keypad. Executives in a far-off boardroom can zoom in on faces and pan the focus group at will. . . . A two-way sound system connects remote viewers to the backroom, focus group room, and directly to the monitor's earpiece. [Recently], while testing new product names in one focus group, the [client's] creative director . . . had an idea and contacted the moderator, who tested the new name on the spot.[12]

Advances in computers and communications have had a large impact on methods of obtaining information. Most research firms now do computer-assisted telephone interviewing (CATI). Professional interviewers call respondents around the country, often using phone numbers drawn at random. When the respondent answers, the interviewer reads a set of questions from a video screen and types the respondent's answers directly into the computer. Some U.S. researchers use completely automated telephone surveys (CATS), which employ voice-response technology to conduct interviews, but the Canadian Radio-television and Telecommunication Commission has banned such devices in Canada.

Other firms are using *computer-assisted interviewing*, in which respondents sit down at a computer, read questions from a screen, and type their own answers into the computer. The Royal Bank of Canada has mastered computer-assisted interviewing without making people actually use a computer. Under a large sign that asks customers to "tell us what you think," customers use a special pen to complete a questionnaire on an electronic board. The information can be downloaded directly into a database for analysis. More and more marketers are turning to the Internet to conduct marketing research (see Marketing at Work 5.2).

Sampling Plan. Marketing researchers usually draw conclusions about large groups of consumers by studying a small sample of the total consumer population. A **sample** is a segment of the population selected to represent the population as a whole. Ideally, the sample should be representative so that the researcher can make accurate estimates of the thoughts and behaviours of the larger population.

Sample A segment of the population selected to represent the population as a whole.

Designing the sample requires three decisions. First, *who* is to be surveyed (what *sampling unit*)? The answer to this question is not always obvious. For example, to study the decision-making process for a family automobile purchase, should the researcher interview the husband, wife, other family members, dealership salespeople, or all of these? The researcher must determine what information is needed and who is most likely to have it.

Second, *how many* people should be surveyed (what *sample size*)? Large samples give more reliable results than small samples. It is not necessary to sample the entire target market or even a large portion to get reliable results, however. If well chosen, samples of less than 1 percent of a population can often give good reliability.

Third, *how* should the people in the sample be chosen (what *sampling procedure*)? Table 5.4 describes different kinds of samples. Using *probability samples*, each population member has a known chance of being included in the sample, and researchers can calculate confidence limits for sampling error. But when probability sampling costs too much or takes too much time, marketing researchers often take *nonprobability samples,* even though their sampling error cannot be measured. These varied ways of drawing samples have different costs and time limitations, as well as different accuracy and statistical properties. Which method is best depends on the needs of the research project.

Marketing at Work | 5.2

Online Marketing Research

As consumers connect to the Internet, an increasing number of marketers are conducting marketing research on the Web. Online research now accounts for 8 percent of all spending on quantitative marketing research. Web research offers two advantages over traditional surveys: speed and low costs.

With online surveys, results are practically instantaneous—survey researchers complete their online studies in a matter of days or weeks. For example, consider a recent online survey by a soft drink company testing teenagers' opinions of new packaging ideas. The 10–15 minute survey presented images of different labels and bottle shapes and asked questions about them. Detailed analysis from the survey was available just five days after all the responses had come in.

Internet research is relatively low in cost. Participants can contribute to a focus group from anywhere in the world, eliminating travel, lodging, and facility costs. Online surveys eliminate most of the postage, phone, labour, and printing costs associated with other approaches. "The cost [of Web research] can be anywhere from 10 percent to 80 percent less," says Tod Johnson, head of NPD Group, a firm that conducts online research. Moreover, sample size has little influence on costs. "There's not a huge difference between 10 and 10 000 on the Web," says Johnson.

One major problem of online research is controlling who's in the sample. To overcome such sample and response problems, many online research firms use opt-in communities and respondent panels. For example, Greenfield Online maintains a 1.3-million-member Internet-based respondent panel, recruited through cooperative marketing arrangements with other sites. Because such respondents opt in and can answer questions whenever they are ready, they yield high response rates. Whereas response rates for telephone surveys have plummeted to less than 14 percent in recent years, online response rates typically reach 40 percent or higher.

But even when you reach the right respondents, online surveys and focus groups lack the dynamics of more personal approaches. "You're missing all of the key things that make a focus group a viable method," says Greenbaum. "You may get people online to talk to

More and more companies are moving their research onto the Web. According to this Greenfield Online ad, in many ways, it "beats the old-fashioned kind."

(continued)

each other and play off each other, but it's very different to watch people get excited about a concept."

Perhaps the most explosive issue facing online researchers concerns consumer privacy. Critics fear that unethical researchers will use the email addresses and confidential responses gathered through surveys to sell products after the research is completed. They are concerned about the use of electronic agents that collect personal information without the respondents' consent. Failure to address such pri-vacy issues could result in less coopera-tive consumers and increased govern-ment intervention.

Although most researchers agree that online research will never com-pletely replace traditional research, some are wildly optimistic about its prospects. Others, however, are more cautious. "Ten years from now, national telephone surveys will be the subject of research methodology folk-lore," proclaims one expert. "That's a little too soon," cautions another. "But in 20 years, yes."

Sources: "Market Trends: Online Research Growing," accessed at www.greenfieldcentral.com/research_solutions/rsrch_solns_main.htm, June 2003; Ian P. Murphy, "Interactive Research," *Marketing News,* January 20, 1997, pp. 1, 17; "NFO Executive Sees Most Research Going to Internet," *Advertising Age,* May 19, 1997, p. 50; Noah Shachtman, "Web Enhanced Market Research," *Advertising Age,* June 18, 2001, p. T18; Thomas W. Miller, "Make the Call: Online Results Are a Mixed Bag," *Marketing News,* September 24, 2001, pp. 30–35; Beth Mack, "Online Privacy Critical to Research Success," *Marketing News,* November 25, 2002, p. 21; and Nina M. Ray and Sharon W. Tabor, "Cybersurveys Come of Age," *Marketing Research,* Spring 2003, pp. 32–37.

Research Instruments. In collecting primary data, marketing researchers have a choice of two main research instruments: the *questionnaire* and *mechanical devices.* The *ques-tionnaire* is by far the most common instrument, whether administered in person, by phone, or online.

Questionnaires are very flexible—there are many ways to ask questions. *Closed-end questions* include all the possible answers, and subjects make choices among them. Examples include multiple-choice questions and scale questions. *Open-end questions* allow respondents to answer in their own words. In a survey of airline users, Westjet might simply ask, "What is your opinion of Westjet Airlines?" Or it might ask people to complete a sentence: "When I choose an airline, the most important consideration is. . . ." These and other kinds of open-end questions often reveal more than closed-end questions, because respondents are not limited in their answers. Open-end questions are especially useful in exploratory research, when the researcher is trying to find out *what* people think but not measuring *how many* people think in a certain way. Closed-end questions provide answers that are easier to interpret and tabulate.

Table 5.4 Types of Samples

Probability Sample	
Simple random sample	Every member of the population has a known and equal chance of selection.
Stratified random sample	The population is divided into mutually exclusive groups (such as age groups), and random samples are drawn from each group.
Cluster (area) sample	The population is divided into mutually exclusive groups (such as blocks), and the researcher draws a sample of the groups to interview.
Nonprobability Sample	
Convenience sample	The researcher selects the easiest population members from which to obtain information.
Judgment sample	The researcher uses his or her judgment to select population members who are good prospects for accurate information.
Quote sample	The researcher finds and interviews a prescribed number of people in each of several categories.

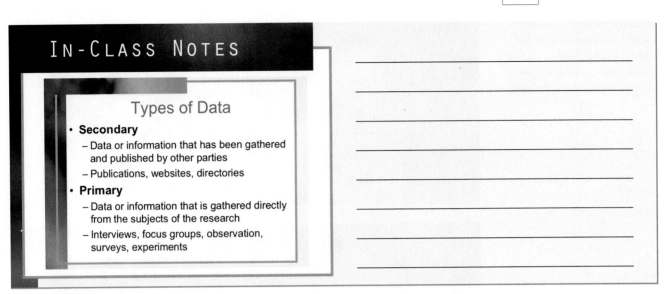

Researchers should also use care in the *wording* and *ordering* of questions. They should use simple, direct, unbiased wording. Questions should be arranged in a logical order. The first question should create interest if possible, and difficult or personal questions should be asked last so that respondents do not become defensive. A carelessly prepared questionnaire usually contains many errors (see Table 5.5).

Although questionnaires are the most common research instrument, *mechanical instruments* such as people meters and supermarket scanners are also used. Another group of mechanical devices measures subjects' physical responses. For example, a galvanometer measures the strength of interest or emotions aroused by a subject's exposure to different stimuli, such as an advertisement or picture. The galvanometer detects the minute degree of sweating that accompanies emotional arousal. Eye cameras are used to study respondents' eye movements to determine on what points their eyes focus first and how long they linger on a given item. Here are examples of new technologies that capture information on consumers' emotional and physical responses:[13]

Table 5.5   A Questionable Questionnaire

Suppose that a summer camp director had prepared the following questionnaire to use in interviewing the parents of prospective campers. How would you assess each question?

1. What is your income to the nearest hundred dollars? *People don't usually know their income to the nearest hundred dollars, nor do they want to reveal their income that closely. Moreover, a researcher should never open a questionnaire with such a personal question.*

2. Are you a strong or a weak supporter of overnight summer camping for your children? *What do "strong" and "weak" mean?*

3. Do your children behave themselves well at a summer camp? Yes ( ) No ( ) *"Behave" is a relative term. Furthermore, are "yes" and "no" the best response options for this question? Besides, will people want to answer this? Why ask the question in the first place?*

4. How many camps mailed literature to you last April? this April? *Who can remember this?*

5. What are the most salient and determinant attributes in your evaluation of summer camps? *What are "salient" and "determinant" attributes? Don't use big words with me!*

6. Do you think it is right to deprive your child of the opportunity to grow into a mature person through the experience of summer camping? *A loaded question. Given the bias, how can any parent answer "yes"?*

Mechanical measures of consumer response: Devices are in the works that will allow marketers to measure facial expressions and adjust their offers or communications accordingly.

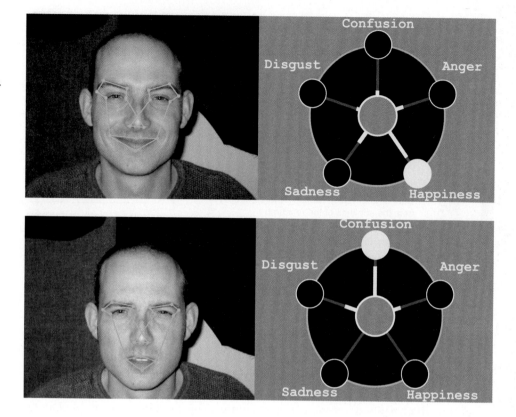

Machine response to facial expressions that indicate emotions will soon be a commercial reality. The technology discovers underlying emotions by capturing an image of a user's facial features and movements—especially around the eyes and mouth—and comparing the image against facial feature templates in a database. Hence, an elderly man squints at a bank machine screen and the font size doubles almost instantly. A woman at a shopping center kiosk smiles at a travel ad, prompting the device to print out a travel discount coupon. Several users at another kiosk frown at a racy ad, leading a store to pull it.

IBM is perfecting an "emotion mouse" that will figure out users' emotional states by measuring pulse, temperature, movement, and galvanic skin response. The company has mapped those measurements for anger, fear, sadness, disgust, happiness, and surprise. The idea is to create a style that fits a user's personality. An Internet marketer, for example, might offer to present a different kind of display if it senses that the user is frustrated.

Implementing the Research Plan After developing the research plan, which includes choosing the best type of data for the plan and the best data collection method, the researcher next puts the marketing research plan into action. This involves collecting, processing, and analyzing the information. Data collection can be carried out by the company's marketing research staff or by outside firms. The data collection phase of the marketing research process is generally the most expensive and the most subject to error. The researcher should watch closely to ensure that the plan is implemented correctly and to guard against problems with contacting respondents, with respondents who refuse to cooperate or who give biased answers, and with interviewers who make mistakes or take shortcuts.

Researchers must process and analyze the collected data to isolate important information and findings. They need to check data for accuracy and completeness and code it

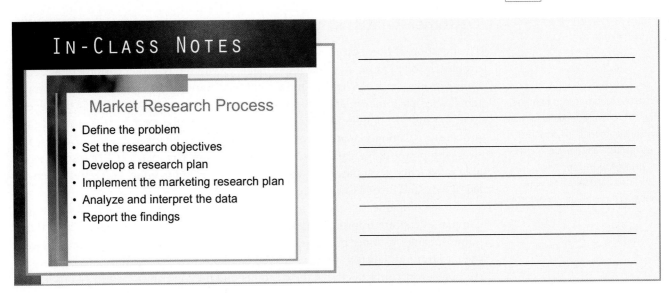

for analysis. The researchers then tabulate the results and compute averages and other statistical measures.

Interpreting and Reporting the Findings The market researcher must now interpret the findings, draw conclusions, and report them to management. The researcher should not try to overwhelm managers with numbers and fancy statistical techniques. Rather, the researcher should present important findings that are useful in the major decisions faced by management.

However, interpretation should not be left only to the researchers. They are often experts in research design and statistics, but the marketing manager knows more about the problem and the decisions that must be made. The best research is meaningless if the manager blindly accepts faulty interpretations from the researcher. Similarly, managers may be biased—they might tend to accept research results that show what they expected and to reject those that they did not expect or hope for. In many cases, findings can be interpreted in different ways, and discussions between researchers and managers will help point to the best interpretations. Thus, managers and researchers must work together closely when interpreting research results, and both must share responsibility for the research process and resulting decisions.

ANALYZING MARKETING INFORMATION

Information gathered in internal databases and through marketing intelligence and marketing research usually requires more analysis, and managers may need help in applying the information to their marketing problems and decisions. This help may include advanced statistical analysis to learn more about both the relationships within a set of data and their statistical reliability. Such analysis allows managers to go beyond means and standard deviations in the data and to answer questions about markets, marketing activities, and outcomes.

Information analysis might also involve a collection of analytical models that will help marketers make better decisions. Each model represents some real system, process, or outcome. These models can help answer the questions of *what if* and *which is best*. Marketing scientists have developed numerous models to help marketing managers make better marketing mix decisions, design sales territories and sales call plans, select sites for retail outlets, develop optimal advertising mixes, and forecast new-product sales.

Customer Relationship Management (CRM)

The question of how best to analyze and use individual customer data presents special problems. Today, most large businesses that deal with thousands of customers, as well as online retailers such as Chapters-Indigo and Cake Beauty, use powerful information systems called **customer relationship management systems (CRM)**. CRM is the generic term for any corporate software system that collects and organizes customer data and provides marketing managers, customer service representatives, and sales representatives with powerful information tools. There are many commercial CRM systems available on the market today, from companies such as On Contact Software, Terrasoft, SalesLogix, and Pivotal Corporation, of Vancouver.

Customer relationship management (CRM) Any corporate software system that collects and organizes customer data and provides marketing managers, customer service representatives, and sales representatives with powerful information tools.

Most companies are awash in information about their customers. In fact, smart companies capture information at every possible customer *touch point*. These touch points include customer purchases, sales force contacts, service and support calls, website registrations, satisfaction surveys, credit and payment interactions, market research studies—every contact between the customer and the company.

The trouble is that this information is usually scattered widely across the organization. It is buried deep in the separate databases, plans, and records of many different company functions and departments. CRM integrates everything that a company's sales, service, and marketing teams know about individual customers to provide a complete view of the customer relationship. It pulls together, analyzes, and provides easy access to customer information from all of the various touch points. Companies use CRM analysis to assess the value of individual customers, identify the best ones to target, and customize their products and interactions to each customer.

CRM analysts develop *data warehouses* and use sophisticated *data mining* techniques to unearth the riches hidden in customer data. A data warehouse is a company-wide electronic storehouse of customer information—a centralized database of finely detailed customer data that needs to be sifted through for gems. The purpose of a data warehouse is not to gather information—many companies have already amassed endless stores of information about their customers. Rather, the purpose is to allow managers to integrate the information the company already has. Then, once the data warehouse brings the data together for analysis, the company uses high-powered data mining techniques to sift through the mounds of data and dig out interesting relationships and findings about customers.

Companies can gain many benefits from customer relationship management. By understanding customers better, they can provide higher levels of customer service and develop deeper customer relationships. They can use CRM to pinpoint high-value customers, target them more effectively, cross-sell their company's products, and create offers tailored to specific customer requirements. Consider the case of FedEx.

FedEx recently launched a multimillion-dollar CRM initiative in an effort to cut costs, improve its customer support, and use its existing customer data to cross-sell and up-sell services to potential or existing customers. Using CRM software from Clarify Inc., the new system

CRM: SAS offers CRM software that provides "a complete view of your customers." So you'll understand their needs, enhance their lifetime value, and achieve greater competitive advantage.

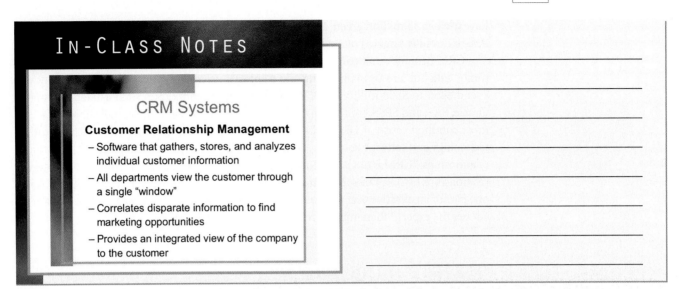

IN-CLASS NOTES

CRM Systems

Customer Relationship Management

– Software that gathers, stores, and analyzes
  individual customer information

– All departments view the customer through
  a single "window"

– Correlates disparate information to find
  marketing opportunities

– Provides an integrated view of the company
  to the customer

gives every member of FedEx's 3300-person sales force a comprehensive view of every customer, detailing each one's needs and suggesting services that might meet those needs. For instance, if a customer who does a lot of international shipping calls to arrange a delivery, a sales rep will see a detailed customer history on his or her computer screen, assess the customer's needs, and determine the most appropriate offering on the spot. Beleaguered sales reps can use such high-tech help. FedEx offers 220 different services—from logistics to transportation to customs brokerage—often making it difficult for salespeople to identify the best fit for customers. The new CRM system will also help FedEx conduct promotions and qualify potential sales leads. The Clarify software will analyze market segments, point out market "sweet spots," and calculate how profitable those segments will be to the company and to individual salespeople.[14]

Most experts believe that good customer data, by itself, can give companies a substantial competitive advantage. Just ask American Express. At a secret location in Phoenix, security guards watch over American Express's 500 billion bytes of data on how customers

Linking the Concepts

Apply the concepts you've examined so far in this chapter.

■ Think about a major purchase you've made recently. What follow-up from the company where you made the purchase did you receive? If none, what customer relationship building techniques would you recommend to the company to ensure that customers are satisfied with their purchases and will buy from that company in future?

■ Pick a company that we've discussed in a previous chapter, such as Canadian Tire, Mountain Equipment Co-op, or Apple, or choose a company that you are a customer of. Visit the company's website and find out whether you can register without purchasing something. Follow the registration process as far as you can, and make a list of all the customer data the company is collecting.

■ Think about Dofasco, which sells its products to carmakers and other businesses that require steel. How would Dofasco's customer relationship strategies differ from a company such as Kraft, which markets products to consumers?

have used its 35 million green, gold, and platinum charge cards. Amex uses the database to design carefully targeted offers in its monthly mailing of millions of customer bills.

CRM benefits don't come without cost or risk, not only in collecting the original customer data but also in maintaining and mining it. Even though Canadian companies will spend $450 to $500 million on CRM software from companies such as Siebel Systems, Oracle, SAS, and SPSS, more than half of all CRM efforts fail to meet their objectives. The most common cause of CRM failures is that companies mistakenly view CRM as only a technology and software solution.[15] But technology alone cannot build profitable customer relationships. "CRM is not a technology solution—you can't achieve . . . improved customer relationships by simply slapping in some software," says a CRM expert. Instead, CRM is just one part of an effective overall *customer relationship management strategy*. "Focus on the *R*," advises the expert. "Remember, a relationship is what CRM is all about."[16]

DISTRIBUTING AND USING MARKETING INFORMATION

Marketing data has no value until it is used to make better marketing decisions. Thus, the marketing information system must make the data available to the managers and others who make marketing decisions or deal with customers daily. In some cases, this means providing managers with regular performance reports, intelligence updates, and reports on the results of research studies.

But marketing managers may also need non-routine information for special situations and on-the-spot decisions. For example, a sales manager having trouble with a large customer may want a summary of the account's sales and profitability over the past year. Or a retail store manager who has run out of a best-selling product may want to know the current inventory levels in the chain's other stores. Increasingly, therefore, information distribution involves entering information into databases and making these available in a user-friendly and timely way. The CRM systems described above are valuable tools to accomplish this goal.

Thanks to modern technology, today's marketing managers can usually access their company's information systems, including the marketing information systems and CRM systems, from their desktop or laptop computer. Marketing managers can obtain information from company databases or outside information services, analyze the information using statistical packages and models, prepare reports using word processing and presentation software, and communicate with others in the network through electronic communications. Such systems allow managers to get the information they need directly and quickly and to tailor it to their own needs.

Conversely, Cake Beauty, for example, uses a back-end customer relationship management system to allow customers to register online, track their purchases, send confirmation emails, and manage the information about customer purchases. Customers can view their account information online and communicate with customer service representatives at the company.

In addition, companies are increasingly allowing key customers and value-network members to access account and product information on *extranets*. Suppliers, customers, and select other network members may access a company's extranet to update their accounts, arrange purchases, and check orders against inventories to improve customer service. For example, one insurance firm allows its 200 independent agents access to a Web-based database of claim information covering 1 million customers. This allows the agents to avoid high-risk customers and to compare claim data with their own customer databases. And Wal-Mart's Retail Link system provides suppliers with up to two years' worth of data on how their products have sold in Wal-Mart stores.[17]

OTHER MARKETING INFORMATION CONSIDERATIONS

This section discusses marketing information in two special contexts: marketing research in small businesses and nonprofit organizations, and international marketing research. To close the chapter, we look at public policy and ethics issues in marketing research.

Marketing Research in Small Businesses and Nonprofit Organizations

Just like their larger counterparts, small organizations need market information. Start-up businesses need information about their industries, competitors, potential customers, and reactions to new market offers. Existing small businesses must track changes in customer needs and wants, reactions to new products, and changes in the competitive environment.

Managers of small businesses and nonprofit organizations often think that marketing research can be done only by experts in large companies with big research budgets. Although large-scale research studies are beyond the budgets of most small businesses, many of the marketing research techniques discussed in this chapter can also be used by smaller organizations in a less formal manner and at little or no expense.

Managers of small businesses and nonprofit organizations can obtain good marketing information simply by observing things around them. For example, retailers can evaluate new locations by *observing* vehicle and pedestrian traffic. They can monitor competitor advertising by collecting ads from local media. They can evaluate their customer mix by recording how many and what kinds of customers shop in the store at different times. In addition, many small business managers routinely visit their rivals and socialize with competitors to gain insights.

Managers can conduct informal *surveys* using small convenience samples. The director of an art museum can learn what patrons think about new exhibits by conducting informal focus groups—inviting small groups to lunch and having discussions on topics of interest. Retail salespeople can talk with customers visiting the store; hospital officials can interview patients. Restaurant managers might make random phone calls during slack hours to interview consumers about where they eat out and what they think of various restaurants in the area. Cake Beauty used an online survey to determine the key selling points of its products (providing information about the points to emphasize in Cake's marketing material), the magazines most often read by their customers (providing information about the media outlets most likely to deliver Cake's marketing message to their target market), and the kinds of new products their customers would like them to create (providing information about new product lines for Cake to consider). To encourage consumers to take part in the survey, Cake entered each respondent's name in a draw for a year's supply of Satin Sugar Hair and Body Refreshing Powder.

Managers also can conduct their own simple *experiments*. For example, by changing the themes in regular fundraising mailings and watching the results, a nonprofit manager can find out much about which marketing strategies work best. By varying newspaper advertisements, a store manager can learn the effects of such things as increasing or decreasing the ad size, moving the position of an ad, including price coupons, and using different types of media.

Small organizations can obtain most of the secondary data available to large businesses. In addition, many associations, local media, chambers of commerce, and government agencies provide special help to small organizations. The Confederation of Independent Business represents more than 100 000 small businesses in Canada and

Industry Canada's Strategis site offers a broad range of information related to establishing and managing a small business, including market research information and links.

provides advice on topics ranging from starting, financing, and expanding a small business to ordering business cards. Another excellent Web resource for small businesses is the Canada Revenue Agency's *Guide for Canadian Small Businesses,* which helps explain everything from setting up a business to importing and exporting regulations and excise taxes. As well, Industry Canada's Strategis site offers a broad range of information related to establishing and managing a small business.

There are also private companies that specialize in consulting and providing information for small businesses, much of it free. One such organization is GDSourcing. The company's website explains its mission clearly: "to help Canadian entrepreneurs with limited research budgets assess their market potential and performance."

The business sections at local libraries can also be a good source of information. They often provide business periodicals as well as access to resources such as the *Financial Post*'s *Canadian Markets, Scott's Directories,* and *Standard and Poor's Industry Surveys* for U.S.-based companies. Local newspapers may provide information on local shoppers and their buying patterns. Finally, small businesses can collect a considerable amount of information at very little cost on the Internet. They can scour competitor and customer websites and use Internet search engines to research specific companies and issues.

In summary, secondary data collection, observation, surveys, and experiments can all be used effectively by small organizations with small budgets. Although these informal research methods are less complex and less costly, they still must be conducted carefully. Managers must think carefully about the objectives of the research, formulate questions in advance, recognize the biases introduced by smaller samples and less skilled researchers, and conduct the research systematically.[18]

International Marketing Research

International marketing researchers follow the same steps as domestic researchers, from defining the research problem and developing a research plan to interpreting and reporting the results. However, these researchers often face more and different problems. Whereas domestic researchers deal with homogeneous markets within a single country, international researchers deal with differing markets in many different countries. These markets often vary greatly in their levels of economic development, cultures and customs, and buying patterns.

In many foreign markets, the international researcher sometimes has a difficult time finding good secondary data. Whereas Canadian marketing researchers can obtain reliable secondary data from dozens of domestic research services, many countries have almost no research services at all.

Because of the scarcity of good secondary data, international researchers often must collect their own primary data. Here again, researchers face problems not found domestically. For example, they may find it difficult simply to develop good samples. And once the sample is drawn, reaching respondents may be difficult. In some countries, few people have phones; for example, there are only 32 phones per thousand people in Argentina. In other countries, like Brazil, the postal system is notoriously unreliable. In many developing countries, poor roads and transportation systems make certain areas hard to reach, making personal interviews difficult and expensive. Finally, few people in developing countries are connected to the Internet.[19]

Cultural differences from country to country cause additional problems for international researchers. Language is the most obvious obstacle. Translating a questionnaire from one language to another is anything but easy. Many idioms, phrases, and statements mean different things in different cultures. For example, a Danish executive suggests that all materials should be checked "by having a different translator put back into English what you've translated from English. You'll get the shock of your life. I remember [an example in which] 'out of sight, out of mind' had become 'invisible things are insane.'"[20]

Consumers in different countries also vary in their attitudes toward marketing research. People in one country may be very willing to respond; in other countries, nonresponse is a major problem. Customs in some countries may prohibit people from talking with strangers. In certain cultures, research questions are often considered too personal. For example, in many Latin American countries, people may feel embarrassed to talk with researchers about their choices of shampoo, deodorant, or other personal care products. Even when respondents are *willing* to respond, they may not be *able* to because of high illiteracy rates.

Despite these problems, the recent growth of international marketing has resulted in a rapid increase in the use of international marketing research. Global companies have little choice but to conduct such research. Although the costs and problems associated with international research may be high, the costs of not doing it—in terms of missed opportunities and mistakes—might be even higher. Once recognized, many of the problems associated with international marketing research can be overcome or avoided.

Public Policy and Ethics in Marketing Research

Most marketing research benefits both the sponsoring company and its consumers. Through marketing research, companies learn more about consumers' needs, resulting in more satisfying products and services. More than 7 million Canadians take part in surveys each year and more than two-thirds of Canadians have participated at some time in a research study and found it a pleasant experience. In fact, 83 percent believe that participation in survey research gives them an opportunity to provide useful feedback to organizations. However, a growing number of Canadians (57 percent) find survey questions too personal.[21]

While many consumers feel positively about marketing research, others strongly resent and even mistrust it. A few consumers fear that researchers might use sophisticated techniques to probe their deepest feelings and then use this knowledge to manipulate their buying. Some are further concerned about the character of the individual to whom they are divulging the information. Some Canadians had a right to be concerned. In 2003, Correctional Services Canada terminated its controversial call centre program, based in three federal penitentiaries. The program offered market research and telemarketing services to private sector clients, but the Solicitor-General ended it after it a number of security breaches were discovered.[22]

Some of the largest international research services operate in many countries. Roper Starch Worldwide provides companies with information resources "from Brazil to Eastern Europe to Cape Town to Beijing."

Fifty-two percent of Canadians state that they have been taken in by previous "research surveys" that actually turned out to be attempts to sell them something. Still others confuse legitimate marketing research studies with telemarketing efforts and say no before an interviewer can even begin. Most, however, simply resent the intrusion. They dislike mail or telephone surveys that are too long, that ask too many personal questions, or that interrupt them at inconvenient times.[23]

With response rates falling throughout North America, increasing consumer resentment has become a major problem for the research industry. It's considering several options for responding to the problem. One is to expand its "Your Opinion Counts" program to educate consumers about the benefits of marketing research and to distinguish it from telephone selling and database building. Another is to provide a toll-free number that people can call to verify that a survey is legitimate.

To guard against inappropriate or harmful research practices in Canada, both the Canadian Marketing Association and the Professional Marketing Research Society (PMRS) publish codes of conduct. Several principles provide the foundation of the code. First is the importance of acting professionally and ensuring that methods used to address research questions are valid and reliable. Next are principles for dealing with research subjects. Subjects are not to be exposed to any risk or harm because of their participation in the research, their voluntary cooperation for participation in the research study must be sought, and their consent attained. Both organizations' codes deal with two major concerns: (1) intrusions on consumer privacy and (2) the misuse of research findings.

Intrusions on Customer Privacy Many consumers worry about the privacy of their personal information and fear that marketers are building huge databases without their knowledge or permission. For example, DoubleClick, a New York–based advertising firm, has profiles of 100 million Web users. Privacy groups have expressed concerns about the possibility of merging such information with offline databases, resulting in a threat to individual privacy. In fact, DoubleClick did combine its data (collected from the browsing habits of individuals viewing its online advertisements) with consumer profiles belonging to another organization, and constructed frighteningly accurate profiles of online consumer behaviour. It stirred up much controversy in Canada and the U.S. when it was announced that DoubleClick would sell about 100 000 of these Web-user profiles to businesses, complete with names and contact information. David Jones, president of Electronic Frontier Canada in Kitchener, Ontario, says that what made DoubleClick's practice especially dubious is that it went on without the consumer being aware of it. "There is not the usual knowledge and consent you should have when someone is collecting personal information." Fearing government investigation and class-action lawsuits, DoubleClick adopted sweeping privacy standards.[24]

Canada's *Personal Information Protection and Electronic Documents Act,* Bill C–6, came into full effect in January 2004. This new law helped resolve many concerns about personal privacy. Under its provisions, organizations must state the reasons why they are collecting information. They must first obtain consumers' consent before they can collect, use, or transfer information about an individual, and they must limit the information collected to the purpose they state at the beginning of the collection process. Moreover, every organization must appoint a privacy officer to ensure compliance with the legislation and to field consumer inquiries and complaints. Organizations also have to ensure that the information they collect is accurate and, upon request, they must

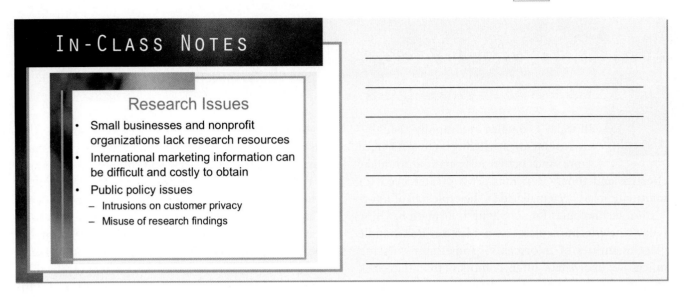

IN-CLASS NOTES

Research Issues

- Small businesses and nonprofit organizations lack research resources
- International marketing information can be difficult and costly to obtain
- Public policy issues
  - Intrusions on customer privacy
  - Misuse of research findings

inform the individual about the information they have on the individual and give him or her access to that information.[25]

In the end, if researchers provide value in exchange for information, customers will gladly supply it. For example, Amazon's customers do not mind if the firm builds a database of individual customer purchases in order to make personalized future product recommendations. This saves the customer time and adds value. Similarly, Bizrate users complete surveys rating online retailers because they have access to the overall ratings of others when making purchase decisions.

Misuse of Research Findings Research studies can be powerful persuasion tools—companies often use study results as claims in their advertising and promotion. Today, however, many research studies appear to be little more than vehicles for pitching the sponsor's products. Few advertisers openly rig their research designs or blatantly misrepresent the findings—most abuses tend to be subtle "stretches." Consider these examples:[26]

- ☐ A study by Chrysler contends that Americans overwhelmingly prefer Chrysler to Toyota after test driving both. However, the study included only 100 people in each of two tests. More important, none of the people surveyed owned a foreign car, so they appear to be favourably predisposed to American produced cars.

- ☐ A poll sponsored by the disposable diaper industry asked: "It is estimated that disposable diapers account for less than 2 percent of the garbage in today's landfills. In contrast, beverage containers, third-class mail, and yard waste are estimated to account for about 21 percent of the garbage in landfills. Given this, in your opinion, would it be fair to ban disposable diapers?" Not surprisingly, 84 percent said no.

Thus, subtle manipulations of the study's sample, or the choice or wording of questions, can greatly affect the conclusions reached. In other cases, so-called independent research studies are paid for by companies with an interest in the outcome.

Each company must accept responsibility for policing the conduct and reporting of its own marketing research to protect consumers' best interests and its own.

LOOKING BACK

In today's complex and rapidly changing environment, marketing managers need more and better information to make effective and timely decisions. This greater need for information has been matched by the explosion of information technologies for supplying information. Using today's new technologies, companies can now handle great quantities of information, sometimes even too much. Yet marketers often complain that they lack enough of the *right* kind of information or have an excess of the *wrong* kind. In response, many companies are now studying their managers' information needs and designing systems that help managers develop and manage market and customer information.

In the previous chapter we discussed the marketing environment. In this chapter, you've studied tools used to gather and manage information that marketing managers and others can use to assess opportunities in the environment and the impact of a firm's marketing efforts. In the next chapter we'll take a closer look at the object of all this activity—the buying behaviour of both consumers and businesses.

REVIEWING THE CONCEPTS

1. Explain the importance of information to the company.

Good products and marketing programs start with a complete understanding of customer needs and wants. Thus, the company needs sound information to produce superior value and satisfaction for customers. The company also requires information on competitors, resellers, and other actors and forces in the marketplace. Increasingly, marketers are viewing information not only as an input for making better decisions but also as an important strategic asset and marketing tool.

2. Define the marketing information system and discuss its parts.

The *marketing information system* consists of people, equipment, and procedures to gather, sort, analyze, evaluate, and distribute needed, timely, and accurate information to marketing decision makers. A well-designed information system begins and ends with users. It first *assesses information needs,* then *develops information* from internal databases, marketing intelligence activities, and marketing research. *Internal databases* provide infor-

mation on the company's own sales, costs, inventories, cash flows, and accounts receivable and payable. Such data can be obtained quickly and cheaply but often need to be adapted for marketing decisions. *Marketing intelligence* activities supply everyday information about developments in the external marketing environment. *Market research* consists of collecting information relevant to a specific marketing problem faced by the company. Lastly, the system *distributes information* gathered from these sources to the right managers in the right form and at the right time to help them make better marketing decisions.

3. Outline the steps in the marketing research process.

The first step in the marketing research process involves *defining the problem and setting the research objectives,* which may be exploratory, descriptive, or causal research. The second step consists of *developing a research plan* for collecting data from primary and secondary sources. The third step calls for *implementing the marketing research plan* by gathering, processing, and analyzing the information. The fourth step consists of *interpreting and reporting the findings.* Additional information analysis helps marketing managers use the information and provides them with sophisticated statistical procedures and models from which to develop more rigorous findings.

Both *internal* and *external* secondary data sources often provide information more quickly and at a lower cost than primary data sources, and they can sometimes yield information that a company cannot collect by itself. However, needed information might not exist in secondary sources, and even if data can be found, they might be largely unusable. Researchers must also evaluate secondary information to ensure that it is *relevant, accurate, current,* and *impartial.* Primary research must also be evaluated for these features. Each primary data collection method—*observational, survey,* and *experiment*—has its own advantages and disadvantages. Each of the various primary research contact methods—mail, telephone, personal interview, and online—also has its own advantages and drawbacks. Similarly, each contact method has its pluses and minuses.

4. Explain how companies analyze and distribute marketing information.

Information gathered in internal databases and through marketing intelligence and marketing research usually requires more analysis. This may include advanced statistical analysis or the application of analytical models that will help marketers make better decisions. In recent years, marketers have paid special attention to the analysis of individual customer data. Many companies have now acquired or developed special software and analysis techniques—called *customer relationship management (CRM)*—that integrate, analyze, and apply the mountains of individual customer data contained in their databases.

Marketing information has no value until it is used to make better marketing decisions. Thus, the marketing information system must make the information available to the managers and others who make marketing decisions or deal with customers. In some cases, this means providing regular reports and updates; in other cases it means making nonroutine information available for special situations and on-the-spot decisions. Thanks to modern technology, today's marketing managers can gain direct access to the information system at any time and from virtually any location.

5. Discuss the special issues some marketing researchers face, including public policy and ethics issues.

Some marketers face special marketing research situations, such as those conducting research in small business, nonprofit, or international situations. Marketing research can be conducted effectively by small businesses and nonprofit organizations with limited budgets. International marketing researchers follow the same steps as domestic researchers but often face more and different problems. All organizations need to respond responsibly to major public policy and ethical issues surrounding marketing research, including issues of intrusions on consumer privacy and misuse of research findings.

KEY TERMS

causal research   *170*
customer relationship management
  (CRM)   *184*
descriptive research   *170*
experimental research   *176*
exploratory research   *170*

focus group   *177*
internal databases   *167*
marketing information system   *165*
marketing intelligence   *168*
marketing research   *169*
observational research   *174*

online databases   *172*
primary data   *171*
sample   *178*
secondary data   *171*
single-source data systems   *175*
survey research   *175*

STUDY GUIDE

After completing this self-test, check your answers against the Answer Key at the back of the book.

MULTIPLE CHOICE

1. As a business, the music industry's response to the Internet and file sharing has revealed them to be inflexible and unable to react when technological and cultural forces have come into play. This inability to react positively indicates a lack of awareness of
   a. Technological advances
   b. How to analyze distributor preference data
   c. Customer wants and perceptions of value
   d. Trends in CD distribution methods
   e. Historical information

2. Hurricane Katrina was a natural force that caused a temporary upheaval in the supply of oil and gasoline. Gas prices rose sharply while energy companies scrambled to overcome the market damage caused by lost production. Hurricane Katrina clearly revealed what research limitation?
   a. It is impossible to predict what information will be needed to deal with unseen future events
   b. Natural disasters can wipe out computer systems and cause the loss of data
   c. Oil production facilities are by nature placed in areas with potential for natural disasters
   d. If there is no time for proper research into an industry's problem, prices tend to rise for that product category
   e. Marketing is an unsure discipline and creativity and seat-of-the-pants thinking can replace disciplined marketing research in many cases

3. The revenue downturn that Nortel suddenly began to experience in 2000 was in large part due to the fact that information being gathered by salespeople on customers and the state of their businesses was not turning into actionable intelligence at the senior levels. This was a direct result of a failure
   a. To capture external information correctly
   b. Of Nortel's marketing information system
   c. To correctly analyze the information and its implications
   d. To pass field information to the right market intelligence groups
   e. All of the above

4. In the early 80s Coca-Cola was losing market share to Pepsi. In response, Coke made a momentous move and changed the taste of Coke in response to marketing research that seemed to reveal a preference for the taste of Pepsi. Consumer reaction was swift and negative. Coke lost even more share before reintroducing the old taste as Coke Classic. Coca-Cola's error was common; it had failed to
   a. Conduct appropriate causal research
   b. Correctly define the problem
   c. Not include primary research in the methodology
   d. Measure results consistently
   e. Include other methods to complement focus group research

5. In the summer of 2005 Tim Hortons heavily promoted its new steeped tea. While all fast-food restaurants serve tea as hot water with the bag in, Tim Hortons' research told it that its customers wanted tea that tasted as good as the coffee, removed the fuss of tea bags, and was prepared "properly." Tim Hortons likely used _____ research to understand this level of detail.
   a. Experimental
   b. Causal
   c. Secondary
   d. Ethnographic
   e. Exploratory

6. Although a long-standing fast-food menu item in Quebec, poutine did not get added to menus across Canada until relatively recently. Before launching poutine as a regular item throughout Canada, most fast-food chains tested the product in several non-francophone cities first. This type of primary research is illustrative of
   a. Controlled sampling
   b. Observational patterning
   c. Experimental research to gather causal information
   d. Mechanical observation
   e. Data mining

7. After correctly identifying the problem and research objective, the next most important aspect of a research project is knowing how to ask the right questions. In the Coleman barbeque example, Sunbeam was able to identify the "nostalgia" association with its product by asking respondents only _____ questions.
   a. Open-ended
   b. Close-ended
   c. Emotional
   d. Observational
   e. Mechanical

8. Most companies use customer relationship management systems as internal tools to analyze customer information and in turn create targeted offerings. However, smart marketers realize that CRM systems can enhance the ongoing relationship with customers even further by
   a. Ensuring that customers never need to be surveyed or otherwise questioned
   b. Providing customers with a way to easily interact with all parts of the company in a consistent, integrated fashion
   c. Providing distribution and channel partners with the same information about their mutual customers
   d. Reducing the amount of data that must be maintained and passing the storage cost savings on to customers in the form of lower prices
   e. Linking CRM systems with financial systems to implement redlining and weblining practices

9. Cognos, a leading maker of business intelligence software, maintains a vast extranet to provide product, customer, pricing, and other information to its large army of software distributor and reseller partners. What is the main reason why Cognos makes large investments to create and maintain such a software system?
   a. Because its competitors do and so Cognos must to remain competitive
   b. Because partners need to find out about customer information from Cognos
   c. Because it's the most inexpensive way to communicate with partners
   d. Because its partners are the main way Cognos sells to customers and are therefore the key link in Cognos's value delivery network
   e. Because Cognos sells business intelligence software and therefore it has to be seen as Web-savvy and as using its own software tools in its own business

10. The layout of a supermarket is deliberate. Produce and deli as you enter look good and smell good, spurring the appetite. Meat is along the back to locate the unpleasant look and odours as far away from the door as possible. Milk and bread are usually located on

opposite sides of the store so that a shopper must walk the entire length of the store for these staples. This style of layout is the result of years of

a. Supermarket shopper surveys
b. Stratified sampling
c. Causal research
d. Focus group research
e. Observational research

TRUE/FALSE

T   F   1. A company should always take advantage of any opportunity to collect raw data because it cannot predict if and when this data will be needed.

T   F   2. It is illegal and ethically wrong to share, sell, or otherwise distribute personal information about customers, but it is generally not illegal or unethical to share or sell aggregated information.

T   F   3. Probability and nonprobability samples provide the researcher with the same level of accuracy and reliability.

T   F   4. The major components of a marketing information system are databases and software analysis tools.

T   F   5. No matter how well data is properly analyzed and synthesized, information is not necessarily usable or actionable.

CONCEPT CHECK

1. A _____ consists of people, equipment, and procedures to gather, sort, analyze, evaluate, and distribute needed, timely, and accurate information to marketing decision makers.

2. The information needed by marketing managers can be obtained from _____, _____, and _____.

3. _____ is a systematic collection and analysis of publicly available information about competitors and developments in the marketing environment.

4. _____ can be defined as the systematic design, collection, analysis, and reporting of data relevant to a specific marketing situation facing an organization.

5. The marketing research process has four steps: _____, _____, _____, and _____.

6. A marketing research project might have any one of three types of objectives. If the objective were to gather preliminary information that would help define the problem and suggest hypotheses, the researcher would use _____ research.

7. _____ data consist of information collected for the specific purpose at hand.

8. Many companies now use _____ research, which combines intensive observation with customer interviews to gain deep insights into how consumers buy and use their products.

9. _____ research is the approach best suited for gathering descriptive information.

10. Of the four research contact methods discussed, _____ is the only one rated as "excellent" with respect to low cost.

11. A researcher is using a _____ sample when he or she selects the easiest population members from which to obtain information.

12. _____ consists of sophisticated software and analytical tools that integrate customer information from all sources, analyze it in depth, and use the results to build stronger customer relationships.

STUDENT MATERIALS

Visit our website at www.pearsoned.ca/armstrong for online quizzes, Internet exercises, and more!

NOTES

_____

_____

_____

_____

_____

_____

_____

_____

_____

_____

DISCUSSING THE ISSUES

1. Many companies build extensive internal databases so that marketing managers can readily access and work with information to identify marketing opportunities and problems, plan programs, and evaluate performance. If you were the marketing manager for a large computer software manufacturer, what type of information would you like to have available in your internal database? Explain.

2. Marketing intelligence has become increasingly important to marketing managers because of its ability to aid them in improving strategic decision making. What other benefits are attributed to a marketing intelligence function? Assuming that you have been hired as a consultant by a company that is developing a new highly caffeinated energy drink, what type of intelligence sleuthing tips would you offer the firm?

3. Name the type of research that would be appropriate in the following situations, and explain why:
   a. Kellogg wants to investigate the impact of young children on their parents' decisions to buy breakfast foods.
   b. Your university bookstore wants to get some insights into how students feel about the store's merchandise, prices, and service.
   c. McDonald's is considering where to locate a new outlet in a fast-growing suburb.
   d. Gillette wants to determine whether a new line of deodorant for children will be profitable.

4. Focus group interviewing is both a widely used and widely criticized research technique in marketing. List the advantages and disadvantages of focus groups. Suggest some kinds of questions that are suitable for exploration by using focus groups. How could focus group research be done via the Internet?

5. Increasingly, companies are turning to customer relationship management (CRM) as a means for integrating and applying the mountains of customer data contained in their databases. Two techniques that analysts use to aid them in applying CRM are data warehousing and data mining. Explain each term and how each is used to improve relationships and "connections." Next, assume that your local grocery store has implemented a store service card. This card allows you to receive special patronage discounts and to cash personal cheques. Beginning with the registration process for the card and moving through its final usage at the checkout stand, discuss all the types of data that could be collected on customers and how this data could eventually be used to build relationships.

MARKETING APPLICATIONS

The Canadian consumer is one of the most researched subjects in the world. Millions of dollars are spent annually to find out what you want, when you want it, and how much you will pay for it. Becoming intimate with consumers is not a luxury, it is a necessity. The desire to become a closer companion to the customer has spurred interest in ethnographic research—which combines intensive observation with customer interviews (see Marketing at Work 5.1 for more details). However, this form of research can often be an expensive pursuit for a company.

Is there a lower cost alternative? Some in marketing believe that one of the oldest forms of research—the consumer poll—is the answer. At one time polling was expensive and often seriously inaccurate. What if the researcher could, however, get the advantages of participatory information results combined with low cost? If this were possible, it would be of great interest. Well, hold onto your questionnaires, the Internet has provided the answer—the online poll.

Although often not scientifically accurate, the online poll has become a great way to get large amounts of preferential information from an interested audience at a low cost. Trends do reveal themselves and, unlike normal polling, those who participate can be recontacted by an interested marketer because a trail is left on the Internet. Ask someone a question in a shopping mall and then he or she is gone. On the Internet this same consumer can be recontacted at a later date with a variety of messages. In fact, many do not mind the recontact at all—it is a "connection" they actually desire. Have you been polled lately? If you want to participate in our society and marketplace, isn't it about time that you were?

THINKING LIKE A MARKETING MANAGER

Websites such as PollingReport.com and The Gallup Organization's www.gallup.com publish the results of some of their polls and questionnaires online. Visit their sites and view some of their poll results.

1. If you were a marketing manager preparing for the launch of a new packaged snack food, which of these polls, if any, would be of interest to you?
2. The vice president of marketing has asked you to set up an online poll on your company's website to conduct market research into the viability of this new packaged snack food. Specify the research objectives of your poll, and develop 10 questions to be asked of visitors to your website.

VIDEO CASE

Go to Pearson Canada's Video Central site (www.pearsoned.ca/highered/videocentral) to view the video and accompanying case for this chapter.

CASE 5 "SLIM CAL": RESEARCHING THE POTENTIAL

Canadians are obsessed with losing weight. Whether it's the Atkins diet, the South Beach diet, or Dr. Phil McGraw's Ultimate Weight Loss Solution, it seems like everyone is on a diet. The website eDiet, which offers a wide variety of weight loss plans personalized to the individual, is so popular that it was the "Number 1 visited Health, Fitness & Nutrition Site," according to research published by Nielsen/NetRatings in April 2004.

In November 2004 AC Nielsen of Canada conducted their first annual weight loss survey. The results indicated that more than half of Canadian adults went on a diet in the first half of 2004. The most popular methods for weight loss were eating smaller portions (26 percent of respondents), low-fat dieting (15 percent), and low-carb dieting (12 percent). The study further indicated that 92 percent of the respondents were "very" or "somewhat" concerned about the health risks of saturated fats and 91 percent were concerned about trans-fatty acids and obesity. Respondents to the survey were also asked what they were doing to alleviate these concerns. The results indicate that 56 percent were cutting back on fat consumption, 47 percent were cutting back on sugar, and 34 percent were cutting salt and sugar intake. Surprisingly, despite the popularity of the low-carb Atkins and related diet programs, the study found that only 26 percent of respondents were lowering their carbohydrate intake.

Major packaged goods companies have responded to the weight-loss trend in a variety of ways. Unilever, the manufacturer of an old diet standby, Slim-Fast, was one of the first companies to commit to the low-carb trend in a major way by launching Carb Options. This comprehensive line of low-carb, low-fat products includes everything from peanut butter to chips to nutrition bars and shakes and condiments. Kraft

Foods offers a "Healthy Living" section on its website that provides a carb-counter and ways to limit carbs while still enjoying many of Kraft's famous brands. The major soft-drink companies continue to offer diet versions of their most popular brands. And in the fall of 2004, General Mills announced that all its major cereal lines would be made with whole grains. The initiative included new packaging with bold, attention-getting "Whole Grain" labelling on every cereal box. Even venerable Snapple, best known for its bottled teas and fruit drinks, has launched a meal replacement beverage called Snapple-A-Day.

In this highly competitive and constantly changing market, how does a small company with a meal replacement concept increase its chances of success?

The company, Symbiotics Ltd., has developed a product called the Slim Cal bar. The product has been formulated under the meal replacement regulations of the *Food and Drugs Act* of Canada. This legislation requires that meal replacements provide the body with the equivalent of a complete, nutritionally balanced meal but with lower caloric content than most regular meals. A Slim Cal bar contains all the essential elements of a complete balanced meal but with less sugar and fat. Slim Cal uses a packaging format and materials that are similar to another Canadian product, Nutribar, but at 75 grams, Slim Cal offers 10 grams more per serving.

Working on the premise that lower caloric intake is a positive contributor to weight loss, Symbiotics has decided to investigate the potential of Slim Cal in a test market. But before reaching this decision the company engaged in considerable consumer research using an external research agency. Initially, the concept of the product and the name Slim Cal were tested in focus groups—the qualitative research method that brings together a small group of consumers to discuss the product and its attributes under the guidance of a trained interviewer. The results of this research were very positive, both in terms of the brand's concept and its proposed name. Management at Symbiotics concluded that, at a minimum, further research was warranted.

The next stage of research was a Pre Market Test (PMT). Personal interviews were conducted with consumers about usage behaviour and attitudes concerning meal replacement products such as bars and shakes. Respondents were exposed to the mock-ups of the product, the packaging, and some proposed print advertising that connected the use of Slim Cal with healthy weight loss. Then the survey respondents were given an opportunity to participate in the next stage of the research, which was actual, in-home usage. Participants used two flavours of Slim Cal—a peanut butter flavour with a crunchy coating and a smooth, yogurt-coated "MultiBerry" flavour—for eight weeks. Respondents were then contacted by telephone and, via a questionnaire, asked about their attitude toward the product, their usage of the product, and their intention to purchase. This quantitative data was incorporated into computer models that included elements of Slim Cal's proposed marketing plan, including pricing, advertising, and distribution intensity. The final output from this stage provided estimates of household trial rates, repeat purchase rates, and average units purchased.

These figures in turn resulted in a first-year sales estimate that indicated the product had solid sales potential. And so, with favourable research results in hand, the decision was made to move Slim Cal into a test market.

Questions

1. What information would you expect Symbiotics Ltd. to have gathered from secondary sources before deciding to develop Slim Cal?

2. What research approach, contact methods, and research instruments were used by Symbiotics in their primary data collection?

3. Develop a research plan for the test market.

4. Aside from the test market, what other means could Symbiotics use to gather information about the likelihood that Slim Cal will succeed?

Sources: www.ckn-inc.com; www.ediets.com/start.cfm?code=17201&media=blank; www.kraftcanada. com/controller?cmd=ARTICLE_VIEW&lang=EN&aid=65008&sid=65005&ctx=2000; www.generalmills. com/corporate/media_center/news_release_detail.aspx?itemID=6816&catID=227; www.carboptions. com, www.nutribar.com, www.powerbar.com; Stephanie Thompson, "Unilever Hedges Bet on Low-Carb Craze," QwikFind ID:AAP78E, Adage Dataplace, July 1, 2004; www.snappleaday.com; www.statcan. ca/Daily/English/041014/d041014d.htm, accessed December 2004.

After reading this chapter, you should be able to

1. *1.* understand the consumer market and the major factors that influence consumer buyer behaviour

2. *2.* identify and discuss the stages in the consumer buyer decision process

3. *3.* describe the adoption and diffusion process for new products

4. *4.* define the business market and identify the major factors that influence business buyer behaviour

5. *5.* list and define the steps in the business buying-decision process

Consumer and Business Buyer Behaviour

6

Looking Ahead

In the previous chapter, you studied how marketers obtain, analyze, and use information to identify marketing opportunities and to assess marketing programs. In this chapter, you'll take a closer look at the most important element of the marketing environment—customers. The aim of marketing is to somehow affect how customers think about and behave toward the organization and its marketing offers. To affect the whats, whens, and hows of buying behaviour, marketers must first understand the *whys*. We look first at *consumer* buying influences and processes and then at the buying behaviour of *business customers*. You'll see that understanding buying behaviour is an essential but very difficult task.

What makes an individual choose one car brand over another? Price is, of course, an important consideration in the buying decision process, but within every price range there are many cars the consumer might choose from. Understanding what makes a consumer choose, say, a Volkswagen Golf instead of a Saturn Ion can make the difference between the success and failure of a new car model. That's why it's so important for auto makers to understand consumer behaviour.

While most automobile manufacturers around the world continue to do what they've done for nearly 100 years—develop new and improved versions of their gasoline and diesel powered cars—one company has jumped out of the box and captured a market segment that the others don't seem to know exists. The Toyota Prius, a hybrid car that runs on both gasoline and electricity, is turning out to be exactly what today's savvy, environmentally conscious consumers want.

The Prius has been in development at Toyota since 1995, when it was code-named 89OT and was the first car to be designed with a hybrid system that combines an internal combustion engine with an electric motor. The company's business-case strategy for 89OT called for all the design and engineering to be done in-house: no partnerships, no contractors, and no suppliers of major components. At a time when most vehicle manufacturers were doing just the opposite, outsourcing as much as possible, Toyota's strategic marketing team felt that the wisest move was for them to do their own product development.

The car was first available in Japan in 1997 and came to the U.S. in 2000. The American market responded with "record-shattering sales," and two years later Toyota announced it would increase production by 31 percent in order to meet consumer demand. Its fast-rising success culminated in the Toyota Prius being named *Motor Trend*'s Car of the Year for 2004. The second generation Prius has 370 patents under its hood. "It's intellectual property transformed into physical product, which is clearly a competitive advantage in the market," says *Motor Trend* magazine.

But consumers don't care about patents; they care about the benefits they get from the car they drive. Consumers want a "real car," not a science project. The second-generation Prius delivers more car for the same price—it's slightly larger, and now falls into the midsize rather than the compact category. It has the lowest emissions of any car on the market, and when the car isn't moving, the engine isn't running. There's more horsepower as a result of a permanent magnet electric motor. And it's the only car on the market that offers consumers a serious alternative propulsion. This car is ready to be driven on the road. It's taken the ideal of alternative fuel and made it a reality for consumers, who do not want to be laboratory mice for auto manufacturers.

The Prius is overwhelmingly popular with movie stars and environmental activists—and with consumers who aspire to be like them. It appeals to geek chic with its high back end and flashy computerized dashboard. "The Prius is a fashion statement," says one expert who studies car buying trends. "It looks different. Other people know the driver is driving a hybrid vehicle. It clearly makes a statement about the person."

"Automobile culture has always been about status," says another expert on popular culture. "With the Prius, you're bringing attention to yourself . . . saying, 'I bought something upscale, something people will talk about.' It is a conversation piece, an attention-getter."

The success of the Prius has sent other car manufacturers scrambling to bring a copycat to market. Toyota's alternative engine, now referred to as the Hybrid Synergy Drive, will be put into an SUV variant of Toyota's upscale Lexus brand, and there are plans to license the technology to other manufacturers. The consumers have spoken, and the automobile manufacturers are listening. According to *Motor Trend*, "The future of the auto industry is not going to be more of the same. It is not going to be the past repackaged."[1]

TEST YOURSELF

Answers to these questions can be found on our website at www.pearsoned.ca/armstrong.

1. Why did Toyota's strategists believe that it was best to do their own product development, including even manufacturing their own components?
   a) Because this technology was so new that no one else could make the parts
   b) Because they would keep it secret and be the first to market, since over time consumers tend to remember the first brand most
   c) Because it was cheaper for Toyota to make everything in-house rather than outsource
   d) Because Toyota always does all its own development in-house, for all their models and makes
   e) Because most companies that provide parts or services to car manufacturers are in North America, and this project was begun in Japan

2. Why would the many patents that Toyota won while creating the Prius be a competitive advantage?
   a) Because consumers tend to trust only those technologies that are heavily patented
   b) Because Toyota received a great deal of publicity as a result of their many successful patents
   c) Because the patents allow Toyota to charge a large price premium for the Prius
   d) Because it prevents other car companies from copying Toyota's technology and so keeps the Prius brand in the forefront of consumers' minds longer
   e) All of the above

3. Why is it so important to Prius's sales success that the car be popular with celebrities?
   a) Because the celebrities were all located in the California area, the first state in which Toyota launched the Prius
   b) Because all these celebrities did endorsements for Toyota Prius in TV commercials
   c) Because celebrities tend to have a lot of money and were willing to pay top dollar for the cars
   d) Because Toyota didn't believe they had a winner until celebrities began to purchase the car
   e) Because when consumers select product brands, they frequently identify with and try to emulate certain celebrities

4. The unique outside design and the flashy dashboard design is distinctive. Why has this look been important to Prius's success?
   a) Because buyers choose cars partly based on status, and the distinctive look instantly proclaims the driver as a trendy, environmentally sensitive owner
   b) Because it makes the car very easy to spot on dealership lots
   c) Because Toyota had originally designed the shape and look of the car for their high-end Lexus line
   d) Because this kind of look is highly popular and common in Japan but unusual in North America
   e) Because as Toyota did all the manufacturing themselves, they could custom-design the car more easily

5. Which of the following best describes the Toyota Prius buyer?
   a) Those who are most concerned about trends and fashion
   b) Those who try out new technologies the instant they're available
   c) Those who are practical but adopt new technologies if they offer a clear benefit
   d) Those who take a "wait and see" attitude to new products
   e) Those who are most influenced by the brands that celebrities prefer

As a marketing manager there is no more important task than knowing who your customers are and trying to understand why they behave the way they do. What influences an organization's customers to make the choices they make is never simple, yet understanding it is the essential task of marketing management. Every organization that markets a product or service does so with a group of customers in mind. Those customers may be other businesses or they may be consumers, or both. But when choosing which pair of shoes, or package of noodles, or car to buy, the choices that *you* make as a consumer are very different from the choices a business buyer must make. In this chapter we explore the dynamics of the consumer market and introduce a model for understanding consumer buyer behaviour. We then examine business markets and the business buying process.

THE CONSUMER MARKET

Consumer buyer behaviour The buying behaviour of consumers—individuals who buy goods and services for their own use or consumption.

Consumer market All individuals in a particular geographic region, who are old enough to have their own money and to choose how to spend it.

Consumer buyer behaviour refers to the buying behaviour of consumers, that is, individuals who buy goods and services for their own use or *consumption*. All individuals, therefore, who are old enough to have their own money and to choose how to spend it, are consumers. Together, they make up the **consumer market**. The Canadian consumer market comprises more than 30 million people who consume billions of dollars' worth of goods and services each year, making it a very attractive market indeed. And the world consumer market comprises more than 6 *billion* people.

Consumers around the world vary tremendously in age, income, education level, and tastes. They also buy an incredible variety of goods and services. How these diverse consumers connect with each other and with other elements of the world around them affects their choices among various goods, services, and companies. Here we examine the fascinating array of factors that affect consumer behaviour.

Model of Consumer Behaviour

Consumers make many buying decisions every day. Most large companies that market consumer products research their target markets in great detail to answer questions about what consumers buy, where they buy, how and how much they buy, when they buy, and why they buy. Marketers can study actual consumer purchases to find out what they buy, where, and how much. But learning about the *whys* of consumer buying behaviour is not so easy—the answers are often locked deep within the consumer's head.

The central question for marketers is this: How do consumers respond to various marketing efforts the company might use? The starting point is the stimulus–response model of buyer behaviour shown in Figure 6.1. This figure shows that marketing and other stimuli enter the consumer's "black box"—that is, the part of the brain that simply takes in and records information—and produce certain responses. Marketing stimuli consist of the four Ps: product, price, place, and promotion. Other stimuli include major forces and events in the buyer's environment: economic, technological, political, and cultural. All these inputs enter the buyer's black box, where they are turned into a set of observable buyer responses: product choice, brand choice, dealer choice, purchase timing, and purchase amount.

Figure 6.1 Model of Buyer Behaviour

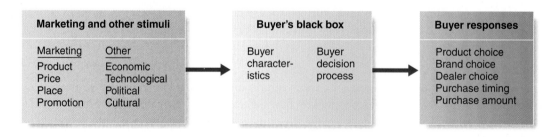

The marketer wants to understand how the stimuli are changed into responses inside the consumer's black box, which has two parts. First, the buyer's characteristics influence how he or she perceives and reacts to the stimuli. Second, the buyer's decision process itself affects the buyer's behaviour. We look first at buyer characteristics as they affect buying behaviour and then discuss the buyer decision process.

Characteristics Affecting Consumer Behaviour

Consumer purchases are influenced strongly by cultural, social, personal, and psychological characteristics, as shown in Figure 6.2. For the most part, marketers cannot control such factors, but they must consider them. To help you understand these concepts, we apply them to the case of a hypothetical consumer—Jennifer Wong, a 26-year-old brand manager working for a multinational packaged-goods company in Toronto. Jennifer was born in Vancouver, but her grandparents came from Hong Kong. She's been in a relationship for two years but isn't married. She has decided that she wants to buy a vehicle but isn't sure she wants to buy a car. She rode a motor scooter while attending university and is now considering buying a motorcycle—maybe even a Harley.

Figure 6.2 Factors Influencing Consumer Behaviour

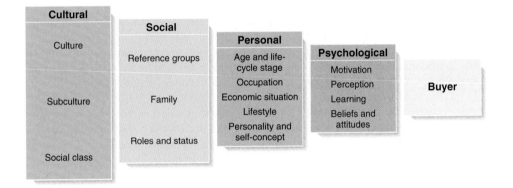

Cultural Factors Cultural factors exert a broad and deep influence on consumer behaviour. The marketer needs to understand the role played by the buyer's *culture, subculture,* and *social class*.

Culture. Culture is the set of basic values, perceptions, wants, and behaviours learned by a member of society from family and other important institutions. As human behaviour is largely learned, culture is the most basic cause of a person's wants and behaviour. Jennifer Wong's cultural background will certainly affect her motorcycle-buying decision. After all, her desire to own a Harley may well result from her being raised in a modern society that has developed motorcycle technology—as well as a whole set of consumer learnings and values.

Maclean's magazine has conducted 20 annual polls of Canadian values and attitudes. They show some core consistencies. For example, the majority of Canadians noted that symbols of our uniqueness include our freedom, the beauty of our natural landscape, our beliefs in respect, equality and fair treatment, our flag, the achievement of prominent Canadians such as artists and scientists, our social safety net, our international role, and our multicultural and multiracial makeup.[2]

Another recent study outlined some other basic values shared by Canadians: "Canada is a country that believes in freedom, dignity, respect, equality and fair treatment, and opportunity to participate. It is a country that cares for the disadvantaged at home and elsewhere, a country that prefers peaceful solutions to disputes. Canada is a country that, for all its diversity, has shared values."[3]

Canadians still see government as the leader in the fight to protect unique Canadian values from the inroads of American influence. Respect for diversity has also long been part of our heritage. Canada had three founding nations: Aboriginal people, Great

Culture The set of basic values, perceptions, wants, and behaviours learned by a member of society from family and other important institutions.

Britain, and France. More than 4 million Canadians report that they can speak both English and French. The proportion of francophones who are bilingual is almost five times that of anglophones who are bilingual. Not surprisingly, Quebec has the largest number of bilingual Canadians (35 percent). New Brunswick is the second most bilingual province.[4] Marketing in Quebec requires marketers to take into account the unique characteristics of Quebec culture (see Marketing at Work 6.1).

Marketing at Work | 6.1

Marketing to Quebec and French-Canadian Consumers

Quebec prides itself on being a "distinct society." And so marketers who want to appeal to Quebec consumers need to do more than communicate in French. They must understand the values, attitudes, and behaviours that are unique to the Quebec population.

Marketers must be aware that Quebec has its own icons and unique media personalities. For example, Bell Canada's long-running Monsieur B campaign is almost unknown in the rest of Canada. However, it has approached legendary status in the province, the way other advertising icons like the Green Giant, Aunt Jemima, and the lonely Maytag repairman have done in the rest of Canada. The Ford Motor Company of Canada also found that it needed Quebec stars if it was to have an impact on the marketplace. During its summer sell-down, Ford used the Tina Turner song "Simply the Best" for its campaign in English-speaking Canada. After discovering that the song didn't resonate in Quebec, Ford used two very prominent Quebec actors—Guy A. Lepage and Sylvie Leonard—in its Quebec campaign.

Quebec also has a distinct business and retail climate. When Home Depot entered the province in 2000, it was faced with a set of competitors different from those in the rest of Canada. Réno-Dépôt and RONA had a loyal set of customers in Quebec. To help Home Depot gain acceptance, Montreal-based Cossette Communications developed an advertising campaign that appealed to Quebecers' unique sense of humour. Rather than creating ads that proclaimed Home Depot's high-quality service, Cossette conducted qualitative research to uncover examples of Quebec consumers' bad shopping experiences. The resulting campaign featured one commercial that showed a clerk literally running away from a client, while in a second ad, a group of clerks chanted, "It is not my department" despite clients' looks of dismay. The campaign not only created awareness of Home Depot, but was listed among Montrealers' favourites in a recent survey.

For a long time, Quebec lagged behind the rest of Canada in terms of Internet adoption and usage. Today, however, more than 60 percent of Quebec adults are online. And there are a growing number of French sites and online services, such as La Toile du Québec, InfinIT, and Le Petit Monde, as well as the French versions of popular portals like Sympatico, Yahoo!, and MSN. Marketers have been quick to leverage this new interconnectivity. Volkswagen, Avon, L'Oréal, and La Senza are some of the Quebec-based companies that have jumped on the bandwagon and are building French versions of their company websites.

Sources: Bernadette Johnson "E-mail Marketing Begins to Flourish in La Belle Province," *Strategy,* May 20, 2002, p. D 10; Sara Minoque, "Sunny Economy Predicted to Grow Spending," *Strategy,* January 13, 2003, p. 10; Nancy Carr, "Does a Distinct Society Need Distinct Creative?" *Strategy,* April 9, 2001, p. 13; Canada Online, "2001 Census Statistics on Languages in Canada," http://canadaonline.about.com/cs/statistics/a/stat-slang.htm#b, accessed June 12, 2003; Helena Katz, "Johnson Sharpens Its Quebec Strategy," *Marketing,* October 12, 1998, p. 3; Retail Council of Canada, "Kids Rule for Back-to-School This Year" (press release), August 30, 2001; Shawna Steinberg, "Only in English Canada, You Say?" *Marketing,* November 12, 1998, p. 10; Danny Kucharsky, "Monsieur's Family," *Marketing,* June 11, 2001, www.marketingmag.ca; Nathalie Fortier, "Building Success: How Cossette Poked Fun at Bad Customer Service to Give Home Depot a Firm Foundation in Quebec," *Marketing,* September 24, 2001, www.marketingmag.ca; Tracey Arial, "Taking Aim at the Giants," *Marketing,* June 11, 2001, www.marketingmag.ca; Government of Quebec website, www.gouv.qc.ca, accessed June 5, 2002).

Marketers are always trying to spot *cultural shifts* in order to discover new products. For example, the cultural shift toward greater concern about health and fitness has created a huge industry for health and fitness services, exercise equipment and clothing, and lower-fat and more natural foods. The shift toward informality has resulted in more demand for casual clothing and simpler home furnishings.

Subculture A group of people with shared value systems based on common life experiences and situations.

Subculture. Each culture contains smaller **subcultures**, or groups of people with shared value systems based on common life experiences and situations. Subcultures include nationalities, religions, racial groups, and geographic regions. Many subcultures make up important market segments, and marketers often design products and marketing programs tailored to their needs. Native Canadians, ethnic consumers, and Internet users are just three of Canada's important subcultures:

1. *Native Canadians.* Native Canadians are making their voices heard both in the political arena and in the marketplace. There are approximately 983 000 Aboriginal Canadians, including Métis and Inuit. Not only do Native Canadians have distinct cultures that influence their values and purchasing behaviour, but they have also profoundly influenced the rest of Canada through their art, appreciation of nature, and concern for the environment.

Banks have been particularly responsive to the unique needs of Aboriginal Canadians. Scotiabank, for example, has maintained its relationship with First Nations people through its three on-reserve branches and 24 Aboriginal banking centres. It also uses grassroots marketing and public relations efforts, including its sponsorship of the Aboriginal Achievement Awards and 10 annual scholarships of $2500 for young Aboriginal entrepreneurs.

2. *Canada's ethnic consumers.* Consumers from ethnic groups represent some of the fastest-growing markets in Canada. In Toronto, for example, the number of Spanish-speaking people has doubled to 250 000 in five years. In Canada today, there are 100 different ethnic groups and they account for billions in consumer spending. And marketing to ethnic communities isn't just an issue for marketers working in Vancouver, Toronto, and Montreal. Even smaller centres, such as Ottawa, Edmonton, and Calgary, have growing ethnic populations. The Canadian Advertising Foundation suggests that visible minorities have as much as $300 billion in purchasing power.[5]

Many ethnic groups believe that they have been neglected or misrepresented by marketers. A Canadian Advertising Foundation study revealed that 80 percent of people belonging to visible minorities believed that advertising has been targeted almost exclusively at "white" people. Yet 46 percent of this group stated that they would be more likely to buy a product if its advertising featured models from visible minority populations.[6]

Let's consider our hypothetical consumer. How will Jennifer Wong's cultural background influence her decision about whether to buy a motorcycle? Jennifer's parents certainly won't approve of her choice. Tied strongly to the values of thrift and conservatism, they believe that she should continue taking the subway instead of purchasing a vehicle. However, Jennifer identifies with her Canadian friends and colleagues as much as she does with her family. She views herself as a modern woman in a society that accepts women in a wide range of roles, both conventional and unconventional. She has female friends who play hockey and rugby. And women riding motorcycles are becoming a more common sight in Toronto.

3. *Internet users.* How does being part of the Internet generation affect Jennifer Wong and her purchase decision? Jennifer is highly computer literate. She uses a computer daily at work, carries a laptop when attending meetings, and has a computer in her apartment. One of the first things she did when considering a motorcycle purchase was to log on to the Internet. She learned a great deal simply by browsing the sites of such manufacturers as Honda, Yamaha, and Harley-Davidson. She especially liked the Harley site and the annual events listed for Harley owners. She was concerned that most of these events took place in the United States, however. Using their response button, she requested information on dealers in her area and information about specific models. Jennifer also found several chat groups and posted questions to members of these groups, especially female riders.

Social Class. Almost every society has some form of social class structure. **Social classes** are society's relatively permanent and ordered divisions of a society into groups whose members share similar values, interests, and behaviours. Social class is determined by a

Social classes Relatively permanent and ordered divisions of a society into groups whose members share similar values, interests, and behaviours

combination of occupation, income, education, wealth, and other variables. In some social systems, members of different classes are reared for certain roles and cannot change their social positions. In Canada, however, the lines between social classes are not fixed and rigid: People can move to a higher social class or drop into a lower one. Marketers are interested in social class because people within a given social class tend to exhibit similar buying behaviour, showing distinct product and brand preferences in areas such as clothing, home furnishings, leisure activity, and automobiles. See Table 6.1 for the Canadian perspective.

Table 6.1 Characteristics of Seven Major Canadian Social Classes

The Upper Class (3 to 5 percent)

Upper uppers (less than 1 percent)	Upper uppers are the social elite who live on inherited wealth and have well-established family backgrounds. They give large sums to charity, own more than one home, and send their children to the finest schools. They are accustomed to wealth and often buy and dress conservatively rather than showing off their wealth.
Lower uppers (about 2 to 4 percent)	Lower uppers have earned high income or wealth through exceptional ability in the professions or business. They usually begin in the middle class. They tend to be active in social and civic affairs and buy for themselves and their children the symbols of status, such as expensive homes, educations, and automobiles. They want to be accepted in the upper-upper stratum, a status more likely to be achieved by their children than by themselves.

The Middle Class (40 to 50 percent)

Upper middles	Upper middles possess neither family status nor unusual wealth. They have attained positions as professionals, independent businesspersons, and corporate managers. They have a keen interest in attaining the "better things in life." They believe in education and want their children to develop professional or administrative skills. They are joiners and highly civic-minded.
Average middles	The middle class is made up of average-pay white- and blue-collar workers who live on the "better side of town" and try to "do the proper things." To keep up with the trends, they often buy products that are popular. Most are concerned with fashion, seeking the better brand names. Better living means owning a nice home in a nice neighbourhood with good schools.

The Working Class (about 33 percent) — The working class consists of those who lead a "working-class lifestyle," whatever their income, school background, or job. They depend heavily on relatives for economic and emotional support, for advice on purchases, and for assistance in times of trouble.

The Lower Class (about 20 percent)

Upper lowers	Upper lowers are working (are not on welfare), although their living standard is just above poverty. Although they strive toward a higher class, they often lack education and perform unskilled work for poor pay.
Lower lowers	Lower lowers are visibly poor. They are often poorly educated and work as unskilled labourers. However, they are often out of work and some depend on public assistance. They tend to live a day-to-day existence.

Sources: Richard P. Coleman, "The Continuing Significance of Social Class to Marketing," *Journal of Consumer Research,* December 1983, pp. 265–280. © Journal of Consumer Research, Inc., 1983; Leon G. Shiffman and Leslie Lazar Kanuk, *Consumer Behavior,* 6th ed. (Upper Saddle River, N.J.: Prentice Hall, 1997), p. 388; Linda P. Morton, "Segmenting Publics by Social Class," *Public Relations Quarterly,* Summer 1999, pp. 45–46; John Macionis and Linda Gerber, *Sociology,* 4th Canadian ed. (Toronto: Pearson Education Canada, 2002), pp. 276–280.

Jennifer Wong's social class may affect her motorcycle decision. Jennifer finds herself frequently buying brand-name products that are fashionable and popular with her friends and extended family.

Social Factors A consumer's behaviour is also influenced by social factors, such as membership in *small groups* and *family,* and *social roles* and *status.*

Groups. A person's behaviour is influenced by many small groups. A **group** consists of two or more people who interact to accomplish individual or mutual goals. Groups that have a direct influence and to which a person belongs are called *membership groups.* Some are *primary groups* with which a person has regular but informal interaction—such as family, friends, neighbours, and co-workers. A person also has less regular interaction with the more formal *secondary groups*—organizations such as religious groups, professional associations, and trade unions.

Reference groups serve as direct (face-to-face) or indirect points of comparison or reference in forming a person's attitudes or behaviour. People are often influenced by reference groups to which they do not belong. For example, an *aspirational group* is one to which the individual wants or aspires to belong. For example, a teenage hockey player hopes to play someday for the Toronto Maple Leafs: He identifies with this group, although there is no face-to-face contact between him and the team. Marketers try to identify the reference groups of their target markets. Reference groups expose a person to new behaviours and lifestyles, influence the person's attitudes and self-concept, and create pressures to conform that may affect the person's product and brand choices.

The importance of group influence varies across products and brands. It tends to be strongest when the product is visible to others whom the buyer respects. Purchases of products that are bought and used privately are not much affected by group influences because neither the product nor the brand will be noticed by others. Manufacturers of products and brands subjected to strong group influence must figure out how to reach **opinion leaders**, people within a reference group who, because of special skills, knowledge, personality, or other characteristics, exert influence on others.

For example, actress Kate Hudson acted as an opinion leader for young women, the consumer market for Cake Beauty's products. When, in 2002, Ms. Hudson stated in a magazine interview that she was planning to give all her friends some "Cake" as part of their Christmas presents, young women who read that magazine, and who admired Ms. Hudson and secretly (or not so secretly) wished they could be like her, might have been influenced to purchase Cake products.

Many marketers try to identify opinion leaders for their products so that they can direct marketing efforts toward them. In other cases, they create advertisements to simulate opinion leadership, thereby reducing the need for consumers to seek advice from others. For example, the hottest trends in teenage music, language, and fashion often start in Canada in major cities then quickly spread to more mainstream youth in the suburbs. Thus, clothing companies that hope to appeal to these fickle and fashion-conscious youth often make a concerted effort to monitor urban opinion leaders' style and behaviour. In other cases, marketers may use buzz marketing, which targets opinion leaders and gets them talking about it to their friends.

Family. Marketers have extensively researched the family, the most important consumer buying organization in society. Since family members can have a strong influence on buyer behaviour, marketers are interested in the roles and influence of the husband, wife, and children on the purchase of different products and services.

Husband–wife involvement depends on product category and on stage in the buying process. Buying roles change with evolving consumer lifestyles. In Canada and the United States, the wife has traditionally been the main purchasing agent for the family,

Group Two or more people who interact to accomplish individual or mutual goals.

Opinion leader A person within a reference group who, because of special skills, knowledge, personality, or other characteristics, exerts influence on others.

especially for food, household products, and clothing. But with 70 percent of women holding jobs outside the home and the willingness of husbands to do more of the family's purchasing, this is changing. For example, women now make or influence 80 percent of car buying decisions and men account for about 40 percent of food-shopping dollars.[7] Such changes in family buying behaviour suggest that marketers who've typically sold their products to only women or only men are now courting the opposite sex. For example, with research showing that women now account for nearly half of all hardware store purchases, home improvement retailers such as Home Depot have turned the once intimidating warehouses into female-friendly outlets that offer bridal registries.

Children can also have a strong influence on family buying decisions. Chevrolet recognizes these influences in marketing its Chevy Venture minivan:

> In an issue of *Sports Illustrated for Kids,* which attracts mostly 8- to 14-year-old boys, the inside cover featured a brightly coloured two-page spread for the Chevy Venture to woo [what it calls] "back-seat consumers." [GM] is sending the minivan into malls and showing previews of Disney's *Hercules* on a VCR inside. "We're kidding ourselves when we think kids aren't aware of brands," says [Venture's brand manager], adding that even she was surprised at how often parents told her that kids played a tie-breaking role in deciding which car to buy.[8]

In the case of expensive products and services, husbands and wives more often make joint decisions. Although Jennifer isn't married, her boyfriend will influence her choice. He purchased a motorcycle last year and loves it. Since he rarely lets Jennifer drive it, she really relates to the slogan on Harley-Davidson ads that feature women proclaiming, "You never took a back seat before!"

Roles and Status. A person belongs to many groups: family, clubs, organizations. The person's position in each group can be defined in terms of both role and status. A *role* comprises the activities that others expect from the person. Each role carries a *status* reflecting the general esteem that society gives it. People often choose products that show their status in society. Jennifer Wong occupies many roles simultaneously. In her role as a daughter, she has lower status than her parents and grandparents, so she often acquiesces to their opinions with respect to family matters. In her role as a brand manager, Jennifer

Children can have a strong influence on family buying decisions. Chevrolet actively woos these "back-seat consumers" with carefully targeted advertising and a Chevy Venture Warner Bros. Edition, complete with a DVD player.

has high status and assumes a leadership role in her brand group. Jennifer also wants to be a leader in her social activities and often organizes group activities. Her desire to be a leader causes her to identify with leading status brands such as Harley-Davidson.

Personal Factors A buyer's decisions are also influenced by personal characteristics such as the buyer's *age and life-cycle stage, occupation, economic situation, lifestyle,* and *personality and self-concept.*

Age and Life-Cycle Stage. People change their preferences in the goods and services they buy over their lifetimes. Tastes in food, clothes, furniture, and recreation are often age related. Buying is also shaped by the stage of the *family life cycle*—the stages through which families might pass as they mature over time. Marketers often define their target markets in terms of life-cycle stage and develop appropriate products and marketing plans for each stage. Traditional family life-cycle stages include young singles and married couples with children. Today, however, marketers are increasingly catering to a growing number of alternative, nontraditional stages such as unmarried couples, singles marrying later in life, childfree couples, same-sex couples, single parents, extended parents (those with young adult children returning home), and those who have recently divorced (see Marketing at Work 6.2).

Marketing at Work 6.2

Targeting Nontraditional Life Stages: Just Divorced, Gone Shopping

Divorcees used to be off limits for marketers. Not any more. Almost 40 percent of all marriages in Canada now end in divorce, down from a peak of 50.6 percent in 1987, shortly after our divorce laws were amended. With more than 70 000 couples splitting up every year and the divorce rate growing at close to 3 percent a year, there are over 1.4 million divorcees in Canada. They represent a distinct market segment in an increasingly expanding life-cycle stage.

There's no doubt that life stages are driving consumers. "They buy when they get married; they buy when they get divorced." Says Dan Couvrette, publisher of *Divorce* magazine, "Next year, at least half of the 2.4 million people who will get divorced in the United States and Canada are going to buy new beds. That's over a million people. You can't find a bigger niche."

Divorcees don't just buy out of necessity; the shopping cure can ease the pain. People going through a

divorce, Couvrette says, "represent a tremendous market potential because they'll spend money to get stuff that makes them feel better." Couvrette

adds, "Even those who suffer financial setbacks—often the case with women leaving long-term marriages—try to treat themselves to the best they can

Life-stage marketing: Marketers are discovering that when couples split, someone goes shopping. Divorcees, much like newlyweds, restock their homes with everything from pots and pans to televisions.

(continued)

afford. . . . [Some] 78 percent of the men bought new entertainment systems, while 69 percent of the women opted for new bedroom furniture."

In response to the growing market, advertisers are testing the waters. Sears launched a television featuring a once-loving couple. After separating their washer and dryer in the settlement, they pass each other in the aisles at Sears, smiling awkwardly while shopping for new appliances. "It was a humorous look at a real-life situation," says a Sears marketer.

Many marketers have shunned the divorcee segment as too downbeat. "Divorce is still a niche market with negative connotations," says one analyst. "Historically, advertisers go with more positive images. But that's going

to change in keeping with the whole trend to go after more targeted groups." Consider this example:

Montauk Sofas was among the first to run an upbeat breakup ad. A smiling woman cozies up in the embrace of a $2400 extra-plush armchair. The text begins in bold type: "He left me. Good Riddance" and ends: "Who cares . . . I kept the sofa." The ad has generated good feelings for Montauk, a Montreal-based furniture manufacturer. "We've gotten an excellent reaction from all walks of life and ages," said Tim Zyto, the owner of Montauk. "Women especially like it. They find it empowering."

Couvrette of *Divorce* magazine thinks it's only a matter of time before the once-taboo D-word comes to stand for "divorce registry." "It's not going to be called a divorce registry," he predicts, "but everyone's going to know that's what it's for."

Sources: Excerpts and quotes from Julie V. Iovine, "Just Divorced, Gone Shopping," *New York Times*, July 12, 2001, p. F1; Pamela Sebastian Ridge, "Tool Sellers Tap Their Feminine Side," *Wall Street Journal*, March 29, 2002, p. B1; Family Facts Canada, "More Canadians Divorcing—StatCan" (news release), December 4–5, 2002, www.fotf.ca/familyfacts/tfn/2002/120402.html; Statistics Canada, "Divorces, 1999 and 2000," *The Daily*, December 2, 2002, www.statcan.ca/Daily/English/021202/td021202. htm; DivorceMagazine.com, "Canadian Divorce Statistics (1998)," www.divorcemag.com/statistics/statsCAN.shtml, accessed June 20, 2003.

Sony recently overhauled its marketing approach in order to target products and services to consumers based on their life stages. It created a new unit called the Consumer Segment Marketing Division, which has identified seven life-cycle segments. They include, among others, Gen Y (under 25), Young Professionals (aged 25–34), Families (35 to 54), and Zoomers (55 and older). Sony's goal is to create brand loyalty early on and to develop long-term relationships. "The goal is to get closer to consumers," says one Sony executive.[9]

Occupation. People's occupations affect the goods and services they buy. Blue-collar workers tend to buy more rugged work clothes, whereas executives buy more business suits. Marketers try to identify the occupational groups that have an above-average interest in their products and services. A company can even specialize in making products needed by a given occupational group. Thus, computer software companies will design different products for brand managers, accountants, engineers, lawyers, and doctors.

Economic Situation. A person's economic situation will affect product choice. Marketers of income-sensitive goods watch trends in personal income, savings, and interest rates. If economic indicators point to a recession, marketers can take steps to redesign, reposition, and reprice their products.

Lifestyle. People coming from the same subculture, social class, and occupation may have quite different lifestyles. A **lifestyle** is a person's pattern of living as expressed in his or her *psychographics*. It involves measuring consumers' major *AIO dimensions: activities* (work, hobbies, shopping, sports, social events), *interests* (food, fashion, family, recreation), and *opinions* (about themselves, social issues, business, products). Lifestyle captures something more than the person's social class or personality. It profiles a person's whole pattern of acting and interacting in the world.

Several research firms have developed lifestyle classifications. The most widely used is the SRI Consulting's *Values and Lifestyles (VALS)* typology. VALS classifies people according to how they spend their time and money. It divides consumers into eight groups based on two major dimensions: self-orientation and resources. Self-orientation

Lifestyle A person's pattern of living as expressed in his or her activities, interests, and opinions.

groups include principle-oriented consumers who buy based on their views of the world; status-oriented buyers who base their purchases on the actions and opinions of others; and action-oriented buyers who are driven by their desire for activity, variety, and risk-taking.

Lifestyle segmentation can also be used to understand Internet behaviour. Forrester developed its "Technographics" scheme, which segments consumers according to motivation, desire, and ability to invest in technology.[10] The framework splits people into 10 categories, such as:

☐ *Fast Forwards:* The biggest spenders on computer technology. Fast Forwards are early adopters of new technology for home, office, and personal use.

☐ *Mouse Potatoes:* Consumers who are dedicated to interactive entertainment and willing to spend for the latest in "technotainment."

☐ *Handshakers:* Older consumers, typically managers, who don't touch computers at work and leave that to younger assistants.

These lifestyle classifications are by no means universal—they can vary significantly among countries. Michael Adams, president of Environics Research Group Ltd., wrote *Sex in the Snow: Canadian Social Values at the End of the Millennium* to capture significant psychographic changes in the Canadian marketplace. He believes that psychographic changes eclipse demographic factors among Canadians. While his classification system begins with demographic factors, he divides the Canadian population along age-based lines into three groups: elders, baby boomers, and Generation Xers. Furthermore, he asserts that 11 value-based "tribes" exist within these broader groups. Table 6.2 provides descriptions of these groups.

When used carefully, the lifestyle concept can help the marketer understand changing consumer values and how they affect buying behaviour. Jennifer Wong falls into Michael Adams's psychographic category of thrill-seeking materialists. Since she values material possessions, recognition, and the idea of living dangerously, owning a motorcycle instead of a traditional car appeals to her. Since her personality is outgoing, daring, and active, she will favour a mode of transportation that projects the same qualities.

Personality and Self-Concept. Each person's distinct personality influences his or her buying behaviour. *Personality* refers to the unique psychological characteristics that lead to relatively consistent and lasting responses to one's own environment. Personality is usually described in terms of traits such as self-confidence, dominance, sociability, autonomy, defensiveness, adaptability, and aggressiveness. Personality can be useful in analyzing consumer behaviour for certain product or brand choices. For example, coffee marketers have discovered that heavy coffee drinkers tend to be high on sociability. Thus, to attract customers, Starbucks, Timothy's, Second Cup, and other coffeehouses create environments in which people can relax and socialize over a cup of steaming coffee.

The idea is that brands have personalities, and that consumers are likely to choose brands whose personalities match their own. A brand personality is the specific mix of human traits that may be attributed to a particular brand. One researcher identifies five brand-personality traits:[11]

Heavy coffee drinkers tend to be high on sociability, so coffeehouses create environments in which people can relax and socialize over a cup of steaming coffee.

Table 6.2 The Social Value Groups of Canada

Groups	% Pop. & Size	Motivators	Values	Exemplar
The Elders:				
Rational Traditionalists	15% 3.5M	Financial independence, stability, and security.	Value safety, reason, tradition, and authority. Religious.	Winston Churchill
Extroverted Traditionalists	7% 1.7M	Traditional communities and institutions.	Value tradition, duty, family, and institutions. Religious.	Jean Chrétien
Cosmopolitan Modernists	6% 1.4M	Traditional institutions. Nomadic, experience-seeking.	Education, affluence, innovation, progress, self-confidence, world perspective.	Pierre Trudeau
The Boomers:				
Disengaged Darwinists	18% 4.3M	Financial independence, stability, and security.	Self-preservation, nostalgia for the past.	Ralph Klein
Autonomous Rebels	10% 2.4M	Personal autonomy, self-fulfillment, and new experiences.	Egalitarian; abhor corruption; personal fulfillment; education. Suspicion of authority and big government.	Michael Moore (*Bowling for Columbine*)
Connected Enthusiasts	6% 1.4M	Traditional and new communities; experience-seeking.	Family, community, hedonism, immediate gratification.	Madonna
Anxious Communitarians	9% 2.1M	Traditional communities, big government, and social status.	Family, community, generosity, duty. Needs self-respect. Fearful.	Oprah Winfrey
The Gen-Xers:				
Aimless Dependents	8% 1.9M	Financial independence, stability, security.	Desire for independence. Disengagement. Fearful.	Eminem, Courtney Love, the Osbournes
Thrill-Seeking Materialists	7% 1.7M	Traditional communities, social status, experience-seeking.	Money, material possessions, recognition, living dangerously.	Richard Branson (Virgin Inc.), *Survivor* participants
Autonomous Postmaterialists	6% 1.4M	Personal autonomy and self-fulfillment.	Freedom, human rights, egalitarian, quality of life.	Naomi Klein (author of *No Logo*), Bono of U2
Social Hedonists	4% 9M	Experience-seeking, new communities.	Esthetics, hedonism, sexual freedom, instant gratification.	Samantha (Kim Cattrall's character on *Sex and the City*)
New Aquarians	4% 9M	Experience-seeking, new communities.	Ecologism, hedonism.	Phoebe (from *Friends*), Sarah McLachlan

Sources: Adapted from Michael Adams, *Sex in the Snow: Canadian Social Values at the End of the Millennium* (Toronto: Viking, 1997), pp. 203–217. See also Michael Adams, "The Demise of Demography," *Globe and Mail*, January 8, 1997, p. D5; and Ann Walmsley, "Canadian Specific," *Report on Business*, March 1997, pp. 15–16.

1. Sincerity (down to earth, honest, wholesome, and cheerful)

2. Excitement (daring, spirited, imaginative, and up to date)

3. Competence (reliable, intelligent, and successful)

4. Sophistication (upper class and charming)

5. Ruggedness (outdoorsy and tough)

The researcher found that a number of well-known brands tended to be strongly associated with one particular trait: Levi's with "ruggedness," MTV with "excitement," CNN with "competence," and Campbell's with "sincerity."

Many marketers use a concept related to personality—a person's *self-concept* (also called *self-image*). The basic self-concept premise is that people's possessions contribute to and reflect their identities; that is, "We are what we have." Thus, to understand consumer behaviour, the marketer must first understand the relationship between consumer self-concept and possessions. For example, the founder and chief executive of Barnes & Noble, one of the largest booksellers in the United States, notes that people buy books to support their self-images:

> People have the mistaken notion that the thing you do with books is read them. Wrong . . . . People buy books for what the purchase says about them—their taste, their cultivation, their trendiness. Their aim . . . is to connect themselves, or those to whom they give the books as gifts, with all the other refined owners of Edgar Allan Poe collections or sensitive owners of Virginia Woolf collections. . . . [The result is that] you can sell books as consumer products, with seductive displays, flashy posters, an emphasis on the glamour of the book, and the fashionableness of the bestseller and the trendy author.[12]

Psychological Factors A person's buying choices are further influenced by four major psychological factors: *motivation, perception, learning,* and *beliefs* and *attitudes.*

Motivation. We know that Jennifer Wong is interested in buying a motorcycle. Why? What is she *really* seeking? What *need* is she trying to satisfy?

A person has many needs at any given time. Some are *biological,* arising from states of tension such as hunger, thirst, or discomfort. Others are *psychological,* arising from the need for recognition, esteem, or belonging. A need becomes a *motive* when it is aroused to a sufficient level of intensity. A **motive (or drive)** is a need that is sufficiently pressing to direct the person to seek satisfaction. Psychologists have developed theories of human motivation. Two of the most popular—the theories of Sigmund Freud and Abraham Maslow—have quite different meanings for consumer analysis and marketing.

Sigmund Freud assumed that people are largely unconscious of the real psychological forces shaping their behaviour. He saw the person as growing up and repressing many urges. These urges are never eliminated or under perfect control; they emerge in dreams, in slips of the tongue, in neurotic and obsessive behaviour, or in psychoses. Thus, Freud suggested that a person does not fully understand his or her motivations. Motivation researchers collect in-depth information from small samples of consumers to uncover the deeper motives for their product choices (see Marketing at Work 6.3).

Abraham Maslow sought to explain why people are driven by particular needs at particular times. Why does one person spend much time and energy on personal safety and another on gaining the esteem of others? Maslow's answer is that human needs are arranged in a hierarchy, as shown in Figure 6.3, from the most pressing at the bottom to

Motive (drive) A need that is sufficiently pressing to direct the person to seek satisfaction of the need.

the least pressing at the top. They include *physiological* needs, *safety* needs, *social* needs, *esteem* needs, and *self-actualization* needs. A person tries to satisfy the most important need first. When that need is satisfied, it will stop being a motivator and the person will then try to satisfy the next most important need. For example, starving people (physiological need) will not take an interest in the latest happenings in the art world (self-actualization needs), nor in how they are seen or esteemed by others (social or esteem needs), nor even in whether they are breathing clean air (safety needs). But as each important need is satisfied, the next most important need will come into play.

Marketing at Work | 6.3

"Touchy-Feely" Research: Psyching Out Consumers

Consumers often don't know or can't describe why they act as they do. Thus, motivation researchers use a variety of probing techniques to uncover underlying emotions and attitudes toward brands and buying situations. These techniques range from free association and inkblot interpretation tests to having consumers form daydreams and fantasies about brands or buying situations.

Shell Oil used motivation research in an attempt to uncover possible reasons behind a decade-long sales slump:

The manager of corporate advertising for Shell Oil, Sixtus Oeschle, called in a consumer researcher who specializes in focus groups conducted under hypnosis. The researcher hypnotized the respondents back to their infancy and asked them about their early experiences in gas stations. After the respondents awoke out of their trance, the researcher asked them whom they'd prefer as a gasoline purveyor. Oeschle says, "What staggered me was that, to a person, it was always linked to that experience in their youth."

Shell is now designing new marketing approaches based on the insights gleaned from the mesmerized motorists. Where Shell had gone wrong, it seems, was in reasoning that, since people don't start buying gas until at least age 16, there was no need to target the tiniest con-

sumers. "They weren't even on Shell's radar," Oeschle laments. "It dawned on us . . . that we'd better figure out how to favourably impact people from an early age."

Similarly, DaimlerChrysler used a dose of deep motivation research to create a successful new concept car:

DaimlerChrysler hired psychologist Clothaire Rapaille to probe consumers' innermost feelings. Rather than convening traditional focus groups, Rapaille used a method known as "archetype research." He had participants lie on soft mats, listen to mood music, and free-associate in the dark.

The PT Cruiser: The phenomenally successful retro style car that's "part 1920s gangster car, part 1950s hot rod, and part London taxicab"—an actual chrome-and-sheet-metal incarnation of the popular will.

(continued)

From this exercise, Rapaille discovered that many of the participants yearned for a time when things seemed simpler and more secure, and when people felt good about themselves. "What that said to us is that people are looking for something that offers protection on the outside, and comfort on the inside. We communicated that to our design team."

The result: the PT Cruiser, DaimlerChrysler's phenomenally successful retro-style car. The PT Cruiser is what one analyst calls "a focus group on wheels—an actual chrome-and-sheet-metal incarnation of the popular will."

Its nostalgic look and protective exterior inspires an emotional reaction from almost everyone. In just two years following its introduction, North American consumers snapped up more than 225,000 PT Cruisers.

Some marketers dismiss such motivation research as mumbo jumbo. However, like Shell and DaimlerChrysler, many companies are now delving into the murky depths of the consumer subconscious. "Such tactics have been worshipfully embraced by even the no-nonsense, jut-jawed captains of industry," claims an analyst. "At companies like Kraft, Coca-Cola, Procter & Gamble, and

DaimlerChrysler, the most sought-after consultants hail not from [traditional consulting firms like McKinsey. They come] from brand consultancies with names like Archetype Discoveries, PsychoLogics, and Semiotic Solutions."

Sources: Ruth Shalit, "The Return of the Hidden Persuaders," *Salon,* September 27, 1999, www.salon.com; Annetta Miller and Dody Tsiantar, "Psyching Out Consumers," *Newsweek,* February 27, 1989, pp. 46–47; Gerry Khermouch, "Consumers in the Mist," *Business Week,* February 26, 2001, pp. 92–94; Alison Stein Wellner, "Research on a Shoestring," *American Demographics,* April 2001, pp. 38–39; Phil Patton, "Car Shrinks," *Fortune,* March 18, 2002, pp. 187–190; "PT Cruiser," *Journal of Business and Design,* Corporate Design Foundation website, www.cdf.org, accessed June 2002.

Figure 6.3   Maslow's Hierarchy of Needs

Source: Adapted from Abraham H. Maslow, *Motivation and Personality,* 2nd ed. © Abraham H. Maslow, 1970. Reprinted by permission of Harper & Row, Publishers, Inc. Reprinted by permission of Addison Wesley Educational Publishers, Inc. Also see Barbara Marx Hubbard, "Seeking Our Future Potentials," *The Futurist,* May 1998, pp. 29–32.

What light does Maslow's theory throw on Jennifer Wong's interest in buying a motorcycle? We can guess that Jennifer has satisfied her physiological, safety, and social needs; they do not motivate her interest in motorcycles. Her interest may come from a strong need for more esteem from others. Or it may come from a need for self-actualization—she may want to be a daring person and express herself through product ownership.

Perception. A motivated person is ready to act. How the person acts is influenced by his or her own perception of the situation. We all learn by using the flow of information through our five senses: sight, hearing, smell, touch, and taste. However, we each receive, organize, and interpret this sensory information in an individual way. **Perception** is the process by which people select, organize, and interpret information to form a meaningful picture of the world.

Perception The process by which people select, organize, and interpret information to form a meaningful picture of the world.

People can form different perceptions of the same stimulus because of three perceptual processes: selective attention, selective distortion, and selective retention. People are exposed to a great amount of stimuli every day. For example, the average person may be exposed to more than 5000 ads in a single day.[13] It is impossible for a person to pay attention to all these stimuli. *Selective attention*—the tendency for people to screen out most of the information to which they are exposed—means that marketers have to work especially hard to attract the consumer's attention.

Even noted stimuli do not always come across in the intended way. Each person fits incoming information into an existing mindset. *Selective distortion* describes the tendency of people to interpret information in a way that will support what they already believe. Selective distortion means that marketers must try to understand the mindsets of consumers and how these will affect interpretations of advertising and sales information.

People also will forget much of what they learn. They tend to retain information that supports their attitudes and beliefs. Because of *selective retention*, Jennifer is likely to remember good points made about Harleys and to forget good points made about competing motorcycles. Because of selective exposure, distortion, and retention, marketers have to work hard to get their messages through. This fact explains why marketers use so much drama and repetition in sending messages to their market.

Learning. When people act, they learn. **Learning** describes changes in an individual's behaviour arising from experience. Learning theorists say that most human behaviour is learned. Learning occurs through the interplay of *drives, stimuli, cues, responses,* and *reinforcement.*

We saw that Jennifer Wong has a drive for self-actualization. A *drive* is a strong internal stimulus that calls for action. Her drive becomes a motive when it is directed toward a particular *stimulus object,* in this case a motorcycle. Jennifer's response to the idea of buying a motorcycle is conditioned by the surrounding cues. *Cues* are minor stimuli that determine when, where, and how the person responds. Seeing motorcycles roaring along the Toronto streets, hearing about Harley's 75th anniversary special edition cycle, and receiving her boyfriend's support for buying her own motorcycle are all *cues* that can influence Jennifer's *response* to her interest in buying a motorcycle.

Suppose Jennifer buys a Harley. If she attends the company's weekend events, makes new friends, and simply enjoys riding the bike around Toronto, her decision will be reinforced. If she decides to upgrade from her first bike to a more upscale model, the probability is greater that she will buy another Harley. The practical significance for marketers of learning theory is that they can create demand for a product by associating it with strong drives, using motivating cues, and providing positive reinforcement.

Beliefs and Attitudes. Through doing and learning, people acquire beliefs and attitudes. These, in turn, influence their buying behaviour. A **belief** is a descriptive thought that a person has about something. These beliefs may be based on real knowledge, opinion, or faith, and may or may not carry an emotional charge.

Marketers are interested in the beliefs that people formulate about specific products and services, because these beliefs make up product and brand images that affect buying behaviour. If some of the beliefs are wrong and prevent purchase, the marketer will want to launch a campaign to correct them.

People have attitudes regarding religion, politics, clothes, music, food, and almost everything else. **Attitude** describes a person's relatively consistent evaluations, feelings, and tendencies toward an object or idea. Attitudes put people into a frame of mind of liking or disliking things, of moving toward or away from them. Attitudes are difficult to change. A person's attitudes fit into a pattern, and to change one attitude may require difficult adjustments in many others. Thus, a company should usually try to fit its products into existing attitudes rather than attempt to change attitudes. Of course, there are exceptions in which the great cost of trying to change attitudes may pay off handsomely.

Learning Changes in an individual's behaviour arising from experience.

Belief A descriptive thought that a person holds about something.

Attitude A person's relatively consistent evaluations, feelings, and tendencies toward an object or idea.

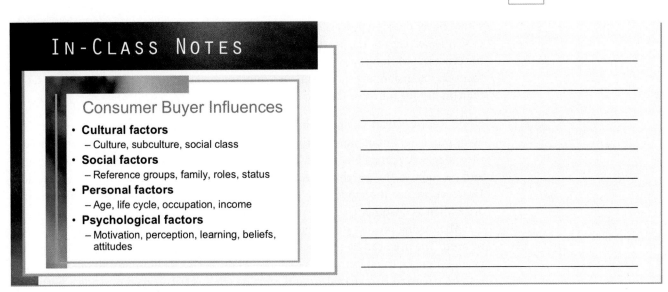

IN-CLASS NOTES

Consumer Buyer Influences

- **Cultural factors**
  - Culture, subculture, social class
- **Social factors**
  - Reference groups, family, roles, status
- **Personal factors**
  - Age, life cycle, occupation, income
- **Psychological factors**
  - Motivation, perception, learning, beliefs, attitudes

An unspoken rule in food marketing is to avoid using newspaper ads. "Given the general standard of newsprint reproduction, that tempting plate of pasta is likely to wind up with all the appetite appeal of a used muffler." But breaking the rules helped the Quebec Milk Producers (La Fédération des Producteurs de Lait du Québec) change the attitude of adults over 30 and get them back into the habit of drinking milk. And non-traditional newspaper advertising proved to be the best way to reach this older target audience on a daily basis. In contrast to other newspaper advertising that tends to be visually clamorous and overloaded with information, the Quebec Milk Producers kept their ads relatively clean and uncluttered, thus giving themselves a better shot at standing out. Since adults already knew the health benefits of milk, creators of the campaign decided to take a different tack and to play upon the consumer's emotional connection with the product. Each ad showed milk in a simple, highly recognized receptacle—a glass, jug, carton, plastic container, and a baby bottle—on a white background. Each photo was overlaid by a catchy phrase. It was these headlines—"What your inner child is thirsting for," "Remember, you used to cry for it," "The mother of all beverages"—that made an emotional connection between these adult consumers and the product. Was the campaign a success? Not only did it win five Coq d'Or awards, it was "the first time in 25 years of working in advertising that I've ever gotten so many calls and letters from people saying they love our campaign," says Nicole Dubé, director of advertising and promotions for the milk marketers at La Fédération des Producteurs de Lait du Québec.[14]

Like the Quebec adults who changed their attitudes about drinking more milk after seeing a great ad campaign, Jennifer Wong responded to the Harley ad discussed earlier in this chapter. The headline grabbed her attention. Like the women shown in the ad photo, Jennifer "never took a back seat before." She is more inclined than ever to go and buy a Harley.

We can now appreciate the many forces acting on consumer behaviour. The consumer's choice is a result of the complex interplay of cultural, social, personal, and psychological factors. Although many of these factors cannot be influenced by the marketer, they can be useful in identifying interested buyers and in shaping products and appeals to serve consumer needs better.

The Consumer Buyer Decision Process

Now that we have looked at the influences on consumer behaviour, we are ready to look at how consumers make buying decisions. Figure 6.4 shows that the con-

What your inner child is thirsting for.

The Quebec Milk Producers' newspaper campaign not only won awards, but also changed adults' attitudes toward milk.

sumer buyer decision process comprises five stages: *need recognition, information search, evaluation of alternatives, purchase decision,* and *postpurchase behaviour.* Clearly, the buying process starts long before actual purchase and continues long after. Marketers need to focus on understanding the consumer's mindset during the entire buying process rather than on just the purchase decision.

Need Recognition The figure implies that consumers pass through all five stages with every purchase. But in more routine purchases, consumers often skip or reverse some of these stages. A woman buying her regular brand of toothpaste would recognize the need and go right to the purchase decision, skipping information search and evaluation. However, we use the model in Figure 6.4 because it shows all the considerations that arise when a consumer faces a new and complex purchase situation.

The buying process starts with need recognition—the buyer recognizes a problem or need. The need can be triggered by *internal stimuli* when one of the person's normal needs—hunger, thirst, sex—rises to a level high enough to become a drive. A need can also be triggered by *external stimuli,* such as when a friend recommends a particular product. At this stage, the marketer should research consumers to find out what kinds of needs or problems arise, what brought them about, and how they led the consumer to this particular product.

Jennifer Wong might answer that she felt the need for more convenience when it came to transportation. Her office recently relocated and is no longer near a subway station. She first considered buying a car, but soon realized that parking in downtown Toronto would pose a problem. The rising cost of gas also concerned her. Thus, her focus turned to another option—a motorcycle. By gathering such information, the marketer can identify the factors that most often trigger interest in the product and can develop marketing programs that involve these factors.

Information Search An interested consumer may or may not search for more information. If the consumer's drive is strong and a satisfying product is near at hand, the consumer is likely to buy it. If not, the consumer may store the need in memory or undertake an information search related to the need. If you are in the market for a camera, you will probably pay more attention to camera ads, cameras used by friends, and camera conversations. Or you may actively look for reading material, phone friends, and gather information in other ways. The amount of searching one does will depend on the strength of their drive, the amount of information you start with, the ease of obtaining more information, the value placed on additional information, and the satisfaction one gets from searching.

The consumer can obtain information from any of several sources. These include *personal sources* (family, friends, neighbours, acquaintances), *commercial sources* (advertising, salespeople, dealers, packaging, displays), *public sources* (mass media, consumer-rating organizations), and *experiential sources* (handling, examining, using the product). The relative influence of these information sources varies with the product and the buyer. Generally, the consumer receives the most information about a product from commercial sources—those controlled by the marketer. The most effective sources, however, tend to be personal. Commercial sources normally *inform* the buyer, but personal sources *legitimize* or *evaluate* products for the buyer.

Figure 6.4   Consumer Buyer Decision Process

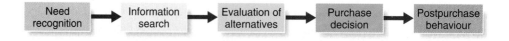

Need recognition can be triggered by advertising. This ad asks an arresting question that alerts parents to the need for a high-quality bike helmet.

As more information is obtained, the consumer's awareness and knowledge of the available brands and features increase. In her information search, Jennifer Wong learned about the many available brands of motorcycles. The information also helped her drop certain brands from consideration. A company must design its marketing mix to make prospects aware of and knowledgeable about its brand. It should carefully identify consumers' sources of information and the importance of each source. Consumers should be asked how they first heard about the brand, what information they received, and what importance they placed on different information sources.

Evaluation of Alternatives We have seen how the consumer uses information to arrive at a set of final brand choices. How does the consumer choose among the alternative brands? The marketer needs to know about alternative evaluation—that is, how the consumer processes information to arrive at brand choices. Unfortunately, consumers do not use a simple and single evaluation process in all buying situations. Instead, several evaluation processes are at work.

The consumer arrives at attitudes toward different brands through some evaluation procedure. How consumers go about evaluating purchase alternatives depends on the individual consumer and the specific buying situation. In some cases, consumers use careful calculations and logical thinking. At other times, the same consumers do little or no evaluating; instead they buy on impulse and rely on intuition. Sometimes consumers make buying decisions on their own; sometimes they turn to friends, consumer guides, or salespeople for buying advice.

Suppose Jennifer has narrowed her choices to four motorcycles. And suppose that she is primarily interested in four attributes—quality, ease of handling, ergonomic design, and price. Jennifer has formed beliefs about how each brand rates on each attribute. The marketer wants to predict which motorcycle Jennifer will buy.

Clearly, if one motorcycle rated best on all the attributes, we could predict that Jennifer would choose it. But the brands vary in appeal. Some buyers will base their buying decision on only one attribute, and their choices are easy to predict. If Jennifer wants ease of handling above everything, she will buy the motorcycle that rates highest on this attribute. But most buyers consider several attributes, each with different importance. If we knew the importance weights that Jennifer assigns to each of the four attributes, we could predict her motorcycle choice more reliably.

Marketers should study buyers to determine how they actually evaluate brand alternatives. If they know what evaluative processes go on, marketers can take steps to influence the buyer's decision. Motorcycle manufacturers that want to appeal directly to female riders can design products to appeal specifically to them. Models such as Harley's Sportster 883 Hugger are lighter in weight than some of their traditional models, with higher seats and easier handling. The company has also moved away from traditional motorcycle colours to power colours such as red. At the same time, the firm has retained traditional features such as Harley's unique engine, so "the streets never sound the same."

Purchase Decision   In the evaluation stage, the consumer ranks brands and forms purchase intentions. Generally, the consumer's purchase decision will be to buy the most preferred brand, but two factors can come between the purchase *intention* and the purchase *decision*. The first factor is the *attitudes of others*. If Jennifer's friends ride Honda motorcycles, chances of her buying a Harley will be reduced.

The second factor is *unexpected situational factors*. The consumer may form a purchase intention based on factors such as expected income, expected price, and expected product benefits. However, unexpected events may change the purchase intention. Jennifer may lose her job, some other purchase may become more urgent, or a friend may report being disappointed in her preferred motorcycle. Thus, preferences and even purchase intentions do not always result in actual purchase choice.

Postpurchase Behaviour   The marketer's job does not end when the product is bought. After purchasing the product, the consumer will be satisfied or dissatisfied and will engage in postpurchase behaviour of interest to the marketer. What determines whether the buyer is satisfied or dissatisfied with a purchase? The answer lies in the relationship between the *consumer's expectations* and the product's *perceived performance*. If the product falls short of expectations, the consumer is disappointed; if it meets expectations, the consumer is satisfied; if it exceeds expectations, the consumer is delighted.

The larger the gap between expectations and performance, the greater the consumer's dissatisfaction. This suggests that sellers should make product claims that faithfully represent the product's performance so that buyers are satisfied. Some sellers might even understate performance levels to boost consumer satisfaction with the product. For example, Boeing's salespeople tend to be conservative when they estimate the potential benefits of their aircraft. They almost always underestimate fuel efficiency—they promise a 5 percent savings that turns out to be 8 percent. Customers are delighted with better-than-expected performance; they buy again and tell other potential customers that Boeing lives up to its promises.

Cognitive dissonance Buyer discomfort caused by postpurchase conflict.

Almost all major purchases result in **cognitive dissonance**, or discomfort caused by postpurchase conflict. After the purchase, consumers are satisfied with the benefits of the chosen brand and are glad to have avoided the drawbacks of the brands not bought. However, every purchase involves compromise. Consumers feel uneasy about acquiring the drawbacks of the chosen brand and about losing the benefits of the brands not purchased. Thus, consumers feel at least some postpurchase dissonance for every purchase.[15]

Why is it so important to satisfy the customer? Such satisfaction is important because a company's sales, whether they are to consumers or to other businesses, come from two basic groups—*new customers* and *retained customers*. As discussed in Chapter 2, it usually costs more to attract new customers than to retain current ones, and the best way to retain current customers is to keep them satisfied. Customer satisfaction is a key to making lasting connections with consumers—to keeping and growing consumers and reaping their customer lifetime value. Satisfied customers buy a product again, talk favourably to others about the product, pay less attention to competing brands and advertising, and buy other products from the company.

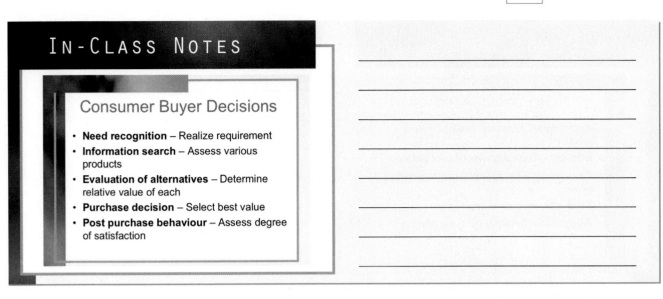

IN-CLASS NOTES

Consumer Buyer Decisions

- **Need recognition** – Realize requirement
- **Information search** – Assess various products
- **Evaluation of alternatives** – Determine relative value of each
- **Purchase decision** – Select best value
- **Post purchase behaviour** – Assess degree of satisfaction

Therefore, a company would be wise to measure customer satisfaction regularly. It cannot simply rely on dissatisfied customers to volunteer their complaints when they are dissatisfied. Some 96 percent of unhappy customers never tell the company about their problem, but they do tell other people about their bad experience. Negative word of mouth travels farther and faster than positive word of mouth and can quickly damage consumer attitudes about a company and its products. Companies should set up systems that *encourage* customers to complain. In this way, the company can learn how well it is doing and how it can improve. The 3M Company, for example, claims that over two-thirds of its new-product ideas come from listening to customer complaints. But listening is not enough—the company also must respond constructively to the complaints it receives.

By studying the overall buyer decision process, marketers may be able to find ways to help persuade potential customers to move through it, to the point of purchase. For example, if individuals are not buying a new product because they do not perceive a need for it, marketing might develop advertising messages that show *how* the product solves customers' problems, and thereby trigger a need for it. If customers know about the product but are not buying because they hold unfavourable attitudes toward it, the marketer must find ways to either change the product or change the attitudes of those potential customers.

The Consumer Buyer Decision Process for New Products

We have looked at the stages consumers go through in trying to satisfy a need. Consumers may pass quickly or slowly through these stages, and some of the stages may even be reversed. Much depends on the nature of the buyer, the product, and the buying situation.

We now look at how consumers approach the purchase of new products. A **new product** is a good, service, or idea that is perceived by some potential customers as new. It may have been around for a while, but our interest is in how consumers learn about products for the first time and make decisions about whether to adopt them. We define the **adoption process** as "the mental process through which an individual passes from first learning about an innovation to final adoption," and *adoption* as the decision by an individual to become a regular user of the product.[16]

Stages in the Adoption Process Consumers go through five stages in the process of adopting a new product:

New product A good, service, or idea that is perceived by some potential customers as new.

Adoption process The mental process through which an individual passes from first hearing about an innovation to final adoption.

IN-CLASS NOTES

New Product Adoption

- **Awareness** – Become aware of new product
- **Interest** – Seek information about product
- **Evaluation** – Decide whether trial makes sense
- **Trial** – Try product on small scale
- **Adoption** – Decide to purchase product

1. *Awareness:* The consumer becomes aware of the new product but lacks information about it.

2. *Interest:* The consumer seeks information about the new product.

3. *Evaluation:* The consumer considers whether trying the new product makes sense.

4. *Trial:* The consumer tries the new product on a small scale to improve his or her estimate of its value.

5. *Adoption:* The consumer decides to make full and regular use of the new product.

This model suggests that the new-product marketer should think about how to help consumers move through these stages. A manufacturer of flat screen televisions or home theatres may discover that many consumers in the interest stage do not move to the trial stage because of uncertainty and the large investment. If these same consumers were willing to use a flat screen television on a trial basis for a small fee, the manufacturer should consider offering a trial-use plan with an option to buy.

Individual Differences in Innovativeness People differ greatly in their readiness to try new products. In each product area, there are "consumption pioneers" and early adopters. Other individuals adopt new products much later. People can be classified into the adopter categories shown in Figure 6.5. After a slow start, an increasing number of people adopt the new product. The number of adopters reaches a peak and then drops off as fewer non-adopters remain. Innovators are defined as the first 2.5 percent of the buyers to adopt a new idea (those beyond two standard deviations from mean adoption time); the early adopters are the next 13.5 percent (between one and two standard deviations); and so forth.

The five adopter groups have differing values. *Innovators* are venturesome—they try new ideas at some risk. *Early adopters* are guided by respect—they are opinion leaders in their communities and adopt new ideas early but carefully. The *early majority* are deliberate—although they rarely are leaders, they adopt new ideas before the average person. The *late majority* are skeptical—they adopt an innovation only after a majority of people have tried it. Finally, *laggards* are tradition bound—they are suspicious of changes and adopt the innovation only when it has become something of a tradition itself.

This adopter classification suggests that an innovating firm should research the characteristics of innovators and early adopters and should direct marketing efforts toward them. In general, innovators tend to be relatively younger, better educated, and

Figure 6.5   Adopter Categorization on the Basis of Relative Time of Adoptions of Innovations

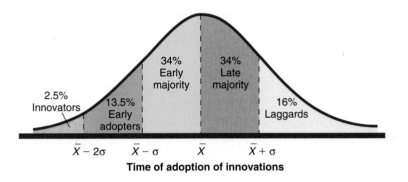

Source: Reprinted with the permission of the Free Press, a Division of Simon & Schuster, from *Diffusion of Innovations,* Fifth Edition, by Everett M. Rogers. Copyright © 2003 by The Free Press.

higher in income than later adopters and non-adopters. They are more receptive to unfamiliar things, rely more on their own values and judgment, and are more willing to take risks. They are less brand loyal and more likely to take advantage of special promotions such as discounts, coupons, and samples.

Influence of Product Characteristics on Rate of Adoption The characteristics of the new product affect its rate of adoption. Some products, like Beanie Babies, catch on almost overnight, whereas others take a long time to gain acceptance, such as high-definition television (HDTV). Five characteristics are especially important in influencing an innovation's rate of adoption. For example, consider the characteristics of HDTV in relation to the rate of adoption:

1. *Relative advantage:* The degree to which the innovation appears superior to existing products. The greater the perceived relative advantage of using HDTV—say, in picture quality and ease of viewing—the sooner such HDTVs will be adopted.

2. *Compatibility:* The degree to which the innovation fits the values and experiences of potential consumers. HDTV, for example, is highly compatible with the lifestyles found in upper-middle-class homes. However, it is not very compatible with the programming and broadcasting systems currently available to consumers.

3. *Complexity:* The degree to which the innovation is difficult to understand or use. HDTVs are not very complex and, therefore, once programming is available and prices come down, will take less time to penetrate Canadian homes than more complex innovations.

4. *Divisibility:* The degree to which the innovation may be tried on a limited basis. HDTVs are still very expensive. To the extent that people can lease them with an option to buy, their rate of adoption will increase.

5. *Communicability:* The degree to which the results of using the innovation can be observed or described to others. Because HDTV lends itself to demonstration and description, its use will spread faster among consumers.

Other characteristics influence the rate of adoption, such as initial and ongoing costs, risk and uncertainty, and social approval. The new-product marketer has to research all these factors when developing the new product and its marketing program.

IN-CLASS NOTES

Adoption Rate Influences

- **Relative advantage** – Compared to existing alternatives
- **Compatibility** – Fit with current values and experiences
- **Complexity** – Ease of understanding
- **Divisibility** – Ability to try out on limited basis
- **Communicability** – Ability to communicate benefits

Consumer Behaviour Across International Borders

Understanding consumer behaviour is difficult enough for companies marketing within the borders of a single country. For companies operating in many countries, however, understanding and serving the needs of consumers can be daunting. Although consumers in different countries may have some things in common, their values, attitudes, and behaviours often vary greatly. International marketers must understand such differences and adjust their products and marketing programs accordingly.

Sometimes the differences are obvious. For example, in Canada and the United States, where most people eat cereal regularly for breakfast, Kellogg focuses its marketing on persuading consumers to select a Kellogg brand rather than a competitor's brand. In France, however, where most people prefer croissants and coffee or no breakfast at all, Kellogg advertising simply attempts to convince people that they should eat cereal for breakfast. Its packaging includes step-by-step instructions on how to prepare cereal. In India, where many consumers eat heavy, fried breakfasts and other consumers skip the meal altogether, Kellogg's advertising attempts to convince buyers to switch to a lighter, more nutritious breakfast diet.

Often, differences across international markets are more subtle. They may result from physical differences in consumers and their environments. For example, Remington makes smaller electric shavers to fit the smaller hands of Japanese consumers and battery-powered shavers for the British market, where few bathrooms have electrical outlets. Other differences result from varying customs. In Japan, for example, where humility and deference are considered great virtues, pushy, hard-hitting sales approaches are considered offensive. Failing to understand such differences in customs and behaviours from one country to another can spell disaster for a marketer's international products and programs.

Marketers must decide on the degree to which they will adapt their products and marketing programs to meet the unique cultures and needs of consumers in various markets. On the one hand, they want to standardize their offerings to simplify operations and take advantage of cost economies. On the other hand, adapting marketing efforts within each country results in products and programs that better satisfy the needs of local consumers. The question of whether to adapt or standardize the marketing mix across international markets has created a lively debate in recent years.

Apply the concepts you've examined in the first part of this chapter.

■ Think about a specific major purchase you've made recently. What buying process did you follow? What factors influenced your decision?

■ Pick a company that we've discussed in a previous chapter—Tim Hortons, Wal-Mart, Volkswagen, Canadian Tire, or a different company. Does the company you chose understand its customers and their buying behaviour?

■ Think about Intel, which sells its computer chips to computer manufacturers such as HP and Dell, not to consumers. Do you think the buyers at HP and Dell, who decide whether to buy Intel's chips or another manufacturer's chips, behave the same way in their purchase decisions as they do when they are at home, acting as consumers? The second part of the chapter deals with this issue.

Business Markets and Business Buyer Behaviour

In one way or another, most large companies sell to other organizations. Many companies, such as Alcan Aluminum, Bombardier, Nortel, Research In Motion, and countless other firms, sell *most* of their products to other businesses. Even large consumer-products companies, which make products *used* by consumers, do not sell those products directly to consumers, and therefore must first sell them to other businesses. For example, Kraft Canada makes many familiar consumer products, including Kraft Dinner, Post cereals, Maxwell House coffee, Jell-O, Kraft Peanut Butter, and Kraft salad dressings, but when you as a consumer want to buy peanut butter you don't go shopping at Kraft's head office. Before these products can reach consumers, Kraft Canada must first sell their products to wholesalers and retailers that serve the consumer market and to specialized food service wholesalers for resale to restaurants.

Business buyer behaviour refers to the buying behaviour of all the organizations that buy goods and services for use in the production of other products and services that are sold, rented, or supplied to others. It also includes retailing and wholesaling firms that acquire goods for the purpose of reselling or renting them to others at a profit.

Business buyer behaviour The buying behaviour of organizations that buy goods and services for use in the production of other products and services that are sold, rented, or supplied to others.

Business Markets

The business market is huge. In fact, business markets involve far more dollars and items than do consumer markets. For example, think about the large number of business transactions involved in the production and sale of a single set of Michelin tires. Various suppliers sell Michelin the rubber, steel, equipment, and other goods that it needs to produce the tires. Michelin then sells the finished tires to retailers, who in turn sell them to consumers. Thus, many sets of *business* purchases were made for only one *consumer* purchase. In addition, Michelin sells tires to automobile manufacturers who install them on new vehicles; as replacement tires to companies that maintain their own fleets of company cars, trucks, buses, or other vehicles; and perhaps to the manufacturers of other wheeled vehicles, such as forklifts and backhoes, golf carts, and baby carriages.

Derived demand: Intel's long-running "Intel Inside" logo advertising campaign boosts demand for Intel chips and for the PCs containing them. Now, most computer makers feature a logo like this one in their ads.

Derived demand Business demand that ultimately comes from (derives from) the demand for consumer goods.

Characteristics of Business Markets In some ways, business markets are similar to consumer markets. Both involve people who assume buying roles and make purchase decisions to satisfy needs. However, business markets differ in many ways from consumer markets. The main differences are in *market structure and demand,* the *nature of the buying unit,* and the *types of decisions and the decision process* involved.

Market Structure and Demand The business marketer normally deals with *far fewer but far larger buyers* than the consumer marketer does. For example, when Michelin's retail partners sell replacement tires to consumers, the potential market includes the owners of the millions of cars currently in use in North America. But Michelin's fate in the business market depends on getting orders from one of only a few large automakers. Even in large business markets, a few buyers normally account for most of the purchasing.

Business markets are also *more geographically concentrated.* More than 70 percent of Canada's manufacturers are located in Ontario and Quebec, and most of these are located within 100 km of the U.S. border. Further, business demand is **derived demand**—it ultimately derives from the demand for consumer goods. General Motors buys steel because consumers buy cars. If consumer demand for cars drops, so will the demand for steel and all the other products used to make cars. Therefore, business marketers sometimes promote their products directly to consumers to increase business demand. For example, Intel's long-running "Intel Inside" advertising campaign sells personal computer buyers on the virtues of Intel microprocessors. The increased demand for Intel chips boosts demand for the PCs containing them, and both Intel and its business partners win. The marketers at Kraft are behind the television commercials for Kraft Peanut Butter, even though the product is not sold directly to the consumer by Kraft but is purchased in grocery stores. In fact, most well-known brands of consumer products control their own marketing—Nike athletic wear, Procter & Gamble household cleaning products, Colgate toothpaste, Highliner seafood products—even though consumers are not their *customers.*

Nature of the Buying Unit Compared with consumer purchases, a business purchase usually involves *more decision participants* and a *more professional purchasing effort.* Often, business buying is done by trained purchasing agents who spend their working lives learning how to buy better. The more complex the purchase, the more likely that several people will participate in the decision-making process. Buying committees made up of technical experts and top management are common in the buying of major goods. As one observer notes, "It's a scary thought: Your customers may know more about your company and products than you do. . . . Companies are putting their best and brightest people on procurement patrol."[17] Therefore, business marketers must have well-trained salespeople to deal with well-trained buyers.

Types of Decisions and the Decision Process Business buyers usually face *more complex* buying decisions than do consumer buyers. Purchases often involve large sums of money, complex technical and economic considerations, and interactions among many people at many levels of the buyer's organization. Because the purchases are more complex, business buyers may take longer to make their decisions.

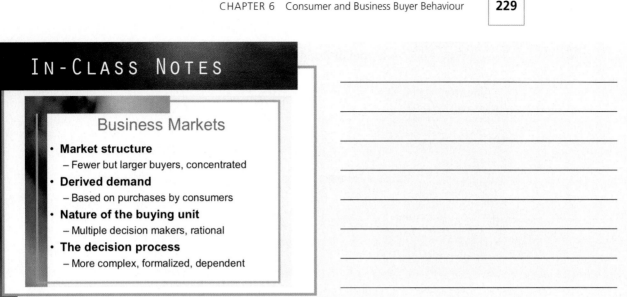

IN-CLASS NOTES

Business Markets

- **Market structure**
  - Fewer but larger buyers, concentrated
- **Derived demand**
  - Based on purchases by consumers
- **Nature of the buying unit**
  - Multiple decision makers, rational
- **The decision process**
  - More complex, formalized, dependent

The business buying process tends to be *more formalized* than the consumer buying process. Large business purchases usually call for detailed product specifications, written purchase orders, careful supplier searches, and formal approval.

Finally, in the business buying process, buyer and seller are often much *more dependent* on each other. Consumer marketers are often at a distance from their customers. In contrast, business-to-business marketers may roll up their sleeves and work closely with their customers during all stages of the buying process—partnering to jointly create solutions to the customer's problems and to support customer operations.

Business Buyer Behaviour

At the most basic level, marketers want to know how business buyers will respond to various marketing stimuli. Figure 6.6 shows a model of business buyer behaviour. In this model, marketing and other stimuli affect the buying organization and produce certain buyer responses. As with consumer buying, the marketing stimuli for business buying consist of the four Ps: product, price, place, and promotion. Other stimuli include major forces in the environment: economic, technological, political, cultural, and competitive. These stimuli enter the organization and are turned into buyer responses: product or service choice; supplier choice; order quantities; and delivery, service, and payment terms. To design good marketing mix strategies, the marketer must understand what happens within the organization to turn stimuli into purchase responses.

Within the organization, buying activity has two major parts: the buying centre, comprising all the people involved in the buying decision, and the buying-decision process. The model shows that the buying centre and the buying-decision process are influenced by internal organizational, interpersonal, and individual factors as well as by external environmental factors.

The model in Figure 6.6 suggests four questions about business buyer behaviour: What types of buying decisions do business buyers make? Who participates in the buying process? What are the major influences on buyers? How do business buyers make their buying decisions?

Major Types of Buying Situations There are three major types of buying situations.[18] At one extreme is the *straight rebuy,* which is a fairly routine decision. At the other extreme is the *new task,* which may call for thorough research. In the middle is the *modified rebuy,* which requires some research.

Figure 6.6   A Model of Business Buyer Behaviour

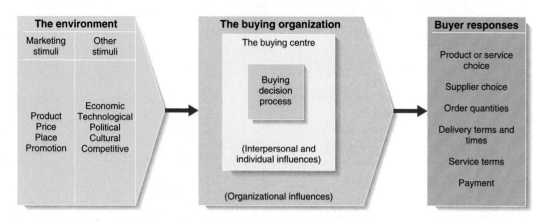

Straight rebuy A business buying situation in which the buyer reorders something without any modifications.

Modified rebuy A business buying situation in which the buyer wants to modify product specifications, prices, terms, or suppliers.

New task A business buying situation in which the buyer purchases a product or service for the first time.

Systems selling Buying a packaged solution to a problem from a single seller, thus avoiding all the separate decisions involved in a complex buying situation.

Buying centre All the individuals and units that participate in the business buying-decision process.

In a **straight rebuy**, the buyer reorders something without any modifications. It is usually handled on a routine basis by the purchasing department. Based on past buying satisfaction, the buyer simply chooses from the various suppliers on its list. "In" suppliers try to maintain product and service quality. They often propose automatic reordering systems so that the purchasing agent will save reordering time. "Out" suppliers try to offer something new or exploit dissatisfaction so that the buyer will consider them.

In a **modified rebuy**, the buyer wants to modify product specifications, prices, terms, or suppliers. The modified rebuy usually involves more decision participants than does the straight rebuy. The in suppliers may become nervous and feel pressured to put their best foot forward to protect an account. Out suppliers may see the modified rebuy situation as an opportunity to make a better offer and gain new business.

A company buying a product or service for the first time faces a **new task** situation. In such cases, the greater the cost or risk, the larger the number of decision participants and the greater their efforts to collect information will be. The new-task situation is the marketer's greatest opportunity and challenge. The marketer not only tries to reach as many key buying influences as possible, but also tries to provide help and information.

Many business buyers prefer to buy a packaged solution to a problem from a single seller, thus avoiding all the separate decisions involved in a complex buying situation. This is called **systems selling**. Instead of buying and putting all the components together, the buyer may ask sellers to supply the components *and* assemble the package or system. The sale often goes to the firm that provides the most complete system meeting the customer's needs. Thus, systems selling is often a key business marketing strategy for winning and holding accounts.

Participants in the Business Buying Process Who does the buying of the trillions of dollars' worth of goods and services needed by business organizations? The decision-making unit of a buying organization is called its **buying centre**: all the individuals and units that participate in the business decision-making process. This group includes the actual users of the product or service, those who make the buying decision, those who influence the buying decision, those who do the actual buying, and those who control buying information.

The buying centre is not a fixed and formally identified unit within the buying organization. It is a set of buying roles assumed by different people for different purchases. Within the organization, the size and makeup of the buying centre will vary for different products and for different buying situations. For some routine purchases, one person—say, a purchasing agent—may assume all the buying centre roles and serve as the only person involved in the buying decision. For more complex purchases, the buying centre may include 20 or 30 people from different levels and departments in the organization.

The buying centre concept presents a major marketing challenge. The business marketer must learn who participates in the decision, each participant's relative influence, and what evaluation criteria each decision participant uses. For example, Baxter International, the large health care products and services company, sells disposable surgical gowns to hospitals. It identifies the hospital personnel involved in this buying decision as the vice president of purchasing, the operating room administrator, and the surgeons. Each participant plays a different role. The vice president of purchasing analyzes whether the hospital should buy disposable gowns or reusable gowns. If analysis favours disposable gowns, then the operating room administrator compares competing products and prices and makes a choice. This administrator considers the gown's absorbency, antiseptic quality, design, and cost, and normally buys the brand that meets requirements at the lowest cost. Finally, surgeons affect the decision later by reporting their satisfaction or dissatisfaction with the brand.

The buying centre usually includes some obvious participants who are involved formally in the buying decision. It may also involve less obvious, informal participants, some of whom may actually make or strongly affect the buying decision. Sometimes, even the people in the buying centre are not aware of all the buying participants.

Major Influences on Business Buyers Business buyers are subject to many influences when they make their buying decisions. Some marketers assume that the major influences are economic. They think buyers will favour the supplier who offers the lowest price or the best product or the most service. They concentrate on offering strong economic benefits to buyers. However, business buyers actually respond to both economic and personal factors. Far from being cold, calculating, and impersonal, business buyers are human and social as well. They react to both reason and emotion.

Today, most business-to-business marketers recognize that emotion plays an important role in business buying decisions. For example, you might expect that an advertisement promoting large trucks to corporate truck fleet buyers would stress objective technical performance and economic factors. However, an ad for Volvo heavy-duty trucks shows two drivers arm wrestling and claims, "It solves all your fleet problems. Except who gets to drive." It turns out that, in the face an industry-wide driver shortage,

Emotions play an important role in business buying: This Volvo truck ad mentions objective factors, such as efficiency and ease of maintenance. But it stresses more emotional factors, such as the raw beauty of the truck and its comfort and roominess—features that make it more appealing to drivers.

the type of truck a fleet provides can help it to attract qualified drivers. The Volvo ad stresses the raw beauty of the truck and its comfort and roominess, features that make it more appealing to drivers. The ad concludes that Volvo trucks are "built to make fleets more profitable and drivers a lot more possessive."

Figure 6.7 lists various groups of influences on business buyers—environmental, organizational, interpersonal, and individual.[19] *Environmental factors* play a major role. For example, buyer behaviour can be heavily influenced by factors in the current and expected economic environment, such as the level of primary demand, the economic outlook, and the cost of money. Another environmental factor is shortages in key materials. Many companies are now more willing to buy and hold larger inventories of scarce materials to ensure adequate supply. Business buyers are also affected by technological, political, and competitive developments in the environment. Finally, culture and customs can strongly influence business buyer reactions to the marketer's behaviour and strategies, especially in the international marketing environment.

Figure 6.7   Major Influences on Business Buyer Behaviour

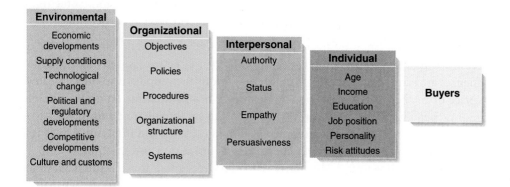

Business buyer behaviour is also influenced strongly by *organizational factors*. Each buying organization has its own objectives, policies, procedures, structure, and systems, and the business marketer must understand these factors well. Questions such as these arise: How many people are involved in the buying decision? Who are they? What are their evaluative criteria? What are the company's policies and limits on its buyers?

The buying centre usually includes many participants who influence each other, so *interpersonal factors* also influence the business buying process. However, it is often difficult to assess such interpersonal factors and group dynamics. As one writer notes, "Managers do not wear tags that say 'decision maker' or 'unimportant person.' The powerful are often invisible, at least to vendor representatives."[20] Nor does the buying centre participant with the highest rank always have the most influence. Participants may influence the buying decision because they control rewards and punishments, are well liked, have special expertise, or have a special relationship with other important participants. Interpersonal factors are often very subtle. Whenever possible, business marketers must try to understand these factors and design strategies that take them into account.

Finally, business buyers are influenced by *individual factors*. Each participant in the business buying-decision process brings in personal motives, perceptions, and preferences. These individual factors are affected by personal characteristics such as age, income, education, professional identification, personality, and attitudes toward risk. Also, buyers have different buying styles. Some may be technical types who make in-depth analyses of competitive proposals before choosing a supplier. Other buyers may be intuitive negotiators who are adept at pitting the sellers against one another for the best deal.

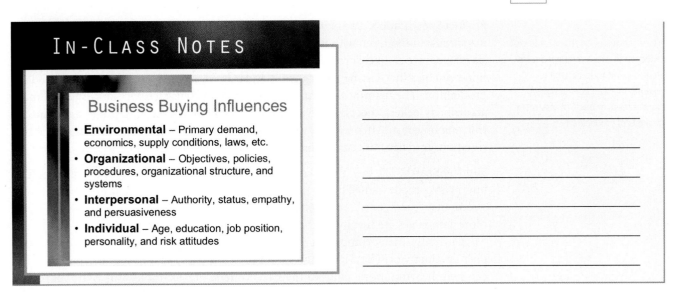

IN-CLASS NOTES

Business Buying Influences

- **Environmental** – Primary demand, economics, supply conditions, laws, etc.
- **Organizational** – Objectives, policies, procedures, organizational structure, and systems
- **Interpersonal** – Authority, status, empathy, and persuasiveness
- **Individual** – Age, education, job position, personality, and risk attitudes

The Business Buying Process Figure 6.8 shows the eight stages of the business buying process and the application of each of the eight steps to the three buying situations.[21] Buyers who face a new task buying situation usually go through all stages of the buying process. Buyers making modified or straight rebuys may skip some of the stages. We will examine these steps for the typical new-task buying situation.

Figure 6.8   Stages of the Business Buying Process

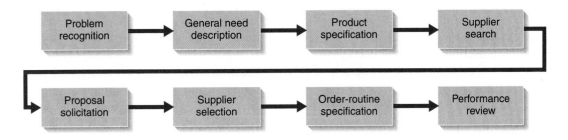

Problem Recognition. The business buying process begins when someone in the company recognizes a problem or need that can be met by acquiring a specific product or service. Problem recognition can result from internal or external stimuli. Internally, the company may decide to launch a new product that requires new production equipment and materials. Or a machine may break down and need new parts. Perhaps a purchasing manager is unhappy with a current supplier's product quality, service, or prices. Externally, the buyer may get some new ideas at a trade show, see an ad, or receive a call from a salesperson who offers a better product or a lower price. In fact, in their advertising, business marketers often alert customers to potential problems and then show how their products provide solutions.

General Need Description. Having recognized a need, the buyer next prepares a general need description that describes the characteristics and quantity of the needed item. For standard items, this process presents few problems. For complex items, however, the buyer may have to work with others—engineers, users, consultants—to define the item. The team may want to rank the importance of reliability, durability, price, and other attributes desired in the item. In this phase, the alert business marketer can help the buyers define their needs and provide information about the value of different product characteristics.

Value analysis An approach to cost reduction in which components are studied carefully to determine whether they can be redesigned, standardized, or made by less costly methods of production.

Product Specification. The buying organization next develops the item's technical product specifications, often with the help of a value analysis engineering team. **Value analysis** is an approach to cost reduction in which components are studied carefully to determine whether they can be redesigned, standardized, or made by less costly methods of production. The team decides on the best product characteristics and specifies them accordingly. Sellers, too, can use value analysis as a tool to help secure a new account. By showing buyers a better way to make an object, outside sellers can turn straight rebuy situations into new task situations that give them a chance to obtain new business.

Supplier Search. The buyer now conducts a supplier search to find the best vendors. The buyer can compile a small list of qualified suppliers by reviewing trade directories, doing a computer search, or phoning other companies for recommendations. Today, more and more companies are turning to the Internet to find suppliers.

Currently, many companies are viewing supplier search more as a process of supplier development. These companies want to develop a system of supplier-partners that can help it bring more value to their customers. For example, Wal-Mart's Supplier Development Department seeks out qualified suppliers and helps them through the complex Wal-Mart buying process. It offers a Supplier Proposal Guide and maintains a website offering advice to suppliers wanting to do business with Wal-Mart. The newer the buying task and the more complex and costly the item, the greater amount of time the buyer will spend searching for and qualifying suppliers. The supplier's task is to get listed in many directories and build a good reputation in the marketplace. Salespeople should watch for companies in the process of searching for suppliers and make certain that their firm is considered.

Proposal Solicitation. In the proposal solicitation stage of the business buying process, the buyer invites qualified suppliers to submit proposals. In response, some suppliers will send only a catalogue or a salesperson. However, when the item is complex or expensive, the buyer will usually require detailed written proposals or formal presentations from each potential supplier.

Business marketers must be skilled in researching, writing, and presenting proposals in response to buyer proposal solicitations. Proposals should be marketing documents, not just technical documents. Presentations should inspire confidence and should make the marketer's company stand out from the competition.

Supplier Selection. The members of the buying centre now review the proposals and select a supplier or suppliers. During supplier selection, the buying centre often will draw up a list of the desired supplier attributes and their relative importance. In one survey, purchasing executives listed the following attributes as most important in influencing the relationship between supplier and customer: quality products and services, on-time delivery, ethical corporate behaviour, honest communication, and competitive prices. Other important factors include repair and servicing capabilities, technical aid and advice, geographic location, performance history, and reputation. The members of the buying centre will rate suppliers against these attributes and identify the best suppliers.

Buyers may attempt to negotiate with preferred suppliers for better prices and terms before making the final selections. In the end, they may select a single supplier or a few suppliers. Many buyers prefer multiple sources of supplies to avoid being dependent on one supplier and to allow for comparisons of prices and performance of several suppliers over time.

Order-Routine Specification. The buyer now prepares an order-routine specification. It includes the final order with the chosen supplier or suppliers and lists items such as technical specifications, quantity needed, expected time of delivery, return policies, and warranties. In the case of maintenance, repair, and operating items, buyers may use *blan-*

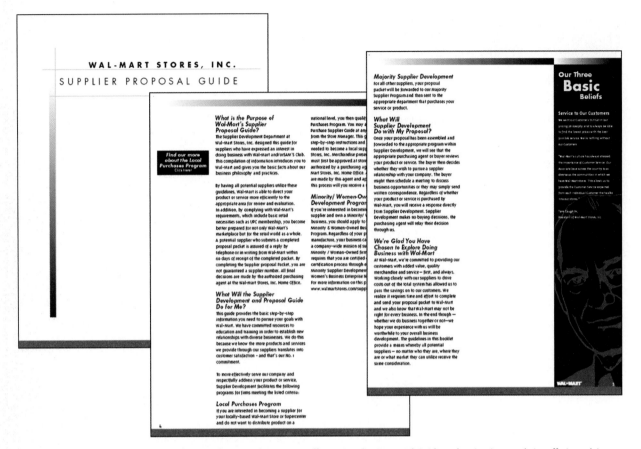

Supplier development: Wal-Mart's Supplier Development department offers a Supplier Proposal Guide and maintains a website offering advice to suppliers wanting to do business with Wal-Mart.

ket contracts rather than periodic purchase orders. A blanket contract creates a long-term relationship in which the supplier promises to resupply the buyer as needed at agreed prices for a set period. A blanket order eliminates the expensive process of renegotiating a purchase each time that stock is required. It also allows buyers to write more, but smaller, purchase orders, resulting in lower inventory levels and carrying costs.

Blanket contracting leads to more single-source buying and to buying more items from that source. This practice locks the supplier in more tightly with the buyer and makes it difficult for other suppliers to break in unless the buyer becomes dissatisfied with prices or service.

Performance Review. In this stage, the buyer reviews supplier performance. The buyer may contact users and ask them to rate their satisfaction. The performance review may lead the buyer to continue, modify, or drop the arrangement. The seller's job is to monitor the same factors used by the buyer to make sure that the seller is giving the expected satisfaction.

We have described the stages that would typically occur in a new-task buying situation. The eight-stage model provides a simple view of the business buying-decision process. The actual process is usually much more complex. In the modified rebuy or straight rebuy situation, some of these stages would be compressed or bypassed. Each organization buys in its own way, and each buying situation has unique requirements. Different buying centre participants may be involved at different stages of the process. Although certain buying process steps usually do occur, buyers do not always follow them in the same order, and they may add other steps. Often, buyers will repeat certain stages of the process. Finally, a customer relationship might involve many different types

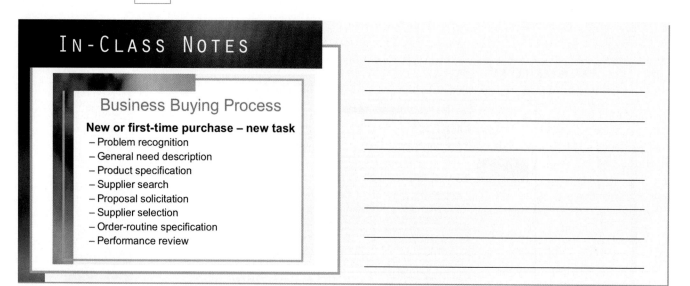

IN-CLASS NOTES

Business Buying Process

New or first-time purchase – new task
- Problem recognition
- General need description
- Product specification
- Supplier search
- Proposal solicitation
- Supplier selection
- Order-routine specification
- Performance review

of purchases ongoing at a given time, all in different stages of the buying process. The seller must manage the total customer relationship, not just individual purchases.

Business Buying on the Internet

Advances in information technology have changed the face of the business-to-business marketing process. Today, most B2B purchasing takes place online, with the buyer being able to log in to the vendor's internal website and place orders, much in the same way that consumers might buy a book or a DVD online. Such "e-procurement" gives buyers access to new suppliers, lowers purchasing costs, and hastens order processing and delivery. In turn, business marketers are connecting with customers online to share marketing information, sell products and services, provide customer support services, and maintain ongoing customer relationships.

So far, most of the online purchasing done by businesses is for MRO materials—maintenance, repair, and operations. The actual dollar amount spent on these MRO items pales in comparison with the amount spent on items like airplane and automotive parts, computer systems, and steel tubing. However, MRO items make up 80 percent of all business orders, and the transaction costs for order processing are high. Thus, companies have much to gain by streamlining the MRO buying process on the Web. To take advantage of this, Business Depot, which operates Staples and Bureau en Gros stores across Canada, is using the Net in a bid to become a one-stop online shop for the growing small business market in Canada.[22] The new site carries the retailer's entire catalogue of supplies—more than 5000 products plus an extended line of technology products and computer equipment. It also offers a variety of time-saving options and personalization features designed to cater primarily to business customers with fewer than four employees. The site has already exceeded the sales goals set for it three-fold, indicating that Canadian small business customers are definitely ready to shop online.

To most consumers, all the buzz about Internet buying has focused on business-to-consumer (B2C) websites selling computers, software, clothing, books, flowers, or other retail goods. However, consumer goods sales via the Web are dwarfed by the Internet sales of business goods. In fact, B2B e-procurement now accounts for a lion's share of the dollar value of all e-commerce transactions.

This rapid-growth business-to-business e-procurement yields many benefits.[23] It shaves transaction costs and results in more efficient purchasing for both buyers and suppliers. A Web-powered purchasing program eliminates the paperwork associated with traditional requisition and ordering procedures. General Electric, one of the world's largest purchasers, plans to buy all of its general operating and industrial supplies online over the next few years. Six years ago, GE set up its Global eXchange Services Network—a central website through which all GE business units could make their purchases. The site was so successful that GE now offers the service to other companies, thus creating a vast electronic e-purchasing clearinghouse. As further evidence of the power of e-procurement, Microsoft has trimmed $833 million from its purchasing costs after implementing its MS Market e-procurement system.[24]

Although e-procurement reduces the time between order and delivery, it also presents some problems. At the same time that the Web makes it possible for suppliers and customers to share business data and even collaborate on product design, it can also erode decades-old customer–supplier relationships. Many firms are using the Web to search for better suppliers. Japan Airlines (JAL) has used the Internet to post orders for in-flight materials such as plastic cups. On its website, it posts drawings and specifications that will attract proposals from any firm that comes across the site, rather than from just the usual Japanese suppliers. In April 2000, JAL's procurement operations were transferred to JALUX Inc., which coordinates procurement for the JAL Group. Finally, e-purchasing can create potential security disasters. More than 80 percent of companies say security is the leading barrier to expanding electronic links with customers and partners.

Although email and home banking transactions can be protected through basic encryption technology, the secure environment that businesses need is still deficient. Companies are spending millions for research on defensive strategies and technologies to reduce the threat posed by hackers. Cisco Systems, for example, specifies the types of routers, firewalls, and security procedures that its partners must use to safeguard extranet connections. The company will also send its own security team to examine a partner's defences and hold the partner liable for any security breach that originates from its computer.

LOOKING BACK

This chapter is the last of three chapters on analyzing marketing opportunities by looking closely at consumers, businesses, and their buying behaviour. The Canadian consumer market comprises more than 30 million people who consume many billions of dollars' worth of goods and services each year. The business market involves far more dollars and items than the consumer market. Consumers and business buyers vary greatly in their characteristics and circumstances. Understanding *consumer* and *business buyer behaviour* is one of the biggest challenges marketers face.

REVIEWING THE CONCEPTS

1. Understand the consumer market and the major factors that influence consumer buyer behaviour.

The *consumer market* comprises all the individuals and households who buy or acquire goods and services for personal consumption. A simple stimulus–response model of consumer behaviour suggests that marketing stimuli and other major forces enter the consumer's "black box." This black box has two parts: buyer characteristics and the buyer's decision process. Once in the black box, the inputs result in observable buyer responses, such as product choice, brand choice, dealer choice, purchase timing, and purchase amount.

Consumer buyer behaviour is influenced by four key sets of buyer characteristics: cultural, social, personal, and psychological. Understanding these factors can help marketers identify interested buyers and shape products and appeals to serve consumer needs better. *Culture* is the most basic determinant of a person's wants and behaviour. People in different cultural, subcultural, and social class groups have different product and brand preferences. *Social factors*—such as small group and family influences—strongly affect product and brand choices, as do *personal characteristics,* such as age, life-cycle stage, occupation, economic circumstances, lifestyle, and personality. Finally, consumer buying behaviour is influenced by four major sets of *psychological factors*—motivation, perception, learning, and beliefs and attitudes. Each of these factors provides a different perspective for understanding the workings of the buyer's black box.

2. Identify and discuss the stages in the consumer buyer decision process.

When making a purchase, the buyer goes through a decision process comprising need recognition, information search, evaluation of alternatives, purchase decision, and postpurchase behaviour. During *need recognition,* the consumer recognizes a problem or need that could be satisfied by a product or service. Once the need is recognized, the consumer moves into the *information search* stage. With information in hand, the consumer proceeds to *alternative evaluation* and assesses brands in the choice set. From there, the consumer makes a *purchase decision* and actually buys the product. In the final stage of the buyer decision process, *postpurchase behaviour,* the consumer takes action based on satisfaction or dissatisfaction. The marketer's job is to understand the buyer's behaviour at each stage and the influences that are operating.

3. Describe the adoption and diffusion process for new products.

The product *adoption process* comprises five stages: awareness, interest, evaluation, trial, and adoption. New-product marketers must think about how to help consumers move through these stages. With regard to the *diffusion process* for new products, consumers respond at different rates depending on consumer and product

characteristics. Consumers may be innovators, early adopters, early majority, late majority, or laggards. Each group may require different marketing approaches. Marketers often try to bring their new products to the attention of potential early adopters, especially those who are opinion leaders.

4. Define the business market and identify the major factors that influence business buyer behaviour.

The *business market* comprises all organizations that buy goods and services for use in the production of other products and services or for the purpose of reselling or renting them to others at a profit. As compared with consumer markets, business markets usually have fewer, larger buyers who are more geographically concentrated. Business demand is derived demand, and the business buying decisions usually involves more, and more professional, buyers.

Business buyers make decisions that vary with the three types of *buying situations:* straight rebuys, modified rebuys, and new tasks. The decision-making unit of a buying organization—the *buying centre*—can comprise many different persons playing many different roles. The business marketer needs to know the following: Who are the major buying centre participants? In what decisions do they exercise influence and to what degree? What evaluation criteria does each decision participant use? The business marketer also needs to understand the major environmental, organizational, interpersonal, and individual influences on the buying process.

5. List and define the steps in the business buying-decision process.

The *business buying-decision process* itself can be quite involved, with eight basic stages: problem recognition, general need description, product specification, supplier search, proposal solicitation, supplier selection, order-routine specification, and performance review. Buyers who face a new-task buying situation usually go through all stages of the buying process. Buyers making modified or straight rebuys may skip some of the stages. Companies must manage the overall customer relationship, which often includes many different buying decisions in various stages of the buying decisions process.

Advances in information technology have given birth to "e-purchasing," by which business buyers are purchasing all kinds of products and services electronically, either through electronic data interchange links (EDI) or on the Internet. Such cyberbuying gives buyers access to new suppliers, lowers purchasing costs, and hastens order processing and delivery. However, it can also erode customer–supplier relationships and create potential security problems. Still, business marketers are increasingly connecting with customers online to share marketing information, sell products and services, provide customer support services, and maintain ongoing customer relationships.

KEY TERMS

adoption process   *223*
attitude   *218*
belief   *218*
business buyer behaviour   *227*
buying centre   *230*
cognitive dissonance   *222*
consumer buyer behaviour   *204*
consumer market   *204*

culture   *205*
derived demand   *228*
group   *209*
learning   *218*
lifestyle   *212*
modified rebuy   *230*
motive (or drive)   *215*
new product   *223*

new task   *230*
opinion leader   *209*
perception   *217*
social classes   *207*
straight rebuy   *230*
subculture   *206*
systems selling   *230*
value analysis   *234*

STUDY GUIDE

After completing this self-test, check your answers against the Answer Key at the back of the book.

MULTIPLE CHOICE

1. Social class is a major factor in brand preferences because
   a. Social class determines how much the buyer can spend on the purchase
   b. Social class determines the status level the buyer seeks
   c. Social class determines whether the buyer tends to buy popular brands or niche brands
   d. Social class often determines the buyer's reference groups
   e. All of the above

2. The marketer of a higher-priced sports car to middle-class males is marketing a status item. In order to influence the buying behaviour of her target market, the marketer may use a formula race car driver to endorse the car in advertising or sponsor the driver in races, an example of using
   a. An opinion leader within a reference group
   b. Aspirational positioning
   c. Reference promotions
   d. A buyer referencer
   e. False advertising

3. A recent radio advertising campaign promoting responsible alcohol consumption featured young children talking about last night's binge and how drunk they were. This type of advertising seeks to accomplish the difficult task of altering consumer _____ about overconsumption.
   a. Complacency
   b. Drivers
   c. Dislike
   d. Attitudes
   e. Learnings

4. A sophisticated woman purchasing a car is more likely to select a Jaguar than a Corvette. Likewise, a male outdoor enthusiastic is more likely to select a Land Rover than a Cadillac SUV. These likelihoods depend on the observed fact that
   a. Price is irrelevant when consumers are seeking status
   b. Consumers never diverge from past brand preferences
   c. Consumers tend to buy brands that reflect their own lifestyle and personalities
   d. Self-actualization is the most powerful need that consumers have
   e. Archetype research can predetermine brand preferences

5. User groups, follow-up phone calls, special discounts on related products, and generous upgrade policies are all tools that marketers use to
   a. Entice customers to buy more products
   b. Reduce the doubt that buyers often experience after making a major purchase
   c. Encourage customers to be more forgiving of poor-quality products
   d. Hamper the competition's ability to scoop the customer later
   e. Charge customers for these additional services and thus increase the customer's lifetime value

6. A car buyer trying to decide what make of SUV to purchase relies on a number of information sources during the buying process. However, the sources most likely to have greatest influence on his decision are
   a. Car dealerships and salespeople
   b. Brochures and other printed literature
   c. Car magazine reviews
   d. Friends and his mechanic
   e. Consumer rating magazines

7. Consumers did not adopt propane and natural gas powered automobiles at the same rate at which they are adopting hybrid cars largely because
   a. These cars were incompatible with consumers' lives since they required costly retrofitting and were in violation of many fire regulations
   b. These cars were pronounced illegal in North America
   c. The cost of natural gas and propane is considerably higher than gasoline
   d. It was very difficult to communicate the environmental benefits to consumers
   e. Consumers were just not ready to make good environmental choices

8. Advertisers face major challenges in getting buyers to behave in certain ways. Perhaps most problematic is the task of getting consumers to pay attention to the ad in the first place. And if the consumer does pay attention, then advertisers still need to overcome the fact that consumers tend to
   a. Be turned off by advertising in general
   b. Be wary of any company that seems to "over-advertise"
   c. Hear only what they already believe and discount anything else
   d. Discount any advertising from a brand unknown to them
   e. Believe that all advertising is inherently dishonest

9. In business-to-business buying situations, it is not one person who makes the purchase decision but more usually a group of people who together comprise a buying centre. The most difficult challenge that sales and marketing people face in dealing with buying centres is
   a. Determining the group's collective understanding of budget allocation for the purchase
   b. Determining who in the group carries what influence and authority
   c. Understanding the role of the purchasing department
   d. Assessing whether the company practises decentralized or centralized purchasing
   e. Identifying whether it is a new-buy or a straight rebuy situation

10. Business-to-business buying on the Internet, called e-procurement, accounts for the bulk of e-commerce. However, the growth of e-procurement continues to be hampered by
    a. Doubt about the security of Internet-based transactions and data
    b. The inability of today's Internet infrastructure to handle the data load
    c. The continuing high cost of Internet access in so many countries
    d. The higher costs of purchasing associated with e-procurement
    e. The loss of traditional supplier–buyer relationships

TRUE/FALSE

T F **1.** Personalities and emotions never play a role in business-to-business buying behaviours.

T F **2.** Despite the cohesion of the North American cultural identity, ethnic background and social class are powerful predictors of consumer buying behaviour.

T F **3.** The number of buying-process steps that a person goes through is largely defined by personality and affinity for detail.

T F **4.** The buying process for the first-time purchase of an existing product type and the process for buying a new, just-released product type are the same.

T F **5.** Age and life-cycle stages once tracked predictably against each other, but in recent times age and life-cycle stages often diverge and are no longer necessarily linked.

CONCEPT CHECK

1. _____ refers to the buying behaviour of consumers—individuals who buy goods and services for personal consumption.

2. _____ is the most basic cause of a person's wants and behaviour.

3. _____ are society's relatively permanent and ordered divisions whose members share similar values, interests, and behaviours.

4. People within a reference group who, because of special skills, knowledge, personality, or other characteristics, exert influence on others are called _____.

5. Lifestyle is a person's pattern of living as expressed in his or her psychographics. It involves measuring consumer's major *AIO* dimensions where
A = _____, I = _____, and
O = _____.

6. Maslow sought to explain why people are driven by particular needs at particular times. He identified five primary need categories, which include _____ needs, _____ needs, _____ needs, _____ needs, and _____ needs.

7. The buyer decision process consists of five stages:
_____,
_____, _____,
_____, and _____.

8. Consumers go through five stages in the process of adopting a new product: _____,
_____, _____,
_____, and _____.

9. Five characteristics are especially important in influencing an innovation's rate of adoption.
_____ is the degree to which the innovation appears superior to existing products.

10. With respect to business buying situations, there are three major types: _____,
_____, and _____.

11. The decision-making unit of a buying organization is called its _____ and it includes all individuals and units that participate in the business decision-making process.

12. The eight stages of the business buying process include problem recognition, general need description, product specification, _____, _____, _____, _____, and performance review.

STUDENT MATERIALS

Visit our website at www.pearsoned.ca/armstrong for online quizzes, Internet exercises, and more!

DISCUSSING THE ISSUES

1. List several factors that you could add to the model shown in Figure 6.1 to make it a more complete description of consumer behaviour. Explain your ideas and reasoning.

2. In designing the advertising for a soft drink, which would you find more helpful, information about consumer demographics or information about consumer lifestyles? Select a new soft drink on the market and give examples of how you would use each type of information.

3. Using Figure 6.4, trace a recent purchase you have made. Examine each of the five stages of the buyer decision process and detail your experiences in each stage. What could the seller have done to make your buying experience better? Did you experience any cognitive dissonance? Explain.

4. Which of the major types of business buying situations is represented by each of the following? (a) Chrysler's purchase of computers that go in cars and adjust engine performance to changing driving conditions. (b) Volkswagen's purchase of spark plugs for its line of vans. (c) Honda's purchase of light bulbs for a new Acura model.

5. Increasingly, business buyers are purchasing all kinds of products and services online. List the benefits of online purchasing. Illustrate your view with an example from the Internet.

MARKETING APPLICATIONS

Performance review is one of the most critical stages in a business buying process. Perhaps nowhere is this more important than in the highly competitive aircraft manufacturing business. Whether the planes are large or small, once a purchase is made, the buyer is tied to the manufacturer for a long time for service and parts requirements. "Air wars" are currently being fought between Europe's Airbus Industrie and America's Boeing. To a lesser extent, the same competitive conflict exists in the smaller personal and corporate aircraft market between Cessna and Lear Jet. Who will eventually win these dramatic competitive struggles is literally "up in the air." Note: For additional information, see www.airbus.com, www.boeing.com, www.cessna.textron.com, and www.learjet.com.

THINKING LIKE A MARKETING MANAGER

1. Apply either of the above two competitive situations to Figure 6.6 and demonstrate the critical factors that might be present in a business buying situation.

2. How would performance review be conducted in either of the above two situations? Who might be responsible for such a performance review?

3. If the review were negative, how might the selling organization overcome this difficulty?
    a. Examine Figure 6.7. Which specific components might be involved in a performance review of aircraft safety?
    b. Find a recent example of "air war" competitiveness and bring the example to class for discussion. How does your example relate to business-to-business marketing and business buying?

VIDEO CASE

Go to Pearson Canada's Video Central site (www.pearsoned.ca/highered/videocentral) to view the video and accompanying case for this chapter.

CASE 6   "TRADING UP" TO NEW LUXURY BRANDS

If you're like most Canadians you probably don't consider yourself to be a consumer of luxury goods. There's no Jaguar in your driveway, no Rolex on your nightstand, and no beluga caviar in your refrigerator. Then again, it depends on how you define luxury goods. According to Michael Silverstein and Neil Fiske, authors of the book *Trading Up: Why Consumers Want New Luxury Goods—and How Companies Create Them*, a growing number of middle-class Canadian consumers are "trading up" for high-end, high-quality, expensive products, and forcing marketers to rethink their conception of the typical consumer of luxury goods. It might surprise you to know that right now the growing trend in consumer behaviour is trading up.

Trading up means being willing, even eager, to pay a premium price for high-end products in certain product categories—the ones that are important to *you*. It doesn't mean that everything you buy is high-end, only certain things. And in exchange for being able to afford those one or two luxuries, we are willing to "trade down" on other items, that is, to buy the lower-cost items in categories that are not important to us.

Before consumers can trade up in a product category, however, there must be high-end brands available for them to buy. Take Jake, for example. Jake is a construction worker who earns $50 000 per year. Jake owns a set of titanium-faced Callaway golf clubs, for which he paid US$3000. Why is he willing to trade up on golf equipment? "The real reason I bought them is that they make me feel rich," he says. "You can run the biggest company in the world and be one of the richest guys in the world, but you can't buy any clubs better than these." Callaway golf clubs are just one of many New Luxury brands now available on the market for consumers who want to trade up.

Trading down is the behaviour of these same consumers when they choose the low-cost alternative in product categories that are of little importance to them. For marketers, that means it is important to offer products in those low-budget price ranges, because if there were no low-cost products available, consumers would not be able to trade up for the luxury products they desire. The end result is that for every product category into which a New Luxury brand enters, that market becomes polarized. Silverstein and Fiske advise marketers that, to be successful, your product must either be the New Luxury brand or the low-cost alternative—anything in the middle will struggle to succeed, and may not even survive.

Distinctive Appliances of Montreal, where a refrigerator can cost as much as $6300, wants to be the New Luxury brand in kitchen appliances. "Consumers are increasingly looking to turn their kitchens into pieces of art," says Michael Benoit, the company's president. "Instead of a white box sticking out of the wall, a consumer might choose a wood-panel fridge or something in stainless steel." Benoit understands the trading up phenomenon in consumer behaviour. Traditional marketing wisdom would have said that no middle-class family with a household income of less than $100 000 would ever spend that much for their fridge, but Benoit has learned that the kitchen is emerging as a room to entertain guests, and as such it must be "decorated" just like the rest of the home.

Consumers of New Luxury brands are a diverse group, but like any market segment they have certain behaviours in common, and the marketer who understands the nature of this consumer group will be able to successfully design a marketing strategy and program to reach them. One of these behaviours is *rocketing*—spending a disproportionate amount of one's income on a single product category. The typical New Luxury consumer will "pay more" for at least one type of product that is important to them, and will have as many as 10 categories in which they will "rocket." New Luxury consumers are highly selective in their buying behaviour. When they make decisions about trading up they do it carefully and deliberately. Empty nesters—married couples whose children no longer live with them—are one segment of the New Luxury consumer. So are working singles in their twenties. Divorced women are another.

How does a New Luxury brand differ from an "old" luxury brand? According to Silverstein and Fiske, it's all about emotional involvement. BMW owners, for example, are emotionally attached to their cars. They wash them more frequently than owners of other car brands, and when they park them on the street they turn back to gaze lovingly at their car before they walk away. Old luxury brands such as Chanel and Cadillac, on the other hand, were not about emotion but about status.

When marketers fail to understand trends in consumer behaviour, the effects can be ravaging. Take Cadillac, for example. Once the epitome of old luxury brands, it provides marketers with a cautionary tale of what can happen when a company rests on its laurels. Up until the 1970s the name Cadillac was synonymous in America with status, achievement, and recognition. It was the car of choice for politicians, Hollywood celebrities, and the wealthy upper class. Believing that they had reached the top with this brand, General Motors reduced its investment in it. The result was that while new brands like Toyota and Honda were entering the market with technical advances in their cars, Cadillac was suffering from increasingly out-of-date styling and only superficial improvements. Between 1975 and 2000 sales declined 2 percent each year, and the Cadillac brand eventually became the butt of jokes on late-night talk shows. Cadillac, it appears, cannot be the New Luxury brand in its category, and has fallen into the dangerous middle market zone.

"When the superpremium model fails to offer technical and functional benefits, it can coast for a while . . . but not for very long," say Silverstein and Fiske. "And no matter how successful—even iconic—a product is, it can swiftly be dethroned by competitors who understand the escalating tastes of consumers. . . . In categories of durable goods, the dethroning can take less than a decade. In consumable goods, it can happen in two years or less."

Questions

1. Are you a consumer who "trades up" to New Luxury Brands? Think of an item you own that is high end in its class. It might be an iPod, or a computer, or perhaps a bicycle. Do you consider this item to be a New Luxury brand? Explain why or why not.

2. Do you believe the authors of the book when they suggest that more and more Canadian consumers engage in "trading up" behaviour? What items do you own that you have traded up for? What product categories do you "trade down" on?

3. The authors claim that modern consumers are emotionally attached to New Luxury brands. Think about some of the brands named in this case. Whether or not you own any products by those brands, are you "emotional" about any of them? What aspirational groups are associated with these New Luxury brands?

4. Think about the most luxurious item you own. Now, describe the buyer decision process you went through when you purchased it.

Sources: Chris Daniels, "Almost Rich," *Marketing*, April 26, 2004; Michael J. Silverstein and Neil Fiske, *Trading Up: Why Consumers Want New Luxury Goods—and How Companies Create Them* (New York: Portfolio (Penguin Group), 2005).

After studying this chapter, you should be able to

1. define the three steps of target marketing: market segmentation, target marketing, and market positioning

2. list and discuss the major approaches for segmenting consumer and business markets

3. explain how companies identify attractive market segments and choose a target marketing strategy

4. discuss how companies position their products for maximum competitive advantage in the marketplace

Segmentation, Targeting, and Positioning: Building the Right Relationships with the Right Customers

7

Looking Ahead

So far you've learned what marketing is and about the complex environments in which it operates. Marketing works with partners inside and outside the company to build profitable customer relationships in a complex and changing marketplace. With that as background, in Part 3 of the book, we'll delve more deeply into marketing strategy and tactics. The key to smart marketing is to build the *right relationships* with the *right customers*. This chapter looks further into key marketing strategy decisions—how to divide up markets into meaningful groups of people (market segmentation), choose which of these groups to serve (target marketing), and create a value proposition that best serves the target segments (positioning). The chapters that follow explore in depth the tactical marketing tools—the *4Ps*—through which marketers bring these strategies to life.

Procter & Gamble is one of the world's premier consumer goods companies. Some 99 percent of all Canadian households use at least one P&G brand, and the typical household regularly buys and uses from one to two *dozen* P&G brands. How many P&G products can you name? Why does this superb marketer compete with itself on supermarket shelves by marketing four different brands of laundry detergent? The P&G story provides a great example of how smart marketers use segmentation, targeting, and positioning.

P rocter & Gamble (P&G) sells four brands of laundry detergent in Canada (Tide, Cheer, Gain, and Ivory Snow). It also sells six brands of shampoo (Head & Shoulders, Herbal Essences, Infusium, Inner Science, Pantene Pro-V, and Pert Plus); five brands of soap (Ivory, Safeguard, Camay, Olay, and Zest); three brands of toilet paper, towels, and tissues (Charmin, Bounty, Puffs); and two brands each of dishwashing detergent (Dawn and Cascade), deodorant (Secret and Old Spice), cosmetics (Cover Girl and Max Factor), skin care potions (Olay and Noxzema), and fabric softener (Downy and Bounce). Moreover, P&G has many additional brands in each category for different international markets. For example, it sells 12 different brands of laundry detergent in Western Europe.

These P&G brands compete with one another on the same supermarket shelves. But why would P&G introduce several brands in one category instead of concentrating its resources on a single leading brand? The answer lies in the fact that different people want different mixes of benefits from the products they buy. Take laundry detergents as an example. People use laundry detergents to get their clothes clean. But they also want other things from their detergents—such as economy, bleaching power, fabric softening, a fresh smell, strength or mildness, and lots of suds or only a few. We all want *some* of every one of these benefits from our detergent, but we may have different *priorities* for each benefit. To some people, cleaning and bleaching power are most important; to others, fabric softening matters most; still others want a mild, fresh-scented detergent. Thus, there are groups—or segments—of laundry detergent buyers, and each segment seeks a special combination of benefits.

Procter & Gamble has identified at least four important laundry detergent segments, along with numerous subsegments, and has developed a different brand designed to meet the special needs of each. The P&G brands are positioned for different segments as follows:

☐ *Tide* keeps laundry "looking clean and new." It's the all-purpose family detergent that "offers powerful cleaning for tough laundry."
☐ *Cheer* is the colour expert. It "helps protect against fading, colour transfer, and fabric wear."
☐ *Gain*, originally P&G's "enzyme" detergent, was repositioned as the detergent with "a unique, fresh scent you'll find irresistible."
☐ *Ivory Snow* is "99-44/100% pure." It provides "gentle cleaning and care for baby items and fine washables."

Within each segment, Procter & Gamble has identified even *narrower* niches. For example, you can buy Tide (in powder or liquid form) or any of several formulations:

☐ *Tide with Bleach* helps "remove tough stains" while keeping colours bright.
☐ *Tide Ultra 2* contains WearCare technology to "help prevent the pills, fuzz, and fading that can make clothes look old before their time."
☐ *Tide High Efficiency* is "specially formulated for high efficiency washers" and prevents oversudsing.
☐ *Tide with a Touch of Downy* "combines the Tide clean you expect with a touch of Downy softness and freshness."
☐ *Tide Free* "provides great cleaning power without any dyes or perfumes."

By segmenting the market and having several detergent brands, Procter & Gamble has an attractive offering for consumers in all important preference groups. As a result, P&G is really cleaning up in the $4.3 billion laundry detergent market. Tide, by itself, captures a whopping 38 percent market share. All P&G brands combined take a 57 percent share of the market—two and one-half times that of nearest rival Unilever and much more than any single brand could obtain by itself.[1]

TEST YOURSELF

Answers to these questions can be found on our website at
www.pearsoned.ca/armstrong.

1. Consider Procter & Gamble's skin care brands Noxzema and Oil of Olay. Why can P&G successfully market these apparently similar products and never directly compete for the same customer?
   a) Because they are sold through different retailers
   b) Because Olay is considerably more expensive than Noxzema
   c) Because Noxzema is carefully targeted at teens and young women while Olay is targeted to women over 50
   d) Because it advertises only the Oil of Olay brand
   e) Because Noxzema is sold only through dermatologists

2. Why does P&G market so many different versions of each brand?
   a) Because while consumers in a segment want the same benefits, there are different priorities within that segment
   b) Because buyers are disloyal and move around from brand to brand
   c) Because P&G cannot decide which target segment to pursue
   d) Because P&G's marketing research has produced conflicting results
   e) Because it is simply practising a deceptive version of mass marketing

3. Why does P&G choose to compete with itself by marketing different brands in the same product category?
   a) Because it creates an aggressive and competitive corporate culture
   b) Because it has never been able to market the P&G brand itself successfully
   c) Because it has different product formulas it wants to use
   d) Because different groups of consumers want different sets of benefits
   e) Because P&G is afraid of any competitor having a segment that P&G could have

4. What is the competitive advantage to P&G in marketing competing brands in a product category?
   a) Economies of scale make it cheaper to manufacture multiple brands than to focus on only one
   b) P&G can capture more share of the total market with multiple brands than with just one brand
   c) Competitors will be unwilling to take on P&G across all segments
   d) If one brand fails, then the others can take over that segment
   e) It gets the same market coverage as it would if it were mass marketing

5. Why does P&G focus on product brands rather than the P&G brand?
   a) Because the words *Procter* and *Gamble* convey no meaning in themselves: They are just surnames
   b) Because it would cost a lot more money to brand P&G across all segments
   c) Because the words *Procter* and *Gamble* are English in origin and have no meaning in many parts of the world
   d) Because its main competitors, Colgate-Palmolive and Johnson & Johnson, do so and P&G wants to be different
   e) Because each brand must be positioned for its target segment, and a single P&G brand cannot have one positioning for all of P&G's segments

Market segmentation Dividing a market into distinct groups with distinct needs, characteristics, or behaviours who might require separate products or marketing mixes.

Target marketing The process of evaluating each market segment's attractiveness and selecting one or more segments to enter.

Market positioning Arranging for a product to occupy a clear, distinctive, and desirable place relative to competing products in the minds of target consumers.

Companies today recognize that they cannot appeal to all buyers in the marketplace, or at least not to all buyers in the same way. Buyers are too numerous, too widely scattered, and too varied in their needs and buying practices. Moreover, the companies themselves vary widely in their abilities to serve different segments of the market. Instead, they must design strategies to build the *right* relationships with the *right* customers. Rather than trying to compete in an entire market, sometimes against superior competitors, each company must identify the parts of the market that it can serve best and most profitably.

Thus, most companies are being choosier about the customers with whom they connect. Most have moved away from mass marketing and toward *market segmentation and targeting*—identifying market segments, selecting one or more of them, and developing products and marketing programs tailored to each. Instead of scattering their marketing efforts (the "shotgun" approach), firms are focusing on the buyers who have greater interest in the values they create best (the "rifle" approach).

Figure 7.1 shows the three major steps in target marketing. The first is **market segmentation**—dividing a market into smaller groups of buyers with distinct needs, characteristics, or behaviours who might require separate products or marketing mixes. The company identifies different ways to segment the market and develops profiles of the resulting market segments. The second step is **target marketing**—evaluating each market segment's attractiveness and selecting one or more of the market segments to enter. The third step is **market positioning**—setting the competitive positioning for the product and creating a detailed marketing mix. We discuss each of these steps in turn.

Figure 7.1   Steps in Market Segmentation, Targeting, and Positioning

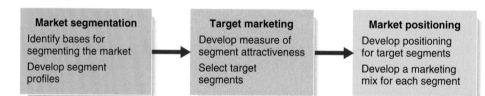

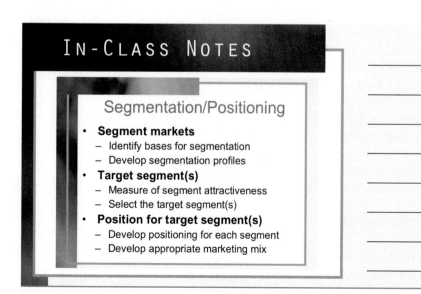

MARKET SEGMENTATION

Markets consist of buyers, and buyers differ in one or more ways. They may differ in their wants, resources, locations, buying attitudes, and buying practices. Through market segmentation, companies divide large, heterogeneous markets into smaller segments that can be reached more efficiently and effectively with products and services that match their unique needs.

For example, Cake Beauty focuses its marketing efforts on a very specific segment: 18- to 34-year-old health-conscious females who are working professionals, have a post-secondary education, and have mid-range spending habits for body care products ($18–$38). Such a well-defined market segment strategy allows Cake Beauty to optimize its product development and maximize its advertising and other marketing expenditures.

In this section we discuss four important segmentation topics: segmenting consumer markets, segmenting business markets, segmenting international markets, and requirements for effective segmentation.

Segmenting Consumer Markets

There is no single way to segment a market. A marketer has to try different segmentation variables, alone and in combination, to find the best way to view the market structure. Table 7.1 outlines the major variables that might be used in segmenting consumer markets. Here we look at the major *geographic, demographic, psychographic,* and *behavioural variables.*

Geographic Segmentation **Geographic segmentation** calls for dividing the market into different geographical units such as nations, regions, provinces, counties, cities, or even neighbourhoods. A company may decide to operate in one or a few geographical areas, or to operate in all areas but pay attention to geographical differences in needs and wants.

Many companies today are localizing their products, advertising, promotion, and sales efforts to fit the needs of individual regions, cities, and even neighbourhoods. For example, Absolut, a maker of vodka, launched a regional advertising campaign aimed at East Coast consumers.[2]

Other companies are seeking to cultivate as-yet untapped geographic territory. For example, many large companies are fleeing the fiercely competitive major cities and suburbs to set up shop in smaller towns. Four-Points Sheraton hotels has opened a chain of smaller format hotels in places like Kingston, Ontario, and Canmore, Alberta, that are too small for its standard-size, more upscale hotels.[3]

In contrast, other retailers are developing new store concepts that will give them access to higher-density urban areas. For example, Home Depot is introducing neighbourhood stores that look a lot like its traditional stores but at about two-thirds the size. It is placing these stores in high-density markets where full-size stores are impractical. Similarly, Wal-Mart is testing Neighbourhood Market grocery stores to complement its supercentres.[4]

Demographic Segmentation **Demographic segmentation** divides the market into groups based on variables such as age, gender, family size, family life cycle, income, occupation, education, religion, race, generation, and nationality. Using demographic factors is the most popular approach for segmenting customer groups. One reason is that consumer needs, wants, and usage rates often vary closely with demographic variables. Another is that demographic variables are easier to measure than

Geographic segmentation
Dividing a market into different geographical units such as nations, regions, provinces, counties, cities, or neighbourhoods.

Demographic segmentation
Dividing the market into groups based on demographic variables such as age, gender, family size, family life cycle, income, occupation, education, religion, race, generation, and nationality.

Geographic segmentation: Many companies are localizing their marketing programs—for example, Absolut launched a campaign aimed at East Coast consumers.

Table 7.1   Major Segmentation Variables for Consumer Markets

Geographic

World region or country	North America, Western Europe, Middle East, Pacific Rim, China, India, Canada, Mexico
Country region	Maritimes, Quebec, Ontario, Prairies, British Columbia, Northern Territories
City or metro size	Up to 5000; 5001–20 000; 20 001–50 000; 50 001–100 000; 100 001–250 000; 250 001–500 000; 500 001–1 000 000; 1 000, 001–4 000 000; more than 4 000 000
Density	Urban, suburban, rural
Climate	Northern, southern, coastal, prairie, mountain

Demographic

Age	Under 6, 6–11, 12–19, 20–34, 35–49, 50–64, 65+
Gender	Male, female
Family size	1–2, 3–4, 5+
Family life-cycle	Young, single; young, married, no children; young, married with children; older, married with children; older, married, no children under 18; older, single; other
Income	Up to $10 000; $10 001–$20 000; $20 001–$30 000; $30 001–$50 000; $50 001–$100, 000; more than $100 000
Occupation	Professional and technical; managers, officials, and proprietors; clerical; sales; craftspeople; supervisors; operatives; farmers; retired; students; homemakers; unemployed
Education	Grade school or less; some high school; high school graduate; college; some university; university graduate; post-graduate
Religion	Catholic, Protestant, Jewish, Muslim, Sikh, Hindu, Buddhist, other
Ethnic Origin	African Canadian, Asian, British, French, German, Scandinavian, Italian, Latin American, First Nations, Middle Eastern, Japanese

Psychographic

Social class	Lower lowers, upper lowers, working class, middle class, upper middles, lower uppers, upper uppers
Lifestyle	Achievers, strivers, strugglers
Personality	Compulsive, gregarious, authoritarian, ambitious

Behavioural

Occasions	Regular occasion; special occasion
Benefits	Quality, service, economy, convenience, speed
User status	Nonuser, ex-user, potential user, first-time user, regular user
User rates	Light user, medium user, heavy user
Loyalty status	None, medium, strong, absolute
Readiness stage	Unaware, aware, informed, interested, desirous, intending to buy
Attitude toward product	Enthusiastic, positive, indifferent, negative, hostile

most other types of variables. Even when market segments are first defined using other approaches, such as benefits sought or behaviour, their demographic characteristics must be known in order to assess the size of the target market and to reach it efficiently.

Age and Life-Cycle Stage. Consumer needs and wants change with age. Some companies use **age and life-cycle segmentation**, offering different products or using different marketing approaches for different age and life-cycle groups. McDonald's targets different age groups—from children to teens to adults and seniors—with different ads and media selection. Its ads aimed at teens feature dance-beat music and a generally fast-paced tone and style, whereas ads for seniors are softer and more sentimental. Procter & Gamble targets its Oil of Olay ProVital moisturizing creams and lotions to women 50+ years of age—where

Age and life-cycle segmentation Dividing a market into different age and life-cycle groups.

the benefit is improving the elasticity and revitalizing the appearance of "maturing skin."[5] Retailer Gap has branched out to appeal to consumers at different life stages with Baby Gap, Gap Kids, and Gap Maternity.

Marketers must be careful to guard against stereotypes when using age and life-cycle segmentation. For example, although some 70-year-olds require wheelchairs, others play tennis. Similarly, whereas some 40-year-old couples are sending their children off to college, others are just beginning new families. Thus, age is often a poor predictor of a person's life cycle; health, work, or family status; needs; and buying power. Companies marketing to mature consumers usually employ positive images and appeals. For example, ads for Olay ProVital feature attractive older spokeswomen and uplifting messages.[6]

Gender. **Gender segmentation** has long been used in clothing, cosmetics, toiletries, and magazines. For example, Procter & Gamble was among the first to use gender segmentation with Secret, a brand of antiperspirant specially formulated for a woman's chemistry, packaged and advertised to reinforce the female image. More recently, other marketers have noticed opportunities for targeting women. Since women make 70 percent of shopping decisions, big-box stores like home-improvement chain RONA are courting women consumers with trendy "paint cafes" and luxurious display kitchens. Owens-Corning aimed a major advertising campaign for home insulation at women after a study showed that two-thirds of all women were involved in materials installation, with 13 percent doing it themselves. Half the women surveyed compared themselves to home improvement guru Bob Vila, whereas less than half compared themselves to Martha Stewart.[7]

Similar thinking was behind Home Depot Canada's new strategy. In 2002 it teamed up with Grocery Gateway, a consumer-direct online service, to offer customers in Greater Toronto and Southern Ontario home delivery of hundreds of home improvement and household items. Home Depot entered the partnership in order to expose its products to a different kind of shopper—people who might not venture into a superstore for a screwdriver or roll of tape. Currently, most Home Depot shoppers are male and are shopping to complete a renovation project, while most Grocery Gateway customers are female and are shopping for consumables and products that are used on an ongoing basis. The partnership enables cross-selling to these different segments.[8]

A growing number of websites also target women. For example, Oxygen Media runs a cable television network and website that targets 18- to 34-year-old women with fresh and hip information, features, and exchanges on a wide variety of topics—from health and fitness, money and work, and style and home to relationships and self-discovery.[9] The W Network offers Canadian women television programming tailored to their interests and issues.

Income. **Income segmentation** has long been used by the marketers of products and services such as automobiles, boats, clothing, cosmetics, financial services, and travel. Many companies target affluent consumers with luxury goods and convenience services. Holt Renfrew specializes in serving affluent, fashion-conscious buyers. To entice consumers to purchase, the stores offer personal shoppers and concierge services.

Neiman Marcus, the upscale U.S. retailer, mails its catalogues to wealthy Canadian consumers, pitching everything from expensive jewellery and fine fashions to glazed Australian apricots priced at $20 a pound. To cater to its best customers, Neiman Marcus created its InCircle Rewards program. Members, who must spend US$5000 a year using their Neiman Marcus credit cards to be eligible, earn points with each purchase—one point for each dollar charged. They then cash in points for anything from a Limited-Edition Emilio Pucci Silk Scarf (5000 points) to a Blue Star Jets Wine Trip (5 million points). InCircle members have an average household income of $606 853 and an average net worth of over $4.5 million.[10]

Gender segmentation Dividing a market into different groups based on gender.

Income segmentation Dividing a market into different income groups.

However, not all companies that use income segmentation target the affluent. The average income (before tax) of unattached individuals in Canada in 2003 was only $25 600 compared with an average income of $64 900 for "economic families" (two or more people in a household). According to Statistics Canada, in 2003 approximately 16 percent of all Canadians and 38 percent of all unattached Canadians were considered to be persons of "low income." Statistics Canada bases its low income definition on the percentage of total income that an individual or household spends on food, shelter, and clothing—and if they are spending approximately 20 percent more than other Canadians on these same basic needs, they are considered to be "lower income."

Greyhound Lines, with its inexpensive nationwide bus network, targets lower-income consumers. Almost half of its revenues come from passengers with annual incomes under $22 000. Many retailers also target this group, including chains such as the Great Canadian Dollar Store and Dollarama. According to AC Nielsen Canada, penetration rates of dollar stores in Canada increased by 5 percent since 2001 to a healthy 77 percent in 2003.

Better merchandising and the direct sourcing of merchandise from overseas manufacturers have enabled these retailers to keep their prices low and to expand their franchises rapidly. And these stores are no longer attracting only the budget conscious. Upscale shoppers are now frequenting their aisles, a fact not missed by competitive retailers such as Wal-Mart and Loblaws that are experimenting with dollar aisles in their stores.[11]

Marketers must be careful to dig deep when they are looking at statistics to make sure they have an accurate picture of a segment—for example, there are no standard measures of poverty across the world and it is easy to wrongly classify the behaviour of a group of consumers based on traditional and subjective definitions. Should a family with plenty of savings and a million-dollar house in the booming real estate market of Vancouver be considered living in poverty because their exceptionally high mortgage means they're spending 20 percent more than other Canadians on food, shelter, and clothing? Many of the households in Canada's richest neighbourhoods would be classified as low income according to the Statistics Canada definition since they spend so much on housing. And yet these same households are definitely lucrative targets for home improvement retailers like RONA and Home Depot. On the other hand, it is sometimes the "asset rich" but "cash-flow poor" like the higher annual income earner with a big mortgage that may be among the most frequent shoppers to a discount retailer like Wal-Mart and even dollar stores.

Psychographic segmentation
Dividing a market into different groups based on social class, lifestyle, or personality characteristics.

Psychographic Segmentation **Psychographic segmentation** divides buyers into different groups based on social class, lifestyle, or personality characteristics. People in the same demographic group can have very different psychographic makeups.

In Chapter 6 we discussed how the products people buy reflect their *lifestyles*. As a result, marketers often segment their markets by consumer lifestyles. For example, Modrobes apparel targets a casual student lifestyle and Lululemon appeals to an athletic chic crowd. One forward-looking grocery store found that segmenting its self-service meat products by lifestyle had a big payoff:

> Walk by the refrigerated self-service meat cases of most grocery stores and you'll usually find the offering grouped by type of meat. Pork is in one case, lamb in another, and chicken in a third. However, one entrepreneurial supermarket decided to experiment and offer groupings of different meats by lifestyle. For instance, the store had a section called "Meals in Minutes," one called "Cookin' Lite," another, filled with prepared products like hot dogs and ready-made hamburger patties, called "Kids Love This Stuff," and one called "I Like to Cook." By focusing on lifestyle needs and not on protein categories, the test store encouraged habitual beef and pork buyers to consider lamb and veal as well. As a result, the five-metre service case has seen a substantial improvement in both sales and profits.[12]

Marketers also have used *personality* variables to segment markets. For example, the marketing campaign for Honda's Reflex and Elite motor scooters *appears* to target hip

Income segmentation: To thank its very best customers, Neiman Marcus created the InCircle Rewards Program. In 2005 members could redeem 5 million points to travel by private jet to California and stay in luxurious accommodations in Sonoma and Napa Valley.

and trendy 22-year-olds. But it is *actually* aimed at a much broader personality group. One ad, for example, shows a delighted child bouncing up and down on his bed while the announcer says, "You've been trying to get there all your life." The ad reminds viewers of the euphoric feelings they got when they broke away from authority and did things their parents told them not to do. It suggests that they can feel that way again by riding a Honda scooter. Thus, Honda is appealing to the rebellious, independent kid in all of us. As Honda notes on its webpage, "Fresh air, freedom, and flair—on a Honda scooter, every day is independence day! When it comes to cool, this scooter is off the charts!" In fact, more than half of Honda's scooter sales are to young professionals and older buyers—15 percent are purchased by the over-50 group. Aging baby boomers, now thrill-seeking middle-agers, caused a 26 percent jump in scooter sales last year.[13]

Behavioural Segmentation   **Behavioural segmentation** divides buyers into groups based on their knowledge, attitudes, uses, or responses to a product. Many marketers believe that behaviour variables are the best starting point for building market segments.

Occasions. Buyers can be grouped according to occasions on which they get the idea to buy, actually make their purchase, or use the purchased item. **Occasion segmentation** can help firms build up product usage. For example, orange juice is most often consumed at breakfast, but orange growers have promoted drinking orange juice as a cool and refreshing drink at other times of the day.

Some holidays, such as Mother's Day and Father's Day, were originally promoted partly to increase the sale of candy, flowers, cards, and other gifts. And many marketers prepare special offers and ads for holiday occasions. For example, Altoids offers a special "Love Tin," the "curiously strong valentine."[14] Hershey wraps its Hershey's Kisses in special holiday colours—75 percent of the demand for Kisses is focused around Valentine's Day, Easter, and other holiday time periods. Butterball, on the other hand, advertises "Happy Thanksgrilling" during the summer to increase the demand for turkeys on non-Thanksgiving occasions.

Kodak, Konica, Fuji, and other camera makers use occasion segmentation in designing and marketing their one-time-use cameras. By mixing lenses, film speeds, and accessories, they have developed special disposable cameras for just about any picture-taking occasion, from underwater photography to baby pictures. The Kodak Water & Sport one-time-use camera is water resistant to 15 metres deep and features a shock-proof

Behavioural segmentation Dividing a market into groups based on consumer knowledge, attitude, use, or response to a product.

Occasion segmentation Dividing the market into groups according to occasions when buyers get the idea to buy, actually make their purchase, or use the purchased item.

Occasion segmentation: For Valentine's Day, Altoids created a special "Love Tin"—a "curiously strong valentine."

frame, a sunscreen and scratch-resistant lens, and 800-speed film. "It survives where your regular camera won't!" claims Kodak.[15]

Benefits Sought. A powerful form of segmentation is to group buyers according to the different *benefits* that they seek from the product. **Benefit segmentation** requires finding the major benefits people look for in the product class, the kinds of people who look for each benefit, and the major brands that deliver each benefit. For example, Procter & Gamble has identified several different laundry detergent segments. Each segment seeks a unique combination of benefits, from cleaning and bleaching to economy, fabric softening, fresh smell, strength or mildness, and lots of suds or only a little.

Benefit segmentation Dividing the market into groups according to the different benefits that consumers seek from the product.

The Champion athletic wear division of Sara Lee Corporation segments its markets according to benefits that different consumers seek from their activewear. For example, "fit and polish" consumers seek a balance between function and style—they exercise for results but want to look good doing it. "Serious sports competitors" exercise heavily and live in and love their activewear—they seek performance and function. By contrast, "value-seeking moms" have low sports interest and low activewear involvement—they buy for the family and seek durability and value. Thus, each segment seeks a different mix of benefits. Champion must target the benefit segment or segments that it can serve best and most profitably using appeals that match each segment's benefit preferences.

User Status. Markets can be segmented into groups of nonusers, ex-users, potential users, first-time users, and regular users of a product. For example, after the tainted blood scandal, Canadians became wary of giving or receiving blood. And with only 3.5 percent of eligible Canadians donating blood out of a potential donor pool of 13 million, Canadian Blood Services used advertising to help meet the demand. When the organization first started using the slogan "It's in you to give," it halted a 10-year decline in blood donations.[16]

In July 2005 the organization released a public service announcement (PSA) to encourage blood donation among youth. Through segmentation, it recognized that, as the donor population ages, it's critical for young people to fill the void. "Even though you can become a blood donor at the age of 17, approximately 80 percent of our donors are over the age of 25," said Dr. Graham Sher, CEO of Canadian Blood Services. "We need to reach out to youth so that they see the value in becoming an everyday hero in their community." The campaign features young adults discussing the extreme lengths they have gone to in order to make a difference in the world and how much easier it is to save a life. The point is made with the tagline "Saving the world isn't easy. Saving a life is. And just one pint of blood can save up to three lives."

An organization's market position also influences its focus. Market share leaders focus on attracting potential users, whereas smaller firms focus on attracting current users away from the market leader.

Usage Rate. Markets can also be segmented into light, medium, and heavy product users. Heavy users are often a small percentage of the market but account for a high percentage of total consumption. Marketers usually prefer to attract one heavy user to their product or service rather than several light users.

For example, in the fast-food industry, heavy users make up only 20 percent of patrons but eat up about 60 percent of all the food served. A single heavy user, typically a single male who doesn't know how to cook, might spend as much as $50 in a day at fast-food restaurants and visit them more than 20 times a month. Heavy users "come more often, they spend more money, and that's what makes the cash registers ring," says a Burger King marketing executive. Interestingly, although fast-food companies such as Burger King, McDonald's, and KFC depend a lot on heavy users and do all they can to keep them satisfied with every visit, these companies often target light users with their ads and promotions. The heavy users "are in our restaurants already," says the Burger King marketer. The company's marketing dollars are more often spent trying to convince light users that they want a burger in the first place.[17]

Loyalty Status. A market can also be segmented by consumer loyalty. Consumers can be loyal to brands (Tide), stores (the Bay), and companies (Ford). Buyers can be divided into groups according to their degree of loyalty. Some consumers are completely loyal—they buy one brand all the time. Others are somewhat loyal—they are loyal to two or three brands of a given product or favour one brand while sometimes buying others. Still other buyers show no loyalty to any brand. They either want something different each time they buy or they buy whatever's on sale.

A company can learn a lot by analyzing loyalty patterns in its market. It should start by studying its own loyal customers. For example, to better understand the needs and behaviour of its core soft drink consumers, Pepsi observed them in places where its products are consumed—in homes, in stores, in movie theatres, at sporting events, and at the beach. "We learned that there's a surprising amount of loyalty and passion for Pepsi's products," says Pepsi's director of consumer insights. "One fellow had four or five cases of Pepsi in his basement and he felt he was low on Pepsi and had to go replenish." The company used these and other study findings to pinpoint the Pepsi target market and develop marketing appeals.[18]

By studying its less loyal buyers, the company can detect which brands are most competitive with its own. If many Pepsi buyers also buy Coke, Pepsi can attempt to improve its positioning against Coke, possibly by using direct-comparison advertising. By looking at customers who are shifting away from its brand, the company can learn about its marketing weaknesses. As for nonloyals, the company may attract them by putting its brand on sale.

Using Multiple Segmentation Bases Marketers rarely limit their segmentation analysis to only one or a few variables. Rather, they use multiple segmentation bases in an effort to identify smaller, better-defined target groups. Thus, a bank may not only identify a group of wealthy retired adults but also, within that group, distinguish several

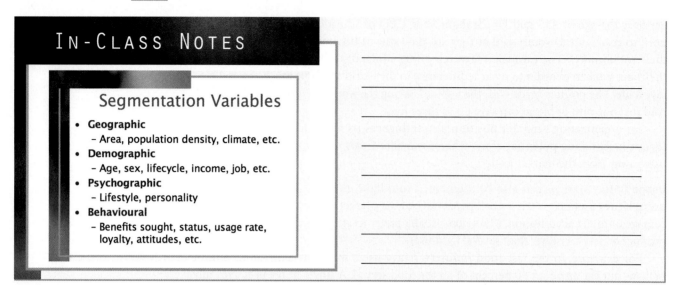

segments based on their current income, assets, savings and risk preferences, and lifestyles. Companies often begin by segmenting their markets using a single base, then expand using other bases. Six Apart, a blog software company, has used multiple segmentation bases with a great deal of success (see Marketing at Work 7.1).

Marketing at Work   7.1

Segmenting Bloggers

The Merriam-Webster dictionary defines a "blog" as a "Web site that contains an online personal journal with reflections, comments, and often hyperlinks provided by the writer." Sounds low-key enough, but this simple concept has become a rapidly growing phenomenon. Blogs help people publish on a worldwide scale anything from what they ate for breakfast to their opinions on a company's stock price or a political issue.

Blogs are having a growing impact on society at large by allowing amateurs to compete with journalists in voicing their opinions and their descriptions of news from the front lines. Blogs are also impacting business—corporations around the world are rushing to jump on the bandwagon, with many having their CEOs write personal blogs on their company websites. Blogs can also keep a company on its toes when it comes to public relations and product development.

In the early days, blogs were built by hackers who developed functionality that they knew intuitively would be good. There was little thought of segmenting the market and targeting specific groups of users. Before long there were literally hundreds of blog software options to choose from, and weblog users, especially beginners, were finding it very challenging to select the best program for their needs.

Six Apart, one of the leading early players that transformed itself from a small basement-based start-up to one of the leading commercial players, was among the first to attempt to segment the blog market. It was launched in 2001 by Mena and Ben Trott, web designers who had lost their jobs after the dot-com crash. Instead of looking for other employment, they decided to try building Movable Type, a software tool to help them create weblogs. Within the first hour of Movable Type's launch, more

than a hundred people downloaded their free software.

Several months after the launch of Movable Type, Mena explained that she and Ben

realized that there were a great number of people who could benefit from a weblogging service as powerful as Movable Type if only it didn't require installation or configuration. We wanted to create a weblogging hosting service that anyone could use, even people who lacked technical experience or desire to fiddle with code. Almost exactly a year from the time we decided to first create Movable Type, Ben and I began work on our hosting service, TypePad. . . . When Ben and I began envisioning TypePad, we imagined a niche service that could run on a couple of servers in a managed hosting environment.

(continued)

October 2003 saw the official launch of TypePad, targeted at light users who wanted to create and manage a weblog but wanted the experience to be simple, requiring no installation and little, if any, configuration. Six Apart's Movable Type product remained for the smaller, but important, developer segment—those wanting extra control of the application and with programming abilities to modify the code base and write their own enhanced features.

Six Apart discovered another market segment when they noticed that many bloggers were not the traditional blog hobbyists—they were webmasters and marketing communications managers with large corporations. They wanted to "harvest" this segment as a potential source of revenue, but they didn't want to alienate the grassroots users who wouldn't be able or interested in paying very much, if anything, for the product.

Six Apart's solution was to set up the pricing and licensing structure based on four segments: personal, commercial, education, and not-for-profit. They further segmented the market based on the number of users who would be accessing their software—an approach that normally means that larger companies with bigger budgets pay more.

At first, the move toward segmented pricing was a disaster. Loyal Movable Type customers were quickly up in arms and migrated to a free open-source product. Six Apart took note and adjusted their segments and pricing strategy to try to discourage their important developer segment from leaving. As Mena Trott explains, "We came back stronger with a powerful new plug-in architecture and API support and a demonstration of our commitment to the developer community with our plug-in contest, through which we awarded $20 000 in prizes to plug-in developers."

In January 2005 Six Apart acquired Danga Interactive, the makers of LiveJournal, in order to target an additional segment of the blog market. "LiveJournal fills a niche in Six Apart's offering as the most community-focused application in the product family," says Mena Trott. "LiveJournal's innovations include friend pages—pages that enable users to easily view the recent journal updates of their LiveJournal friends. Additionally, with LiveJournal, users can have custom control over who can view their journal posts as well as join interest-based communities. Paying members have access to additional features including additional image uploads, fast-lane access, and the ability to post by email or phone."

With the consumer, developer, corporate, and community blog segments covered, Six Apart is in an excellent strategic position. And as the blog market continues to grow and evolve, Six Apart will no doubt continue to identify new segments and adapt their offerings to accommodate them.

Source: www.sixapart.com.

One good example of multivariable segmentation is "geodemographic" segmentation. Several business information services have arisen to help marketing planners link Canadian and U.S. census data with lifestyle patterns to better segment their markets down to postal codes, neighbourhoods, and even city blocks. One of the leading lifestyle segmentation systems in Canada is PSYTE Canada Advantage by MapInfo. Based on Canadian Census data, this system classifies Canadian neighbourhoods into 65 mutually exclusive and unique lifestyle groups, or "clusters," developed from select indicators of consumer behaviour, key demographics, media preferences, lifestyle, and location.

Such systems provide a powerful tool for segmenting markets, refining demand estimates, selecting target markets, and shaping promotion messages. Since birds of a feather tend to flock together, knowing a customer's postal code can reap a goldmine of useful segmentation information. In fact, many organizations such as Ikea and Winners routinely ask their shoppers at the point of purchase for their postal code to start leveraging this information. Marketers must be careful not to be overzealous with their attempts to capture segmentation information, however. New privacy legislation in Canada requires customers be told why they're being asked for personal information.

Segmenting Business Markets

Consumer and business marketers use many of the same variables to segment their markets. Business buyers can be segmented geographically, demographically (industry, company size), or by benefits sought, user status, usage rate, and loyalty status. But business marketers use some additional variables, such as customer *operating characteristics, purchasing approaches, situational factors,* and *personal characteristics.*

By going after segments instead of the whole market, companies have a much better chance to deliver value to customers and to receive maximum rewards for close attention to their needs. Hewlett-Packard's Computer Systems Division targets specific industries that promise the best growth prospects, such as telecommunications and financial services. Its "red team" sales force specializes in developing and serving major customers in these targeted industries.[19] Within the chosen industry, a company can further segment by *customer size* or *geographic location*. For example, Hewlett-Packard's "blue team" telemarkets to smaller accounts and to those that don't fit neatly into the strategically targeted industries on which HP focuses.

A company might also set up separate systems for dealing with larger or multiple-location customers. For example, Steelcase, a major producer of office furniture, first segments customers into 10 industries, including banking, insurance, and electronics. Next, company salespeople work with independent Steelcase dealers to handle smaller, local, or regional Steelcase customers in each segment. But many national, multiple-location customers, such as Exxon/Mobil or IBM, have special needs that may reach beyond the scope of individual dealers. So Steelcase uses national accounts managers to help its dealer networks handle its national accounts.

Within a given target industry and customer size, the company can segment by purchase approaches and criteria. As in consumer segmentation, many marketers believe that *buying behaviour* and *benefits* provide the best basis for segmenting business markets.[20]

Segmenting International Markets

Few companies have either the resources or the will to operate in all, or even most, of the countries that dot the globe. Although some large companies, such as Coca-Cola or Sony, sell products in hundreds of countries, most international firms focus on a smaller set. Operating in many countries presents new challenges. Different countries, even those that are close together, can vary greatly in their economic, cultural, and political makeup. Thus, just as they do within their domestic markets, international firms need to group their world markets into segments with distinct buying needs and behaviours.

Companies can segment international markets using one or a combination of several variables. They can segment by *geographic location*, grouping countries by regions such as Western Europe, the Pacific Rim, the Middle East, or Africa. Geographic segmentation assumes that nations close to one another will have many common traits and behaviours. Although this is often the case, there are many exceptions. For example, although Canada and the United States have much in common, overlooking differences between the two countries can be dangerous. Furthermore, both differ culturally and economically from neighbouring Mexico. And even within a region consumers can differ widely. For example, many marketers think that all Central and South American countries are the same, including their 400 million inhabitants. However, the Dominican Republic is no more like Brazil than Italy is like Sweden. Many Latin Americans don't speak Spanish, including 140 million Portuguese-speaking Brazilians and the millions in other countries who speak a variety of Indian dialects.

World markets can also be segmented on the basis of *economic factors*. For example, countries might be grouped by population income levels or by their overall level of economic development. Some countries, such as Canada, the United States, Britain, France, Germany, Japan, Italy, and Russia, have established, highly industrialized economies. Other countries have newly industrialized or developing economies (China, India, Singapore, Taiwan, Korea, Brazil, Mexico). Still others are less developed or have a patchy record of development (many African and Central American countries, Haiti, North Korea). A country's economic structure shapes its population's product and service needs and, therefore, the marketing opportunities it offers.

Countries can be segmented by *political and legal factors* such as the type and stability of government, receptivity to foreign firms, monetary regulations, and the amount of bureaucracy. Such factors can play a crucial role in a company's choice of which countries to enter and how. *Cultural factors* can also be used, grouping markets according to common languages, religions, values and attitudes, customs, and behavioural patterns.

Segmenting international markets on the basis of geographic, economic, political, cultural, and other factors assumes that segments should consist of clusters of countries. However, many companies use a different approach called **intermarket segmentation**. Using this approach, they form segments of consumers who have similar needs and buying behaviour even though they are located in different countries. For example, Mercedes-Benz targets the world's well-to-do, regardless of their country.

Intermarket segmentation
Forming segments of consumers who have similar needs and buying behaviour even though they are located in different countries.

And MTV, MuchMusic, and other music channels target the world's teenagers. The world's teens have a lot in common: They study, shop, and sleep. They are exposed to many of the same major issues: love, crime, homelessness, ecology, and working parents. In many ways, they have more in common with each other than with their parents. "Last year I was in 17 different countries," says one expert, "and it's pretty difficult to find anything that's different, other than language, among a teenager in Japan, a teenager in the U.K., and a teenager in China." Says another, "Global teens in Buenos Aires, Beijing, and Bangalore swing to the beat of MTV while sipping Coke." MTV bridges the gap between cultures, appealing to what teens around the world have in common. Sony, Reebok, Nike, Swatch, and many other firms also actively target global teens.[21]

Requirements for Effective Segmentation

Clearly, there are many ways to segment a market, but not all segmentations are effective. For example, buyers of table salt could be divided into blond and brunette customers. But hair colour obviously does not affect the purchase of salt. Furthermore, if all salt buyers bought the same amount of salt each month, believed that all salt is the same, and wanted to pay the same price, the company would not benefit from segmenting this market.

To be useful, market segments must be

☐ *Measurable:* The size, purchasing power, and profiles of the segments can be measured. Certain segmentation variables are difficult to measure. For example, there are around 4 million left-handed people in Canada—which is 15 percent of the population. Yet few products are targeted toward this left-handed segment. The major problem may be that the segment is hard to identify and measure. There are

Intermarket segmentation: Teens show surprising similarity no matter where in the world they live. For instance, these two teens could live almost anywhere. Thus, many companies target teenagers with worldwide marketing campaigns.

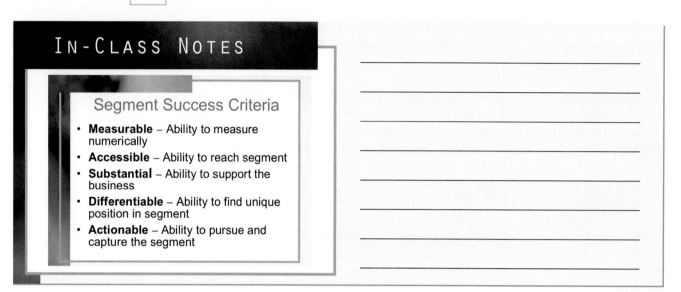

IN-CLASS NOTES

Segment Success Criteria

- **Measurable** – Ability to measure numerically
- **Accessible** – Ability to reach segment
- **Substantial** – Ability to support the business
- **Differentiable** – Ability to find unique position in segment
- **Actionable** – Ability to pursue and capture the segment

---

no data on the demographics of lefties, and Statistics Canada does not keep track of left-handedness in its surveys. Private data companies keep reams of statistics on other demographic segments but not on left-handers. As a result, only market nichers like Anything Left-Handed in the U.K. target this segment.

☐ *Accessible:* The market segments can be effectively reached and served. Suppose a fragrance company finds that heavy users of its brand are single men and women who stay out late and socialize a lot. Unless this group lives or shops at certain places and is exposed to certain media, its members will be difficult to reach.

☐ *Substantial:* The market segments are large or profitable enough to serve. A segment should be the largest possible homogeneous group worth pursuing with a tailored marketing program. It would not pay, for example, for an automobile manufacturer to develop cars especially for people whose height is greater than seven feet.

☐ *Differentiable:* The segments are conceptually distinguishable and respond differently to different marketing mix elements and programs. If married and unmarried women respond similarly to a sale on perfume, they do not constitute separate segments.

☐ *Actionable:* Effective programs can be designed for attracting and serving the segments. For example, although one small airline identified seven market segments, its staff was too small to develop separate marketing programs for each segment.

Linking the Concepts

How do the companies you do business with employ the segmentation concepts you're reading about here?

■ Can you identify specific companies, other than the examples already discussed, that practise the different types of segmentation just discussed?

■ Using the segmentation bases you've just read about, segment the Canadian footwear market. Describe each of the major segments and subsegments. Keep these segments in mind as you read the next section on target marketing.

TARGET MARKETING

Market segmentation reveals the firm's market segment opportunities. The firm now has to evaluate the various segments and decide how many and which segments it can serve best. We now look at how companies evaluate and select target segments.

Evaluating Market Segments

In evaluating different market segments, a firm must look at three factors: segment size and growth, segment structural attractiveness, and company objectives and resources.

Segment Size and Growth   The company must first collect and analyze data on current segment sales, growth rates, and expected profitability for various segments. It will be interested in segments that have the right size and growth characteristics. But "right size and growth" is a relative matter. The largest, fastest-growing segments are not always the most attractive ones for every company. Smaller companies may lack the skills and resources needed to serve the larger segments. Or they may find these segments too competitive. Such companies may select segments that are smaller and less attractive, in an absolute sense, but that are potentially more profitable for them.

Segment Structural Attractiveness   The company also needs to examine major structural factors that affect long-run segment attractiveness.[22] For example, a segment is less attractive if it already contains many strong and aggressive *competitors*. The existence of many actual or potential *substitute products* may limit prices and the profits that can be earned in a segment. The relative *power of buyers* also affects segment attractiveness. Buyers with strong bargaining power relative to sellers will try to force prices down, demand more services, and set competitors against one another—all at the expense of seller profitability. Finally, a segment may be less attractive if it contains *powerful suppliers* who can control prices or reduce the quality or quantity of ordered goods and services.

Company Objectives and Resources   Even if a segment has the right size and growth and is structurally attractive, the company must consider its own objectives and resources in relation to that segment. Some attractive segments could be dismissed quickly because they do not mesh with the company's long-run objectives. The company must consider whether it possesses the skills and resources needed to succeed in that segment. If the company lacks the needed strengths and cannot readily obtain them, it should not enter the segment. Even if the company possesses the *required* strengths, it needs to employ skills and resources *superior* to those of the competition in order to really win in a market segment. The company should enter only those segments in which it can offer superior value and gain advantages over competitors.

Selecting Target Segments

After evaluating different segments, the company must now decide which and how many segments it will target. A **target market** consists of a set of buyers who share common needs or characteristics that the company decides to serve.

Because buyers have unique needs and wants, a seller could potentially view each buyer as a separate target market. Ideally, then, a seller might design a separate marketing program for each buyer. However, although some companies do attempt to serve buyers individually, most face larger numbers of smaller buyers and do not find individual targeting worthwhile. Instead, they look for broader segments of buyers. More generally, target marketing can be carried out at several different levels. Figure 7.2 shows that companies can target very broadly (undifferentiated marketing), very narrowly (micromarketing), or somewhere in between (differentiated or concentrated marketing).

Target market A set of buyers sharing common needs or characteristics that the company decides to serve.

Figure 7.2   Target Marketing Strategies

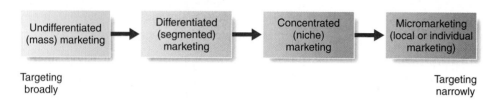

Undifferentiated (mass) marketing A market-coverage strategy in which a firm decides to ignore market segment differences and go after the whole market with one offer.

Undifferentiated Marketing

Using an **undifferentiated marketing** (or **mass marketing**) strategy, a firm might decide to ignore market segment differences and target the whole market with one offer. This mass-marketing strategy focuses on what is *common* in the needs of the market rather than on what is *different*. The company designs a product and a marketing program that will appeal to the largest number of buyers. It relies on mass distribution and mass advertising, and it aims to give the product a superior image in people's minds.

As noted earlier in the chapter, most modern marketers have strong doubts about this strategy. Difficulties arise in developing a product or brand that will satisfy all consumers. Moreover, mass marketers often have trouble competing with more focused firms that do a better job of satisfying the needs of specific segments and niches.

Differentiated (segmented) marketing A market-coverage strategy in which a firm decides to target several market segments and designs separate offers for each.

Differentiated Marketing

Using a **differentiated marketing** (or **segmented marketing**) strategy, a firm decides to target several market segments and designs separate offers for each. General Motors tries to produce a car for every "purse, purpose, and personality." Nike offers athletic shoes for a dozen or more different sports, from running, fencing, golf, and aerobics to baseball and bicycling. Weston Foods appeals to the needs of different shopper segments by offering different retail banners such as No Frills, Loblaws, Zehrs, and Fortinos for different shopper segments. Cadbury Chocolate Canada targets its Mr. Big candy bar to teenagers, Crispy Crunch to young adults, and Time Out bars to harried businesspeople.

By offering product and marketing variations to segments, companies hope for higher sales and a stronger position within each market segment. Developing a stronger position within several segments creates more total sales than undifferentiated marketing across all segments. Procter & Gamble gets more total market share with seven brands of laundry detergent than it could with only one. And Estée Lauder's combined brands give it a much greater market share than any single brand could. The Estée Lauder and Clinique brands alone reap a combined 40 percent share of the prestige cosmetics market.

But differentiated marketing also increases the costs of doing business. A firm usually finds it more expensive to develop and produce 10 units of 10 different products than 100 units of one product. Developing separate marketing plans for the separate segments requires extra marketing research, forecasting, sales analysis, promotion planning, and channel management. And trying to reach different market segments with different advertising increases promotion costs. Thus, the company must weigh increased sales against increased costs when deciding on a differentiated marketing strategy.

Concentrated (niche) marketing A market-coverage strategy in which a firm goes after a large share of one or a few segments, or niches.

Concentrated Marketing

A third market-coverage strategy, **concentrated marketing** (or **niche marketing**), is especially appealing when company resources are limited. Instead of going after a small share of a large market, the firm goes after a large share of one or a few segments or niches. For example, Oshkosh Truck is the world's largest producer of airport rescue trucks and front-loading concrete mixers. Tetra sells 80 percent of the world's tropical fish food, and Steiner Optical captures 80 percent of the world's military binoculars market.

Whereas segments are fairly large and normally attract several competitors, niches are smaller and may attract only one or a few competitors. Through concentrated marketing, the firm achieves a strong market position because of its greater knowledge of consumer needs in the niches it serves and the special reputation it acquires. It can market more *effectively* by fine-tuning its products, prices, and programs to the needs of carefully defined segments. It can also market more *efficiently*, targeting its products or services, channels, and communications programs toward only the consumers that it can serve best and most profitably.

Niching offers smaller companies an opportunity to compete by focusing their limited resources on serving niches that may be unimportant to or overlooked by larger competitors. WestJet began operations in 1996 to

Niching: Rather than competing head-on with other PC makers, Apple has invested in research and development, creating a loyal base of consumers who are willing to pay more for Apple's cutting edge products.

provide low-cost air travel to a restricted number of smaller Canadian markets. And consider Apple Computer. Although it once enjoyed a better than 13 percent market share, Apple is now a market niche player, capturing only about 3 percent of the personal computer market in 2004. Rather than competing head-on with other PC makers as they slash prices and focus on volume, Apple invests in research and development, making it the industry trendsetter. Such innovation has created a loyal base of consumers who are willing to pay more for Apple's cutting edge products, such as the iPod.[23] The growing popularity of the iPod is expected to result in more Apple computer sales and a market share increase to 5 percent in 2005.

Today, the low cost of setting up shop on the Internet makes it even more profitable to serve seemingly minuscule niches. Small businesses in particular are realizing riches from serving small niches on the Web. Here is a "Webpreneur" who achieved astonishing results:

> Whereas Internet giants like Amazon.com have yet to even realize a consistent profit, Steve Warrington is earning a six-figure income selling ostriches—and every product derived from them—online (www.ostrichesonline.com). Launched for next to nothing on the Web in 1996, Ostrichesonline.com now boasts that it sends newsletters to more than 55,000 subscribers and sells 20,000 ostrich products to more than 34,000 satisfied clients in more than 125 countries. The site tells visitors everything they ever wanted to know about ostriches and much, much more—it supplies ostrich facts, ostrich pictures, an ostrich farm index, and a huge ostrich database and reference index. Visitors to the site can buy ostrich meat, feathers, leather jackets, videos, eggshells, and skin care products derived from ostrich body oil.[24]

Concentrated marketing can be highly profitable. At the same time, it involves higher-than-normal risks. Companies that rely on one or a few segments for all of their business will suffer greatly if the segment experiences an economic downturn. Or larger competitors may decide to enter the same segment. California Cooler's early success in the wine cooler segment attracted many large competitors, causing the original owners to sell to a larger company that had more marketing resources. For these reasons, many companies prefer to diversify in several market segments.

Micromarketing   Differentiated and concentrated marketers tailor their offers and marketing programs to meet the needs of various market segments and niches. At the

Micromarketing The practice of tailoring products and marketing programs to the needs and wants of specific individuals and local customer groups—includes *local marketing* and *individual marketing.*

Local marketing Tailoring brands and promotions to the needs and wants of local customer groups—cities, neighbourhoods, and even specific stores.

same time, however, they do not customize their offers to each individual customer. **Micromarketing** is the practice of tailoring products and marketing programs to suit the tastes of specific individuals and locations. Rather than seeing a customer in every individual, micromarketers see the individual in every customer. Micromarketing includes *local marketing* and *individual marketing.*

Local Marketing. **Local marketing** involves tailoring brands and promotions to the needs and wants of local customer groups—cities, neighbourhoods, and even specific stores. Retailers such as Sears and Wal-Mart routinely customize each store's merchandise and promotions to match its local clientele. And Kraft helps supermarkets identify specific cheese assortments and shelf-positioning that will optimize cheese sales in low, middle, and high-income stores in ethnic communities.

Local marketing has some drawbacks. It can drive up manufacturing and marketing costs by reducing economies of scale. It can also create logistics problems, as companies try to meet the varied requirements of different regional and local markets. Furthermore, a brand's overall image might be diluted if the product and message vary too much in different localities.

Still, as companies face increasingly fragmented markets, and as new supporting technologies develop, the advantages of local marketing often outweigh the drawbacks. Local marketing helps a company to market more effectively in the face of pronounced regional and local differences in demographics and lifestyles. It also meets the needs of the company's first-line customers—retailers—who prefer more fine-tuned product assortments for their neighbourhoods.

Individual marketing Tailoring products and marketing programs to the needs and preferences of individual customers—also labelled "markets-of-one marketing," "customized marketing," and "one-to-one marketing."

Collaborative filtering The method of making automatic predictions about the interests of an individual user by collecting taste information from many users.

Individual Marketing. In the extreme, micromarketing becomes **individual marketing**—tailoring products and marketing programs to the needs and preferences of individual customers. Individual marketing has also been labelled *one-to-one marketing, customized marketing,* and *markets-of-one marketing.*

The growing use of information technology has enabled and fuelled the growth of micromarketing. Customer information can be stored in large databases and data warehouses and detailed purchase history can be "data mined" to come up with compelling offers for individual customers. **Collaborative filtering** is the method of making automatic predictions about the interests of an individual user by collecting taste information from many users. The underlying assumption of the approach is that those who agreed in the past tend to agree again in the future. For example, a collaborative filtering or recommendation system for music tastes could make predictions about which music a user should like given a partial list of that user's tastes (likes or dislikes). One of the most successful examples of this is Amazon.com's use of collaborative filtering—providing suggestions of books that a customer would likely be interested in buying based on the sales records and feedback from other customers that have a similar purchase history. The personalized suggestions are remarkably relevant—millions of records are searched for patterns to provide the recommendations, something that would just not be possible without information technology.

The widespread use of mass marketing has obscured the fact that for centuries consumers were served as individuals: The tailor custom-made the suit, the cobbler designed shoes for the individual, the cabinetmaker made furniture to order. Today, however, new technologies are permitting many companies to return to customized marketing in a more productive fashion. More powerful computers, detailed databases, robotic production and flexible manufacturing, and interactive communication media such as email and the World Wide Web—all have combined to foster "mass customization." *Mass customization* is the process through which firms interact one-to-one with masses of customers to design products and services tailor-made to individual needs. This approach doesn't work so well in all situations—it's difficult for a cereal manufacturer to mass customize its products to individual customers and remain profitable. But for a company with easy-to-configure options such as a telecommunications player offering cell phone service and associated services, one-to-one marketing enables it to offer seamless, custom packages instead of a one size fits all.

Perhaps the most important factor driving the trend toward one-to-one marketing is the Internet. It ties it all together and makes it easy for a company to interact with customers and respond to their preferences. Indeed, the Internet appears to be the ultimate one-to-one medium. Unlike mass production, which eliminates the need for human interaction, mass customization has made relationships with customers more important than ever.

Dell Computer, for example, delivers computers to individual customers loaded with customer-specified hardware and software. Dell's mass customization approach has paid off very well—it was the leading PC maker in the world in 2004, with about 18 percent of the worldwide market. And it's not just manufacturers that are taking advantage of one-to-one marketing—leading service players like Ritz-Carlton Hotels are creating custom-designed experiences to delight their guests:

> Check into any Ritz-Carlton hotel around the world, and you'll be amazed at how well the hotel's employees anticipate your slightest need. Without ever asking, they seem to know that you want a nonsmoking room with a king-size bed, a non-allergenic pillow, and breakfast with decaffeinated coffee in your room. How does Ritz-Carlton work this magic? The hotel employs a system that combines information technology and flexible operations to customize the hotel experience. At the heart of the system is a huge customer database, which contains information gathered through the observations of hotel employees. Each day, hotel staffers—from those at the front desk to those in maintenance and housekeeping—discreetly record the unique habits, likes, and dislikes of each guest on small "guest preference pads." These observations are then transferred to a corporate-wide "guest preference database." Every morning, a "guest historian" at each hotel reviews the files of all new arrivals that have previously stayed at a Ritz-Carlton and prepares a list of suggested extra touches that might delight each guest. Guests have responded strongly to such markets-of-one service. Since inaugurating the guest-history system, Ritz-Carlton has boosted guest retention by 23 percent. An amazing 95 percent of departing guests report that their stay has been a truly memorable experience.[25]

Business-to-business marketers are also finding new ways to customize their offerings. For example, Becton-Dickinson, a major medical technology supplier, offers to customize almost anything for its hospital customers. It offers custom-designed labelling, individual packaging, customized quality control, customized computer software, and customized billing. And John Deere manufactures seeding equipment that can be configured in more than 2 million versions to individual customer specifications. The seeders are produced one at a time, in any sequence, on a single production line.[26]

The move toward individual marketing mirrors the trend in consumer *self-marketing*. Increasingly, individual customers are taking more responsibility for determining which products and brands to buy. Consider two business buyers with two different purchasing styles. The first sees several salespeople, each trying to persuade him to buy his or her product. The second sees no salespeople but rather logs on to the Internet. She searches for information on available products; interacts electronically with various suppliers, users, and product analysts; and then makes up her own mind about the best offer. The second purchasing agent has taken more responsibility for the buying process, and the marketer has had less influence over her buying decision.

As the trend toward more interactive dialogue and less advertising monologue continues, self-marketing will grow in importance. As more buyers look up consumer

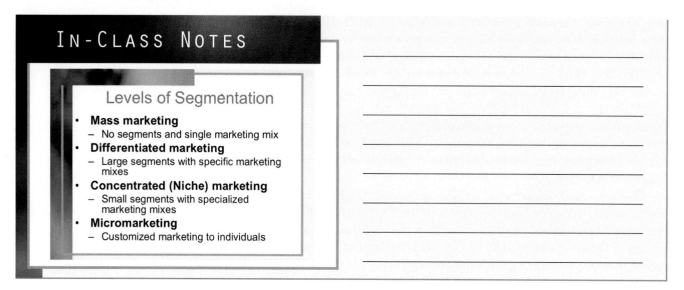

IN-CLASS NOTES

Levels of Segmentation

- **Mass marketing**
  - No segments and single marketing mix
- **Differentiated marketing**
  - Large segments with specific marketing mixes
- **Concentrated (Niche) marketing**
  - Small segments with specialized marketing mixes
- **Micromarketing**
  - Customized marketing to individuals

reports, join Internet product discussion forums, and place orders via phone or online, marketers will have to influence the buying process in new ways. Many companies now practise *customerization*.[27] They combine operationally driven mass customization with customized marketing to empower consumers to design products and services to their own preferences. They involve customers more in all phases of the product development and buying processes, increasing opportunities for buyers to practise self-marketing.

Choosing a Target-Marketing Strategy Companies need to consider many factors when choosing a target-marketing strategy. Which strategy is best depends on *company resources*. When the firm's resources are limited, concentrated marketing makes the most sense. The best strategy also depends on the degree of *product variability*. Undifferentiated marketing is more suited for uniform products such as grapefruit or steel. Products that can vary in design, such as cameras and automobiles, are more suited to differentiation or concentration.

The *product's life-cycle stage* also must be considered. When a firm introduces a new product, it may be practical to launch only one version, and undifferentiated marketing or concentrated marketing may make the most sense. In the mature stage of the product life cycle, however, differentiated marketing begins to make more sense. Another factor is *market variability*. If most buyers have the same tastes, buy the same amounts, and react the same way to marketing efforts, undifferentiated marketing is appropriate. Finally, *competitors' marketing strategies* are important. When competitors use differentiated or concentrated marketing, undifferentiated marketing can be disastrous. Conversely, when competitors use undifferentiated marketing, a firm can gain an advantage by using differentiated or concentrated marketing.

Socially Responsible Target Marketing

Smart targeting helps companies be more efficient and effective by focusing on the segments that they can satisfy best and most profitably. Targeting also benefits consumers—companies reach specific groups of consumers with offers carefully tailored to satisfy their needs. However, target marketing sometimes generates controversy and concern. Issues usually involve the targeting of vulnerable or disadvantaged consumers with controversial or potentially harmful products.

For example, over the years, the cereal industry has been heavily criticized for its marketing efforts directed toward children. Critics worry that premium offers and high-powered advertising appeals presented through the mouths of lovable animated characters will overwhelm children's defences. The marketers of toys and other children's products have been similarly battered, often with good justification.

Other problems arise when the marketing of adult products spills over into the kid segment—intentionally or unintentionally. For example, regulators and citizen action groups have accused Molson of targeting children with their beer advertising. And a recent U.S. study found that 80 percent of R-rated movies and 70 percent of video games with a mature rating were targeted to children under 17.[28] Some critics have even called for a complete ban on advertising to children. To encourage responsible advertising to children, the Canadian Association of Broadcasters and the Advertising Standards Council have partnered to develop the Broadcast Code for Advertising to Children. This code is designed to complement the general principles for ethical advertising outlined in the Canadian Code of Advertising Standards.

Fast-food marketers have also generated much controversy in recent years by their attempts to target vulnerable consumers. For example, McDonald's and other chains have drawn criticism for pitching their high-fat, salt-laden fare to low-income people. McDonald's has faced lawsuits alleging that its marketing practices are responsible for teenage obesity. *Super Size Me*, a popular documentary produced in 2004 and directed by Morgan Spurlock, takes an irreverent look at obesity in America and blames fast food corporations as one of its primary sources. McDonald's has since phased out its super-sizing—the practice of offering customers discounts for buying larger portions—and has introduced a number of healthier choices. McDonald's has also successfully associated itself with healthy athletes through its long-term sponsorship of the Olympic Games.

The meteoric growth of the Internet and other carefully targeted direct media has raised fresh concerns about potential targeting abuses. The Internet allows increasing refinement of audiences and, in turn, more precise targeting. This might help makers of questionable products or deceptive advertisers to more readily victimize the most vulnerable audiences. As one expert observes, "In theory, an audience member could have tailor-made deceptive messages sent directly to his or her computer screen."[29]

Not all attempts to target children, minorities, or other special segments draw such criticism. In fact, most provide benefits to targeted consumers. For example, Colgate makes a large selection of toothbrushes and toothpaste flavours and packages for children—from Colgate Barbie Sparkling Bubble Fruit, Colgate Barney Mild Bubble Fruit, and Colgate Looney Tunes Tazmanian Devil Wild Mint toothpastes to Colgate Pokemon and Disney Monsters, Inc. character toothbrushes. Such products help make tooth brushing more fun and get children to brush longer and more often.

Nacara Cosmétiques markets cosmetics for "ethnic women who have a thirst for the exotic." The line is specially formulated to complement the darker skin tones of black women and dark-skinned women of Latin American, First Nations, and Caribbean origins.

Thus, in target marketing, the issue is not really *who* is targeted but rather *how* and for *what*. Controversies arise when marketers attempt to profit at the expense of targeted segments—when they unfairly target vulnerable segments or target them with questionable products or tactics. Socially responsible marketing calls for segmentation and targeting that serve not just the interests of the company but also the interests of those targeted.

Deciding on the Global Marketing Program

Companies that operate in one or more foreign markets must decide how much, if at all, to adapt their marketing mixes to local conditions. At one extreme, some global companies avoid regional segmentation and instead use a **standardized marketing mix**, pri-

Standardized marketing mix An international marketing strategy for using basically the same product, advertising, distribution channels, and other elements of the marketing mix in all of the company's international markets.

Most target marketing benefits both the marketer and the consumer. Nacara Cosmétiques, a Canadian company founded in 1999, meets the specific needs of consumers of African, North African, Iberian, Caucasian, and mixed-race heritage.

Adapted marketing mix An international marketing strategy for adjusting the marketing mix elements to each international target market, bearing more costs but hoping for a larger market share and return.

marily selling the same products and using the same marketing approaches worldwide. At the other extreme, some companies use an **adapted marketing mix** and adjust its elements to each regional target market segment, bearing more costs but hoping for a larger market share and return.

How does a firm choose whether to adapt or standardize the marketing mix? The marketing concept holds that marketing programs will be more effective if tailored to the unique needs of each targeted customer group. If this concept applies within a country, it should apply even more in international markets. Consumers in different countries have widely varied cultural backgrounds, needs and wants, spending power, product preferences, and shopping patterns. Because these differences are hard to change, most marketers adapt their products, prices, channels, and promotions to fit consumer desires in each country.

However, some global marketers are bothered by what they see as too much adaptation, which raises costs and dilutes global brand power. As a result, many companies have created so-called world brands—more or less the same product sold the same way to all consumers worldwide. Marketers at these companies believe that advances in communication, transportation, and travel are turning the world into a common marketplace.

Proponents of global standardization claim that international marketers should adapt products and marketing programs only when local wants cannot be changed or avoided. Standardization results in lower production, distribution, marketing, and management costs, and thus lets the company offer consumers higher quality and more reliable products at lower prices. In fact, some companies have successfully marketed global product formats—for example, Coca-Cola soft drinks, McDonald's hamburgers, Black & Decker tools, and Sony Walkmans.

However, even for these "global" brands, companies make some adaptations. For example, MTV, with its largely global programming, has retrenched along more local lines. Pummelled by dozens of local music channels in Europe, such as Germany's Viva, Holland's The Music Factory, and Scandinavia's ZTV, MTV Europe has had to drop its pan-European programming, which featured a large amount of American and British pop along with local European favourites. In its place, the division created regional channels broadcast by four separate MTV stations—MTV: UK & Ireland, MTV: Northern Europe, MTV: Central Europe, and MTV: Southern Europe. Each of the four channels shows programs tailored to music tastes of its local market, along with more traditional pan-European pop selections. Within each region, MTV further subdivides its programming. For example, within the United Kingdom, MTV offers sister stations M2 and VH-1, along with three new digital channels: MTV Extra, MTV Base, and VH-1 Classic. Says the head of MTV Europe, "We hope to offer every MTV fan something he or she will like to watch any time of the day."

Which approach is best—global standardization or adaptation and reliance on regional segments? Clearly, global standardization is not an all-or-nothing proposition but rather a matter of degree. Companies should look for more standardization to help keep down costs and prices and to build greater global brand power. But they must not replace long-run marketing thinking with short-run financial thinking. Although standardization saves money, marketers must make certain that they offer consumers in each country what they want.

Linking the Concepts

Review the main concepts of what you've read so far:

■ Previously, you segmented the Canadian footwear market. Refer to Figure 7.2 and select two companies that serve this market. Describe their segmentation and targeting strategies. Can you come up with one that targets many different segments versus another that focuses on only one or a few segments?

■ How does each company you chose differentiate its marketing offer and image? Has each done a good job of establishing this differentiation in the minds of targeted consumers? The final section in this chapter deals with such positioning issues.

POSITIONING FOR COMPETITIVE ADVANTAGE

Beyond deciding which segments of the market it will target, the company must decide what positions it wants to occupy in those segments. A **product's position** is the way the product is *defined by consumers* on important attributes—the place the product occupies in consumers' minds relative to competing products. Positioning involves implanting the brand's unique benefits and differentiation in customers' minds.

Tide is positioned as a powerful, all-purpose family detergent; Ivory Snow is positioned as the gentle detergent for fine washables and baby clothes. In the automobile market, the Toyota Echo and Ford Focus are positioned on economy, Mercedes and Cadillac on luxury, and Porsche and BMW on performance. Volvo positions itself powerfully on safety. And Toyota positions its fuel-efficient hybrid Prius as a high-tech solution to the energy shortage. "How far will you go to save the planet?" it asks.

Consumers are overloaded with information about products and services. They cannot reevaluate products every time they make a buying decision. To simplify the buying process, consumers organize products, services, and companies into categories and "position" them in their minds. A product's position is the complex set of perceptions, impressions, and feelings that consumers have for the product compared with competing products.

Consumers position products with or without the help of marketers. But marketers do not want to leave their products' positions to chance. They must *plan* positions that will give their products the greatest advantage in selected target markets, and they must design marketing mixes to create these planned positions.

Product position The way the product is defined by consumers on important attributes—the place the product occupies in consumers' minds relative to competing products.

Positioning Maps

In planning their positioning strategies, marketers often prepare *perceptual positioning maps,* which show consumer perceptions of their brands versus competing products on important buying dimensions. Figure 7.3 shows a positioning map for the large luxury sport utility vehicle market.[30] The position of each circle on the map indicates the brand's perceived positioning on two dimensions—price and orientation (luxury versus performance). The size of each circle indicates the brand's relative market share. Thus, customers view the market-leading Cadillac Escalade as a moderately priced large luxury SUV with a balance of luxury and performance.

Figure 7.3 Positioning Map: Large Luxury SUVs

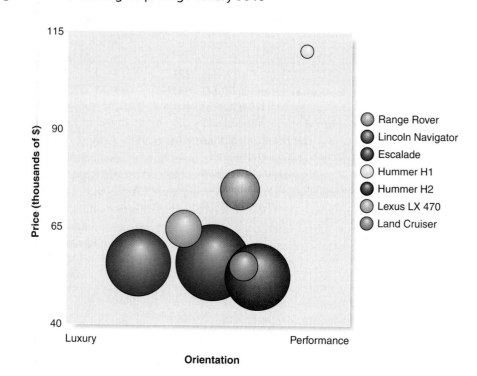

The original Hummer H1 was positioned as a very high performance SUV with a price tag to match. Hummer targets the H1 toward a small segment of well-off rugged individualists. According to the H1 website, "The H1 was built around one central philosophy: function. Every aspect of the H1 was created to allow it to go where cars and trucks just aren't supposed to go. [It] gives you an incredible sense of freedom and allows you to experience the world and your place in it." By contrast, although also oriented toward performance, the Hummer H2 is positioned as a more luxury-oriented and more reasonably priced luxury SUV. The H2 is targeted toward a larger segment of urban and suburban professionals. "In a world where SUVs have begun to look like their owners, complete with love handles and mushy seats, the H2 proves that there is still one out there that can drop and give you twenty," says the H2 website. The H2 "strikes a perfect balance between interior comfort, on-the-road capability, and off-road capability."

Choosing a Positioning Strategy

Some firms find it easy to choose their positioning strategy. For example, a firm well known for quality in certain segments will go for this position in a new segment if there are enough buyers seeking quality. But in many cases, two or more firms will go after the same position. Then, each will have to find other ways to set itself apart. Each firm must differentiate its offer by building a unique bundle of benefits that appeals to a substantial group within the segment.

The positioning task consists of three steps: identifying a set of possible competitive advantages on which to build a position, choosing the right competitive advantages, and selecting an overall positioning strategy. The company must then effectively communicate and deliver the chosen position to the market.

Identifying Possible Competitive Advantages The key to winning customers and building profitable relationships with them is to understand their needs better than competitors do and to deliver more value. To the extent that a company can position itself as providing superior value, it gains **competitive advantage**. But solid positions cannot be built on empty promises. If a company positions its product as *offering* the best quality and service, it must then *deliver* the promised quality and service. Thus, positioning begins with actually *differentiating* the company's marketing offer so that it will give consumers more value than competitors' offers do.

To find points of differentiation, marketers must think through the customer's entire experience with the company's product or service. An alert company can find ways to differentiate itself at every point where it comes in contact with customers. In what specific ways can a company differentiate its offer from those of competitors? A company or market offer can be differentiated along the lines of *product, services, channels, people,* or *image.*

Product differentiation takes place along a continuum. At one extreme we find physical products that allow little variation: chicken, steel, aspirin. Yet even here some meaningful differentiation is possible. For example, Maple Leaf Foods claims that its Maple Leaf Prime Naturally branded chickens are better—fresher and more tender—and gets a price premium based on this differentiation. At the other extreme are products that can be highly differentiated, such as automobiles, clothing, and furniture. Such products can be differentiated on features, performance, or style and design. Thus, Volvo provides new and better safety features; Whirlpool designs its dishwasher to run more quietly; Bose positions its speakers on their striking design characteristics. Similarly, companies can differentiate their products on attributes such as consistency, durability, reliability, or repairability.

Beyond differentiating its physical product, a firm can also differentiate the services that accompany the product. Some companies gain *services differentiation* through speedy, convenient, or careful delivery. For example, CIBC partnered with Loblaws to form President's Choice Banking, opening branches in Weston's store (Loblaws and SuperStore) and thus providing location convenience along with Saturday, Sunday, and weekday-evening hours.

Installation can also differentiate one company from another, as can repair services. Many an automobile buyer will gladly pay a little more and travel a little farther to buy a car from a dealer that provides top-notch repair services. Some companies differentiate their offers by providing customer training service or consulting services—data, information systems, and advising services that buyers need. McKesson Corporation, a major drug wholesaler, consults with its 12 000 independent pharmacists to help them set up accounting, inventory, and computerized ordering systems. By helping its customers compete better, McKesson gains greater customer loyalty and sales.

Firms that practise *channel differentiation* gain competitive advantage through the way they design their channel's coverage, expertise, and performance. Caterpillar's success in the construction-equipment industry is based on superior channels. Its dealers, such as Finning in Canada, are renowned for their first-rate service. ING Direct Banking, Amazon, and Dell Computer similarly distinguish themselves by their high-quality direct channels.

Competitive advantage An advantage over competitors gained by offering greater value, either through lower prices or by providing more benefits that justify higher prices.

Companies can gain a strong competitive advantage through *people differentiation*—hiring and training better people than their competitors do. Disney people are known to be friendly and upbeat. Singapore Airlines enjoys an excellent reputation largely because of the grace of its flight attendants. IBM positions itself as a "solutions provider" to businesses and takes pride in its consultants' high level of skills. In short, people differentiation requires that a company select its customer-contact people carefully and train them well. For example, Toronto's Four Seasons Hotel is famous for its people and the service it provides to business travellers.

Even when competing offers look the same, buyers may perceive a difference based on company or brand *image differentiation*. A company or brand image should convey the product's distinctive benefits and positioning. Developing a strong and distinctive image calls for creativity and hard work. A company cannot develop an image in the public's mind overnight using only a few advertisements. If Four Seasons means quality, this image must be supported by everything the company says and does. Symbols—such as the McDonald's golden arches, the Prudential rock, the Nike swoosh, the Intel Inside logo, or the Pillsbury doughboy—can also provide strong company or brand recognition and image differentiation. The company might build a brand around a famous person, as Nike did with its Air Jordan basketball shoes and Tiger Woods golfing products. Some companies even become associated with colours, such as IBM (blue), Campbell (red and white), or UPS (brown). The chosen symbols, characters, and other image elements must be communicated through advertising that conveys the company's or brand's personality.

Choosing the Right Competitive Advantages   Suppose a company is fortunate enough to discover several potential competitive advantages. It now must choose the ones on which it will build its positioning strategy. It must decide *how many* differences to promote and *which ones*.

How Many Differences to Promote?   Many marketers think that companies should aggressively promote only one benefit to the target market. Ad man Rosser Reeves, for example, has said that a company should develop a *unique selling proposition* (USP) for each brand and stick to it. Each brand should pick an attribute and tout itself as "number one" on that attribute. Buyers tend to remember number one better, especially in an overcommunicated society. Thus, Crest toothpaste consistently promotes its anticavity protection and Volvo promotes safety. A company that hammers away at one of these positions and consistently delivers on it will probably become best known and remembered for it.

Other marketers think that companies should position themselves on more than one differentiator. This may be necessary if two or more firms are claiming to be best on the same attribute. Today, in a time when the mass market is fragmenting into many small segments, companies are trying to broaden their positioning strategies to appeal to more segments. For example, Unilever introduced the first three-in-one bar soap—Lever 2000—offering cleansing, deodorizing, *and* moisturizing benefits. Clearly, many buyers want all three benefits. The challenge was to convince them that one brand can deliver all three. Judging from Lever 2000's outstanding success, Unilever easily met the challenge.

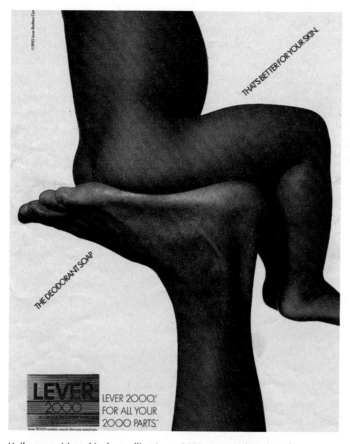

Unilever positioned its bestselling Lever 2000 soap on three benefits in one: cleansing, deodorizing, and moisturizing benefits. It's good "for all your 2000 parts."

However, as companies increase the number of claims for their brands, they risk disbelief and a loss of clear positioning.

In general, a company needs to avoid three major positioning errors. The first is *underpositioning*—failing ever to really position the company at all. Some companies discover that buyers have only a vague idea of the company or that they do not really know anything special about it. The second error is *overpositioning*—giving buyers too narrow a picture of the company. Thus, a consumer might think that the Steuben glass company makes only fine art glass costing $1600 and up, when in fact it makes affordable fine glass starting at around $90.

Finally, companies must avoid *confused positioning*—leaving buyers with a confused image of a company. For example, Wal-Mart has consistently positioned itself forcefully as offering "Always low prices. Always!" In contrast, Zellers has gone through a series of different advertising messages that have left many shoppers confused.

Which Differences to Promote? Not all brand differences are meaningful or worthwhile; not every difference makes a good differentiator. Each difference has the potential to create company costs as well as customer benefits. Therefore, the company must carefully select the ways in which it will distinguish itself from competitors. A difference is worth establishing to the extent that it satisfies the following criteria:

- ☐ *Important:* The difference delivers a highly valued benefit to target buyers.
- ☐ *Distinctive:* Competitors do not offer the difference, or the company can offer it in a more distinctive way.
- ☐ *Superior:* The difference is superior to other ways that customers might obtain the same benefit.
- ☐ *Communicable:* The difference is communicable and visible to buyers.
- ☐ *Preemptive:* Competitors cannot easily copy the difference.
- ☐ *Affordable:* Buyers can afford to pay for the difference.
- ☐ *Profitable:* The company can introduce the difference profitably.

Many companies have introduced differentiations that failed one or more of these tests. The Westin Stamford hotel in Singapore advertises that it is the world's tallest hotel, a distinction that is not important to most tourists—in fact, it turns many off. Polaroid's Polarvision, which produced instantly developed home movies, bombed too. Although Polarvision was distinctive and even preemptive, it was inferior to another

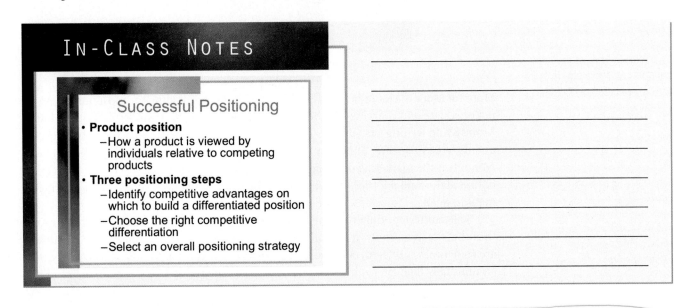

IN-CLASS NOTES

Successful Positioning
- **Product position**
  - How a product is viewed by individuals relative to competing products
- **Three positioning steps**
  - Identify competitive advantages on which to build a differentiated position
  - Choose the right competitive differentiation
  - Select an overall positioning strategy

way of capturing motion, namely, camcorders. When Pepsi introduced clear Crystal Pepsi some years ago, cola drinkers were unimpressed. Although the new drink was distinctive, consumers didn't see "clarity" as an important benefit in a cola drink. Thus, choosing competitive advantages on which to position a product or service can be difficult, yet such choices may be crucial to success.

Selecting an Overall Positioning Strategy Buyers typically choose products and services that give them the greatest value. Thus, marketers want to position their brands on the key benefits that they offer relative to competing brands. The full positioning of a brand is called the brand's **value proposition**—the full mix of benefits on which the brand is positioned. It is the answer to the customer's question "Why should I buy your brand?" Volvo's value proposition hinges on safety but also includes reliability, roominess, and styling, all for a price that is higher than average but seems fair for this mix of benefits.

Figure 7.4 shows possible value propositions on which a company might position its products. In the figure, the five blue cells represent winning value propositions—positioning that gives the company competitive advantage. The red cells represent losing value propositions. The centre yellow cell represents at best a marginal proposition. In the following sections, we discuss the five winning value propositions on which companies can position their products: more for more, more for the same, the same for less, less for much less, and more for less.[31]

> **Value proposition** The full positioning of a brand—the full mix of benefits on which it is positioned.

Figure 7.4   Possible Value Propositions

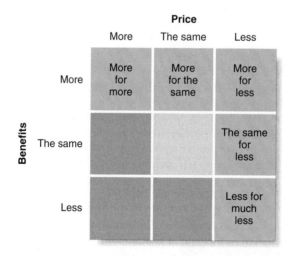

More for More. "More for more" positioning involves providing the most upscale product or service and charging a higher price to cover the higher costs. Ritz-Carlton Hotels, Mont Blanc writing instruments, Mercedes-Benz automobiles—each claims superior quality, craftsmanship, durability, performance, or style and charges a price to match. Not only is the marketing offer high in quality, it also gives prestige to the buyer. It symbolizes status and a loftier lifestyle. Often, the price difference exceeds the actual increment in quality.

Sellers offering "only the best" can be found in every product and service category, from hotels, restaurants, food, and fashion to cars and kitchen appliances. Consumers are sometimes surprised, even delighted, when a new competitor enters a category with an unusually high-priced brand. Starbucks coffee entered as a very expensive brand in a largely commodity category; Häagen-Dazs came in as a premium ice cream brand at a price never before charged.

In general, companies should be on the lookout for opportunities to introduce a "much-more-for-much-more" brand in any underdeveloped product or service category. Yet "more-for-more" brands can be vulnerable. They often invite imitators who claim the same quality but at a lower price. And luxury goods that sell well during good times may be at risk during economic downturns when buyers become more cautious in their spending.

More for the Same. Companies can attack a competitor's more-for-more positioning by introducing a brand offering comparable quality but at a lower price. For example, Toyota introduced its Lexus line with a "more-for-the-same" value proposition. Its headline read: "Perhaps the first time in history that trading a $90,000 car for a $44,000 car could be considered trading up." It communicated the high quality of its new Lexus through rave reviews in car magazines and through a widely distributed videotape showing side-by-side comparisons of Lexus and Mercedes automobiles. It published surveys showing that Lexus dealers were providing customers with better sales and service experiences than were Mercedes dealerships. Many Mercedes owners switched to Lexus, and the Lexus repurchase rate has been 60 percent, twice the industry average.

Before we knew it we were having Häagen~Dazs.

Fall deeply in Häagen~Dazs.

"Much more for much more" value proposition: Häagen-Dazs offers its superpremium ice cream at a price never before charged.

The Same for Less. Offering "the same for less" can be a powerful value proposition—everyone likes a good deal. For example, Dell Computer offers equivalent-quality computers at a lower "price for performance." Discounts stores such as Wal-Mart and "category killers" such as Future Shop/Best Buy and Sportmart also use this positioning. They don't claim to offer different or better products. Instead, they offer many of the same brands as department stores and specialty stores but at deep discounts based on superior purchasing power and lower-cost operations. Other companies develop imitative but lower-priced brands in an effort to lure customers away from the market leader. For example, AMD makes less expensive versions of Intel's market-leading microprocessor chips.

Less for Much Less. A market almost always exists for products that offer less and therefore cost less. Few people need, want, or can afford "the very best" in everything they buy. In many cases, consumers will gladly settle for less than optimal performance or give up some of the bells and whistles in exchange for a lower price. For example, many travellers seeking lodgings prefer not to pay for what they consider unnecessary extras, such as a pool, attached restaurant, or mints on the pillow. Motel chains such as Motel 6 and Holiday Inn Express suspend some of these amenities and charge less accordingly.

"Less for much less" positioning involves meeting consumers' lower performance or quality requirements at a much lower price. For example, Dollarama and Buck or Two stores offer more affordable goods at very low prices. Sam's Club and Costco warehouse stores offer less merchandise selection and consistency, and much lower levels of service; as a result, they charge rock-bottom prices. WestJet, the nation's most profitable air carrier, also practises less for much less positioning. It charges incredibly low prices by not serving free food, not assigning seats, and not using travel agents (see Marketing at Work 7.2).

Marketing at Work | 7.2

WestJet: "Less for Less" Strategy at Work

WestJet was founded on a strategy of "less for less." By researching other successful airlines in North America—and in particular low-cost carriers—the founders of WestJet followed the primary examples of Southwest Airlines and Morris Air and determined that a similar concept could be successful in western Canada.

Southwest Airlines had pioneered, developed, and successfully exploited the low-fare airline model for 25 years before WestJet's creation. Southwest began in 1971 with three aircraft servicing three cities in Texas. It became known over time as an employee-oriented, somewhat irreverent, work-hard-play-hard company. It has also been the most consistently profitable airline in the world.

The actual business model differed from traditional airlines in several ways:

☐ Low-cost-producer strategy: From the outset, the company adopted a low-cost, no-frills strategy

☐ Target market focus: Price-sensitive passengers

☐ Single-class service focus: Short haul, point-to-point routes

Southwest's communications strategy emphasized that the airline operated as a complement to traditional airlines and targeted travellers who might otherwise drive or travel by bus or train.

WestJet adopted much of Southwest's successful model. WestJet is employee owned, and in keeping with the "less for less" philosophy, it offers a single class of service, without ticket offices at points other than airports. Nor does it offer baggage transfer services with other airlines, in-flight meals, frequent flier promotions, or such special passenger privileges as business-class lounges.

WestJet focuses on short-haul, point-to-point service. It has chosen to service both traditional and nontradi-

tional routes, where it can increase flight service frequency and where its jet service has a competitive advantage over the regional turbo-prop planes. And even though it's focused on minimizing costs and prices, WestJet has maintained respect for its customers and rightfully takes pride in its customer service.

The Air Travel Complaints Commission began tracking complaints from air travellers in mid-2000. To the end of December 2001, 3912 complaints had been laid. Of this total, 2597 complaints had been lodged against Air Canada and their regional carriers while only 13 had been registered against WestJet. Even considering Air Canada's dominance of the Canadian airline market, WestJet's performance in this area is testimony to its commitment to customers and totally consistent with WestJet's values and spirit.

A critical element in WestJet's communications strategy is retaining the

airline's consistent image as "a low-cost, pretzel kind of carrier." Siobhan Vinish, the airline's director of public relations and communications, says, "We don't want to be perceived as another monolithic airline. Our advertising has to reinforce our image as an easygoing, fun airline."

WestJet is an excellent example of the success possible with the "less for less" model. In WestJet's case, "less service for less money" is defined as fewer routes and fewer amenities for a lower fare, *not* less customer service. And with WestJet's focus on performance and excellent customer service, you could even argue that this exemplifies a "more for less" strategy!

Sources: WestJet Annual Report 2001, March 20, 2002, www.westjet.com, accessed May 2002; *Southwest Airlines Fact Sheet, June 2001*, www.southwest.com, accessed May 2002; Peter Verburg, "Reach for the Bottom," *Canadian Business*, 2000; Helena Katz, "Peanuts and Pretzels Fly East," *Marketing*, March 6, 2000; Norma Ramage, "WestJet Fuels up Advertising Effort," *Marketing*, March 12, 2001.

WestJet provides less in terms of frills, but offers more in terms of unique customer service. Here, a WestJet employee reads her poetry to the passengers.

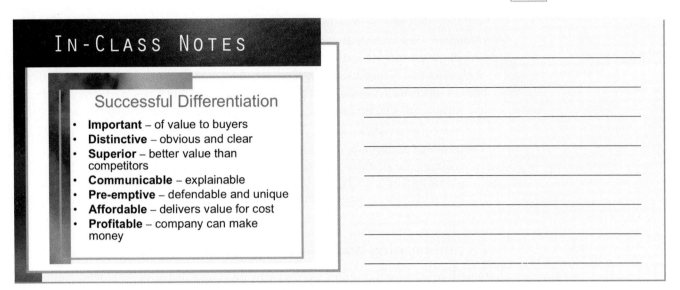

More for Less. Of course, the winning value proposition would be to offer "more for less." Many companies claim to do this. For example, Dell Computer claims to have better products *and* lower prices for a given level of performance. Procter & Gamble claims that its laundry detergents provide the best cleaning *and* everyday low prices. In the short run, some companies can actually achieve such lofty positions. For example, when it first opened for business, Home Depot had arguably the best product selection, the best service, *and* the lowest prices compared with local hardware stores and other home improvement chains.

Yet, in the long run, companies will find it very difficult to sustain such best-of-both positioning. Offering more usually costs more, making it difficult to deliver on the "for less" promise. Companies that try to deliver both may lose out to more focused competitors. For example, facing determined competition from Wal-Mart stores, Zellers must now decide whether it wants to compete primarily on superior service or on lower prices.

In the end, each brand must adopt a positioning strategy designed to serve the needs and wants of its target markets. "More for more" will draw one target market, "less for much less" will draw another, and so on. Thus, in any market, there is usually room for many different companies, each successfully occupying different positions.

The important thing is that each company must develop its own winning positioning strategy, one that makes it special to its target consumers. Offering only "the same for the same" provides no competitive advantage, leaving the firm in the middle of the pack. Companies offering one of the three losing value propositions—"the same for more," "less for more," and "less for the same"—will inevitably fail. Customers soon realize that they've been underserved, tell others, and abandon the brand.

Developing a Positioning Statement Company and brand positioning should be summed up in a **positioning statement**. The statement should follow the following form: *To (target segment and need) our (brand) is (concept) that (point-of-difference).*[32] For example: "To *busy professionals who need to stay organized, Palm Pilot is an electronic organizer that allows you to back up files on your PC more easily and reliably than competitive products.*" Sometimes a positioning statement is more detailed:

> To young, active soft-drink consumers who have little time for sleep, Mountain Dew is the soft drink that gives you more energy than any other brand because it has the highest level of caffeine. With Mountain Dew, you can stay alert and keep going even when you haven't been able to get a good night's sleep.[33]

Positioning statement A statement that summarizes company or brand positioning—it takes this form: *To (target segment and need) our (brand) is (concept) that (point-of-difference).*

Note that the positioning first states the product's membership in a category (Mountain Dew is a soft drink) and then shows its point-of-difference from other members of the category (has more caffeine). Placing a brand in a specific category suggests similarities that it might share with other products in the category. But the case for the brand's superiority is made on its points of difference. Sometimes marketers put a brand in a surprisingly different category before indicating the points of difference:

> Kraft's Delissio frozen pizza offers a variation called Rising Crust pizza. Instead of putting it in the frozen pizza category, the marketers positioned it in the delivered pizza category. Their ad shows party guests asking which pizza delivery service the host used. But, says the host, "It's not delivery, its Delissio!" This helped highlight Delissio's fresh quality and superior taste over the normal frozen pizza.

Communicating and Delivering the Chosen Position

Once it has chosen a position, the company must take strong steps to deliver and communicate the desired position to the target market segment. All the company's marketing mix efforts must support the positioning strategy. Positioning the company calls for concrete action, not just talk. If the company decides to build a position on better quality and service, it must first *deliver* that position. Designing the marketing mix—product, price, place, and promotion—involves working out the tactical details of the positioning strategy. Thus, a firm that seizes on a more-for-more position knows that it must produce high-quality products, charge a high price, distribute through high-quality dealers, and advertise in high-quality media. It must hire and train more service people, find retailers who have a good reputation for service, and develop sales and advertising messages that broadcast its superior service. This is the only way to build a consistent and believable more-for-more position.

Companies often find it easier to come up with a good positioning strategy than to implement it. Establishing a position or changing one usually takes a long time. In contrast, positions that have taken years to build can quickly be lost. Once a company has built the desired position, it must take care to maintain the position through consistent performance and communication. It must closely monitor and adapt the position over time to match changes in consumer needs and competitors' strategies. However, the company should avoid abrupt changes that might confuse people. Instead, a product's position should evolve gradually as it adapts to the ever-changing marketing environment.

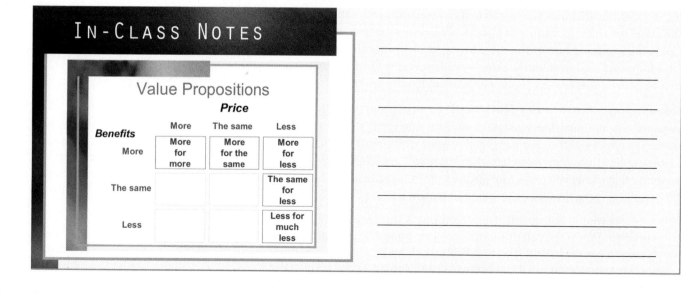

LOOKING BACK

In this chapter, you've learned about the major elements of marketing strategy: segmentation, targeting, and positioning. Marketers know that they cannot appeal to all buyers in their markets, or at least not to all buyers in the same way. Buyers are too numerous, too widely scattered, and too varied in their needs and buying practices. Therefore, most companies today are moving away from mass marketing. Instead, they practise target marketing—identifying market segments, selecting one or more of them, and developing products and marketing mixes tailored to each. In this way, sellers can develop the right product for each target market and adjust their prices, distribution channels, and advertising to reach the target market efficiently.

REVIEWING THE CONCEPTS

1. Define the three steps of target marketing: market segmentation, target marketing, and market positioning.

Target marketing involves designing strategies to build the *right relationships* with the *right customers*. *Market segmentation* is the act of dividing a market into distinct groups of buyers with different needs, characteristics, or behaviours who might require separate products or marketing mixes. Once the groups have been identified, *target marketing* evaluates each market segment's attractiveness and selects one or more segments to serve. *Market positioning* consists of deciding how to best serve target customers—setting the competitive positioning for the product and creating a detailed marketing plan.

2. List and discuss the major approaches for segmenting consumer and business markets.

There is no single way to segment a market. Therefore, the marketer tries different variables to see which give the best segmentation opportunities. For consumer marketing, the major segmentation variables are geographic, demographic, psychographic, and behavioural. In *geographic segmentation*, the market is divided into different geographical units such as nations, regions, provinces, counties, cities, or neighbourhoods. In *demographic segmentation*, the market is divided into groups based on demographic variables, including age, gender, family size, family life cycle, income, occupation, education, religion, race, generation, and nationality. In *psycho-graphic segmentation*, the market is divided into different groups based on social class, lifestyle, or personality characteristics. In *behavioural segmentation*, the market is divided into groups based on consumers' knowledge, attitudes, uses, or responses to a product.

Business marketers use many of the same variables to segment their markets. But business markets also can be segmented by business *demographics* (industry, company size), *operating characteristics, purchasing approaches, situational factors,* and *personal characteristics*. The effectiveness of segmentation analysis depends on finding segments that are *measurable, accessible, substantial, differentiable,* and *actionable*.

3. Explain how companies identify attractive market segments and choose a target marketing strategy.

To target the best market segments, the company first evaluates each segment's size and growth characteristics, structural attractiveness, and compatibility with company objectives and resources. It then chooses one of four target marketing strategies—ranging from very broad to very narrow targeting. The seller can ignore segment differences and target broadly using *undifferentiated (or mass) marketing*. This involves mass producing, mass distributing, and mass promoting about the same product in about the same way to all consumers. Or the seller can adopt *differentiated marketing*—developing different market offers for several segments. *Concentrated marketing* (or *niche marketing*) involves focusing on only one or a few market segments. Finally, *micromarketing* is the practice of tailoring products and marketing programs to suit the tastes of specific individuals and locations. Micromarketing includes *local marketing* and *individual marketing*. Which targeting strategy is best depends on company resources, product variability, product life-cycle stage, market variability, and competitive marketing strategies.

4. Discuss how companies position their products for maximum competitive advantage in the marketplace.

Once a company has decided which segments to enter, it must decide on its *market positioning* strategy—on which positions to occupy in its chosen segments. The positioning task consists of three steps: identifying a set of possible competitive advantages on which to build a position, choosing the right competitive advantages, and selecting an overall positioning strategy. The brand's full positioning is called its *value proposition*—the full mix of benefits on which the brand is positioned. In general, companies can choose from one of five winning value propositions on which to position its products: more for more, more for the same, the same for less, less for much less, or more for less. Company and brand positioning are summarized in positioning statements that state the target segment and need, positioning concept, and specific points of difference. The company must then effectively communicate and deliver the chosen position to the market.

KEY TERMS

adapted marketing mix   *270*
age and life-cycle segmentation   *252*
behavioural segmentation   *255*
benefit segmentation   *256*
collaborative filtering   *266*
competitive advantage   *273*
concentrated (niche) marketing   *264*
demographic segmentation   *251*
differentiated (segmented) marketing   *264*

gender segmentation   *253*
geographic segmentation   *251*
income segmentation   *253*
individual marketing   *266*
intermarket segmentation   *261*
local marketing   *266*
market positioning   *250*
market segmentation   *250*
micromarketing   *266*
occasion segmentation   *255*

positioning statement   *279*
product position   *271*
psychographic segmentation   *254*
standardized marketing mix   *269*
target market   *263*
target marketing   *250*
undifferentiated (or mass) marketing   *264*
value proposition   *276*

STUDY GUIDE

After completing this self-test, check your answers against the Answer Key at the back of the book.

MULTIPLE CHOICE

1. The market segmentation strategies of Red Bull Energy Drink and Gatorade are largely based on what segmentation criteria?
   a. Price and sweetness
   b. Availability and packaging
   c. Gender and self-actualization
   d. Lifestyle and personality
   e. Macro and niche

2. Consider the following product category brands: Dasani bottled water, diet caffeine-free Coke, and Clearly Canadian. Each of these brands illustrates a type of segmentation. Select the set that most closely matches these brands respectively:
   a. Mass, specific, and micro
   b. Common, specialized, and patriotic
   c. Undifferentiated, differentiated, and niche
   d. Physical, lifestyle, and psychographic
   e. Normalized, specialized, and individualized

3. Although loyal and heavy users of a brand generate the most revenue, marketers generally target advertising at nonusers or light users. Why is this so?

   a. Because heavy users do not need the reinforcement of brand advertising and stay loyal as a result of ongoing customer satisfaction
   b. Because studies show that heavy users do not respond well to advertising
   c. Because most light users will turn into heavy users if they are exposed to enough advertising
   d. Because the media used to advertise to heavy users is much more costly than that used for light users
   e. Because it is virtually impossible to lure a competitor's heavy users away through advertising

4. An undifferentiated segmentation strategy in the business-to-business market is illustrated by makers of standard printer paper. A differentiated segmentation strategy in the business-to-business market is best illustrated by
   a. IBM
   b. Home Depot
   c. Staples
   d. 3M
   e. All of the above

5. Intermarket segmentation takes the approach of finding mass similarities in what are otherwise dissimilar groups of people from different countries. An example of intermarket segmentation might be
   a. Marketing textbooks to schools
   b. Marketing cell phones to businesspeople
   c. Marketing beer and wine to consumers
   d. Marketing birth control pills to young women
   e. None of the above

6. Mass marketing, the idea that one brand can be successfully sold to an entire market with no segmentation, is far less common than it was a hundred years ago. However, certain product categories still lend themselves well to mass marketing approaches, for example:
   a. Book matches
   b. Lawn fertilizers
   c. Batteries
   d. Cat litter
   e. Bottled mineral water

7. A marketer of athletic shoes may have seven different brands and three versions of each brand—clearly a case of segmented marketing. However, this maker now wants to offer a shoe that's made to order based on a footprint impression taken at the store. For this new brand, the marketer must reformulate his marketing mix to suit which segmentation strategy?
   a. Concentrated segmentation
   b. One-on-one marketing
   c. Collaborative filtering
   d. Micromarketing
   e. Niche marketing

8. When portable phones were first introduced in the late 70s and early 80s, the manufacturers and the cellular service providers had to collaborate on an important strategic decision in order to achieve a successful market entry. They had to determine
   a. How revenues would be shared between the phone makers and the service providers
   b. The right initial target segment
   c. Whether the phone would be car-mounted or handheld
   d. Whether the market was price sensitive
   e. Whether North Americans would accept the idea of "talking and walking"

9. One way of determining positioning is to identify a particular value proposition for the brand. The value proposition that best reflects President's Choice "Too Good to Be True" products is
   a. Price leadership
   b. Less for less
   c. Maximum value delivery
   d. Quality vs. price
   e. More for less

10. Dell Computer established a significant market share in the business computer market by establishing a unique position based on
    a. Customization and direct-to-consumer distribution
    b. Messaging vehicles
    c. Technology innovation
    d. Lowest possible price
    e. Most powerful machines

TRUE/FALSE

T F 1. The increased prevalence of segmentation and targeting is leading to the end of traditional mass marketing.

T F 2. Generally, segments comprise consumers who exhibit similar buying behaviours.

T F 3. As a criterion for determining a segment's value as a target segment, "substantial" dictates that the largest possible segment is the correct target.

T F 4. If a desired market position is already owned by another brand, it is possible to compete by deliberately shifting that brand's position in the minds of consumers.

T F 5. Marketers are beginning to lose control of consumers, as the latter search for brand and product information online and make purchase decisions without ever viewing advertising or interacting with a salesperson.

CONCEPT CHECK

1. The first step in target marketing is _____— dividing a market into smaller groups of buyers with distinct needs, characteristics, or behaviours who might require separate products or marketing mixes.

2. According to the chapter, the three major steps in target marketing are market segmentation, _____, and _____.

3. The following statements symbolize which levels of market segmentation: (a) Henry Ford offered Model Ts to customers "in any colour as long as it was black." This market segmentation level equals _____; (b) GM has designed specific models of cars for different income and age groups. This market segmentation level equals _____; (c) An auto insurance company sells "nonstandard" auto insurance to high-risk drivers with a record of auto accidents or drunkenness. This market segmentation level equals _____; (d) A microbrewery tailors its products and marketing programs to suit the tastes of specific individuals and locations. This market segmentation level equals _____.

4. The major variables that might be used in segmenting consumer markets include: _____, _____, _____, and _____ variables.

5. _____ segmentation divides the market into groups based on variables such as age, gender, family size, family life cycle, income, occupation, education, religion, race, and nationality.

6. Proctor & Gamble was practising _____ segmentation when it designed Secret deodorant, a brand specially formulated for a woman's chemistry and packaged and advertised to reinforce the female image.

7. There are several requirements for effective segmentation. To be useful, market segments must be _____, _____, _____, _____, and _____.

8. A _____ consists of a set of buyers who share common needs or characteristics that the company decides to serve.

9. Nike is using a _____ marketing strategy when it offers athletic shoes for a dozen or more different sports, from running, fencing, and aerobics to bicycling and baseball.

10. In general, a company needs to avoid three major positioning errors: _____ positioning, _____ positioning, and _____ positioning.

11. In considering which differences to promote, a difference is worth establishing to the extent that it satisfies the following criteria: important, distinctive, _____, _____, _____, _____, and profitable.

12. The full positioning of a brand is called the brand's _____—the full mix of benefits on which the brand is positioned.

STUDENT MATERIALS

Visit our website at www.pearsoned.ca/armstrong for online quizzes, Internet exercises, and more!

NOTES

_____

_____

_____

_____

_____

_____

DISCUSSING THE ISSUES

1. What are the differences between mass marketing, segment marketing, niche marketing, and micro marketing? Discuss actual products that use each of these market segmentation levels.

2. For each of these three products—DVD player, shoes, and salsa—consider each of the segmentation variables listed in Table 7.1 and assess the degree to which it is useful to segment the market for the product based on that variable.

3. Describe the student market segments for your college or university. To what extent are these segments measurable, accessible, substantial, differentiable, and actionable?

4. The George Foreman Grilling Machine is a compact cooking appliance with a double-sided cooking surface that is angled to allow fat to drip off the food and out of the grill. Describe a likely target market for this product. How does this target market rate with respect to size, growth, and structural attractiveness?

5. Discuss how Mountain Dew has differentiated itself from other soft drink brands on the basis of product, services, channels, people, and image differentiation.

6. Study Figure 7.4. Give examples of a hotel chain that falls into each of the five value propositions. What does each hotel you selected do on the benefits dimension to offer more, the same, or less than competitors?

MARKETING APPLICATIONS

Recent events suggest that marketers are increasingly moving beyond demographics in their segmentation efforts. Demographics have not been replaced but have instead been merged with psychographic and behavioural variables. For example, many companies today appear to be tailoring their products, promotions, and strategies to two tiers of consumers. Some call this the "Tiffany/Wal-Mart" approach. In automobiles, several General Motors divisions are selling record numbers of new SUVs to upscale consumers (those seeking more features at higher prices). At the same time, GM's Saturn division is selling record numbers of pre-owned cars to downscale consumers (those seeking value and low cost). In clothing, Gap's Banana Republic stores sell upscale jeans for $50 or more, whereas its Old Navy stores sell value jeans for $20 or less. During the past decade, marketers have seen the wealthiest 5 percent of consumers grow richer while the average Canadian's income has remained relatively stagnant.

THINKING LIKE A MARKETING MANAGER

1. What other examples of two-tier marketing can you find?
2. How does a two-tier (upscale versus downscale) consumer economy affect a marketing manager's marketing strategy?
3. What geographic, demographic, psychographic, or behavioural variables would be most important in designing appeals for the upscale and downscale markets found in a two-tier economy?
4. One organization that focuses on changing income and spending levels is the Canadian Association of Retired Persons (CARP). Visit the CARP website at www.50plus.com for additional data. Also investigate *Fifty-Five Plus* magazine at www.fifty-five-plus.com. What effect does a two-tier market have on seniors? Give an example of a company that seems to be approaching seniors with a two-tier market strategy.
5. Assume that you are the marketing manager for (a) a Wal-Mart store, (b) an Indigo bookseller store, and (c) a Sears department store. Design a marketing strategy for attracting (a) upscale consumers, (b) downscale consumers, or (c) both to your store. Can strategies for these two distinctly different markets coexist for each of these stores?

VIDEO CASE

Go to Pearson Canada's Video Central site (www.pearsoned.ca/highered/videocentral) to view the video and accompanying case for this chapter.

CASE 7   THE 2010 WINTER OLYMPICS

Nothing gets a country's athletes as motivated and excited as the chance to compete in an Olympic Games on home turf. Likewise, nothing gets a region's economic development and business players as galvanized as the hosting of an Olympic Games in their home market. When Vancouver-Whistler was selected in July 2003 by the International Olympic Committee to host the 2010 Winter Olympics, British Columbia began one of its biggest marketing projects ever.

British Columbia Premier Gordon Campbell describes the Games as a "once-in-a-lifetime opportunity to promote our province, our communities, and our entrepreneurial excellence around the world." A lot of smaller businesses across B.C. feel that the economic opportunities of the Games are accessible only to the top-tier multinationals like Kodak, VISA, and McDonald's or large domestic sponsors like Bell and the Hudson Bay Company. However, Premier Campbell believes the Games offer "tremendous potential for prosperity for *every* community in B.C." and encourages businesses and communities across British Columbia, large and small, to "plan for the possibilities."

This is where Brian Krieger, director of the 2010 Commerce Centre, plays a critical role. The 2010 Commerce Centre is the single point of contact related to the business opportunities associated with the 2010 Games—and its website provides research and resources to help businesses and communities recognize these opportunities.

There are several unique aspects of the segmentation for the 2010 Commerce Centre target audience. A private sector company could relatively easily segment based on the market segments most likely to contribute the most profit to the shareholders. But, as a government organization, the 2010 Commerce Centre faces certain challenges. There are multiple stakeholders that must be satisfied, including business sectors and the general public. There are also social objectives along with the business objectives—the Secretariat's responsibilities include ensuring that the social opportunities associated with hosting the Olympics are accessible to all British Columbians. And since British Columbians are contributing such an investment in the Games, there's a strong desire to see significant and tangible local economic development returns.

The 2010 Commerce Centre has limited funds for advertising and promotion—despite the enormous scope of its mission and goals, the Centre operates on a relatively lean budget with a small handful of staff.

A shotgun approach to marketing would be costly, since more than 98 percent of all businesses in B.C. are characterized as small businesses—those with less than 50 employees. Micro-businesses—those with fewer than five employees—comprise approximately 84 percent of these small businesses. Trying to reach such a fragmented market with a universal marketing approach is likely impossible. Clearly, segmentation is important, but what is not so clear is *how* the Centre should segment its market.

Should the 2010 Commerce Centre try to segment based on business size, market sector, region, or international exporting capability? Brian Krieger believes that it's not such a textbook case of segmentation. If the Centre segments too broadly, it might waste valuable marketing resources and time focusing on companies with no interest or ability to leverage 2010 marketing opportunities. And while it's possible to structure the Commerce Centre website by industry sector, Krieger believes that this might add unnecessary cost and actually do businesses a disservice by making faulty assumptions about what the segments should be. If the Centre selected only businesses with a certain sales volume or number of employees, or from specific region, they would likely miss the mark. "If there's a small company in Fort St. John that believes they can be successful in bidding on a Games contract, we want them to be engaged," says Krieger. "If we segment too rigidly by company size or region, we might start leaving important people out. We know we can't be all things to all people but we must do our best to keep everyone engaged."

Krieger does believe that their segmenting should be primarily focused on small and medium sized businesses, companies that "don't have $50 million to become a top-tier sponsor" and that may not have a lot of experience developing Expressions of Interest (EOIs) and responding to Requests for Quotations (RFQs) and Requests for Proposals (RFPs). In other words, companies that could really benefit from the Centre's help. "The larger companies are sophisticated and already have their networks in place . . . they have their project managers . . . and usually don't need help to find the opportunities."

Initially, the Centre is relying in part on self-selection or self-segmentation based on level of interest, enthusiasm, skills, and knowledge. And it's communicating its message to a broad audience by hosting 2010 Procurement Workshops across British Columbia in partnership with Industry Canada and Western Economic Diversification. The workshops help local businesses identify 2010 procurement opportunities, interpret bid opportunities, and create successful bids.

As businesses start attending these workshops and signing up for their email newsletter, the Centre will be able to develop more targeted segmentation and focused marketing based on both "levels of interest, skills and abilities" and by the industry sectors that emerge.

However, the Centre doesn't want to rely exclusively on self-selection of the businesses that are most enthusiastic. Given British Columbia's strong economy, many businesses may not be overly aggressive in pursuing opportunities that might not materialize until 2010 or shortly before. Some organizations with significant potential may need to be given a gentle nudge before really understanding the Games' opportunities.

Because the Games are such a unique event, little marketing research exists to help with segmentation. Adding to the complexity is the fact that the Games' support organizations are still being established—for example, a dedicated organization focused on helping support the tourism sector won't be put in place until after the Commerce Centre has already had to determine much of its segmentation approach.

Some of the best secondary research is the experiences of other stakeholders involved in hosting Olympic Games in other regions. Krieger points to the Sydney 2000 Olympic Games as an example of an effective and successful approach to segmentation. The Sydney Games segmented their business market, not by sector, but by level of interest and sophistication of global networks. Krieger says that in the past, governments would often select sectors they thought had potential: "We have a few biotech firms, or venture capitalists, or manufacturing companies, so let's support these organizations in hopes of building a cluster of similar firms and capabilities." But in Sydney, they "went out to their network of contacts and formed relationships with businesses around the world with Australian connections and desire to develop their capabilities," says Krieger. Their aim was to "improve Australia's business image from one of 'Crocodile Dundee' to that of a sophisticated international player, in time zone proximity to important Asian markets."

Staging a successful Olympics can indeed transform a city and a country, according to Andrew Gilkes, chief executive of Australasian Access, an organization that evolved from Investment 2000 and the Sydney 2000 Olympic Games and that now promotes Australasia as an increasingly important regional business location. Gilke notes that the Games repositioned Australia and Sydney in the eyes of the global business community and generated $6.5 billion in economic activity: "Over 80 percent of the [Australian] companies dealt with were small- to medium-size businesses, making or considering their first move outside of their home market."

The 2010 Olympics has similar potential for British Columbia and, like Australia, a lot of the lasting economic development will likely come from small and medium sized companies. A study in 2002 by InterVISTAS Consulting Inc. forecast that, when combined with independently measured impacts from an expanded Vancouver Convention and Exhibition Centre, hosting the 2010 Games could generate $6.1 billion to $10.7 billion in economic activity, create the equivalent of 126 000 to 244 000 full-time jobs, and result in tax revenues of $1.4 billion to $2.6 billion.

When Canadians are glued to their televisions or actually at the Olympic facilities watching the Canadian hockey team, skiers, skaters, and other athletes compete for Gold at the 2010 Games, they will likely be unaware of the work of the 2010 Commerce Centre behind the scenes. Nevertheless, the work of this organization, including how it decides to segment its target markets, may be equally if not more important to the development of pride in Canada's capability. The Centre will no doubt be the unheralded gold medal winner in the sport of international business—one that will contribute enormously to the region's economic development and employment opportunities benefiting Canadians for years to come.

Questions

1. If you were the general manager of the 2010 Commerce Centre, how would you segment your marketplace? How would the segmentation differ if the Centre was a private sector company?

2. What is the danger of an overly granular segmentation of the marketplace? What is the danger of segmenting too loosely?

3. How do you think the Centre will be able to segment its marketplace based on "level of interest"?

Olympics and Olympic Games are protected marks of the Canadian Olympic Committee.

hope in a bottle®

philosophy®: where there is hope there can be faith. where there is faith, miracles can occur. science can give us better skin. only humanity can give us better days. 2 fl. oz. - 59.2ml

for adult acne

hope and a prayer™

philosophy®: hope is desperation, faith is relaxation.
100%
topical vitamin c powder
0.31 oz. - 8.75 g.

hope in a jar®

philosophy®: where there is hope there can be faith. where there is faith miracles can occur.

therapeutic moisturizer for aging skin
2 oz. - 56.7 g

After studying this chapter, you should be able to

1. define *product* and the major classifications of goods and services

2. describe the decisions companies make regarding their individual goods and services, product lines, and product mixes

3. discuss branding strategy—the decisions companies make in building and managing their brands

4. identify the four characteristics that affect the marketing of a service

5. discuss social responsibility and international issues related to products

Product and
Branding Strategy

8

Looking Ahead   Now that you've had a good look at marketing strategy, we'll look at the marketing mix—the tactical tools that marketers use to implement their strategies. In this and the next chapter, we'll study how companies develop and manage products. Then, in the chapters that follow, we'll look at pricing, distribution, and marketing communication tools. The product is usually the first and most basic marketing consideration. How well firms manage their individual brands and their overall product offerings has a major impact on their success in the marketplace.

And the cosmetics industry, for one, shows why. After all, what, really, *are* cosmetics? Cosmetics makers like Aveda know that when a woman buys cosmetics, she buys much, much more than scented ingredients in fancy bottles.

E ach year, cosmetics companies sell billions of dollars' worth of potions, lotions, and fragrances to consumers around the world, part of a $160 billion global beauty industry. In one sense, these products are no more than careful mixtures of oils and chemicals that have nice scents and soothing properties. But the cosmetics companies know that they sell much more than just mixtures of ingredients—they sell the promise of what these concoctions will do for the people who use them.

What *is* the promise of cosmetics? The following account by a *New York Times* reporter suggests the extent to which cosmetics take on meaning far beyond their physical makeup.

Last week I bathed in purple water (*I Trust* bubble bath, made by Philosophy) and powdered up with pink powder (*Rebirth*, by 5S, "to renew the spirit and recharge the soul"). My moisturizer was *Bliss* (Chakra VII by Aveda, for "the joyful enlightenment and soaring of the spirit"); my nail polish was *Spiritual* (by Tony and Tina, "to aid connection with the higher self"). My teeth were clean, my heart was open—however, my bathroom counter was so crowded with bottles and brochures, the latest tools and totems from the human potential movement, that I could hardly find my third eye. Still, my "Hope in a Jar" package (from Philosophy) pretty well summed it up: "Where there is hope there can be faith. Where there is faith miracles can occur."

If you are looking for enlightenment in all the wrong places, cosmetics companies are eager to help. Because today, feeling good is the new religion. And cosmetics companies are the newest of the new prophets, turning the old notion of hope in a jar on its head.

"Cosmetics are our satellite to the divine!" This is what you'll hear from Tony and Tina, for example. Tony and Tina (Anthony Gillis and Cristina Bornstein) are nice young artists. He's from London, she grew up in New York. Chakra nail polish, which they invented for an installation at the Gershwin Gallery in Manhattan two years ago, was intended as an ironic commentary on the beauty business. But then a friend suggested they get into the beauty business, and now Tony and Tina have a $2 million cosmetics company with a mission statement: "To aid in the evolution of human consciousness." Their products include nail polishes (Vibrational Remedies) in colors meant to do nice things to your chakras, as well as body glitter and hair mascara, lipstick and eyeshadow. "We think color therapy is going to be the new medicine," said Tony.

Rainbows are proliferating as rapidly in the New Age as angels once did. Philosophy, an Arizona company, makes a sort of head/heart kit—"a self-help program," the company insists—called the *Rainbow Connection*. You pay $45 for seven bottles of colored bubble bath in a metal box. "Choose your colored bath according to the area of your emotional life that needs attention, i.e. self-love, self-worth," the brochure reads. "My role as I see it," said Christina Carlino, Philosophy's founder, "is to help you stay on your destiny path. It's not about what you look like. Beauty is defined by your deeds."

5S, a sprout of the Japanese cosmetics company Shiseido, offers a regimen that plays, the company says, on the "fundamental and mythical significance of 5" (Five Pillars of Islam, Five Classics of Confucianism, and so on), and which is organized into emotional rather than physical categories. At the 5S store in SoHo, you don't buy things for dry skin, you buy things that are "energizing" or "nurturing" or "adoring." The company also believes in color therapy. Hence, *Rebirth*, products tinted "nouveau pink" (the color of bubble gum). A customer can achieve rebirth with 5S pink soap, pink powder, and pink toner.

Here are products that are not intended to make you look better, but to make you act better, feel better, and be a better person. You don't need a month's visit to India to find your higher self; you need only buy this bubble bath, that lipstick, this night cream. The beauty business' old come-on (trap your man!) has been swept away in favor of a new pitch. I don't have wrinkles anymore. I've got a chakra blockage.

Of course, who knew about chakras before Aveda? In 1989, the plant-based, eco-friendly cosmetics company Aveda trademarked Chakras I through VII to use as titles for moisturizers and scents. Chakra products were perhaps a little ahead of their time back then. However, the purchase of Aveda in 1997 by the Estée Lauder Companies, the General Motors of the cosmetics world, suggests that the pendulum of history has finally caught up. "Aveda isn't a marketing idea," says Jeanette Wagner, the vice chairman of Estée Lauder. "It is a passionately held belief. From my point of view, the appeal is first the spirituality, and then the products."

Similarly, Canadian cosmetics company Cake Beauty believes in the value and importance of indulgence. As its website notes, "Women everywhere deserve a moment in their lives to indulge . . . our goal is to transform that moment to everyday. Cake Beauty products ensure a complete and specific experience that accommodates the modern woman—a woman who knows what she wants and deserves." Thus, one of its tactics is to bring the spa to the comfort of users' homes. Take, for example, its new product, Milk Made Smoothing Hand & Cuticle Buffer. The company promises that it will give your hands a spa-like treatment, making them look "perfectly polished in just seconds."

The success of such brands affirms that products really are more than just the physical entities. When a woman buys cosmetics, she really does buy much, much more than just oils, chemicals, and fragrances. The cosmetic's image, its promises and positioning, its ingredients, its name and package, the company that makes it, the stores that sell it—all become a part of the total cosmetic product. When Aveda, Philosophy, Cake Beauty, and 5S sell cosmetics, they sell more than just tangible goods. They sell lifestyle, self-expression, exclusivity, and spirituality; achievement, success, and status; romance, passion, and fantasy; memories, hopes, and dreams.[1]

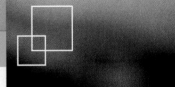

TEST YOURSELF

Answers to these questions can be found on our website at www.pearsoned.ca/armstrong.

1. How does Chakra's brand positioning contribute to the product itself?
   a. There is no relationship because no physical product can provide spiritual renewal
   b. None, since brand is simply the name and logo that goes onto a product
   c. The spiritual renewal promised by the brand's position is what the consumer actually buys; the physical product is secondary
   d. The brand positioning is unbelievable, and so it has a detrimental effect on how consumers will view the product
   e. The product contains an assortment of highly exotic and expensive ingredients in order to bring about spiritual renewal

2. How important are the physical properties of the cosmetics to their positioning of spiritual renewal?
   a. Irrelevant, because consumers won't notice the physical characteristics of the products
   b. Critical, because consumers will expect physical product performance beyond anything they've used before
   c. Important, because the focus on spiritual renewal means that the cosmetic makers can save money by devoting fewer resources to delivering high quality
   d. Somewhat important, because consumers will expect fragrance, texture, consistency, and other qualities to suggest the possibility of spiritual renewal
   e. None of the above

3. What role do the names of the cosmetic brands play in their positioning?
   a. Good brand names strengthen the brand by evoking the promised benefit and the brand's main position
   b. None, since name is irrelevant to perceptions of brand
   c. Since the brand names are protected by copyright, no other cosmetic manufacturer can attempt to use the same positioning
   d. Names and logos have to match the style of packaging used
   e. Neutral brand names allow the cosmetics makers to launch other products with different positioning under the same name, thus saving money and resources

4. Why have these cosmetics manufacturers chosen spirituality as a brand positioning for products that are traditionally supposed to deliver physical changes to skin and hair?
   a. Because no other manufacturers will be able to position on that benefit
   b. Because their products don't perform well physically, so this was the only benefit open to them
   c. Because physical benefits have to be provable, whereas "spiritual" benefits do not
   d. Because it costs far less in research and development to make products that don't promise an actual physical change
   e. Because the cosmetics market is saturated with "look younger" positioning, and these companies needed a compelling brand differentiation that sets them noticeably apart

5. Why are otherwise intelligent consumers flocking to cosmetic products that promise spirituality rather than clearer skin?
   a. Because the advertising promoting these products is deceptive
   b. Because the products are relatively low priced and consumers buy them simply because they are cheaper
   c. Because cosmetics that promise physical benefits do not work either
   d. Because the most powerful branding position is to appeal to consumers' need for self-actualization and their psychological beliefs
   e. Because consumers will generally try anything at least once, and these cosmetics companies are milking the market until consumers move on to the next fad

This chapter begins with that deceptively simple question: *What is a product?* After answering this question, we look at ways to classify products in consumer and business markets. Then we discuss the important decisions that marketers make regarding individual products, product lines, and product mixes. Next, we look into the critically important issue of how marketers build and manage brands. Finally, we examine the characteristics and marketing requirements of a special form of product—services.

WHAT IS A PRODUCT?

Product Anything that can be offered to a market for attention, acquisition, use, or consumption that might satisfy a want or need.

A Sony DVD player, a Ford Taurus, a Costa Rican vacation, a Caffé Mocha at Starbucks, Fidelity online investment services, and advice from your family doctor—all are products. We define a **product** as anything that can be offered to a market for attention, acquisition, use, or consumption and that might satisfy a want or need. Products include more than just tangible goods. Broadly defined, products include physical objects, services, events, persons, places, organizations, ideas, or mixes of these entities. Thus, throughout this book, we use the term *product* broadly to include any or all of these entities.

Service Any activity or benefit that one party can offer to another that is essentially intangible and does not result in the ownership of anything.

Because of their growth and strategic importance in the world economy, we give special attention to services. **Services** are a form of product that consists of activities, benefits, or satisfactions offered for sale that are essentially intangible and do not result in the ownership of anything. Examples are banking, hotel, airline, retail, tax preparation, and home repair services. We will look at services more closely later in this chapter.

Goods, Services, and Experiences

A product is a key element in the *market offering*; it is one of the 4Ps of the marketing mix. Marketing-mix planning begins with formulating an offering that brings value to target customers and satisfies their needs. This offering becomes the basis on which the company builds profitable relationships with customers.

A company's market offering often includes both tangible goods and services. Each component can be a minor or a major part of the total offer. At one extreme, the offer may consist of a *pure tangible good*, such as soap, toothpaste, or salt—no services accompany the product. At the other extreme are *pure services*, for which the offer consists primarily of a service. Examples include a doctor's exam or financial services. Between these two extremes, however, many goods-and-services combinations are possible, such as a fast-food restaurant that provides intangible service items like convenience, fast turnaround, and clean seating areas and washrooms, along with the more tangible products of the actual food provided.

Today, as goods and services become more and more commoditized, many companies are moving to a new level in creating value for their customers. To differentiate their offers, beyond simply making goods and delivering services, companies are staging, marketing, and delivering memorable customer *experiences*. Whereas goods are tangible and services are intangible, experiences are memorable. Whereas goods and services are external, experiences are personal and take place in the minds of individual consumers.

Experiences have always been important in the entertainment industry—Disney has long manufactured memories through its movies and theme parks. Today, however, all kinds of firms are recasting their traditional goods and services to create experiences. For example, restaurants create value well beyond the food they serve. Starbucks patrons are paying for more than just coffee. The company treats customers to poetry on its wallpaper, apron-clad performers behind espresso machines, and a warm but modern interior ambience that leaves them feeling more affluent and fulfilled.

Garnier, a division of L'Oréal Paris, even used a contest to enhance customers' experiences with their products. In the summer of 2005 it partnered with concert promoters House of Blues to offer Canadian consumers a chance to win the ultimate VIP Concert Experience. This promotion was designed as part of the brand's entertainment marketing strategy, and "is a bull's-eye for its core psychographic segment," says one analyst. The winning concert goer, along with three of her friends, also had the chance to participate in the "Green Room Experience" where they could all get a makeover backstage. This, combined with product placement at the concert, reinforced the brand's image among its young demographic.[2]

Many retailers also stage experiences. Niketown stores create "shoppertainment" by offering interactive displays, engaging activities, and promotional events in a stimulating shopping environment. And at stores such as HMV and Best Buy, people play with the latest gadgets, listen to music, and often enjoy the shopping experience as much as the merchandise. Companies that market experiences realize that customers are really

IN-CLASS NOTES

Products Defined

- **Product:** any market offering that is intended to satisfy a want or need.
- **Service:** a type of product that is intangible and does not result in the ownership of anything.
- **Experience:** a type of product that combines a service or physical product with a memorable experience.

buying much more than just goods and services. They are buying what those offers will *do* for them.[3]

Levels of Goods and Services   Product planners need to think about goods and services on three levels (see Figure 8.1). Each level adds more customer value. The most

---

Figure 8.1   Three Levels of Product

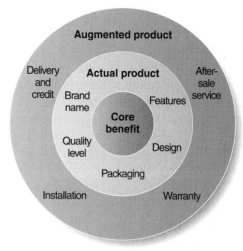

basic level is the *core benefit*, which addresses the question *What is the buyer really buying?* When designing products, marketers must first define the core problem-solving benefits or services that consumers seek. A woman buying lipstick buys more than lip colour. Charles Revson of Revlon saw this early: "In the factory, we make cosmetics; in the store, we sell hope." Charles Schwab does more than sell financial services—it promises to fulfill customers' "financial dreams." When customers buy a soft drink from a vending machine, they are really buying convenience, not just a beverage.

At the second level, product planners must turn the core benefit into an *actual product.* They need to develop product and service features, design, a quality level, a brand name, and packaging. For example, a Sony camcorder is an actual product. Its name, parts, styling, features, packaging, and other attributes have all been combined carefully to deliver the core benefit—a convenient, high-quality way to capture important moments.

Finally, product planners must build an *augmented product* around the core benefit and actual product by offering additional consumer services and benefits. Sony must offer more than just a camcorder. It must provide consumers with a complete solution to their picture-taking problems. Thus, when consumers buy a Sony camcorder, Sony and its dealers also might give buyers a warranty on parts and workmanship, instructions on how to use the camcorder, quick repair services when needed, and a toll-free telephone number to call if they have problems or questions.

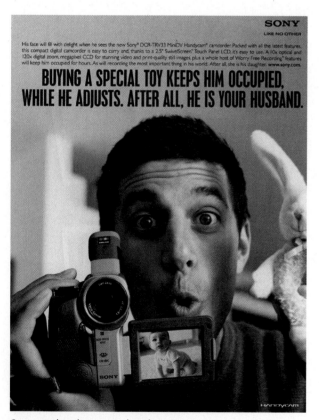

Core, actual, and augmented product: Consumers perceive this Sony Handycam as a complex bundle of intangible features and services that deliver a core benefit—a convenient, high-quality way to capture important moments.

In some product categories like automobiles and real estate, marketers even need to deal with "buyer's remorse" by marketing to their recent, *existing* customers to reinforce in the buyer's mind that they made the right decision and that the three levels of value were indeed worthwhile.

In sum, consumers see products as complex bundles of benefits that satisfy their needs. When developing products, marketers first must identify the *core* consumer needs the product will satisfy. They must then design the *actual* product and find ways to *augment* it in order to create the bundle of benefits that will provide the most satisfying customer experience.

Goods and Services Classifications

Goods and services fall into two broad classes based on the types of consumers that use them—*consumer products* and *industrial products*. Broadly defined, products also include other marketable entities such as experiences, organizations, places, and ideas.

Consumer Products **Consumer products** are goods and services bought by individuals for personal consumption. Marketers usually classify these products further based on how consumers go about buying them. Consumer products include *convenience products*, *shopping products*, *specialty products*, and *unsought products*. These products differ in the ways consumers buy them and therefore in how they are marketed (see Table 8.1).

Convenience products are consumer goods and services that the customer usually buys frequently, immediately, and with a minimum of comparison and buying effort. Examples include soap, candy, newspapers, and fast food. Convenience products are usually low priced, and marketers place them in many locations to make them readily available when consumers need them.

Shopping products are less frequently purchased consumer goods and services that people compare carefully on suitability, quality, price, and style. When buying shopping products, consumers spend much time and effort in gathering information and making comparisons. Examples include furniture, clothing, used cars, major appliances, and hotel and airline services. Shopping products marketers usually distribute their products through fewer outlets but provide deeper sales support to help consumers in their comparison efforts.

Consumer product Product bought by individuals for personal consumption.

Convenience product Consumer product that the individual usually buys frequently, immediately, and with a minimum of comparison and buying effort.

Shopping product Consumer product that people, in the process of selection and purchase, characteristically compares on bases such as suitability, quality, price, and style.

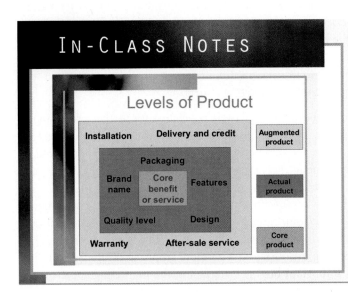

Table 8.1	**Marketing Considerations for Consumer Products**			
Marketing Considerations	**Type of Consumer Product**			
	Convenience	**Shopping**	**Specialty**	**Unsought**
Buyer behaviour	Frequent purchase, little planning, little comparison or shopping effort, low customer involvement	Less frequent purchase, much planning and shopping effort, comparison of brands on price, quality, style	Strong brand preference and loyalty, special purchase effort, little comparison of brands, low price sensitivity	Little product awareness, knowledge (or, if aware, little or even negative interest)
Price	Low price	Higher price	High price	Varies
Distribution	Widespread distribution, convenient locations	Selective distribution in fewer outlets	Exclusive distribution in only one or a few outlets per market area	Varies
Promotion	Mass promotion by the producer	Advertising and personal selling by both producer and resellers	More carefully targeted promotion by both producer and resellers	Aggressive advertising and personal selling by producer and resellers
Examples	Toothpaste, magazines, laundry detergent	Major appliances, televisions, furniture, clothing	Luxury goods, such as Rolex watches or fine crystal	Life insurance, blood donations, funeral services

Specialty product Consumer product with unique characteristics or brand identification for which a significant group of buyers is willing to make a special purchase effort.

Specialty products are consumer goods and services with unique characteristics or brand identification for which a significant group of buyers is willing to make a special purchase effort. Examples include specific brands and types of cars, high-priced photographic equipment, designer clothes, and the services of medical or legal specialists. A Lamborghini automobile, for example, is a specialty product because buyers are usually willing to travel great distances to buy one. Buyers normally do not compare specialty products. They invest only the time needed to reach dealers carrying the wanted products.

Unsought product Consumer product that the consumer either does not know about or knows about but does not normally think of buying.

Unsought products are consumer products that the consumer either does not know about or knows about but does not normally think of buying. Most major new innovations are unsought until the consumer becomes aware of them through advertising. Classic examples of known but unsought goods and services are life insurance, cemetery plots, and blood donations. By their very nature, unsought products require a lot of advertising, personal selling, and other marketing efforts.

Industrial product Product bought by individuals and organizations for further processing or for use in conducting a business.

Industrial Products   **Industrial products** are those purchased for further processing or for use in conducting a business. Industrial products are also referred to as business-to-business or B2B products. Thus, the distinction between a consumer product and an industrial product is based on the *purpose* for which the product is bought. If a person buys a lawn mower for use around home, the lawn mower is a consumer product. If the same person buys the same lawn mower for use in a landscaping business, the lawn mower is an industrial product. The motivation behind the purchase of industrial products is usually focused on helping an organization save money by operating more efficiently or increasing revenues by expanding the business. With more emphasis on the bottom line, return on investment is an important buying criteria and the marketing approach for industrial products is significantly different from the marketing of consumer products.

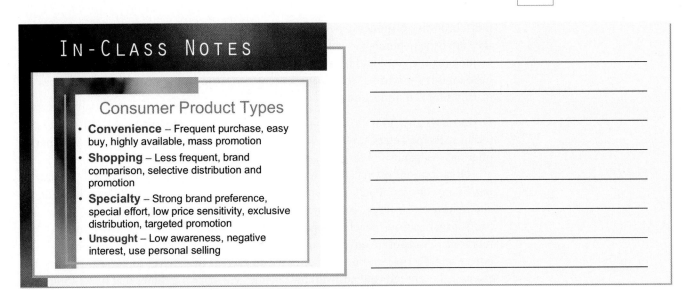

The three groups of industrial goods and services include materials and parts, capital items, and supplies and services. *Materials and parts* include raw materials and manufactured materials and parts. Raw materials consist of farm products (wheat, cotton, livestock, fruits, vegetables) and natural products (fish, lumber, crude petroleum, iron ore). Manufactured materials and parts consist of component materials (iron, yarn, cement, wires) and component parts (small motors, tires, castings). Most manufactured materials and parts are sold directly to industrial users. Price and service are the major marketing factors; branding and advertising tend to be less important.

Capital items are industrial products that aid in the buyer's production or operations, including installations and accessory equipment. Installations consist of major purchases such as buildings (factories, offices) and fixed equipment (generators, drill presses, large computer systems, elevators). Accessory equipment includes portable factory equipment and tools (hand tools, lift trucks) and office equipment (computers, fax machines, desks). They have a shorter life than installations and simply aid in the production process.

The final group of business products is *supplies and services.* Supplies include operating supplies (lubricants, coal, paper, pencils) and repair and maintenance items (paint,

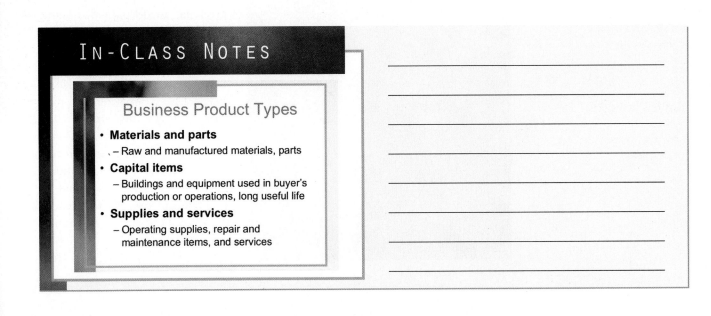

nails, brooms). Supplies are the convenience products of the industrial field because they are usually purchased with a minimum of effort or comparison. Business services include maintenance and repair services (window cleaning, computer repair) and business advisory services (legal, management consulting, advertising). Such services are usually supplied under contract.

Organizations, Places, and Ideas In addition to tangible goods and services, in recent years marketers have broadened the concept of a product to include other market offerings—organizations, places, and ideas.

Organizations often carry out activities to "sell" the organization itself. *Organization marketing* consists of activities undertaken to create, maintain, or change the attitudes and behaviour of target consumers toward an organization. Both profit and not-for-profit organizations kids practise organization marketing. Business firms sponsor public relations or corporate advertising campaigns to polish their images. *Corporate image advertising* is a major tool companies use to market themselves to various publics. For example, Lucent puts out ads with the tag line "We make the things that make communications work." IBM wants to establish itself as the company to turn to for "e-Business Solutions." And General Electric stands for "imagination at work." Similarly, nonprofit organizations, such as churches, colleges, charities, museums, and performing arts groups, market their organizations in order to raise funds and attract members or patrons.

Place marketing involves activities undertaken to create, maintain, or change attitudes or behaviour toward particular places. Cities, provinces, regions, and even entire nations compete to attract tourists, new residents, conventions, and company offices and factories. Travel Canada challenges Canadians and prospective tourists from around the world to "Discover Our True Nature." Newfoundland describes itself as the place where "land, water and sky embrace like old friends . . . the edge of North America [that] holds an adventure as big as the sky." The Irish Development Agency has attracted more than 1200 companies to locate their plants in Ireland. At the same time, the Irish Tourist Board has built a flourishing tourism business by advertising ". . . a different life: friendly, beautiful, relaxing." And the Irish Export Board has created attractive markets for Irish exports.[4]

The growth in globalization and travel has made place marketing even more important. However, it is becoming increasingly challenging to make one city, region, or country stand out amidst all the marketing chatter. The cutthroat and well-publicized competitions among cities around the world to host the Olympics—and thus reap their economic benefits and international exposure—epitomizes this trend.

Ideas can also be marketed. In one sense, all marketing is the marketing of an idea, whether it be the general idea of brushing your teeth

Covenant House, Canada's largest youth shelter, won awards for its hard-hitting campaign that brought attention to the problem of homeless youth.

or the specific idea that Crest toothpastes "create smiles every day." Here, however, we narrow our focus to the marketing of *social ideas*. This area has been called **social marketing,** defined by the Social Marketing Institute as the use of commercial marketing concepts and tools in programs designed to influence individuals' behaviour to improve their well-being and that of society.[5]

Social marketing programs include public health campaigns to reduce smoking, alcoholism, drug abuse, and overeating. Other social marketing efforts include environmental campaigns to promote wilderness protection, clean air, and conservation. Still others address issues such as family planning, human rights, and racial equality. For example, Toronto-based Covenant House, Canada's largest youth shelter, used an award-winning poster campaign to bring home the message that many kids are homeless. And the Canadian Landmine Foundation used a TV campaign and event marketing titled the "Night of a Thousand Dinners." During the annual one-night event, individuals host dinner parties to raise funds for the Adopt-a-Minefield program. This Canadian-led initiative is now used in more than 30 countries.

But social marketing involves much more than just advertising—the Social Marketing Institute encourages the use of a broad range of marketing tools. "Social marketing goes well beyond the promotional '*P*' of the marketing mix to include every other element to achieve its social change objectives," says the SMI's executive director.[6]

Social marketing The design, implementation, and control of programs seeking to increase the acceptability of a social idea, cause, or practice among a target group.

PRODUCT DECISIONS

Marketers make product decisions at three levels: individual product decisions, product line decisions, and product mix decisions. We discuss each in turn.

Individual Product Decisions

Figure 8.2 shows the important decisions in the development and marketing of individual goods and services. We will focus on decisions about *product attributes*, *branding*, *packaging*, *labelling*, and *product support services*.

Figure 8.2   Individual Product Decisions

Product Attributes   Developing a product involves defining the benefits that it will offer. These benefits are communicated and delivered by product attributes such as *quality*, *features*, and *style and design*.

Product Quality.   Product quality is one of the marketer's major positioning tools. Quality has a direct impact on product performance; thus, it is closely linked to customer value and satisfaction. In the narrowest sense, quality can be defined as "freedom from defects." But most customer-centred companies go beyond this narrow definition. Instead, they define quality in terms of customer satisfaction or "fitness of use"—does the offering do what the customer expected? The American Society for Quality defines quality as the characteristics of a good or service that bear on its ability to satisfy stated or implied customer needs. Similarly, Siemens defines quality this way: "Quality is when our customers come back and our products don't."[7] These customer-focused definitions suggest that quality begins with customer needs and ends with customer satisfaction.

Product quality The ability of a product to perform its functions; it includes the product's overall durability, reliability, precision, ease of operation and repair, and other valued attributes.

Total quality management (TQM) is an approach in which all the company's people are involved in constantly improving the quality of goods, services, and business processes. During the past two decades, companies large and small have credited TQM with greatly improving their market shares and profits. Recently, however, the total quality management movement has drawn criticism. Too many companies viewed TQM as a magic cure-all and created token total quality programs that applied quality principles only superficially. Still others became obsessed with narrowly defined TQM principles and lost sight of broader concerns for customer value and satisfaction. As a result, many such programs failed, causing a backlash against TQM.

When applied in the context of creating customer satisfaction, however, *total quality* principles remain a requirement for success. Although many firms don't use the TQM label any more, for most top companies customer-driven quality has become a way of doing business. Today, companies are taking a "return on quality" approach, viewing quality as an investment and holding quality efforts accountable for bottom-line results.[8]

Product quality has two dimensions—level and consistency. In developing a product, the marketer must first choose a *quality level* that will support the product's position in the target market. Here, product quality means *performance quality*—the ability of a product to perform its functions. For example, a Rolls-Royce provides higher performance quality than a Chevrolet: It has a smoother ride, handles better, and lasts longer. Companies rarely try to offer the highest possible performance quality level—few customers want or can afford the high levels of quality offered in products such as a Rolls-Royce automobile, a Sub-Zero refrigerator, or a Rolex watch. Instead, companies choose a quality level that matches target market needs and the quality levels of competing products.

Beyond quality level, high quality also can mean high levels of quality *consistency*. Here, product quality means *conformance quality*—freedom from defects and *consistency* in delivering a targeted level of performance. All companies should strive for high levels of conformance quality. In this sense, a Chevrolet can have just as much quality as a Rolls-Royce. Although a Chevy doesn't perform as well as a Rolls, it can as consistently deliver the quality that customers pay for and expect.

Many companies today have turned customer-driven quality into a potent strategic weapon. They create customer satisfaction and value by consistently and profitably meeting customers' needs and preferences for quality.

Product Features. A product can be offered with varying features. A stripped-down model, one without any extras, is the starting point. The company can create higher-level models by adding more features. Features are a competitive tool for differentiating the company's product from competitors' products. Being the first producer to introduce a needed and valued new feature is one of the most effective ways to compete.

How can a company identify new features and decide which ones to add to its product? The company should periodically survey buyers who have used the product and ask these questions: How do you like the product? Which specific features of the product do you like most? Which features could we add to improve the product? The answers provide the company with a rich list of feature ideas. The company can then assess each feature's *value* to customers versus its *cost* to the company. Features that customers value little in relation to costs should be dropped; those that customers value highly in relation to costs should be added.

Product Style and Design. Another way to add customer value is through distinctive *product style and design*. Design is a larger concept than style. *Style* simply describes the appearance of a product. A sensational style may grab attention and produce pleasing aesthetics, but it does not necessarily make the product *perform* better. Unlike style, *design* is more than skin deep—it goes to the very heart of a product. Good design contributes to a product's usefulness as well as to its looks.

Good style and design can attract attention, improve product performance, cut production costs, and give the product a strong competitive advantage in the target market. Here is an example:

> Apple's original iMac—which featured a sleek, egg-shaped monitor and hard drive, all in one unit, in a futuristic translucent turquoise casing—redefined the look and feel of the personal computer. There was no clunky tower or desktop hard drive to clutter up your office area. Featuring one-button Internet access, this machine was designed specifically for cruising the Internet (that's what the "i" in "iMac" stands for). The dramatic iMac won raves for design and lured buyers in droves. Within a year, it had sold more than a million units, marking Apple's reemergence in the personal computer industry. Before it was over, Apple had sold more than 10 million of the original iMacs. "If they had not done that," says an industry insider, "they probably would have gone under. It captured the world's attention and put Apple back on the map." Four years later, Apple did it again with a stunning new iMac design—a clean, futuristic machine featuring a flat-panel display that seems to float in the air. Within only three months, Apple-lovers had snapped up nearly one-quarter million of these eye-pleasing yet functional machines.[9]

Branding   Perhaps the most distinctive skill of professional marketers is their ability to create, maintain, protect, and enhance brands of their products. A **brand** is a name, term, sign, symbol, or design, or a combination of these, that identifies the maker or seller of a good or service. Consumers view a brand as an important part of a product, and branding can add value to a product. For example, most consumers would perceive a bottle of Obsession perfume as a high-quality, expensive product. But the same perfume in an unmarked bottle would likely be viewed as lower in quality, even if the fragrance were identical.

Branding has become so strong that today hardly anything goes unbranded. Salt is packaged in branded containers, common nuts and bolts are packaged with a distributor's label, and automobile parts—spark plugs, tires, filters—bear brand names that differ from those of the auto makers. Even meats, fruits, and vegetables are branded— Maple Leaf Prime chicken, McCain French fries, Sunkist oranges, Dole pineapples, and Chiquita bananas.

Branding helps buyers in many ways. Brand names help consumers identify products that might benefit them. Brands also tell the buyer something about product quality. Buyers who always buy the same brand know that they will get the same features, benefits, and quality each time they buy. Branding also gives the seller several advantages. The brand name becomes the basis on which a whole story can be built about a

Brand A name, term, sign, symbol, or design, or a combination of these intended to identify the goods or services of one seller or group of sellers and to differentiate them from those of competitors.

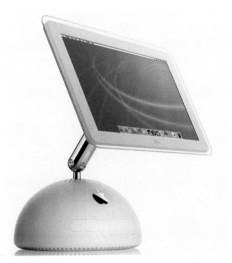

Product design: The design of the dramatic iMac helped reestablish Apple as a legitimate contender in the PC industry.

product's special qualities. The seller's brand name and trademark provide legal protection for unique product features that otherwise might be copied by competitors. And branding helps the seller to segment markets. For example, General Mills can offer Cheerios, Total, Lucky Charms, Trix, and many other cereal brands, not just one general product for all consumers.

Building and managing brands is perhaps the marketer's most important task. We will discuss branding strategy in more detail later in the chapter.

Packaging **Packaging** involves designing and producing the container or wrapper for a product. The package includes a product's primary container (the tube holding Colgate Total toothpaste). It may also include a secondary package that is thrown away when the product is about to be used (the cardboard box containing the tube of Colgate). Finally, it can include a shipping package necessary to store, identify, and ship the product (a corrugated box carrying six dozen tubes of Colgate). Labelling, printed information appearing on or with the package, is also part of packaging.

Traditionally, the primary function of the package was to contain and protect the product. In recent times, however, numerous factors have made packaging an important marketing tool. Increased competition and clutter on retail store shelves means that packages must now perform many sales tasks—from attracting attention, to describing the product, to making the sale.

Companies are realizing the power of good packaging to create instant consumer recognition of the company or brand. For example, in an average supermarket, which stocks 15 000 to 17 000 items, the typical shopper passes by some 300 items per minute, and more than 60 percent of all purchases are made on impulse. In this highly competitive environment, the package may be the seller's last chance to influence buyers. "Not long ago, the package was merely the product's receptacle, and the brand message was elsewhere—usually on TV," says a packaging expert. But changes in the marketplace environment are now "making the package itself an increasingly important selling medium."[10]

Innovative packaging can give a company an advantage over competitors. Consumer packaged goods firms have recently upped their investments in packaging research to develop package designs that grab more shelf attention or make life easier for consumers. Notable examples include Skippy Squeez'It peanut butter, dispensed from tubes for on-the-go families, and Coca-Cola beverage packs designed to fit neatly onto refrigerator shelves. Dutch Boy recently came up with a long overdue innovation—paint in plastic containers with twist-off caps.

> How did Dutch Boy Paint stir up the paint business? Imagine a paint can that's easy to carry, doesn't take a screwdriver to pry open, doesn't dribble when pouring, and doesn't take a hammer to bang closed again. It's here—in the form of Dutch Boy's new Twist and Pour paint container. The new container is an all-plastic gallon container with a twist-off lid, side handle, and pour spout. It's lighter weight than a can and rust-proof, too. "It's so much easier to use," says Dutch Boy's marketing director. "You can hold it like a cup of coffee." It kind of makes you wonder: Why did it take so long to come up with an idea like this? The new containers cost a dollar or two more than traditional cans, but consumers don't seem to mind. More than 50 percent of Dutch Boy's customers are now buying the plastic containers, and new stores, like Wal-Mart, are now carrying it. "It's an amazing innovation. Worth noticing," says one observer. "Not only did the new packaging increase sales, but it also got them more distribution at a higher retail price!"[11]

In contrast, poorly designed packages can cause headaches for consumers and lost sales for the company (see Marketing at Work 8.1). For example, a few years ago, Planters Lifesavers Company attempted to use innovative packaging to create an association between fresh-roasted peanuts and fresh-roasted coffee. It packaged its Fresh Roast Salted Peanuts in vacuum-packed "Brik-Pacs," similar to those used for ground

Packaging The activities of designing and producing the container or wrapper for a product.

coffee. Unfortunately, the coffeelike packaging worked too well: Consumers mistook the peanuts for a new brand of flavoured coffee and ran them through supermarket coffee-grinding machines, creating a gooey mess, disappointed customers, and lots of irate store managers.[12]

Developing a good package for a new product requires making many decisions. First, the company must establish the *packaging concept,* which states what the package should *be* or *do* for the product. Should it mainly offer product protection, introduce a new dispensing method, suggest certain qualities about the product, or do something else? Decisions then must be made on specific elements of the package, such as size, shape, materials, colour, text, and brand mark. These elements must work together to support the product's position and marketing strategy.

In recent years, product safety has also become a major packaging concern. We have all learned to deal with hard-to-open "childproof" packages. And after the rash of product tampering scares during the 1980s, most drug producers and food makers now put their products in tamper-resistant packages. In making packaging decisions, the company also must heed growing environmental concerns. Fortunately, many companies have gone "green" by reducing their packaging and using environmentally responsible packaging materials. For example, P&G eliminated outer cartons from its Secret and Sure deodorants, saving 3.4 million pounds of paperboard per year.

Labelling Labels may range from simple tags attached to products to complex graphics that are part of the package.

Innovative packaging: Dutch Boy recently came up with a long overdue innovation—paint in plastic containers with twist-off caps. Imagine a paint can that's easy to carry, doesn't take a screwdriver to pry open, doesn't dribble when pouring, and doesn't take a hammer to bang closed again.

They perform several functions. At the very least, the label *identifies* the product or brand, such as the name Sunkist stamped on oranges. The label might also *describe* several things about the product—who made it, where it was made, when it was made, its contents, how it is to be used, and how to use it safely. Finally, the label might *promote* the product through attractive graphics.

There has been a long history of legal and ethical concerns about labels. Labels have the potential to mislead consumers, fail to describe important ingredients, and fail to include needed safety warnings. Labelling regulations depend on the type of product being sold. Canada's *Consumer Packaging and Labelling Act,* which covers many non-food products, protects consumers from labelling or packaging that is false or misleading. The *Weights and Measures Act* deals with the units of measurement on labels. The Government of Canada's "Consumer Packaging and Labelling" page (see www.strategis. ic.gc.ca) details the requirements for the principal display panel of prepackaged, non-food consumer products.

Consumer advocates have long lobbied for additional legislation that would require more informative food labelling, and the efforts have finally met with success. Starting in January 2003, Canadians saw a lot more information on food packaging labels as a result of new government legislation. It became mandatory for food labels to display *Nutrition Facts,* a table that lists calories and 13 key nutrients. Specifically, labels must list the amount of fat, saturated and trans fats, cholesterol, sodium, carbohydrate, fibre, sugars, protein, vitamins A and C, calcium, and iron in a specified amount of food. "Nutritional information is essential to helping Canadians make informed choices for healthy living," Health Minister Anne McLellan noted. "The *Nutrition Facts*

Marketing at Work   8.1

Those Frustrating, Not-So-Easy-to-Open Packages

Some things, it seems, will never change. This classic letter from an angry consumer to Robert D. Stuart, then chairman of Quaker Oats, beautifully expresses the utter frustration all of us have experienced in dealing with so-called easy-opening packages.

Dear Mr. Stuart:

I am an 86-year-old widow in fairly good health. (You may think of this as advanced age, but for me that description pertains to the years ahead. Nevertheless, if you decide to reply to this letter I wouldn't dawdle, actuarial tables being what they are.)

As I said, my health is fairly good. Feeble and elderly, as one understands these terms, I am not. My two Doberman Pinschers and I take a brisk 3-mile walk every day. They are two strong and energetic animals and it takes a bit of doing to keep "brisk" closer to a stroll than a mad dash. But I manage because as yet I don't lack the strength. You will shortly see why this fact is relevant.

I am writing to call your attention to the cruel, deceptive, and utterly [false] copy on your Aunt Jemima buttermilk complete pancake and waffle mix. The words on your package read, "to open—press here and pull back."

Mr. Stuart, though I push and press and groan and strive and writhe and curse and sweat and jab and push, poke and ram . . . whew!—I have never once been able to do what the package instructs—to "press here and pull back" the [blankety-blank]. It can't be done! Talk about failing strength! Have you ever tried and succeeded?

My late husband was a gun collector who among other lethal weapons kept a Thompson machine gun in a locked cabinet. It was a good thing that the cabinet was locked. Oh, the number of times I was tempted to give your package a few short bursts.

That lock and a sense of ladylike delicacy kept me from pursuing that vengeful fantasy. Instead, I keep a small cleaver in my pantry for those occasions when I need to open a package of your delicious Aunt Jemima pancakes.

For many years that whacking away with my cleaver served a dual purpose. Not only to open the [blankety-blank] package but also to vent my fury at your sadists who willfully and maliciously did design that torture apparatus that passes for a package.

Sometimes just for the [blank] of it I let myself get carried away. I don't stop after I've lopped off the top. I whack away until the package is utterly destroyed in an outburst of rage, frustration, and vindictiveness. I wind up with a floorful of your delicious Aunt Jemima pancake mix. But that's a small price to pay for blessed release. (Anyway, the Pinschers lap up the mess.)

So many ingenious, considerate (even compassionate) innovations in package closures have been designed since Aunt Jemima first donned her red bandana. Wouldn't you consider the introduction of a more humane package to replace the example of marketing malevolence to which you resolutely cling? Don't you care, Mr. Stuart?

I'm really writing this to be helpful and in that spirit I am sending a copy to Mr. Tucker, president of Container Corp. I'm sure their clever young designers could be of immeasurable help to you in this matter. At least I feel it's worth a try.

Really, Mr. Stuart, I hope you will not regard me as just another cranky old biddy. I am The Public, the source of your fortunes.

Ms. Roberta Pavloff
Malvern, Pa.

Source: This letter was reprinted in "Some Designs Should Just Be Torn Asunder," *Advertising Age*, January 17, 1983, p. M54.

An easy to open package?

table will allow Canadians to compare products more easily, assess the nutritional value of more foods, and better manage special diets." Labels also must be in an easy-to-read, standardized format.[13]

Product Support Services Customer service is another element of product strategy. A company's offer to the marketplace usually includes some support services, which can be a minor or a major part of the total offering. Later in the chapter, we will discuss services as products in themselves. Here, we discuss services that augment tangible goods.

The first step is to survey customers periodically to assess the value of current services and to obtain ideas for new ones. For example, Cadillac holds regular focus group interviews with owners and carefully watches complaints that come into its dealerships. From this careful monitoring, Cadillac has learned that buyers are very upset by repairs that are not done correctly the first time.

Once the company has assessed the value of various support services to customers, it must next assess the costs of providing these services. It can then develop a package of services that will both delight customers and yield profits to the company. Based on its consumer interviews, Cadillac has set up a system directly linking each dealership with a group of 10 engineers who can help walk mechanics through difficult repairs. Such actions helped Cadillac jump, in one year, from 14th to 7th in independent rankings of service. For the past several years, Cadillac has rated at or near the top of its industry on the American Customer Satisfaction Index.[14]

Many companies are now using a sophisticated mix of phone, email, fax, Internet, and interactive voice and data technologies to provide support services that were not possible before. Consider the following example:

> It's February 14, and you've just remembered that it's Valentine's Day. There's no time for florist shops, so you jump online to www.1800FLOWERS.com. Then you pause. Red roses? Boxed or in a vase? One dozen or two? Just as your head starts to pound, you notice a button on the Web site. Click on it, and you're connected to a customer service rep at the call center who can help sniff out your options. A chat page opens on your screen, allowing a real-time dialog with the agent. The service rep even "pushes" pages to your browser so you can see different floral arrangements and how much they cost. In minutes, you have placed your order online, with a little hand-holding. Like 1-800-Flowers, many e-marketers now offer live interaction with service reps. Some feature real-time chat sessions, others voice-over-Web capabilities. In the future, a "call cam" will even let consumers see an agent on their computer screen.[15]

Product Line Decisions

Beyond decisions about individual goods and services, product strategy also calls for building a product line. A **product line** is a group of products that are closely related because they function in a similar manner, are sold to the same customer groups, are marketed through the same types of outlets, or fall within given price ranges. For example, Nike produces several lines of athletic shoes and apparel, Nokia produces several lines of telecommunications products, and Charles Schwab produces several lines of financial services.

The major product line decision involves *product line length*—the number of items in the product line. The line is too short if the manager can increase profits by adding items; the line is too long if the manager can increase profits by dropping items. The company should manage its product lines carefully. Product lines tend to lengthen over time, and most companies eventually need to prune unnecessary or unprofitable items from their lines to increase overall profitability.

Product line length is influenced by company objectives and resources. For example, one objective might be to allow for up-selling. Thus, BMW wants to move cus-

Product line A group of products that are closely related because they function in a similar manner, are sold to the same customer groups, are marketed through the same types of outlets, or fall within given price ranges.

tomers up from its 3-series models to 5- and 7-series models. Another objective might be to allow cross-selling: Hewlett-Packard sells printers as well as cartridges. Still another objective might be to protect against economic swings: Gap runs several clothing-store chains (Gap, Old Navy, Banana Republic) covering different price points.

A company can lengthen its product line in two ways: by *line stretching* or by *line filling*. *Product line stretching* occurs when a company lengthens its product line beyond its current range. The company can stretch its line downward, upward, or both ways.

Companies located at the upper end of the market can stretch their lines *downward*. A company may stretch downward to plug a market hole that otherwise would attract a new competitor or to respond to a competitor's attack on the upper end. Or it may add low-end products because it finds faster growth taking place in the low-end segments. DaimlerChrysler stretched its Mercedes line downward for all these reasons. Facing a slow-growth luxury car market and attacks by Japanese auto makers on its high-end positioning, it successfully introduced its Mercedes C-Class cars. These models sell at less than $30 000 without harming the firm's ability to sell other Mercedes for $100 000 or more. Similarly, Rolex launched its Rolex Tudor watch retailing for about $1350, compared with a Rolex Submariner, usually priced at $3875.

Companies at the lower end of a market can stretch their product lines *upward*. Sometimes, companies stretch upward in order to add prestige to their current products. Or they may be attracted by a faster growth rate or higher margins at the higher end. For example, each of the leading Japanese auto companies introduced an upmarket automobile: Toyota launched Lexus; Nissan launched Infinity; and Honda launched Acura. They used entirely new names rather than their own.

Companies in the middle range of the market may decide to stretch their lines in *both directions*. Marriott did this with its hotel product line. Along with regular Marriott hotels, it added the Renaissance Hotel line to serve the upper end of the market and the TownePlace Suites line to serve the moderate and lower ends. Each branded hotel line is aimed at a different target market. Renaissance aims to attract and please top executives; Marriotts, upper and middle managers; Courtyards, salespeople and other "road warriors"; and Fairfield Inns, vacationers and business travellers on a tight travel budget. ExecuStay by Marriott provides temporary housing for those relocating or away on long-term assignments of 30 days or longer. Marriott's Residence Inn provides a relaxed, residential atmosphere—a home away from home for people who travel for a living.

Product line stretching: Marriott offers a full line of hotel brands, each aimed at a different target market.

Marriott TownePlace Suites provide a comfortable atmosphere at a moderate price for extended-stay travellers.[16] The major risk with this strategy is that some travellers will trade down after finding that the lower-price hotels in the Marriott chain give them pretty much everything they want. However, Marriott would rather capture its customers who move downward than lose them to competitors.

An alternative to product line stretching is *product line filling*—adding more items within the present range of the line. There are several reasons for product line filling: reaching for extra profits, satisfying dealers, using excess capacity, being the leading full-line company, and plugging holes to keep out competitors. Sony filled its Walkman line by adding solar-powered and waterproof Walkmans, an ultralight model that attaches to a sweatband for exercisers, the MiniDisc Walkman, the CD Walkman, and the Memory Stick Walkman, which enables users to download tracks straight from the Net. To add to their original product line, Cake Beauty has created Dessert's On Me Whipped Body Spread, Desserted Island Moisturizing Body Glaze, and Cake Kiss Silky Smooth Lip Butter. However, line filling is overdone if it results in cannibalization and customer confusion. The company should ensure that new items are noticeably different from existing ones.

Product Mix Decisions

An organization with several product lines has a product mix. A **product mix** (or **product assortment**) consists of all the product lines and items that a particular seller offers for sale. Avon's product mix consists of five major product lines: beauty products, wellness products, jewellery and accessories, gifts, and "inspirational" products (inspiring gifts, books, music, and home accents). Each product line consists of several sublines. For example, the beauty line breaks down into makeup, skin care, bath and beauty, fragrance, and outdoor protection products. Each line and subline has many individual items. Altogether, Avon's product mix includes 1300 items. In contrast, a typical Kmart stocks 15 000 items, 3M markets more than 60 000 products, and General Electric manufactures as many as 250 000 items.

A company's product mix has four important dimensions: width, length, depth, and consistency. Product mix *width* refers to the number of different product lines the company carries. Procter & Gamble markets a fairly wide product mix consisting of 250 brands organized into many product lines. These lines include fabric and home care; baby, feminine, and family care; beauty care; health care; and food and beverage products. Product mix *length* refers to the total number of items the company carries within its product lines.

Product mix (or product assortment) The set of all product lines and items that a particular seller offers for sale.

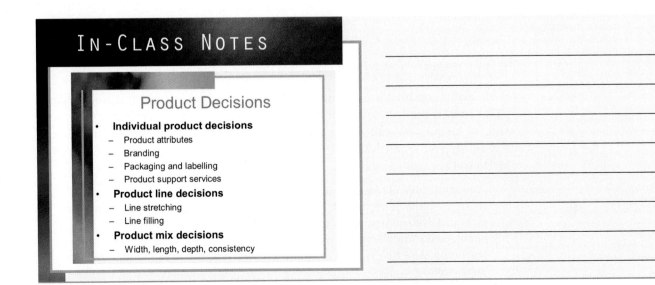

IN-CLASS NOTES

Product Decisions

- **Individual product decisions**
  - Product attributes
  - Branding
  - Packaging and labelling
  - Product support services
- **Product line decisions**
  - Line stretching
  - Line filling
- **Product mix decisions**
  - Width, length, depth, consistency

P&G typically carries many brands within each line. For example, it sells seven laundry detergents, six hand soaps, five shampoos, and four dishwashing detergents.

Product line *depth* refers to the number of versions offered of each product in the line. P&G's Crest toothpaste comes in 13 varieties, ranging from Crest Multicare, Crest Cavity Protection, and Crest Tartar Protection to Crest Sensitivity Protection, Crest Dual Action Whitening, Crest Whitening Plus Scope, Kid's Cavity Protection, and Crest Baking Soda & Peroxide Whitening formulations.[17]

Finally, the *consistency* of the product mix refers to how closely related the various product lines are in end use, production requirements, distribution channels, or some other way. P&G's product lines are consistent insofar as they are consumer products that go through the same distribution channels. The lines are less consistent insofar as they perform different functions for buyers.

These product mix dimensions provide the handles for defining the company's product strategy. The company can increase its business in four ways. It can add new product lines, widening its product mix. In this way, its new lines build on the company's reputation in its other lines. The company can lengthen its existing product lines to become a more full-line company. Or it can add more versions of each product and thus deepen its product mix. Finally, the company can pursue more product line consistency—or less—depending on whether it wants to have a strong reputation in a single field or in several fields.

Linking the Concepts

To get a better sense of how large and complex a company's product offering can become, investigate Procter & Gamble's product mix.

- Using P&G's website (www.pg.com), its annual report, or other sources, develop a list of all the company's product lines and individual products. What surprises you about this list of products?
- Is P&G's product mix consistent? What overall strategy or logic appears to have guided the development of this product mix?
- Try the same exercise with Tim Hortons (www.timhortons.com), Canada's top brand. How has Tim Hortons' product line evolved over the years?

BRANDING STRATEGY: BUILDING STRONG BRANDS

Some analysts see brands as *the* major enduring asset of a company, outlasting the company's specific products and facilities. John Stewart, co-founder of Quaker Oats, once said, "If this business were split up, I would give you the land and bricks and mortar, and I would keep the brands and trademarks, and I would fare better than you." The CEO of McDonald's agrees:[18]

> A McDonald's board member who worked at Coca-Cola once talked to us about the value of our brand. He said if every asset we own, every building, and every piece of equipment were destroyed in a terrible natural disaster, we would be able to borrow all the money to replace it very quickly because of the value of our brand. And he's right. The brand is more valuable than the totality of all these assets.

Thus, brands are powerful assets that must be carefully developed and managed. In this section, we examine the key strategies for building and managing brands.

Brand Equity

Brands are more than just names and symbols. Brands represent people's perceptions and feelings about a product and its performance—everything that the good or service *means* to consumers. In the final analysis, brands exist in the minds of consumers. Thus, the real value of a strong brand is its power to capture consumer preference and loyalty.

Brands vary in the amount of power and value they have in the marketplace. Some brands—such as Coca-Cola, Tide, Nike, Harley-Davidson, Volkswagen, and others—become larger-than-life icons that maintain their power in the market for years, even generations. "These brands win competitive battles not [just] because they deliver distinctive benefits, trustworthy service, or innovative technologies," notes a branding expert. "Rather, they succeed because they forge a deep connection with the culture."[19] In December of 2004, *Canadian Business* magazine published a list of Canada's top brands. Companies listed in the top 10 were the Royal Bank of Canada, Bell Canada, Loblaws, TD Bank, CIBC, Bank of Nova Scotia, Bank of Montreal, Sun Life, Canadian Tire, and Bombardier.[20]

A powerful brand has high *brand equity*. **Brand equity** is the positive differential effect that knowing the brand name has on customer response to the product. A measure of a brand's equity is the extent to which people are willing to pay more for the brand. One study found that 72 percent of consumers would pay a 20 percent premium for their brand of choice relative to the closest competing brand; 40 percent said they would pay a 50 percent premium.[21] Tide and Heinz lovers are willing to pay a 100 percent premium. Loyal Coke drinkers will pay a 50 percent premium and Volvo users a 40 percent premium. A badly mismanaged brand can actually have negative brand equity, meaning that customers would have such low expectations of the brand that they would be willing to pay less, not more for a branded product over a generic one.

Brand equity The usually positive but sometimes negative differential effect that knowing the brand name has on customer response to the product.

A brand with strong brand equity is a very valuable asset. *Brand valuation* is the process of estimating the total financial value of a brand. Measuring such value is difficult. However, according to one estimate, the brand value of Coca-Cola is $67 billion, Microsoft is $61 billion, and IBM is $54 billion. Other brands rating among the world's most valuable include General Electric, Intel, Disney, McDonald's, Nokia, and Toyota.[22]

High brand equity provides a company with many competitive advantages. A powerful brand enjoys a high level of consumer brand awareness and loyalty. Because consumers expect stores to carry the brand, the company has more leverage in bargaining with resellers. Because the brand name carries high credibility, the company can more easily launch line and brand extensions, as when Coca-Cola used its well-known brand to

A strong brand is a valuable asset. How many familiar brands and brand symbols can you find in this picture?

introduce Diet Coke and Vanilla Coke, and when Procter & Gamble introduced Ivory dishwashing detergent. A powerful brand offers the company some defence against fierce price competition.

Above all, a powerful brand forms the basis for building strong and profitable customer relationships. Therefore, the fundamental asset underlying brand equity is *customer equity*—the value of the customer relationships that the brand creates. A powerful brand is important, but what it really represents is a set of loyal customers. The proper focus of marketing is building customer equity, with brand management serving as a major marketing tool.[23]

Building Strong Brands

Branding poses challenging decisions to the marketer. Figure 8.3 shows that the major brand strategy decisions involve brand positioning, brand name selection, brand sponsorship, and brand development.

Figure 8.3   Major Brand Strategy Decisions

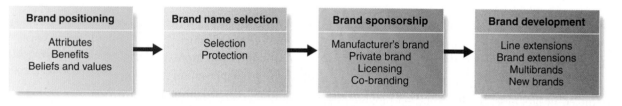

Brand Positioning   Marketers need to position their brands clearly in target customers' minds. They can position brands at any of three levels.[24] At the lowest level, they can position the brand on *product attributes*. Thus, marketers of Dove soap can talk about the product's attribute of one-quarter moisturizing lotion. However, attributes are the least desirable level for brand positioning. Competitors can easily copy attributes. More important, customers are not interested in attributes as such; they are interested in what the attributes will do for them.

A brand can be better positioned by associating its name with a desirable *benefit*. Thus, Dove marketers can go beyond the brand's moisturizing lotion attribute and talk about the resulting benefit of softer skin. Some successful brands positioned on benefits are Volvo (safety), Hallmark (caring), Harley-Davidson (adventure), FedEx (guaranteed overnight delivery), Nike (performance), and Lexus (quality).

The strongest brands go beyond attribute or benefit positioning. They are positioned on strong *beliefs and values*. These brands pack an emotional wallop. Thus, Dove's marketers can talk not just about moisturizing lotion attributes and softer skin benefits, but about how these will make you more attractive. Dove has gone beyond the traditional, and often shallow, view of beauty with its Campaign for Real Beauty, whose aim is to "change the status quo and offer in its place a broader, healthier, more democratic view of beauty." Their initiatives include the creation of a forum for woman to participate in a dialogue and debate about the definition and standards of beauty in society, and self-esteem workshops with young girls in schools to help them foster a healthy relationship with and confidence in their bodies and their looks. Brand expert Marc Gobe argues that successful brands must engage customers on a deeper level, touching a universal emotion.[25] His brand design agency, which has worked on brands such as Starbucks, Victoria's Secret, Godiva, Versace, and Lancôme, relies less on a product's tangible attributes and more on creating surprise, passion, and excitement surrounding a brand.

When positioning a brand, the marketer should establish a mission for the brand and a vision of what the brand must be and do. A brand is the company's promise to deliver a specific set of features, benefits, services, and experiences consistently to the buyers. It can be thought of as a contract to the customer regarding how the good or service will deliver value and satisfaction. The brand contract must be simple and honest. Motel 6, for example, offers clean rooms, low prices, and good service but does not promise expensive furniture or large bathrooms. In contrast, Fairmont Hotels, such as the Banff Springs, offer luxurious rooms and a truly memorable experience but does not promise low prices.

Brand Name Selection   A good name can add greatly to a product's success. However, finding the best brand name is a difficult task. It begins with a careful review of the product and its benefits, the target market, and proposed marketing strategies.

Desirable qualities for a brand name include the following: (1) It should suggest something about the product's benefits and qualities. Examples: Beautyrest, Craftsman, Snuggle, Merrie Maids, OFF! bug spray. (2) It should be easy to pronounce, recognize, and remember. Short names help. Examples: Tide, Crest, Puffs. But longer ones are sometimes effective. Examples: "Love My Carpet" carpet cleaner, "I Can't Believe It's Not Butter" margarine. (3) The brand name should be distinctive. Examples: Taurus, Kodak, Oracle. (4) It should be extendable: Amazon.com began as an online bookseller but chose a name that would allow expansion into other categories. (5) The name should translate easily into foreign languages. Before spending $100 million to change its name to Exxon, Standard Oil of New Jersey tested several names in 54 languages in more than 150 foreign markets. It found that the name Enco referred to a stalled engine when pronounced in Japanese. (6) It should be capable of registration and legal protection. A brand name cannot be registered if it infringes on existing brand names.

Once chosen, the brand name must be protected. Many firms try to build a brand name that will eventually become identified with the product category. Brand names such as Kleenex, Levi's, Jell-O, Scotch Tape, Formica, Ziploc, and Fiberglass have succeeded in this way. However, their very success may threaten the company's rights to the name. Many originally protected brand names—such as cellophane, aspirin, nylon, kerosene, linoleum, yo-yo, trampoline, escalator, thermos, and shredded wheat—are now generic names that any seller can use.

Brand Sponsorship   A manufacturer has four sponsorship options. The product may be launched as a *manufacturer's brand* (or national brand), as when Kellogg and Sony sell their output under their own manufacturer's brand names. Or the manufacturer may sell to resellers who give it a *private brand* (also called a *store brand* or *distributor brand*). Although most manufacturers create their own brand names, others market *licensed brands*. Finally, two companies can join forces and *co-brand* a product.

Manufacturer's Brands Versus Private Brands.   Manufacturers' brands have long dominated the retail scene. In recent times, however, an increasing number of retailers and wholesalers have created their own **private brands** (or *store brands*). For example, Sears has created several names—DieHard batteries, Craftsman tools, Kenmore appliances, and Weatherbeater paints. Private brands can be hard to establish and costly to stock and promote. However, they also yield higher profit margins for the reseller. And they give resellers exclusive products that cannot be bought from competitors, resulting in greater store traffic and loyalty.

Private (or store) brand A brand created and owned by a reseller of a product.

In the so-called *battle of the brands* between manufacturers' and private brands, retailers have many advantages. They control what products they stock, where they go on the shelf, what prices they charge, and which ones they will feature in local circulars. Retailers price their store brands lower than comparable manufacturers' brands, thereby appealing to budget-conscious shoppers, especially in difficult economic times. And most shoppers believe that store brands are often made by one of the larger manufacturers anyway.

Most retailers also charge manufacturers slotting fees—payments demanded by retailers before they will accept new products and find "slots" for them on the shelves. Store brands have the advantage of not having to pay these fees, which have to be paid by all other food manufacturers. Vancouver coffee roaster and fair-trade coffee marketer Roy Hardy is one person who has a bitter taste in his mouth as a result of these fees. He couldn't afford to get his product on store shelves because of such payments. While one supermarket was willing to take his coffee on a trial basis, it demanded that Hardy provide 40 pounds (18 kg) of free coffee per store as an incentive for providing shelf space. Hardy just couldn't afford even this version of a slotting fee.

Like Hardy, many claim that slotting fees favour large manufacturers and effectively shut out the small players. Slotting fees can range from a few hundred dollars to $25 000 per item or up to $3 million per supermarket chain. Canadian grocery manufacturers face demands for slotting fees ranging from "pay-to-play," staying fees ("pay-to-stay"), and failure fees. In other words, stores can charge a company for access to shelf space, to keep their place on the shelf, or to remove a dud product. Because ownership of Canada's grocery stores rests in the hands of a few companies, Canada's Competition Bureau has been studying the issue.[26]

As store brands improve in quality and as consumers gain confidence in their store chains, store brands are posing a strong challenge to manufacturers' brands. Consider the case of Loblaws.

Loblaws' President's Choice Decadent Chocolate Chip Cookies brand is now the leading cookie brand in Canada. Its private label President's Choice cola racks up 50 percent of Loblaws' canned cola sales. Based on this success, the private label powerhouse has expanded into a wide range of food and even nonfood categories. For example, it now offers more than 3,500 items under the President's Choice label, ranging from frozen desserts, paper, prepared foods, and boxed meats to pet foods, beauty care, and lawn and garden items. And the company launched PC Financial, a Web-based bank that offers no-fee bank accounts and mortgages. The President's Choice brand has become so popular that Loblaws now licenses it to retailers across the United States and fifteen other countries where Loblaws has no stores of its own.[27]

Private-label products control almost a quarter of the Canadian grocery market and the drug store market. In some categories, private-label sales are even higher. For example, in the paper and wrap category, private-label goods account for 45.7 percent of the market. They control 36 percent of the frozen food marketplace and almost 29 percent of the pet product market.[28] To fend off private brands, leading brand marketers will have to invest in R&D to bring out new brands, new features, and continuous quality improvements. They must design strong advertising programs to maintain high awareness and preference. They must also find

Store brands: Loblaws' President's Choice brand has become so popular that the company licenses it to retailers across the United States and in 15 other countries where Loblaws has no stores of its own.

ways to partner with major distributors in a search for distribution economies and improved joint performance.

Licensing. Most manufacturers take years and spend millions to create their own brand names. However, some companies license names or symbols previously created by other manufacturers, names of well-known celebrities, or characters from popular movies and books. For a fee, any of these can provide an instant and proven brand name.

Apparel and accessories sellers pay large royalties to adorn their products—from blouses to ties, and linens to luggage—with the names or initials of well-known fashion innovators such as Calvin Klein, Tommy Hilfiger, Gucci, or Armani. Sellers of children's products attach an almost endless list of character names to clothing, toys, school supplies, linens, dolls, lunch boxes, cereals, and other items. Licensed character names range from classics such as *Sesame Street*, Disney, Peanuts, Winnie the Pooh, the Muppets, Scooby Doo, and Dr. Seuss characters to the more recent Teletubbies, Pokemon, Powerpuff Girls, Rugrats, Blue's Clues, and Harry Potter characters. Almost half of all retail toy sales come from products based on television shows and movies such as *Scooby Doo, SpongeBob SquarePants, The Rugrats Movie, The Lion King, Batman, Star Trek, Star Wars, Spider-Man, Men in Black,* or *Harry Potter.*[29]

Name and character licensing has grown rapidly in recent years. Annual retail sales of licensed products in Canada and the United States has grown from only $4 billion in 1977 to $55 billion in 1987 and more than $71 billion today. Licensing can be a highly profitable business for many companies. For example, Warner Brothers has turned *Looney Tunes* characters into one of the world's most sought-after licences. More than 225 licensees generate $6 billion in annual retail sales of products sporting Bugs Bunny, Daffy Duck, Foghorn Leghorn, or one of more than 100 other *Looney Tunes* characters. Warner Brothers has yet to tap the full potential of many of its secondary characters. The Tazmanian Devil, for example, initially appeared in only five cartoons. But through cross-licensing agreements with organizations such as Harley-Davidson and the NFL, Taz has become something of a pop icon. Warner Brothers sees similar potential for Michigan Frog or Speedy Gonzales for the Hispanic market.[30]

The fastest-growing licensing category is corporate brand licensing, as more and more for-profit and not-for-profit organizations are licensing their names to generate additional revenues and brand recognition. Coca-Cola, for example, has some 320 licensees in 57 countries producing more than 10 000 products, ranging from baby clothes and boxer shorts to earrings, a Coca-Cola Barbie doll, and even a fishing lure shaped like a tiny Coke can. Each year, licensees sell more than $1 billion worth of licensed Coca-Cola products.[31]

Co-Branding. Although companies have been **co-branding** products for many years, there has been a recent resurgence in co-branded products. Co-branding occurs when two established brand names of different companies are used on the same product. For example, Nabisco joined forces with Pillsbury to create Pillsbury Oreo Bars baking mix, and Kellogg joined with ConAgra to co-brand Healthy Choice from Kellogg's cereals. Ford and Eddie Bauer co-branded a sport utility vehicle—the Ford Explorer, Eddie Bauer edition. General Electric worked with Culligan to develop its Water by Culligan Profile Performance refrigerator with a built-in Culligan water-filtration system. Mattel teamed with Coca-Cola to market Soda Fountain Sweetheart Barbie. In most co-branding situations, one company licenses another company's well-known brand to use in combination with its own.

Co-branding offers many advantages. Because each brand dominates in a different category, the combined brands create broader consumer appeal and greater brand equity. Co-branding also allows a company to expand its existing brand into a category it might otherwise have difficulty entering alone. For example, by licensing its Healthy

Co-branding The practice of using the established brand names of two different companies on the same product.

Choice brand to Kellogg, ConAgra entered the breakfast segment with a solid product. In return, Kellogg could leverage the broad awareness of the Healthy Choice name in the cereal category.

Co-branding also has limitations. Such relationships usually involve complex legal contracts and licences. Co-branding partners must carefully coordinate their advertising, sales promotion, and other marketing efforts. Finally, when co-branding, each partner must trust that the other will take good care of its brand. For example, consider the marriage between Kmart and the Martha Stewart housewares brand. When Kmart declared bankruptcy, it cast a shadow on the Martha Stewart brand. In turn, when Martha Stewart was convicted of obstructing justice and lying to investigators in 2004, it created negative associations for Kmart. As one Nabisco manager put it, "Giving away your brand is a lot like giving away your child—you want to make sure everything is perfect."[32]

Brand Development   A company has four choices when it comes to developing brands (see Figure 8.4). It can introduce *line extensions* (existing brand names extended to new forms, sizes, and flavours of an existing product category), *brand extensions* (existing brand names extended to new product categories), *multibrands* (new brand names introduced in the same product category), or *new brands* (new brand names in new product categories).

Figure 8.4   Brand Development Strategies

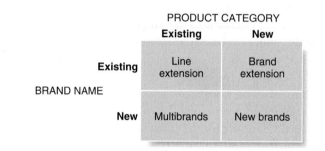

Line Extensions.   **Line extensions** occur when a company introduces additional items in a given product category under the same brand name, such as new flavours, forms, colours, ingredients, or package sizes. Thus, Danone introduced several line extensions, including seven new yogurt flavours, a fat-free yogurt, and a large, economy-size yogurt. The vast majority of all new-product activity consists of line extensions.

A company might introduce line extensions as a low-cost, low-risk way to introduce new products. Or it might want to meet consumer desires for variety, to use excess capacity, or simply to command more shelf space from resellers. However, line extensions involve some risks. An overextended brand name might lose its specific meaning, or heavily extended brands can cause consumer confusion or frustration. For example, a consumer buying cereal at the local supermarket will be confronted by more than 150 brands, including up to 30 different brands, flavours, and sizes of oatmeal alone. By itself, Quaker offers its original Quaker Oats, several flavours of Quaker instant oatmeal, and several dry cereals such as Oatmeal Squares, Toasted Oatmeal, and Toasted Oatmeal-Honey Nut.

Another risk is that sales of an extension may come at the expense of other items in the line. For example, the original Nabisco Fig Newtons cookies have now morphed into a full line of Newtons Fruit Chewy Cookies, including Cranberry Newtons, Blueberry Newtons, and Apple Newtons. Although all are doing well, the original Fig Newton brand now seems like just another flavour. A line extension works best when it takes sales away from competing brands, not when it cannibalizes the company's other items.

Line extension Using a successful brand name to introduce additional items in a given product category under the same brand name, such as new flavours, forms, colours, added ingredients, or package sizes.

Too many line extensions can confuse or frustrate consumers. A shopper at a local supermarket may be confronted by 30 different brands, flavours, and sizes of oat cereal alone.

Brand Extensions. A **brand extension** involves the use of a successful brand name to launch new or modified products in a new category. Mattel has extended its enduring Barbie Doll brand into new categories ranging from Barbie home furnishings, Barbie cosmetics, and Barbie electronics to Barbie books, Barbie sporting goods, and even a Barbie band—Beyond Pink. Honda uses its company name to cover different products such as its automobiles, motorcycles, snowblowers, lawn mowers, marine engines, and snowmobiles. This allows Honda to advertise that it can fit "six Hondas in a two-car garage." Swiss Army brand sunglasses, Disney Cruise Lines, Cosmopolitan low-fat dairy products, Century 21 Home Improvements, and Brinks home security systems—all are brand extensions.

A brand extension gives a new product instant recognition and faster acceptance. It also saves the high advertising costs usually required to build a new brand name. At the same time, a brand extension strategy involves some risk. Brand extensions such as Bic pantyhose, Heinz pet food, LifeSavers gum, and Clorox laundry detergent met early deaths. The extension may confuse the image of the main brand. And if a brand extension fails, it may harm consumer attitudes toward the other products carrying the same brand name. Furthermore, a brand name may not be appropriate to a particular new product, even if it is well made and satisfying—would you consider buying Sunoco milk or Alpo chili? A brand name may lose its special positioning in the consumer's mind through overuse. Companies that are tempted to transfer a brand name must research how well the brand's associations fit the new product.[33]

Multibrands. Companies often introduce additional brands in the same category. Thus, P&G markets many different brands in each of its product categories. *Multibranding* offers a way to establish different features and appeal to different buying motives. It also allows a company to lock up more reseller shelf space. Or the company may want to protect its major brand by setting up *flanker* or *fighter brands*. Seiko uses different brand names for its higher-priced watches (Seiko Lasalle) and lower-priced watches (Pulsar) to protect the flanks of its mainstream Seiko brand.

A major drawback of multibranding is that each brand might obtain only a small market share, and none may be very profitable. The company may end up spreading its resources over many brands instead of building a few brands to a highly profitable level. These companies should reduce the number of brands they sell in a given category and set up tighter screening procedures for new brands.

Brand extension Using a successful brand name to launch a new or modified product in a new category.

New Brands. A company might believe that the power of its existing brand name is waning and a new brand name is needed. Or a company may create a new brand name when it enters a new product category for which none of the company's current brand names is appropriate. For example, Honda created the Acura brand to differentiate its luxury car from the established Honda line. Japan's Matsushita uses separate names for its different families of products: Technics, Panasonic, National, and Quasar.

As with multibranding, offering too many new brands can result in a company spreading its resources too thin. And in some industries, such as consumer packaged goods, consumers and retailers have become concerned that there are already too many brands, with too few differences between them. Thus, Procter & Gamble, Frito-Lay, and other large consumer-product marketers are now pursuing *megabrand* strategies— weeding out weaker brands and focusing their marketing dollars only on brands that can achieve the number one or number two market share positions in their categories.

Managing Brands

Companies must carefully manage their brands. First, the brand's positioning must be continuously communicated to consumers. Major brand marketers often spend huge amounts on advertising to create brand awareness and to build preference and loyalty. For example, AT&T spends almost a billion dollars annually to promote its brands. McDonald's spends more than $600 million.[34]

Such advertising campaigns can help to create name recognition and brand knowledge and increase brand preference. However, the fact is that brands are not maintained by advertising but by the *brand experience.* Today, customers come to know a brand through a wide range of contacts and touch points. These include advertising, but also personal experience with the brand, word of mouth, personal interactions with company people, telephone interactions, company websites, and many others. Any of these experiences can have a positive or negative impact on brand perceptions and feelings. The company must put as much care into managing these touch points as it does into producing its ads.

The brand's positioning will not take hold fully unless everyone in the company lives the brand. Therefore the company needs to train its people to be customer-centred. Even better, the company should build pride in its employees regarding their products and services so that their enthusiasm will spill over to customers. Companies such as Mountain Equipment Co-op, Lexus, Dell, and Harley-Davidson have succeeded in turn-

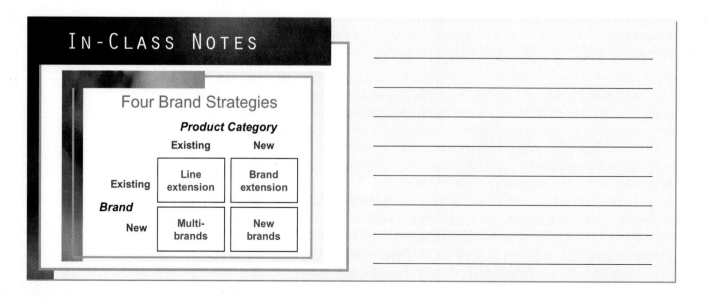

ing all of their employees into enthusiastic brand builders. Companies can carry on internal brand building to help employees understand, desire, and deliver on the brand promise. Many companies go even further by training and encouraging their distributors and dealers to serve their customers well.

All of this suggests that managing a company's brand assets can no longer be left only to brand managers. Brand managers do not have enough power or scope to do all the things necessary to build and enhance their brands. Moreover, brand managers often pursue short-term results, whereas managing brands as assets calls for longer-term strategy. Thus, some companies are now setting up brand asset management teams to manage their major brands. Canada Dry and Colgate-Palmolive have appointed *brand equity managers* to maintain and protect their brands' images, associations, and quality, and to prevent short-term actions by overeager brand managers from hurting the brand. Similarly, Hewlett-Packard has appointed a senior executive in charge of the customer experience in each of its two divisions, consumer and B2B. Their job is to track, measure, and improve the customer relationship with HP products. They report directly to the presidents of their respective divisions.

Finally, companies need to periodically audit their brands' strengths and weaknesses.[35] They should ask: Does our brand excel at delivering benefits that customers truly value? Is the brand properly positioned? Do all of our customer touch points support the brand's positioning? Do the brand's managers understand what the brand means to our customers? Does the brand receive proper, sustained support?

The brand audit may turn up brands that need to be repositioned because of changing customer preferences or new competitors. Some cases may call for completely *rebranding* a product, service, or company. The Clarica brand was born, for example, when Mutual Life of Canada became a public company and its business model transformed. The new name was chosen to portray the power of clear dialogue in making personal financial choices. The recent wave of corporate mergers and acquisitions has set off a flurry of corporate rebranding campaigns. A prime example is American telecommunications brand Verizon Communication, created by the merger of Bell Atlantic and GTE. The company decided that neither of the old names properly positioned the new company. "We needed a master brand to leave all our old names behind," says Verizon's senior vice president of brand management and marketing services. The old names created too much confusion, conjured up an image of old-fashioned phone companies, and "held us back from marketing in new areas of innovation—high speed Internet and wireless services." The new branding effort appears to have worked. Verizon Wireless is now the leading provider of wireless phone services, with better than a 21 percent market share. Number two is Cingular Wireless, another new brand created through a joint venture between Bell South and SBC Communications.[36]

However, building a new image and re-educating customers can be a huge undertaking. The cost of Verizon's brand overhaul included tens of millions of dollars just for a special four-week advertising campaign to announce the new name, followed by considerable ongoing advertising expenses. And that was only the beginning. The company had to repaint its fleet of 70 000 trucks, along with its garages and service centres. The campaign also required relabelling 250 000 pay phones, redesigning 91 million customer billing statements, and producing videos and other in-house employee educational materials.

SERVICES MARKETING

Services have grown dramatically in recent years. As of 2004, the service sector accounted for 69 percent of Canada's GDP. Service industries in Canada have grown faster than both goods-producing industries and the economy as a whole. The services sector is also a much larger employer than the goods-producing sector. Almost 12 million Canadians were employed in the service sector compared with the 4 million people working in the goods-producing sector. And the biggest service sector employer is the retail industry, with 132 000 workers.[37]

Service industries vary greatly. *Governments* offer services through courts, employment services, hospitals, military services, police and fire departments, postal services, and schools. *Private not-for-profit organizations* offer services through museums, charities, churches, colleges, foundations, and hospitals. A large number of *business organizations* offer services—airlines, banks, hotels, insurance companies, consulting firms, medical and law practices, entertainment companies, real estate firms, advertising and research agencies, and retailers.

Nature and Characteristics of a Service

A company must consider four special service characteristics when designing marketing programs: *intangibility*, *inseparability*, *variability*, and *perishability* (see Figure 8.5).

Figure 8.5 **Four Service Characteristics**

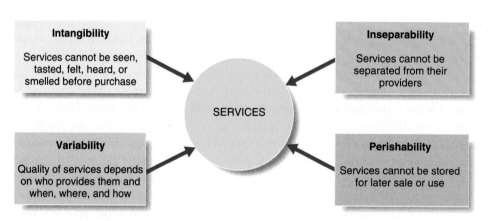

Intangibility
Services cannot be seen, tasted, felt, heard, or smelled before purchase

Inseparability
Services cannot be separated from their providers

SERVICES

Variability
Quality of services depends on who provides them and when, where, and how

Perishability
Services cannot be stored for later sale or use

Service intangibility A major characteristic of services—they cannot be seen, tasted, felt, heard, or smelled before they are bought.

Service intangibility means that services cannot be seen, tasted, felt, heard, or smelled before they are bought. For example, people undergoing cosmetic surgery cannot see the result before the purchase. Airline passengers have nothing but a ticket and the promise that they and their luggage will arrive safely at the intended destination, hopefully at the same time. To reduce uncertainty, buyers look for "signals" of service quality. They draw conclusions about quality from the place, people, price, equipment, and communications that they can see.

Therefore, the service provider's task is to make the service tangible in one or more ways and to send the right signals about quality. One analyst calls this *evidence management,* in which the service organization presents its customers with organized, honest evidence of its capabilities. The Mayo Clinic practises good evidence management:[38]

> Nobody likes going to the hospital. The experience is at best unnerving and often frightening. What's more, it's very hard for the average patient to judge the quality of the "product." You can't try it on, you can't return it if you don't like it, and you need an advanced degree to understand it. And so, when we're considering a medical facility, most of us unconsciously turn detective, looking for evidence of competence, caring, and integrity. The Mayo Clinic doesn't leave that evidence to chance. By carefully managing a set of visual and experiential clues, Mayo offers patients and their families concrete evidence of its strengths and values. For example, staff people at the clinic are trained to act in a way that clearly signals its patient-first focus. "My doctor calls me at home to check on how I am doing," marvels one patient. "She wants to work with what is best for my schedule." Mayo's

physical facilities also send the right signals. They've been carefully designed to relieve stress, offer a place of refuge, create positive distractions, convey caring and respect, signal competence, accommodate families, and make it easy to find your way around. The result? Exceptionally positive word-of-mouth and abiding customer loyalty, which have allowed Mayo Clinic to build what is arguably the most powerful brand in health care—with very little advertising.

Physical goods are produced, then stored, later sold, and still later consumed. In contrast, services are first sold, then produced and consumed at the same time. **Service inseparability** means that services cannot be separated from their providers, whether the providers are people or machines. If a service employee provides the service, then the employee is a part of the service. Because the customer is also present as the service is produced, *provider–customer interaction* is a special feature of services marketing. Both the provider and the customer affect the service outcome.

Service variability means that the quality of services depends on who provides them as well as when, where, and how they are provided. For example, some hotels—say, Marriott—have reputations for providing better service than others. Still, within a given Marriott hotel, one registration-desk employee may be cheerful and efficient, whereas another standing just a couple of metres away may be unpleasant and slow. Even the quality of a single Marriott employee's service varies according to his or her energy and frame of mind at the time of each customer encounter.

Service perishability means that services cannot be stored for later sale or use. Some dentists charge patients for missed appointments because the service value existed only at that point and disappeared when the patient did not show up. The perishability of services is not a problem when demand is steady. However, when demand fluctuates, service firms often have difficult problems. For example, because of rush-hour demand, public transportation companies have to own much more equipment than they would if demand were even throughout the day. Thus, service firms often design strategies for producing a better match between demand and supply. Hotels and resorts charge lower prices in the off-season to attract more guests. And restaurants hire part-time employees to serve during peak periods.

Service inseparability A major characteristic of services—they are produced and consumed at the same time and cannot be separated from their providers, whether the providers are people or machines.

Service variability A major characteristic of services—their quality may vary greatly, depending on who provides them and when, where, and how.

Service perishability A major characteristic of services—they cannot be stored for later sale or use.

Marketing Strategies for Service Firms

Just like manufacturing businesses, good service firms use marketing to position themselves strongly in chosen target markets. WestJet Airlines positions itself as a no-frills,

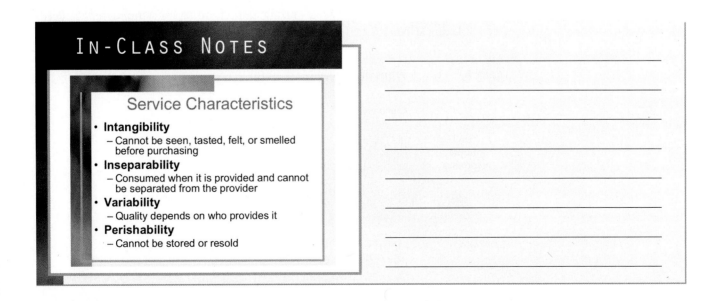

IN-CLASS NOTES

Service Characteristics

- **Intangibility**
  – Cannot be seen, tasted, felt, or smelled before purchasing
- **Inseparability**
  – Consumed when it is provided and cannot be separated from the provider
- **Variability**
  – Quality depends on who provides it
- **Perishability**
  – Cannot be stored or resold

short-haul airline charging very low fares. Wal-Mart promises "Always Low Prices, Always." Ritz-Carlton Hotels positions itself as offering a memorable experience that "enlivens the senses, instills well-being, and fulfills even the unexpressed wishes and needs of our guests." At the Mayo Clinic, "the needs of the patient come first." These and other service firms establish their positions through traditional marketing mix activities.

However, because services differ from tangible goods, they often require additional marketing approaches. In a business that sells tangible goods, products are fairly standardized and can sit on shelves waiting for customers. But in a service business, the customer and front-line service employee *interact* to create the service. Thus, service providers must interact effectively with customers to create superior value during service encounters. Effective interaction, in turn, depends on the skills of front-line service employees and on the support processes backing these employees.

The Service-Profit Chain Successful service companies focus their attention on *both* their customers and their employees. They understand the **service-profit chain**, which links service firm profits with employee and customer satisfaction. This chain consists of five links:[39]

- □ *Internal service quality:* superior employee selection and training, a quality work environment, and strong support for those dealing with customers, which results in . . .
- □ *Satisfied and productive service employees:* more satisfied, loyal, and hardworking employees, which results in . . .
- □ *Greater service value:* more effective and efficient customer value creation and service delivery, which results in . . .
- □ *Satisfied and loyal customers:* satisfied customers who remain loyal, repeat purchase, and refer other customers, which results in . . .
- □ *Healthy service profits and growth:* superior service firm performance.

Therefore, reaching service profits and growth goals begins with taking care of those who take care of customers.

Thus, service marketing requires more than just traditional external marketing using the four Ps. Figure 8.6 shows that service marketing also requires *internal marketing* and *interactive marketing*. **Internal marketing** means that the service firm must effectively train and motivate its customer-contact employees and supporting service people to work as a *team* to provide customer satisfaction. Marketers must get everyone in the organization to be customer-centred. In fact, internal marketing must *precede* external marketing. Ritz-Carlton orients its employees carefully, instills in them a sense of pride, and motivates them by recognizing and rewarding outstanding service deeds (see Marketing at Work 8.2).

Service-profit chain The chain that links service firm profits with employee and customer satisfaction.

Internal marketing Marketing by a service firm to train and effectively motivate its customer-contact employees and all the supporting service people to work as a team to provide customer satisfaction.

Figure 8.6 Three Types of Service Marketing

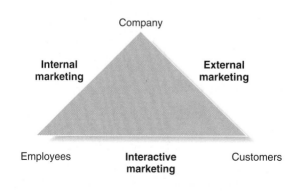

Marketing at Work   8.2

Ritz-Carlton: Taking Care of Those Who Take Care of Customers

Ritz-Carlton, a chain of luxury hotels renowned for outstanding service, caters to the top 5 percent of corporate and leisure travellers. The company's Credo sets lofty customer service goals: "The Ritz-Carlton Hotel is a place where the genuine care and comfort of our guests is our highest mission. We pledge to provide the finest personal service and facilities for our guests, who will always enjoy a warm, relaxed yet refined ambience."

The Credo is more than just words on paper—Ritz-Carlton delivers on its promises. In surveys of departing guests, some 95 percent report that they've had a truly memorable experience. Since its incorporation in 1983, the company has received virtually every major award that the hospitality industry bestows. More importantly, service quality has resulted in high customer retention. More than 90 percent of Ritz-Carlton customers return. And despite its hefty room rates, the chain enjoys a 70 percent occupancy rate, almost nine points above the industry average.

Most of the responsibility for keeping guests satisfied falls to Ritz-Carlton's customer-contact employees. Thus, the hotel chain takes great care in finding just the right personnel.

"We don't hire or recruit, we select," says Ritz-Carlton's director of human resources. Once selected, new employees attend a two-day orientation, in which top management drums into them the "20 Ritz-Carlton Basics."

Employees are taught to do everything they can never to lose a guest. "There's no negotiating at Ritz-Carlton when it comes to solving customer problems," says the quality executive. Staff learn that *anyone* who receives a customer complaint *owns* that complaint until it's resolved. They are trained to drop whatever they're doing to help a customer—no matter what they're doing or what their department. Ritz-Carlton employees are empowered to handle problems on the spot, without consulting higher-ups. Each employee can spend up to $2000 to redress a guest grievance. And each is allowed to break from his or her routine for as long as needed to make a guest happy.

Ritz-Carlton recognizes and rewards employees who perform feats of outstanding service. Outstanding performers are nominated by peers and managers, and winners receive plaques at dinners celebrating their achievements. For on-the-spot recognition, managers award Gold

Standard Coupons, redeemable for items in the gift shop and free weekend stays at the hotel. Ritz-Carlton further motivates its employees with events such as Super Sports Day and an employee talent show. As a result, employee turnover is less than 30 percent a year, compared with 45 percent at other luxury hotels.

Ritz-Carlton's success is based on a simple philosophy: To take care of customers, you must first take care of those who take care of customers. Satisfied employees deliver high service value, which then creates satisfied customers. Satisfied customers, in turn, create sales and profits for the company.

Sources: Edwin McDowell, "Ritz-Carlton's Keys to Good Service," *New York Times,* March 31, 1993, p. D1; Howard Schlossberg, "Measuring Customer Satisfaction Is Easy to Do—Until You Try," *Marketing News,* April 26, 1993, pp. 5, 8; Ginger Conlon, "True Romance," *Sales & Marketing Management,* May 1996, pp. 85–90; "The Ritz-Carlton, Half Moon Bay," *Successful Meetings,* November 2001, p. 40; Ritz-Carlton website at www.ritzcarlton.com, accessed August 2003; Patricia Sheehan, "Back to Bed: Selling the Perfect Night's Sleep," *Lodging Hospitality,* March 15, 2001, pp. 22–24; Nicole Harris, "Can't Sleep? Try the Eye Gel in the Minibar—Hotels Roll Out Products to Help Tired Travelers Snooze," *Wall Street Journal,* June 20, 2002, p. D1; and Scott Neuman, "Relax, Put Your Feet Up," *Far Eastern Economic Review,* April 17, 2003, p. 36.

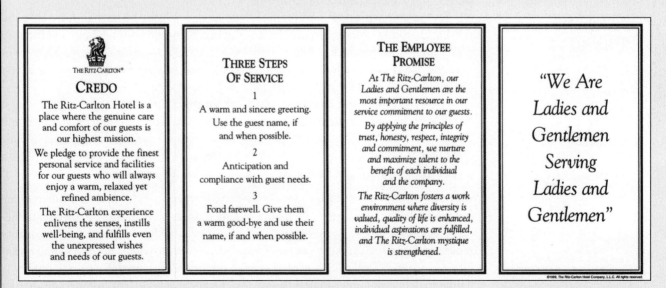

The credo and employee promise: Ritz-Carlton knows that to take care of customers, you must first take care of those who take care of the customers.

Interactive marketing Marketing by a service firm that recognizes that perceived service quality depends heavily on the quality of buyer–seller interaction.

Interactive marketing means that service quality depends heavily on the quality of the buyer–seller interaction during the service encounter. When marketing goods, product quality often depends little on how the good is obtained. But in services marketing, service quality depends on both the service deliverer and the quality of the delivery. Service marketers, therefore, have to master interactive marketing skills. Thus, Ritz-Carlton selects only "people who care about people" and instructs them carefully in the fine art of interacting with customers to satisfy their every need.

In today's marketplace, companies must know how to deliver interactions that are not only "high-touch" but also "high-tech." For example, if you look any Canadian earnestly in the eye and spout the phrase "Save your money!" they will instantly think of ING Direct. This is quite a feat given that the online bank has been operating in Canada for only a short period of time. Although ING has been in Canada since the 1950s, the launch of the new branchless bank in 1997 has become the subject of marketing legend as one of the all-time greatest service launches. While Canadians had long socked their money away in the big six banks, valuing them for their safety and stability, research told ING that Canadians had a "love-hate relationship with the big banks." Thus, ING positioned itself carefully against its rivals, offering a distinct online service, a price advantage, and simplicity. The strategy has been a huge success. In 2005, ING Direct Canada provided financial services to almost 1 million customers and held over $14 billion in assets.[40]

Today, as competition and costs increase and productivity gains are more difficult to find and exploit, more service marketing sophistication is needed. Service companies face three major marketing tasks: They want to increase their *competitive differentiation*, *service quality*, and *productivity*.

Managing Service Differentiation In these days of intense price competition, service marketers often complain about the difficulty of differentiating their services from those of competitors. To the extent that customers view the services of different providers as similar, they care less about the provider than the price.

The solution to price competition is to develop a differentiated offer, delivery, and image. The *offer* can include innovative features that set one company's offer apart from competitors' offers. Some hotels offer car rental, banking, and business centre services in their lobbies. Airlines introduced innovations such as in-flight movies, advance seating, air-to-ground telephone service, and frequent flyer award programs to differentiate their offers. British Airways even offers international travellers beds and private "demi-cabins," hot showers, and cooked-to-order breakfasts.

Service companies can differentiate their service *delivery* by having more able and reliable customer-contact people, by developing a superior physical environment in which the service product is delivered, or by designing a superior delivery process. For example, many banks offer their customers Internet banking as a better way to access banking services than having to drive, park, and wait in line.

Finally, service companies also can work on differentiating their *images* through symbols and branding. Royal Bank's stylized "Leo the Lion" symbolizes strength and power—desirable qualities of a large bank. Other well-known service symbols include Canadian National Railway's CN symbol, Air Canada's maple leaf, TD Canada Trust's green armchair, and Bell Canada's swirl and stylized face symbol.

Managing Service Quality One of the major ways a service firm can differentiate itself is by delivering consistently higher quality than its competitors do. Like manufacturers before them, most service industries have now joined the customer-driven quality movement. And like marketers of tangible goods, service providers need to identify what target customers expect concerning service quality. Unfortunately, service quality is harder to define and judge than is the quality of a tangible good. For instance, it is harder to agree on the quality of a haircut than on the quality of a hair dryer. Customer retention is perhaps the best measure of quality—a service firm's ability to hang onto its customers depends on how consistently it delivers value to them.[41]

Top service companies are customer obsessed and set high service quality standards. They watch service performance closely, both their own and that of competitors. They do not settle for merely good service; they aim for 100 percent defect-free service. A 98 percent performance standard may sound good, but using this standard, 64 000 FedEx packages would be lost each day, 10 words would be misspelled on each printed page, 400 000 prescriptions would be misfilled daily, and drinking water would be unsafe 8 days a year.[42]

Unlike goods manufacturers, who can adjust their machinery and inputs until everything is perfect, service quality will always vary, depending on the interactions between employees and customers. As hard as they try, even the best companies will have an occasional late delivery, burned steak, or grumpy employee. However, good *service recovery* can turn angry customers into loyal ones. In fact, good recovery can win more customer purchasing and loyalty than if things had gone well in the first place. Therefore, companies should take steps not only to provide good service every time but also to recover from service mistakes when they do occur.

The first step is to *empower* front-line service employees—to give them the authority, responsibility, and incentives they need to recognize, care about, and tend to customer needs. At Marriott, for example, well-trained employees are given the authority to do whatever it takes, on the spot, to keep guests happy. They are also expected to help management ferret out the cause of guests' problems and to inform managers of ways to improve overall hotel service and guests' comfort.

Managing Service Productivity With their costs rising rapidly, service firms are under great pressure to increase service productivity. They can do so in several ways. They can train current employees better or hire new ones who will work harder or more skillfully. Or they can increase the quantity of their service by giving up some quality. The provider can "industrialize the service" by adding equipment and standardizing production, as in McDonald's assembly-line approach to fast-food retailing. Finally, the service provider can harness the power of technology. Although we often think of technology's power to save time and costs in manufacturing companies, it also has great—and often untapped—potential to make service workers more productive.

Canada Post's newest service, Fetch, is one example. It uses wireless technology to directly connect marketers with individual consumers while protecting shoppers' privacy. Advertisers decide on a special offer they want to make to a particular market segment. Canada Post convinces consumers to register their contact information on the Fetch website. Then, once the consumer sees a "Fetch-enabled" ad, they call, text, or email the site. The consumer is then sent the special offer—usually a discount coupon or a product sample. And all the while the consumer's contact information is kept private. Advertisers are delighted, since they pay Canada Post only when someone "fetches" their product.[43]

However, companies must avoid pushing productivity so hard that doing so reduces quality. Attempts to industrialize a service or to cut costs can make a service company more efficient in the short run. But they can also reduce its longer-run ability to innovate, maintain service quality, or respond to consumer needs and desires. In short, they can take the "service" out of service.

ADDITIONAL PRODUCT CONSIDERATIONS

Here, we discuss two additional product policy considerations: social responsibility in product decisions and issues of international product and services marketing.

Product Decisions and Social Responsibility

Product decisions have attracted much public attention. Marketers should carefully consider public policy issues and regulations concerning acquiring or dropping products, patent protection, product quality and safety, and product warranties.

Canadian manufacturers must navigate a complex web of government departments and legislation when considering their product policies. Agriculture Canada, the Canadian Food Inspection Agency, and the Consumer Products Division of Health Canada, for example, govern food and product safety. The Competition Bureau regulates many aspects of the marketing of products. The *Competition Act*'s provisions cover pricing and advertising, not just the maintenance of a competitive marketplace. When considering a merger that would give a firm access to new products, a company has to be aware that the government may invoke the *Competition Act* if it thinks the merger would lessen competition. Companies dropping products must be aware that they have legal obligations, written or implied, to their suppliers, dealers, and customers who have a stake in the discontinued product. Companies must also obey patent laws when developing new products. A company cannot make its product illegally similar to another company's established product. Firms may also have to be aware of legislation controlled by Environment Canada and the Department of Transport.

Federal statutes cover product safety (except electrical equipment), competition, labelling, and weights and measures. The *Hazardous Products Act,* for example, controls the marketing of dangerous or potentially dangerous consumer and industrial products; the *Food and Drugs Act* covers safety of cosmetics as well as food and drugs. Both acts can be found on the Canadian Department of Justice website (http://canada.justice.gc.ca).[44] Provincial statutes deal with such matters as conditions of sale, guarantees, and licensing, as well as unfair business practices.

Consumers who have been injured by a defectively designed product can sue the manufacturer or dealer. The number of product liability suits has been increasing, and settlements often run in the millions of dollars. This, in turn, has resulted in huge increases in the cost of product liability insurance premiums. Some companies pass these higher rates along to consumers by raising prices. Others are forced to discontinue high-risk product lines.

International Product and Services Marketing

International product marketers face special challenges. First, they must figure out what goods and services to introduce and in which countries. Then, they must decide how much to standardize or adapt their products for world markets. Take the case of Mega Bloks of Montreal, which is the world's second largest maker of educational construction toys. Exports make up about 90 percent of its sales, and it markets its building blocks to children in over 100 countries. Named Exporter of the Year in 2003, Marc Bertrand, president and CEO says, "To succeed internationally, you need a core product with universal appeal, an affordable price range, innovative retail partnerships, dynamic and dedicated local sales teams, and a step-by-step approach to international expansion."[45]

In general, companies would like to standardize their offerings. Standardization helps a company develop a consistent worldwide image. It also lowers manufacturing costs and eliminates duplication of research and development, advertising, and product design efforts. **Straight product extension** is marketing a product in a foreign market without any change. Top management tells its marketing people: "Take the product as is and find customers for it." The first step, however, should be to find out whether foreign consumers use that product and what form they prefer.

Straight extension has been successful in some cases and disastrous in others. Coca-Cola, Kellogg cereals, Heineken beer, and Black & Decker tools are all sold successfully in

Straight product extension
Marketing a product in a foreign market without any change.

about the same form around the world. But General Foods introduced its standard pow-dered Jell-O in the British market only to find that British consumers prefer a solid-wafer or cake form. Straight extension is tempting because it involves no additional product development costs, manufacturing changes, or new promotion. But it can be costly in the long run if products fail to satisfy foreign consumers and fail to acknowl-edge that consumers around the world differ in their cultures, attitudes, and buying behaviours. And markets vary in their economic conditions, competition, legal require-ments, and physical environments.

Product adaptation involves changing the product to meet local conditions or wants. For example, Procter & Gamble's Vidal Sassoon shampoos contain a single fra-grance worldwide, but the amount of scent varies by country—less in Japan, where sub-tle scents are preferred, and more in Europe. Gerber serves the Japanese baby food fare that might turn the stomachs of many Western consumers: Local favourites include flounder and spinach stew, cod roe spaghetti, mugwort casserole, and sardines ground up in white radish sauce. Finnish cellular phone superstar Nokia customized its 6100 series phone for every major market. Developers built in rudimentary voice recognition for Asia, where keyboards are a problem, and raised the ring volume so that the phone could be heard on crowded Asian streets.[46] And even something as simple as an electri-cal outlet can create big product problems:

> Those who have traveled across Europe know the frustration of electrical plugs, different voltages, and other annoyances of international travel. . . . Philips, the electrical appliance manufacturer, has to produce 12 kinds of irons to serve just its European market. The problem is that Europe does not have a universal [electri-cal] standard. The ends of irons bristle with different plugs for different countries. Some have three prongs, others two; prongs protrude straight or angled, round or rectangular, fat, thin, and sometimes sheathed. There are circular plug faces, squares, pentagons, and hexagons. Some are perforated and some are notched. One French plug has a niche like a keyhole. Looking for a fix? One online travel service sells an elaborate 10-piece adapter plug set for international travelers for $65.00.[47]

Packaging also presents new challenges for international marketers. Packaging issues can be subtle. For example, names, labels, and colours may not translate easily from one country to another. A firm using yellow flowers in its logo might fare well in Canada but meet with disaster in Mexico, where a yellow flower symbolizes death or dis-respect. Similarly, although Nature's Gift might be an appealing name for gourmet mushrooms in North America, it would be deadly in Germany, where *gift* means poison. Packaging may also have to be tailored to meet the physical characteristics of consumers in various parts of the world. For instance, soft drinks are sold in smaller cans in Japan to fit the smaller Japanese hand better. Thus, although product and package standard-ization can produce benefits, companies must usually adapt their offerings to the unique needs of specific international markets.

In some instances, products must also be adapted to local superstitions or spiritual beliefs. In Asia, the supernatural world often relates directly to sales. Hyatt Hotels' expe-rience with feng shui is a good example:[48]

> A practice widely followed in China, Hong Kong, and Singapore (and which has spread to Japan, Vietnam, and Korea), feng shui means "wind and water." Practitioners of feng shui, or geomancers, will recommend the most favorable conditions for any venture, particularly the placement of office buildings and the arrangement of desks, doors, and other items within. To have good feng shui, a building should face the water and be flanked by mountains. However, it should not block the view of the mountain spirits. The Hyatt Hotel in Singapore was designed without feng shui in mind and, as a result, had to be redesigned to boost business. Originally the front desk was parallel to the doors and road, and this was

Product adaptation Adapting a product to meet local conditions or wants in foreign markets.

thought to lead to wealth flowing out. Furthermore, the doors were facing northwest, which easily let undesirable spirits in. The geomancer recommended design alterations so that wealth could be retained and undesirable spirits kept out.

Product invention Creating new products for foreign markets.

The **product invention** strategy, creating something new for the foreign market, can take two forms. It may mean reintroducing earlier product forms that happen to be well adapted to the needs of a given country. For example, the National Cash Register Company reintroduced its crank-operated cash register at half the price of a modern cash register and sold large numbers in Asia, Latin America, and Spain. Or a company can create a new product to meet a need in another country. For example, an enormous need exists for low-cost, high-protein foods in less developed countries. Companies such as Maple Leaf Foods, McCain, Quaker Oats, Swift, and Monsanto are researching the nutrition needs of these countries, creating new foods, and developing advertising campaigns to gain product trial and acceptance. Product invention can be costly, but the payoffs are worthwhile.

Service marketers also face special challenges when going global. Some service industries have a long history of international operations. For example, the commercial banking industry was one of the first to grow internationally. Banks had to provide global services in order to meet the foreign exchange and credit needs of their home country clients wanting to sell overseas. In recent years, many banks have become truly global. Germany's Deutsche Bank, for example, serves customers in 75 countries. For its clients around the world who wish to grow globally, Deutsche Bank can raise money not only in Frankfurt but also in Zurich, London, Paris, and Tokyo.[49]

Professional and business services industries such as accounting, management consulting, and advertising have only recently globalized. The international growth of these firms followed the globalization of the client companies they serve. For example, as their clients began to employ worldwide marketing and advertising strategies, advertising agencies responded by globalizing their own operations. Cossette Communications, the largest advertising agency in Canada, is among the top 15 agencies in North America and the top 30 in the world. It serves major clients as diverse as McDonald's, General Motors Canada, Coca-Cola, Bell, and BMO Financial Group. Cossette's main offices are in Montreal, Toronto, and New York, and the company employs approximately 1400 people.[50]

Retailers are among the latest service businesses to go global. As their home markets become saturated, retailers such as Wal-Mart, Toys "R" Us, Office Depot, and Disney are expanding into faster-growing markets abroad. For example, Wal-Mart's international division's sales reached $47.5 billion in fiscal year ending 2004, a 16.6 percent increase over the previous year, and operating profits rose to $2.3 billion, an increase of 18.6 percent.

Service companies wanting to operate in other countries are not always welcomed with open arms. Whereas manufacturers usually face straightforward tariff, quota, or currency restrictions when attempting to sell their products in another country, service providers are likely to face more subtle barriers. In some cases, rules and regulations affecting international service firms reflect the host country's traditions. In others, they appear to protect the country's own fledgling service industries from large global competitors with greater

Retailers are among the latest service businesses to go global. Here Asian shoppers buy North American products in a Dutch-owned Makro store in Kuala Lumpur.

resources. In still other cases, however, the restrictions seem to have little purpose other than to make entry difficult for foreign service firms.

Despite such difficulties, the trend toward growth of global service companies will continue, especially in banking, airlines, telecommunications, and professional services. Today, service firms are no longer simply following their manufacturing customers. Instead, they are taking the lead in international expansion.

LOOKING BACK

A product is more than a simple set of tangible features. In fact, many marketing offers consist of combinations of both tangible goods and services, ranging from *pure tangible goods* at one extreme to *pure services* at the other. Each good or service offered to customers can be viewed on three levels. The *core product* consists of the core problem-solving benefits that consumers seek when they buy a product. The *actual product* exists around the core and includes the quality level, features, design, brand name, and packaging. The *augmented product* is the actual product plus the various services and benefits offered with it, such as warranty, free delivery, installation, and maintenance.

REVIEWING THE CONCEPTS

1. Define *product* and the major classifications of goods and services.

Broadly defined, a *product* is anything that can be offered to a market for attention, acquisition, use, or consumption that might satisfy a want or need. Products include physical objects but also services, events, persons, places, organizations, ideas, or mixes of these entities. *Services* are products that consist of activities, benefits, or satisfactions offered for sale that are essentially intangible, such as banking, hotel, tax preparation, and home repair services.

Goods and services fall into two broad classes based on the types of consumers that use them. *Consumer products*—those bought by individuals for their personal use—are usually classified according to consumer shopping habits (convenience products, shopping products, specialty products, and unsought products). *Industrial products*—purchased for further processing or for use in conducting a business—include materials and parts, capital items, and supplies and services. Other marketable entities—such as organizations, persons, places, and ideas—can also be thought of as products.

2. Describe the decisions companies make regarding their individual goods and services, product lines, and product mixes.

Individual product decisions involve product attributes, branding, packaging, labelling, and product support services. *Product attribute* decisions involve product quality, features, and style and design. *Branding* decisions include selecting a brand name and developing a brand strategy. *Packaging* provides many key benefits, such as protection, economy, convenience, and promotion. Package decisions often include designing *labels*, which identify, describe, and possibly promote the product. Companies also develop *product support services* that enhance customer service and satisfaction and safeguard against competitors.

Most companies produce a product line rather than a single product. A *product line* is a group of products that are related in function, customer-purchase needs, or distribution channels. *Line stretching* involves extending a line downward, upward, or in both directions to occupy a gap that might otherwise be filled by a competitor. In contrast, *line filling* involves adding items within the present range of the line. The set of product lines and items offered to customers by a particular seller make up the *product mix*. The mix can be described by four dimensions: width, length, depth, and consistency. These dimensions are the tools for developing the company's product strategy.

3. Discuss branding strategy—the decisions companies make in building and managing their brands.

Some analysts see brands as *the* major enduring asset of a company. Brands are more than just names and symbols—they embody everything that the product *means* to consumers. *Brand equity* is the positive differential effect that knowing the brand name has on customer response to the product. A brand with strong brand equity is a very valuable asset.

In building brands, companies need to make decisions about brand positioning, brand name selection, brand sponsorship, and brand development. The most powerful *brand positioning* builds around strong consumer beliefs and values. *Brand name selection* involves finding the best brand name based on a careful review of product benefits, the target market, and proposed marketing strategies. A manufacturer has four *brand sponsorship* options: It can launch a *manufacturer's brand* (or national brand), sell to resellers who use a *private brand*, market *licensed brands*, or join forces with another company to *co-brand* a product. A company also has four choices when it comes to developing brands. It can introduce *line extensions, brand extensions, multibrands,* or *new brands* (new brand names in new product categories).

Companies must build and manage their brands carefully. The brand's positioning must be continuously communicated to consumers. Advertising can help, but brands are not maintained by advertising but by the *brand experience*. Customers come to know a brand through a wide range of contacts and interactions. The company must put as much care into managing these touch points as it does into producing its ads. Thus, managing a company's brand assets can no longer be left only to brand managers. Some companies are now setting up brand asset management teams to manage their major brands. Finally, companies must periodically audit their brands' strengths and weaknesses. In some cases, brands may need to be repositioned because of changing customer preferences or new competitors. Other cases may call for completely *rebranding* a good, service, or company.

4. Identify the four characteristics that affect the marketing of a service.

Services are characterized by four key characteristics; they are *intangible, inseparable, variable,* and *perishable.* Each characteristic poses problems and marketing requirements. Marketers work to find ways to make the service more tangible, to increase the productivity of providers who are inseparable from their products, to standardize quality in the face of variability, and to improve demand movements and supply capacities in the face of service perishability.

Good service companies focus attention on *both* customers and employees. They understand the *service-profit chain*, which links service firm profits with employee and customer satisfaction. Services marketing strategy calls not only for external marketing but also for *internal marketing* to motivate employees and *interactive marketing* to create service delivery skills among service providers. To succeed, service marketers must create *competitive differentiation*, offer high *service quality*, and find ways to increase *service productivity.*

5. Discuss social responsibility and international issues related to products.

Marketers must consider two additional product issues. The first is *social responsibility*. These include public policy issues and regulations involving acquiring or dropping products, patent protection, product quality and safety, and product warranties. The second involves the special challenges facing international product marketers. International marketers must decide how much to standardize or adapt their offerings for world markets.

KEY TERMS

brand *303*
brand equity *311*
brand extension *317*
co-branding *315*
consumer product *297*
convenience product *297*
industrial product *298*
interactive marketing *324*
internal marketing *322*
line extension *316*

packaging *304*
private (or store) brand *313*
product *294*
product adaptation *327*
product invention *328*
product line *307*
product mix (or product assortment) *309*
product quality *301*
service *294*

service inseparability *321*
service intangibility *320*
service perishability *321*
service-profit chain *322*
service variability *321*
shopping product *297*
social marketing *301*
specialty product *298*
straight product extension *326*
unsought product *298*

STUDY GUIDE

After completing this self-test, check your answers against the Answer Key at the back of the book.

MULTIPLE CHOICE

1. While Home Depot sells gallons of different brands of wall paint to do-it-yourselfers, Home Depot also provides the _____ by offering how-to guides, workshops, professional decorating advice, and a no-hassle return policy.
   a. Augmented product
   b. Extended product
   c. Perceived product
   d. Core product
   e. In-filled product

2. A Sherlock-Manning piano can deliver the same customer satisfaction as a Steinway because
   a. A Sherlock-Manning piano has the same quality as a Steinway for less money
   b. It has the same level of quality and the same price
   c. Each piano's brand is appropriately priced and positioned for its level of quality
   d. Steinway does not position its brand on a "highest quality" platform
   e. Sherlock-Manning pianos are poor quality and buyers don't expect much

3. President's Choice "Memories of" sauces include such versions as Szechwan, Kobe, and Loire. Each time President's Choice adds a new sauce, the Memories sub-brand has further filled its
   a. Brand offering
   b. Price points
   c. Product life cycle
   d. Business portfolio
   e. Product line

4. How does the packaging of ready-to-eat puddings reinforce the product's core benefit?
   a. Reinforces rationale for higher price point
   b. Reinforces convenience
   c. Reinforces high quality
   d. Reinforces less nutrition
   e. Reinforces serving suggestion

5. General Motors' goal is to market a car for every person. In order to achieve this, General Motors must maintain
   a. Interchangeable brands
   b. Low price points
   c. A wide product mix
   d. Extensive dealer networks
   e. Tight product lines

6. Although the Toyota Prius uses hybrid technology and saves on fuel, the brand's strength lies partly in conferring the status of fashionable environmentalist on its owner, again proving that positioning on _____ is stronger than positioning on product attributes or benefits.
   a. Beliefs and values
   b. Celebrity endorsements
   c. Perceived benefit
   d. Augmentation
   e. Customer value

7. P&G's Crest brand, known for toothpastes, recently launched a new product called Crest Whitestrips for whitening teeth. Launching this new product in a new product category under the Crest brand is illustrative of
   a. Line stretching
   b. Multibranding
   c. Brand extension
   d. Co-branding
   e. Brand association

8. One of the key drivers behind Wal-Mart's highly successful service brand is the customer orientation of its employees, the result of
   a. Strong union relations
   b. Services marketing
   c. Collective brand building
   d. Reward/punishment systems
   e. Internal marketing

9. A manufacturer of baby formula attempted to market concentrated formula to emerging third world countries. The attempt was a failure because mothers were using unsafe drinking water to make up the formula. This manufacturer failed to consider the need for
   a. Better instructions
   b. Product adaptation
   c. Clearer packaging
   d. Lower global standards
   e. Product invention

10. The importance of inseparability and provider–customer interaction in services marketing is best illustrated by what service industry?
    a. Dry cleaners
    b. Cinemas
    c. Hotels
    d. Driveway scalers
    e. Car washes

TRUE/FALSE

T F 1. A physical product or a service can be marketed as an experience.

T F 2. Unsought products are those that are so common that they are readily accessible.

T F 3. Higher quality is a product element that can always be successfully used to create more expensive products in the same brand.

T F 4. Line stretching and line filling do not mean the same thing.

T F 5. National Grocers' well-known generic product line in their instantly recognized yellow packaging enjoys a significant amount of brand equity.

CONCEPT CHECK

1. The text defines a _____ as anything that can be offered to a market for attention, acquisition, use, or consumption and that might satisfy a want or need.

2. _____ are a form of product that consist of activities, benefits, or satisfactions offered for sale that are essentially intangible and do not result in the ownership of anything.

3. Product planners need to think about goods and services on three levels: the _____, the _____ product, and the _____ product.

4. Three groups of industrial goods and services include _____, _____, and _____.

5. A(n) _____ is a name, term, sign, symbol, or design, or a combination of these, that identifies the maker or seller of a good or service.

6. Desirable qualities for a brand name include: (a) It should suggest something about the product's _____; (b) It should be easy to _____, _____, and _____; (c) The brand name should be _____; (d) It should be _____; and (e) It should translate easily into foreign languages.

7. _____ occur when a company introduces additional items in a given category under the same brand name, such as new flavours, forms, colours, ingredients, or package sizes.

8. Product mix _____ refers to the number of different product lines the company carries.

9. A company must consider four special service characteristics when designing marketing programs: _____, _____, _____, and _____.

10. A company's service-profit chain consists of five links: Internal service quality; _____; _____; _____; and healthy service profits and growth.

STUDENT MATERIALS

Visit our website at www.pearsoned.ca/armstrong for online quizzes, Internet exercises, and more!

NOTES

_____

_____

_____

_____

_____

_____

_____

DISCUSSING THE ISSUES

1. Brand equity is the positive differential effect that knowing the brand name has on customer response to the product. Name three firms that you feel have high brand equity. How does having high brand equity help them compete against rival companies?

2. Visit a grocery store and look at the packages for competing products in two or three different product categories. Which packages are the best? Why? What functions do the packages perform?

3. Visit the Kraft Foods company website (www.kraftCanada.com) and examine its list of different brands. Evaluate the company's product mix on the dimensions of width, length, depth, and consistency.

4. Consider how Cheerios cereal has been positioned in terms of product attributes, desired benefits, and strong beliefs and values.

5. What issues should a manufacturer of canned green beans consider when deciding between selling the product as a manufacturer's brand, store brand, licensed brand, or co-branded product?

6. Discuss how the products offered by a dry cleaning company are different from the products offered by an auto parts store in terms of intangibility, inseparability, variability, and perishability.

MARKETING APPLICATIONS

Which company has the world's strongest brand? To find the answer, what questions would you ask? Is brand strength determined by sales volume, a global presence, innovation, reputation, amount of advertising, success on the Internet, positive public relations, stock value, or all of these things? Marketing managers know that strong brand equity is the key to entering new markets and successfully penetrating old ones. Brand image also shapes corporate strategy, advertising campaigns, and overall marketing effort. Alliances are encouraged or dropped based on brand reputation and confidence. Strong brands can command premium prices. Hence, the brand is a company's most important asset and profit producer. In contrast, loss of confidence in a brand, such as the recent Ford and Firestone public relations nightmare, can affect not only the companies involved but also all of the distributors, service providers, and secondary publics that are affiliated with the industry. However, when a strong brand faces difficulty, its reputation can help earn it a second chance. So, what is the world's strongest brand? According to recent studies, the vote goes to Coca-Cola, followed by Microsoft, IBM, GE, and Nokia. Were these your picks? Do you buy products from these companies? Many people around the world do.

THINKING LIKE A MARKETING MANAGER

1. What makes a strong brand? How would you go about measuring brand equity?

2. What makes Coca-Cola the number one brand in the world? What characteristics do the company and its brand possess that competitors do not?

3. With all of its legal difficulties, how can Microsoft be considered the second strongest global brand? Does its status help it overcome public relations and legal problems? Explain.

4. Examine the websites for the brands listed above: www.cocacola.com, www.microsoft.com, www.ibm.com, www.ge.com, and www.nokia.com. Based on your answers to question 1 above, construct a grid that evaluates each of these brands. How does your evaluation match the order suggested above?

5. Go to the Internet and examine another brand that you perceive to be superior. Discuss the characteristics of the brand you value. How could its brand equity be improved?

6. Assuming that you were the marketing manager for a new dot.com start-up, develop a branding strategy that would match the characteristics of "great" global brands to your enterprise. Discuss your proposal with the class.

VIDEO CASE

Go to Pearson Canada's Video Central site (www.pearsoned.ca/highered/videocentral) to view the video and accompanying case for this chapter.

CASE 8   KRAVE'S CANDY COMPANY

Winnipeg-based Krave's Candy Company produces Clodhoppers, a small candy made of cashews and graham wafers in white or milk chocolate.

Started in 1995 by entrepreneurs Chris Emery and Larry Finnson, the company has already undergone a complete brand image makeover, packaging redesign, and a major international expansion in its short history. All these changes are aimed at increasing the company's sales and capturing more of the total market for boxed chocolates.

The confectionery industry is highly concentrated in Canada—the leading eight companies compose 87 percent of the value of total shipments. Further, 60 percent of industry shipments are done by foreign-controlled organizations such as Hershey Foods and Nestlé. The majority of chocolate operations in Canada are dedicated to three product categories: (1) boxed chocolates, (2) chocolate bars, and (3) seasonal novelties.

Boxed chocolates and novelty items are purchased primarily as gifts for birthdays, anniversaries, religious holidays, Valentine's Day, and Mother's Day. The chocolate bar market is highly fragmented: a 4 percent to 5 percent share of the market places a product in the top 10 brands. Firms in the chocolate industry compete on the basis of brand name, advertising, sales promotion, quality, and cost, depending on the market segment. The baby boomer segment, for example, is very quality oriented.

The Confectionery Manufacturers Association of Canada (www.confectioncanada.com) estimates that its members spend $55 million annually on advertising and sales promotion. From a consumption perspective, the CMAC estimates that the average Canadian consumes 10.3 kg of chocolate annually, with per capita annual spending on the category of $68. The total chocolate market is valued at approximately $1.4 billion per year and the boxed chocolate segment at between $160 million and $200 million.

Despite market complexities and large multinational competitors, Krave's Candies has had considerable success. Sales are already in the millions, and the company was named one of Canada's top 10 food companies by *Food in Canada* magazine. The key to maintaining that success will be effectively managing both the brand's identity and the company's growth through product line extensions and increased geographic distribution.

The original Clodhopper brand identity was built around the fictitious Krave family, which even has its own coat of arms. The first page of the original Krave's website claimed, "From their secluded castle high in the European Alps, secret recipes have been handed down from generation to generation." The family was used to help establish an image of quality for the Clodhopper product, which, according to the Krave's family tradition, was made "using only the finest ingredients from around the world." In reality, the Clodhopper product does have some family tradition behind it, since it originated with the grandmother of one of the founding partners.

Emery and Finnson learned the importance of packaging in establishing a brand identity early in the company's history. The original 300-g plastic jar that they used created shelving problems for retailers. Based on the packaging, retailers tended to place the product in the snack aisles, near the popcorn products. Since Clodhoppers were $6 a jar, the price was inconsistent with the lower-priced snacks. The plastic jar also made the product look cheap, and because the product settles over time, a four-centimetre gap appeared at the top of the jar, making it look half empty to consumers.

Emery and Finnson repackaged the product so that it fit into the upscale boxed chocolate product category, which includes the major players in the category, Black Magic and Pot of Gold. The quality image of the candy was reinforced by using a black package with gold and red trim that included an image of the Alps (to tie in with the Krave family) in the background. Consistent with the high-quality image, a gold foil bag was used on the inside of the package, which also helped establish the product as being appropriate as a gift. But even though the new packaging helped product placement—retailers began to place it in the boxed chocolate section of stores—it did not do a good job of differentiating the product from its competitors.

Searching for a more distinctive identity, Emery and Finnson revised the entire positioning of the brand. The fictitious Krave family was replaced by the entrepreneurs themselves as the trade characters for the product. The brand was renamed Chris and Larry's Clodhoppers, and both the retro-style packaging and the website feature cartoon characters of Chris and Larry.

A large part of Krave's success has been its ability to sell the brand to important retailers in Canada. Clodhoppers are available in Wal-Mart, Shoppers Drug Mart, Zellers, Loblaws, and regional chains such as Sobeys, Safeway, and Save-On-Foods. However, one of the most important distribution arrangements for the future growth of Krave's is in the U.S. market. During a trade show in Toronto in 2000, Emery and Finnson met Wal-Mart U.S.A. president and CEO Lee Scott and secured a deal that expanded their distribution into Wal-Mart stores in the United States. Chris and Larry are trying to achieve a large volume in the United States through aggressive pricing. The 212-g box sells at U.S. Wal-Marts for US$1.97, compared with its Canadian retail price of $5.87 for a 300-g box.

December is the most important time of the year for Krave's, with 85 percent of its sales occurring at this time. To reinforce the brand during the holidays, the company runs promotional sampling programs, giving away free samples to consumers in stores. In the future, Emery and Finnson would like to reduce the seasonality of the business by establishing the brand name at other times of the year. As an example of their marketing efforts, in April 2001 Dairy Queen introduced the Clodhoppers Blizzard after a successful test market.

Chris and Larry have relied on public relations more than advertising to create brand recognition and consumer positioning, partly because of their limited budget. However, recognizing the importance of consumer awareness for this product category, the company embarked on its first television campaign in May 2001.

Consistent with the company's strategy to reduce its reliance on seasonal box chocolate sales, Chris and Larry decided to launch Clodhoppers in a new line of small bags, targeted at consumers looking for a quick snack rather than a take-home product or a gift like the chocolate line. The new line was launched in 45-g and 225-g packages, as well as in three flavours. And by focusing on retailers with high-volume potential through consumers' impulse purchasing, the company has gained respectable distribution for the line.

Chris and Larry are now considering further expansion of their product line and have test formulas available on line extensions. And with trade restrictions reduced through the NAFTA process, Canadian chocolate manufacturers are finding that the U.S. market is a promising source of new business. Chris and Larry are evaluating the potential for further U.S. and international expansion.

Questions

1. In what product classification does the original Clodhoppers product fall? How would you classify the new snack line?

2. What distribution strategy is appropriate for Clodhoppers boxed chocolate line? for the bagged snack products?

3. Is the Clodhoppers brand name consistent with consumer expectations in the boxed chocolate category? What image does it project relative to the category leaders?

4. What further recommendations can you make for reducing the company's reliance on seasonal sales for its boxed chocolate product?

5. What business building programs could you recommend for (a) the current Clodhoppers product, and (b) the new line extensions in bags?

Sources: Agriculture Canada's website, www.agr.gc.ca, accessed November 21, 2002; Confectionery Manufacturers Association of Canada's website, www.confectioncanada.com, accessed November 21, 2002; Krave's website, www.clodhoppers.tv.

After studying this chapter, you should be able to

1. explain how companies find and develop new product ideas

2. list and define the steps in the new product development process

3. describe the stages of the product life cycle

4. explain how marketing strategies change during the product's life cycle

New Product Development and Product Life Cycle Strategies

9

Looking Ahead In the previous chapter, you learned about decisions that marketers make in managing brands and product mixes. In this chapter, we'll expand on the principles of product and brand management by examining how marketers develop new products for the market, and how they manage those products through the product life cycle. New products are the lifeblood of an organization. Companies must continually improve their products and develop new ones in order to keep their customers satisfied; however, new product development is risky, and many new products fail. The first part of this chapter describes the process for creating new products. The second part of the chapter illustrates the concept of the product life cycle. You'll see that every product, small or large, simple or complicated, passes through a life cycle, beginning with its introduction to the market. Each stage of the product life cycle poses challenges to the marketer and requires its own marketing strategies and tactics.

Did you know that Coca-Cola markets over 400 brands in more than 200 countries around the world? In Canada, Minute Maid is a Coca-Cola company, and recently a Minute Maid product was chosen as the best new product of 2005 by Canadian consumers. It's a good illustration of how a seemingly familiar product—orange juice—can be made new again.

t the second annual Best New Products Awards in March 2005 Canadians chose 50 new products as the best innovations in their category. The overall winner, claiming the coveted "Best of Show" prize, was Minute Maid Simply Orange.

New products aren't always new inventions, or what marketers call "new to the world" products. New products can be new to the company; for example, Unilever's Dove brand soaps have been on the market for many years, but Dove shampoo and conditioner are new products—for Unilever. A new product can be a variation on an existing product, such as Cracker Jack's new Butter Toffee flavour. A new product can be a redesign or repackaging of an old product. For example, every few years Ford redesigns its classic Mustang, and calls it the "new Mustang." The shape may change slightly, new features might be added, and the colours offered will vary with the fashion of the time, but a Mustang is still a Mustang.

When marketers are developing a new product they must consider level of quality, features, and design. Simply Orange is made from fresh oranges, not from concentrate, and has no added water, sugar, or preservatives. It is therefore positioned as a high quality orange juice compared to lower quality juices from concentrate. Another key feature of the product is added calcium. In a press release announcing the new product, Coca-Cola Ltd. said,

> Each 250-ml serving provides an equivalent amount of calcium to that found in a 250-ml serving of milk, along with a full day's supply of vitamin C. Changing demographics, consumer demand and dietary need are driving interest in calcium-rich beverage options, particularly among mature adults. Canadians (ages 50+) now make up nearly one-third of the population and are among the greatest consumers of juice. Mature Canadians may require added dietary sources of calcium, particularly as milk consumption and the body's ability to absorb calcium both decrease with age.

Minute Maid group brand manager Bobby Patton was responsible for the launch of the new product. "Focus groups and market research had revealed that consumers these days tend to think that simple, pure and honest products come from smaller companies," he said, "So all branding throughout the campaign focused on the product name as Simply Orange Juice."

Simply Orange is not only a new product, it's also a new brand. A website was created at SimplyOrangeJuice.com, and neither the Minute Maid nor the Coca-Cola brand is visible on the site. In fact, it's the oranges themselves that are the stars of the brand's personality: "Near the town of Apopka, Florida, something refreshing is happening. Oranges, left to their own devices, are ripening in the sun. When they've convinced us beyond all doubt that they're truly, sweetly ready, we pluck them from the trees and gently wash them."

What did Canadians like about Minute Maid Simply Orange? The consumer judges commented on the easy-to-use bottle design, and the fact that the carafe bottle shape set it apart from other juices. Bobby Patton would be pleased. In designing the new product he wanted the packaging to be different from anything else in stores. Most ready-to-drink orange juice comes in a carton or a white plastic jug, so he put Simply Orange in a clear plastic bottle that resembles a carafe. There's nothing like it in the orange juice section of the grocery store.

So, what does it take to be a successful new product in Canada? Based on the responses from the consumer judges, BrandSpark International, which founded and sponsors the awards, created a checklist. New product marketers, take note: A successful product must

☐ be healthy, if it's a food product
☐ be convenient, easy to use, and save time
☐ be kid-approved
☐ appeal to the senses
☐ have efficient and, for food products, transparent packaging
☐ deliver what it promises
☐ incorporate new technologies
☐ have a positive brand reputation

There's no new technology involved in making orange juice, but clearly Simply Orange has what it takes to succeed as a new product in the Canadian market.[1]

TEST YOURSELF

Answers to these questions can be found on our website at www.pearsoned.ca/armstrong.

1. Look at Simply Orange Juice's website and that of the Ethical Bean Company (www.ethicalbean.com). How do these sites help position their respective products?
   a) Both sites give the impression of a small, independent, caring company
   b) Both sites educate the consumer about the product
   c) Both sites use language that directly addresses the consumer
   d) Both sites emphasize the all-natural quality of their products
   e) All of the above

2. What was one of the main reasons for Simply Orange's choice of packaging?
   a) The carafe is refillable
   b) The carafe is inexpensive
   c) The carafe communicates "high quality"
   d) The carafe keeps the orange juice fresher longer
   e) The carafe is unbreakable

3. There are other 100% orange juice products on the market, some with added calcium. Why is Simply Orange more successful?
   a) Because Simply Orange has been branded by claiming the high-quality "pure" position
   b) Because the brand is associated with the well-known Minute Maid brand
   c) Because Simply Orange had a much bigger advertising and promotion budget
   d) Because the other brands have unmemorable packaging
   e) Because Simply Orange was launched only in the United States

4. Why was Coca-Cola careful to dissociate its brand from Simply Orange Juice?
   a) Because the Simply Orange brand is already associated with Minute Maid
   b) Because consumers associate Coca-Cola with sugary soft drinks, not with natural juices
   c) Because Coca-Cola never reveals its ownership of other brands
   d) Because Coca-Cola technically does not have the legal right to sell juice outside of the United States
   e) Because Coca-Cola wants to avoid an internal war between Minute Maid and Simply Orange

5. Why would Minute Maid create a completely separate brand when it could have less expensively leveraged the well-known Minute Maid brand?
   a) Because Coca-Cola already owns Minute Maid
   b) Because Minute Maid would have been in contravention of patents
   c) Because consumers would have presumed that Simply Orange has the same mid-range quality as Minute Maid products
   d) Because orange growers currently contracted to supply Minute Maid with juice could not legally increase their supply
   e) Because Minute Maid is already a declining brand

NEW PRODUCT DEVELOPMENT IN CANADA

Whether it's a new type of credit card from the Bank of Montreal or a new snowmobile from Bombardier, Canadians have a long history as inventors of new products. McIntosh apples, Pablum, frozen fish, and instant mashed potatoes are food products that all originated in Canada. Canadians are responsible for developing such sports and leisure activities as basketball, five-pin bowling, table hockey, and Trivial Pursuit. Many Canadian inventions spawned entire industries. Reginald Fessenden, born near Sherbrooke, Quebec, was known as the father of radio after he invented amplitude modulation (AM) radio and transmitted his first broadcast in 1900. In 1844 Nova Scotia's Charles Fenerty developed the product we now call newsprint, which is made from wood pulp. Modern air travel was made possible by another Canadian, Wallace Rupert Turnbull, who developed the variable-pitch propeller.

Dr. Cluny McPherson, of St. John's, Newfoundland, invented the gas mask used to save the lives of many Allied soldiers in World War I. A quintessentially Canadian tool, the snowblower, was invented in 1925 by Quebec resident Arthur Sicard. Olivia Poole, an Aboriginal woman from Manitoba, invented the Jolly Jumper, the internationally popular baby seat, in the 1950s, and Steve Pacjack of Vancouver invented the beer case with a tuck-in handle that helps you lug your beer home. Three Canadian Olympic sailors—Bruce Kirby, Hans Fogh, and Ian Bruce—designed the world-class Laser sailboat in 1970. Wendy Murphy, a medical research technician in Toronto, developed the Weevac 6—so named because it can carry six wee babies. Her idea was born when she realized, during the devastation of the 1985 Mexico City earthquake, that no apparatus existed to evacuate young children. Dr. Dennis Colonello designed the Abdomenizer in 1986 while practising as a chiropractor in northern Ontario. Before you laugh, note that he has rung up more than $100 million in sales. Dr. Frank Gunston, of Brandon, Manitoba, may have been one of the most philanthropic inventors. After developing and building a total knee-joint replacement, he decided not to patent his invention. This made it freely available to manufacturers and allowed patients needing the joint to benefit quickly from the technology and walk without pain. He received the prestigious Manning Principal Award in 1989 for his efforts.[2]

Canadians are leaders in technology and e-commerce as well. Most Canadians are aware that the modern communications industry was born with the invention of the telephone by Alexander Graham Bell. That tradition has continued in companies like Nortel, with its Internet networking products for businesses; Research In Motion (RIM), BlackBerry and Open Text Corporation which, long before Google, had the Internet's first full-text search engine, The Open Text Index. Toronto's IMAX revolutionized the art and science of 3D image recording and projection. Air Canada was the first major airline to operate an e-commerce website that allowed consumers to purchase airline tickets online, and Canada's banks were the first in the world to offer online banking.

In order to survive and be successful a company has to be good at developing and managing new products. Every product, from the safety pin to the coffee maker to the Porsche Carrera, goes through a life cycle: It is born, it grows, it matures, and eventually it dies, as newer products come along that better serve consumer needs. This product life cycle presents two major challenges. First, because all products eventually decline, marketers must continually develop new products to replace aging ones (the problem of *new product development*). Second, marketers must be good at adapting their marketing

The newest products in the BlackBerry product line from Canada's Research In Motion make up the 8100 series, which combines wireless phone, email, and data services.

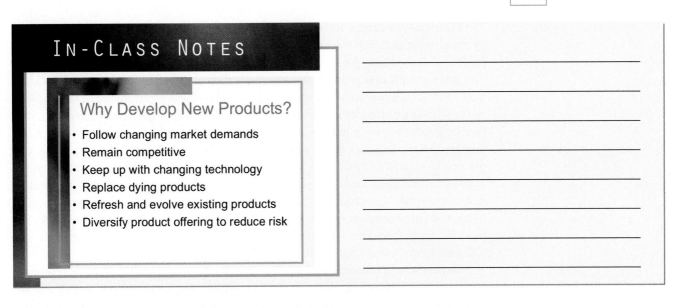

strategies in the face of changing tastes, technologies, and competition, as products pass through these life cycle stages (the problem of *product life cycle strategies*). We first look at the problem of finding and developing new products and then at the problem of managing them successfully over their life cycles.

NEW PRODUCT DEVELOPMENT STRATEGY

Given the rapid changes in consumer tastes, technology, and competition, companies must develop a steady stream of new products and services. A firm can obtain new products in two ways. One is through *acquisition*—by buying a whole company, a patent, or a licence to produce someone else's product. The other is through **new product development**, or the development of original products, new brands, and product improvements and modifications, through the firm's own research and development (R&D) efforts. In this chapter, we concentrate on new product development.

A new product isn't necessarily a new invention or what marketers call a "new to the world" product. It can be an improvement or modification to an existing product. See what Maple Leaf foods has done:

> Maple Leaf won praise as the developer of one of the 2004 Best New Products with its Prime Naturally chicken. The product was acclaimed because of its lean, clean, and additive-free branding. Since the product tapped into Canadians' health and nutrition concerns, it became a surefire hit. Moreover, its clear packaging allows the consumers to see the quality of the chicken. As one consumer noted, "I trust the name 'Maple Leaf' and I like knowing that my foods aren't fed a bunch of chemicals."[3]

Innovation can be very risky, especially in highly competitive markets. Texas Instruments lost a staggering $920 million before withdrawing from the home computer business, and IBM, once synonymous with home computing, announced in 2004 the withdrawal of its ubiquitous PC from the market. The telex machine, the electric typewriter, the Polaroid camera, the Sony Betamax, the VCR, and the fax machine are just a few products that have disappeared, or are on the verge of disappearing, from the market. Other products that failed shortly after being launched: Cracker Jack cereal, Fruit of the Loom laundry detergent, buttermilk and yogurt shampoos of the 1970s, Polarvision instant movies, Clorox detergent—and, more recently, Pepsi Blue and a whole host of unpopular new menu items from McDonald's. (Do you remember when McDonald's made pizza in the 1990s?).

New product development The development of original products, new brands, and product improvements and modifications, through the firm's own research and development (R&D) efforts.

Coca-Cola chairman Roberto Goizueta, when asked whether he was embarrassed by the number of failed new products his company had launched since the very successful Diet Coke, replied, "No, you only stumble when you're moving."

Every month new products arrive on the shelves of your local grocery store, drug store, hardware store, and department store, and just as quickly, many of them disappear. Why do so many new products fail?[4] There are many reasons. Although an idea may be good, the target market may have been inappropriately defined or evaluated. Perhaps the product was not designed as well as it should have been, or maybe it was priced too high for its level of quality. It may have been incorrectly positioned in the market, or not given sufficient advertising support. Sometimes marketers or product developers create new products simply because they can, or because they themselves like them, and fail to conduct market research to determine whether a market exists for the product. Sometimes the costs of product development are higher than expected, and sometimes competitors fight back harder than expected.

Because so many new products fail, and because new products are normally years in development, which is time consuming and expensive, companies are anxious to learn how to improve their chances of success. One way is to study successful new products and try to figure out what they have in common. Another is to study new product failures to see what lessons can be learned. Cake Beauty uses research to identify the specific features and benefits that the target market segment values. This research will be used to inform future decisions on product development, branding, pricing, distribution, and promotion. Various studies suggest that new product success depends on developing a *unique superior product,* one with higher quality, new features, and higher value in use. Another key success factor is a *well-defined product concept* before development, in which the company carefully defines and assesses the target market, the product requirements, and the benefits before proceeding. Other success factors have also been suggested: senior management commitment, relentless innovation, and a smoothly functioning new product development process. In all, to create successful new products, a company must understand its consumers, markets, and competitors and develop products that deliver superior value to customers.

So companies face a problem. They must continually develop new products, but the odds weigh heavily against the success of any new product launch. The solution lies in strong new product planning and in setting up a systematic *new product development process* for finding and growing new products.

The major stages in the new product development process are

1. Idea generation
2. Idea screening

IN-CLASS NOTES

Some Succeed, but Most Fail

- **Successful new products**
  - Offer a unique superior product
  - Have a well-defined product concept
- **Failed new products**
  - Market size may have been overestimated
  - Poor quality or design
  - Incorrect positioning, pricing, or promotion
  - Do not deliver superior value

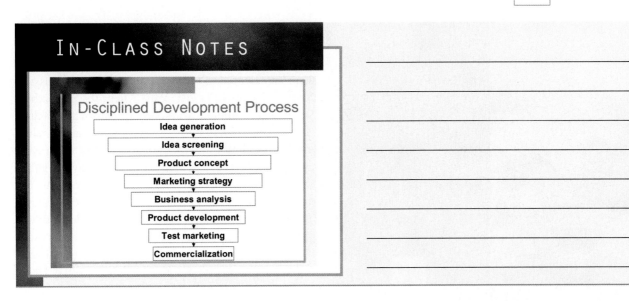

IN-CLASS NOTES

Disciplined Development Process

- Idea generation
- Idea screening
- Product concept
- Marketing strategy
- Business analysis
- Product development
- Test marketing
- Commercialization

3. Concept development and testing

4. Marketing strategy development

5. Business analysis

6. Product development and testing

7. Test marketing

8. Commercialization

Let's look at each of these stages in more detail.

Stage 1: Idea Generation

New product development starts with **idea generation**—the systematic search for new product ideas. A company typically has to generate many ideas in order to find a few good ones. According to one well-known management consultant, "For every 1,000 ideas, only 100 will have enough commercial promise to merit a small-scale experiment, only ten of those will warrant substantial financial commitment, and of those, only a couple will turn out to be unqualified successes."[5] His conclusion? "If you want to find a few ideas with the power to enthrall customers, foil competitors, and thrill investors, you must first generate hundreds and potentially thousands of unconventional strategic ideas."

Major sources of new product ideas include internal sources, customers, competitors, distributors and suppliers, and others. Using internal sources, the company can find new ideas through formal research and development. It can pick the brains of its executives, scientists, engineers, manufacturing, and salespeople. Some companies have developed successful "intrapreneurial" programs that encourage employees to think up and develop new product ideas. For example, 3M has a "15 percent rule" that allows employees to spend 15 percent of their time "bootlegging"—working on projects of personal interest whether those projects directly benefit the company or not. The spectacularly successful Post-it notes evolved out of this program. Similarly, Texas Instruments' IDEA program provides funds for employees who pursue their own ideas. Among the successful new products to come out of the IDEA program was TI's Speak 'n' Spell, the first children's toy to contain a microchip. Many other speaking toys followed, ultimately generating several hundred million dollars for TI.[6]

Good new product ideas also come from watching and listening to *customers*. The company can analyze questions and complaints to find new products that better solve customer problems, whether those customers are other businesses or individual consumers.

Idea generation The systematic search for new product ideas.

Avon capitalized on new uses discovered by users of its Skin-So-Soft bath oil and moisturizer by developing a complete line of Skin-So-Soft Bug Guard products.

Company engineers or salespeople can meet with and work alongside customers to get suggestions and ideas. The company can conduct surveys or focus groups with ordinary people to learn about consumer needs and wants. Heinz did just that when its researchers approached children, who consume more than half of the ketchup sold, to find out what would make ketchup more appealing to them. "When we asked them what would make the product more fun," says a Heinz spokesperson, "changing the color was among the top responses." So Heinz developed and launched EZ Squirt, green ketchup that comes in a soft, squeezable bottle targeted at kids. The bottle's special nozzle also emits a thin ketchup stream, "so tykes can autograph their burgers (or squirt someone across the table, though Heinz neglects to mention that)."[7]

Finally, customers often create new products and uses on their own, and companies can benefit by finding these products and putting them on the market. Customers can also be a good source of ideas for new product uses that can expand the market for and extend the life of current products. For example, Avon capitalized on new uses discovered by individual consumers who used its Skin-So-Soft bath oil and moisturizer. For years, these consumers had been spreading the word that Skin-So-Soft bath oil is also a terrific bug repellent. Whereas some people were content simply to bathe in water scented with the fragrant oil, others carried it in their backpacks to mosquito-infested campsites or kept a bottle on the deck of their cottages. Now, Avon offers a complete line of Skin-So-Soft Bug Guard products, including Bug Guard Mosquito Repellent Moisturizing Towelettes and Bug Guard Plus, a combination moisturizer, insect repellent, and sunscreen.[8]

Competitors are another good source of new product ideas. Companies watch competitors' ads and other communications to get clues about their new products. They buy competing new products, take them apart to see how they work, analyze their sales, and decide whether they should bring out a new product of their own. Finally, *distributors and suppliers* contribute many good new product ideas. Resellers are close to the market and can pass along information about consumer problems and new product possibilities. Suppliers can tell the company about new concepts, techniques, and materials that can be used to develop new products. Other idea sources include trade magazines, trade shows, and seminars; government agencies; new product consultants; advertising agencies; marketing research firms; university and commercial laboratories; and inventors.

The search for new product ideas should be systematic rather than haphazard. Otherwise, few new ideas will surface and many good ideas will sputter and die. Top management can avoid these problems by installing an *idea management system* that directs the flow of new ideas to a central point where they can be collected, reviewed, and evaluated. In setting up such a system, the company can do any or all of the following:[9]

☐ Appoint a respected senior person to be the company's idea manager.

☐ Create a multidisciplinary idea management committee consisting of people from R&D, engineering, purchasing, operations, finance, and sales and marketing to meet regularly and evaluate proposed new product and service ideas.

☐ Set up a toll-free number for anyone who wants to send a new idea to the idea manager.

☐ Encourage all company stakeholders—employees, suppliers, distributors, dealers—to send their ideas to the idea manager.

☐ Set up formal recognition programs to reward those who contribute the best new ideas.

The idea manager approach yields two favourable outcomes. First, it helps create an innovation-oriented company culture. It shows that top management supports, encourages, and rewards innovation. Second, it will yield a larger number of ideas among which will be found some especially good ones. As the system matures, ideas will flow more freely. No longer will good ideas wither for the lack of a sounding board or a senior product advocate.

Stage 2: Idea Screening

While the purpose of the idea generation stage of the new product development process is to come up with as many ideas as possible, the purpose of the **idea screening** stage is to reduce that number. Screening ideas is like screening anything else—the goal is to sort through the pile, identify the good ideas, and separate them from the not-so-good ideas. Product development, as we have already seen, is costly and time consuming. Companies spend years in R&D before a new product is ready for the market, so it only makes good business sense to select the "go-ahead" ideas carefully.

Idea screening: Sorting through new product ideas to identify good ideas, and separate them from the not-so-good ideas.

Many companies require their executives to write up new product ideas on a standard form that can be reviewed by a new product committee. The write-up describes the product, the target market, and the competition. It makes some rough estimates of market size, product price, development time and costs, manufacturing costs, and rate of return. The committee then evaluates the idea against a set of general criteria. For example, at Kao Company, the large Japanese consumer-products company, the committee asks questions such as these: Is the product truly useful to consumers and society? Is it good for our particular company? Does it mesh well with the company's objectives and strategies? Do we have the people, skills, and resources to make it succeed? Does it deliver more value to customers than do competing products? Is it easy to advertise and distribute? Many companies have well-designed systems for rating and screening new product ideas.

Stage 3: Concept Development and Testing

Once the marketing managers have generated, then screened, new product ideas, the next step is to develop those ideas into a product concept. Whereas a product idea is an idea for a possible product that the company can potentially offer to the market, a **product concept** is a detailed description, drawing, or prototype of that idea that can be shown to potential customers. That product concept must be then be **developed and tested**, that is, the new product idea is developed in various alternative forms, and tested with a group of potential customers.

Product concept A detailed version of the new product idea that can be shown to potential customers.

Concept development and testing Developing the new product idea into various alternative forms and testing the concepts with a group of potential customers.

DaimlerChrysler AG has been working on the development of fuel cell vehicles for more than a decade. A fuel cell-powered vehicle runs on liquid hydrogen rather than gasoline, and produces only water as a byproduct. It is highly fuel efficient and extremely environmentally friendly. DaimlerChrysler AG introduced the first NECAR (New Electric Car) in 1994, built on the basis of a Mercedes-Benz Transporter van. Since then, DaimlerChrysler has advanced fuel cell technology and publicly presented 20 fuel cell concept vehicles.[10]

These vehicles are now in the product development and testing stage (as we'll see shortly), but before they got to that stage the concept for the vehicles was developed and tested. At the concept development and testing stage, DaimlerChrysler's task was to

Between 2003 and 2007 DaimlerChrysler is conducting on-road, real driving conditions tests with F-cell vehicles in San Francisco, Sacramento, Los Angeles, and Detroit.

develop this new product into alternative product concepts, then test each concept with a group of potential customers to find out how attractive each concept is, and be able choose the best one for each of its target markets. For example, one concept, let's call it Concept A, for the F-Cell vehicle was a moderately priced subcompact designed to be a family's second car. Concept B was the F-Cell SUV, a sport utility vehicle. Concept C was the F-Cell bus designed for use by public transportation providers.

In the early stages of concept testing, product concepts may be presented to potential customers only symbolically, through pictures or words. For example, Concept A of the F-Cell vehicle might have been described to prospective customers like this: "An efficient, fun-to-drive, fuel-cell-powered subcompact car that seats four. This high-tech wonder runs on liquid hydrogen, providing practical and reliable transportation with virtually no pollution. It goes up to 90 miles per hour and, unlike battery-powered electric cars, it never needs recharging. It's priced, fully equipped, at $20 000."

For some concept tests, a word or picture description might be sufficient. However, a more concrete and physical presentation of the concept will increase the reliability of the concept test. A prototype is a full scale model or sample of the product that may be partially functional. It allows prospective customers to examine, touch, and possibly use the product. Virtual reality is increasingly being used to test product concepts. Virtual reality is a computer-based, or Web-based, program that allows a customer to "virtually" experience a product. They can examine it in three dimensions, view the various colours and options, and hear it if necessary. Many real estate agents offer online virtual reality tours of their available properties. Most automobile websites today offer some form of virtual reality experience to consumers, allowing them to build their own car, choose its options, then save and price their choice. Ikea's website features a Kitchen Planner that allows you to design your own kitchen, save and print your design, and calculate the cost of your dream kitchen. On the L'Oréal Paris website consumers can upload a photograph of themselves, then virtually try on new hair colours.

After showing the product concept to the potential customers, and allowing them to experience it, the marketers will then ask the test consumers questions about their experience. An example of questions the marketers of the Mercedes F-Cell cars might ask are shown in Table 9.1. The answers will help the company decide which concept has the strongest appeal. For example, the last question asks about the consumer's intention to buy. Suppose 10 percent of the test consumers said they definitely would buy, and 5 percent said they probably would buy. The company could use those percentages to estimate the number of "real" consumers in the target market who would definitely or probably buy the car.

Table 9.1   **Questions for Potential Customers of the F-Cell Vehicle**
1.   Do you understand the concept of a fuel cell-powered vehicle?
2.   Do you believe the claims about the vehicle's performance?
3.   What do you believe are the major benefits of the F-Cell vehicle compared with a conventional vehicle?
4.   What are the advantages of an F-Cell vehicle compared with a battery-powered electric vehicle?
5.   What improvements in the F-Cell vehicle's features would you suggest?
6.   For what uses might you prefer an F-Cell vehicle to a conventional vehicle?
7.   What do you feel would be a reasonable price to charge for the car?
8.   Who would be involved in your decision to buy such a vehicle?
9.   Would you say you would definitely, probably, probably not, or definitely not buy this vehicle?

Stage 4: Marketing Strategy Development

After the product concept has been tested with members of the target market, and their opinions about the concept have been collected, the next step in the product development process is to design the marketing strategy. **Marketing strategy development** involves designing an initial marketing strategy for a new product based on the product concept. The strategy must answer questions about how, when, where, and to whom the product will be introduced.

Let's imagine that DaimlerChrysler has decided that the inexpensive subcompact version of the F-Cell car (Concept A) is the most likely concept to succeed in the market. Their marketing strategy must begin by describing the target market and the product's positioning. For example:

> The target market for the F-Cell subcompact is a 20- to 35-year-old man or woman, well-educated, with a moderate to high income. He or she may be single or married, and may have one small child. This person is seeking practical, reliable transportation. Most importantly, the target market for the F-Cell subcompact is someone who cares about the environment and strives, in their consumer decisions, to be environmentally responsible. The car will be positioned as more economical to operate, more fun to drive, less polluting than today's internal combustion engine or hybrid cars, and less restricting than battery-powered electric cars, which must be recharged regularly.

Marketing strategy development Designing an initial marketing strategy for a new product based on the product concept.

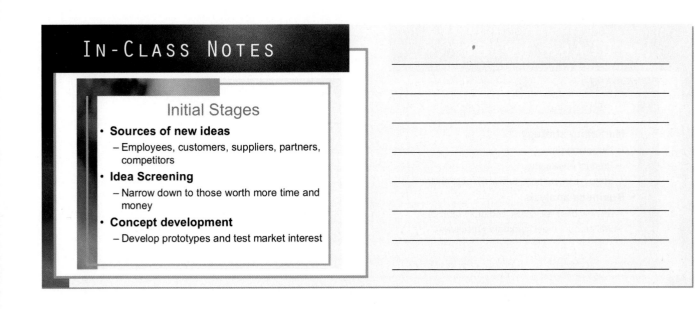

IN-CLASS NOTES

Initial Stages

- **Sources of new ideas**
  - Employees, customers, suppliers, partners, competitors
- **Idea Screening**
  - Narrow down to those worth more time and money
- **Concept development**
  - Develop prototypes and test market interest

Next, sales goals must be stated:

> Our goal is to sell 100 000 cars in the first year, at a loss of not more than $15 million. In the second year, sales will increase to 120 000 cars and generate a profit of $25 million. In the first five years sales are projected to increase by 20 percent each year.

Next, the marketing strategy must outline the product's price, distribution channels, and marketing budget:

> The F-Cell subcompact basic model will retail for $20 000. Air conditioning and other options will be offered at an additional charge. In year one we will offer our dealers special incentives to encourage them to meet quota. The advertising budget of $20 million for year one is based on 15 percent of projected year one sales. During the first year, $100 000 will be spent on marketing research to find out who is buying the car and their satisfaction levels.

Finally, the marketing strategy must describe the longer term goals and the marketing mix strategy:

> DaimlerChrysler intends to capture a 3 percent long-run share of the total auto market and realize an after-tax return on investment of 15 percent. To achieve this, product quality will start high and be improved over time. Price will be raised in the second and third years if competition permits. The total advertising budget will be raised each year by about 10 percent. Marketing research will be reduced to $60 000 per year after the first year.

Stage 5: Business Analysis

The product concept has been tested and the marketing strategy has been set. The next step is to evaluate the business attractiveness of the new product within the larger context of the company's corporate strategy, financial goals, and other products. At the **business analysis** stage, a review is conducted of the sales, cost, and profit projections for the new product to determine whether the company's objectives will be met. The new product must not only succeed in the market, but must satisfy the company's objectives.

Business analysis A review of the sales, cost, and profit projections for a new product to determine whether the company's objectives will be met.

In the business analysis stage of the new product development process, management studies the projected costs of bringing the new product to market and weighs them against the marketing team's estimates of sales and revenue. This is not to say that a product must be profitable in its first year. It is at the business analysis stage that management must decide whether to allow the product to operate in the red, and if so, for how long.

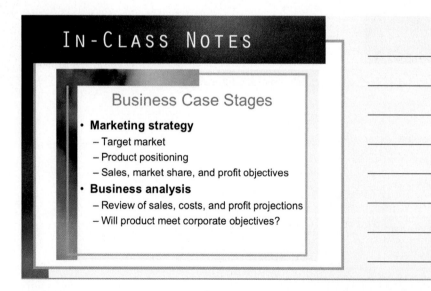

IN-CLASS NOTES

Business Case Stages

- **Marketing strategy**
  - Target market
  - Product positioning
  - Sales, market share, and profit objectives
- **Business analysis**
  - Review of sales, costs, and profit projections
  - Will product meet corporate objectives?

It is normally the marketing manager's task to estimate sales and to present those estimates to senior management. A wise marketer will present minimum and maximum sales projections, so that senior management can fully assess the range of risk. Senior managers then compare these sales forecasts to the expected costs and profits for the product, and make a decision about whether to go ahead with bringing the new product to market.

Stage 6: Product Development and Testing

Up to this stage the product has existed only as a concept, that is, a design, an image, a virtual reality construct, or perhaps a prototype. If the new product concept passes the business analysis stage, the next step is to plan the development and production of the product.

During the **product development and testing** stage of the new product development process, a real working version of the product is built and subjected to a variety of tests. (This is not to be confused with test marketing, which we'll get to next.) At this stage of the process, the product is tested for endurance, wear, breaking points, and usability.

Product development and testing Developing the product concept into a real working version of the product and subjecting it to a variety of tests.

The product development and testing stage calls for a major investment by the company. This is the stage in which financial, human, and marketing resources are devoted to the new product—and the product concept becomes a real product.

For example, DaimlerChrysler has been testing its F-cell vehicles for several years, beginning in 2000 when the company released as a test car the Jeep Commander 2, a fuel cell–powered luxury SUV. In 2003 buses powered by fuel cells were tested in 10 European cities, and the following year 100 F-Cell vehicles were delivered to drivers in Europe, the U.S., Japan, and Singapore for a two-year consumer testing period. Then, in November 2004, DaimlerChrysler research and development engineers conducted endurance tests on a number of F-Cell vehicles at a test track near Barcelona.

All new products must pass through the product development and testing phase, even—or perhaps especially—toys.

> A scuba-diving Barbie doll must swim and kick for 15 straight hours to satisfy Mattel that she will last at least one year. But because Barbie may find her feet in small owners' mouths rather than in the bathtub, Mattel has devised another, more torturous test: Barbie's feet are clamped by two steel jaws to make sure that her skin doesn't crack—and potentially choke—her young owners.[11]

Test marketing Testing the product and marketing program in real, but limited, market conditions.

> Shaw Industries, a manufacturer of carpet and hardwood flooring, hires temporary workers to pace up and down long rows of Shaw's products all day. During an average day's work these professional walkers walk 15–20 km. Shaw Industries counts the walkers' steps and figures that 20,000 steps equal several years of average carpet wear.[12]

Stage 7: Test Marketing

If the new product passes the product development and testing phase where, it is hoped, all the bugs are discovered and fixed, the product is ready to go into mass production. At this point many companies opt to conduct **test marketing**, where the product and marketing program are tested in real, but limited, market conditions, usually in a small geographic area.

Shaw Industries tests its product by paying temporary workers to walk on it.

Some marketers are now using virtual reality to test new products (see Marketing at Work 9.1). The purpose of test marketing a product is to see how the market responds to it. If the response is favourable, then the new product will be *rolled out* to the larger market—sections of the country, or the entire country. New product rollout is an expensive proposition. If it is discovered after rollout that something needs to be changed in the product itself, or its packaging, or its promotion, the marketers may have to recall the product and rethink their distribution strategy. Test marketing allows the marketers to discover and correct potential problems before they become too big to handle.

The scale of, and time required for, test marketing varies by company and by product within the company. Many products are not test marketed at all. The time it takes to test market a product may allow competitors to gain advantages. When the costs of developing and introducing the product are low, or when management is already confident about the new product, the company may do little or no test marketing. For example, a product that is a line extension, such as Dove shampoos, or a product that is similar to an existing, successful product, is not likely to be test marketed. However, when introducing a new product requires a big investment, or when management isn't sure of the product or marketing program, a company may do a lot of test marketing. For instance, Lever spent two years testing its highly successful Lever 2000 bar soap before introducing it internationally. Frito-Lay did 18 months of testing in three markets on at least five formulations before introducing its Baked Lays line of low-fat snacks.[13]

The Nokia N-Gage—a combination cell phone, game console, MP3 player, and radio—was released in late 2003. Nokia encouraged journalists to review its new product, and the company test-marketed the N-Gage extensively in London, England, before introducing it worldwide. The Nokia N-Gage console is now available in Canada, and the companion website for Canadian players is offered in both French and English. On the website players can download upgrades and accessories for their N-Gage console, register to receive news and updates via email, and play online against other players around the world. In September 2004, Nokia announced it had shipped 1 million N-Gage consoles around the world.[14]

Though the costs of test marketing can be high, they may be small when compared with the costs of making a major mistake. In the 1980s, based on the success of Teddy Grahams, teddy-bear-shaped graham crackers, Nabisco decided to develop a new product called Breakfast Bears Graham Cereal. When the product came out consumers didn't like the taste, so the product developers went back to the kitchen and modified the formula. Unfortunately, they didn't test it, and the result was a disaster. Although the cereal may have tasted better, it no longer stayed crunchy in milk and left a gooey mess of graham mush on the bottom of cereal bowls. Supermarket managers refused to restock the cereal, and Nabisco executives decided it was too late to reformulate the product again.[15] So a promising new product was killed through haste to get it to market.

Canada is becoming the ultimate test market for many U.S.-based multinationals that also have operations in Canada. And Canadians are testing not only new products but the marketing campaigns that support their launches. The strategy of such firms is to "let the Canadian subsidiary come up with something a little more innovative and daring. Then, if it

The Nokia N-Gage console was test marketed in London, England, before being rolled out to global markets.

Marketing at Work   9.1

Virtual Reality Test Marketing: The Future Is Now

Virtual reality is the wave of the future for test marketing and concept-testing research. A company called Gadd International Research has developed a tool called Simul-Shop, a software product that allows researchers to create virtual shopping experiences to test consumers' reactions to new products.

Suppose General Mills wants to test reactions to a new Cheerios package design and store shelf positioning. Using Simul-Shop, the marketers create a virtual store and "place" the product on the shelves. Then, test shoppers sit down at a computer. They click to enter the virtual store and are guided to the appropriate store section. Once there, they can scan the shelf, pick up various cereal packages, rotate them, study the labels—even look around to see what's on the shelf behind them. The virtual shopping trip includes full sound and video, along with a guide who directs users through the experience and answers their questions.

A company called Elumens has created a virtual reality amphitheatre called the VisionDome. The VisionDome is like an IMAX theatre, but with one big difference—it's interactive. "When you use a computer to generate an image . . . you have the advantage of making that image interactive," comments an Elumens executive. When conducting research on a car, he suggests, "we can go into a VisionDome, see that car in three dimensions, look at it from every angle, take it out for a test drive, and allow the customer to configure that car exactly the way he wants it." Caterpillar sees enormous potential for VisionDome. "We can put one of our tractors in a VisionDome and actually have a customer sit in it and test it under whatever conditions they would use it for," says a Caterpillar design engineer. "The ability to immerse people in the product makes it a phenomenal [research and sales] tool."

Virtual reality is relatively inexpensive compared to traditional market research—a firm can conduct a Simul-Shop study for about $25 000. Another advantage is flexibility. A virtual reality store can display an almost infinite variety of products, sizes, styles, and flavours in response to consumers' desires and needs. Research can be conducted in almost any simulated surroundings, ranging from food store interiors and new car showrooms to farm fields or the open road.

Virtual reality also makes it much easier to conduct international research. Researchers can create virtual stores in different countries and regions using the appropriate local products, shelf layouts, and currencies. Once the stores are online, a product concept can be quickly tested across locations. When the studies are completed, the results are communicated to headquarters electronically.

The analysis reveals which markets offer the greatest opportunity for a successful launch.

Virtual reality research does have its limitations, since it's only a simulation of the shopping experience, not the real thing. Though testers can see and hear a product, they can't taste and touch it. Still, as a marketing research tool, virtual reality has great potential.

Sources: Quotes and extracts from Raymond R. Burke, "Virtual Shopping: Breakthrough in Marketing Research," *Harvard Business Review,* March–April, 1996, pp. 120–131; Tom Dellacave Jr., "Curing Market Research Headaches," *Sales and Marketing Management,* July 1996, pp. 84–85; Brian Silverman, "Get 'Em While They're Hot," *Sales and Marketing Management,* February 1997, pp. 47–48, 52; and Mike Hoffman, "Virtual Shopping," *Inc.,* July 1998, p. 88. Also see Sara Sellar, "The Perfect Trade Show Rep," *Sales and Marketing Management,* April 1999, p. 11; Christopher Ryan, "Virtual Reality in Marketing," *Direct Marketing,* April 2001, pp. 57–62; www.elumens.com/products/products.html www.elumens.com/products, accessed February 27, 2005.

The wave of the future for concept testing is virtual reality, such as Elumens' VisionStation, a 3-D immersive viewing system.

works here, roll it out in the U.S." New York–based Pfizer and its Montreal-based subsidiary are setting the pace with this type of test marketing. Their award-winning "Good Morning" and "Champions" ads for Viagra (developed by Taxi Advertising of Toronto), as well as the launch of Listerine PocketPaks and Benylin DM Medicated Freezer Pops for children, were test marketed first in Canada.[16]

Stage 8: Commercialization

Commercialization The full-scale introduction of the new product into the market.

The final step in the new product development process is **commercialization**, or the full-scale introduction of the product into the market. If test marketing is conducted, it is done on a small scale, keeping costs relatively low and allowing the company to back out of a full-scale market rollout if the test marketing fails. But once the company decides to go ahead with commercialization, it will necessarily face high costs. The company will have to expand its manufacturing facilities to accommodate the new product, and it may have to spend, in the case of a new consumer packaged good, between $16 million and $300 million for advertising, sales promotion, and other marketing efforts in the first year.

The company launching a new product must first decide on the timing of the market introduction. Competitive products, the economy, the company's financial situation, and the possible cannibalization of the company's own products are all factors that must be taken into consideration. Being first to market has its advantages; however, as we saw in the Teddy Grahams cereal example, rushing to market too soon can result in a failed product.

Next, the company must decide where to launch the new product; in other words, which geographic markets to target. Few companies have the confidence, capital, and capacity to launch new products into full national or international distribution immediately. Instead, they plan a market rollout over time. Small companies, with fewer resources, may decide to enter a few cities or regions one at a time, while larger companies may quickly introduce new products into several regions at once, or into the full national market.

Companies with international distribution systems may introduce new products to all their markets worldwide simultaneously or in very fast sequence. Colgate-Palmolive used to follow a "lead-country" strategy. For example, it launched its Palmolive Optims shampoo and conditioner first in Australia, the Philippines, Hong Kong, and Mexico, then rapidly rolled it out into Europe, Asia, Latin America, and Africa. And when the company introduced its Actibrush battery-powered toothbrush it did so in 50 countries in a one-year period, generating US$115 million in sales. Such rapid worldwide expansion solidified the brand's market position before foreign competitors could react.[17]

IN-CLASS NOTES

Commercialization Stage

- **Test marketing**
  - Test product in selected markets
  - Can include virtual testing
- **Launch product**
  - Full market distribution at once or in stages
  - Often heavy and costly promotion
  - Measure market acceptance
  - Adjust to meet launch sales objectives

Organizing for New Product Development

Companies that organize their new product development process into the sequence of eight stages, from idea generation to commercialization, are following a **sequential product development** approach, where one company department or team works to complete its stage of the process before passing the new product along to the next group and stage. This orderly, step-by-step process can help bring control to the otherwise complex and risky process of developing new products for the market. The danger, however, is that it can be dangerously slow. In fast-changing, highly competitive markets, such slow-but-sure product development can result in product failures, lost sales and profits, and crumbling market positions. Speed to market and reducing new product development cycle time have become pressing concerns to companies in all industries.

In order to get their new products to market more quickly, many companies are adopting a faster, team-based or collaborative approach called **simultaneous product development**. Under this approach, the company departments involved in the new product development process work closely together through cross-functional teams, overlapping the steps in the process and carrying them out simultaneously. Needless to say, when done properly this approach can save time and increase effectiveness. Instead of passing the new product from department to department, the company assembles a team of people from various departments that stays with the new product from start to finish. Such teams usually include people from the marketing, finance, design, manufacturing, and legal departments, and may even involve suppliers and customers.

Top management gives the product development team general strategic direction but no clear-cut product idea or work plan. It challenges the team with stiff and seemingly contradictory goals—"turn out carefully planned and superior new products, but do it quickly"—and then gives the team whatever freedom and resources it needs to meet the challenge. In the sequential process, a bottleneck at one phase can seriously slow the entire project. In the simultaneous approach, if one functional area hits snags, it works to resolve them while the team moves on.

Allen-Bradley, a division of Rockwell Automation, designs and manufactures industrial control and automation products such as circuit breakers and switches. The company markets thousands of different products and has found that simultaneous product development is much more efficient, less expensive, and results in faster time-to-market than its old sequential system. Today, all the company's departments, from design engineering to manufacturing to marketing, work together to develop new products.

The simultaneous team-based approach does have some limitations. Superfast product development can be riskier and more costly than the slower, more orderly sequential approach. Moreover, it often creates increased organizational tension and confusion. And the company must take care that rushing a product to market doesn't adversely affect its quality—the objective is not only to create products faster, but to create them *better* and faster.

Despite these drawbacks, in rapidly changing industries facing increasingly shorter product life cycles, the rewards of fast and flexible product development far exceed the risks. Companies that get new and improved products to the market faster than competitors often gain a dramatic competitive edge. They can respond

Sequential product development A new product development approach in which one company department works to complete its stage of the process before passing the new product along to the next department and stage.

Simultaneous product development A new product development approach in which various company departments work closely together, overlapping the steps in the product-development process to save time and increase effectiveness.

Rockwell Automation's Allen-Bradley UL489 circuit breakers are just one of thousands of products developed using the simultaneous product development approach.

more quickly to emerging consumer tastes and charge higher prices for more advanced designs. As one auto industry executive states, "What we want to do is get the new car approved, built, and in the consumer's hands in the shortest time possible. . . . Whoever gets there first gets all the marbles."[18]

So we can see that developing a successful new product requires more than simply thinking up a good idea, turning it into a product, and finding customers for it. It requires a systematic approach for finding new ways to create value for those customers. Furthermore, successful new product development requires a total company commitment.

Linking the Concepts

Think about new products and how companies find and develop them.

- What new products have you seen or heard about in the past year?
- Every year, *Business Week* magazine holds a contest to recognize the best new products of the year. The judges are members of the Industrial Designers Society of America. In 2004 the Apple iPod Mini, the Chevrolet Super Sport Roadster, and the Nokia 7600 cell phone were recognized. Suppose you were on the panel of judges. Which new product would get your vote as the best new product of the year, and why?
- Try to find out what you can about the new product development process for the product you nominated.
- Come up with an idea for a new snack food product. Now, sketch out a plan for bringing your new product to market. Describe the product concept. Consider what needs to be tested in the product development and testing stage. What will your marketing strategy be? Will you conduct test marketing?

PRODUCT LIFE CYCLE STRATEGIES

It goes without saying that after launching a new product the company wants that product to enjoy a long and happy life. Although it does not expect the product to sell forever, the company wants to earn a profit sufficient to cover all the effort and risk that went into launching it. Marketing managers are aware, however, that all new products, no matter how innovative, or how common, have a limited life. The lifespan of a new product, from its development to its eventual (and unavoidable) decline, is called the **product life cycle**, or PLC.

Product life cycle (PLC) The lifespan of a new product, from its development to its eventual decline.

Figure 9.1 shows the five stages of the product life cycle, and the corresponding course that the product's sales and profits take. The product life cycle has five distinct stages:

1. *Product development* begins when the company finds and develops a new product idea. During product development, sales are zero and the company's investment costs mount.

2. *Introduction* is a period of slow sales growth as the product is introduced in the market. Profits are nonexistent in this stage because of the heavy expenses of product introduction.

3. *Growth* is a period of rapid market acceptance and increasing profits.

Figure 9.1   Sales and Profits Over the Product's Life from Inception to Decline

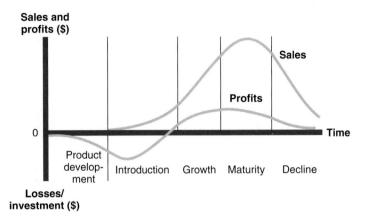

4. *Maturity* is a period of slowdown in sales growth because the product has achieved acceptance by most potential buyers. Profits level off or decline because of increased marketing outlays to defend the product against competition.

5. *Decline* is the period when sales fall off and profits drop.

The length of time a product takes to pass through each of these stages varies greatly. Some products are introduced and then decline quickly; others stay in the mature stage for a long, long time. Some products enter the decline stage and are then cycled back into the growth stage through strong promotion or repositioning.

The PLC concept can describe a *product class* (gasoline-powered automobiles), a *product form* (the SUV), or a *brand* (the Volkswagen Jetta). The PLC concept applies differently in each case. Product classes have the longest life cycles—the sales of many product classes stay in the mature stage for a long time. Product forms, in contrast, tend to have the standard PLC shape. Product forms such as dial telephones, videotapes, and VCRs passed through a regular history of introduction, rapid growth, maturity, and decline.

A specific brand's life cycle can change quickly because of changing competitive attacks and responses. For example, although laundry soaps (product class) and powdered detergents (product form) have enjoyed long life cycles, the life cycles of specific brands have tended to be much shorter. Today's leading brands of powdered laundry soap are Tide and Cheer; the leading brands 75 years ago were Fels Naptha, Octagon, and Kirkman.[19]

We looked at the product development stage of the product life cycle in the first part of the chapter. We now look at strategies for each of the other stages of the product life cycle.

The Product Life Cycle: Introduction Stage

The **introduction stage** of the PLC starts when the new product is first launched into the market. Introduction takes time, and sales growth during this time will be slow. Well-known products such as instant coffee, frozen orange juice, and powdered coffee creamers lingered in the introduction stage for many years.

In this stage, as compared with other stages, profits are negative or low because of the low sales and high distribution and promotion expenses. Much money is needed to attract distributors and build their inventories. Promotion spending is relatively high to inform potential customers of the new product and to encourage them to try it. Because

Introduction stage The product life cycle stage in which the new product is first launched into the market.

the market is not generally ready for product refinements at this stage, the company and its few competitors produce basic versions of the product. These firms focus their selling on those customers who are the most ready to buy.

During the introduction stage of the PLC, the company must choose a launch strategy that is consistent with the product's positioning. It should realize that the initial strategy is just the first step in the marketing plan for the product's entire life cycle. If the company is first to market with the new product it may try to maximize profits by pricing the product high. If the product is positioned as a prestige product such a strategy could be successful, but if the product is positioned as a value product, a too high price might result in market failure. As the product moves through later stages of the PLC, the marketers will have to continually formulate new pricing, promotion, and other marketing strategies.

The Product Life Cycle: Growth Stage

Growth stage The product life cycle stage in which a product's sales start climbing quickly.

If the new product satisfies the market, it will enter a **growth stage**, in which sales will start climbing quickly. The early adopters will continue to buy, and later buyers will start following their lead, especially if they hear favourable word of mouth. Attracted by the opportunities for profit, new competitors will enter the market. They will introduce new product features, and the market will expand. The increase in competitors leads to an increase in the number of distribution outlets, and sales jump just to build reseller inventories. Prices remain where they are or fall only slightly. Companies keep their promotion spending at the same high level as during the introduction stage. Educating the market remains a goal, but now the company must also meet the competition.

Profits increase during the growth stage, as promotion costs are spread over a large volume and unit manufacturing costs fall. The firm uses several strategies to sustain rapid market growth as long as possible. It improves product quality and adds new product features and models. It enters new market segments and new distribution channels. It shifts its promotional goals from building product awareness to building product conviction and encouraging purchase, and it lowers prices at the right time to attract more buyers.

In the growth stage, the firm faces a trade-off between high market share and high current profit. By spending a lot of money on product improvement, promotion, and distribution, the company can capture a dominant position. In doing so, however, it gives up maximum current profit, which it hopes to make up in the next stage.

The Product Life Cycle: Maturity Stage

Maturity stage The stage in the product life cycle in which sales growth slows, then levels off.

At some point the product's sales growth will slow, then level off, and the product will enter the **maturity stage**. This stage normally lasts longer than the previous stages, and it poses strong challenges to marketing management. Most products that are available in the market at any given time are in the maturity stage of their life cycle, and therefore most of marketing management deals with the mature product.

The slowdown in sales growth results in many producers with many products to sell. In turn, this overcapacity leads to greater competition. Competitors begin marking down prices, increasing their advertising and sales promotions, and upping their R&D budgets to find better versions of the product. These steps lead to a drop in profit. Some of the weaker competitors start dropping out, and the industry eventually contains only well-established competitors.

Although many products in the mature stage appear to remain unchanged for long periods, most successful ones are actually evolving to meet changing market needs (see Marketing at Work 9.2). Product managers should do more than simply maintain and

Marketing at Work 9.2

Age-Defying Products or Just Skillful PLC Management?

Some products are born and die quickly. Others, however, seem to defy the product life cycle, enduring for decades or even generations. It's skillful product life cycle management that keeps these mature products fresh, relevant, and appealing to customers.

Take Kraft Dinner. Canadians consume an incredible 246 000 boxes of "KD" a day. It's the country's number-one-selling grocery item, holding a 75 percent share of the market. Not bad for a product that's been on the market in Canada since 1937. But senior brand manager Gannon Jones says, "You can't sit back and simply expect the brand to continue to be popular without trying to keep it relevant with consumers." But how, you might ask, can you get Canadians to eat even more of the stuff?

Well, rather than just talking to kids, the KD brand now reaches out to adults. Kraft conducted market research to ask Canadians why they love Kraft Dinner, and discovered that everyone has their own "KD truths." The first TV spot that resulted was "Laundry Night." It featured a group of university-age guys filing into a laundromat, where one of them uses a washing machine to prepare KD. When another patron gives him a look, he shrugs and says, "My night to cook." Kraft has also developed new versions of the product, such as the microwaveable, single-serving Easy Mac. Its TV campaign, entitled "Dog Gone Girl," features a young man returning home and finding nothing in his apartment but his dog. Not overly concerned about his girlfriend's abandonment, he's hungry and manages to make Easy Mac in the dog's dish.

Binney & Smith's Crayola crayons are another household staple.

Available in more than 60 countries around the world, they haven't changed much since 1903, when the crayons were sold in an eight-pack for a nickel. But Binney & Smith has actually made many adjustments to keep the brand out of decline. It's also extended the Crayola brand to new markets—markers, watercolour paints, themed stamps and stickers, and stencils—and licensed it for use on everything from lunch boxes to house paints. And the company strengthens its customer relationships through such initiatives as *Crayola Kids* magazine and the Crayola Web.

In 1990, to make room for more modern colours, the company retired eight colours from the time-honoured box of 64—and unleashed a groundswell of protest from loyal Crayola users. "We were aware of the loyalty and nostalgia surrounding Crayola crayons," a flabbergasted

spokesperson said, "but we didn't know we [would] hit such a nerve." The company reissued the old standards in a special collector's tin, and sold 2.5 million units.

Through smart product life cycle management, Binney & Smith, now a subsidiary of Hallmark, has dominated the crayon market for almost a century.

Sources: John Heinzl, "Kraft Dinner Serves up a New Look," *The Globe and Mail,* January 13, 1999, p. B30; Lara Mills, "Kraft Builds Ads Around 'KD Truths,'" *Marketing On-Line,* April 26, 1999; "Easy Mac Simplifies Kraft Dinner," *Marketing On-Line,* September 6, 1999; Michael Cavanaugh, "The Digital Eye," *Marketing On-Line,* March 13, 2000; Kathleen Deslauriers, "Easy Mac Stirs Up Awareness," *Strategy,* March 13, 2000, p. 18; "Hue and Cry over Crayola May Revive Old Colors," *The Wall Street Journal,* June 14, 1991, p. B1; Margaret O. Kirk, "Coloring Our Children's World Since '03," *Chicago Tribune,* October 29, 1986, pp. 5, 1; Becky Ebenkamp, "Crayola Heritage Tack Continues with $6-7M," *Brandweek,* February 1, 1999, p. 5; www.crayola.com, accessed February 2000; Gene Del Vecchio, "Keeping It Timeless, Trendy," *Advertising Age,* March 23, 1998, p. 24.

Some products seem to defy the product life cycle. Over the years the Crayola brand has added a steady stream of new colours, forms, and packages.

defend their mature products. They must always be keenly aware of the market, the product, and the marketing mix, and consider how they might make modifications that will delay for as long as possible the product's decline.

In *modifying the market,* the company tries to increase the consumption of the current product. It looks for new users and market segments, as when Johnson & Johnson targeted the adult market with its baby powder and shampoo. The manager also looks for ways to increase usage among present customers. This is Bell's strategy in continually offering new voice, Internet, and satellite communications services (i.e., products) to consumers, and in "bundling" new products with old, familiar ones such as long distance.

The WD-40 Company has shown a real knack for expanding the market by finding new uses for its popular substance. In 2000, the company launched a search to uncover 2000 unique uses for WD-40. After receiving 300 000 individual submissions, it narrowed the list to the best 2000 and posted it on the company's website. Some consumers suggest simple and practical uses. One teacher uses WD-40 to clean old chalkboards in her classroom. "Amazingly, the boards started coming to life again," she reports. "Not only were they restored, but years of masking and Scotch tape residue came off as well." Others, however, report some pretty unusual applications. One man uses WD-40 to polish his glass eye; another uses it to remove a prosthetic leg. And did you hear about the nude burglar who had wedged himself in a vent at a café in Denver? The fire department extracted him with a large dose of WD-40. Or how about the Mississippi naval officer who used WD-40 to repel an angry bear? Then there's the student who wrote to say that a friend's nightly amorous activities in the next room were causing everyone in his dorm to lose sleep—he solved the problem by treating the squeaky bedsprings with WD-40. There's even a WD-40 Fan Club on the company's website, where individuals can submit their favourite WD-40 story, and sign up to receive tips for using WD-40 via email.[20]

The company might also try *modifying the product*—changing characteristics such as quality, features, or style to attract new users and to inspire more usage. It might improve the product's quality and performance—its durability, reliability, speed, taste. It can improve the product's styling and attractiveness. Thus, car manufacturers restyle their cars to attract buyers who want a new look. The makers of consumer food and household products introduce new flavours, colours, ingredients, or packages to revitalize consumer buying. Or the company might add new features that expand the product's usefulness, safety, or convenience.

Apple Computer's portable music storage and playing device, the iPod, was launched into the market as a new product in October 2001. It grew quickly in popularity, and today could be considered in the early part of the maturity stage; however, Apple isn't content to coast on its past success—the company is continually improving the product. The second generation iPod was released in July 2002; the third generation in May 2003. Each new version improved the storage size, features, and functionality. In January 2004, Apple announced the release of the iPod Mini, a smaller version of the iPod, available in five colours. In October 2004, two new iPods were introduced: the iPod photo, promoted with the tagline, "Why should your ears have all the fun?" and the iPod U2 Special Edition, a limited edition black and orange iPod autographed by the members of the band and, in 2005, the iPod Nano, the smallest iPod yet, was introduced to the market.[21]

Finally, the company can try *modifying the marketing mix*—improving sales by changing one or more marketing mix elements. It can cut prices to attract new users and competitors' customers. It can launch a better advertising campaign or use aggressive sales promotions—trade deals, cents-off, premiums, and contests. In can move into larger or different market channels, using mass merchandisers, if these channels are growing. Marketers can't simply sit back and expect a product to be popular forever. They must continually modify the marketing mix to keep sales from decreasing over time.

The Product Life Cycle: Decline Stage

Although products can remain for many years in the maturity stage of the PLC, eventually the product inevitably declines. In the **decline stage** the product's sales begin to decrease. This decline may be slow, as in the case of oatmeal cereal and electric typewriters, or rapid, as in the case of phonograph records and videotapes. Sales may plunge to zero, or they may drop to a low level where they continue for many years.

Decline stage The product life cycle stage in which a product's sales begin to decrease.

Sales decline for many reasons, including technological advances, shifts in people's tastes, and increased competition. As sales and profits decline, some firms may reduce their number of product offerings, or may withdraw from the market altogether. They may drop markets from their distribution channels, or they may cut back on the promotion budget. The marketer's goal when a product is in decline is to reduce expenditures and "milk the brand," that is, get what they can out of it with minimum or no investment.

Carrying a weak product can be very costly to a firm. A weak product may take up too much of management's time, require frequent price and inventory adjustments, and consume an advertising budget that might be better used to make stronger products more profitable. Keeping weak products delays the search for replacements, creates a lopsided product mix, hurts current profits, and weakens the company's foothold on the future. The firm must identify those products that are entering the decline stage by regularly reviewing sales, market shares, costs, and profit trends. Then, management must decide whether to maintain, harvest, or drop each of these declining products.

Management may decide to *maintain* its brand without change in the hope that competitors will leave the industry. For example, Procter & Gamble made good profits by remaining in the declining liquid soap business as others withdrew. Or management may decide to reposition or reformulate the brand in hopes of moving it back into the growth stage of the product life cycle. Frito-Lay did this with the classic Cracker Jack brand:

When Cracker Jack passed the 100-year-old mark, it seemed that the timeless brand was running out of time. By the time Frito-Lay acquired the classic snack-food brand from Borden Foods in 1997, sales and profits had been declining for five straight years. Frito-Lay set out to reconnect the box of candy-coated popcorn, peanuts, and a prize with a new generation of kids. "We made the popcorn bigger and fluffier with more peanuts and bigger prizes, and we put it in bags, as well as boxes," says Frito Lay's Chris Neugent. New promotional programs shared a connection with baseball and fun for kids, featuring

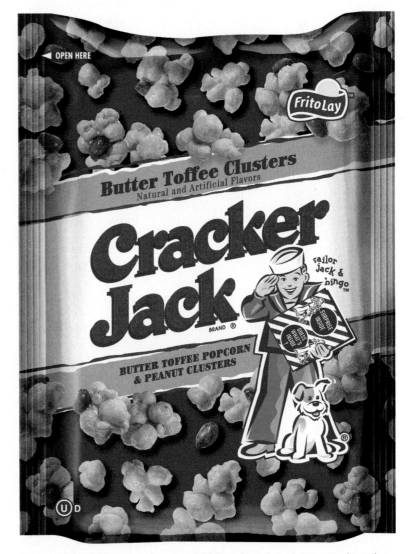

When 100-year-old Cracker Jack went into decline, Frito Lay's marketers revived it. Today, new products such as Cracker Jack Butter Toffee Clusters have joined the product line.

Table 9.2 Summary of Product Life Cycle Characteristics, Objectives, and Strategies

	Introduction	Growth	Maturity	Decline
Characteristics				
Sales	Low sales	Rapidly rising sales	Peak sales	Declining sales
Costs	High cost per customer	Average cost per customer	Low cost per customer	Low cost per customer
Profits	Negative	Rising profits	High profits	Declining profits
Customers	Innovators	Early adopters	Middle majority	Laggards
Competitors	Few	Growing number	Stable number beginning to decline	Declining number
Marketing objectives	Create product and trial	Maximize market share	Maximize profit while defending market share	Reduce expenditure and milk the brand
Strategies				
Product	Offer a basic product	Offer product extensions, service, warranty	Diversify brand and models	Phase out weak items
Price	Use cost-plus formula	Price to penetrate market	Price to match or best competitors	Cut price
Distribution	Build selective distribution	Build intensive distribution	Build more intensive distribution	Go selective: Phase out unprofitable outlets
Advertising	Build product awareness among early adopters and dealers	Build awareness and interest in the mass market	Stress brand differences and benefits	Reduce to level needed to retain hard-core loyals
Sales promotion	Use heavy sales promotion to entice trial	Reduce to take advantage of heavy consumer demand	Increase to encourage brand switching	Reduce to minimal level

Source: Philip Kotler, *Marketing Management: Analysis, Planning, Implementation, and Control*, 11th ed. (Upper Saddle River, NJ: Prentice Hall, 2003), Chapter 10.

baseball star Mark McGwire, Rawlings Sporting Goods trading cards, and Pokemon and Scooby Doo characters. The revitalized marketing pulled Cracker Jack out of decline. Sales more than doubled during the two years following the acquisition and the brand has posted double-digit increases each year since.[22]

Harvest (a product) To reduce various costs in hopes that sales hold up.

Management may decide to **harvest** a product, which means reducing various costs (plant and equipment, maintenance, R&D, advertising, sales force) and hoping that sales hold up. If successful, harvesting will increase the company's profits in the short run. Or management may decide to *drop* the product from the line. It can sell it to another firm or simply liquidate it at salvage value. If the company plans to find a buyer, it won't want to run down the product through harvesting.

Styles, Fashions, and Fads

The PLC concept also can be applied to styles, fashions, and fads, though the shape of their life cycles is very different, as you can see in Figure 9.2.

Figure 9.2   Styles, Fashions, and Fads

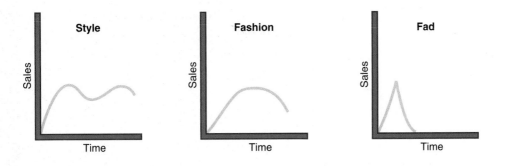

A **style** is a basic and distinctive mode of expression. For example, styles appear in homes (colonial, ranch, transitional), clothing (formal, casual), and art (realist, surrealist, abstract). Once a style is invented, it may last for generations, passing in and out of vogue. A style has a cycle showing several periods of renewed interest.

A **fashion** is a currently accepted or popular style in a given field. We're all familiar with fashions in clothing and hairstyles, but television programming also has its fashions. For example, prime-time game shows were fashionable television programming for much of the 1990s, but they slowly gave way to the wildly popular reality shows of today. Fashions tend to grow slowly, remain popular for a while, then decline slowly.

A **fad** is a new product that enters the market quickly, is adopted with great zeal, peaks early, and declines very quickly. Most fads don't survive for long because they normally don't satisfy a strong need or satisfy it well.

Take the case of the low-carb diet craze. While some marketers claimed it wasn't a fad at all but permanent social change, others were more cautious. Remember, it's not always clear whether a new trend will become entrenched in society or whether it will disappear. But following the relaunch of Dr. Robert Atkins's book in 1997 the market for low-carb products grew by stellar proportions—and many marketers jumped on the bandwagon. Giant food manufacturing companies from around the world spent millions of dollars developing, testing, and launching more than 2800 low-carb products, only to withdraw many of them as the market collapsed in 2004. Kellogg CEO Carlos Gutierrez was the first to publicly admit that the abundance of low-carb products, including some introduced by Kellogg, had created "a bit of a glut" in the market. Other firms, such as Kraft, a company that relies on lines of carb-rich products, celebrated.[23]

Style A basic and distinctive mode of expression.

Fashion A currently accepted or popular style in a given field.

Fad A fashion that enters quickly, is adopted with great zeal, peaks early, and declines very quickly.

In-Class Notes

Product Life Cycle

- **Development** – No customers, no profits, heavy spending
- **Introduction** – Early adopter customers, no profits, high launch costs
- **Growth** – Early majority customers, rapid sales growth and revenues
- **Maturity** – Late majority customers, flat sales, declining profits
- **Decline** – Laggard customers, declining sales, replaced by new products

LOOKING BACK

New products are the lifeblood of every company. Marketers must continuously strive to invent, improve, or acquire products. Not every new product is necessarily a new invention, however.

New product marketing and product management are challenging tasks for marketers because a high percentage of new products fail in the market. Therefore, to improve their chances of success, marketers follow an eight-step new product development process that begins with idea generation and ends with commercialization of the product.

After the product is developed and launched into the marketplace its life cycle must be managed. Every product goes through a product life cycle, from development, to introduction, to growth, to maturity, to decline. Some products mature and decline quickly, and disappear from the market. Others, like Cracker Jack, have been around for 100 years. Clever marketers, recognizing that a product is in the decline stage, can revitalize the product and re-introduce it to the market, beginning the product life cycle all over again.

REVIEWING THE CONCEPTS

1. Explain how companies find and develop new product ideas.

Companies find and develop new product ideas from a variety of sources. Many new product ideas stem from internal sources. Companies conduct formal research and development, pick the brains of their employees, and brainstorm at executive meetings. By conducting surveys and focus groups and analyzing customer questions and complaints, companies can generate new product ideas that will meet specific consumer needs. Companies track competitors' offerings and inspect new products, dismantling them, analyzing their performance, and deciding whether to introduce a similar or improved product. Distributors and suppliers are close to the market and can pass along information about consumer problems and new product possibilities.

2. List and define the steps in the new product development process.

The new product development process consists of eight stages, which can be performed sequentially, or simulta-

neously. The process starts with *idea generation*. Next comes *idea screening*, which reduces the number of ideas based on the company's own criteria. Ideas that pass the screening stage continue through *concept development and testing*, in which a detailed version of the new product idea is stated in meaningful consumer terms, then new product concepts are tested with a group of target consumers to determine whether the concepts have consumer appeal. Strong concepts proceed to *marketing strategy development*, in which strategic plans are made for taking the finished product to market. In the *business analysis* stage, a review of the sales, costs, and profit projections for a new product is conducted to determine whether the new product is likely to satisfy the company's objectives. If the new product is determined to make good business sense, *development* of the actual working product, with all its features, is undertaken. When the product is ready, the marketers may decide to conduct *test marketing* in a limited area before rolling the product out to the entire market in the final *commercialization* stage.

3. Describe the stages of the product life cycle.

After product development is complete and the product is available in the market, it will go through a *product life cycle* consisting of five distinct stages, each marked by a changing set of problems and opportunities. The first stage is the *product development stage* when the company finds and develops a new product idea. The *introduction stage* is when the new product is introduced to the market. Next, the product enters a *growth stage*, where it may remain for weeks or months. During the growth stage an increasing number of customers are buying and trying the product. Sales and profits grow. This rapid stage of sales growth eventually slows, and the product enters the *maturity stage*. In this stage, the product is known to the market, and competition will increase. A product may remain in the maturity stage for many years, but eventually it will enter the *decline stage* in which sales and profits dwindle. The company's task during this stage is to recognize the decline and decide whether it should maintain, harvest, or drop the product.

4. Explain how marketing strategies change during the product's life cycle.

In the introduction stage, the company must choose a launch strategy consistent with its intended product positioning. Heavy investment in promotion, both to the customers in the target market and to the channel members, must be made.

In the growth stage, companies must continue to promote the new product, but may face challenges in terms of managing demand. Feedback from the market may lead to new product features, improved product quality, or changes in packaging or distribution channels. Promotional goals change from raising awareness and encouraging trial to building long-term customer relationships. Competitors typically enter the market during this stage, and the marketers' strategy may have to adapt to new situations.

In the maturity stage, companies continue to invest in maturing products and consider modifying the market, the product, and the marketing mix. When modifying the market, the company attempts to increase the consumption of the current product. When modifying the product, the company changes some of the product's characteristics—such as quality, features, or style—to attract new users or inspire more usage. When modifying the marketing mix, the company works to improve sales by changing one or more of the marketing mix elements.

Once the company recognizes that a product has entered the decline stage, management must decide whether to maintain the brand without change, hoping that competitors will drop out of the market; harvest the product, reducing costs and trying to maintain sales; or drop the product, selling it to another firm or liquidating it at salvage value.

KEY TERMS

business analysis *350*
commercialization *354*
concept development and
  testing *347*
decline stage *361*
fad *363*
fashion *363*
growth stage *358*
harvest (a product) *362*
idea generation *345*

idea screening *347*
introduction stage *357*
marketing strategy development
  349
maturity stage *358*
new product development *343*
product concept *347*
product development and testing
  351

product life cycle (PLC) *356*
sequential product development
  355
simultaneous product development
  355
style *363*
test marketing *351*

STUDY GUIDE

After completing this self-test, check your answers against the Answer Key at the back of the book.

MULTIPLE CHOICE

1. The decision to move to the next stage of the new product development process always carries some risk, and more risk with some products than others. For complex products companies, such as technology or electronics, the most critical point is the decision to move into the _____ stage.
   a. Development and testing
   b. Test marketing
   c. Market research
   d. Partnering
   e. e-Business

2. Marketing-driven companies are not put off by new product failures, because they understand that
   a. It is a valuable tool in misleading the competition
   b. Every failure garners them additional coverage in the media
   c. Most failed products can be modified and turned into successes
   d. Without trying out new products in the market they cannot have successes
   e. Loyal customers are very forgiving

3. Many technologically advanced products that today's consumers use and enjoy were first introduced decades ago and failed. Reintroduced more recently, these now-successful products are testaments to the importance of _____ when commercializing new product ideas.
   a. Pricing
   b. Timing
   c. Customer tolerance
   d. Doubt and uncertainty
   e. Market suspicion

4. Kleenex, Tylenol, Aspirin, Jacuzzi, Scotch tape, and Jell-O are all brands that dominate their product category. Which critical characteristic do these different products all share that made them so successful?
   a. They were all launched in the United States
   b. They were all heavily advertised
   c. They were all low-priced
   d. They were all launched initially to do something else
   e. They were all the first to be commercialized in that product category

5. As the iPod entered the growth stage several years ago, Apple had to wrestle with a key growth stage problem. In the end, Apple chose to
   a. Maximize promotional spending to capture a leading market share position rather than harvest maximum profit
   b. Retire the product early
   c. Harvest maximum profit rather than capture a majority market share
   d. Price the product high in order to skim off early, high peak demand
   e. Recall the product in order to fix quality problems

6. The Dodge Caravan, a minivan, has introduced several modifications over the years, including backseat cupholders, dual side doors, and onboard video and DVD players. These types of modifications are typical of
   a. A declining product that must be retired soon
   b. Companies that want to raise the price of existing brands
   c. Companies who want to "bury" quality problems with loads of features
   d. Evolving a highly mature product class to keep it relevant in the market
   e. American-style "pushy" marketing

7. You are looking up movies in your hometown and you hop onto the website of Cinema World to check out the listings. You see a link that says "Take a tour of our new Cinema World design." You click and you enter an online tour of a very cool new cinema with all the bells and whistles. At the end of the tour, you're asked to answer some questions about what you thought in exchange for an online discount coupon. You have just participated in
   a. A virtual reality product
   b. Virtual test marketing
   c. An interactive advertisement
   d. A sales promotion
   e. None of the above

8. Since laptop computers are in the mature life-cycle stage, new buyers of these types of computers fall into what adopter category?
   a. Innovators
   b. Price sensitive
   c. Risk averse
   d. Laggards
   e. Non-technical

9. Distribution can be a key part of the marketing mix when commercializing new products. Which brand below used distribution as a differentiator for its products?
   a. Dell
   b. Nabisco
   c. Sony
   d. Coca-Cola
   e. Hyundai

10. Pet rocks and hula hoops had very short product life cycles, typical of
    a. Trends
    b. Styles
    c. Takers
    d. Fads
    e. Market makers

TRUE/FALSE

T   F   1. Test marketing should continue to be treated sequentially even in a simultaneous product development process.

T   F   2. Companies never remove already commercialized new products from the market for modification.

T   F   3. The increased use of simultaneous product development has caused a significant relative rise in the number of new product failures.

T   F   4. The hybrid car product category is now entering the maturity phase of the product life cycle.

T   F   5. Mature products undergoing feature evolution still need to go through the new product development process.

CONCEPT CHECK

1. New-to-the-world products, product improvements, product modifications, and new brands that the firm develops through its own research and development efforts can all be called _____.

2. The eight steps in the new product development process are idea generation, _____, concept development and testing, _____, business analysis, _____, test marketing, and _____.

3. A _____ is a detailed version of the idea stated in meaningful consumer terms.

4. A marketing strategy statement consists of three parts. Part one describes the target market, the planned product positioning, and the sales, market share, and profit goals for the first few years. Part two outlines the product's planned price, distribution, and marketing budget for the first year. Part three describes _____, _____, and _____.

5. _____ introduces the product to the market under limited conditions before going to the expense of a full-scale product rollout.

6. The four stages of the product life cycle following product development are _____, _____, _____, and _____.

7. Most products are in the _____ stage of the life cycle and, therefore, most marketing management deals with this type of product.

8. Virtual reality simulations are useful to marketers in the _____ stage of new product development.

9. A product that experiences a short but extreme growth period followed almost immediately by decline is called a _____.

10. Clever marketers can revitalize a product in the decline stage and re-enter the PLC in the _____ stage.

STUDENT MATERIALS

Visit our website at www.pearsoned.ca/armstrong for online quizzes, Internet exercises, and more!

NOTES

DISCUSSING THE ISSUES

1. Choose a company whose products you are familiar with. What specific sources might you turn to for new product ideas? Assuming the company has a website, how might it be used to interact with the market to generate new product ideas? Brainstorm your own new product ideas for this company.

2. Choose three of the products mentioned in this chapter. Which stage of the product life cycle is each of these products in? Explain how you were able to identify the stage. How long do you think it will be before each product enters the next stage of the life cycle?

3. Yoplait recently introduced a new product to the market called Go-GURT. Described as a "portable yogurt," its target market is children. Visit the Yoplait website and learn about this product. Now, assume the position of the product manager responsible for Go-GURT. You have been asked to modify the market for this product.

Do you think this product can be adapted for the adult market? Devise a plan for testing the product concept with 25- to 45-year-olds. What factors would be critical to your test? What questions would you ask the testers?

4. Pick a soft drink, car, fashion, food product, or electronic device and trace the product's life cycle. Do appropriate research to make your timeline and application as accurate as possible. Explain how you separated the stages of the product's development. Project when the product might enter its decline stage.

5. Visit a large department store, drugstore, or grocery store and find a product you believe is an example of a fad. What evidence can you find—through research, online, or by asking people you know who have experience with the product—that supports your theory? Explain why you believe the product won't last in the market.

MARKETING APPLICATIONS

Is it just a fad? Is it a fashion? Or will it become the next Rollerblade? The newest footwear product for teens is the Heely. Heelys look like thick-soled sneakers, but they have a wheel embedded in each heel that allows the wearer to switch from walking mode to rolling or skating mode simply by shifting weight. Texas-based Heeling Sports Limited, which produces these unique shoes, is still in the early stages of its product marketing strategy. The product is not yet widely available in retail stores, but can be purchased from a dozen online retailers.

THINKING LIKE A MARKETING MANAGER

1. Visit the Heelys website and find out whether the product is available in Canada. If it is, try to find a local store that carries the product so that you can examine it. What stage of the PLC are Heelys currently in? Do you think they're a fad, a fashion, or a style? Explain.

2. Briefly describe the target market for Heelys in terms of its demographic, psychographic, geographic, and behavioural characteristics. What new market segments do you think might be developed for this product?

VIDEO CASE

Go to Pearson Canada's Video Central site (www.pearsoned.ca/highered/videocentral) to view the video and accompanying case for this chapter.

CASE 9   PRODUCT INNOVATION AT THE GILLETTE COMPANY

Gillette is the most recognizable brand in shaving. Whether you're male or female, if you're over 16 you're a member of the target market for Gillette's shaving products. The Gillette brand has been in existence for over a hundred years, but it doesn't rest on the laurels of its past successes. As you'll see, the company behind the brand owes much of its success to a passion for innovation and new product development.

The Gillette Company was founded in 1901, and acquired by consumer products giant Procter & Gamble in 2005 for $57 billion U.S. When Gillette reported its third-quarter results in October 2004, CEO James M. Kilts recognized the importance of new products to the company's success: "Our record third-quarter and nine-month results reflect the strong performance of our existing products plus the largest introduction of new products in recent years." That year the company launched several new products, including the M3Power razor for men, Venus Divine razor for women, and two new electric toothbrushes, the Professional Care 8000 and the Sonic Complete.

Since Gillette's founding in 1901, its heavy commitment to innovation has kept the company razor sharp. Gillette is best known for its absolute dominance of the wet shaving, dry shaving, and personal grooming markets, but did you know the company also owns the Duracell brand, with its market-leading alkaline batteries, and the Oral-B brand of oral hygiene products? In fact, each division of the company is profitable, fast-growing, number one worldwide in its markets, and anchored by a steady flow of innovative new product offerings.

Every year sees new Gillette products introduced into the market. The year 2004 began with the introduction of the M3Power men's shaving system, "a revolutionary powered wet shaving system that delivers the world's best shave and a totally new shaving experience."

In December 2004 Gillette introduced two new women's razors under its highly popular Venus brand. In a company press release, blades and razors president Peter K. Hoffman said that "The introduction of Venus Vibrance and Venus Disposable reflects Gillette's commitment to product innovations that drive category growth. With Venus Vibrance, we are offering the world's best shaving performance through our power wet shaving technology, while Venus Disposable offers the category's best technology in a disposable razor. These new products reinforce Gillette's leadership position in female shaving."

New products don't just happen at Gillette. New product success starts with a companywide culture that supports innovation. Whereas many companies try to protect their successful existing products, Gillette encourages innovations that will cannibalize its established product hits. The company also accepts blunders and dead ends as a normal part of creativity and innovation. It knows that it must generate dozens of new product ideas to get just one success in the marketplace. Gillette strongly encourages its people to take creative risks in applying cutting-edge technologies to find substantial improvements that make life easier for customers.

New product development is complex and expensive, but Gillette's mastery of the process has put the company in a class of its own. For example, Gillette spent $275 million on designing and developing its Sensor family of razors, garnering 29 patents along the way. And it spent an incredible $1.5 billion on the development of Sensor's successor, the triple-bladed MACH3, and applied for 35 more patents. Competing brands Bic and Wilkinson have managed to claim significant shares of the disposable-razor market, and Norelco and Remington compete effectively in electric razors with Gillette's Braun unit. But Gillette, with its stunning technological superiority, operates with virtually no competition worldwide in the burgeoning cartridge-razor sector. Backed by Gillette's biggest new product launch up to that point, the MACH3 strengthened the company's stranglehold on this market. Within only a few months of its introduction, MACH3 razors and blades were number-one sellers. The new M3Power system is the evolution of the MACH3 product line, and when it was introduced Hoffman declared, "We expect this new system to substantially fuel the value of the blade and razor category, in the same way that MACH3Turbo has driven growth over the past two years."

At Gillette, it seems that almost everyone gets involved in one way or another with new product development. Even people who don't participate directly in the product design and development are likely to be pressed into service testing prototypes. Every working day at Gillette, 200 volunteers from various departments come to work unshaven and troop to the second floor of the company's gritty South Boston manufacturing and research plant. The male volunteers enter small booths with a sink and mirror and take instructions from technicians on the other side of a small window as to which razor, shaving cream, or aftershave to use. The volunteers evaluate razors for sharpness of blade, smoothness of glide, and ease of handling. When finished, they enter their judgments into a computer. In a nearby shower room, women perform the same ritual on their legs and underarms.

Gillette simply excels at bringing new products to market. The company understands that, once introduced, fledgling products need generous manufacturing and marketing support to thrive in the hotly competitive consumer products marketplace. To deliver the required support, Gillette has devised a formula that calls for R&D, capital investment, and advertising expenditures—which it refers to collectively as "growth drivers."

In addition to being an innovative product marketer, Gillette is a sports marketing pioneer. The company partners with NASCAR through its "Young Guns" program. The Gillette Company Young Guns are racecar drivers Kurt Busch, Dale Earnhardt, Jr., Kevin Harvick, Jimmie Johnson, Matt Kenseth, and Ryan Newman. The company's sponsorship of sporting events dates back to 1910, when baseball players were featured in advertisements for the original Gillette Safety Razor. And in Massachusetts, the home of the NFL's New England Patriots is called "Gillette Stadium." Gillette also maintains a close relationship with Major League baseball, World Cup soccer, the PGA Tour, and the National Hockey League.

Thus, over the decades, superior new products combined with innovative marketing programs have been the cornerstone of Gillette's amazing success. In February 2005 the company reported record annual and fourth-quarter results with double-digit percentage increases in net sales. CEO James Kilts attributes the successful year to the company's new product achievements: "Gillette posted excellent results across the board, fueled by our largest and most successful new products effort ever. Key successes included M3Power, the first battery powered wet shaving system; the Venus Divine premium system for women; the Oral B Professional Care 8000 power rechargeable toothbrush; and the Sonic Complete, the Company's first entry in the sonic segment of brushing. We look forward to another very good year in 2005. It promises to again be our most active year for new products, with the ongoing international roll out of M3Power and several Oral Care products and the introduction of several major new trade-up products, including Venus Vibrance, our powered wet shaving system for women, and Venus Disposable, the most advanced women's disposable razor."

It's success stories like these that made Gillette a desirable acquisition for Procter & Gamble. The deal to acquire Gillette is, to date, the largest acquisition in the history of P&G.

Sources: Press release from the Procter & Gamble website, January 28, 2005, "P&G Signs Deal to Acquire The Gillette Company"; Press releases from The Gillette Company's website, www.gillette-news.com, accessed February 2005: "The Gillette Company: Over 100 Years of Shaving Innovation," "Gillette Introduces Two New High-Performance Venus Razors," "Gillette Reports Record Fourth-Quarter and Full-Year Results"; Lawrence Ingrassia, "Taming the Monster: How Big Companies Can Change," *The Wall Street Journal,* December 10, 1992, pp. A1, A6; William H. Miller, "Gillette's Secret to Sharpness," *Industry Week,* January 3, 1994, pp. 24–30; Linda Grant, "Gillette Knows Shaving—And How to Turn out Hot New Products," *Fortune,* October 14, 1996, pp. 207–210; and Dana Canedy, "Gillette's Strengths in Razors Undone by Troubles Abroad," *The New York Times,* June 19, 1999, p. 3. Also see William C. Symonds, "Would You Spend $1.50 for a Razor Blade?" *Business Week,* April 27, 1998, p. 46; James Heckman, "Razor Sharp: Adding Value, Making Noise with Mach3 Intro," *Marketing News,* 29 March 1999, pp. E4, E13; and William C. Symonds, "The Big Trim at Gillette," *Business Week,* November 8, 1999, p. 42.

Questions

1. The Gillette brand is the most recognized name in wet shaving products—razors and razor blades. New products in this product category will almost certainly continue to be developed. If you were a Gillette product manager in charge of developing new-to-the-company products, what type of product would you recommend as an extension of the Gillette brand?

2. Find out more about the merger of Gillette and Procter & Gamble. Visit your local drugstore or grocery store, and examine the Gillette products on the shelves. Have the products changed since the acquisition? If so, how?

3. A product marketing manager must be acutely aware of all the competing products on the market. Choose one product category, either men's wet shaving non-disposable razors or women's wet shaving non-disposable razors. Make a list of all the Gillette products (any and all variations, different sizes of packages, pricing, etc.) and at least three competitive products. Then, make a checklist or grid of all the product features, and check off which brand and product has which features. Write a competitive analysis report of how your products compare with those of the competition.

1. identify and explain the internal and external factors affecting a firm's pricing decisions

2. contrast the three general approaches to setting prices

3. describe the major strategies for pricing new products

4. explain how companies find a set of prices that maximizes the profits from the total product mix

5. discuss how companies adjust their prices to take into account different types of customers and situations

6. discuss the key issues related to initiating and responding to price changes

Pricing Considerations and Strategies

Looking Ahead We will now look at a second major marketing mix tool—pricing. According to one pricing expert, "If effective product development, promotion, and distribution sow the seeds of business success, effective pricing is the harvest."[1] Good pricing, he continues, "involves finding a balance between the customer's desire to obtain good value and the firm's need to cover costs and earn profits." Yet, despite its importance, many firms do not handle pricing well. In this chapter, we'll examine factors that affect pricing decisions, general pricing approaches, and specific pricing strategies. We will also look at how dynamic pricing, facilitated by information systems, is continuing to challenge traditional pricing strategies and structures.

In just over a decade, Wal-Mart has gone from being an American brand to becoming as entrenched in the Canadian psyche and landscape as The Bay. But which retailer—and the different pricing strategies each represent—will ultimately capture Canadians' mindshare and wallet in the longer run?

I n 1962 Sam Walton and his brother opened the first Wal-Mart discount store in small-town Rogers, Arkansas. It was a big, flat warehouse-like store that sold everything from apparel to automotive supplies to small appliances at very low prices. Experts gave the fledgling retailer little chance—yet from these modest beginnings, the chain exploded onto the global retailing scene. Today, Wal-Mart's annual sales of $275 billion—more than the GDP of British Columbia and Alberta combined—makes it the world's largest company. In 2002 Wal-Mart's sales grew by the equivalent of the annual sales of one Microsoft, two Coca-Colas, or three Nikes. It also accounts for approximately 10 percent of all imports to America from China.

In March of 1994, 32 years after Wal-Mart's modest beginnings, Wal-Mart Canada was founded with the acquisition of the Woolco division of Woolworth Canada Inc. A total of 122 Woolco stores were converted in less than eight months to the Wal-Mart format. By 2005, Wal-Mart Canada had grown to more than 235 stores employing more than 70 000 people. Wal-Mart has committed to continue to aggressively open new stores across Canada. And each of these stores offers apparel, home fashions, household goods, toys, hardware, paint, wallpapers, automotive accessories, furniture, horticulture, cosmetics, jewellery, and convenience food items—close to 80 000 different products.

Canadians might not all be aware of just how big Wal-Mart is, but one thing almost every Canadian knows is that Wal-Mart is all about low prices. In fact, EDLP—"everyday low prices"—has been the heart of Wal-Mart's strategy that has helped capture more than 51 percent of the Canadian retail market in just 11 years, making Wal-Mart the largest Canadian retailer.

In contrast, the Hudson Bay Company (HBC) with its Zellers discount stores and The Bay, its higher-end department store, has mostly avoided an EDLP strategy. Instead, it tries to maintain relatively high regular prices and attract customers through a promotions discounting and differentiation strategy. For example, The Bay holds regular "Bay Days," when certain items are offered at sale prices, and "Customer Appreciation Days" when HBC credit card holders can get 10–15 percent discounts on merchandise throughout the store. HBC got into hot water in 1998 over its pricing approach when a fine of $600 000—one of the highest ever for a misleading advertising offence under the *Competition Act*—was imposed by the Ontario Court. The charges related to The Bay's marketing of a range of bicycles sold during the 1980s and early 1990s. According to the Competition Bureau, The Bay misled Canadians by representing that its bicycles would be offered at a sale price for a certain limited period of time when in fact the sale continued for a much longer period. The misrepresentations were in the form of flyers, newspaper advertisements, and in-store displays. "Consumers can be easily misled by sales promotions that create a general impression of urgency, especially when these relate to items as commonly purchased as bicycles," said Konrad von Finckenstein, director of Investigation and Research.

The Competition Bureau has also challenged HBC on what constitutes the "sale" and "regular" price for some of its product lines. Customers had become so accustomed to waiting for the next Scratch-and-Save-Day or Bay Day that in some product categories, the majority of the total sales came during these promotional periods rather than during the rest of the year's regular pricing. The sales promotion pricing had in effect become the ordinary selling price, leading regulators to challenge HBC on whether the product really could legally be advertised as being on sale—a practice known as "false or misleading ordinary selling price representations" under the *Competition Act*.

Although these legal concerns led HBC to re-examine its pricing strategy, Wal-Mart's entry into Canada represented a far greater source of change to Canadian retail pricing. The world's biggest retailer didn't have to worry about the semantics of a promotional sale with its EDLP strategy, and Canadians started to get used to the idea of always having low prices instead of having to wait until the next sale at The Bay.

How does Wal-Mart sustain its EDLP strategy? Quite simply, it keeps its costs down. While retailers were spending hundreds of millions of dollars in advertising, battling it out for customers in the major urban markets, Wal-Mart was slowly but surely locating in more rural, low-population areas, opening stores in places that were unattractive to the other leading retailers. Rather than extensive advertising spending, Wal-Mart invested heavily in information technology and logistics, hooking up individual stores into a well-tuned supply chain network—a hyper-efficient retail ecosystem.

Its information technology and operations management were extremely successful, and have become a model for best practices in the retail sector and beyond. With its infrastructure and economies of scale in place, Wal-Mart then expanded from its rural locations to the top markets, attracting customers with its "hard to beat" low prices and in the process knocking out many of the retail incumbents.

"It the most loved, most hated, most admired and most sued corporation in the country—and its customers now arrive in everything from city buses to Mercedes-Benz," says Steve Biggerstaff, brand strategist with the U.S.-based Brand Consultancy.

Wal-Mart earned a reputation for wielding its growing power to bring the lowest possible prices to consumers. In fact, on many products, the price Wal-Mart will pay and will charge shoppers must drop every year. Gib Carey, a partner at global management consulting firm Bain & Co. who is leading a year-long study of how to do business with Wal-Mart, says, "For any product that's the same as what you sold them last year, Wal-Mart will say, 'Here's the price you gave me last year. Here's what I can get a competitor's product for. Here's what I can get a private-label version for. I want to see a better value that I can bring to my shoppers this year. Or else I'm going to use that shelf space differently.'"

Some industry observers think that a focus on low pricing can sustain a brand for only so long, and that inevitably Wal-Mart will have to move to a new pricing and branding strategy. Wal-Mart is also facing negative publicity around social issues, with some activists accusing it of strong-armed reaction to unionization attempts and others criticizing its negotiation practices with suppliers. Communities, such as those in British Columbia that recently refused to allow Wal-Mart to set up operations, have also been looking into the "Wal-Mart effect" whereby smaller, locally based stores may have to go out of business shortly after Wal-Mart's arrival in an area.

But Wal-Mart's relentless drive to reduce operating costs has undoubtedly benefited consumers. According to consulting firm McKinsey & Company, Wal-Mart was single-handedly responsible for about 12 percent of the entire U.S. economy's productivity gains in the second half of the 1990s. It has forced suppliers to improve the efficiency of their operations in order to maintain profit margins while giving Wal-Mart customers lower prices each year.

One thing is clear. As long as Wal-Mart continues to keep a close eye on its cost structure and passes on this advantage to customers through low prices, consumers will continue to fill the parking lots and pass by the Wal-Mart greeter. And retailers like HBC will be playing a game of catch up—if they can continue playing the retail game in Canada at all.[2]

TEST YOURSELF

Answers to these questions can be found on our website at www.pearsoned.ca/armstrong.

1. Why does Wal-Mart work so hard to keep its supply costs as low as possible?
   a) Because the company's payroll is very large, Wal-Mart must economize elsewhere
   b) Because it frees up additional money for Wal-Mart's aggressive advertising campaigns
   c) Because it is low supply costs that allow Wal-Mart to maintain its Everyday Low Pricing (EDLP) strategy
   d) Because it saves money and therefore increases the value of Wal-Mart's shares
   e) None of the above

2. Why does Wal-Mart's EDLP strategy win against competitors who use an event-driven promotions discount strategy, even when the latter may have lower prices than Wal-Mart at times?
   a) Because consumers never know when the deep discount promotions are happening
   b) Because shoppers distrust that promotion discounts are actually sale prices and not regular prices
   c) Because the deep discounts are usually on products that consumers rarely demand
   d) Because rural buyers cannot travel to the retailers who offer promotional discounting
   e) Because a constant approach to low price positioning is more successful at establishing consistent customer relationships and loyalty

3. Why does Wal-Mart insist that suppliers be able to provide the same product at a lower price year over year?
   a) Because Wal-Mart is driven to provide increased customer value by ever lower prices
   b) Because Wal-Mart wants to use new suppliers all the time and this approach causes suppliers to drop away
   c) Because Wal-Mart believes that on the whole its suppliers are already over-charging
   d) Because Wal-Mart believes that if it doesn't lower its prices each year it will lose customers to retailers who practise promotional deep discounting
   e) Because Wal-Mart eventually wants to launch its own line of privately branded products at much lower prices

4. Why did Wal-Mart focus on the rural town market in the early days?
   a) Because they were afraid of the strong competition from established retailers in urban areas
   b) Because the rural market was unserved by most other retailers, allowing Wal-Mart to capture that market without incurring heavy advertising and competition costs
   c) Because sophisticated urban people would be less inclined to buy the low-quality prices offered by Wal-Mart
   d) Because land and buildings were cheaper to get in rural areas
   e) Because the Waltons were rural people and they wanted to serve their own first

5. Why would Wal-Mart never offer promotional discounts as well to augment its EDLP approach?
   a) Because by maintaining a consistent pricing level, Wal-Mart can forecast its revenues and clearly understand its operating budget
   b) Because it would erode the EDLP positioning of the Wal-Mart brand
   c) Because it has been shown to be a less successful strategy by other retailers
   d) Because they would need to offer too many products at below cost to make it worthwhile
   e) All of the above

Companies today face a fierce and fast-changing pricing environment. Increasing globalization and related competitive pressures have put many companies in a "pricing vice." One analyst sums it up this way: "They have virtually no pricing power. It's impossible to raise prices, and often, the pressure to slash them continues unabated." It seems that almost every company is slashing prices, and that is hurting their profits.[3]

Yet, cutting prices is often not the best answer. Reducing prices unnecessarily can lead to lost profits and damaging price wars. It can signal to customers that price is more important than brand. Instead, companies should usually "sell value, not price."[4] They should persuade customers that paying a higher price for the company's brand is justified by the greater value it delivers. The challenge is to find the price that will let the company make a fair profit by harvesting the customer value it creates.

WHAT IS A PRICE?

Price The amount of money charged for a product or service, or the sum of the values that buyers exchange for the benefits of having or using the product or service.

In the narrowest sense, **price** is the amount of money charged for a product or service. More broadly, price is the sum of all the values that buyers exchange for the benefits of having or using the product or service. Historically, price has been the major factor affecting buyer choice. However, non-price factors such as service and warranty are also an important factor in buyer-choice behaviour. So for many products, such as computers, photocopiers, and cars, pricing is more effectively measured in terms of "total cost of ownership," where the buyer considers such non-price factors as after-sales support and maintenance. When calculating total cost of ownership, buyers can truly compare the "price" of one computer vendor's offering to another's—and the least expensive sticker price often ends up being the higher one if ongoing support and maintenance costs are going to be high. Marketers such as Pitney Bowes, Canon, Xerox, and Hewlett-Packard promote the total cost of ownership approach to pricing so that buyers don't automatically migrate to less expensive, generic computer brands that may mean a lower capital investment but larger overall price down the road.

Throughout most of history, prices were set by negotiation between buyers and sellers. *Fixed price* policies—setting one price for all buyers—is a relatively modern idea that arose with the development of large-scale retailing at the end of the 19th century. Now, more than a hundred years later, many companies are reversing the fixed pricing trend. They are taking us back to an era of **dynamic pricing**—charging different prices depending on individual customers and situations (see Marketing at Work 10.1).

The Internet, corporate networks, and wireless communications are connecting sellers and buyers as was never possible before. Dynamic pricing online means that an online bookseller such as Indigo can change the price of a new bestseller immediately in response to a lower price offer by competitor Amazon.com. Websites such as Price Grabber allow consumers to compare prices quickly and easily, and online services such as Red Flag Deals and Hotels.com list and link to discounts and special offers in a directory format. As well, online auction sites such as eBay make it easy for buyers and sellers to negotiate prices on thousands of items—from collector hockey cards to backhoes and bulldozers. American travel site Priceline.com even lets customers set their own prices. Finally, new technologies allow sellers to collect detailed data about customers' buying habits, preferences—and even spending limits—so that they can tailor their products and prices.[5]

Dynamic pricing Charging different prices depending on individual customers and situations.

Marketing at Work | 10.1

Back to the Future: Dynamic Pricing on the Web

The Internet is more than simply a new "marketspace"—it's actually changing the rules of commerce.

Sellers Can . . .

Charge lower prices, reap higher margins. Web buying and selling can sometimes result in much lower costs, allowing online sellers to charge lower prices and still make higher margins. Reduced inventory and distribution costs can also add to the savings. For example, by selling made-to-order computers online, Dell Computer greatly reduces inventory costs and eliminates retail markups. It shares the savings with buyers in the form of the "lowest price per performance." Amazon.com sells thousands of items

in dozens of product categories direct to consumers, often brokering the shipment directly from manufacturers or other distributors and thus eliminating the need to handle inventory itself.

Monitor customer location and behaviour and tailor offers to individuals. When Canadian Tire first began selling merchandise online, it charged one price regardless of the location of the buyer. But problems ensued between Canadian Tire Retail and Canadian Tire's online division, as store managers complained that the website was undercutting their local promotions. Today, Canadian Tire's website asks visitors to enter their postal code, then presents prices that have been set for that geographic region.

In theory, marketers with access to databases with detailed information about each customer, including that customer's purchases, preferences, and amounts spent, could personalize pricing offers, presenting a "best price offer" to the customer each time he or she logs on. It is not known whether any online retailers actually do so, however. Furthermore, although it is perfectly legal for a retailer to charge different prices for the same good or service to different customers, the practice is likely to lead to customer complaints, should those customers discover it.

Change prices on the fly according to changes in demand or costs. Just ask online catalogue retailers such as

(continued)

Mountain Equipment Co-op (www.mec.ca) or Tilley's (www.tilley.com). With printed catalogues, a price is a price, at least until the next catalogue is printed. Online sellers, however, can change prices for specific items on a day-by-day or even hour-by-hour basis, adjusting quickly to changing costs and merchandise movement. Dell also uses dynamic online pricing. "If the price of memory or processors decreases, we pass those savings along to the customer almost in real time," says a Dell spokesperson.

Both Sellers and Buyers Can . . .

Negotiate prices in online auctions and exchanges. Suddenly the centuries-old art of haggling is back in vogue. Of the dozens of Internet auction sites, eBay and Amazon are the largest. eBay began when founder and chairman Pierre Omidyar used the Web to find a market for his girlfriend's vintage Pez dispenser collection. Now, on any given day, it lists more than 10 million items across thousands of categories, generating more than $34 billion in trades annually from a network of more than 150 million registered members. Buyers like auctions because, quite simply, they like the bargains they find. Sellers—both individuals and

companies—like auctions because, over the Internet, the cost per transaction can drop dramatically and they can quickly clear slow-moving inventory. Thus, it becomes practical and profitable to auction an item for mere dollars rather than thousands of dollars.

Buyers Can . . .

Get instant price comparisons from thousands of vendors. The Internet gives consumers unprecedented access to data about products and prices. Online comparison guides such as Price Grabber, BizRate, and Kelkoo give product and price comparisons at the click of a mouse.

Find and negotiate lower prices. With market information and access comes buyer power. In addition to finding the vendor with the best price, customers armed with price information can often negotiate lower prices. Business buyers have also learned the price advantages of shopping the Web. For example, hoping to save some money, United Technologies Corporation tried something new last year. Instead of the usual haggling with dozens of individual vendors to secure printed circuit boards for various subsidiaries worldwide, UTC

posted the contract on FreeMarkets, an online marketplace for industrial goods that was purchased by leading e-procurement player, Ariba, in 2004. To the company's delight, bids poured in from 39 suppliers, saving UTC $12 million of its initial $29 million estimate. Will dynamic pricing sweep the marketing world? "Not entirely," says *Business Week*'s Robert Hof. "It takes a lot of work to haggle—which is why fixed prices happened in the first place." However, he continues, "Pandora's E-box is now open, and pricing will never be the same. For many . . . products, millions of buyers figure a little haggling is a small price to pay for a sweet deal."

Sources: Robert D. Hof, "Going, Going, Gone," *Business Week*, April 12, 1999, pp. 30–32; Hof, "The Buyer Always Wins," *Business Week*, March 22, 1999, pp. EB26–EB28; Mui Kung, Kent B. Monroe, and Jennifer L. Cox, "Pricing on the Internet," *The Journal of Product and Brand Management*, 2002, pp. 274–287; Stephen Manes, "Off-Web Dickering," *Forbes*, April 5, 1999, p. 134; Walter Baker, Mike Marn, and Craig Zawada, "Price Smarter on the Net," *Harvard Business Review*, February 2001, pp. 122–127; Charles Fishman, "Which Price Is Right?" *Fast Company*, March 2003, pp. 92–102; Faith Keenan, "The Price Is Really Right," *Business Week*, March 31, 2003, pp. 60–67; "eBay Inc. Announces Fourth Quarter and Full Year 2004 Financial Results," eBay Press Release, Jan. 19, 2005; "Ariba and FreeMarkets Announce Strategic Merger Agreement," Ariba Press Release, Jan. 23, 2004.

In the current environment, pricing is the number one problem facing many marketing executives. Yet, many companies do not handle pricing well. One frequent problem is that companies are too quick to reduce prices in order to get a sale rather than convincing buyers that their products are worth a higher price. Other common mistakes include pricing that is too cost oriented rather than customer-value oriented and pricing that does not take the rest of the marketing mix into account.

In this chapter, we focus on the process of setting prices. We look first at the factors marketers must consider when setting prices and at general pricing approaches. Then, we examine pricing strategies for new-product pricing, product mix pricing, price adjustments for buyer and situational factors, and price changes.

FACTORS TO CONSIDER WHEN SETTING PRICES

A company's pricing decisions are affected by both internal company factors and external environmental factors (see Figure 10.1).[6]

Internal Factors Affecting Pricing Decisions

Internal factors affecting pricing include the company's marketing objectives, marketing mix strategy, costs, and organizational considerations.

Figure 10.1   Factors Affecting Pricing Decisions

Marketing Objectives Before setting price, the company must decide on its strategy for the product. If the company has selected its target market and positioning carefully, then its marketing mix strategy, including price, will be fairly straightforward. For example, when Honda and Toyota decided to develop their Acura and Lexus brands to compete with European luxury-performance cars in the higher-income segment, they had to charge a high price. In contrast, Motel 6 has positioned itself as a motel that provides economical rooms for budget-minded travellers, a position that requires charging a low price. Thus, pricing strategy is largely determined by decisions on market positioning.

At the same time, the company may seek additional general or specific objectives. General objectives include survival, current profit maximization, market share leadership, and product quality leadership. At a more specific level, a company can set prices low to prevent competition from entering the market or set prices at competitors' levels to attempt to stabilize the market. Prices can be set to keep the loyalty and support of resellers or to avoid government intervention. Prices can be reduced temporarily to create excitement for a product or to draw more customers into a retail store. One product may even be priced to help the sales of other products in the company's line. Thus, pricing may play an important role in helping to accomplish the company's objectives at many levels.

Target costing Pricing that starts with an ideal selling price, then targets costs that will ensure the price is met.

Marketing Mix Strategy Price is only one of the marketing mix tools that a company uses to achieve its marketing objectives. Price decisions must be coordinated with product design, distribution, and promotion decisions to form a consistent and effective marketing program. Decisions made for other marketing mix variables may affect pricing decisions. For example, producers using many resellers who are expected to support and promote their products may have to build larger reseller margins into their prices. The decision to position the product on high-performance quality will mean that the seller must charge a higher price to cover higher costs. If a seller wants to brand a product as being of high quality, a low price might actually lead to fewer sales, instead of more.

Companies often position their products on price and then tailor other marketing mix decisions to the prices they want to charge. Here, price is a crucial product-positioning factor that defines the product's market, competition, and design. Many firms support such price-positioning strategies with a technique called **target costing**, a potent strategic weapon. Target costing reverses the usual process of first designing a new product, determining its cost, and then asking, "Can we sell it for

Product quality leadership: Four Seasons starts with very high-quality service—"We await you with the perfect sanctuary." It then charges a price to match.

that?" Instead, it starts with an ideal selling price based on customer considerations, then targets costs that will ensure the price is met.

P&G used target costing to price and develop its highly successful Crest SpinBrush electric toothbrush:

> P&G usually prices its goods at a premium. But with Crest SpinBrush, P&G reversed its usual thinking. It started with an attractive low market price, and then found a way to make a profit at that price. SpinBrush's inventors first came up with the idea of a low-priced electric toothbrush while walking through their local Wal-Mart, where they saw Sonicare, Interplak, and other electric toothbrushes priced at more than $60. These pricy brushes held only a fraction of the overall toothbrush market. A less expensive electric toothbrush, the designers reasoned, would have huge potential. They decided on a target price of just $10, batteries included, and set out to design a brush they could sell at that price. Every design element was carefully considered with the targeted price in mind. To meet the low price, P&G passed on the usual lavish new-product launch campaign. Instead, to give SpinBrush more point-of-sale impact, it relied on "Try Me" packaging that allowed consumers to turn the brush on in stores. Target cost pricing has made Crest SpinBrush one of P&G's most successful new products ever. It has now become a best-selling toothbrush with a more than 40 percent share of the American electric toothbrush market.[7]

Other companies de-emphasize price and use other marketing mix tools to create *non-price* positions. Often, the best strategy is not to charge the lowest price, but rather to differentiate the marketing offer to make it worth a higher price. For example, Sony builds more value into its consumer electronics products and charges a higher price than many competitors. Customers recognize Sony's higher quality and are willing to pay more to get it.

Thus, marketers must consider the total marketing mix when setting prices. If the product is positioned on non-price factors, then decisions about quality, promotion, and distribution will strongly affect price. If price is a crucial positioning factor, then price will strongly affect decisions made about the other marketing mix elements. But even when featuring price, marketers need to remember that customers rarely buy on price alone. Instead, they seek products that give them the best value in terms of benefits received for the price paid.

Costs Costs set the floor for the price that the company can charge. The company wants to charge a price that both covers all its costs for producing, distributing, and selling the product, and delivers a fair rate of return for its effort and risk. A company's costs may be an important element in its pricing strategy. Many companies work to become the "low-cost producers" in their industries. Companies with lower costs can set lower prices that usually result in greater sales and profits.

Fixed costs Costs that do not vary with production or sales level.

A company's costs take two forms, fixed and variable. **Fixed costs** (also known as overhead) are costs that do not vary with production or sales level. For example, a company must pay each month's bills for rent, heat, interest, and executive salaries, regardless of the company's output. **Variable costs** vary directly with the level of production. Each personal computer produced by Compaq involves a cost of computer chips, wires, plastic, packaging, and other inputs. These costs tend to be the same for each unit produced. They are called variable because their total varies with the number of units produced. **Total costs** are the sum of the fixed and variable costs for any given level of production. Management wants to charge a price that will at least cover the total costs.

Variable costs Costs that vary directly with the level of production.

Total costs The sum of the fixed and variable costs for any given level of production.

The company must watch its costs carefully. If it costs the company more than it costs competitors to produce and sell its product, the company will have to charge a higher price or make less profit, putting it at a competitive disadvantage, especially in the longer term.

Organizational Considerations Management must decide who within the organization should set prices. Companies handle pricing in a variety of ways. In small companies, prices are often set by top management rather than by the marketing or sales departments. In large companies, pricing is typically handled by divisional or product-line managers. In industrial markets, salespeople may be allowed to negotiate with customers within certain price ranges. Even so, top management normally sets the pricing objectives and policies, and it often approves the prices proposed by lower-level management or salespeople.

In industries in which pricing is a key factor (aerospace, steel, railroads, oil companies), companies often have a pricing department to set the best prices or help others in setting them. This department reports to the marketing department or top management. Others who have an influence on pricing include sales managers, production managers, finance managers, and accountants. The growth of information technology has empowered junior managers to set pricing in real time without as much need for executive approval. The dynamic prices can be immediately monitored and can be quickly changed if the objectives of the pricing strategy are not being met.

External Factors Affecting Pricing Decisions

External factors that affect pricing decisions include the nature of the market and demand, competition, and other environmental elements.

The Market and Demand Whereas costs set the lower limit of prices, the market and demand set the upper limit. Both consumer and industrial buyers balance the price of a product or service against the benefits of owning it. Thus, before setting prices, the marketer must understand the relationship between price and demand for its product. In this section, we explain how the price–demand relationship varies for different types of markets and how buyer perceptions of price affect the pricing decision. We then discuss methods for measuring the price–demand relationship.

Pricing in Different Types of Markets. The seller's pricing freedom varies with different types of markets. Economists recognize four main types of markets, each presenting a different pricing challenge.

Under *pure competition*, the market consists of many buyers and sellers trading in a uniform commodity such as wheat, copper, or financial securities. No single buyer or seller has much effect on the going market price. A seller cannot charge more than the going price, because buyers can obtain as much as they need at this price. Nor would sellers charge less than the market price, because they can sell all they want at this price. If price and profits rise, new sellers can easily enter the market. In a purely competitive market, marketing research, product development, pricing, advertising, and sales promotion play little or no role. Thus, sellers in these markets do not spend much time on marketing strategy.

Under *monopolistic competition*, the market consists of many buyers and sellers who trade over a range of prices rather than a single market price. A range of prices occurs because sellers can differentiate their offers to buyers. Either the physical product can be varied in quality, features, or styles, or the accompanying services can be varied. Buyers see differences in sellers' products and will pay different prices for them. Sellers try to develop differentiated offers for different customer segments and, in addition to price, freely use branding, advertising, and personal selling to set their offers apart. For example, Kinko's differentiates its offer through strong branding and advertising, reducing the impact of price. Because there are many competitors in such markets, each firm is less affected by competitors' pricing strategies than in oligopolistic markets.

Under *oligopolistic competition*, the market consists of a few sellers who are highly sensitive to each other's pricing and marketing strategies. The product can be uniform

Monopolistic competition: Bick's sets its pickles apart from other brands by using both price and nonprice factors.

(steel, aluminum) or non-uniform (cars, computers). There are few sellers because it is difficult for new sellers to enter the market. Each seller is alert to competitors' strategies and moves. If a steel company slashes its price by 10 percent, buyers will quickly switch to this supplier. The other steelmakers must respond by lowering their prices or increasing their services.

In a *pure monopoly*, the market consists of one seller. The seller may be a government monopoly (Canada Post), a private regulated monopoly (a power company like BC hydro), or a private non-regulated monopoly (DuPont when it introduced nylon). Pricing is handled differently in each case. In a regulated monopoly, the government permits the company to set rates that will yield a "fair return," one that will let the company maintain and expand its operations as needed. Non-regulated monopolies are free to price at what the market will bear. However, they do not always charge the full price for a number of reasons: a desire not to attract competition, a desire to penetrate the market faster with a low price, or a fear of increased government regulation.

Perceptions of Price and Value. In the end, the buyer will decide whether a product's price is right. Pricing decisions, like other marketing mix decisions, must be buyer oriented. When people buy a product, they exchange something of value (the price) to get something of value (the benefits of having or using the product). Effective, buyer-oriented pricing involves understanding how much value customers place on the benefits they receive from the product and setting a price that fits this value.

A company often finds it hard to measure the values customers will attach to its product. For example, calculating the cost of ingredients in a meal at a fancy restaurant is relatively easy. But assigning a value to other satisfactions such as taste, environment, relaxation, conversation, and status is more difficult. And these values will vary both for different consumers and different situations. Still, people will use these values to evaluate a product's price. If customers perceive that the price is greater than the product's value, they will not buy the product. If they perceive that the price is below the product's value, they will buy it, but the seller loses profit opportunities.

Analyzing the Price–Demand Relationship. Each price the company might charge will lead to a different level of demand. The relationship between the price charged and the resulting demand level is shown in the demand curve in Figure 10.2. The **demand curve** shows the number of units the market will buy in a given time period at different prices that might be charged. In the normal case, demand and price are inversely related; that is, the higher the price, the lower the demand. Thus, the company would sell less if it

Demand curve A curve that shows the number of units the market will buy in a given time period at different prices that might be charged.

Figure 10.2   Demand Curve

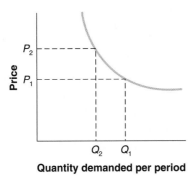

raised its price from P_1 to P_2. In short, buyers with limited budgets will probably buy less of something if its price is too high.

In the case of prestige goods, the demand curve sometimes slopes upward. Consumers usually believe that higher prices mean better quality. For example, Gibson Guitar Corporation recently toyed with the idea of lowering its prices to compete more effectively with Japanese rivals such as Yamaha and Ibanez. To its surprise, Gibson found that its instruments didn't sell as well at lower prices. "We had an inverse [price–demand relationship]," noted Gibson's chief executive officer. "The more we charged, the more product we sold." At a time when other guitar manufacturers have chosen to build their instruments more quickly, cheaply, and in greater numbers, Gibson still promises guitars that "are made one at a time, by hand. No shortcuts. No substitutions." It turns out that low prices simply aren't consistent with "Gibson's century-old tradition of creating investment-quality instruments that represent the highest standards of imaginative design and masterful craftsmanship."[8] Still, if the company charges too high a price, the level of demand will be lower.

Most companies try to measure their demand curves by estimating demand at different prices. The type of market makes a difference. In a monopoly, the demand curve shows the total market demand resulting from different prices. If the company faces competition, its demand at different prices will depend on whether competitors' prices stay constant or change with the company's own prices.

Price elasticity A measure of the sensitivity of demand to changes in price.

Price Elasticity of Demand. Marketers also need to know **price elasticity**—how responsive demand will be to a change in price. If demand hardly changes with a small change in price, we say demand is *inelastic.* If demand changes greatly, we say the demand is *elastic.* For example, demand for gasoline is inelastic—when the price of gas decreases, not many people will buy more gas; when the price of gas increases, not many people will stop buying gas since they still need it to travel by car. International vacation packages are an example of elastic demand—when the price goes up, a lot of people will

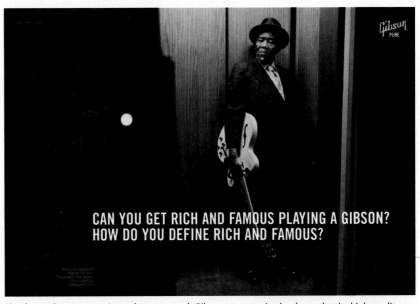

The demand curve sometimes slopes upward: Gibson was surprised to learn that its high-quality instruments didn't sell as well at lower prices.

decide to choose a less expensive domestic travel option instead; when the price goes down, purchases of international vacation packages will increase significantly.

What determines the price elasticity of demand? Buyers are less price sensitive when the product they are buying is unique or when it is high in quality, prestige, or exclusiveness. They are also less price sensitive when substitute products are hard to find or when they cannot easily compare the quality of substitutes. Finally, buyers are less price sensitive when the total expenditure for a product is low relative to their income or when the cost is shared by another party.[9]

If demand is elastic rather than inelastic, sellers will consider lowering their price. A lower price will produce more total revenue. This practice is effective as long as the extra costs of producing and selling more do not exceed the extra revenue. At the same time, most firms want to avoid pricing that turns their products into commodities—undifferentiated offerings purchased primarily on price. In recent years, forces such as deregulation and the instant price comparisons afforded by the Internet and other technologies have increased consumer price sensitivity, turning products ranging from telephones and computers to new automobiles into commodities in consumers' eyes. Marketers need to work harder than ever to differentiate their offerings when a dozen competitors are selling virtually the same product at a comparable or lower price. More than ever, companies need to understand the price sensitivity of their customers and prospects and the trade-offs people are willing to make between price and product characteristics. In the words of marketing consultant Kevin Clancy, those who target only the price sensitive are "leaving money on the table."

Competitors' Costs, Prices, and Offers Another external factor affecting the company's pricing decisions is competitors' costs and prices and possible competitor reactions to the company's own pricing moves. A consumer who is considering the purchase of a Sony digital camera will evaluate Sony's price and value against the prices and values of comparable products made by Nikon, Kodak, and others. In addition, the company's pricing strategy may affect the nature of the competition it faces. Air Canada has been accused by its rivals, such as WestJet and Transat, of using price to drive them out of the market. To defend itself, Air Canada needed to benchmark its costs and value against competitors' costs and value. It was then able to use these benchmarks as a starting point for its own pricing.

Other External Factors When setting prices, the company must also consider other factors in its external environment. *Economic conditions* can have a strong impact on the

---

IN-CLASS NOTES

Demand and Elasticity

- **Demand** – The relationship between price changes and the number of units sold
- **Elasticity** – A way of measuring how sensitive the market is to price changes
  - **Inelastic** – Minimal change in demand as price increases
  - **Elastic** – Significant drop in demand as price increases

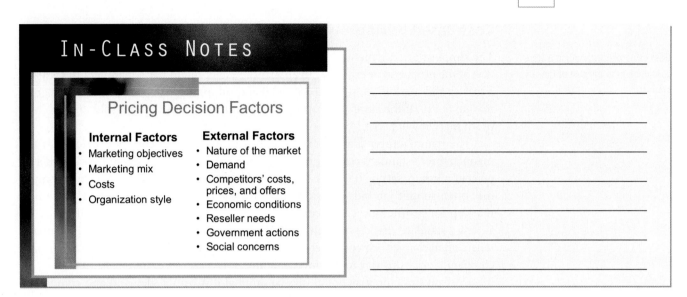

firm's pricing strategies. Economic factors such as boom or recession, inflation, and interest rates affect pricing decisions because they affect both the costs of producing a product and market perceptions of the product's price and value. The company must also consider what impact its prices will have on other parties in its environment. How will *resellers* react to various prices? The company should set prices that give resellers a fair profit, encourage their support, and help them to sell the product effectively. The *government* is another important external influence on pricing decisions. Finally, *social concerns* may have to be taken into account. In setting prices, a company's short-term sales, market share, and profit goals may have to be tempered by broader societal considerations.

GENERAL PRICING APPROACHES

The price the company charges will be somewhere between one that is too low to produce a profit and one that is too high to produce any demand. Figure 10.3 summarizes the major considerations in setting price. Product costs set a floor to the price; market perceptions of the product's value set the ceiling. The company must consider competitors' prices and other external and internal factors to find the best price between these two extremes.

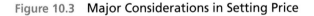

Figure 10.3   Major Considerations in Setting Price

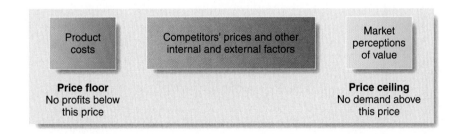

Companies set prices by selecting a general pricing approach that includes one or more of these three sets of factors. We will examine the following approaches: the *cost-based approach* (cost-plus pricing, break-even analysis, and target profit pricing), the *buyer-based approach* (value-based pricing), and the *competition-based approach* (going-rate and sealed-bid pricing).

Cost-Based Pricing

Cost-plus pricing Adding a standard markup to the cost of the product.

The simplest pricing method is **cost-plus pricing**—adding a standard markup to the cost of the product. For example, an appliance retailer might pay a manufacturer $20 for a toaster and mark it up to sell at $30, a 50 percent markup on cost. The retailer's gross margin is $10. If the store's operating costs amount to $8 per toaster sold, the retailer's profit margin will be $2.

The manufacturer that made the toaster probably used cost-plus pricing. If the manufacturer's standard cost of producing the toaster was $16, it might have added a 25 percent markup, setting the price to the retailers at $20. Similarly, construction companies often submit job bids by estimating the total project cost and adding a standard markup for profit. Lawyers, accountants, and other professionals typically price by adding a standard markup to their costs. Where costs are difficult to accurately estimate, sellers often charge their customers cost plus a specified markup; for example, aerospace companies price this way to the government.

Cost-plus pricing may not always be optimal if it ignores demand and competitor prices; however, this pricing approach remains popular and effective in many sectors. One advantage is that sellers are more certain about costs than about demand, and so markup-based pricing is less risky. By tying the price to cost, sellers also simplify pricing—they do not have to make frequent adjustments as demand changes. Another advantage is that when all firms in the industry use this pricing method, prices tend to be similar, and price competition is thus minimized. Finally, many people feel that cost-plus pricing is fairer to both buyers and sellers. Sellers earn a fair return on their investment but do not take advantage of buyers when buyers' demand becomes great.

Break-even pricing (target profit pricing) Setting price to break even on the costs of making and marketing a product; or setting price to make a target profit.

Another cost-oriented pricing approach is **break-even pricing**, or a variation called target profit pricing. The firm tries to determine the price at which it will break even or make the target profit it is seeking. Target pricing uses the concept of a *break-even chart*, which shows the total cost and total revenue expected at different sales volume levels. Figure 10.4 shows a break-even chart for the toaster manufacturer discussed here. Here, fixed costs are $300 000 regardless of sales volume, and variable costs are $10 per unit. Variable costs are added to fixed costs to form total costs, which rise with each unit sold. The slope of the total revenue curve reflects the price. Here, the price is $20 (for example, the company's revenue is $1 million on 50 000 units, or $20 per unit).

Figure 10.4   Break-Even Chart for Determining Target Price

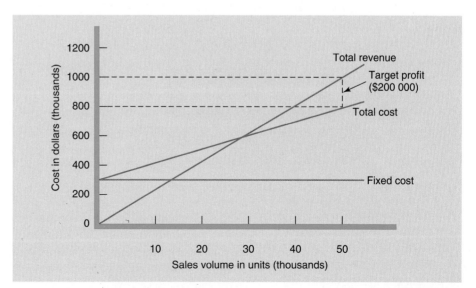

At the $20 price, the company must sell at least 30 000 units to *break even*—that is, at this level, total revenues will equal total costs of $600 000. If the company wants a target profit of $200 000, it must sell at least 50 000 units to obtain the $1 million of total revenue needed to cover the costs of $800 000 plus the $200 000 of target profits. In contrast, if the company charges a higher price, say $25, it will not need to sell as many units to break even or to achieve its target profit. In fact, the higher the price, the lower the company's break-even point will be.

However, as the *price* increases, *demand* decreases, and the market may not buy even the lower volume needed to break even at the higher price. Much depends on the relationship between price and demand. For example, suppose the company calculates that given its current fixed and variable costs, it must charge a price of $30 for the product in order to earn its desired target profit. But marketing research shows that few buyers will pay more than $25. In this case, the company will have to trim its costs in order to lower the break-even point so that it can charge the lower price customers expect.

Thus, although break-even analysis and target profit pricing can help the company determine minimum prices needed to cover expected costs and profits, they do not take the price–demand relationship into account. When using this method, the company must also consider the impact of price on sales volume needed to realize target profits and the likelihood that the needed volume will be achieved at each possible price.

Value-Based Pricing

An increasing number of companies are basing their prices on the product's perceived value. **Value-based pricing** uses buyers' perceptions of value, not the seller's cost, as the key to pricing. Value-based pricing means that the marketer cannot design a product and marketing program and then set the price. Price is considered along with the other marketing mix variables *before* the marketing program is set.

Value-based pricing Setting price based on buyers' perceptions of value rather than on the seller's cost.

Figure 10.5 compares cost-based pricing with value-based pricing. Cost-based pricing is product driven. The company designs what it considers to be a good product, totals the costs of making the product, and sets a price that covers costs plus a target profit. Marketing must then convince buyers that the product's value at that price justifies its purchase. If the price turns out to be too high, the company must settle for lower markups or lower sales, both resulting in disappointing profits.

Value-based pricing reverses this process. The company sets its target price based on customer perceptions of the product value. The targeted value and price then drive decisions about product design and what costs can be incurred. As a result, pricing begins

Figure 10.5 Cost-Based Versus Value-Based Pricing

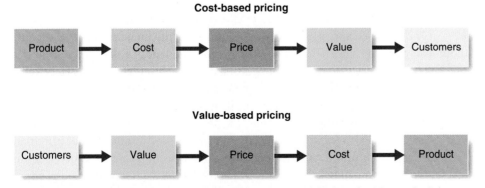

Source: Thomas T. Nagle and Reed K. Holden, *The Strategy and Tactics of Pricing*, 3rd ed. (Upper Saddle River, NJ: Prentice Hall, 2002), p. 4.

A Steinway takes you places you've never been.

Call 1-800-346-5086 for a complimentary color catalog and the name of your nearest Steinway dealer. Or visit us at www.steinway.com

Perceived value: A less expensive piano might play well, but would it take you places you've never been?

Value pricing Offering just the right combination of quality and good service at a fair price.

Everyday low pricing (EDLP) Charging a constant, everyday low price with few or no temporary discounts.

with analyzing consumer needs and value perceptions, and the price is set to match consumers' perceived value. It's important to remember that "good value" is not the same as "low price." For example, a Steinway piano sells at a higher price than many competing brands. But to those who buy one, it's a great value. For them, as a recent ad proclaims, "a Steinway takes you places you've never been."

A company using value-based pricing must find out what value buyers assign to different competitive offers. However, measuring perceived value can be difficult. Sometimes, companies conduct market research to find out what price the target market is willing to pay for a basic product and for each benefit added to the offer. Or a company might conduct experiments to test the perceived value of different product offers.

During the past decade, marketers have noted a fundamental shift in people's attitudes toward price and quality. Many companies have changed their pricing approaches to bring them into line with changing economic conditions and consumer price perceptions. More and more, marketers have adopted **value pricing** strategies—offering just the right combination of quality and good service at a fair price. In many cases, this has involved introducing less expensive versions of established, brand name products. Campbell introduced its Great Starts Budget frozen-food line, Holiday Inn opened several Holiday Express budget hotels, Holt Renfrew launched an extensive private label line, offered at prices less than designer brands, and fast-food restaurants such as Taco Bell and McDonald's offered "value menus." In other cases, value pricing has involved redesigning existing brands to offer more quality for a given price or the same quality for less.

An important type of value pricing at the retail level is **everyday low pricing (EDLP)**. EDLP involves charging a constant, everyday low price with few or no temporary price discounts. In contrast, *high-low pricing* involves charging higher prices on an everyday basis but running frequent promotions to lower prices temporarily on selected items. Employing the EDLP strategy has proven to be enormously successful for Wal-Mart; however, when Eatons tried the same approach to pricing in the late 1990s, it eventually led to the company's demise.

In many marketing situations, the challenge is to build the company's *pricing power*—its power to escape price competition and to justify higher prices and margins without losing market share. To do this, many companies adopt *value-added* strategies. Rather than cutting prices to match competitors, they attach value-added services to differentiate their offers and thus support higher margins (see Marketing at Work 10.2). Cake Beauty, for example, differentiates itself by using high-quality ingredients and pretty packaging and by adding personal touches to products in the form of handwritten notes. These extra features allow Cake to price its products at a higher price than generic or drug-store products. With growing globalization, however, differentiation strategies are becoming increasingly difficult for incumbents as shoppers find products with similar quality yet significantly lower prices from companies operating in lower-cost environments.

Marketing at Work   10.2

Pricing Power: The Value of Value-Added

When a company finds its major competitors offering a similar product at a lower price, the natural tendency is to try to match or beat that price. While the idea of undercutting competitors' prices and watching customers flock to you is tempting, there are dangers. Successive rounds of price cutting can lead to price wars that erode the profit margins of all competitors in an industry. Or worse, discounting a product can cheapen it in the minds of customers, greatly reducing the seller's power to maintain profitable prices in the long term. "It ends up being a losing battle," notes one marketing executive. "You focus away from quality, service, prestige—the things brands are all about."

So, how can a company keep its pricing power when a competitor undercuts its price? Often, the best strategy is not to price below the competitor, but rather to price above and convince customers that the product is worth it. The company should ask, "What is the value of the product to the customer?" and then stand up for what the product is worth. In this way, the company shifts the focus from price to value.

Caterpillar is a master at charging premium prices for its heavy construction and mining equipment and convincing customers that its products and service justify every additional cent—or, rather, the extra tens of thousands of dollars. Caterpillar typically reaps a 20 to 30 percent price premium over competitors. When a

large potential customer says "I can get it for less from a competitor," rather than discounting the price, the Caterpillar dealer explains that, even at the higher price, Cat offers the best value. Caterpillar equipment is designed with modular components that can be removed and repaired quickly, minimizing machine downtime. Caterpillar dealers carry an extensive parts inventory and guarantee delivery within 48 hours anywhere in the world, again minimizing downtime. Cat's products are designed to be rebuilt, providing a second life that competitors cannot match. As a result, Caterpillar used-equipment prices are often 20 percent to 30 percent higher.

And most customers seem to agree with Caterpillar's value proposition—the company dominates its markets, with a more than 40 percent worldwide market share.

Sources: Jim Morgan, "Value Added: From Cliché to the Real Thing," *Purchasing,* April 3, 1997, pp. 59–61; James E. Ellis, John Jesitus, "Close Connections," *Industry Week,* October 6, 1997, pp. 28–34; James C. Anderson and James A. Narus, "Business Marketing: Understand What Customers Value," *Harvard Business Review,* November–December 1998, pp. 53–65; Tom Nagle, "How to Pull It Off," *Across the Board,* March 1999, pp. 53–56; Robert B. Tucker, "Adding Value Profitably," *American Salesman,* April 2001, pp. 17–20; Erin Stout, "Keep Them Coming Back for More," *Sales & Marketing Management,* February 2002, pp. 51–52; Pioneer website, www.pioneer.com, accessed July 2002.

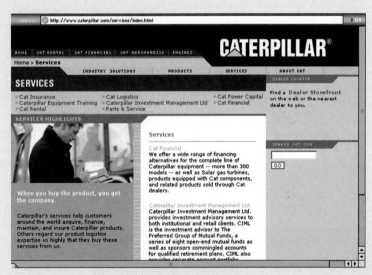

Value added: Caterpillar offers its dealers a wide range of value-added services—from guaranteed parts delivery to investment management advice and equipment training. Such added value supports a higher price.

Competition-Based Pricing

Buyers will base their judgments of a product's value on the prices that competitors charge for similar products. One form of **competition-based pricing** is *going-rate pricing,* in which a firm bases its price largely on competitors' prices, with less attention paid to its own costs or to demand. The firm might charge the same as, more than, or less than its major competitors. In oligopolistic industries that sell a commodity such as steel, paper, or fertilizer, firms normally charge the same price. The smaller firms follow

Competition-based pricing
Setting prices based on the prices that competitors charge for similar products.

Linking the Concepts

The concept of value is critical to good pricing and to successful marketing in general. Take a minute to be certain that you appreciate what value really means.

- A few years ago, Buick pitched its top-of-the-line Park Avenue model as "the best car value." Does this fit with your idea of value?
- Pick two competing brands from a familiar product category (watches, perfume, consumer electronics, restaurants)—one low priced and the other high priced. Which, if either, offers the greatest value?
- Does "value" mean the same thing as "low price"? How do these concepts differ?

the leader: They change their prices when the market leader's prices change, rather than when their own demand or costs change. Some firms may charge a bit more or less, but they hold the amount of difference constant. Thus, minor gasoline retailers usually charge a few cents less than the major oil companies, without letting the difference increase or decrease.

Going-rate pricing is quite popular. When demand elasticity is hard to measure, firms feel that the going price represents the collective wisdom of the industry concerning the price that will yield a fair return. They also feel that holding to the going price will prevent harmful price wars.

Competition-based pricing is also used in a business-to-business setting when firms *bid* for jobs. Using *sealed-bid pricing,* a firm bases its price on how it thinks competitors will price rather than on its own costs or on the demand. The firm wants to win a contract, and winning the contract requires pricing lower than other firms. Yet the firm cannot set its price below a certain level. It cannot price below cost without harming its position. In contrast, the higher the company sets its price above its costs, the lower its chance of getting the contract.

No matter what general pricing approach the company uses, pricing decisions are subject to an incredibly complex array of environmental and competitive forces. A company sets not a single price, but rather a pricing structure that covers different items in its line. This pricing structure changes over time as products move through their life cycles.

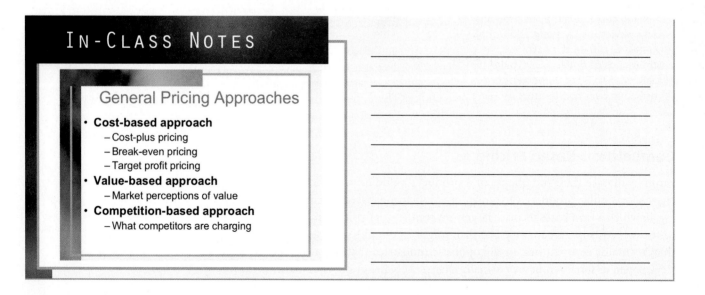

IN-CLASS NOTES

General Pricing Approaches

- **Cost-based approach**
  - Cost-plus pricing
  - Break-even pricing
  - Target profit pricing
- **Value-based approach**
  - Market perceptions of value
- **Competition-based approach**
  - What competitors are charging

The company adjusts product prices to reflect changes in costs and demand and to account for variations in buyers and situations. As the competitive environment changes, the company considers when to initiate price changes and when to respond to them.

We now examine the major dynamic pricing strategies available to management. In turn, we look at *new-product pricing strategies* for products in the introductory stage of the product life cycle, *product mix pricing strategies* for related products in the product mix, *price-adjustment strategies* that account for customer differences and changing situations, and strategies for initiating and responding to *price changes*.[10]

NEW-PRODUCT PRICING STRATEGIES

Pricing strategies usually change as the product passes through its life cycle. The introductory stage is especially challenging. Companies bringing out a new product face the challenge of setting prices for the first time. They can choose between two broad strategies: *market-skimming pricing* and *market-penetration pricing*.

Market-Skimming Pricing

Many companies that invent new products use **market-skimming pricing**, where they set high prices initially to "skim" revenues layer by layer from the market. For example, when York University's Schulich School of Business joined forces with Northwestern University to offer a new MBA program, it used market-skimming pricing. Sony frequently uses this strategy. When it introduced the world's first high-definition television (HDTV) to the Japanese market in 1990, the high-tech sets cost $52 000. These televisions were purchased only by customers who could afford to pay a high price for the new technology. Sony rapidly reduced the price over the next several years to attract new buyers. By 1993, a 28-inch HDTV cost a Japanese buyer just over $7000. In 2001, a Japanese consumer could buy a 40-inch HDTV for about $2400, a price that many more customers could afford. An entry-level HDTV set now sells for just $1000 in the United States. In this way, Sony skimmed the maximum amount of revenue from the various segments of the market.[11]

Market skimming makes sense only under certain conditions. First, the product's quality and image must support its higher price, and enough buyers must want the product at that price. Second, the costs of producing a smaller volume cannot be so high that they cancel the advantage of charging more. Finally, competitors should not be able to enter the market easily and undercut the high price.

Market-skimming pricing Setting a high price for a new product to skim maximum revenues layer by layer from the segments willing to pay the high price; the company makes fewer but more profitable sales.

Market-Penetration Pricing

Rather than setting a high initial price to skim off small but profitable market segments, some companies use **market-penetration pricing**. They set a low initial price in order to *penetrate* the market quickly and deeply—to attract a large number of buyers quickly and win a large market share. The high sales volume results in falling costs, allowing the company to cut its price even further. For example, Wal-Mart used penetration pricing to rapidly expand its network of stores and become the world's largest retailer. And Dell used penetration pricing to enter the personal computer market, selling high-quality computer products through lower-cost direct channels. Its sales soared when IBM, Apple, and other competitors selling through retail stores could not match its prices.

Several conditions must be met for this low-price strategy to work. First, the market must be highly price sensitive so that a low price produces more market growth. Second, production and distribution costs must fall as sales volume increases. Finally, the low

Market-penetration pricing Setting a low price for a new product in order to attract a large number of buyers and a large market share.

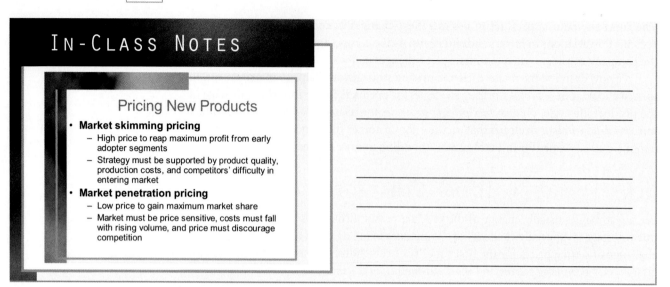

IN-CLASS NOTES

Pricing New Products

- **Market skimming pricing**
  - High price to reap maximum profit from early adopter segments
  - Strategy must be supported by product quality, production costs, and competitors' difficulty in entering market
- **Market penetration pricing**
  - Low price to gain maximum market share
  - Market must be price sensitive, costs must fall with rising volume, and price must discourage competition

price must help keep out the competition, and the penetration pricing organization must maintain its low-price position—otherwise, the price advantage may be only temporary. For example, Dell faced difficult times when IBM and other competitors established their own direct distribution channels. However, through its dedication to low production and distribution costs, Dell has retained its price advantage and established itself as the industry's number one personal computer maker.

PRODUCT MIX PRICING STRATEGIES

The strategy for setting a product's price often has to be changed when the product is part of a product mix. In this case, the firm looks for a set of prices that maximizes the profits on the total product mix. Pricing is difficult because the various products have related demand and costs and face different degrees of competition. We now take a closer look at five product mix pricing situations: product line pricing, optional-product pricing, *product bundle pricing*, *captive-product pricing*, and *by-product pricing*.

Product Line Pricing

Companies usually develop product lines rather than single products. For example, Toro makes many different lawn mowers, ranging from simple walk-behind versions priced at $259.95, $299.95, and $399.95, to elaborate riding mowers and lawn tractors priced at $1000 or more. Each successive lawn mower in the line offers more features. Sony offers not just one type of television, but several lines of televisions, each containing many models. It offers everything from Watchman portable colour TVs starting at $119.95, to flat-screen Trinitrons ranging from $200 to $1500, to its top-of-the-line plasma WEGA flat-panel sets running from $3000 to $5000. And Gramophone makes a complete line of high-quality sound systems, ranging in price from $6000 to $150 000. Notes the company, "Mozart sacrificed his life to create beautiful music. Surely you can afford $10,000." In **product line pricing**, management must decide on the price steps to set between the various products in a line.

Product line pricing Setting the price steps between various products in a product line based on cost differences between the products, customer evaluations of different features, and competitors' prices.

The price steps should take into account cost differences between the products in the line, customer evaluations of their different features, and competitors' prices. In many industries, sellers use well-established *price points* for the products in their line. Thus, men's clothing stores might carry men's suits at three price levels: $185, $325, and $495. The customer will probably associate low-, average-, and high-quality suits with the three price points. Even if the three prices are raised a little, men normally will buy suits at their own preferred price points. The seller's task is to establish perceived quality differences that support the price differences.

Optional-Product Pricing

Many companies use **optional-product pricing**—offering to sell optional or accessory products along with their main product. For example, a car buyer may choose to order power windows, cruise control, and a CD changer. Refrigerators come with optional ice makers.

> **Optional-product pricing** The pricing of optional or accessory products along with a main product.

Pricing these options is a sticky problem. Automobile companies have to decide which items to include in the base price and which to offer as options. Until recent years, General Motors' normal pricing strategy was to advertise a stripped-down model at a base price to pull people into showrooms and then to devote most of the showroom space to showing option-loaded cars at higher prices. The economy model was stripped of so many comforts and conveniences that most buyers rejected it. Then, GM and other North American car makers followed the example of the Japanese and German automakers and included in the sticker price many useful items previously sold only as options. Most advertised prices today represent a well-equipped car. However, during periods of economic downturn, auto companies often move some features back into the "options" category in order to reduce the prices of standard models.

Product Bundle Pricing

Using **product bundle pricing**, sellers often combine several of their products and offer the bundle at a reduced price. For example, theatres and sports teams sell season tickets at less than the cost of single tickets; hotels sell specially priced weekend packages that include room, meals, and entertainment; computer makers include attractive software packages with their personal computers; and Internet service providers sell packages that include Web access, Web hosting, email, and an Internet search program. Some marketers price bundle the offerings of other organizations. For example, Telus and Rogers bundle various combinations of wireless phone and Internet services to provide consumers with an overall lower price. Price bundling can promote the sales of products consumers might not otherwise buy, but the combined price must be low enough to get them to buy the bundle.[12]

> **Product bundle pricing** Combining several products and offering the bundle at a reduced price.
>
> **Captive-product pricing** Setting a price for products that must be used along with a main product, such as blades for a razor and film for a camera.

Captive-Product Pricing

Companies that make products that must be used along with a main product are using **captive-product pricing**. Examples of captive products are razor blades, camera film, video games, and printer cartridges. Producers of the main products (razors, cameras, video game consoles, and printers) often price them low and set high markups on the supplies. Thus, Gillette sells low-priced razors but makes money on the replacement cartridges. U-Haul rents out trucks at low rates but commands high margins on accessories such as boxes, pads, insurance, and storage space rental. HP makes very low margins on its printers but very high margins on printer cartridges and other supplies. Captive products are almost always highly consumable and must be purchased constantly in order to make the original product useable.

Captive product pricing: Makers of game consoles such as Microsoft's X-box make significantly higher profit margins on the "captive" products, such as the games

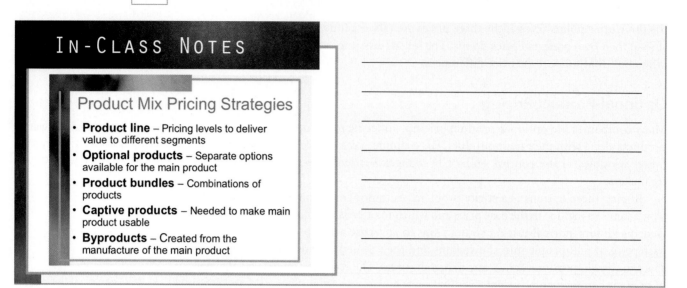

Nintendo sells its game consoles at low prices and makes money on video games. In fact, whereas Nintendo's margins on its consoles run a mere 1 to 5 percent, margins on its game cartridges run close to 45 percent. Video game sales contribute more than half of the company's profits. Similarly, Sony loses money on sales of its PlayStation 2 game console. But the games themselves, while accounting for only 17 percent of sales, generate more than a third of Sony's profits.[13]

In the case of services, this strategy is called *two-part pricing*. The price of the service is broken into a *fixed fee* plus a *variable usage rate*. Thus, amusement parks charge admission plus fees for food, midway attractions, and rides over a minimum. Theatres charge admission, then generate additional revenues from concessions. And cell phone companies charge a flat rate for a basic calling plan, then charge for minutes over what the plan allows. The service firm must decide how much to charge for the basic service and how much for the variable usage. The fixed amount should be low enough to induce use of the service; profit can be made on the variable fees.

Byproduct Pricing

In producing processed meats, petroleum products, chemicals, and other products, there are often byproducts. If the byproducts have no value and if getting rid of them is costly, this will affect the pricing of the main product. Using **byproduct pricing**, the manufacturer will seek a market for these byproducts and should accept any price that covers more than the cost of storing and delivering them.

Byproduct pricing Setting a price for byproducts in order to make the main product's price more competitive.

Byproducts can even turn out to be profitable. For example, many lumber mills sell bark chips and sawdust profitably as decorative mulch for home and commercial landscaping. EcoStrat, a consulting firm in Canada, takes the idea further. The firm partnered with WoodworkingSite.com to give wood product companies a place to sell their chips, shavings, dust, and other byproducts. To find buyers, a manufacturer can log on to WoodworkingSite.com, answer a few questions, and hit "send." EcoStrat does the rest.[14]

PRICE-ADJUSTMENT STRATEGIES

Companies usually adjust their basic prices to account for various market differences and changing situations. Here we examine the six price adjustment strategies: *discount and allowance pricing, segmented pricing, psychological pricing, promotional pricing, geographical pricing*, and *international pricing*.

Discount and Allowance Pricing

Most companies adjust their basic price to reward customers for certain responses, such as early payment of bills, volume purchases, and off-season buying. These price adjustments—called *discounts* and *allowances*—can take many forms.

The many forms of discounts include a cash **discount**, a price reduction to buyers who pay their bills promptly. A typical example is "2/10, net 30," which means that although payment is due within 30 days, the buyer can deduct 2 percent if the bill is paid within 10 days. A *quantity discount* is a price reduction to buyers who buy large volumes. A typical example might be "$10 per unit for less than 100 units, $9 per unit for 100 or more units." Such discounts provide an incentive to the customer to buy more from one given seller rather than from many different sources.

A *functional discount* (also called a *trade discount*) is offered by the seller to trade-channel members who perform certain functions, such as selling, storing, and record keeping. A *seasonal discount* is a price reduction to buyers who buy merchandise or services out of season. For example, lawn and garden equipment manufacturers offer seasonal discounts to retailers during the fall and winter months to encourage early ordering in anticipation of the heavy spring and summer selling seasons. Seasonal discounts allow the seller to keep production steady during an entire year.

Allowances are another type of reduction from the list price. For example, *trade-in allowances* are price reductions given for turning in an old item when buying a new one. Trade-in allowances are most common in the automobile industry but are also given for other durable goods. *Promotional allowances* are payments or price reductions to reward dealers for participating in advertising and sales support programs.

Discount A straight reduction in price on purchases during a stated period of time.

Allowance Promotional money paid by manufacturers to retailers in return for an agreement to feature the manufacturer's products in some way.

Segmented Pricing

Companies will often adjust their basic prices to allow for differences in customers, products, and locations. In **segmented pricing**, the company sells a product or service at two or more prices, even though the difference in prices is not based on differences in costs.

Segmented pricing takes several forms. Under *customer-segment pricing*, different customers pay different prices for the same product or service. Museums, for example, may charge a lower admission for students and senior citizens. Under *product-form pricing*, different versions of the product are priced differently but not according to differences in their costs. For instance, the most expensive Black & Decker iron is priced at $64.95, which is $15 more than the price of the next most expensive Black & Decker iron. The top model has a self-cleaning feature, yet this extra feature costs only a few more dollars to make.

Using *location pricing*, a company charges different prices for different locations, even though the cost of offering each location is the same. For instance, theatres vary their seat prices because of audience preferences for certain locations, and universities and colleges charge higher tuition for out-of-country students. Finally, using *time pricing*, a firm varies its price by the season, the month, the day, and even the hour. Some public utilities vary their prices to commercial users by time of day and weekend versus weekday. Resorts give weekend and seasonal discounts.

For segmented pricing to be effective, certain conditions must exist. It must be possible to segment the market, and the segments must show differences of degree of demand. Members of the segment paying the lower price should not be able to turn around and resell the product to the segment paying a higher price. Competitors should not be able to undersell the firm in the segment being charged the higher price. Nor should the costs of segmenting and watching the market exceed the extra revenue obtained from the price difference. The segmented pricing must also be legal. And given

Segmented pricing Selling a product or service at two or more prices, where the difference in prices is not based on differences in costs.

our focus on the long-term relationships with customers, the price difference should reflect real differences in customers' perceived value. Otherwise, in the long run, the practice will lead to customer ill-will.

Segmented pricing and yield management aren't really new ideas. For instance, Marriott Corporation used "seat-of-the-pants" yield-management approaches long before it installed its current sophisticated system.

> Back when Bill Marriott was a young man working at the family's first hotel, the Twin Bridges in Washington, D.C., he sold rooms from a drive-up window. As Bill tells it, the hotel charged a flat rate for a single occupant, with an extra charge for each additional person staying in the room. When room availability got tight on some nights, Bill would lean out the drive-up window and assess the cars waiting in line. If some of the cars were filled with passengers, Bill would turn away vehicles with just a single passenger to sell his last rooms to those farther back in line who would be paying for multiple occupants. He might have accomplished the same result by charging a higher rate at peak times, regardless of the number of room occupants.[15]

Psychological Pricing

Psychological pricing A pricing approach that considers the psychology of prices and not simply the economics; the price is used to say something about the product.

Price says something about the product. For example, many people use price to judge quality. A $100 bottle of perfume may contain only $3 worth of scent, but some people are willing to pay the $100 because this price indicates something special.

In using **psychological pricing**, sellers consider the psychology of prices and not simply the economics. For example, consumers and business buyers usually perceive higher-priced products as having higher quality. When they can judge the quality of a product by examining it or by calling on past experience with it, they use price less to judge quality. But when they cannot judge quality because they lack the information or skill, price becomes an important quality signal:

Psychological pricing: What do the prices marked on this tag suggest about the product and buying situation?

Heublein produces Smirnoff, America's leading vodka brand. Some years ago, Smirnoff was attacked by another brand. Wolfschmidt, priced at one dollar less per bottle, claimed to have the same quality as Smirnoff. To hold on to market share, Heublein considered either lowering Smirnoff's price by one dollar or holding Smirnoff's price but increasing advertising and promotion expenditures. Either strategy would lead to lower profits, and it seemed that Heublein faced a no-win situation. At this point, however, Heublein's marketers thought of a third strategy. They *raised* the price of Smirnoff by one dollar! Heublein then introduced a new brand, Relska, to compete with Wolfschmidt. Moreover, it introduced yet another brand, Popov, priced even *lower* than Wolfschmidt. This clever strategy positioned Smirnoff as the elite brand and Wolfschmidt as an ordinary brand, producing a large increase in Heublein's overall profits. The irony is that Heublein's three brands are pretty much the same in taste and manufacturing costs. Heublein knew that a product's price signals its quality. Using price as a signal, Heublein sells roughly the same product at three different quality positions.

Another aspect of psychological pricing is **reference prices**—prices that buyers carry in their minds and refer to when looking at a given product. The reference price might be formed by noting current prices, remembering past prices, or assessing the buying situation. Sellers can influence or use these consumers' reference prices when setting price. For example, a company could display its product next to more expensive ones in order to imply that it belongs in the same class. Department stores often sell women's clothing in separate departments differentiated by price: Clothing found in the more expensive department is assumed to be of better quality. Companies can also influence buyers' reference prices by stating high manufacturer's suggested prices, by indicating that the product was originally priced much higher, or by pointing to a competitor's higher price.

Even small differences in price can suggest product differences. Consider a stereo priced at $300 compared to one priced at $299.95. The actual price difference is only five cents, but the psychological difference can be much greater. For example, some consumers will see the $299.95 as a price in the $200 range rather than the $300 range. The $299.95 will more likely be seen as a bargain price, whereas the $300 price suggests more quality. Some psychologists argue that each digit has symbolic and visual qualities that should be considered in pricing. Thus, 8 is round and even and creates a soothing effect, whereas 7 is angular and creates a jarring effect.[16]

Reference prices Prices that buyers carry in their minds and refer to when they look at a given product.

Promotional Pricing

With **promotional pricing**, companies will temporarily price their products below list price and sometimes even below cost to create buying excitement and urgency. Promotional pricing takes several forms. Supermarkets and department stores will price a few products as **loss leaders**—products priced below their cost to attract customers to the store in the hope that they will buy other items at normal markups. For example, supermarkets often sell disposable diapers at less than cost in order to attract family buyers who make larger average purchases per trip. Sellers will also use *special-event pricing* in certain seasons to draw more customers. Thus, linens are promotionally priced every January to attract weary Christmas shoppers back into stores.

Manufacturers sometimes offer *cash rebates* to consumers who buy the product from dealers within a specified time; the manufacturer sends the rebate directly to the customer. Rebates have been popular with auto makers and producers of durable goods and small appliances, but they are also used with consumer packaged goods. Some manufacturers offer *low-interest financing*, *longer warranties*, or *free maintenance* to reduce the buyer's "price." This practice has become a favourite of the auto industry. Or, the seller may simply offer *discounts* from normal prices to increase sales and reduce inventories.

Promotional pricing Temporarily pricing products below the list price, and sometimes even below cost, to increase short-run sales.

Loss leaders Products priced below their cost to attract customers to the store in the hope that they will buy other items at normal markups.

Promotional pricing: Companies offer promotional prices to create buying excitement and urgency.

Promotional pricing, however, can have adverse effects. When used too frequently and copied by competitors, price promotions can create "deal-prone" customers, who wait until brands go on sale before buying them. Or, constantly reduced prices can erode a brand's value in the eyes of the target market. Marketers sometimes use price promotions as a quick fix instead of sweating through the difficult process of developing effective longer-term strategies for building their brands. In fact, one observer notes that price promotions can be downright addictive to both the company and the customer: "Price promotions are the brand equivalent of heroin: easy to get into but hard to get out of. Once the brand and its customers are addicted to the short-term high of a price cut it is hard to wean them away to real brand building. . . . But continue and the brand dies by 1,000 cuts."[17]

The frequent use of promotional pricing can also lead to industry price wars. Such price wars usually play into the hands of only one or a few competitors—those with the most efficient operations. For example, until recently, the computer industry avoided price wars. Computer companies, including Hewlett-Packard and Gateway, showed strong profits as their new technologies were snapped up by eager consumers. When the market cooled, however, many competitors began to unload PCs at discounted prices. In response, Dell, the industry's undisputed low-cost leader, started a price war. With its incredibly efficient operations, Dell was assured a victory.

Linking the Concepts

Think about some of the companies and industries you deal with that are "addicted" to promotional pricing.

■ Many industries have created "deal-prone" shoppers through the heavy use of promotional pricing—fast food, automobiles, airlines, tires, furniture, and others. Pick a company in one of these industries and suggest ways that it might deal with this problem.

■ How does the concept of value relate to promotional pricing? Does promotional pricing add to or detract from customer value?

Geographical Pricing

A company must also decide how to price its products for markets located in different parts of the country or world. Should the company risk losing the business of more-distant customers by charging them higher prices to cover the higher shipping costs? Or should the company charge all customers the same prices regardless of location? We will look at five geographical pricing strategies for the following hypothetical situation:

> Peerless, a B.C.-based paper manufacturing company, sells paper products to customers all over North America. The cost of freight is high and affects the companies from whom customers buy their paper. Peerless wants to establish a geographical pricing policy. It is trying to determine how to price a $100 order to three specific customers: Customer A (Vancouver), Customer B (Winnipeg), and Customer C (Tampa, Florida).

One option is for the company to ask each customer to pay the shipping cost from the B.C. factory to the customer's location. All three customers would pay the same factory price of $100, with Customer A paying, say, $10 for shipping; Customer B, $15; and Customer C, $35. Called *FOB-origin pricing*, this practice means that the goods are placed *free on board* (hence, *FOB*) a carrier. At that point the title and responsibility pass to the customer, who pays the freight from the factory to the destination. Because each customer picks up their own cost, supporters of FOB pricing feel that this is the fairest way to assess freight charges. The disadvantage, however, is that the manufacturer will be a high-cost firm for distant customers.

Uniform-delivered pricing is the opposite of FOB pricing. Here, the company charges the same price plus freight to all customers, regardless of their location. The freight charge is set at the average freight cost. Suppose this is $20. Uniform-delivered pricing therefore results in a higher charge to the Vancouver customer (who pays $20 freight instead of $10) and a lower charge to the Tampa-based customer (who pays $20 instead of $35). Although the Vancouver customer would prefer to buy paper from another local paper company that uses FOB-origin pricing, the company has a better chance of winning over the Tampa customer. Other advantages of uniform-delivered pricing are that it is fairly easy to administer and it lets the firm advertise its price nationally.

Zone pricing falls between FOB-origin pricing and uniform-delivered pricing. The company sets up two or more zones. All customers within a given zone pay a single total price; the more distant the zone, the higher the price. For example, the paper company might set up a West Zone and charge $10 freight to all customers in this zone, a Midwest Zone in which it charges $15, and a Southeast Zone in which it charges $35. In this way, the customers within a given price zone receive no price advantage from the company. For example, customers in Vancouver and Seattle pay the same total price. The complaint, however, is that the Vancouver customer is paying part of the Seattle customer's freight cost.

Using *basing-point pricing*, the seller selects a given city as a "basing point" and charges all customers the freight cost from that city to the customer location, regardless of the city from which the goods are actually shipped. For example, the paper manufacturer might set Winnipeg as the basing point and charge all customers the freight from Winnipeg to their locations. This means that a Vancouver customer pays the freight cost from Winnipeg to Vancouver, even though the goods may be shipped from Vancouver. If all sellers used the same basing-point city, delivered prices would be the same for all customers and price competition would be eliminated. Industries such as sugar, cement, steel, and automobiles used basing-point pricing for years, but this method has become less popular today. Some companies set up multiple basing points to create more flexibility: They quote freight charges from the basing-point city nearest to the customer.

Finally, the seller who is anxious to do business with a certain customer or geographical area might use *freight-absorption pricing*. Using this strategy, the seller absorbs all or part of the actual freight charges in order to get the desired business. The seller might reason that if it can get more business, its average costs will fall and more than compensate for its extra freight cost. Freight-absorption pricing is used for market penetration and to hold on to increasingly competitive markets.

International Pricing

Companies that market their products internationally must decide what prices to charge in the different countries in which they operate. In some cases, a company can set a uniform worldwide price. For example, Boeing sells its jetliners at about the same price everywhere, whether in the United States, Europe, or a third-world country. However, most companies adjust their prices to reflect local market conditions and cost considerations.

The price that a company should charge in a specific country depends on many factors, including economic conditions, competitive situations, laws and regulations, and development of the wholesaling and retailing system. Consumer perceptions and preferences also may vary from country to country, calling for different prices. Or the company may have different marketing objectives in various world markets, which require changes in pricing strategy. For example, Panasonic might introduce a new product into mature markets in highly developed countries with the goal of quickly gaining mass-market share—this would call for a penetration-pricing strategy. In contrast, it might enter a less developed market by targeting smaller, less price-sensitive segments; in this case, market-skimming pricing makes sense.

For example, Campbell's found that distribution in the United Kingdom cost 30 percent more than in the United States. U.S. retailers typically purchase soup in large quantities—48-can cases of a single soup by the dozens or hundreds. In contrast, English grocers purchase soup in small quantities—typically in 24-can cases of *assorted* soups. Each case must be hand-packed for shipment. To handle these small orders, Campbell's had to add a costly extra wholesale level to its European channel. The smaller orders also mean that English retailers order two or three times as often as their U.S. counterparts, bumping up billing and order costs. These and other factors caused Campbell's to charge much higher prices for its soups in the United Kingdom.[18]

Makers of Feathercraft kayaks also discovered the problem of increased distribution costs and price escalation as they marketed into Japan. Even though the kayaks cost the Japanese consumer twice as much as they do Canadian purchasers, the firm makes its lowest margins on Japanese sales. The problem results from Japan's multilevel distribution system. A kayak may have to pass through five intermediaries before reaching the consumer, and each intermediary gets a cut of the price pie.

Another problem involves setting a price for goods that a company ships to its foreign subsidiaries. If the company charges a foreign subsidiary too much, it may end up

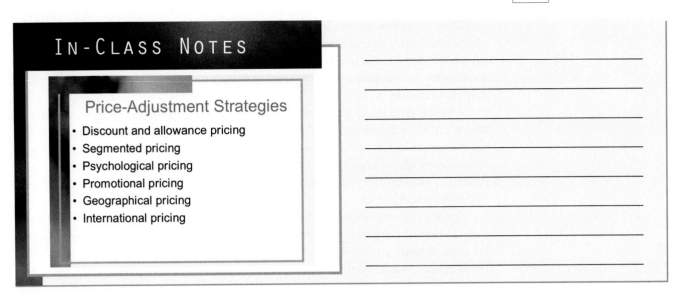

paying higher tariff duties even while paying lower income taxes in that country. If the company charges its subsidiary too little, it can be charged with *dumping*—charging less than the good costs or less than it charges in its home market. Harley-Davidson accused Honda and Kawasaki of dumping motorcycles on the U.S. market.[19] Canadian farmers have been charged with dumping wheat on the U.S. market. The U.S. International Trade Commission also ruled recently that Japan was dumping computer memory chips in the United States and laid stiff duties on future imports. Various governments are always watching for dumping abuses, and often force companies to set the price charged by other competitors for the same or similar products. Anti-dumping legislation, while usually highly politicized, is intended in theory to protect domestic players from unfair international competition.

Recent economic and technological changes have had an impact on global pricing. In the European Union, 12 countries now use a single currency, the euro. Use of this common currency is reducing the amount of price differentiation. In 1998, for instance, a bottle of Gatorade cost 3.5 euros in Germany but only about 0.9 in Spain. Today, the adoption of the euro has helped harmonize prices across the countries in the EU.

The Internet also makes global price differences more obvious. When firms sell their wares over the Internet, customers can see how much products sell for in different countries. They may even be able to order a product directly from the company location or dealer offering the lowest price. This may force companies to standardize international pricing.[20]

PRICE CHANGES

After developing their pricing structures and strategies, companies often face situations in which they must initiate price changes or respond to price changes by competitors.

Initiating Price Changes

In some cases, the company may find it desirable to initiate either a price cut or a price increase. In both cases, it must anticipate possible buyer and competitor reactions.

Initiating Price Cuts Several situations may lead a firm to consider cutting its price. One such circumstance is excess capacity. In this case, the firm needs more business and cannot get it through increased sales effort, product improvement, or other measures. It may drop its "follow-the-leader pricing"—charging about the same price as its leading competitor—and aggressively cut prices to boost sales. But as the airline, construction equipment, fast-food, and other industries have learned in recent years, cutting prices in an industry loaded with excess capacity may lead to price wars, as competitors try to hold on to market share.

Another situation leading to price changes is falling market share in the face of strong price competition. Several North American industries—automobiles, consumer electronics, cameras, watches, and steel, for example—lost market share to Japanese competitors whose high-quality products carried lower prices than did their North American counterparts. In response, North American companies resorted to more-aggressive pricing action.

A company may also cut prices in a drive to dominate the market through lower costs. Either the company starts with lower costs than its competitors, or it cuts prices in the hope of gaining market share that will further cut costs through larger volume. The North American auto manufacturers have been aggressively using rebates and low-interest loans to increase demand in a market that is experiencing share increases from Asian and European competitors.

Initiating Price Increases A successful price increase can greatly increase profits. For example, if the company's profit margin is 3 percent of sales, a 1 percent price increase will increase profits by 33 percent if sales volume is unaffected. A major factor in price increases is cost inflation. Rising costs squeeze profit margins and lead companies to pass cost increases along to customers. Another factor leading to price increases is over-demand: When a company cannot supply all that its customers need, it can raise its prices, ration products to customers, or both.

Companies can increase their prices in a number of ways to keep up with rising costs. Prices can be raised almost invisibly by dropping discounts and adding higher-priced units to the line. Or prices can be pushed up openly. In passing price increases on to customers, the company must avoid being perceived as a "price gouger." Companies also need to think of who will bear the brunt of increased prices. Customers have long memories, and they will eventually turn away from companies or even whole industries that they perceive as charging excessive prices.

This happened to the cereal industry in the 1990s. Industry leader Kellogg covered rising costs and preserved profits by steadily raising prices without also increasing customer value. Eventually, frustrated consumers retaliated with a quiet fury by shifting away from branded cereals toward cheaper private-label brands. Worse, many consumers switched to less expensive, more portable handheld breakfast foods, such as bagels, muffins, and breakfast bars. Thus, customers paid the price in the short run but Kellogg paid the price in the long run.[21]

There are some techniques for avoiding this problem. One is to maintain a sense of fairness surrounding any price increase. Price increases should be supported by company communications telling customers why prices are being increased. Making low-visibility price moves first is also a good technique: Some examples include eliminating discounts, increasing minimum order sizes, and curtailing production of low-margin products. The company sales force should help business customers find ways to economize.

Wherever possible, the company should consider ways to meet higher costs or demand without raising prices. For example, it can consider more cost-effective ways to produce or distribute its products. It can shrink the product instead of raising the price, as candy bar manufacturers often do. It can substitute less expensive ingredients or remove certain product features, packaging, or services. Or it can "un-bundle" its products and services, removing and separately pricing elements that were formerly part of the offer. IBM, for example, now offers training and consulting as separately priced services.

Buyer Reactions to Price Changes Whether the price is raised or lowered, the action will affect buyers, competitors, distributors, and suppliers and may interest government as well. Customers do not always interpret prices in a straightforward way. For example, what would you think if you saw a bottle of Chanel No. 5 for sale in a Giant Tiger store for $10? You would likely assume that something was wrong with it, or that it wasn't the real Chanel No. 5 at all. And if you were shopping for a new car and the sales representative offered you a $500 discount on a particular car on the lot, you'd think that was a great deal—but if that same representative offered you a $5000 discount, you'd become suspicious.

Similarly, a price increase, which would normally lower sales, may have some positive meaning for buyers. What would you think if Apple raised the price of its latest iPod? On the one hand, you might think it must be hot and may be unobtainable unless you buy it soon. Or you might think this newest version is an unusually good value. On the other hand, you might think Apple is greedy and charging what the market will bear.

Competitor Reactions to Price Changes A firm considering a price change has to worry about the reactions of its competitors as well as those of its customers. Competitors are most likely to react when the number of firms involved is small, when the product is uniform, and when the buyers are well informed.

How can the firm anticipate the likely reactions of its competitors? The problem is complex because, like the customer, the competitor can interpret a company price cut in many ways. It might think the company is trying to grab a larger market share, or that it's doing poorly and trying to boost its sales. Or it might think that the company wants the whole industry to cut prices to increase total demand.

The company must guess each competitor's likely reaction. If all competitors behave alike, this amounts to analyzing only a typical competitor. In contrast, if the competitors do not behave alike—perhaps because of differences in size, market shares, or policies—then separate analyses are necessary. However, if some competitors will match the price change, there is good reason to expect that the rest will also match it.

Responding to Price Changes

Here we reverse the question and ask how a firm should respond to a price change by a competitor. The firm needs to consider several issues: Why did the competitor change the price? Was it to take more market share, to use excess capacity, to meet changing cost conditions, or to lead an industrywide price change? Is the price change temporary or permanent? What will happen to the company's market share and profits if it does not respond? Are other companies going to respond? And what are the competitor's and other firms' responses to each possible reaction likely to be?

Besides these issues, the company must make a broader analysis. It has to consider its own product's stage in the life cycle, the product's importance in the company's product mix, the intentions and resources of the competitor, and the possible consumer reactions to price changes. The company cannot always make an extended analysis of its alternatives at the time of a price change, however. The competitor may have spent much time preparing this decision, but the company may have to react within hours or days. About the only way to cut down reaction time is to plan ahead for both possible competitor's price changes and possible responses.

Figure 10.6 shows the ways a company might assess and respond to a competitor's price cut. Suppose the company learns that a competitor has cut its price and decides that this price cut is likely to harm company sales and profits. It might simply decide to hold its current price and profit margin. The company might believe that it will not lose too much market share, or that it would lose too much profit if it reduced its own price.

Or it might decide that it should wait and respond when it has more information on the effects of the competitor's price change. The argument against this holding strategy, however, is that the competitor may get stronger and more confident as its sales increase and that your company might wait too long to act.

Figure 10.6 Assessing and Responding to Competitor Price Changes

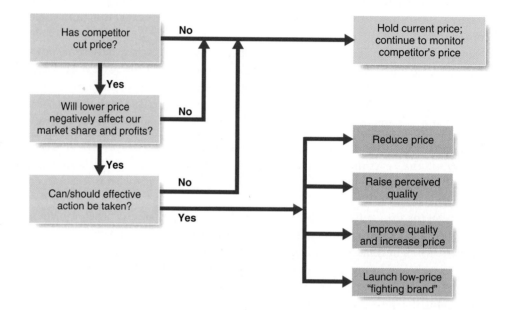

If the company decides that effective action can and should be taken, it might make any of four responses. First, it could *reduce its price* to match the competitor's price. It may decide that the market is price sensitive and that it would lose too much market share to the lower-priced competitor. Or it might worry that recapturing lost market share later would be too hard. Cutting the price will reduce the company's profits in the short run. Some companies might also reduce their product quality, services, and marketing communications to retain profit margins, but this will ultimately hurt long-run market share. The company should try to maintain its quality as it cuts prices.

Alternatively, the company might maintain its price but raise the *perceived value* of its offer. It could improve its communications, stressing the relative quality of its product over that of the lower-price competitor. The firm may find it cheaper to maintain price and spend money to improve its perceived value than to cut price and operate at a lower margin.

Or, the company might *improve quality and increase price*, moving its brand into a higher-price position. The higher quality justifies the higher price, which in turn preserves the company's higher margins. Or the company can hold price on the current product and introduce a new brand at a higher-price position.

Finally, the company might *launch a low-price "fighting brand"*—adding a lower-price item to the line or creating a separate lower-price brand. This is necessary if the particular market segment being lost is price sensitive and will not respond to arguments of higher quality. Thus, when challenged on price by store brands and other low-price entrants, Procter & Gamble turned a number of its brands into fighting brands, including Luvs disposable diapers, Joy dishwashing detergent, and Camay beauty soap.

PUBLIC POLICY AND PRICING

Price competition is a core element of our free-market economy. In setting prices, however, companies are not usually free to charge whatever prices they wish. Legal issues surrounding pricing are outlined in Sections 34, 36, and 38 of the *Competition Act*. Canadian pricing legislation was designed with two goals in mind: to foster a competitive environment and to protect consumers. Although pricing decisions made by firms do not generally require regulatory approval, Canadian marketers should be aware of three areas of concern: price fixing, price discrimination. and deceptive pricing (often referred to as "misleading price advertising").[22]

Figure 10.7 shows the major public policy issues in pricing. These include potentially damaging pricing practices within a given level of the channel (price fixing and predatory pricing) and across levels of the channel (retail price maintenance, discriminatory pricing, and deceptive pricing).[23]

Figure 10.7   Public Policy Issues in Pricing

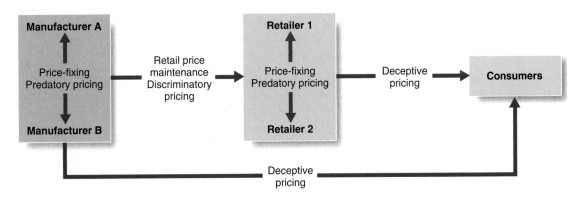

Price Fixing

Federal legislation on *price fixing* states that sellers must set prices without talking to competitors. Otherwise, price collusion is suspected. Price fixing is illegal per se—that is, the government does not accept any excuses for price fixing. Even a simple conversation between competitors can have serious consequences. The legal charge under the *Competition Act* for offences of this nature is conspiracy. Six Ottawa hotels were each fined from $60 000 to $80 000 after they were convicted of colluding to fix prices offered to government employees.

Bid rigging—any activity to suppress and eliminate competition in the bid process— is another form of price fixing and is an indictable offence under the clauses pertaining to price fixing. Examples of bid rigging include bid suppression, where bidders that would be expected to bid on a contract refrain from bidding to help another company secure a contract, and bid rotation, where conspirators agree to take turns being the lowest bidder. A number of cases in the construction industry have resulted in heavy fines being levied when competitors have been found guilty of rigging the prices of their bids. These cases have made most executives very reluctant to discuss prices in any way with competitors. In obtaining information on competitor's pricing, they rely only on openly published materials, such as trade association surveys and competitors' catalogues.

Predatory Pricing

Predatory pricing is the practice of a dominant firm selling a product at a loss in order to drive competitors out of the market or to create a barrier to entry into the market for potential new competitors. When the dominant firm sells below its cost, the other firms in the market must lower their prices in order to compete, causing them to lose money and eventually driving them bankrupt. The predatory pricer then has fewer competitors or even a monopoly, allowing it to raise its prices above what the market would otherwise bear.

Predatory pricing Selling a product at a loss to drive competitors out of the market.

Price Discrimination

Section 34 of the *Competition Act* seeks to ensure that sellers offer the same price terms to a given level of trade. For example, every retailer is entitled to the same price terms whether the retailer is Sears or a small, local bike shop. However, *price discrimination* is allowed if the seller can prove that its costs are different when selling to different retailers—for example, that it costs less per unit to sell a large volume of bicycles to Sears than it does to sell a few bicycles to a smaller local store. In other words, quantity discounts are legal in Canada. However, marketers must be careful about discriminatory promotional allowances (those not offered on proportional terms to all other competing customers), which are illegal. Thus, large competitors cannot negotiate special discounts, rebates, and price concessions that are not made proportionally available to smaller competitors.

Functional discounts (offering a larger discount to wholesalers than to retailers) are legal in the United States, but are illegal in Canada. In Canada, retailers and wholesalers are seen to be competing customers who must receive proportionally equal promotional allowances. Often, Canadian marketers working for multinational firms must explain the differences in the law to their U.S. counterparts. Canadian marketers must also keep in mind that it is illegal for a buyer to knowingly benefit from any form of price discrimination. Price differentials may be used to "match competition" in "good faith," provided the firm is trying to meet competitors at its own level of competition and the price discrimination is temporary, localized, and defensive rather than offensive.

Canadian marketers are allowed to offer *price breaks* for one-shot deals such as store-opening specials, anniversary sales, and stock clearance sales. However, regional price differentials that limit competition are illegal. Canadian firms cannot price products unreasonably low in one part of the country with the intent of driving out competition.

Finally, *retail price maintenance* is illegal. Canadian manufacturers can only suggest prices; it is illegal to require retailers to sell at a stipulated manufacturers' price.

Deceptive Pricing

Section 36 of the *Competition Act* covers areas where pricing and advertising practices converge. For example, firms cannot advertise a product at a low price, carry limited stock, and then tell shoppers that they are out of the product and attempt to manipulate the customer to switch to a higher priced product. This is referred to as "bait and switch" advertising and is illegal in Canada. Past actions by individuals and consumer groups

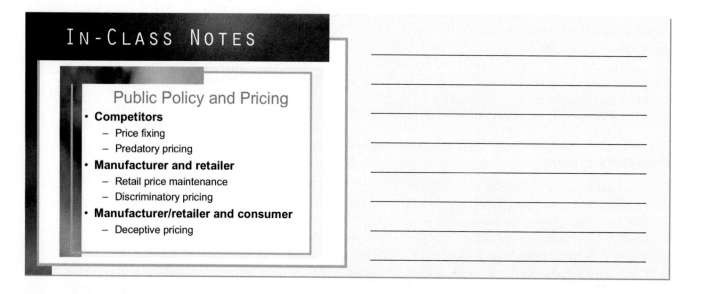

IN-CLASS NOTES

Public Policy and Pricing
- **Competitors**
  - Price fixing
  - Predatory pricing
- **Manufacturer and retailer**
  - Retail price maintenance
  - Discriminatory pricing
- **Manufacturer/retailer and consumer**
  - Deceptive pricing

against this practice, especially unscrupulous retailers, is the reason why in print advertising, especially for large-scale price-based promotions, the actual quantity of specific products that will be made available during the promotion are printed in the ad.

Deceptive pricing occurs when a seller states prices or price savings that are not actually available to consumers. Some deceptions are difficult for consumers to discern, such as when an airline advertises a low, one-way fare that is available only with the purchase of a round-trip ticket, or when a retailer sets artificially high "regular" prices, then announces "sale" prices close to the previous everyday prices.

ETHICAL ISSUES IN PRICING

Compliance with the law is considered the minimum standard when judging whether pricing practices are ethical. For example, although charging inordinately high prices is not illegal, such a practice can lead to ethical concerns. Ethical criticisms have been levelled at grocery stores, mainly chains, when higher prices are charged in poor areas of towns and cities where consumers have limited access to transportation and have few choices of alternative retail outlets.

Other ethical questions relate to whether the consumer can understand prices and realistically make comparisons. For example, consumer advocates have condemned many car-leasing contracts, since the legal language used in the contracts prevents consumers from fully understanding the price they are paying for the car.

Ethical concerns about pricing also arise when consumers must negotiate prices. Often, those who can least afford to pay a higher price (the poor, elderly, very young, or disabled) have the least ability to negotiate prices. These concerns arise when prices are not fixed. This is the case when people purchase cars, houses, or professional services. Many consumers are unaware that even when prices appear fixed, they may be subject to negotiation. For example, many consumers don't know they can negotiate with their bank for a more favourable interest rate on a consumer loan or mortgage.

LOOKING BACK

Price can be defined as the sum of the values that consumers exchange for the benefits of having and using the product or service. It is the only marketing mix element that produces revenue; all other elements represent costs. Even so, many companies are not good at handling pricing. Pricing decisions are subject to an incredibly complex array of environmental and competitive forces.

REVIEWING THE CONCEPTS

1. Identify and explain the internal and external factors affecting a firm's pricing decisions.

Many internal factors influence the company's pricing decisions, including the firm's marketing objectives, marketing mix strategy, costs, and organization for pricing. Common pricing objectives include survival, current profit maximization, market share leadership, and product quality leadership. The pricing strategy is largely determined by the company's target market and positioning objectives. Pricing decisions affect and are affected by product design, distribution, and promotion decisions and must be carefully coordinated with these other marketing mix variables. Costs set the floor for the company's price—the price must cover all the costs of making and selling the product, plus a fair rate of return. Finally, in order to coordinate pricing goals and decisions, management must decide who within the organization is responsible for setting price.

External factors that influence pricing decisions include the nature of the market and demand; competitors' costs, prices, and offers; and factors such as the economy, reseller needs, and government actions. The seller's pricing freedom varies with different types of markets. Ultimately, the consumer decides whether the company has set the right price. The consumer weighs the price against the perceived values of using the product—if the price exceeds the sum of the values, consumers will not buy. Therefore, demand and consumer value perceptions set the ceiling for prices. Consumers also compare a product's price to the prices of competitors' products. As a result, a company must learn the price and quality of competitors' offers.

2. Contrast the three general approaches to setting prices.

A company can select one or a combination of three general pricing approaches: the cost-based approach (cost-plus pricing, break-even analysis, and target profit pricing); the value-based approach; and the competition-based approach (going-rate pricing, sealed-bid pricing). Cost-based pricing sets prices based on the seller's cost structure, whereas value-based pricing relies on consumer perceptions of value to drive pricing decisions. Competition-based pricing involves setting prices based on what competitors are charging or are expected to charge.

3. Describe the major strategies for pricing new products.

Pricing strategies usually change as a product passes through its life cycle. In pricing innovative new products, a company can follow a skimming policy by initially setting high prices to "skim" the maximum amount of revenue from various segments of the market. Or it can use penetration pricing by setting a low initial price to penetrate the market deeply and win a large market share.

4. Explain how companies find a set of prices that maximizes the profits from the total product mix.

When the product is part of a product mix, the firm searches for a set of prices that will maximize the profits from the total mix. In product line pricing, the company decides on price steps for the entire set of products it offers. In addition, the company must set prices for optional products (optional or accessory products included with the main product), captive products (products that are required for use of the main product), byproducts (waste or residual products produced when making the main product), and product bundles (combinations of products at a reduced price).

5. Discuss how companies adjust their prices to take into account different types of customers and situations.

Companies apply a variety of price-adjustment strategies to account for differences in consumer segments and situations. One is discount and allowance pricing, whereby the company establishes cash, quantity, functional, or seasonal discounts, or varying types of allowances. A second strategy is segmented pricing, whereby the company sells a product at two or more prices to accommodate different customers, product forms, locations, or times. Sometimes companies consider more than economics in their pricing decisions, using psychological pricing to better communicate a product's intended position. In promotional pricing, a company offers discounts or temporarily sells a product below list price as a special event, sometimes even selling below cost as a loss leader. Another approach is geographical pricing, whereby the company decides how to price to near and distant customers. Finally, international pricing means that the company adjusts its price to meet conditions and expectations in different world markets.

6. Discuss the key issues related to initiating and responding to price changes.

When a firm considers initiating a price change, it must consider customers' and competitors' reactions. There are different implications to initiating price cuts and initiating price increases. Buyer reactions to price changes are influenced by the meaning customers see in the price change. Competitors' reactions flow from a set reaction policy or a fresh analysis of each situation. There are also many factors to consider in responding to a competitor's price changes. The company that faces a price change initiated by a competitor must try to understand the competitor's intent as well as the likely duration and impact of the change. If a swift reaction is desirable, the firm should preplan its reactions to different possible price actions by competitors. When facing a competitor's price change, the company might sit tight, reduce its own price, raise perceived quality, improve quality and raise price, or launch a fighting brand.

In general, marketers are free to charge whatever prices they wish, so long as they operate within the guidelines and regulations established by the government in the market they are serving.

The major public policy issues in pricing include potentially damaging pricing practices within a given level of the channel (price fixing and predatory pricing) and across levels of the channel (retail price maintenance, discriminatory pricing, and deceptive pricing).

KEY TERMS

allowance   *395*

break-even pricing (target profit pricing)   *386*

byproduct pricing   *394*

captive-product pricing   *393*

competition-based pricing   *389*

cost-plus pricing   *386*

demand curve   *382*

discount   *395*

dynamic pricing   *377*

everyday low pricing (EDLP)   *388*

fixed costs   *380*

loss leaders   *397*

market-penetration pricing   *391*

market-skimming pricing   *391*

optional-product pricing   *393*

predatory pricing   *405*

price   *376*

price elasticity   *383*

product bundle pricing   *393*

product line pricing   *392*

promotional pricing   *397*

psychological pricing   *396*

reference prices   *397*

segmented pricing   *395*

target costing   *379*

total costs   *380*

value pricing   *388*

value-based pricing   *387*

variable costs   *380*

STUDY GUIDE

After completing this self-test, check your answers against the Answer Key at the back of the book.

MULTIPLE CHOICE

1. The rapid, sometimes hourly changes in gasoline prices as supply and demand predictions fluctuate is an older and non-Internet-based example of
   a. Deceptive pricing
   b. Dynamic pricing
   c. Value pricing
   d. Wave pricing
   e. Geographic pricing

2. Several years ago General Motors launched a new, smaller Cadillac priced well below normal Cadillac levels in the hope of enticing younger buyers. The experiment was a disaster for Cadillac because
   a. The new Cadillac design and pricing opened up a healthy market in full-sized used Cadillacs instead
   b. Lower pricing compromised Cadillac's luxury status, causing a large drop in sales of Cadillac's high-end cars
   c. The new Cadillac was incorrectly promoted to the traditional Cadillac buyer, not the intended target
   d. The new price was still not low enough to attract younger buyers
   e. All of the above

3. In terms of the main types of pricing markets, home furniture belongs to
   a. Skimming markets
   b. Price-competitive markets
   c. Price-insensitive markets
   d. Oligopolistic-competition markets
   e. Monopolistic-competition markets

4. Of all the pricing approaches, value pricing aligns most closely with what marketing philosophy?
   a. Selling concept marketing
   b. Sense-of-mission marketing
   c. Cost-plus marketing
   d. Pure competition marketing
   e. Marketing concept marketing

5. Toyota's market offers range from the expensive luxury Lexus to the economical Tercel. This range of offers illustrates what type of product mix pricing strategy?
   a. Captive pricing
   b. Product line pricing
   c. Value-added pricing
   d. Differentiated pricing
   e. Line stretch pricing

6. Although not manufactured by the makers of the main product with which they are used, products such as gasoline, pool chemicals, and dishwasher detergent are priced as
   a. Captive products with high margins
   b. Byproducts at low prices to offset the high cost of the original products
   c. Product line pricing to match the margins of the original products
   d. Commodity products priced the same everywhere
   e. None of the above

7. A manufacturer's second highest snowblower model costs $750 to make and retails for $1950. The highest model has only one added feature: an electric self-start that adds $25 to the manufacturing costs but which raises the model's cost to $2495. In this case, the snowblower maker is practising
   a. Functional pricing because the additional price is warranted by additional functionality
   b. Price stretching because the price has been stretched well beyond the more popular model
   c. Seasonal pricing because the bulk of buyers will purchase the product in the late autumn months
   d. Product-form segmented pricing because a certain segment places a high value on the self-start
   e. Deceptive pricing because the one added feature is unfairly marked up

8. The text discusses an example in which Gatorade sells for 3.5 euros in Germany but only 0.9 euros in Spain. Although both countries use the same currency and belong to the European Union, Gatorade's use of geographic pricing could be valued as a result of what conditions:
   a. Higher per capita incomes in Germany than in Spain
   b. More aggressive advertising in Germany and thus higher retail prices
   c. Higher distribution costs in Germany than in Spain
   d. Greater demand and greater perceived value for Gatorade in Germany than in Spain
   e. All of the above

9. President's Choice ketchup offers similar quality to Heinz ketchup but at a lower price. Likewise, President's Choice popcorn takes on Orville Redenbacher at a lower price, and PC salad dressings take on Kraft's Signature brand. President's Choice has taken a _____ pricing approach to competing with the main national brands.
   a. Feature-for-feature
   b. Fighting brand
   c. Equal quality
   d. Plus-minus
   e. Less-for-less

10. A Canadian electronics retailer distributed a print flyer that advertised an attractive sale price on portable DVDs with small print stating "while quantities last." The sale applied to three stores in the area. When the first customer in a particular store came to buy the advertised DVD, she discovered that the store had only one unit. Thus, subsequent customers would not be able to purchase the sale unit. What form of unethical pricing did this retailer practise, and is it legal in Canada?
    a. Predatory pricing (illegal)
    b. Pricing discrimination (legal)
    c. Deceptive pricing (illegal)
    d. Price fixing (legal)
    e. Price maintenance (illegal)

TRUE/FALSE

T   F   1. Total Cost of Ownership should be a key consideration when purchasing a car.

T   F   2. The nature of dynamic pricing always demands negotiation between seller and consumer.

T   F   3. Pharmaceutical research companies enjoy a nonregulated, pure monopoly for their brand drugs until patents expire.

T   F   4. Milk is price elastic while filet mignon is highly price inelastic.

T   F   5. If Ferrari were to lower its price, its demand curve would likely run backwards.

CONCEPT CHECK

1. With _____ pricing, different prices are charged, depending on individual customers and situations.

2. Common objectives with respect to pricing include survival, _____, _____, and _____.

3. Economists recognize four types of markets, each presenting a different pricing challenge: _____; _____; _____; and, _____.

4. Price elasticity measures how responsive demand will be to a change in price. If demand changes greatly, we say the demand is _____.

5. The simplest pricing method is _____, where the marketer adds a standard markup to the cost of the product.

6. _____ pricing means that the marketer cannot design a product and marketing program and then set the price. Price is considered along with the other marketing-mix variables before the marketing program is set.

7. _____-based pricing is used when firms bid for jobs. Versions of this pricing form would be going-rate pricing and sealed-bid pricing.

8. If a company chooses to set a low initial price in order to go into the market quickly and deeply (to attract a large number of buyers quickly and win a large market share), the company would be using a _____ pricing strategy.

9. Examples of products that would use _____ pricing would include razor blades, camera film, video games, and computer software.

10. A typical example of a _____ discount is "2/10, net 30," which means that although payment is due within 30 days, the buyer can deduct 2 percent if the bill is paid within 10 days.

11. Consumers usually perceive higher-priced products as having higher quality. This would be a case where _____ pricing was used.

12. If a customer is asked to pay the entire cost of freight from the factory to the customer's destination (distant customers will have to pay more), the company is most likely using the _____ pricing form of geographical pricing.

STUDENT MATERIALS

Visit our website at www.pearsoned.ca/armstrong for online quizzes, Internet exercises, and more!

NOTES

_____

_____

_____

_____

_____

_____

_____

_____

_____

_____

_____

_____

DISCUSSING THE ISSUES

1. Assume you are the vice president for financial affairs at a major university. For the past three years, enrollments and revenues have declined steadily at a rate of about 10 percent per year. You are under great pressure to raise tuition to compensate for the falling revenues. However, you suspect that raising tuition might only make matters worse. What internal and external pricing factors should you consider before you make your decision? Explain.

2. Discuss the typical pricing objectives outlined in the chapter. Which of these objectives do you believe (a) is the most commonly used, (b) is the most difficult to achieve, (c) has the greatest potential for long-term growth of the organization, and (d) is most likely to be a pricing objective used by an e-commerce company? Explain.

3. Your company is about to launch a new brand of paper towels that are more absorbent and durable than paper towels currently being sold. Your boss wants you to con-

sider both market-skimming and market-penetration pricing strategies. What factors should you consider in making your decision?

4. After examining Figure 10.5, compare and contrast cost-based pricing and value-based pricing. What situations favour each pricing method?

5. Think of a consumer product that you believe is priced according to a market-skimming pricing strategy, and a consumer product that you believe is priced according to a market-penetration pricing strategy. Explain what evidence leads you to believe that this is the strategy being employed.

6. Formulate rules that might govern (a) initiating a price cut, (b) initiating a price increase, (c) a negative reaction on the part of buyers to a price change by your company, (d) a competitor's response to your price change, and (e) your response to a competitor's price change. State the assumptions underlying your proposed rules.

MARKETING APPLICATIONS

The printer industry is intensively competitive with respect to pricing. The first home printers, marketed by companies such as Epson and Hewlett-Packard, were almost as expensive as the computer itself. But like most technology products, as technology improves and features are added the price is forced down. Today, consumers can choose from a wide range of desktop printers for home use—from high-end colour laser printers that print on photo-quality paper, to multiple-use printer/fax/copier/scanner machines, to inexpensive printers for occasional use such as Canon's line of Bubblejet printers.

THINKING LIKE A MARKETING MANAGER

1. What role does pricing play in a consumer's selection of a home printer? What about a buyer selecting an office printer? Or a travelling sales manager selecting a portable printer to take on business trips?

2. Visit your local office supply store and examine the brand names, features, and prices of various printers. Do all the printers seem to be following the same pricing strategy, or are different manufacturers employing different pricing strategies? Explain.

3. Assume that you are the marketing manager of a company introducing a new line of colour printers and seeking quick entry into the small printer market. Your products are comparable to those of primary competitors, and you have the funds necessary to compete with industry leaders. Design a pricing strategy for capturing business in the home computer, home office, and mobile office markets. What factors would be critical to your product's success? How would you combat competitive reaction to your entry?

VIDEO CASE

Go to Pearson Canada's Video Central site (www.pearsoned.ca/highered/videocentral) to view the video and accompanying case for this chapter.

CASE 10 GOOGLE: DYNAMIC PRICING OF ONLINE ADVERTISING

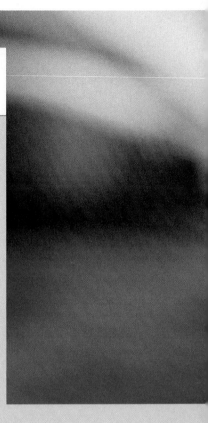

It's difficult to pick up a business magazine or newspaper without reading about the latest success of Google, the world's most popular Internet search engine. Deloitte Touche Tohmatsu named Google the fastest growing technology company in North America, with a five-year growth rate of 437 115 percent, moving from revenues of US$220 000 in 1999 to more than US$961 million in 2003. By April 2005, Google's market capitalization had reached more than $61 billion and its share price hovered around US$200, up 73 percent from a year earlier and more than 90 percent from its IPO debut. First-quarter revenue in 2005 doubled to $1.26 billion from the previous year.

Fuelling this growth, Google has been launching such innovative offerings as Google AdWords, Google Answers, and Gmail BETA at a speed that would make race car driver Mario Andretti look like he was going on a Sunday drive. And while Google's success is no secret, many aren't aware that at the heart of the dizzying financials is its innovative approach to pricing.

Google AdWords

In 2001 Google launched AdWords—text-based ads that would be displayed next to search listings in the context of the topics being searched for. According to Google, the purpose of AdWords was to "reach people when they are actively looking for information about your products and services online and send targeted visitors directly to what you are offering." A user searching for a car would see car-related ads, not ads for dog food. By 2002, payment for AdWords would not follow the traditional impressions model but would instead be based on "click-through"—how many times users clicked on the ad to reach the advertiser's destination website. "With AdWords' cost-per-click pricing, it's easy to control costs—and you only pay when people click on your ad."

Following the lead of e-marketplaces like eBay, buying advertising space on Google followed an auction model where advertisers bid on keywords. The goal of advertisers was to bid high enough to ensure their keywords were displayed close to the top of the first page of search results, a function of bid price combined with click-through conversion rate (percentage of the ads clicked on by search engine visitors). This new advertising marketplace is truly dynamic, with bid prices and placement changing in real time. Advertisers can submit a maximum spending per day limit, but there are no guarantees for how many "click-throughs" they will receive and no guarantees that another organization won't outbid them at any time. One company could bid $10.00 for the "mortgage" keyword one second, only to get outbid the next second by another advertiser willing to bid the same amount plus a penny. Buying AdWords was more like day-trading stocks than the customary practice of buying from a static rate sheet. But despite the learning curve required to jump aboard, the approach is taking off with professional marketers and amateurs alike.

Keyword prices are driven up by bidding for the most popular words. The average price paid per keyword has increased from $US1.37 in September 2004 to $US1.75 in March 2005, according to Fathom Online, a company that tracks 500 generic keywords across more than 50 search engines. "Much like the stock market, PPC (pay per click) ads are bought and sold in auctions and are affected by supply and demand," says Chris Churchill, Fathom Online CEO. "The latest increase in demand for keywords suggests that advertisers are continuing to get the ROI out of their search spend." And unlike many forms of traditional advertising, it's easy to track and to measure the effectiveness of keyword advertising, leading to optimal AdWords pricing decisions. It appears that the new dynamic pricing models for keywords are here to stay.

Google Answers

Google's innovative approach to pricing doesn't stop with its AdWords offering. Google Answers is also using dynamic pricing to turn conventional marketing research pricing on its head. Do you have a difficult question that's taking too much time and money to find the answer to? With Google Answers you can submit a question to one of the many Google researchers and name your price. The researchers will look at your offering price, determine how much effort is required, and let you know if they will proceed to find an answer. Not happy with the answer to your questions? You can ask for a refund, and will get your money back minus a small processing fee. Pleasantly surprised by the answer they found for you? You can leave a tip! The fact that a number of Google Answers customers do indeed go beyond the negotiated price to leave a tip is a testament to the success and popularity of the service.

Google Answers is only in the early stages of development, but the impact it could have on such information sectors as consulting and marketing research is enormous. The client that used to pay several thousand dollars to the business consultant and wait a few weeks for her to research the size of the soft drink market in northern Brazil can now get the answer for less than the cost of a pizza—and in just days, if not hours.

Gmail

Not content to put all its eggs in its search engine and network advertising basket, Google created a buzz across the Internet with its launch in April 2004 of Gmail, a Web-based email service and one of the hottest new offerings on the Net. It was so popular that users were profiting by auctioning off their extra, BETA-trial memberships on eBay. When Gmail launched, it gave its BETA users an unprecedented one-gigabyte (1000 megabytes) of storage compared to Hotmail's five megabytes. While Hotmail was forced to raise its free storage to 250 megabytes, Gmail quickly regained its lead by offering its users two gigabytes starting on April Fools' Day, 2005. Many assumed it was a joke, but the increased storage was serious, and remained. In fact, available storage is constantly growing, with Google promising users that they will "never need to delete another message." And just to remind users that they are getting more and more value every day, Google has a ticker on the Gmail homepage indicating how much additional Web storage is available each second—the ultimate example of value-based pricing (no cost, and perceived value increasing by the second).

The Future

The Google offerings aren't perfect. Some experts estimate that more than 20 percent of all AdWords' click-throughs are fraudulent—for example, someone clicking on their competitors' ads to drive up their advertising costs. Google Answers currently displays paid answers publicly, leading some critics to wonder about the true value of the answers if potential competitors can see them. And Google's Gmail BETA offering is attracting a lot of concern over privacy, since individual emails are scanned by Google's indexing program to generate context-appropriate AdWords advertising. The idea of storing many gigabytes of personal data with an external company also raises concerns of an overly powerful Big Brother.

Despite these potential problem areas, Google's offerings provide a useful glimpse into the future model of dynamic pricing. It will likely no longer be sufficient for an organization to ask itself, "Should we have a market-penetration pricing strategy or should we go with a skimming pricing strategy?" Increasingly, organizations will instead have to decide, "What type of dynamic pricing model will best work for our offering?" In many cases, this means not making a pricing decision at all, but rather letting the market decide what it will pay in real time. Pricing, often not the most glamorous of the four marketing Ps, is becoming increasingly critical—and with such products as Gmail, pricing becomes a key factor in defining the offering.

Google co-founders Larry Page and Sergey Brin hold to this philosophy: "Always deliver more than expected. Google does not accept being the best as an endpoint, but a starting point. Through innovation and iteration, Google takes something that works well and improves upon it in unexpected ways." In addition to launching numerous innovative products, Google has elevated the importance of creative and dynamic pricing to a new level. Future marketers will be increasingly transforming fixed-based pricing to auction-based pricing, and will be pricing by the second rather than by the quarter. The opportunities are limitless. Many marketers—including pricing specialists caught in pricing ruts—are just beginning to take notice and realize that many of the pricing theory and lessons they've previously relied on are now up for grabs.

Questions

1. How do you think Google's approach to pricing might affect the pricing of traditional media advertising?

2. How can Google offer its Gmail service for free? What are the true costs to consumers?

3. An individual can purchase AdWords from Google with the same pricing process as a large multinational company. Do you think this democratization of the online pricing market will continue? Does the auction approach to sell AdWords maximize Google's revenues and profit?

4. How does the pricing of keywords differ with Google's competitor, Yahoo's Overture network? What pricing approach do you think is better?

Sources: http://searchenginewatch.com/reports/article.php/2156431, accessed April 29, 2005; www.deloitte.com/dtt/press_release/0,1014,sid%253D1018%2526cid%253D63294,00.html, accessed April 29, 2005; http://money.cnn.com, accessed April 30, 2005; www.cbc.ca/story/business/national/2004/07/26/google_040726.html, accessed April 29, 2005; www.google.ca/ads, accessed April 30, 2005; gmail.google.com, accessed April 30, 2005; www.webpronews.com/insiderreports/marketinginsider/wpn–5020050421HowClickFraudImpactsHonestPublishers.html, accessed April 30, 2005; www.fathomonline.com, accessed April 30, 2005; www.bizonline-content.com/BizResourceOnline/harris/displayarticle.asp?id=192&clientid=4&categoryid=2, accessed April 29, 2005.

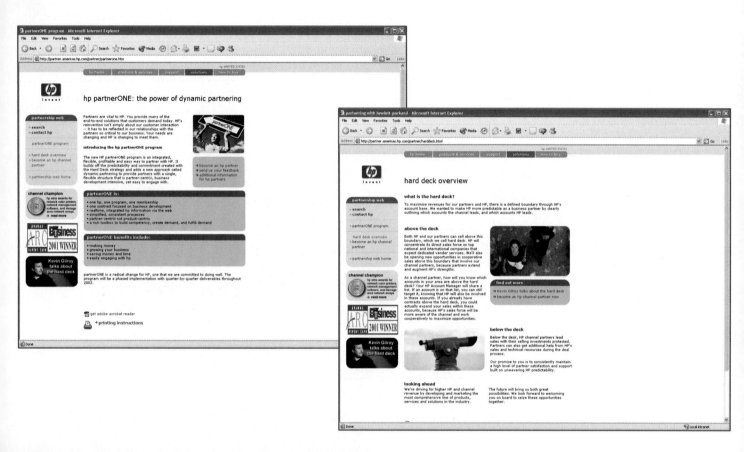

1. explain why companies use distribution channels and discuss the functions these channels perform, particularly those of retailers and wholesalers

2. discuss how channel members interact and how they organize to perform the work of the channel

3. identify the major channel alternatives open to a company

4. explain how companies select, motivate, and evaluate channel members

5. discuss the nature and importance of marketing logistics and integrated supply chain management

Marketing Channels and Supply Chain Management

11

Looking Ahead   We now arrive at the third marketing mix tool: distribution. Firms rarely work alone in bringing value to customers. Instead, most are only a single link in a larger supply chain or distribution channel. As such, an individual firm's success depends not only on how well it performs, but also on how well its entire distribution channel competes with competitors' channels. For example, an automobile manufacturer can make the world's best cars but still will not do well if its dealers perform poorly in sales and service compared to the dealers of Toyota, GM, Chrysler, Ford, or Honda. The manufacturer must choose its channel partners carefully and work with them effectively. As Coca-Cola CEO Roberto Goizueta once said, "You let me have the bottling plants and the trucks and the highly efficient systems, and I'll let you have the TV commercials. I'll beat you to a pulp over time."[1]

The first part of this chapter explores the nature of distribution channels, including their two best-known components: retailing and wholesaling. We then examine the marketer's channel design and management decisions, and the important area of physical distribution, or logistics.

While you're getting ready to think about channel relationships, we'll look at Hewlett-Packard. Its success rests on more than just quality computers and a reputation for service. Part of what makes HP so successful is its strong relationship with both its customers and its channel partners. Read on and see why.

Hewlett-Packard has a long history of working *with* its channel partners, rather than *through* them or *against* them. It understands the great value these partners add, both for HP and for customers. "Partners are core to HP's business go-to-market strategy," says Webb McKinney, president of HP's Business Customer Organization. "[Only by working closely] with our channel partners can we meet the diverse needs of our customers." Channel partners extend HP's reach far beyond its own capacity. They have a clear understanding of customers' needs and have the resources needed to build customer relationships and provide hands-on support. Managing channel relationships is one of the most important things HP does. "Put simply, it's a partnering world," adds Kevin Gilroy, general manager for HP's channel program.

A few years back, however, HP faced a difficult decision. Given competitor Dell's incredible success at selling direct to customers, HP had to decide whether it would do the same. Not only could direct selling reduce costs and increase profits, but some customers actually prefer to deal directly with HP. Carly Fiorina, who was then HP's CEO, says, "The reality is there are some customers who prefer to order through a direct distribution capability *à la* Dell, and we have to satisfy those customers." So HP really had no choice: It had to go direct. The problem? By selling direct, HP would be competing directly with its traditional distribution channel partners. This in turn would threaten HP's prized, and profitable, relationships with its distributors. "Two thirds of our business comes as a direct result of our collaboration with our partners and our channel," says Fiorina.

Thus, HP had to find a way to both sell direct to customers *and* build support and trust among its traditional partners. To solve the problem, the company has developed a direct sales program that avoids infringing on its partners' turf. Whereas HP's competitors take business from their distributors through direct sales to even the smallest customers, HP has "drawn a line in the sand," Gilroy says. Its direct sales program, sometimes referred to as the "hard deck" program, clearly limits which accounts the company will target with direct selling.

"Hard deck" is an aviation term that defines a boundary under which there is a "no-fly zone." For HP, it means that the company will sell direct only to potential customers that exceed established specifications. To date, that includes about 1000 large accounts. Customers falling below the specifications—those in the "no-fly zone"—are off limits to HP for direct sales. Such an arrangement allows HP to concentrate its direct sales force on the largest national and international companies, those that expect dedicated supplier service. At the same time, it creates a market for channel partners, below the hard deck, that's free from direct selling competition.

HP also goes out of its way to help its partners sell the company's products and services. When HP sales reps get leads on accounts in the no-fly zone, they pass the information along to HP distributors, who make the sale and provide service and support. In addition, HP dedicates sales and technical resources to help channel members find the best customer solutions.

The day-to-day management of relationships with more than 20 000 channel partners, who sell everything from computer networks to pocket calculators, presents an immense challenge. Something as simple as distributing sales leads collected through various HP marketing campaigns—everything from business cards dropped in fish bowls at trade shows to requests for product information from HP's Internet site—can be a daunting task. To manage these tasks, HP set up an integrated partner relationship management (PRM) system that links HP directly with its channel partners and helps coordinate channel-wide marketing efforts. Using a secure website, channel partners can log on at any time to obtain leads that have been generated for them. While at the site, they can also order literature and sales support materials, check product specifications, and obtain pricing information. In addition, HP communicates with channel members regularly, offering training seminars and promotional materials to support sales. In fact, many partners receive one or two emails a day offering information, resources, and support.

The PRM system not only provides strong support for channel partners, it improves their effectiveness and provides feedback to HP. Under the old system, says an HP manager, "we would generate a mass-mailing campaign, send it off to who knows where, out it would go, and we'd hope it would work. Now we can generate a targeted campaign, see when the opportunities start coming back, and . . . the channel partner tells us what happened. . . . It's changing the way we do campaigns."

The results of HP's partner relationship marketing efforts speak for themselves. HP has won multiple awards for its support of and relationships with channel members. It swept almost every category it was eligible for in the 2004 Channel Champions awards sponsored by *CRN*, a technology-focused trade journal. In surveys administered to determine the winners, one channel member said "You won't find a support network out there that's better. Overall, HP is a step above the rest." Referring to the support HP reps provide to channel partners, another distributor commented, "We treat our HP reps more like our sales managers. HP has high integrity. In a gray area, HP will always default to its partners." Adds Fiorina, "Our success is measured on what we can achieve together with our partners."[2]

TEST YOURSELF

Answers to these questions can be found on our website at
www.pearsoned.ca/armstrong.

1. Why does Hewlett-Packard (HP) choose to give up margin to channel partners?
   a) Because HP does not have the budget or resources to advertise and market directly to customers
   b) Because HP can sell its computers for less if it sells through channel partners
   c) Because the value that those channel partners provide in support, service, and access to customers is greater to HP than any increase in margins
   d) Because HP's channel partners are flexible and don't mind if HP sells to their customers directly as well
   e) Because IBM has the same channel partners and so HP has to compete through margins

2. Why did HP choose to sell direct only to its 1000 largest accounts instead of selling directly to small players and leaving the large accounts to the channel partners?
   a) Because HP's channel partners were not servicing those large accounts adequately
   b) Because it's large companies that want personal, dedicated service from suppliers and that tend to want the savings of dealing direct because of the large orders they place
   c) Because HP wanted to compete directly with Dell's customized Web and telephone-based direct model
   d) Because HP wanted to own those accounts directly in case its channel partners decided to switch to other computer makers
   e) All of the above

3. Why does HP put as much effort and money into its partner relationship management (PRM) system as some companies put into their customer relationship management (CRM) systems?
   a) Because HP doesn't have any direct customers, only partners
   b) Because HP is a developer and marketer of PRM systems and therefore wants to be seen using its own products
   c) Because for HP its channel partners are among their first-line customers and so it uses software tools to integrate with them as closely as possible
   d) Because the CRM systems belong to partners who are the only ones that have the contact with customers
   e) None of the above

4. Why does HP pass on to its channel partners all sales leads that qualify as below the "hard deck"?
   a) Because the well-being of HP depends on not competing with its channel
   b) Because HP does not understand how to sell to smaller accounts
   c) Because HP is not interested in the smaller profits generated by selling directly to small accounts
   d) Because HP does not have the infrastructure to handle custom direct sales to smaller accounts
   e) Because HP maintains greater control over its channel partners by making them dependent on HP for sales leads

5. HP developed its direct sales strategy in response to Dell's success in direct selling. How has HP's hybrid model given the company a strong competitive advantage against Dell and its single-model direct strategy?
   a) By forcing Dell to develop a channel sales strategy
   b) By using its channel to deliver more value to those customers who want personal or custom service
   c) By forcing Dell to cut its prices even further to complete
   d) By significantly reducing the amount of margin that HP must give up to its distributors
   e) By confusing the market and positioning Dell as a discount PC provider

Channel decisions are among the most important decisions management faces. A company's channel decisions are linked with every other marketing decision. The company's pricing depends on whether it sells its product through mass merchandisers or high-quality specialty stores. Sales force and advertising decisions depend on how much persuasion, training, motivation, and support the dealers need. Whether a company develops or acquires certain new products may depend on how well those products fit the capabilities of its channel members.

Moreover, many companies have used imaginative distribution systems to gain a competitive advantage. FedEx's creative and imposing distribution system made it the leader in the small-package delivery industry. General Electric gained a strong advantage in selling its major appliances by supporting its dealers with a sophisticated computerized order-processing and delivery system. Dell Computer revolutionized its industry by selling personal computers directly to consumers rather than through retail stores. And Charles Schwab & Company pioneered the delivery of financial services via the Internet.

Distribution channel decisions often involve long-term commitments to other firms. For example, companies such as Ford, IBM, or McDonald's can easily change their advertising, pricing, or promotion programs. They can scrap old products and introduce new ones as market tastes demand. But when they set up distribution channels through contracts with franchisees, independent dealers, or large retailers, they cannot readily replace these channels with company-owned stores or websites if conditions change. And the decision to cut out a long-time channel partner has an ethical element as well, since even partnerships that are not cemented with legal paperwork carry expectations of mutual support. Therefore, management must design its channels carefully, with an eye on tomorrow's likely selling environment as well as today's.

This chapter examines four major questions concerning distribution channels: What is the nature of distribution channels? How do channel firms interact and organize to do the work of the channel? What decisions do companies need to make to design and manage their channels? What role do physical distribution and supply chain management play in attracting and satisfying customers?

THE NATURE OF DISTRIBUTION CHANNELS

Most producers use intermediaries to bring their products to market. They try to forge a **distribution channel**—a set of interdependent organizations involved in the process of making a product or service available for use or consumption by the consumer or business user.[3] The two terms *marketing channel* and *distribution channel* are usually used interchangeably. In this textbook we will generally use the term *distribution channel*. The term **supply chain** refers more broadly to a collection of organizations that in a collaborative manner handles production, marketing, and logistics for a product.

Distribution channel A set of interdependent organizations involved in the process of making a product or service available for use or consumption by the consumer or business user.

Supply chain A collection of organizations that in a collaborative manner handles production, marketing, and logistics for a product.

Why Are Marketing Intermediaries Used?

Why do producers give some of the selling job to intermediaries? After all, doing so means giving up some control over how and to whom the products are sold. The use of intermediaries results from their greater efficiency in making goods available to target markets. Through their contacts, experience, specialization, and scale of operation, intermediaries usually offer the firm more than it can achieve on its own.

Figure 11.1 shows how using intermediaries can provide economies. Figure 11.1A shows three manufacturers each using direct marketing to reach three customers. This system requires nine different contacts. Figure 11.1B shows the three manufacturers working through one distributor, which contacts the three customers. This system requires only six contacts. In this way, intermediaries reduce the amount of work that must be done by both producers and consumers.

From the economic system's point of view, the role of marketing intermediaries is to match supply and demand. Producers make narrow assortments of products in large quantities, but consumers want broad assortments of products in small quantities. In the

---

Figure 11.1   How Marketing Intermediaries Reduce the Number of Channel Transactions

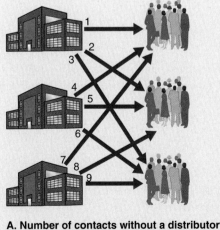
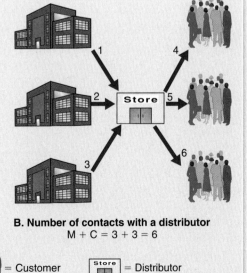

A. Number of contacts without a distributor
$M \times C = 3 \times 3 = 9$

B. Number of contacts with a distributor
$M + C = 3 + 3 = 6$

= Manufacturer   = Customer   = Distributor

distribution channels, intermediaries buy large quantities from many producers and break them down into the smaller quantities and broader assortments wanted by consumers.

Distribution Channel Functions

The distribution channel moves goods and services from producers to consumers. It overcomes the major time, place, and possession gaps that separate goods and services from those who would use them. Members of the channel perform many key functions, such as

☐ *Information function:* Gathering and distributing marketing research and intelligence information about actors and forces in the marketing environment needed for planning and aiding exchange; finding and communicating with prospective buyers.

☐ *Product function:* Shaping and fitting the offer to the buyer's needs, including activities such as manufacturing, grading, assembling, and packaging.

☐ *Price function:* Reaching an agreement on price and other terms of the offer so that ownership or possession can be transferred.

☐ *Place function:* Transporting and storing goods.

☐ *Promotion function:* Developing and spreading persuasive communications about an offer.

☐ *Ownership function:* Acquiring and using funds to cover the costs of the channel work; assuming the risks of carrying out the channel work.

The question is not whether these functions need to be performed—they must be—but rather who will perform them. If the manufacturer performs these functions, its costs go up and its prices have to be higher. When functions are shifted to intermediaries, the producer's costs and prices may be lower, but the intermediaries must charge more to cover the costs of their work. In dividing the work of the channel, the various functions should be assigned to the channel members who can perform them most efficiently and effectively to provide satisfactory assortments of goods to target market segments.

Number of Channel Levels

Distribution channels can be described by the number of channel levels involved. Each layer of marketing intermediaries that performs some work in bringing the product and its ownership closer to the final buyer is a **channel level**. Because the producer and the final consumer both perform some work, they are part of every channel. We use the number of intermediary levels to indicate the length of a channel. Figure 11.2A shows several consumer distribution channels of different lengths.

Channel 1, called a **direct distribution channel**, has no intermediary levels. It consists of a company selling directly to consumers. For example, Avon, Amway, and Tupperware sell their products door to door or through home and office sales parties; Rogers and Bell sell their cell phones through their own stores; and Dell sells computers direct through telephone selling and its website. The remaining channels in Figure 11.2A are **indirect distribution channels**, which contain one or more intermediary levels. Channel 2 contains one intermediary level. In consumer markets, this level is typically a retailer. For example, the makers of televisions, cameras, tires, furniture, major appliances, and many other products sell their goods directly to large retailers such as Wal-Mart and Sears, which then sell the goods to consumers. Channel 3 contains two intermediary levels, a wholesaler and a retailer. This channel is often used by small manufacturers of food, drugs, hardware, and other products. Channel 4 contains three intermediary levels. In the meatpacking industry, for example, jobbers buy from wholesalers and sell to smaller retailers who are not generally served by larger wholesalers. Distribution channels with

Channel level A layer of intermediaries that performs some work in bringing the product and its ownership closer to the final buyer.

Direct distribution channel A marketing channel that has no intermediary levels.

Indirect distribution channel Channel containing one or more intermediary levels.

even more levels are sometimes found, but less often, at least domestically. Internationally, Japan typically has many channel levels. From the producer's point of view, a greater number of levels means less control and greater channel complexity.

Figure 11.2B shows some common business distribution channels. The business marketer can use its own sales force to sell directly to business customers. It can also sell to industrial distributors, who in turn sell to business customers. It can sell through manufacturer's representatives or its own sales branches to business customers, or it can use these representatives and branches to sell through industrial distributors. Thus, business markets commonly include multilevel distribution channels.

Figure 11.2   Consumer and Business Distribution Channels

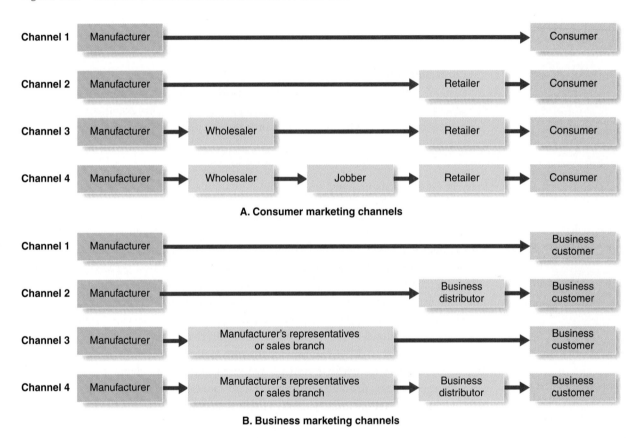

even more levels are sometimes found, but less often, at least domestically. Internationally, Japan typically has many channel levels. From the producer's point of view, a greater number of levels means less control and greater channel complexity.

A. Consumer marketing channels

B. Business marketing channels

All the institutions in the channel are connected by several types of flows. These include the physical flow of products, the flow of ownership, the payment flow, the information flow, and the promotion flow. These flows can make even channels with only one or a few levels very complex.

WHOLESALING

Wholesaling includes all activities involved in selling goods and services to those buying for resale or business use. **Wholesalers** are firms engaged *primarily* in wholesaling activity.

Wholesalers buy mostly from producers and sell mostly to retailers, industrial consumers, and other wholesalers. But why are wholesalers used at all? For example, why would a producer use wholesalers rather than selling directly to retailers or consumers? Quite simply, wholesalers are often better at performing one or more of the following channel functions:

Wholesaling All activities involved in selling goods and services to those buying for resale or business use.

Wholesaler A firm engaged *primarily* in wholesaling activity.

> □ *Information function:* Wholesalers give information to suppliers and customers about competitors, new products, and price developments. Wholesalers often help retailers train their salesclerks, improve store layouts and displays, and set up accounting and inventory control systems.
>
> □ *Product function:* Wholesalers can select items and build assortments needed by their customers, saving the consumers work because they do not have to go to many different places to find what they want.
>
> □ *Price function:* Wholesalers can reach many small customers at a low cost and save their customers money by buying in carload lots and breaking bulk (breaking large lots into small quantities).
>
> □ *Place function:* Wholesalers can provide quicker delivery to buyers because they are closer than the producers.
>
> □ *Promotion function:* The wholesaler often has more contacts and is more trusted by the buyer than the distant manufacturer.
>
> □ *Ownership function:* Wholesalers hold inventories, thereby reducing the inventory costs of suppliers and customers. They absorb risk by taking title and bearing the cost of theft, damage, spoilage, and obsolescence. Wholesalers also finance their customers by giving credit, and they finance their suppliers by ordering early and paying bills on time.

Types of Wholesalers

Merchant wholesaler
Independently owned business that takes title to the merchandise it handles.

Wholesalers fall into three major groups (see Table 11.1): *merchant wholesalers, agents and brokers,* and *manufacturers' sales branches and offices.* **Merchant wholesalers** are independently owned businesses that take title to the merchandise they handle. They are the largest single group of wholesalers, accounting for roughly 50 percent of all wholesaling. Merchant wholesalers include two broad types: *Full-service wholesalers* who provide a full set of services and *limited-service wholesalers* who offer fewer services to their suppliers and customers. The several different types of limited-service wholesalers perform varied specialized functions in the distribution channel.

Broker A wholesaler who does not take title to goods and whose function is to bring buyers and sellers together and assist in negotiation.

Brokers and *agents* differ from merchant wholesalers in two ways: They do not take title to goods, and they perform only a few functions. Like merchant wholesalers, they generally specialize by product line or customer type. A **broker** brings buyers and sellers together and assists in negotiation. **Agents** represent buyers or sellers on a more permanent basis. *Manufacturers' agents* (also called manufacturers' representatives) are the most common type of agent wholesaler.

Agent A wholesaler who represents buyers or sellers on a relatively permanent basis, performs only a few functions, and does not take title to goods.

The third major type of wholesaling is that done in **manufacturers' sales branches and offices** by sellers or buyers themselves rather than through independent wholesalers.

Manufacturers' sales branches and offices Wholesaling by sellers or buyers themselves rather than through independent wholesalers.

Wholesaler Marketing Decisions

Wholesalers have experienced growing competitive pressures in recent years. The industry remains vulnerable to one of the most enduring trends of the past decade—fierce resistance to price increases and the winnowing out of suppliers based on cost and quality. They have also faced new sources of competition, more demanding customers, new technologies, and more direct-buying programs on the part of large industrial, institutional, and retail buyers. Progressive wholesalers constantly watch for better ways to meet the changing needs of their suppliers and customers. They recognize that, in the long run, their only reason for existence comes from adding value by increasing the efficiency and effectiveness of the entire channel. As a result, they too have had to improve their strategic decisions on target markets and positioning, and

Table 11.1 Major Types of Wholesalers

Type	Description
Merchant Wholesalers	Independently owned businesses that take title to the merchandise they handle. In different trades, they are known as *jobbers, distributors,* or *mill supply houses.* They include full-service wholesalers and limited-service wholesalers.
Full-service wholesalers	Provide a full line of services: carrying stock, maintaining a sales force, offering credit, making deliveries, and providing management assistance. They include wholesale merchants and industrial distributors.
Limited-service wholesalers	Offer fewer services than full-service wholesalers; they are of several types:
Cash-and-carry wholesalers	Carry a limited line of fast-moving goods and sell to small retailers for cash. Normally do not deliver.
Truck wholesalers (or truck jobbers)	Perform primarily a selling and delivery function.
Drop shippers	Do not carry inventory or handle the product. Upon receiving an order, they select a manufacturer, who ships the merchandise directly to the customer. The drop shipper assumes title and risk and operates in such bulk industries as coal, lumber, and heavy equipment.
Rack jobbers	Serve grocery and drug retailers, mostly in non-food items. They send delivery trucks to stores, where the delivery people set up toys, paperbacks, hardware items, health and beauty aids, or other items. They price goods, keep them fresh, set up point-of-purchase displays, and keep inventory records. Rack jobbers retain title to the goods and bill the retailers only for the goods sold to consumers.
Producers' cooperatives	Owned by farmer members, they assemble farm produce to sell in local markets. The co-op's profits are distributed to members at the end of the year.
Mail-order wholesalers	Send catalogues to retail, industrial, and institutional customers featuring jewellery, cosmetics, specialty foods, and other small items. Maintain no outside sales force.
Brokers and Agents	Do not take title to goods. Main function is to facilitate buying and selling, for which they earn a commission.
Brokers	Chief function is bringing buyers and sellers together and assisting in negotiation. They do not carry inventory, provide financing, or assume risk. Examples: food, real estate, and insurance brokers.
Agents	Represent either buyers or sellers on a more permanent basis than brokers do. There are several types:
Manufacturers' agents	Represent two or more manufacturers of complementary lines. Often used in apparel, furniture, and electrical goods. Hired by small manufacturers who cannot afford their own field sales forces, and by large manufacturers to open or cover territories that cannot support full-time salespeople.
Selling agents	Have contractual authority to sell a manufacturer's entire output. Found in such product areas as textiles, industrial machinery, coal, chemicals, and metals.
Purchasing agents	Generally have a long-term relationship with buyers and make purchases for them, often receiving, inspecting, warehousing, and shipping the merchandise to the buyers.
Commission merchants	Take physical possession of products and negotiate sales, usually on a short-term basis. Used most often in agricultural marketing. The commission merchant takes a truckload of commodities to a central market, sells it for the best price, deducts a commission and expenses, and remits the balance to the producer.
Manufacturers' and Retailers' Branches and Offices	Wholesaling operations conducted by sellers or buyers themselves rather than through independent wholesalers.
Sales branches and offices	Set up by manufacturers to improve inventory control, selling, and promotion. *Sales branches* carry inventory and are found in such industries as lumber and automotive parts. *Sales offices* do not carry inventory and are found in dry goods and notions industries.
Purchasing offices	Perform a role similar to that of brokers or agents but are part of the buyer's organization.

on the marketing mix—product assortments and services, price, promotion, and place (see Figure 11.3).

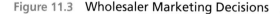

Figure 11.3 Wholesaler Marketing Decisions

Wholesalers must define their target markets and position themselves effectively—they cannot serve everyone. They can choose a target group by size of customer (only large retailers), type of customer (convenience stores only), need for service (customers who need credit), or other factors. Within the target group, they can identify the more profitable customers, design stronger offers, and build better relationships with them. They can propose automatic reordering systems, set up management-training and advising systems, or even sponsor a voluntary chain. They can discourage less profitable customers by requiring larger orders or adding service charges to smaller ones.

Wholesalers must also decide on product assortment and services, prices, promotion, and place. The wholesaler's "product" is the assortment of *goods* and *services* that it offers. Wholesalers are under great pressure to carry a full line and to stock enough for immediate delivery. But this practice can damage profits. Wholesalers today are cutting down on the number of lines they carry, choosing to carry only the more profitable ones. Wholesalers are also rethinking which services count most in building strong customer relationships and which should be dropped or charged for. The key is to find the mix of services most valued by their target customers.

Price is also an important wholesaler decision. Wholesalers usually mark up the cost of goods by a standard percentage—say, 20 percent. Expenses may run 17 percent of the gross margin, leaving a profit margin of 3 percent. In grocery wholesaling, the average profit margin is often lower than 2 percent. And so wholesalers are trying new pricing approaches. They may cut their margin on some lines to win important new customers. They may ask suppliers for special price breaks when they can turn them into an increase in the supplier's sales.

Although *promotion* can be critical to wholesaler success, most wholesalers are not promotion minded. Their use of trade advertising, sales promotion, personal selling, and public relations is largely scattered and unplanned. Many are behind the times in personal selling—they still see selling as a single salesperson talking to a single customer instead of as a team effort to sell, build, and service major accounts. Wholesalers also need to adopt some of the non-personal promotion techniques used by retailers. They need to develop an overall promotion strategy and to make greater use of supplier promotion materials and programs.

Finally, *place* is important—wholesalers must choose their locations and facilities carefully. Wholesalers typically locate in low-rent, low-tax areas and tend to invest little money in their buildings, equipment, and systems. As a result, their materials-handling and order-processing systems are often outdated. Recently, however, large and progressive wholesalers have been reacting to rising costs by investing in automated warehouses and online ordering systems. Orders are fed from the retailer's system directly into the wholesaler's computer, and the items are picked up by mechanical devices and automatically taken to a shipping platform where they are assembled. Most large wholesalers use computers to carry out accounting, billing, inventory control, and forecasting. Modern wholesalers are adapting their services to the needs of target customers and finding cost-reducing methods of doing business.

Such developments as the North American Free Trade Agreement mean that many large wholesalers are now going global. Geographic expansion will require that distributors learn how to compete effectively over wider and more diverse areas. As more manufacturers attempt to control their market share by owning the intermediaries that bring their goods to market, consolidation will significantly reduce the number of wholesaling firms. Surviving wholesalers will grow larger, primarily through acquisition, merger, and geographic expansion.

RETAILING

We all know that The Bay, Zellers, and Wal-Mart are retailers, but so are TD and Royal Banks, Avon representatives, the local Holiday Inn, a doctor seeing patients, and companies selling products and services to consumers through direct mail, catalogues, telephone, home TV shopping shows, home and office parties, door-to-door contact, vending machines, online services, and Internet marketing. **Retailing** includes all the activities involved in selling goods or services directly to consumers for their personal, nonbusiness use. **Retailers** are businesses whose sales come primarily from retailing. This section focuses on retailing done in retail stores. Non-store retailing includes selling to consumers through direct mail, catalogues, telephone, home TV shopping shows, home and office parties, door-to-door contact, vending machines, and the Internet, and other direct retailing approaches.

What functions do retailers serve? Why don't all producers simply sell their products directly to consumers? In some cases, it is practical for producers to do their own selling, but in many cases, using retailers just makes sense in terms of both cost and expertise. Retailers can perform many of the channel functions discussed earlier, and in many cases they can perform them better and for less cost than the manufacturer could. These functions include

☐ *Information function:* Retailers can collect information about consumers in their particular geographic area, interpret buyer preferences as seen by their sales staff, or communicate the proper use of a product to a prospective customer.

☐ *Product function:* Retailers may advise manufacturers on necessary changes in product design, as learned from front-line interaction with consumers; they may make arrangements with manufacturers to provide private-label or store-label goods.

☐ *Price function:* Retailers offer a smaller volume of goods for the typical consumer to purchase; it's cheaper to make 5000 golf balls, but since most consumers buy them five at a time, retailers help reduce prices for the ordinary consumer. Retailers may also make decisions about when to mark an item down for sale, and work to improve productivity in order to avoid raising prices.

☐ *Place function:* Retailers offer a variety of products in one location so that customers don't have to visit separate stores for each item; they make products available when the customer wants them; and they make decisions about which new products will be offered shelf space.

☐ *Promotion function:* Retailers can run their own ads to feature certain items, or team up with the manufacturer in joint promotions. They arrange in-store display of

Retailing All activities involved in selling goods and services directly to consumers for their personal, non-business use.

Retailer A business whose sales come primarily from retailing.

products, and can direct customers to particular products in the store and engage in personal selling.

☐ *Ownership function:* Retailers are the final step in the consumer actually taking title to the product, but they also absorb risk by taking title and bearing the cost of theft, damage, spoilage, and obsolescence.

Types of Retailers

Retail stores come in all shapes and sizes, and new retail types keep emerging. They can be classified in terms of *amount of service* offered, breadth and depth of *product lines,* the *relative prices* they charge, and how they are *organized.* Table 11.2 shows how the major types of retailers compare on service, product line, and price.

Self-service retailers increased rapidly in Canada during the Great Depression of the 1930s. Customers were willing to perform their own "locate-compare-select" process to save money. Today, self-service is the basis of all discount operations, and is typically used by sellers of convenience goods (such as supermarkets) and nationally branded, fast-moving shopping goods (such as Future Shop).

Limited-service retailers, such as Sears or The Bay, provide more sales assistance because they carry more goods about which customers need information. Their increased operating costs result in higher prices. In *full-service retailers,* such as specialty stores and first-class department stores, salespeople assist customers in every phase of the shopping process. Full-service stores usually carry more specialty goods for which customers like to be "waited on." These increased services result in much higher operating costs, which are passed along to customers as higher prices.

Product Line Retailers also can be classified by the length and breadth of their product assortments. Some retailers, such as **specialty stores,** carry narrow product lines with deep assortments within those lines. The increasing use of market segmentation, market targeting, and product specialization has resulted in a greater need for stores that focus on specific products and segments.

In contrast, **department stores** carry a wide variety of product lines. In recent years, department stores have been squeezed between more focused and flexible specialty stores on the one hand, and more efficient, lower-priced discounters on the other. In

Specialty store A retail store that carries a narrow product line with a deep assortment within that line.

Department store A retail organization that carries a wide variety of product lines—typically clothing, home furnishings, and household goods; each line is operated as a separate department managed by specialist buyers or merchandisers.

Table 11.2 How Major Types of Retailers Compare on Three Major Factors

	Amount of Service	Product Line	Relative Prices
Specialty store	Full-service	Narrow and deep	High
Department store	Limited-service	Wide but not deep	Average to High
Supermarket	Self-service	Wide but not deep	Average
Convenience store	Self-service	Limited	High
Superstore	Self-service	Very wide	Low to Average
Category killer	Limited-service	Very deep	Average
Discount store	Self-service	Varies	Low
Off-price retailer	Self-service	Varies	Low
Factory outlet	Self-service	Varies	Low
Warehouse club	Self-service	Very wide	Low

response, many have added "bargain basements" and promotional events to meet the discount threat. Others have set up store brand programs, "boutiques" and "designer shops" (such as Tommy Hilfiger or Polo shops within department stores), and other store formats that compete with specialty stores. Still others are trying mail-order, telephone, and website selling. Service remains the key differentiating factor.

Supermarkets are large, low-cost, low-margin, high-volume, self-service stores that carry a wide variety of food, laundry, and household products. Chains such as Sobey's, A&P, and Loblaws account for most of the supermarket sales in Canada, and this channel is rapidly consolidating. Most chains now operate fewer but larger stores. They practise "scrambled merchandising," and carry many nonfood items—beauty aids, housewares, toys, prescriptions, appliances, video cassettes, sporting goods, garden supplies—hoping to find high-margin lines to improve profits. They are also improving their facilities and services to attract more customers. Many supermarkets are "moving upscale," providing "from-scratch" bakeries, gourmet deli counters, and fresh seafood departments. Others are cutting costs, establishing more efficient operations, and lowering prices to compete more effectively with food discounters.

> **Supermarket** Large, low-cost, low-margin, high-volume, self-service store that carries a wide variety of food, laundry, and household products.

Convenience stores are small stores that carry a limited line of high-turnover convenience goods. These stores are located near residential areas and are open long hours, seven days a week. When supermarkets won the right to open for business on Sundays, and drugstore chains and gas station boutiques began selling groceries and snack foods, convenience stores lost their monopoly on their key differentiating variable—*convenience*. The result has been a huge industry shakeout. Whereas once these stores sold over-priced emergency goods, they now offer a wide range of convenience items that are competitively priced, as well as services such as bank machines and photocopying. And although many of the "mom-and-pop" stores that once dominated the industry are closing, others are being opened by the huge chains, such as Couche-Tard, which includes Mac's, Becker's, Mike's Mart, and Daisy Mart.

> **Convenience store** A small store located near a residential area that is open long hours seven days a week and carries a limited line of high-turnover convenience goods.

Superstores are much larger than regular supermarkets. They carry a large assortment of routinely purchased food and nonfood items and offer services such as dry cleaning, post offices, photo finishing, cheque cashing, bill paying, lunch counters, car care, and pet care. The Real Canadian Superstore, for example, has locations all across Canada. These stores carry everything from telephones and children's apparel to fresh fruits and seafood, and even provide in-store President's Choice Financial Services.

> **Superstore** A store much larger than a regular supermarket that carries a large assortment of routinely purchased food and nonfood items and offers services such as dry cleaning, post offices, photo finishing, cheque cashing, bill paying, lunch counters, car care, and pet care.

Recent years have seen the advent of superstores that are actually giant specialty stores, the so-called **category killers.** Many of these "big-box" retailers are megastores that have crossed the border from the United States. As big as airplane hangars, the stores carry a wide assortment of a particular line and have a knowledgeable staff. American big-box retailers Sleep Country, Home Depot, and The Sports Authority have entered the Canadian market, and Canadian big-box retailers such as Chapters and Rona followed suit.

> **Category killer** Giant specialty store that carries a very deep assortment of a particular line and is staffed by knowledgeable employees.

Finally, for some retailers, the product line is actually a service. **Service retailers** include hotels and motels, banks, airlines, colleges and universities, hospitals, movie theatres, tennis clubs, bowling alleys, restaurants, repair services, hair care shops, and dry cleaners. Today, service retailers in Canada are growing faster than product retailers.

> **Service retailers** Retailers that sell services rather than goods.

Relative Prices Retailers can also be classified according to the prices they charge. Most retailers charge regular prices and offer normal-quality goods and customer service. Others offer higher-quality goods and service at higher prices. The retailers that feature low prices are discount stores and "off-price" retailers.

A **discount store** sells standard merchandise at lower prices by accepting lower margins and selling higher volume. The early discount stores, like Zellers, cut expenses by offering few services and operating in warehouse-like facilities in low-rent, heavily travelled districts. In recent years, facing intense competition from other discounters like

> **Discount store** A retail institution that sells standard merchandise at lower prices by accepting lower margins and selling at higher volume.

Wal-Mart and department stores, many discount retailers have "traded up." They have improved decor, added new lines and services, and opened suburban branches, which have led to higher costs and prices.

When the major discount stores traded up, a new wave of off-price retailers moved in to fill the low-price, high-volume gap. Ordinary discounters buy at regular wholesale prices and accept lower margins to keep prices down. In contrast, **off-price retailers**, like the dollar stores, buy at less-than-regular wholesale prices and charge consumers less than retail. Off-price retailers can be found in all areas, from food, clothing, and electronics to no-frills banking and discount brokerages.

The three main types of off-price retailers are *independents, factory outlets,* and *warehouse clubs.* **Independent off-price retailers** are either owned and run by entrepreneurs or are divisions of larger retail corporations. Although many off-price operations are run by smaller independents, most large off-price retailer operations are owned by bigger retail chains. Winners, for example, is owned by U.S.-based TJX.

Factory outlets are off-price retailing operations that are owned and operated by a manufacturer and that normally carry the manufacturer's surplus, discontinued, or irregular goods. Factory outlets sometimes group together in *factory outlet malls,* which have become one of the hottest growth areas in retailing. The malls are now moving upscale—and even dropping "factory" from their descriptions—narrowing the gap between factory outlet and more traditional forms of retailers.

Warehouse clubs (or *wholesale clubs* or *membership warehouses*), such as Costco, sell a limited selection of brand-name grocery items, appliances, clothing, and a hodgepodge of other goods at deep discounts to members who pay annual membership fees. They operate in huge warehouse-like facilities and offer few frills. Customers themselves must wrestle furniture, heavy appliances, and other large items to the checkout line. Such clubs make no home deliveries and often accept no credit cards. However, they do offer ultra-low prices and surprise deals on selected brand merchandise. Warehouse clubs took the country by storm in the 1980s and early 1990s, but their growth has slowed considerably of late because of the emergence of Wal-Mart and strong competitive reactions by supermarket chains.

Retail Organizations Although many retail stores are independently owned, an increasing number are banding together under some form of corporate or contractual organization. There are four major types of retail organizations—*corporate chains, voluntary chains* and *retailer cooperatives, franchise organizations,* and *merchandising conglomerates.*

Chain stores are two or more outlets that are commonly owned and controlled, have central buying and merchandising, and sell similar lines of merchandise. They have many advantages over independents. Their size allows them to buy in large quantities at lower prices. They can afford to hire corporate-level specialists to deal with areas such as pricing, promotion, merchandising, inventory control, and sales forecasting. And corporate chains gain promotional economies because their advertising costs are spread over many stores and over a large sales volume. Unique government owned and operated chain stores are found in parts of Canada; for example, the LCBO and The Beer Store control the distribution of liquor, wine, and beer in Ontario.

The great success of corporate chains caused many independents to band together in one of two forms of contractual associations. One is the **voluntary chain**—a wholesaler-sponsored group of independent retailers that engages in group buying and common merchandising. Examples include True Value Hardware and Independent Grocers Alliance (IGA). The other form of contractual association is the **retailer cooperative**—independent retailers that band together to set up a jointly owned, central wholesale operation and conduct joint merchandising and promotion efforts. Ace Hardware is an example. These organizations give independents the buying and promotion economies they need to meet the prices of corporate chains.

Off-price retailer Retailer that buys at below wholesale prices and sells at less than retail. Examples are factory outlets, independents, and warehouse clubs.

Independent off-price retailer Off-price retailer that is either owned and run by entrepreneurs or is a division of a larger retail corporation.

Factory outlet Off-price retailing operation that is owned and operated by a manufacturer and that normally carries the manufacturer's surplus, discontinued, or irregular goods.

Warehouse club Off-price retailer that sells a limited selection of brand-name grocery items, appliances, clothing, and a hodgepodge of other goods at deep discounts to members who pay annual membership fees.

Chain stores Two or more outlets that are owned and controlled in common, have central buying and merchandising, and sell similar lines of merchandise.

Voluntary chain A wholesale-sponsored group of independent retailers that engages in group buying and common merchandising.

Retailer cooperative Independent retailers banded together for central buying and promotion.

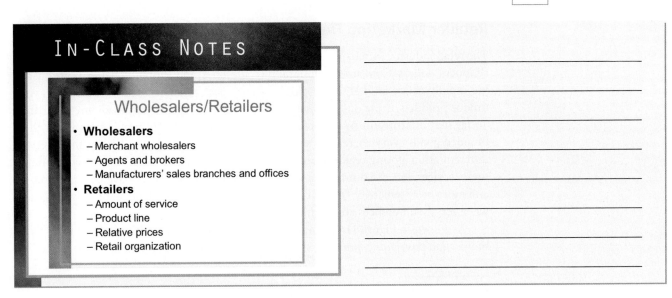

IN-CLASS NOTES

Wholesalers/Retailers

- **Wholesalers**
  - Merchant wholesalers
  - Agents and brokers
  - Manufacturers' sales branches and offices
- **Retailers**
  - Amount of service
  - Product line
  - Relative prices
  - Retail organization

Merchandising conglomerates are corporations that combine several retailing forms under central ownership and share some distribution and management functions. The Venator Group, for example, operates a number of specialty chains, including Northern Reflections, Northern Traditions, Northern Elements, and Northern Getaway, as well as Foot Locker (sports shoes). Diversified retailing, which provides superior management systems and economies that benefit all the separate retail operations, is likely to increase.

> **Merchandising conglomerates** A free-form corporation that combines several diversified retailers under central ownership.

Another form of contractual retail organization is a **franchise**, where a contractual association exists between a manufacturer, wholesaler, or service organization (a franchiser) and independent businesspeople (franchisees) who buy the right to own and operate one or more units in the franchise system. The main difference between franchise organizations and other contractual systems (voluntary chains and retail cooperatives) is that franchise systems are normally based on some unique product or service; on a method of doing business; or on the trade name, goodwill, or patent that the franchiser has developed. Franchising has been prominent in fast-food restaurants, video stores, health or fitness centres, haircutting, auto rentals, motels, travel agencies, real estate, and dozens of other product and service areas. A notable Canadian example is Canadian Tire.

> **Franchise** A contractual association between a manufacturer, wholesaler, or service organization (a franchiser) and independent businesspeople (franchisees) who buy the right to own and operate one or more units in the franchise system.

Linking the Concepts

Think about all the different kinds of retailers you deal with regularly, many of which overlap in the products they carry.

- Pick a product: a camera, microwave oven, hand tool, or something else you are familiar with. Shop for this product at two very different store types, say a discount store or category killer on the one hand, and a department store or smaller specialty store on the other. Compare the stores on product assortment, services, and prices. If you were going to buy the product, where would you buy it and why?
- What does your shopping trip suggest about the futures of the competing store formats you sampled?

Retailer Marketing Decisions

The retail industry suffers from chronic overcapacity, resulting in fierce competition for shoppers' dollars. Consumer demographics, lifestyles, and shopping patterns are changing rapidly, as are retailing technologies. In the past, retailers attracted customers with unique products, more or better services than their competitors offered, or credit cards. Today, national-brand manufacturers, in their drive for volume, have placed their branded goods everywhere, and as a result stores are looking increasingly alike. Service differentiation among retailers has also eroded; many department stores have trimmed their services and discounters have increased theirs. Consumers have become smarter and more price sensitive. They see no reason to pay more for identical brands, especially when service differences are shrinking.

As shown in Figure 11.4, retailers face major marketing decisions about their *target market* and *positioning, product assortment and services, price, promotion,* and *place.*

Figure 11.4   Retailer Marketing Decisions

Retailers first must define their target markets and then decide how they will position themselves in these markets. Should the store focus on upscale or downscale shoppers? Do they want to serve those shoppers through variety, depth of assortment, convenience, or low prices? Until they define and profile their markets, retailers cannot make all the other decisions that must support their positions.

The retailer's *product assortment* should match the target market's expectations. In its quest to differentiate itself from competitors, a retailer can offer a narrow and shallow assortment (small lunch counter), a narrow and deep assortment (delicatessen), a wide and shallow assortment (cafeteria), or a wide and deep assortment (large restaurant). Another product assortment element is the *quality* of the goods: The consumer is interested not only in the range of choice but also in the quality of the products available.

Retailers also must decide on a *services mix* to offer customers. The old mom-and-pop grocery stores offered home delivery, credit, and conversation—services that today's supermarkets ignore. The services mix is one of the key tools of nonprice competition for setting one store apart from another.

The store's *atmosphere* is another element in its product arsenal. Every store has a physical layout that makes moving around in it either hard or easy. Each store has a certain feel; one store is cluttered, another charming, a third plush. The store must have a planned atmosphere that suits the target market and moves shoppers to buy.

A retailer's price policy is another crucial positioning factor and must be decided in relation to its target market, its product and service assortment, and its competition. All retailers would like to charge high markups and achieve high volume, but the two seldom go together. Most retailers seek *either* high markups on lower volume (most specialty stores) *or* low markups on higher volume (mass merchandisers and discount stores). Thus, Winnipeg-based Hanford Drewitt prices men's suits starting at $1000 and shoes at $400—it sells a low volume but makes a hefty profit on each sale. At the other extreme, Winners sells brand-name clothing at discount prices, settling for a lower margin on each sale but selling a much higher volume.

Retailers use the normal marketing communications tools—advertising, personal selling, sales promotion, public relations, and direct marketing—to reach consumers. They advertise in newspapers, magazines, radio, and television. Advertising may be supported by newspaper inserts and direct-mail pieces. Personal selling requires careful training of salespeople in how to greet customers, meet their needs, and handle their complaints. Sales promotions may include in-store demonstrations, displays, contests, and visiting celebrities. Public relations activities, such as press conferences and speeches, store openings, special events, newsletters, magazines, and public service activities, are always available to retailers. Most retailers also have websites, offering customers information and other features and often selling merchandise directly.

Retailers often cite three critical factors in retailing success: *location, location,* and *location!* A retailer's location is key to its ability to attract customers. And the costs of building or leasing facilities have a major impact on the retailer's profits. Thus, site-location decisions are among the most important the retailer makes. Small retailers may have to settle for whatever locations they can find or afford. Large retailers usually employ specialists who select locations using advanced methods. One of the savviest location experts in recent years has been the toy-store giant Toys "R" Us. Most of their new locations are in rapidly growing areas where the population closely matches their customer base.

The life cycle of new retail forms is getting shorter. Department stores took about 100 years to reach the mature stage of the life cycle; more recent forms, such as warehouse stores, reached maturity in about 10 years. In such an environment, seemingly solid retail positions can crumble quickly. One of Canada's most venerable retailers, Eaton's, learned this the hard way. The fall of the 127-year-old retailing veteran shows that retailers can no longer sit back and rely on a once-successful formula—they must keep adapting.

Many retailing innovations are partially explained by the wheel of retailing concept (see Figure 11.5), which states that new types of retailers usually begin as low-margin, low-price, low-status operations but later evolve into higher-priced, higher-service

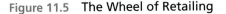

Figure 11.5   **The Wheel of Retailing**

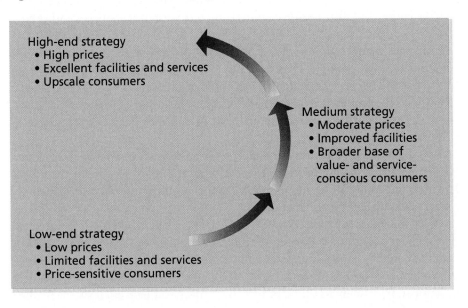

operations, eventually becoming like the conventional retailers they replaced.[4] The cycle begins again when still newer types of retailers evolve with lower costs and prices. The wheel of retailing concept seems to explain the initial success and later troubles of department stores, supermarkets, and discount stores, and the recent success of off-price retailers. At the start of that wheel now may be the new array of alternative retail outlets, including mail order, television, phone, and online shopping.

Retailers with unique formats and strong brand positioning are increasingly moving into other countries. Many are expanding internationally to escape mature and saturated home markets. Over the years, several giant retailers—McDonald's, The Gap, Toys "R" Us—have become globally prominent because of their great marketing prowess. Others, such as Wal-Mart, are rapidly establishing a global presence. Wal-Mart, which now operates 1300 stores in nine countries abroad, sees exciting global potential. Its international division racked up fiscal 2002 sales of US$35.4 billion. Still other companies are taking advantage of increasingly liberalized tariffs among many countries worldwide. For example, January 2005 legislation eliminated the tariff on textiles imported from China to the United States. This has in turn increased Chinese interest in acquiring a share of Canadian businesses in order to better reach even more markets.

CHANNEL BEHAVIOUR AND ORGANIZATION

Distribution channels are more than simple collections of firms tied together by various flows. They are complex behavioural systems in which people and companies interact to accomplish individual, company, and channel goals. Some channel systems consist only of informal interactions among loosely organized firms; others consist of formal interactions guided by strong organizational structures. Moreover, channel systems do not stand still—new types of intermediaries emerge and completely new channel systems evolve. Here we look at channel behaviour and at how members organize to do the work of the channel.

Channel Behaviour

A distribution channel comprises firms that work together to move the product from its point of origin to the hands of the final customer. For example, a Ford dealer depends on the Ford Motor Company to design cars that meet consumer needs. In turn, Ford depends on the dealer to attract consumers, persuade them to buy Ford cars, and service cars after the sale. In fact, the success of individual Ford dealers depends on how well the entire Ford distribution channel competes with the channels of other auto manufacturers.

Each channel member plays a role in the channel and specializes in performing one or more functions. For example, HP's role is to produce personal computers that consumers will like and to create demand through national advertising. Future Shop's role is to display these HP computers in convenient locations, to answer buyers' questions, and to close sales. The channel will be most effective when each member is assigned the tasks it can do best.

Because the success of individual channel members depends on overall channel success, all channel firms should understand and accept their roles, coordinate their goals and activities, and cooperate to attain overall channel goals in order to more effectively sense, serve, and satisfy the target market.

However, individual channel members rarely take such a broad view. They are usually more concerned with their own short-run goals and their dealings with those firms closest to them in the channel. Cooperating to achieve overall channel goals sometimes means giving up individual company goals. Although channel members are dependent on one another, they often act alone in their own short-run best interests. They often disagree on the roles each should play—on who should do what and for what rewards. Such disagreements over goals and roles generate **channel conflict**.

Horizontal conflict occurs among firms at the same level of the channel. For instance, Future Shop might complain that Best Buy, another retailer that sells HP computers, is being too aggressive in their advertising and sales promotion.

Vertical conflict, conflict among different levels of the same channel, is even more common. A recent instance took place when dealerships decided to wage war on Ford Canada:

> Car dealerships are among Canada's largest small businesses; they depend on a single supplier for their inventory, and minor disputes are frequent. However, in an unprecedented letter written in March 2000 sent to all Ford dealers in Canada, the president of the Canadian Automobile Dealers Association lashed out at Ford Canada for its "unilateral, autocratic and confrontational" actions that pose a "threat to the Canadian dealer network." The letter was written as a result of dealer complaints that arose out of Ford Canada's new retail strategy called Ford Retail Networks (FRN). Ford wants to limit dealer autonomy and institute more customer-friendly sales tactics such as single-price selling. To accomplish this, Ford Canada hopes to become a 40 percent shareholder in the dealers' operations. Dealers believe they are being forced to sell out to Ford, and as a result, dialogue between Ford and its retailers has broken down.[5]

Sometimes conflict occurs because of differences in the way things are done in different countries. For example, national pricing norms have been the subject of a long battle between U.S. giant manufacturer Procter & Gamble and the huge combination food/non-food consumer goods stores in France called hypermarchés. Since the 1950s the hypermarchés have had a system of negotiating their margins with producers that involves delaying a percentage of the margin until they see how well the producers' brands actually sell in the stores. P&G, unaccustomed to such resistance from retailers, has lost millions in revenue while the hypermarchés boycott their goods. P&G is betting that, through the power of their brands, they will ultimately end the practice known as "delayed margins."[6]

Sometimes conflict in the channel may be merely a difference in perception rather than true conflict. Japanese supermarkets resist selling Coca-Cola in vending machines, fearing it will take business away from their stores, but Coke tries to convince them that the machines are selling to the same people, just on different purchase occasions.[7]

Some conflict in the channel takes the form of healthy competition. Such competition can be good for the channel—without it, the channel could become passive and non-innovative. But if it gets out of hand, conflict can disrupt channel effectiveness and cause lasting harm to channel relationships. For the channel as a whole to perform well, each channel member's role must be specified and channel conflict must be managed. Cooperation, role assignment, and conflict management in the channel are attained through strong channel leadership with the power to assign roles and manage conflict. A **Channel Captain** may be formally chosen by members of a channel, but more often simply rises to the position by virtue of demonstrated skills to help the channel deal with a particular issue of conflict. Global electronic communication has in many ways greatly helped in the management of channels, as managers working around the world can instantaneously contact each other and all members of the supply chain.

Channel conflict Disagreement among channel members on goals and roles—who should do what and for what rewards.

Channel Captain A leader, whether formally chosen or rising to the role by virtue of demonstrated skills, who helps the channel deal with conflict.

Vertical Marketing Systems

Historically, distribution channels have been loose collections of independent companies, each showing little concern for overall channel performance. One of the biggest channel developments has been the vertical marketing systems that have emerged over the years to challenge conventional distribution channels. Figure 11.6 contrasts the two types of channel arrangements.

Figure 11.6 Comparison of Conventional Distribution Channel with Vertical Marketing System

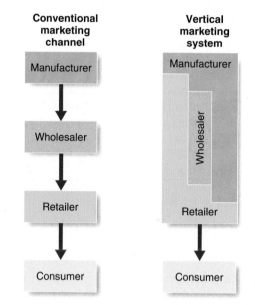

Conventional distribution channel A channel consisting of one or more independent producers, wholesalers, and retailers, each a separate business seeking to maximize its own profits even at the expense of profits for the system as a whole.

Vertical marketing system (VMS) A distribution channel structure in which producers, wholesalers, and retailers act as a unified system. One channel member owns the others, has contracts with them, or has so much power that they all cooperate.

A **conventional distribution channel** consists of one or more independent producers, wholesalers, and retailers. Each is a separate business seeking to maximize its own profits, even at the expense of profits for the system as a whole. No channel member has much control over the other members, and no formal means exists for assigning roles and resolving channel conflict. In contrast, a **vertical marketing system (VMS)** consists of producers, wholesalers, and retailers acting as a unified system. One channel member owns the others, has contracts with them, or wields so much power that they must all cooperate. For example, Sears buys more than 50 percent of its goods from companies that it partly or wholly owns. George Weston Inc., owner of Loblaws, operates a soft-drink bottling operation, an ice-cream-making plant, and a bakery that supplies stores with everything from bagels to birthday cakes.

Franchises are special types of vertical marketing systems that link several stages in the production–distribution process. Canada has more than 65 000 franchise operations (four times more per capita than the United States) that ring up more than $90 billion in sales annually. In fact, 40 percent of every dollar spent on retail items is spent at a franchise.[8] Almost every kind of business has been franchised—from motels and fast-food restaurants to dental centres and dating services, and from wedding consultants and maid services to funeral homes and fitness centres.

Horizontal Marketing Systems

Horizontal marketing system A channel arrangement in which two or more companies at one level join together to follow a new marketing opportunity.

Another channel development is the **horizontal marketing system**, in which two or more companies at one level combine their capital, production capabilities, or marketing resources to follow a new marketing opportunity. Companies might join forces with competitors or noncompetitors. They might work with each other temporarily or permanently, or they may create a separate company.

Forming successful horizontal marketing systems is essential in an era of global business and travel. For example, the merger of Canada's two largest wineries, T.G. Bright &

Canada has more than 65 000 franchise operations that ring up more than $90 billion in sales annually. In fact, 40 percent of every dollar spent on retail items is spent at a franchise.

Co. Ltd. and Cartier & Inniskillin Vintners Inc., once major competitors, placed them in the top 10 of North American wine makers and gave them the economies of scale and resources necessary to export into the U.S. market. And Air Canada is now part of the Star Alliance, whose partners include United Airlines, Lufthansa, SAS, and Thai Airways International. It battles other alliances, such as the one formed by American Airlines, British Airways, Japan Airlines, and Qantas. This partnership allows Air Canada to offer flights to 642 U.S. cities and to provide passengers with shorter layovers, more convenient connections, and less hassle transferring their baggage.[9]

Hybrid Marketing Systems

In the past, many companies used a single channel to sell to a single market or market segment. Today, with the proliferation of market segments and channel possibilities, more and more companies have adopted multichannel distribution systems—often called **hybrid marketing systems.** Such multichannel marketing occurs when a single firm sets up two or more channels to reach one or more customer segments. The use of hybrid channel systems has recently increased significantly.

    Figure 11.7 shows a hybrid system. In the figure, the producer sells directly to consumer segment 1 using direct-mail catalogues, telemarketing, and the Internet and directly to consumer segment 2 through retailers. It sells indirectly to business segment 1 through distributors and dealers and directly to business segment 2 through its own sales force.

    IBM used such a hybrid system effectively. For years it sold computers only through its own sales force, which sold large systems to business customers. To meet the demands of a huge market for computers and information technology with dozens of segments and niches, IBM added 18 new channels in fewer than 10 years. It also sold through a comprehensive network of distributors and value-added resellers. Consumers could buy IBM personal computers from specialty computer stores or any of several large retailers, including Wal-Mart, Future Shop, and Staples. IBM used telemarketing to service the needs of small and medium-size business. And both business and final consumers were able to buy online from the company's IBM Store website. In December of 2004, however, IBM sold its PC division to a mainland China firm, Lenovo. The PC Division had

Hybrid marketing system
Multichannel distribution system in which a single firm sets up two or more channels to reach one or more customer segments.

Figure 11.7   Hybrid Marketing System

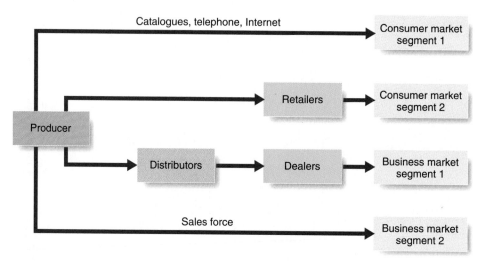

been losing money for a number of years, and this sale provided IBM with an entry to the huge mainland China market.

Hybrid systems, then, offer many advantages to companies facing large and complex markets. But such hybrid systems are harder to control, and they generate conflict as more channels compete for customers and sales. For example, when IBM began selling directly to customers through catalogues, telemarketing, and its own website, many of its retail dealers cried "unfair competition" and threatened to drop the IBM line or to give it less emphasis.

Changing Channel Organization

Disintermediation The displacement of traditional resellers from a distribution channel by radical new types of intermediaries or by product and service producers going directly to final buyers.

Changes in technology and the explosive growth of direct and online marketing are having a profound impact on the nature and design of distribution channels. One major trend is toward disintermediation—a big term with a clear message and important consequences. **Disintermediation** is the displacement of traditional resellers from a distribution channel by radical new types of intermediaries or by product and service producers going directly to final buyers.

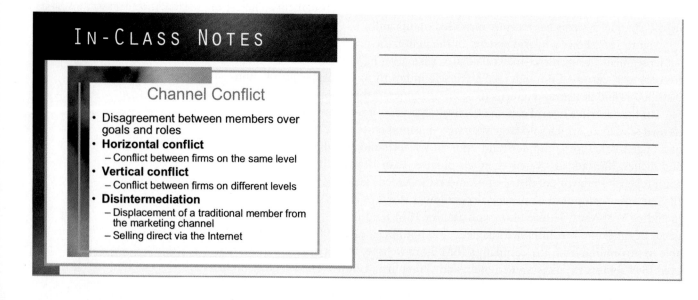

Figure 11.8 Disintermediation of a Marketing Channel

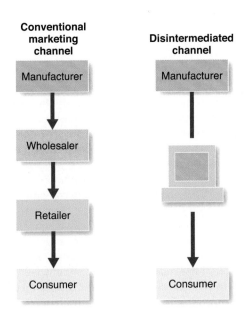

Thus, in some industries, traditional intermediaries are dropping by the wayside. WestJet sells directly to final buyers, eliminating the retail travel agency from its distribution channels. Online retailing has taken business from traditional brick-and-mortar retailers.

Disintermediation presents problems and opportunities for both producers and intermediaries (see Marketing at Work 11.1). To avoid being swept aside, traditional intermediaries must find new ways to add value in the supply chain. Some distribution chains that had previously disintermediated are already reintermediating, although with different kinds of members of the channel. For example, some years ago the airlines attempted to sell directly to consumers online, allowing them to bypass the traditional brick-and-mortar travel agencies that had once served as an intermediary. But companies like Expedia.com and Travelocity.ca have re-intermediated the channel as online

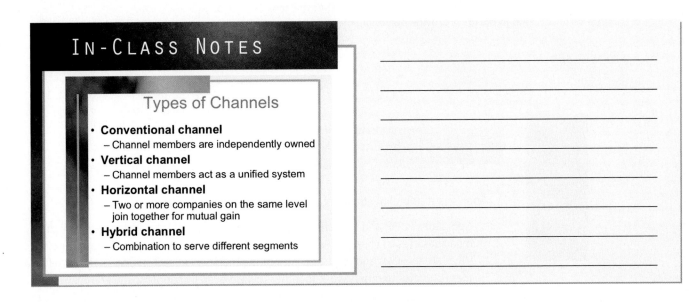

In-Class Notes

Types of Channels

- **Conventional channel**
  - Channel members are independently owned
- **Vertical channel**
  - Channel members act as a unified system
- **Horizontal channel**
  - Two or more companies on the same level join together for mutual gain
- **Hybrid channel**
  - Combination to serve different segments

Marketing at Work | 11.1

Disintermediation: A Fancy Word but a Clear Message

Bayridge Travel in Kingston, Ontario, typifies the kind of business most threatened by the increase in Internet selling. Giant online travel supersites like Expedia and Travelocity let consumers surf the Web for rock-bottom ticket prices, and even the airlines operate websites to sell seats. Similarly, Chapters/Indigo, with its huge inventories and low prices, has displaced the traditional small bookshop, and sites like Amazon.ca and the superstores' own website are displacing traditional bricks-and-mortar retailers.

We call this elimination of a layer of intermediaries from a distribution channel *disintermediation*. Bob Westrope, director of the electronic markets group with KPMG in Toronto, believes that disintermediation represents "a shift in the structure of our economy not seen since the dawning of the industrial age." By facilitating direct contact between buyers and sellers, the Internet is displacing channels in industries ranging from books, apparel, toys, drugs, and consumer electronics to travel, stock brokerage, and real estate services. However, disintermediation can involve almost any new form of channel competition, for example bypassing retailers through telephone and mail-order selling.

Disintermediation works only when a new channel form succeeds in bringing greater value to consumers. If the Internet sites weren't giving buyers greater convenience, selection, and value, they would not succeed. Their huge success suggests they are bringing greater value to significant segments of consumers.

From a producer's viewpoint, disintermediation poses some difficult choices. If the producers create a direct electronic link to the consumer, they risk losing valuable wholesale and retail partners, but if they don't, they risk losing sales to competitors who do.

For many businesses, the major question often is not whether to move to a new, high-growth channel but how quickly and what to do with the already established channels. Despite the risks, most companies know that when more effective channels come along, they must change; traditional producers can't afford to wait very long to rid their distribution channels of inefficiencies.

How can traditional resellers avoid being shut out? By continually looking for new ways to create real customer value, often using the Web. Bayridge Travel now deemphasizes airline ticket sales and specializes in a market niche: cruises. The owner plans to do what computers can't: She'll get to know her customers so well that she can provide personal advice on the cruises

she books. And she'll use a website to launch this new business.

Discount brokerage Charles Schwab & Company, facing a horde of price-cutting e-commerce competitors, jumped onto the Internet, plying customers with a wealth of financial and company information and helping them manage their accounts. Schwab now ranks number one online with a 28 percent share of the online market, twice the share of nearest competitor E*Trade.

Disintermediation is a big word, but the meaning is clear. Those who continually seek new ways to add real value for customers have little to fear; those who fall behind in adding value risk being swept aside by their customers and channel partners.

Sources: Quotes from Rochelle Garner, "Mad as Hell," *Sales & Marketing Management,* June 1999, pp. 55–61; and Maricris G. Briones, "What Technology Wrought: Distribution Channel in Flux," *Marketing News,* February 1, 1999, pp. 3, 15. Also see "Special Report: Technology and Communications Tools for Marketers: Disintermediation: No More Middleman," *Strategy,* March 1, 1999, p. 21; Evan I. Schwartz, "How Middlemen Can Come out on Top," *Business Week,* February 9, 1998, p. ENT4-7; James Champy, "How to Fire Your Dealers," *Forbes,* June 14, 1999, p. 141; Stewart Alsop, "Is There an Amazon.com for Every Industry?" *Fortune,* January 11, 1999, pp. 159–160; and Daniel Roth, "E*Trade's Plan for World Domination," *Fortune,* August 2, 1999, pp. 95–98.

Linking the Concepts

Apply the distribution channel concepts we've discussed so far.

- Compare the HP and Dell channels. Draw a diagram that shows the types of intermediaries in each channel. What kind of channel system does each company use?
- What are the roles and responsibilities of the members in each channel? How well do these channel members work together toward overall channel success?

travel agencies, bringing together in one place a website, all the information a traveller needs to successfully book a business or vacation trip, and the kind of service that used to be offered by brick-and-mortar travel agencies.

To remain competitive, goods and services producers must develop new channel opportunities. However, developing these new channels often brings them into direct competition with their established channels, resulting in conflict. To ease this problem, companies often look for ways to make going direct work for both the company and its channel partners, as we saw in the case of Hewlett-Packard at the start of this chapter.

CHANNEL DESIGN DECISIONS

We now look at several channel decisions that manufacturers face. In designing distribution channels, manufacturers struggle between what is ideal and what is practical. For example, a new firm like Cake Beauty with limited capital usually begins by selling in a limited market area. Cake started out in small boutiques, and once it was successful there, branched out to reach retail agreements with Caban and Holt Renfrew. Eventually, it expanded to international distribution and online sales.

Channel systems often evolve to meet market opportunities and conditions, but for maximum effectiveness, channel analysis and decision making should be more purposeful. Designing a channel system calls for analyzing customer service needs, setting channel objectives and constraints, identifying major channel alternatives, and evaluating them.

Analyzing Consumer Service Needs

Designing the distribution channel starts with finding out what the target market wants from the channel. But providing the fastest delivery, greatest assortment, and most services may not be possible or practical. The company and its channel members may not have the resources or skills needed to provide all the desired services. The company must balance customer service needs not only against the feasibility and costs of meeting these needs, but also against customer price preferences. The success of off-price and discount retailing shows that consumers are often willing to accept lower service levels if this means lower prices.

Setting Channel Objectives and Constraints

Channel objectives should be stated in terms of the desired service level of the target market. The company then decides which segments to serve and the best channels to use in each case in order to minimize the total channel cost of meeting customer service requirements.

The company's channel objectives are also influenced by the nature of the company, its products, its marketing intermediaries, its competitors, and the environment. For example, the company's size and financial situation determine which marketing functions it can handle itself and which it must give to intermediaries. Companies selling perishable products may require more direct marketing to avoid delays and too much handling. And in some cases, a company may want to compete in or near outlets that carry competitors' products, or producers may avoid the channels used by competitors. Avon, for example, uses door-to-door selling rather than going head to head with other cosmetics makers for scarce positions in retail stores. Environmental factors such as economic conditions and legal constraints may also affect channel objectives and design. For example, in a depressed economy, producers want to distribute their goods in the most economical way, using shorter channels and dropping unneeded services that add to the final price of the goods.

Product characteristics affect channel decisions: Fresh flowers must be delivered quickly, with a minimum of handling.

Identifying Major Alternatives

When the company has defined its channel objectives, it should next identify its major channel alternatives in terms of types of intermediaries, the number of intermediaries, and the responsibilities of each channel member.

Types of Intermediaries A firm should identify the types of channel members available to carry out its channel work. For example, suppose a manufacturer of test equipment has developed an audio device that detects poor mechanical connections in machines with moving parts. Company executives think this product would have a market in all industries in which electric, combustion, or steam engines are made or used. The company's current sales force is small, and the problem is how best to reach these different industries. The following channel alternatives might emerge from management discussion:

☐ *Company sales force:* Expand the company's direct sales force. Assign outside salespeople to territories and have them contact all prospects in the area or develop separate company sales forces for different industries. Or, add an inside telesales operation in which telephone salespeople handle small or midsize companies.

☐ *Manufacturer's agency:* Hire manufacturer's agents—independent firms whose sales forces handle related products from many companies—in different regions or industries to sell the new test equipment.

☐ *Industrial distributors:* Find distributors in the different regions or industries who will buy and carry the new line. Give them exclusive distribution, good margins, product training, and promotional support.

Number of Marketing Intermediaries Companies must also determine the number of channel members to use at each level. Three strategies are available: intensive distribution, exclusive distribution, and selective distribution.

Producers of convenience products and common raw materials typically seek **intensive distribution**—a strategy in which they stock their products in as many outlets as possible. These goods must be available where and when consumers want them. For example, toothpaste, candy, and other similar items are sold in millions of outlets to provide maximum brand exposure and consumer convenience. Kraft, Coca-Cola, Kimberly-Clark, and other consumer goods companies distribute their products in this way.

Intensive distribution Stocking the product in as many outlets as possible.

By contrast, some producers purposely limit the number of intermediaries handling their products. The extreme form of this practice is **exclusive distribution**, in which the producer gives only a limited number of dealers the exclusive right to distribute its products in their territories. Exclusive distribution is often found in the distribution of new automobiles and prestige women's clothing. For example, Rolls-Royce dealers are rare—even large cities may have only one or two dealers. By granting exclusive distribution, Rolls-Royce gains stronger distributor selling support and more control over dealer prices, promotion, credit, and services. Exclusive distribution also enhances the car's image and allows for higher markups.

Exclusive distribution Giving a limited number of dealers the exclusive right to distribute the company's products in their territories.

Between intensive and exclusive distribution lies **selective distribution**—the use of more than one, but fewer than all, of the intermediaries who are willing to carry a company's products. Most television, furniture, and small-appliance brands are distributed in this manner. For example, Maytag, Whirlpool, and General Electric sell their major appliances through dealer networks and selected large retailers. By using selective distribution, they do not have to spread their efforts over many outlets, including many marginal ones. They can develop good working relationships with selected channel members and expect a better-than-average selling effort.

Selective distribution The use of more than one, but fewer than all, of the intermediaries who are willing to carry the company's products.

Responsibilities of Channel Members The producer and intermediaries need to agree on price policies, conditions of sale, territorial rights, and responsibilities of each party. For example, McDonald's provides franchisees with promotional support, a record-keeping system, training at Hamburger University, and general management assistance. In turn, franchisees must meet company standards for physical facilities, cooperate with new promotion programs, provide requested information, and buy specified food products. The producer should establish a list price and a fair set of discounts for intermediaries. It must define each channel member's territory, and it should be careful about where it places new resellers.

Evaluating the Major Alternatives

Suppose a company has identified several channel alternatives and wants to select the one that will best satisfy its long-run objectives. Each alternative should be evaluated against economic, control, and adaptive criteria.

Using *economic criteria*, a company compares the likely profitability of different channel alternatives. It estimates the sales that each channel would produce and the costs of selling different volumes through each channel. The company must also consider *control issues*. Using intermediaries usually means giving them some control over the marketing of the product, and some intermediaries take more control than others. Other things being equal, the company prefers to keep as much control as possible. Finally, the company must apply *adaptive criteria*. Channels often involve long-term commitments to other firms, making it hard to adapt the channel to the changing marketing environment. The company wants to keep the channel as flexible as possible. Thus, to be considered, a channel involving long-term commitment should be greatly superior on economic and control grounds.

Exclusive distribution: Luxury car makers sell exclusively through a limited number of dealerships. Such limited distribution enhances the car's image and generates stronger dealership support.

DESIGNING INTERNATIONAL DISTRIBUTION CHANNELS

International marketers face many additional complexities in designing their channels. First, the company must determine the best mode of entry. Figure 11.9 shows three market-entry strategies—*exporting, joint venturing,* and *direct investment*—along with the options each one offers. As the figure shows, each succeeding strategy involves more commitment and risk, but also more control and potential profits.

Figure 11.9   Market Entry Strategies

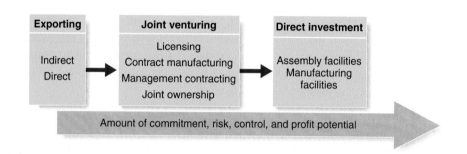

Exporting

Exporting Entering a foreign market by sending products and selling them through international marketing intermediaries (indirect exporting) or through the company's own department, branch, or sales representatives or agents (direct exporting).

The simplest way to enter a foreign market is through **exporting**. The company can passively export its surpluses periodically, or it can make an active commitment to expand exports to a particular market. In either case, the company produces all its goods in its home country, possibly modifying them for the export market. Exporting involves the least change in the company's product lines, organization, investments, or mission.

Companies typically start with *indirect exporting,* working through independent international marketing intermediaries. Indirect exporting involves less investment because the firm does not require an overseas sales force or set of contacts. It also involves less risk. International marketing intermediaries—domestic-based export merchants or agents, cooperative organizations, and export-management companies—bring know-how and services to the relationship, so the seller normally makes fewer mistakes.

Sellers may eventually move into *direct exporting* and handle their own exports. The investment and risk are somewhat greater in this strategy, but so is the potential return. A company can conduct direct exporting in several ways. It can set up a domestic export department that carries out export activities. It can set up an overseas sales branch that handles sales, distribution, and perhaps promotion; the sales branch gives the seller more presence and program control in the foreign market and often serves as a display centre and customer service centre. The company can also send home-based salespeople abroad at certain times to find business. Finally, the company can do its exporting either through foreign-based distributors who buy and own the goods or through foreign-based agents who sell the goods on behalf of the company.

How do you know when you are ready to export? Knowing when your company has both the right product and the capacity to compete on a global scale involves thinking about the resources and knowledge your organization has at its disposal. Your first step is to think about the resources and knowledge your business already has. Team Canada Inc., a network of government departments and agencies that works to help Canadian business compete in a global marketplace, recommends examining the following:

Expectations: Do you have

- ☐ clear and achievable export objectives;
- ☐ a realistic idea of what exporting entails;
- ☐ an openness to new ways of doing business; and
- ☐ an understanding of what is required to succeed in the international marketplace?

Human resources: Do you have

- ☐ the capacity to handle the extra demand associated with exporting;
- ☐ a senior management committed to exporting;
- ☐ efficient ways of responding quickly to customer inquiries;
- ☐ personnel with culturally-sensitive marketing skills; and
- ☐ ways of dealing with language barriers?

Financial and legal resources: Can you

- ☐ obtain enough capital or lines of credit to produce the product or service;
- ☐ find ways to reduce the financial risks of international trade;
- ☐ find people to advise you on the legal and tax implications of exporting;
- ☐ deal effectively with different monetary systems; and
- ☐ ensure protection of your intellectual property?

Competitiveness: Do you have

- ☐ the resources to do market research on the exportability of your product or service;
- ☐ proven, sophisticated market-entry methods; and
- ☐ a product or service that is potentially viable in your target market?[10]

Joint Venturing

A second method of entering a foreign market is **joint venturing**—joining with domestic or foreign companies to produce or market products or services. Joint venturing differs from exporting in that the company joins with a partner to manufacture or market abroad. It differs from direct investment in that an association is formed with someone in the foreign country. The four types of joint ventures are licensing, contract manufacturing, management contracting, and joint ownership.

Licensing **Licensing** is a simple way for a manufacturer to enter international marketing. The company forms an agreement with a licensee in the foreign market. For a fee or royalty, the licensee buys the right to use the company's manufacturing process, trademark, patent, trade secret, or other item of value. The company gains entry into the market at little risk; the licensee gains production expertise or a well-known product or name without having to start from scratch. For example, Tokyo Disneyland is owned and operated by Oriental Land Company under licence from the Walt Disney Company: The 45-year licence gives Disney licensing fees plus 10 percent of admissions and 5 percent of food and merchandise sales.

Licensing has potential disadvantages, however. The firm has less control over the licensee than it would over its own production facilities. If the licensee is very successful, the firm has given up these profits, and when the contract ends, it may find it has created a competitor.

Joint venturing Entering foreign markets by joining with foreign companies to produce or market a product or service.

Licensing A method of entering a foreign market in which the company enters into an agreement with a licensee in the foreign market, offering the right to use a manufacturing process, trademark, patent, trade secret, or other item of value for a fee or royalty.

Contract manufacturing A joint venture in which a company contracts with manufacturers in a foreign market to produce the product.

Contract Manufacturing With **contract manufacturing**, the company contracts with manufacturers in the foreign market to produce its product or provide its service. The drawbacks of contract manufacturing are the decreased control over the manufacturing process and the loss of potential profits on manufacturing. The benefits are the chance to start faster, with less risk, and the later opportunity to either form a partnership with or buy out the local manufacturer.

Management contracting A joint venture in which the domestic firm supplies the management expertise to a foreign company that supplies the capital; the domestic firm exports management services rather than products.

Management Contracting Under **management contracting**, the domestic firm supplies management expertise to a foreign company that supplies the capital. The domestic firm exports management services rather than products.

Management contracting is a low-risk method of getting into a foreign market, and it yields income from the beginning. The arrangement is even more attractive if the contracting firm has an option to buy some share in the managed company later on. The arrangement is not sensible, however, if the company can put its scarce management talent to better uses or if it can make greater profits by undertaking the whole venture. Management contracting also prevents the company from setting up its own operations for a time.

Joint ownership A joint venture in which a company joins investors in a foreign market to create a local business in which the company shares joint ownership and control.

Joint Ownership **Joint ownership** ventures consist of one company joining forces with foreign investors to create a local business in which they share ownership and control. A company can buy an interest in a local firm, or the two parties can form a new business venture. Joint ownership may be needed for economic or political reasons. The firm may lack the financial, physical, or managerial resources to undertake the venture alone, or a foreign government may require joint ownership as a condition for entry.

Joint ownership has drawbacks. The partners may disagree over investment, marketing, or other policies. Whereas many Canadian firms like to reinvest earnings for growth, local firms often like to take out these earnings; whereas Canadian firms emphasize the role of marketing, local investors may rely on selling.

Direct-Investment

Direct investment Entering a foreign market by developing foreign-based assembly or manufacturing facilities.

The greatest involvement in a foreign market comes through **direct investment**—the development of foreign-based assembly or manufacturing facilities. If a company has gained experience in exporting and if the foreign market is large enough, foreign production facilities offer many advantages. The firm may have lower costs in the form of cheaper labour or raw materials, foreign government investment incentives, and freight savings. The firm may improve its image in the host country because it creates jobs. Generally, a firm develops a deeper relationship with government, customers, local suppliers, and distributors, allowing it to better adapt its products to the local market. Finally, the firm keeps full control over the investment and can, therefore, develop manufacturing and marketing policies that serve its long-term international objectives. The main disadvantage of direct investment is the many risks: restricted or devalued currencies, falling markets, or government takeovers.

Whole-Channel View

Whole-channel view Designing international channels that take into account all the necessary links in distributing the seller's products to final buyers, including the seller's headquarters organization, channels between nations, and channels within nations.

Companies who enter the international market will find that each country has its own unique distribution system that has evolved over time and changes very slowly. These channel systems can vary widely from country to country. Global marketers, then, must take a **whole-channel view** of distributing products to customers.

Figure 11.10 shows the three major links between the seller and the buyer. The first link, the *seller's headquarters organization,* supervises the channels and is part of the channel itself. The second link, *channels between nations,* moves the products to the borders of the foreign nations. The third link, *channels within nations,* moves the products

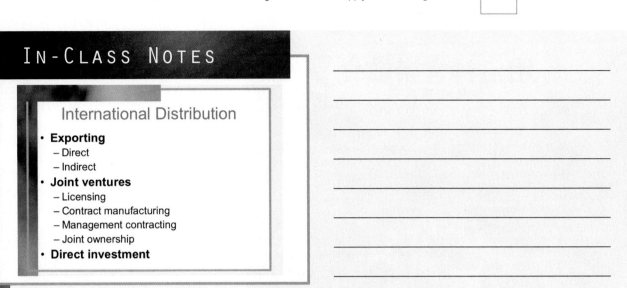

from their foreign entry point to the customers. Some Canadian manufacturers may think their job is done once the product leaves their hands, but they would do well to pay attention to its handling within foreign countries.

Figure 11.10 Whole-Channel Concept for International Marketing

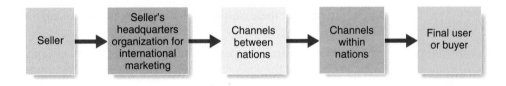

Global marketers, after all, must usually adapt their channel strategies to the existing structures within each country. And in some markets, the distribution system is complex and hard to penetrate, consisting of many layers and large numbers of intermediaries. Consider Japan:

> The Japanese distribution system stems from the early seventeenth century when cottage industries and a [quickly growing] urban population spawned a merchant class. . . . Despite Japan's economic achievements, the distribution system has remained remarkably faithful to its antique pattern. . . . [It] encompasses a wide range of wholesalers and other agents, brokers, and retailers, and myriad tiny retail shops, many more than a North American executive would think necessary. For example, soap may move through three wholesalers plus a sales company after it leaves the manufacturer before it ever reaches the retail outlet. . . . The distribution network . . . reflects the traditionally close ties among many Japanese companies . . . [and places] much greater emphasis on personal relationships with users. . . . Although [these channels appear] inefficient and cumbersome, they seem to serve the Japanese customer well. . . . Lacking much storage space in their small homes, most Japanese homemakers shop several times a week and prefer convenient [and more personal] neighborhood shops.[11]

Many Western firms have had great difficulty breaking into the closely knit, tradition-bound Japanese distribution network.

At the other extreme, distribution systems in developing countries may be scattered and inefficient, or altogether lacking. For example, China and India appear to be huge mar-

The Japanese distribution system is remarkably traditional: A profusion of tiny retail shops is supplied by an even greater number of small wholesalers.

kets, each with populations in the hundreds of millions. In reality, because of inadequate distribution systems in both countries, most companies can profitably access only a small portion of the population located in each country's most affluent cities.[12]

Another major problem that companies face in international distribution is the question of whose ethical framework will dictate behaviour. A Canadian firm selling its product in a foreign country may suddenly find a local expectation of payment for placement of their goods on store shelves that conflicts with the home office's policy on such payments. At home, such an expectation might be considered a bribe, and unethical. Abroad, in a different country, such fees may be considered simply part of doing business. And in between are examples where expectations of a distributor's role are simply different in different countries. In France, wholesalers don't want to promote a product. They ask their retailers what they want and deliver it. So if a Canadian company, for example, were to build its strategy around its French wholesaler's cooperation in promotions, it is likely to fail.

CHANNEL MANAGEMENT DECISIONS

Once the company has reviewed its channel alternatives and decided on the best channel design, it must implement and manage the chosen channel. Channel management calls for selecting and motivating individual channel members and evaluating their performance over time.

Selecting Channel Members

Producers vary in their ability to attract qualified marketing intermediaries. When Toyota first introduced its Lexus line, it had no trouble attracting new dealers for its much sought-after vehicle. But at the other extreme are producers who have to work hard to line up enough qualified intermediaries. For example, when distributors were approached in 1986 about an unknown new game called Nintendo, many refused to carry it because they had recently been burned by the failure of Atari. But a Canadian electronics distributor called Beamscope, which at the time had over 7000 retail customers in Canada, decided to take it on. Not a bad move considering that within one year of that decision, their sales went from next to nothing to $24 million![13]

When selecting intermediaries, the company should evaluate each channel member's years in business, other lines carried, growth and profit record, cooperativeness, and reputation. If the intermediaries are sales agents, the company will want to evaluate the number and character of other lines carried and the size and quality of the sales force. If the intermediary is a retail store that wants exclusive or selective distribution, the company will want to evaluate the store's customers, location, and future growth potential.

Motivating Channel Members

Once selected, channel members must be continuously motivated to do their best. Most companies see their intermediaries as first-line customers. Some use the carrot-and-stick approach: At times they offer *positive* motivators such as higher margins, special deals, premiums, cooperative advertising allowances, display allowances, and sales contests. At other times they use *negative* motivators, such as threatening to reduce margins, to slow down delivery, or to end the relationship altogether. A producer using this approach usually has not done a good job of studying the needs, problems, strengths, and weaknesses of its distributors.

More advanced companies try to forge long-term partnerships with their channel partners. In managing its channels, a company must convince distributors that they can succeed better by working together as a part of a cohesive value delivery system.[14] Many companies are now developing *partner relationship management (PRM)* systems to coordinate their whole-channel marketing efforts, as we saw with Hewlett-Packard at the opening of this chapter. GE Appliances also works closely with its independent dealers to help them succeed in selling the company's products (see Marketing at Work 11.2).

Marketing at Work   11.2

General Electric Adopts a "Virtual Inventory" System to Support Its Dealers

Before the late 1980s, General Electric sold through its dealers rather than to them or with them. GE operated a traditional system of trying to load up the channel with GE appliances, on the premise that "loaded dealers are loyal dealers." Loaded dealers would have less space to feature other brands and would recommend GE appliances to reduce their high inventories. To load its dealers, GE would offer the lowest price when the dealer ordered a full truckload of its appliances.

GE eventually realized that this approach created many problems, especially for smaller independent appliance dealers who could not afford to carry a large amount of stock. These dealers were hard-pressed to meet price competition from larger multibrand dealers. Rethinking its strategy from the point of view of creating dealer satisfaction and profitability, GE created an alternative distribution model called the Direct Connect system. Under this system, GE dealers carry only display models and rely on a "virtual inventory" to fill orders. Dealers can access GE's order-processing system 24 hours a day, check on model availability, and

place orders for next-day delivery. Using the Direct Connect system, dealers can also get GE's best price, financing from GE Credit, and no interest charges for the first 90 days.

Dealers benefit by having much lower inventory costs while still having a large virtual inventory available to satisfy their customers' needs. In exchange for this benefit, dealers must commit to selling nine major GE product categories, generating 50 percent of their sales from GE products, opening their books to GE for

Using GE's CustomerNet system, dealers can access GE's order-processing system 24 hours a day, check on model availability, and place orders for next-day delivery.

(continued)

review, and paying GE every month through electronic funds transfer.

As a result of Direct Connect, dealer profit margins have skyrocketed. And GE has benefited as well. Its dealers are now more committed to and dependent on GE, and the new order-entry system has saved GE substantial clerical costs. GE now knows the actual sales of its goods at the retail level, which helps it to schedule its production more accurately. And it can now produce in response to demand rather than having to meet inventory replenishment rules. Finally, GE has been able to simplify its warehouse locations and deliver appliances to 90 percent of its customers within 24 hours. Thus, by forging a partnership, GE has helped both its dealers and itself.

Source: See Michael Treacy and Fred Wiersema, "Customer Intimacy and Other Discipline Values," *Harvard Business Review,* January–February 1993, pp. 84–93.

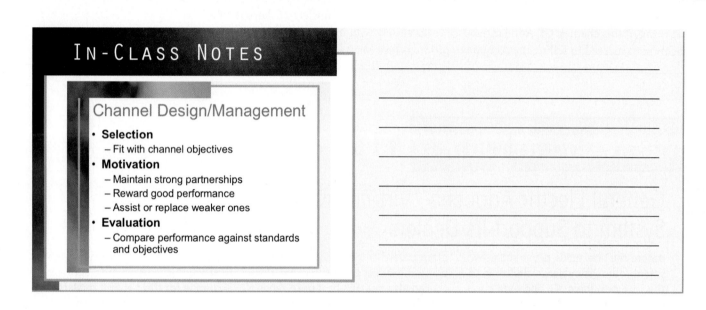

IN-CLASS NOTES

Channel Design/Management

- **Selection**
  - Fit with channel objectives
- **Motivation**
  - Maintain strong partnerships
  - Reward good performance
  - Assist or replace weaker ones
- **Evaluation**
  - Compare performance against standards and objectives

Evaluating Channel Members

The producer must regularly check channel member performance against standards such as sales quotas, average inventory levels, customer delivery time, treatment of damaged and lost goods, cooperation in company promotion and training programs, and services to the customer. The company should recognize and reward intermediaries who are performing well and providing value to customers. Those who are performing poorly should be assisted or, as a last resort, replaced.

Finally, manufacturers need to be sensitive to their dealers. Those who treat their dealers poorly risk not only losing dealer support, but also causing some legal problems. The next section describes various rights and duties pertaining to manufacturers and their channel members.

Linking the Concepts

Compare the HP and GE Appliances channel systems.

- Diagram the HP and GE Appliances systems. How do they compare in terms of channel levels, types of intermediaries, channel member roles and responsibilities, and other characteristics. How well is each system designed?
- Assess how well HP and GE Appliances have managed and supported their channels. With what results?

Public Policy and Distribution Decisions

For the most part, companies are legally free to develop whatever channel arrangements suit them. In fact, the laws affecting channels seek to prevent the exclusionary tactics of some companies that might keep another company from using a desired channel. Most channel law deals with the mutual rights and duties of the channel members once they have formed a relationship.

As discussed earlier in the chapter, some producers and wholesalers like to develop *exclusive distribution* for their products. When the seller requires that these dealers not handle competitors' products, its strategy is called *exclusive dealing*. Both parties can benefit from exclusive arrangements: The seller obtains more loyal and dependable outlets, and the dealers obtain a steady source of supply and stronger seller support. But of course exclusive arrangements also exclude other producers from selling to these dealers. This situation brings exclusive dealing contracts under the scope of the *Competition Act*. They are legal as long as they do not substantially lessen competition or create a monopoly and as long as both parties enter into the agreement voluntarily.

Exclusive dealing often includes *exclusive territorial agreements*. The producer may agree not to sell to other dealers in a given area, or the buyer may agree to sell only in its own territory. The first practice is normal under franchise systems as a way to increase dealer enthusiasm and commitment. It is also legal—a seller has no legal obligation to sell through more outlets than it wants. The second practice, whereby the producer tries to keep a dealer from selling outside its territory, has become a major legal issue.

Producers of a strong brand sometimes sell it to dealers only if the dealers will take some or all of the rest of the line. This is called full-line forcing. Such *tying agreements* are not necessarily illegal, but they do violate the *Competition Act* if they lessen competition substantially. The practice may prevent consumers from freely choosing among competing suppliers of other brands.

Finally, producers are free to select their dealers, but their right to terminate dealers is somewhat restricted. In general, sellers can drop dealers "for cause." However, they cannot drop dealers if, for example, the dealers refuse to cooperate in a doubtful legal arrangement, such as exclusive dealing or tying agreements, or in an unethical but legal practice. Unethical practices can be more difficult to handle; the law may be quite clear on what a company can and cannot do, while ethical practices may differ from one country to another, or even from one distribution chain to another.[15]

Marketing Logistics and Supply Chain Management

In today's global marketplace, selling a product is sometimes easier than getting it to customers. Companies must decide on the best way to store, handle, and move their products and services so that they are available to customers in the right assortments, at the right time, and in the right place. Physical distribution and logistics effectiveness has a major impact on both customer satisfaction and company costs. Here we consider the nature and importance of logistics management in the supply chain, goals of the logistics system, major logistics functions, and the need for integrated supply chain management.

Nature and Importance of Marketing Logistics

To some managers, marketing logistics means only trucks and warehouses. But modern logistics is much more than this. **Marketing logistics**—also called **physical distribution**—involves planning, implementing, and controlling the physical flow of goods, services, and related information from points of origin to points of consumption

Marketing logistics (physical distribution) The tasks involved in planning, implementing, and controlling the physical flow of materials, final goods, and related information from points of origin to points of consumption to meet customer requirements at a profit.

to meet customer requirements at a profit. In short, it involves getting the right product to the right customer in the right place at the right time.

Traditional physical distribution typically started with products at the plant and then tried to find low-cost solutions to get them to customers. However, today's marketers prefer customer-centred logistics thinking, which starts with the marketplace and works backward to the factory, or even to sources of supply. Marketing logistics addresses not only *outbound distribution* (moving products from the factory to resellers and ultimately to customers) but also *inbound distribution* (moving products and materials from suppliers to the factory) and *reverse distribution* (moving broken, unwanted, or excess products returned by consumers or resellers). That is, it involves entire **supply chain management**—managing value-added flows of materials, final goods, and related information between suppliers, the company, resellers, and final users. Thus, the logistics manager's task is to coordinate activities of suppliers, purchasing agents, marketers, channel members, and customers. These activities include forecasting, information systems, purchasing, production planning, order processing, inventory, warehousing, and transportation planning.

Companies can gain a powerful competitive advantage by using improved logistics to give customers better service or lower prices, and improved logistics can yield tremendous cost savings to both the company and its customers. About 15 percent of an average product's price is accounted for by shipping and transport alone. Shaving off even a small fraction of these costs can mean substantial savings.

The explosion in product variety has created a need for improved logistics management. For example, in 1911 the typical A&P grocery store carried only 270 items. The store manager could keep track of this inventory on about 10 pages of notebook paper stuffed in a shirt pocket. Today, the average A&P carries a bewildering stock of more than 16 700 items.

Improvements in information technology have created opportunities for major gains in distribution efficiency. Using sophisticated supply chain management software, Web-based logistics systems, point-of-sale scanners, uniform product codes, satellite tracking, and electronic data interchange (EDI) and electronic funds transfer (EFT), companies can quickly and efficiently manage the flow of goods, information, and finances through the supply chain.

Goals of the Logistics System

No logistics system can both maximize customer service and minimize distribution costs. Maximum customer service implies rapid delivery, large inventories, flexible assortments, liberal return policies, and other services—all of which raise distribution costs. In contrast, minimum distribution costs imply slower delivery, smaller inventories, and larger shipping lots—which represent a lower level of overall customer service. The goal of marketing logistics should be to provide a targeted level of customer service at the least cost.

Major Logistics Functions

Given a set of logistics objectives, the company is ready to design a logistics system that will minimize the cost of attaining these objectives. The major logistics functions include order processing, warehousing, inventory management, and transportation.

Order Processing Orders can be submitted in many ways—through salespeople, by mail or telephone, via the Internet, or through electronic data interchange (EDI), the electronic exchange of data between companies. Both the company and its customers benefit when order processing is carried out quickly and efficiently.

Many large retailers—such as Wal-Mart and Home Depot—work closely with major suppliers such as Procter & Gamble or Black & Decker to set up *vendor-managed inventory (VMI) systems* (or collaborative planning, forecasting, and replenishment [CPFR] systems, if you're looking for an even fancier name).[16] Using VMI, the customer shares real-time data on sales and current inventory levels with the supplier. The supplier then takes full responsibility for managing inventories and deliveries. Such systems require close cooperation between the buyer and seller.

Warehousing Production and consumption cycles rarely match, so most companies must store their tangible goods until they are sold. For example, Snapper, Toro, and other lawn mower manufacturers run their factories all year long and store up products for the heavy spring and summer buying seasons.

A company must decide how many and what types of warehouses it needs and where they will be located. The company might use storage warehouses for goods that need to be stored for moderate to long periods of time. Or the company might use **distribution centres**, which are large, highly automated warehouses designed to move goods rather than just store them. For example, Wal-Mart operates a network of 62 huge U.S. distribution centres and another 37 around the globe. Almost 84 percent of the merchandise shipped to Wal-Mart stores is routed through one of its own distribution centres, giving Wal-Mart tremendous control over inventory management. One centre, which serves the daily needs of 165 Wal-Mart stores, contains some 11 hectares of space under a single roof. Laser scanners route as many as 190 000 cases of goods per day along 11 kilometres of conveyer belts, and the centre's 1000 workers load or unload 310 trucks daily.[17]

Like almost everything else, warehousing has seen dramatic changes in technology in recent years. Older, multi-storey warehouses with outdated materials-handling methods are being replaced by newer, single-storey automated warehouses with advanced, computer-controlled materials-handling systems, replacing employees with computers and scanners.

Inventory Management Inventory levels also affect customer satisfaction. Here, managers must maintain the delicate balance between carrying too much inventory and carrying too little, balancing the costs of carrying larger inventories against possible loss of sales and profits. Many companies have greatly reduced their inventories and related costs through *just-in-time* logistics systems, where producers and retailers carry only enough inventory of parts or merchandise for a few days of operations. For example, Dell Computer, a master just-in-time producer, carries just 5 days of inventory, whereas competitors might carry 40 days or even 60.[18] Just-in-time systems require accurate forecasting along with fast, frequent, and flexible delivery so that new supplies will be available when needed. However, these systems result in substantial savings in inventory-carrying and handling costs.

Transportation The choice of transportation carriers affects the pricing of products, delivery performance, and condition of the goods when they arrive—all of which will affect customer satisfaction. In shipping goods to its warehouses, dealers, and customers, the company can choose among five transportation modes: rail, truck, water, pipeline, and air.

Rail. Because most of Canada's population is contained in a belt that is only 300 km wide but 6400 km long, rail still carries most of the country's freight. Railways are one of the most cost-effective modes for shipping large amounts of bulk products—coal, sand, minerals, farm, and forest products—over long distances. In addition, railways recently have begun to increase their customer services. Both CN and CP have designed new equipment to handle special categories of goods, provided flatcars for carrying truck trailers by rail (piggyback), and provided in-transit services such as the processing or diversion of shipped goods to other destinations en route.

Distribution centre A large, highly automated warehouse designed to receive goods from various plants and suppliers, take orders, fill them efficiently, and deliver goods to customers as quickly as possible.

Information At The Speed Of Light

In today's business environment speed is critical.
Roadway Express moves your shipment around the clock
and communicates your shipment's location at the speed of light.
Continuously tracked by satellite, our new sleeper tractors
keep your shipment on the road and on time.
You get reliable service and reliable information.

*Just some of the ways we're changing to offer you
exceptional service...with no exceptions.*

ROADWAY.
Roadway Express

Roadway Express and other trucking firms have added many services in recent years, such as satellite tracking of shipments and sleeper tractors that keep freight moving around the clock.

Intermodal transportation
Combining two or more modes of transportation.

Integrated supply chain management The logistics concept that emphasizes teamwork, both inside the company and among all the channel organizations, to maximize the performance of the entire distribution system.

Third-party logistics (3PL) provider An independent logistics provider that performs any or all of the functions required to get its clients' product to market.

Truck. Trucks now account for 25 percent of total cargo and account for the largest portion of transportation *within* cities. Trucks are highly flexible in their routing and time schedules. They can move goods door to door, saving the need to transfer goods between truck and rail, and can usually offer faster service. Roadway Express now offers satellite tracking of shipments and sleeper tractors that move freight around the clock.

Water. Many goods are moved by ships and barges on coastal and inland waterways. Water transportation is inexpensive but slow, and subject to changes in weather. Many goods are shipped across the Great Lakes and through the St. Lawrence Seaway in the warmer months, but these routes are impassable in the winter.

Pipeline. Pipelines are used for shipping petroleum, natural gas, and chemicals from sources to markets. Pipeline shipment costs less than rail shipment but more than water shipment.

Air. Although air carriers transport less than 1 percent of the nation's goods, they are becoming more important as a transportation mode. Air-freight rates are much higher than rail or truck rates, but air freight is ideal when speed is needed or distant markets have to be reached. Among the most frequently air-freighted products are perishables (fresh fish, cut flowers) and high-value, low-bulk items (technical instruments, jewellery).

Increasingly, shippers are using **intermodal transportation**—combining two or more modes of transportation. *Piggyback* describes the use of rail and trucks; *fishyback,* water and trucks; *trainship,* water and rail; and *airtruck,* air and trucks. Combining modes provides advantages that no single mode can deliver.

In choosing a transportation mode for a product, shippers must balance many considerations: speed, dependability, availability, cost, and others. Thus, if a shipper needs speed, air and truck are the prime choices. If the goal is low cost, then water or pipeline might be best.

Integrated Supply Chain Management

Today, more and more companies are adopting the concept of **integrated supply chain management** with the goal of harmonizing all of the company's logistics decisions in order to create high market satisfaction at a reasonable cost. Because distribution activities involve strong tradeoffs, decisions by different functions must be coordinated. Companies do this through logistics committees, special management positions, or sophisticated, system-wide supply chain management software, now available through Oracle and other software providers.[19] Many companies have created cross-functional, cross-company teams. For example, Procter & Gamble has a team of almost 100 people living in Bentonville, Arkansas, home of Wal-Mart. The P&Gers work jointly with their counterparts at Wal-Mart to find ways to squeeze costs out of their distribution system.

One company's distribution system is another company's supply system. The success of each channel member depends on the performance of the entire supply chain. For example, Zellers can charge the lowest prices at retail only if its entire supply chain—consisting of thousands of merchandise suppliers, transport companies, warehouses, and service providers—operates at maximum efficiency.

Most businesses perform their own logistics functions, but a growing number of firms now outsource some or all of their logistics to **third-party logistics (3PL)**

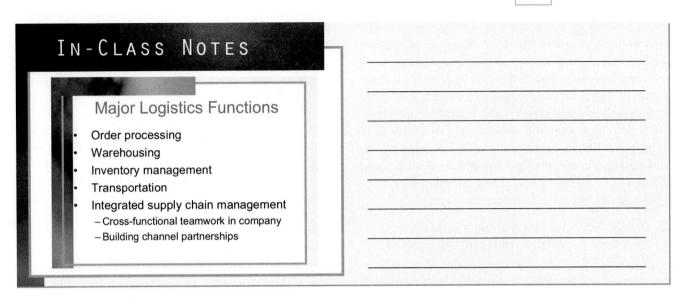

In-Class Notes

Major Logistics Functions

- Order processing
- Warehousing
- Inventory management
- Transportation
- Integrated supply chain management
  - Cross-functional teamwork in company
  - Building channel partnerships

providers such as UPS Worldwide Logistics, FedEx Logistics, or Roadway Logistics Services. Such integrated logistics companies perform any or all of the functions required to get their clients' product to market. The Japanese company Fujitsu's personal computer division recently made use of FedEx's experience with Dell in the field of assembling computers to expand their facilities to create customized laptop computers in Memphis, Tennessee, instead of bringing over fully completed computers.[20]

LOOKING BACK

So, what have you learned about distribution channels and integrated supply chain management? We have seen that channel decisions are among the most important decisions that management faces. A company's channel decisions affect not only every other marketing decision, but corporate strategy as well. Each marketing channel has its own costs, produces its own revenues, and reaches a different segment of the market. Management must make channel decisions carefully, incorporating today's needs with tomorrow's likely marketing environment. Some companies pay too little attention to their marketing channels, but others have used imaginative distribution systems to gain competitive advantage.

REVIEWING THE CONCEPTS

1. Explain why companies use distribution channels and discuss the functions these channels perform, particularly those of retailers and wholesalers.

Most producers use intermediaries to bring their products to market. They try to forge a *distribution channel*— a set of interdependent organizations involved in the process of making a product or service available for use or consumption by the consumer or business user. Through their contacts, experience, specialization, and scale of operation, intermediaries usually offer the firm more than it can achieve on its own. Distribution channels perform many key functions, including *gathering and distributing information; developing and spreading persuasive communications about an offer; finding and communicating with prospective buyers; matching the offer to the buyer's needs;* and *negotiating.* Other functions help fulfill the completed transactions by offering physical distribution—*transporting and storing goods; financing*— acquiring and using funds to cover the costs of the channel work; and *risk taking*—assuming the risks of carrying out the channel work.

Retailers can be classified as *store retailers* and *nonstore retailers.* Nonstore retailing has been growing much faster than has store retailing. Store retailers can be further classified by the *amount of service* they provide, *product line* sold, and *relative prices*. Today, many retailers are banding together in corporate and contractual *retail organizations*. Wholesalers fall into three groups. First, *merchant wholesalers* take possession of the goods. They include *full-service wholesalers* and *limited-service wholesalers*. Second, *brokers* and *agents* do not take possession of the goods but are paid a commission for aiding buying and selling. Finally, *manufacturers' sales branches and offices* are wholesaling operations conducted by non-wholesalers to bypass the wholesalers.

2. Discuss how channel members interact and how they organize to perform the work of the channel.

The channel will be most effective when each member is assigned the tasks it can do best. Ideally, because the success of individual channel members depends on overall channel success, all channel firms should work together smoothly. They should understand and accept their roles, coordinate their goals and activities, and cooperate to attain overall channel goals. By cooperating, they can more effectively sense, serve, and satisfy the target market. In a large company, the formal organization structure assigns roles and provides needed leadership. But in a distribution channel made up of independent firms, leadership and power are not formally set. Traditionally, distribution channels have lacked the leadership needed to assign roles and manage conflict. Recently, however, new types of channel organizations have appeared that provide stronger leadership and improved performance.

3. Identify the major channel alternatives open to a company.

Each firm identifies alternative ways to reach its market. Available means vary from direct selling to using one, two, three, or more intermediary *channel levels*. Distribution channels face continuous and sometimes dramatic change. Three of the most important trends are the growth of *vertical, horizontal,* and *hybrid marketing systems*. These trends affect channel cooperation, conflict, and competition. *Channel design* begins with assessing customer channel service needs and company channel objectives and constraints. The company then identifies the major channel alternatives in terms of the *types* of intermediaries, the *number* of intermediaries, and the *channel responsibilities* of each. Each channel alternative must be evaluated according to economic, control, and adaptive criteria. Channel management calls for selecting qualified intermediaries and motivating them. Individual channel members must be evaluated regularly.

4. Explain how companies select, motivate, and evaluate channel members.

Producers vary in their ability to attract qualified marketing intermediaries. Some producers have no trouble signing up channel members. Others have to work hard to line up enough qualified intermediaries. When selecting intermediaries, the company should evaluate each channel member's qualifications and select those who best fit its channel objectives. Once selected, channel members must be continually motivated to do their best. The company must sell not only *through* the intermediaries, but also *to* them. It should work to forge long-term partnerships with its channel partners to create a marketing system that meets the needs of both the manufacturer *and* the partners. The company must also regularly check channel member performance against established performance standards, rewarding intermediaries who are performing well and assisting or replacing weaker ones.

5. Discuss the nature and importance of marketing logistics and integrated supply chain management.

More business firms are paying attention to *marketing logistics* (or *physical distribution*), an area of potentially high cost savings and improved customer satisfaction. Marketing logistics involves entire supply chain management—managing value-added flows between suppliers, the company, resellers, and final users. No logistics system can both maximize customer service and minimize distribution costs. Instead, the goal of logistics management is to provide a targeted level of service at the least cost. The major logistics functions include *order processing, warehousing, inventory management,* and *transportation*.

The *integrated supply chain management* concept recognizes that improved logistics requires teamwork in the form of close working relationships across functional areas inside the company and across various organizations in the supply chain. Companies can achieve logistics harmony among functions by creating functions and positions within the company, or through cross-company teams, shared projects, and information sharing systems. Today, some companies are outsourcing their logistics functions to *third-party logistics (3PL) providers* to save costs, increase efficiency, and gain faster and more effective access to global markets.

Key Terms

agent *424*
broker *424*
category killer *429*
chain stores *430*
channel captain *435*
channel conflict *435*
channel level *422*
contract manufacturing *446*
convenience store *429*
conventional distribution channel *436*
direct investment *446*
department store *428*
direct distribution channel *422*
discount store *429*
disintermediation *438*
distribution centre *453*
distribution channel *421*
exclusive distribution *443*
exporting *444*

factory outlet *430*
franchise *431*
horizontal marketing system *436*
hybrid marketing system *437*
independent off-price retailer *430*
indirect distribution channel *422*
integrated supply chain management *454*
intensive distribution *442*
intermodal transportation *454*
joint ownership *446*
joint venturing *445*
licensing *445*
management contracting *446*
manufacturers' sales branches and offices *424*
marketing logistics (physical distribution) *451*
merchandising conglomerates *431*
merchant wholesaler *424*

off-price retailer *430*
retailer *427*
retailer cooperative *430*
retailing *427*
selective distribution *443*
service retailer *429*
specialty store *428*
supermarket *429*
superstore *429*
supply chain *421*
supply chain management *452*
third-party logistics (3PL) provider *454*
vertical marketing system (VMS) *436*
voluntary chain *430*
warehouse club *430*
whole-channel view *446*
wholesaler *423*
wholesaling *423*

STUDY GUIDE

After completing this self-test, check your answers against the Answer Key at the back of the book.

Multiple Choice

1. The text defines wholesalers as companies that sell mostly to retailers. Which example below best illustrates a circumstance in which wholesalers do not sell just to retailers?
   a. When wholesalers sell directly to consumers under certain conditions and rules, such as those that are open to the public
   b. When a wholesaler turns itself into a warehouse club
   c. When a wholesaler owns the retailer directly
   d. When a wholesale in turn sells to jobbers
   e. A and D

2. Wholesaling is in many ways an old-fashioned industry in which progress in modern marketing methods has been slow. The smart wholesaler looking for competitive advantage should focus on what particular aspect of the marketing mix?

   a. Pricing
   b. Mission marketing
   c. Promotion
   d. Re-intermediation
   e. Distribution

3. Independent Grocers are franchisee-owned supermarkets that are sponsored by the major grocery wholesaler National Grocers. Independent Grocers is an example of what type of chain?
   a. Retail cooperative
   b. Voluntary chain
   c. Captive chain
   d. Direct control
   e. Conglomerate

4. A religious bookstore represents which retail assortment levels?
   a. Narrow and shallow
   b. Wide and deep
   c. Wide and shallow
   d. Narrow and deep
   e. None of the above

5. Some retailers do not operate retail locations but rather sell directly to consumers. Avon sells door-to-door through salespeople who are in essence running their own small independent businesses. Avon recently began selling its products directly on its own website. Why might this Web-based addition change Avon's larger distribution strategy later?
   a. Shipping costs will force Avon to go back to agent-based selling
   b. Customers will start bypassing agents in favour of buying directly from the website
   c. Products on the site are priced higher and are therefore more profitable
   d. Agents will re-intermediate by launching their own competing websites
   e. Avon's competitors will move away from agent-based selling too

6. Experts have stated that Wal-Mart will need to evolve from its current "discounter" position in order to survive over time. This opinion is founded on what retailing philosophical concept?
   a. Wheel of retailing
   b. Societal marketing
   c. Intermediation
   d. Off-price retailing
   e. Discount erosion

7. Hewlett-Packard, in its decision to go direct for certain target segments, evolves into what type of channel marketing system?
   a. Conventional
   b. Direct
   c. Hybrid
   d. Vertical
   e. Disintermediated

8. Several years ago, Microsoft came under scrutiny for instituting punitive measures to prevent PC manufacturers from including competing software products on new machines being shipped out to retailers and customers. Of all the types of distributor arrangements, the one practised by Microsoft in this case is the most open to abuse because to be legal it required the voluntary participation of both parties. This type of arrangement is known as

   a. Predatory distribution
   b. Intensive distribution
   c. Exclusive dealings
   d. Exclusive distribution
   e. Controlled handling

9. In general, a small company seeking to enter a country with a significantly different language, culture, and business environment would initially select what form of international distribution channel?
   a. Joint venture
   b. Manufacturer's agent
   c. Jobbers
   d. Contract manufacturing
   e. Indirect export

10. An integrated supply chain means that all members of the inbound and outbound distribution network work cooperatively to make the operation as efficient as possible. Of all the factors that go into making an integrated supply chain work, the most critical is
    a. Integrated exchange of real-time information
    b. Tying agreements
    c. Third-party logistics providers
    d. Contractual relationships
    e. Intermodal transportation

TRUE/FALSE

T F 1. Warehouse clubs like Costco compete directly with big-box category killers.

T F 2. There appears to be a direct relationship between the complexity and price of the product and the number of distributors that carry it.

T F 3. A Canadian company seeking to expand into India with a full manufacturing capability would have the greatest amount of control by choosing direct investment rather than joint venturing.

T F 4. Wal-Mart's low price advantage is partially maintained by just-in-time systems.

T F 5. The nature of Canada's demographic settlement patterns is a major factor in how goods are shipped.

CONCEPT CHECK

1. A _____ is a set of interdependent organizations involved in the process of making a product or service available for use or consumption by the consumer or business user.

2. Members of the distribution channel perform many key functions. Chief among these are _____, _____, _____, _____, _____, physical distribution, financing, and risk taking.

3. A _____ distribution channel has no intermediary levels.

4. _____ includes all the activities involved in selling goods or services directly to final consumers for their personal, nonbusiness use.

5. _____ includes all activities involved in selling goods and services to those buying for resale or business use.

6. Disagreements over goals and roles generate channel conflict. McDonald's recently had a form of _____ conflict with some of its dealers when its aggressive expansion plans called for placing new stores in areas that took business from existing locations.

7. Changes in technology have caused traditional distribution to undergo changes such as _____, where more and more product and service producers are bypassing intermediaries and going directly to final buyers, or where radically new types of channel intermediaries are emerging to displace traditional ones.

8. Companies must determine the number of channel members to use at each level. Producers of convenience products and common raw materials typically seek _____ distribution—a strategy in which they stock their products in as many outlets as possible.

9. According to the _____ concept, many new types of retailing forms begin as low-margin, low-price, low-status operations.

10. Another term used to describe physical distribution is _____.

11. Managing value-added flows of materials, final goods, and related information between suppliers, the company, resellers, and final users is called _____ management.

12. The major logistics functions include _____, _____, _____, and _____.

STUDENT MATERIALS

Visit our website at www.pearsoned.ca/armstrong for online quizzes, Internet exercises, and more!

DISCUSSING THE ISSUES

1. List and briefly discuss the channel functions that are involved in completing and fulfilling transactions. Which function applies most in each of the following situations? (a) A retailer puts in a rush reorder for a needed holiday item that is in short supply. (b) An Internet marketer seeks ways to identify and contact its market. (c) A small retailer wants to expand its order size but does not currently have funds to pay for the expanded order. (d) A business buyer attends a large trade show looking for higher-quality products on a limited budget.

2. What is "disintermediation?" Give an example other than those discussed in the chapter. What opportunities and problems does disintermediation present for traditional retailers? Explain.

3. Compare the basic marketing decisions made by retailers and wholesalers to those made by manufacturers.

Give examples that show the similarities and differences in marketing decisions made by these groups.

4. Which distribution strategy—intensive, selective, or exclusive—is used for the following products and why? (a) Piaget watches, (b) Acura automobiles, and (c) Snickers chocolate bars.

5. Regarding outsourcing: (a) Why would a company choose to outsource its distribution function? (b) What major factors contribute to a successful outsourcing relationship? What are the potential dangers of such a relationship? (c) Give an example of a company that could benefit from outsourcing its logistics and suggest some practical outsourcing alternatives for the company. (For additional information on outsourcing, see the Outsourcing Institute's website at www. outsourcing.com.)

MARKETING APPLICATIONS

You know about the Internet but have you ever heard of an "extranet"? An extranet occurs when a company opens its own internal network (or intranet) to selected business partners. Trusted suppliers, distributors, and other special users can then link into the company's network without having to go through traditional red tape. The connecting company can use the Internet or virtual private networks for communication. Once inside the company's intranet, the outside company (or partner) can view whatever data the company makes available.

What types of data? A supplier might analyze a customer's inventory needs: Boeing booked $100 million in spare parts from airline customers in one year. Partners might swap customer lists for interrelated products and services or share purchasing systems to gain savings through more efficient purchasing: General Electric claims that $500 million can be saved in purchasing costs by using an extranet. Imagine the strategic advantages created when "virtual" partners move information to one another in seconds about shifting supply and demand situations, customer requests and opportunities, and just-

in-time inventory needs. Purchase processing times can be reduced from weeks to minutes at enormous cost savings that can be passed along to consumers.

THINKING LIKE A MARKETING MANAGER

1. What role might an extranet play in distribution decisions for (a) retailers, (b) wholesalers, and (c) manufacturers?
2. What are the potential dangers of an extranet system?
3. What areas of a marketing organization's intranet would be most interesting to a partner using the extranet?
4. Assume that you are the marketing manager of Cisco Systems (investigate this master of e-commerce and networking at www.cisco.com). How could an extranet help you to better assist resellers? How could costs be saved by using an extranet? How does an extranet work with an outsourcing concept (if at all)? After examining the advantages and disadvantages of using an extranet, write a short position paper that outlines your thoughts on the subject and its future in marketing commerce.

VIDEO CASE

Go to Pearson Canada's Video Central site (www.pearsoned.ca/highered/videocentral) to view the video and accompanying case for this chapter.

CASE 11   THE GLOBAL SUPPLY CHAIN OF A SINGLE COMPUTER

The following is an excerpt from Thomas Friedman's *The World Is Flat: A Brief History of the Globalized World in the 21st Century* (published by Allen Lane).

Let me tell you a little bit about the computer I am writing this on. It's a Dell Inspiron 600m notebook, service tag number 9ZRJP41. As part of the research for my book, I visited the management team at Dell, near Austin, Texas. I shared with them the ideas in this book and in return I asked for one favor: I asked them to trace the entire global supply chain that produced my Dell notebook. Here is their report.

My computer was conceived when I phoned Dell's 800 number on April 2 2004, and was connected to sales representative Mujteba Naqvi. He typed in both the type of notebook I ordered as well as the special features I wanted, along with my personal information, shipping address, billing address and credit card information. My credit card was verified by Dell through its work-flow connection with Visa, and my order was then released to Dell's production system. Dell has six factories around the world—in Limerick, Ireland; Xiamen, China; Eldorado do Sul, Brazil; Nashville, Tennessee; Austin, Texas; and Penang, Malaysia.

My order went out by email to the Dell notebook factory in Malaysia, where the parts for the computer were immediately ordered from the supplier logistics centers (SLCs) next to the Penang factory. Surrounding every Dell factory in the world are these supplier logistics centers, owned by the different suppliers of Dell parts. These SLCs are like staging areas.

If you are a Dell supplier anywhere in the world, your job is to keep your SLC full of your specific parts so they can constantly be trucked over to the Dell factory for just-in-time manufacturing. "In an average day, we sell 140,000 to 150,000 computers," explained Dick Hunter, one of Dell's three global production managers. "The orders come in over www.Dell.com or over the telephone. As soon as these orders come in, our suppliers know about it. They get a signal based on every component in the machine you ordered, so the supplier knows just what he has to deliver. If you are supplying power cords for desktops, you can see minute by minute how many power cords you are going to have to deliver."

Every two hours, the Dell factory in Penang sends an email to the various SLCs nearby, telling each one what parts and what quantities of those parts it wants delivered within the next 90 minutes—and not one minute later. Within 90 minutes, trucks from the various SLCs around Penang pull up to the Dell manufacturing plant and unload the parts needed for all those notebooks ordered in the last two hours. This goes on all day, every two hours. As soon as those parts arrive at the factory, it takes 30 minutes for Dell employees to unload the parts, register their barcodes, and put them into the bins for assembly. "We know where every part in every SLC is in the Dell system at all times," said Hunter.

So where did the parts for my notebook come from?

To begin with, he said, the notebook was co-designed in Austin, Texas, and in Taiwan by a team of Dell engineers and a team of Taiwanese notebook designers. It happened that when my notebook order hit the Dell factory in Penang, one part—the wireless card—was not available due to a quality-control issue, so the assembly of the notebook was delayed for a few days.

Then the truck full of good wireless cards arrived. On April 13, at 10.15am, a Dell Malaysia worker pulled the order slip that automatically popped up once all my parts had arrived from the SLCs at the Penang factory. Another Dell Malaysia employee then took out a "traveler"—a special carrying tote designed to hold and protect parts—and started plucking all the parts that went into my notebook.

Where did those parts come from? Dell uses multiple suppliers for most of the 30 key components that go into its notebooks. That way, if one supplier breaks down or cannot meet a surge in demand, Dell is not left in the lurch. So here are the key suppliers for my Inspiron 600m notebook: the Intel microprocessor came from an Intel factory either in the Philippines, Costa Rica, Malaysia or China. The memory came from a Korean-owned factory in Korea (Samsung), a Taiwanese-owned factory in Taiwan (Nanya), a German-owned factory in Germany (Infineon), or a Japanese-owned factory in Japan (Elpida). My graphics card was shipped from either a Taiwanese-owned factory in China (MSI) or a Chinese-run factory in China (Foxconn). The cooling fan came from a Taiwanese-owned factory in Taiwan (CCI or Auras). The motherboard came from either a Korean-owned factory in Shanghai (Samsung), a Taiwanese-owned factory in Shanghai (Quanta), or a Taiwanese-owned factory in Taiwan (Compal or Wistron). The keyboard came from either a Japanese-owned company in Tianjin, China (Alps), a Taiwanese-owned factory in Shenzen, China (Sunrex), or a Taiwanese-owned factory in Suzhou, China (Darfon). The LCD display was made in either South Korea (Samsung or LG Philips LCD), Japan (Toshiba or Sharp), or Taiwan (Chi Mei Optoelectronics, Hannstar Display, or AU Optronics). The wireless card came from either an American-owned factory in China (Agere) or Malaysia (Arrow), or a Taiwanese-owned factory in Taiwan (Askey or Gemtek) or China (USI). The modem was made by either a Taiwanese-owned company in China (Asustek or Liteon) or a Chinese-run company in China (Foxconn). The battery came from an American-owned factory in Malaysia (Motorola), a Japanese-owned factory in Mexico or Malaysia or China (Sanyo), or a South Korean or Taiwanese factory in either of those two countries (SDI or Simplo). The hard-disk drive was made by an American-owned factory in Singapore (Seagate), a Japanese-owned company in Thailand (Hitachi or Fujitsu), or a Japanese-owned factory in the Philippines (Toshiba). The CD/DVD drive came from a South Korean-owned company with factories in Indonesia and the Philippines (Samsung); a Japanese-owned factory in China or Malaysia (NEC); a Japanese-owned factory in Indonesia, China, or Malaysia (Teac); or a Japanese-owned factory in China (Sony).

The notebook carrying bag was made by either an Irish-owned company in China (Tenba) or an American-owned company in China (Targus, Samsonite or Pacific Design). The power adaptor was made by either a Thai-owned factory in Thailand (Delta) or a Taiwanese, Korean or American-owned factory in China (Liteon, Samsung or Mobility). The power cord was made by a British-owned company with factories in China, Malaysia and India (Volex). The removable memory stick was made by either an Israeli-owned company in Israel (M-System) or an American-owned company with a factory in Malaysia (Smart Modular).

This supply chain symphony—from my order over the phone to production to delivery to my house—is one of the wonders of what I have called the flat world.

"We have to do a lot of collaborating," said Hunter. "Michael [Dell] personally knows the CEOs of these companies, and we are constantly working with them on process improvements and real-time demand/supply balancing."

Demand shaping goes on constantly, said Hunter. What is "demand shaping"? It works like this: at 10am Austin time, Dell discovers that so many customers have ordered notebooks with 40-gigabyte hard drives since the morning, its supply chain will run short in two hours. That signal is automatically relayed to Dell's marketing department and to Dell.com and to all the Dell phone operators taking orders.

If you happen to call to place your Dell order at 10.30am, the Dell representative will say to you, "Tom, it's your lucky day! For the next hour we are offering 60-gigabyte hard drives with the notebook you want—for only $10 more than the 40-gig drive. And if you act now, Dell will throw in a carrying case along with your purchase, because we so value you as a customer." In an hour or two, using such promotions, Dell can reshape the demand for any part of any notebook or desktop to correspond with the projected supply in its global supply chain.

Picking up the story of my notebook, on April 13, at 11.29am, all the parts had been plucked from the just-in-time inventory bins in Penang, and the computer was assembled there by A Sathini, a team member "who manually screwed together all of the parts from kitting as well as the labels needed for Tom's system," said Dell in their production report to me. "The system was then sent down the conveyor to go to burn, where Tom's specified software was downloaded." Dell has huge server banks stocked with the latest in Microsoft, Norton Utilities, and other popular software applications, which are downloaded into each new computer according to the specific tastes of the customer.

"By 2.45pm, Tom's software had been successfully downloaded, and [was] manually moved to the boxing line. By 4.05pm, Tom's system [was] placed in protective foam and a shuttle box, with a label, which contains his order number, tracking code, system type, and shipping code. By 6.04pm, Tom's system had been loaded on a pallet with a specified manifest, which gives the Merge facility visibility to when the system will arrive, what pallet it will be on (out of 75+ pallets with 152 systems per pallet), and to what address Tom's system will ship. By 6.26pm, Tom's system left [the Dell factory] to head to the Penang, Malaysia airport."

Six days a week Dell charters a China Airlines 747 out of Taiwan and flies it from Penang to Nashville via Taipei. Each 747 leaves with 25,000 Dell notebooks that weigh altogether 110,000kg. It is the only 747 that ever lands in Nashville, except for Air Force One, when the president visits. "By April 15 2004, at 7.41am, Tom's system arrived at [Nashville] with other Dell systems from Penang and Limerick. By 11.58am, Tom's system [was] inserted into a larger box, which went down the boxing line to the specific external parts that Tom had ordered."

That was 13 days after I'd ordered it. Had there not been a parts delay in Malaysia when my order first arrived, the time between when I phoned in my purchase, when the notebook was assembled in Penang, and its arrival in Nashville would have been only four days. Hunter said the total supply chain for my computer, including suppliers of suppliers, involved about 400 companies in North America, Europe, and primarily Asia, but with 30 key players. Somehow, though, it all came together. My computer was delivered to Bethesda, outside Washington DC, on April 19 2004.

Questions

1. Which of the channel functions are performed in this story, either by Dell or by one of the suppliers involved?

2. What are the pros and cons of using suppliers from so many different countries?

3. Which retailer and wholesaler functions are performed by Dell? Which are performed by its network of suppliers?

4. How does Dell motivate its suppliers to do their best? Do you think this is the best way to build a supply-chain team?

5. What do you think made Dell decide to sell its product this way instead of through a brick-and-mortar store?

Hampton Beach

Nouveau-Brunswick

Nouveau ⚜ Brunsv

After studying this chapter, you should be able to

1.   explain why it is important for organizations to integrate their marketing communications

2.   describe and discuss the major decisions involved in developing an advertising program

3.   list the major marketing communications goals achieved through sales promotions

4.   list and describe the steps in the personal selling process

5.   identify and discuss the major forms of direct response marketing

6.   explain how companies use public relations to communicate with their publics

Integrated Marketing Communications

12

Looking Ahead
We'll forge ahead now into the last of the marketing mix tools: promotion. You'll find that promotion, or, as it is more frequently called today, *marketing communications*, is not a single tool but rather a collection of several tools that work together to communicate a consistent message about the organization and its products. This is the concept of *integrated marketing communications*. We'll begin by introducing you to marketing communications, and discussing the need for integrated marketing communications. Then, we'll look in detail at the five major elements of marketing communications: advertising, sales promotion, public relations, personal selling, and direct marketing.

To begin, let's look at how a Canadian marketer, Tourism New Brunswick, developed a strategic integrated marketing communications plan to persuade Quebecers to vacation there rather than in the United States.

How do you convince your next-door neighbours to visit you during their summer vacation? This was the challenge faced by Tourism New Brunswick in the 1990s. Although New Brunswick registered the highest growth rate of any tourist destination in Canada between 1984 and 1995 (up 56 percent), only 22 percent of visitors were from Quebec. This was less than the percentage of visitors from the Atlantic provinces (29 percent), the U.S. (25 percent), and Ontario (24 percent). Tourism New Brunswick saw great potential in the Quebec market, and so in 1996 it hired Montreal marketing communications agency LG2 and put it in charge of the campaign to attract Quebecers to New Brunswick.

LG2 knew that the majority of Quebecers named Quebec as their number one summer travel destination, followed by the American beaches of Maine and Massachusetts. In order to create a successful marketing campaign, LG2 needed to find out what benefits of a New Brunswick vacation would appeal to Quebecers. The agency conducted surveys of Quebecers visiting New Brunswick and found that these vacationers were very satisfied with their choice of destination. After all, French is spoken in most of the province. As well, Quebecers in general prefer to vacation at a beach, and New Brunswick boasts the warmest salt-water beaches north of Virginia. And since few Quebecers were aware of the warmth of New Brunswick's beaches, this became the focus of LG2's campaign.

Tourism New Brunswick's campaign to draw tourists from Quebec lasted four years, from 1997 to 2001, and was carefully planned, timed, and executed. LG2's objective for the campaign was to increase visitor levels from Quebec by dominating advertising awareness and then generating inquiries, interest, and action. Timing was a key factor in the campaign strategy. Research had shown that Quebecers typically begin planning their summer vacations in May, and that Tourism Quebec ran its advertising campaigns from May through August. So LG2 ran the Tourism New Brunswick ads in March and April, getting Quebecers to think about their vacations well before Tourism Quebec's advertising would begin.

Supersized outdoor billboards were used throughout the campaign, with three new creative executions developed each year. The billboards were all visually similar; they were split into two panels, the left in a bluish tone to signify the cold waters of the American East Coast and the right in a yellowish tone to portray the warmth of the water at New Brunswick beaches. Each billboard featured one element reacting in very different ways to the temperature of the water in each vacation destination. For example, one ad shows a foot timidly dipping one toe into the frigid water of Cape Cod on the left panel and the same foot relaxing in the warm water of New Brunswick on the right panel. Other visual elements included people, bathing suits, fish, money, birds, and hermit crabs.

The billboards succeeded in generating awareness of New Brunswick as a tourist destination, setting the stage for the second part of the campaign. It was critical to LG2's campaign that the interest in the billboards be converted into action. When people plan a vacation they want information, so the second part of the plan was to create a multi-media campaign whose every ad included a toll free number to call or a postcard to fill out and mail to request a New Brunswick vacation planner. The campaign included

- 60-second television spots, similar in look and concept to the billboard ads
- double-page spreads in women's magazines, with a postcard that could be sent in for a vacation planner
- direct mail sent to previous inquirers inviting them to order the free planner

As well as traditional media placement, LG2 set up a marketing partnership between Tourism New Brunswick and the CAA. In exchange for including New Brunswick tourism information in CAA materials, Tourism New Brunswick gave the CAA logo placement in its ads and posters to place in CAA's Quebec offices. And, throughout the four years of the campaign, LG2 delivered a consistent marketing message across all of its media vehicles: "New Brunswick offers the warmest salt-water beaches north of Virginia."

Was the campaign successful? Yes! During the four years of the campaign New Brunswick went from seventh to first position in Quebecers' advertising awareness of vacation destinations. Before the campaign, interest in visiting New Brunswick was at 20 percent. After, it was 32 percent. As well, unaided awareness of the warm salt-water positioning jumped from 17 percent to 39 percent, and inquiries from Quebecers increased by 57 percent. LG2 also evaluated the campaign in terms of its return on investment, and found that every dollar spent on advertising resulted in $18 to $23 in revenue for New Brunswick over the course of the campaign.[1]

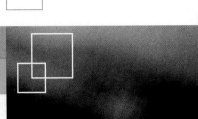

TEST YOURSELF
Answers to these questions can be found on our website at
www.pearsoned.ca/armstrong.

1. Before entering the creative phase, LG2 went through a critical process that was the greatest contributing factor to the overall success of the campaign. What was that process?
   a) It decided to time its ads earlier than those of Tourism Quebec
   b) It investigated and clearly understood Tourism New Brunswick's available budget
   c) It researched Quebecers, their vacationing habits, and the preferences they had when selecting vacation spots
   d) Tourism New Brunswick and LG2 established what the measurable goals for the campaign were
   e) It tested the temperature of New Brunswick's beaches

2. Why did LG2 decide to use the same message and the same look in the billboards, the television spots, and the magazine ads?
   a) Because using the same creative radically reduces the cost of the campaign
   b) Because sending a consistent brand message across all media has a greater and more memorable impact
   c) Because people would not understand that it was all part of the same campaign
   d) Because it could produce the ads all at once and roll them out as needed
   e) Because it was able to test the entire campaign at once with the same set of focus groups

3. The ads in the second half of the campaign included a phone number or another way for the viewer or reader to request a vacation planner. Why was this important?
   a) Because it was a way of measuring how compelling the campaign was to Quebecers
   b) Because they would be able to tell what areas of Quebec were responding best to the campaign
   c) Because Tourism New Brunswick and LG2 knew that if people used the planner they would be more likely to actually vacation there
   d) A call to action turns the viewer's initial interest into the next step along the sales path
   e) All of the above

4. What key benefit did Tourism New Brunswick get from forging a marketing partnership with the Canadian Automobile Association?
   a) The CAA's "endorsement" of New Brunswick would have carried significance for Quebecers
   b) The CAA would provide money to help fund the campaign
   c) Tourism New Brunswick would be assured of a way to get its planner distributed
   d) The CAA would not be able to similarly partner with Tourism Quebec
   e) The CAA uses LG2 as their advertising agency and they combined forces

5. Why did LG2 and Tourism New Brunswick keep track of the increase in interest and the additional tourism money spent in New Brunswick?

a) Because LG2's billing was dependent on how much extra money New Brunswick made in tourism revenue

b) Because the success of a promotional campaign must be constantly measured so that adjustments can be made and objectives met

c) Because LG2 would then be able to use the same style of campaign for other provinces more easily

d) Because Tourism New Brunswick was uncertain that it had delivered a successful campaign

e) None of the above

Modern marketing calls for more than just developing a good product, pricing it attractively, and making it available to the market. Companies must also *communicate* with current and prospective customers, and what they communicate should not be left to chance. All of their communications efforts must be blended into a consistent and coordinated communications program. Just as good communication is important in building and maintaining any kind of relationship, it is a crucial element in a company's efforts to build customer relationships.

THE ELEMENTS OF MARKETING COMMUNICATIONS

A company's total **marketing communications mix**—also called its **promotion mix**—consists of the specific blend of advertising, sales promotion, public relations, personal selling, and direct-marketing tools that the company uses to pursue its advertising and marketing objectives. Definitions of the five major promotion tools follow:[2]

> **Advertising:** Any paid form of nonpersonal presentation and promotion of ideas, goods, or services by an identified sponsor. The paid placement of a promotional message in the mass media.
>
> **Sales promotion:** Short-term incentives, usually presented at the point of purchase, designed to encourage the immediate purchase of a product or service.
>
> **Personal selling:** Personal presentation by the firm's sales representatives for the purpose of making sales and building customer relationships.
>
> **Direct response marketing:** Direct communications with carefully targeted customers (consumers or businesses) that request an immediate, measurable response and cultivate lasting customer relationships.
>
> **Public relations:** Building good relations with the company's various publics by obtaining favourable publicity, building a good corporate image, and handling or heading off unfavourable rumours, stories, and events.

Each element of the marketing communications mix requires its own delivery medium, that is, a method or vehicle through which the members of the target market can receive the communications. For example, advertising uses print, broadcast, and out-of-home media; sales promotion includes point-of-purchase displays, premiums, and coupons; personal selling makes use of sales presentations and trade shows; direct marketing can be conducted through catalogues, telemarketing, direct mail, and online; and public relations delivers communications through press releases and events.

Though these are the five major tools of marketing communications, the marketer must realize that everything the organization does communicates a message to the mar-

---

Marketing communications mix (promotion mix) The specific blend of advertising, sales promotion, public relations, personal selling, and direct marketing tools a company uses to pursue its advertising and marketing objectives.

Advertising Any paid form of nonpersonal presentation and promotion of ideas, goods, or services by an identified sponsor.

Sales promotion Short-term incentives designed to encourage the purchase of a product or service.

Personal selling Personal presentation by the firm's sales representatives for the purpose of making sales and building customer relationships.

Direct response marketing Direct communications with carefully targeted customers to obtain an immediate response.

Public relations Building good relations with the company's various publics by obtaining favourable publicity, building a good corporate image, and handling or heading off unfavourable rumours, stories, and events.

ket: the product's design, its price, the shape and colour of its package, the choice of retail outlets that will carry it, and the functionality and content of the organization's website. Thus, in addition to the marketing communications mix, the company's entire marketing mix—promotion *and* product, price, and place—must be coordinated.

THE NEED FOR INTEGRATED MARKETING COMMUNICATIONS (IMC)

Early in the history of marketing, companies developed the art of mass marketing—selling standardized products to masses of customers. In the process, they perfected mass media advertising techniques to support their mass marketing strategies. Canada's top mass media advertisers include Bell Canada Enterprises (BCE Canada), Procter & Gamble, General Motors, Hudson's Bay Company, Sears, Wendy's International Inc. (which includes Tim Hortons), McCain Foods, Molson, Rogers Communications Inc., and the Government of Canada.[3] They spend millions of dollars on advertising, reaching tens of millions of customers with a single ad. The marketing communications manager of today, however, faces some new challenges.

Figure 12.1 **Integrated Marketing Communications**

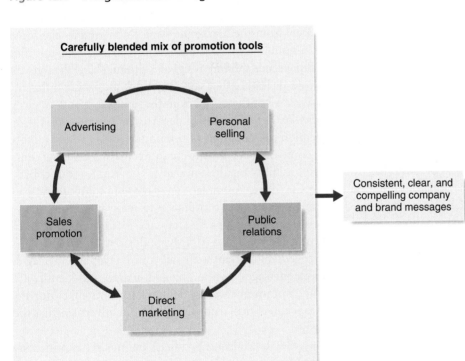

Two major factors are changing marketing communications. First, as mass markets have fragmented, marketers are finding they must develop more focused and targeted marketing communications in order to reach customers in more narrowly defined market segments. Second, marketers are no longer limited to one-to-many mass marketing communications, since such technologies as database management software, websites, email, and text messaging via cell phones allow marketers to *interact* with the market and provide one-to-one, personalized, communications messages.

Given this new marketing environment, marketers must rethink their marketing communications strategies and tactics. Market fragmentation has resulted in *media fragmentation*—in an explosion of more focused media that better match today's targeting strategies. For example, where there were once a handful of major network television stations on which advertisers might place their messages, today there are hundreds of specialty channels, allowing advertisers to more precisely target their audience. Why wouldn't Home Depot, for example, choose to advertise on TLC, the Canadian cable channel that airs popular home renovation programs such as *Trading Spaces*, instead of "wasting" its advertising on mass market major network programming?

Advertisers are also making increased use of other highly targeted media, including specialty magazines, CD catalogues, Web coupons, airport kiosks, and floor decals in drugstore aisles. In all, companies are doing less *broadcasting* and more *narrowcasting*.

But the shift from mass marketing to targeted marketing, and the corresponding use of a larger, richer mix of communication channels and promotion tools, pose a problem for marketers. Consumers don't distinguish among message sources the way marketers do. In the consumer's mind, all advertising messages, regardless of the delivery media, become part of a single message about the company. If these messages are not carefully coordinated, or *integrated*, the result is a confused company image and brand position.

You might think that it would be only common sense for a company to integrate its messages; however, large companies often have an advertising agency, a separate public relations agency, perhaps another firm designing their packaging, and yet another managing their website. And the company itself might contain a corporate communications department that operates separately from the marketing department and a sales force that's located in another city. As a result, it's not uncommon to see advertisements that say one thing, a price promotion that sends a different signal, a product label that creates still another message, company sales literature that says something altogether different, and a website that seems unrelated to all of these—all from the same company.

Until very recently, no one person in the marketing department was responsible for thinking through the communication roles of all these promotion tools and coordinating them. Today, however, many companies are appointing a director of marketing communications who has overall responsibility for the company's communications efforts. These organizations are adopting the concept of **integrated marketing communications (IMC)**, under which the company integrates and coordinates its many communications channels and delivers a clear, consistent, and compelling message about the organization and its products.[4] As one marketing executive puts it, "IMC builds a strong brand identity in the marketplace by tying together and reinforcing all your images and messages. IMC means that all your corporate messages, positioning and images, and identity are coordinated across all [marketing communications] venues. It means that your PR materials say the same thing as your direct mail campaign, and your advertising has the same look and feel as your Web site."[5]

For example, in a rare move, in 2003 Molson Canadian's online agency, ninedots, worked closely with Molson's traditional media agency, Bensimon Byrne, to craft an integrated marketing campaign featuring hockey celebrity Don Cherry. Cherry's image appeared on specially marked cases of Molson Canadian; on the iam.ca website, and in all traditional media ads. The campaign also used public relations to raise money for Rose Cherry's Home.

IMC calls for recognizing all contact points or *touchpoints* where the customer may encounter the company, its products, and its brands. Each *brand contact* will deliver a message to the audience—so the company must strive to make those messages strong, positive, and consistent.

Integrated marketing communications (IMC) The approach under which a company carefully integrates and coordinates its many communications channels to deliver a clear, consistent, and compelling message about the organization and its products.

Molson Canadian's 2003 integrated marketing campaign featured Don Cherry in its television, radio, and outdoor ads; on its website; and in its public relations activities.

Marketing Communications Agencies

Another change in the marketing environment that has facilitated companies' ability to integrate their marketing communications programs is the changing nature of advertising agencies.

In small and medium-sized companies, marketing communications management is typically handled by the marketing department. Most large companies, however, retain one or more agencies to produce and deliver their communications programs. In the not too distant past, a large company like Ford or General Motors might have several differ-

---

IN-CLASS NOTES

IMC

- Response to fragmented mass markets and new technologies
- Allows promotions to be more targeted
- Integrated means "fits together"
  - Message is consistent across all channels
  - Generate leverage through repetition and multiple sources with the same message
- Promotional mix must be coordinated with other marketing mix elements

ent agencies working on its marketing communications materials: one to create the ads, one to buy the media, and another to manage public relations. Agencies consider themselves competitors of one another, and they do not work together, hence the too-often appearance of *dis*-integrated marketing communications.

Some very large international agencies, such as Ogilvy & Mather, and Young & Rubicam, have been around for decades. They started out simply as advertising agencies and grew into enormous international conglomerates that provide companies with every type of marketing communications assistance. There are also smaller, "boutique" agencies, such as Toronto's Taxi, which handles all the advertising for Telus. Regardless of size, most of these firms now refer to themselves as "communications agencies."

Cossette Communication Group is a case in point. Starting out as a small advertising agency in Quebec City in the 1970s, it has grown to become a publicly traded company listed on the TSX. Cossette is the biggest marketing communications firm in Canada, with 1400 employees and offices in six cities in Canada, New York, and London. Today's Cossette offers the gamut of communications services: strategic planning, media planning and buying, direct marketing, database management, sales promotions, public relations, brand identity, graphic design, sports marketing, and interactive marketing services. The company's first major client was McDonald's, but they were given limited account responsibilities, serving only eastern Quebec. Today, Cossette's clients are all A-list companies: Bell, General Motors, Shopper's Drug Mart, General Mills, Nike, Coca-Cola, and Molson. And yes, McDonald's is still a Cossette client.

The IMC Process

Integrated marketing communications involves identifying the target audience and shaping a well-coordinated program to elicit the desired audience response. Too often, traditional marketing communications focus on simply creating awareness in the target market. But this approach to communication is shortsighted. Today, marketers are moving toward viewing communications as *managing the customer relationship over time*, during the preselling, selling, purchasing, and post-purchase stages. Because market segments differ in their demographic and psychographic composition, communications programs need to be developed specifically for the target market, and even, in some cases, for individuals in that market. As companies learn how to effectively integrate online communications with traditional communications, they are asking not only "How can we reach our customers?" but also "How can we let our customers reach us?"

Thus, the communications process should start with an audit of all the potential contacts members of the target market may have with the company and its brands. For example, a consumer in the market for a new cell phone may talk to others, see television ads, read articles in newspapers and magazines, search for information online, and visit a retail store. The marketer needs to assess what influence each of these communications experiences will have at different stages of the buying process. This understanding will help marketers allocate their communication dollars more efficiently and effectively (see Marketing at Work 12.1).

The concept of integrated marketing communications suggests that the company must blend all the elements into a coordinated mix. But how does the company determine which elements of marketing communications it will use? Companies within the same industry differ greatly in the design of their communications mixes. For example,

Marketing at Work 12.1

Integrated Communications Create Brand Personality for Mini

When BMW of North America launched the Mini Cooper in the U.S.A., its advertising agency, Crispin Porter + Bogusky, created an award-winning integrated marketing campaign.

A shining example of the strategic use of integrated marketing communications was the campaign to launch the Mini Cooper in the United States in 2001. The comprehensive campaign, created by Crispin Porter + Bogusky, used every element of marketing communications and then some, all carefully integrated to deliver a high-impact brand message to a new market.

"We wanted to be as different as we could because the car is so different from anything out there," says a Mini marketer. The creative "big idea" behind the campaign was to imbue the Mini with personality.

It began with a teaser campaign. Billboards showed only a website address and cryptic, humourous messages such as, "Soon small will mean huge the way bad means good." Later in the campaign, less traditional forms of out-of-home advertising were employed, such as the entire outer wall of a parking garage that featured a bright yellow Mini and the tagline, "Parking. How sad." and wild postings that showed brightly coloured Minis juxtaposed with similarly shaped objects: a red Mini and a

red boxing glove; a yellow Mini and a bumble bee.

A television spot featured a man driving a Mini being pulled over by a British "Bobby," who tells the driver he's on the wrong side of the road. "This is America!" the driver replies. Traditional print advertising was used in innovative ways: A Mini was the centrefold in *Playboy* magazine, and a two-page spread in *Rolling Stone* had a Mini "slaloming" around specially-created orange staples.

Public relations played a major role in the launch. "Mission Mini" was a staged event that took place in Barcelona in 2002. BMW's German marketing team headed the effort, but each international division of the company, and their agencies, was involved. Teams from 17 countries were invited to Spain, given the use of a Mini, trained in racecar driving techniques, and spent a week playing a game called "Mission Mini." Teams from the U.S. were chosen from entrants into an online competition.

Dozens of "guerilla marketing" tactics were dreamed up by the very creative people at CP+B. There was the

"Mini Ride" display, which was made of an actual Mini but looked like a children's ride. "Rides $16,850. Quarters only, please" the sign read. Advertising "installations" in airports featured oversized but functional newspaper vending machines, waste baskets, and pay phones next to posters showing the diminutive Mini and proclaiming, "Makes everything else seem a little too big." Minis were "sat" in the stands at football games, their headlights pointed toward the game, and driven around on top of SUVs painted with the question, "What are you doing this weekend?" Product placement, a relatively new form of marketing communications, was used later in the ongoing branding campaign. BMW gave the producers of the 2003 film *The Italian Job* 30 Minis to use any way they wanted in the movie.

What was the effect of the campaign? In the U.S.A., BMW dealers were deluged with orders. Within a year of the start of the campaign the company was selling Minis faster than it could make them. The offbeat marketing campaign scooped up numerous advertising industry awards. Not bad, considering that three years earlier, only 2 percent of Americans had even heard of Mini. Today, Mini enjoys a 67 percent brand awareness. And the Mini brand certainly has personality. "Mini is inherently interesting," says BMW communications manager Michael McHale. "It's anthropomorphic—it is such a character it comes to life. I feel sorry for marketers who have boring brands to work with."

Sources: "Creating Max Buzz for New BMW Mini," *Advertising Age*, June 17, 2002, p. 12; Joan Voight, "Mini's Wild Ride," *Adweek*, June 2, 2003, pp. 24–26; "Calling All Countries," *Promo* magazine, Feb. 1, 2003; Examples of Mini advertising found on the Crispin Porter + Bogusky Web site, http://www.cpbmiami.com/. Information about "Mission Mini" taken from CityTV program, *Media Television*.

Avon spends most of its promotion funds on personal selling and direct marketing, whereas Revlon spends heavily on mass media advertising.

When designing their marketing communications mix, marketers must take into consideration previous marketing decisions about product, price, and distribution, as well as the characteristics of the target market and the stage of the product life cycle.

Promotion Mix Strategies: Push vs. Pull

Push strategy A promotion strategy that calls for using the sales force and trade promotion to push the product through channels.

Pull strategy A promotion strategy that calls for using advertising and consumer promotion to build consumer demand.

Marketers can choose from two basic promotion mix strategies: *push* promotion or *pull* promotion. Figure 12.2 contrasts the two strategies. A **push strategy** uses the sales force and trade promotion to push the product through its distribution channels to the consumer. The producer directs its marketing activities at channel members to induce them to carry the product and to promote it. The producer promotes the product to wholesalers, the wholesalers promote to retailers, and the retailers promote to consumers. Using a **pull strategy**, the producer uses advertising and consumer promotion to build consumer demand. If the pull strategy is effective, consumers will then demand the product from channel members, who will in turn demand it from producers.

Figure 12.2   Push Versus Pull Promotion Strategy

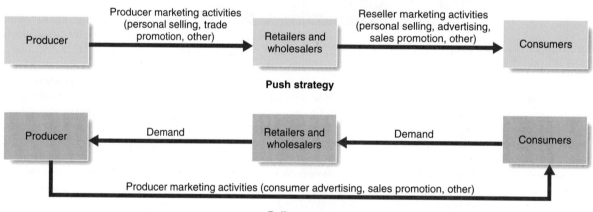

Consumer products companies usually "pull" more, putting more of their marketing budget into advertising, sales promotion, and public relations. In contrast, B2B marketers tend to "push" more, putting more of their budget into personal selling and trade promotion. Generally, personal selling is used in the marketing of expensive and risky products, and in markets with fewer and larger sellers.

Some B2B marketers use only push strategies; some direct marketing companies use only pull. However, most large companies use some combination of both. For example, Kraft uses mass-media advertising and consumer promotions to pull its products, and a large sales force and trade promotions to push its products through the channels.

Setting the Marketing Communications Budget

How does a company decide how much to spend on advertising? What percentage of its budget to allocate to sales promotions? Whether to invest in a direct response marketing campaign? Marketing managers typically set their marketing communications budget at the beginning of each fiscal year. Four methods are commonly used.[6]

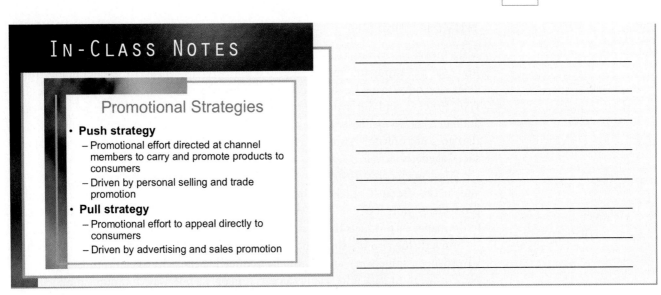

Some companies use the **affordable method**: They set the budget at the level they think the company can afford. Small businesses often use this method, reasoning that the company cannot spend more on promotions than it has. Unfortunately, this method places marketing communications last among spending priorities, even in situations in which promoting a new product is critical to the firm's success. It leads to an uncertain annual budget, which makes long-range market planning difficult. Although the affordable method can result in overspending on promotions, it more often results in underspending.

Other companies use the **percentage-of-sales method**, setting their promotion budget at a certain percentage of current or forecast sales—typically between 5 and 15 percent. Or they budget a percentage of the unit sales price. The percentage-of-sales method is simple to use and helps management think about the relationships among marketing communications spending, selling price, and profit per unit. The difficulty with this method is that it wrongly views sales as the *cause* of promotion rather than as the *result*. Studies often show positive correlations between advertising and brand performance; however, it is also usually the case that brands with higher sales can afford bigger marketing communications budgets. Because the percentage of sales budget is based on availability of funds rather than on opportunities, it may prevent the increased spending sometimes needed to turn around falling sales.

Companies that use the **competitive parity method** set their marketing communications budget to match competitors' outlays. They monitor competitors' advertising campaigns, or get industry promotion spending estimates from publications or trade associations, and then set their budgets based on the industry average. Beer companies tend to use this method, especially for advertising expenditures. They believe that parity in advertising spending helps prevent promotion wars. In reality, of course, there are no grounds for believing that the competition has a better idea of what a company should be spending on advertising than does the company itself.

The most logical budget-setting method is the **objective-and-task method**, whereby the company sets its marketing communications budget based on what it wants those communications to accomplish. Unfortunately, this is also the most difficult method to use, because it forces the marketing manager to spell out assumptions about the relationship between dollars spent and communications results. The objective-and-task method entails (1) defining specific communications and promotional objectives, (2) determining the tasks needed to achieve these objectives, and (3) estimating the costs of performing these tasks. The sum of these costs is the proposed budget.

Affordable method Setting the budget at the level management thinks the company can afford.

Percentage-of-sales method Setting the budget at a certain percentage of current or forecast sales or as a percentage of the unit sales price.

Competitive parity method Setting the budget to match competitors' outlays.

Objective-and-task method Setting the budget by (1) defining specific objectives, (2) determining the tasks that must be performed to achieve these objectives, and (3) estimating the costs of performing these tasks.

ADVERTISING

Mass media advertising reaches large numbers of geographically dispersed buyers at a low cost per exposure, and enables the marketer to repeat a message many times. Television advertising has the greatest reach, with audience sizes for popular shows like *CSI*, *The O.C.*, and *Survivor* numbering in the millions. "If you want to get to the mass audience," says a media services executive, "broadcast TV is where you have to be."[7] And that goes not only for businesses, but for nonprofit organizations and professional and social agencies as well.

Mass media advertising says something positive about the seller's size, popularity, and success. Because of advertising's public nature, consumers tend to view advertised products as more legitimate. Advertising is also very expressive—it allows the company to dramatize its products through the artful use of visuals, print, sound, and colour.

Advertising also has some shortcomings. Although it reaches many people quickly, advertising is impersonal and cannot be as directly persuasive as can company salespeople. For the most part, advertising can carry on only a one-way communication with the audience, and the audience does not feel that it has to pay attention or respond. In addition, advertising can be very costly.

Marketing communications managers must make four important decisions when developing an advertising program. They must set advertising objectives, make budget decisions, develop an advertising strategy, and then evaluate the campaign. And if the company operates internationally, the marketing communications manager must make decisions about international advertising.

Setting Advertising Objectives

Advertising objective A specific communication task to be accomplished with a specific target audience during a specific time.

An **advertising objective** is a specific communication task to be accomplished with a specific target audience during a specific time. Advertising objectives can be classified by primary purpose: to *inform*, *persuade*, or *remind*. Table 12.1 lists examples of each of these objectives.

Informative advertising is typically used when introducing a new product to the market. The goal is to build primary demand, but first, the marketers must inform the target market of the existence of the new product.

Persuasive advertising becomes more important as competition increases; that is, when the product enters the growth stage of the product life cycle. Here, the goal is to build selective demand. A marketer such as Sony, for example, wishes to persuade consumers that its brand of DVD player offers the best quality for their money. Persuasive advertising may even compare the advertiser's brand to the competition, in order to highlight the advantages of the advertiser's brand.

Reminder advertising is typically used for products in the mature stage of the product life cycle. The goal is to keep consumers from "forgetting" about the product; to keep demand steady, and prevent it from decreasing.

Developing Advertising Strategy

Advertising strategy consists of creating advertising *messages* and selecting advertising *media*. In the past, companies often viewed media planning as secondary to the message-creation process. The creative team first created the ads, then the media planners selected the best media for carrying these advertisements to desired target audiences. But today marketers are realizing that advertising strategy is only one aspect of a marketing communications strategy. Advertising may be a critical component of an IMC program, or it may not be included at all. For example, Cake Beauty's IMC strategy calls

Table 12.1 **Possible Advertising Objectives**	
Informative Advertising	
Telling the market about a new product	Describing available services
Suggesting new uses for a product	Correcting false impressions
Informing the market of a price change	Reducing consumers' fears
Explaining how the product works	Building a company image
Persuasive Advertising	
Building brand preference	Persuading consumer to purchase now
Encouraging switching to your brand	Persuading consumer to receive a sales call
Changing consumers' perception of product attributes	
Reminder Advertising	
Reminding consumer that the product may be needed in the near future	Keeping it in consumer's mind during off seasons
Reminding consumer where to buy it	Maintaining top-of-mind awareness

for a focus on public relations, not mass media advertising. Meanwhile, one of the beauty industry's largest corporations, L'Oréal, has a totally different strategy, focusing on mass media such as radio, television, and the Internet:

> L'Oréal Canada was named *Marketing* magazine's 2004 Marketer of the Year because it is among the best at integrating all aspects of its marketing communications—as it proved with its L'Oréal Paris brand's comprehensive sponsorship of CTV's *Canadian Idol* television show. According to Dominique De Celles, general manager of L'Oréal Paris in Montreal, sales of the L'Oréal Paris brand grew by more than 30 percent following the first *Canadian Idol* competition in 2003. And Ron Szekely, director of marketing for L'Oréal, points out that the goal of the *Canadian Idol* sponsorship was to reach a younger demographic.
>
> When the third contest began on May 31, 2005, the first commercial was for L'Oréal True Match powder and featured Beyoncé as its spokesmodel. L'Oréal's sponsorship includes 30-second brand sell spots and opening and closing billboards on each episode; a major presence on the *Canadian Idol* website, including large logos at both the top and bottom of the homepage; and sponsorship announcements during on-air promotion. And during the final few weeks of the show, when individual contestants are filmed as their hair and makeup are done, those makeup attendants wear L'Oréal Paris T-shirts. At retail points of purchase for L'Oréal products there are also contests and signs. But the real marketing coup for L'Oréal is the inclusion of its products in several in-show segments. For example, a segment featuring L'Oréal's EasyColor interactive application allowed visitors to the L'Oréal Paris website to upload pictures of themselves and create new looks.[8]

Creating the Advertising Message   No matter how big the budget, advertising can succeed only if the ads communicate effectively. But advertisers face a significant challenge in today's media-saturated world. How can they cut through the clutter and get their message heard? After all, Canada boasts 128 broadcast television stations and 2000 radio stations. There are two national newspapers, *The Globe and Mail* and *National Post*, and almost every city, small or large, has a daily newspaper. There are hundreds of specialty magazines about everything from fitness to knitting. And all of these major media sell advertising space to marketers.

So today's advertising messages must be better planned and more entertaining than ever before. "Today we have to entertain and not just sell, because if you try to sell directly and come off as boring or obnoxious, people are going to press the remote on you," points out one advertising executive. "When most TV viewers are armed with remote channel switchers, a commercial has to cut through the clutter and seize the viewers in one to three seconds, or they're gone," comments another.[9] And today viewers have other ways of avoiding the message altogether, such as Rogers Personal TV television-on-demand service.[10]

Message Strategy. The first step in creating an effective advertising message is to decide on a *message strategy.* The purpose of advertising is to get consumers to think about or react to the product or company in a certain way. And since people will react only if they believe they will benefit from doing so, developing an effective message strategy begins with identifying customer *benefits* that can be used as advertising appeals.

Next, the advertiser must develop a compelling *creative concept*—or "*big idea*"—that will bring the message strategy to life in a distinctive and memorable way. The creative concept will guide the choice of specific appeals to be used in an advertising campaign. These *appeals* should have three characteristics: First, they should be *meaningful,* pointing out benefits that make the product more desirable or interesting to consumers. Second, appeals must be *believable*—consumers must believe that the product or service will deliver the promised benefits. Appeals should also be *distinctive*—they should tell how the product is better than the competing brands. For example, the most meaningful benefit of owning a wristwatch is that it keeps accurate time, yet few watch ads feature this benefit. Instead, based on the distinctive benefits they offer, watch advertisers might select any of a number of advertising themes. For years, Timex has been the affordable watch that "Takes a lickin' and keeps on tickin'." In contrast, Swatch has featured style and fashion, whereas Rolex stresses luxury and status.

Message Execution. The *execution* of the message refers to the particular way in which the message is presented. The advertiser must carefully choose the best style, tone, and words for executing the message. Here are some examples:

☐ *Slice of life:* This style shows one or more "typical" people using the product in a normal setting.

☐ *Lifestyle:* This style shows how a product fits in with a particular lifestyle.

☐ *Fantasy:* This style creates a fantasy around the product or its use. Ads for the Ontario Lottery Corporation, for example, show what you might do with your winnings, allowing consumers to vicariously live the fantasy.

☐ *Mood or image:* This style builds a mood or image around the product, such as beauty, love, or serenity. No claim is made about the product except through suggestion. Billboards showing images of sunny Cuba during a Canadian February accomplish this.

☐ *Musical:* This style shows people or characters singing about the product.

☐ *Personality symbol:* This style creates a character that represents the product. There are many examples: Tony the Tiger, the Pillsbury Doughboy, The Man from Glad.

☐ *Technical expertise:* This style shows the company's expertise in making the product.

☐   *Scientific evidence:* This style presents survey or scientific evidence that the brand is better or better liked than one or more other brands. Advertisements for medicines frequently use this style.

☐   *Testimonial evidence or endorsement:* This style features a highly believable or likable source endorsing the product. It could be ordinary people saying how much they like the product, or a celebrity endorsing it.

The advertiser also must choose a *tone* for the ad. The tone could be humorous, or serious, or instructive (as a parent or teacher explaining something to a child), or suspenseful, or shocking (as many of the advertisements created by MADD, Mothers Against Drunk Driving, are).

Successful advertisements usually state the message in powerful, memorable words or phrases. Consider Volkswagen's "Drivers Wanted" and London Life's "Freedom 55."

Selecting Advertising Media

The major forms of media for advertising are print (newspaper and magazine), broadcast (television and radio), out-of-home, direct mail, and online (websites and email). When selecting advertising media the advertiser must consider not only choice of media, but reach, frequency, and impact; specific media vehicles; and timing of the media placement.

Deciding on Reach, Frequency, and Impact. *Reach* is a measure of the percentage of people in the target market who are exposed to the ad campaign during a given period. An advertiser might set a goal of reaching 70 percent of the target market during the first three months of a campaign. *Frequency* is a measure of how many *times* the average person in the target market is exposed to the message. The media planner must decide on the desired media *impact*—the qualitative value of a message exposure through a given medium. For example, for products that need to be demonstrated, messages on television will have more impact than messages on radio because television uses sight *and* sound.

Choosing Among Major Media Types. The media planner has to know the reach, frequency, and impact of each of the major media types. The advantages and limitations of each medium are outlined in Table 12.2.

Media planners consider many factors when choosing advertising media. They will typically meet with media sales representatives from newspapers, magazines, and television and radio stations, and ask questions about the size and demographics of the audience. Then, they must decide if the audience characteristics of that medium are similar in nature to the target market for their product.

The nature of the product also affects media choices; for example, food and clothing are best represented through high-quality images, therefore magazines are a better choice than newspapers. Newspapers are the best choice when the message strategy is to provide information about the product, therefore marketers of computers and cell phones often choose this medium. For products that are not highly differentiated, such as beer, television is chosen because of its ability to appeal to our senses and play to our emotions, much as a television program or movie can. Television is also favoured by car marketers because it allows them to show the product in action.

The choice of media must also reflect the marketers' strategy and goals. Radio is most effective at reaching a local audience, and is frequently the medium of choice for local events such as concerts and theatre. Direct mail is effective when the marketer has

Table 12.2	Profiles of Major Media Types	

Medium	Advantages	Limitations
Newspapers	Flexibility; timeliness; local market coverage; acceptability; credibility	Short life; poor image quality; little or no pass-along readership
Magazines	Geographic and demographic selectivity; credibility and prestige; high-quality images; long life; pass-along readership	Long lead time for purchasing ad space; high cost; no guarantee of position
Television	Mass market coverage; low cost per exposure; combines sight, sound, and motion; appeals to senses	High production and placement costs; clutter; fleeting exposure; audience avoidance
Radio	Local market coverage; geographic and demographic selectivity; low cost	Audio only; fleeting exposure; low attention paid by audience
Out-of-Home	Flexibility; repeat exposure; low cost; low message competition; geographic selectivity; positional selectivity	Little audience selectivity; creative limitations
Direct Mail	Audience selectivity; flexibility; personalization	High cost per exposure; "junk mail" image
Online	Audience selectivity; low cost; immediacy; personalization; interactivity	Relatively low impact; audience controls exposure

a specific offer to make to the audience, such as signing up for a new credit card. Out-of-home advertising is typically used when the marketer's goal is precise geographic targeting. Online advertising is the best choice when the marketer's goal is to entice the consumer to pursue further information. For example, most major car marketers place advertising on websites such as CNN and *The Globe and Mail* to entice readers to click on the ads and visit the car manufacturer's site for more information. Air Canada frequently advertises on Yahoo! Canada, with large banner ads announcing seat sales.

Different types of messages also require different media; for example, a local retailer announcing a major sale tomorrow will choose radio or newspapers. Conversely, a marketer that's presenting detailed technical information to a business customer—who requires time to consider a major purchase such as network hardware—will choose a business or trade magazine.

Cost is another major factor in media choice. Once the marketer has set the marketing communications budget, the choice of media must be made with budget constraints in mind. Network television, national newspapers, and magazines are all very expensive. Local newspapers, radio, and limited out-of-home advertising cost much less but also reach a much smaller audience. And the marketer must also consider the costs of producing the ads (the *creative*) for different media. Television ads, not surprisingly, are the most expensive to produce. National brand advertisers pay, on average, $450 000 to produce a single 30-second television commercial.

Finally, as well as the major forms of mass media available to advertisers, many new forms of advertising media are becoming available. These don't fit into any of the traditional categories and so are collectively referred to as "alternative media" (see Marketing at Work 12.2).

Selecting Media Vehicles. The media buyer, working under the direction of the media planner, is normally the person in the company's marketing department or at the advertising agency whose job it is to choose the *media vehicles*. A media vehicle is the specific newspaper, magazine, television program, radio station, or website that will carry the advertising message.

Marketing at Work   12.2

Advertisers Seek Alternative Media

Cabs in Toronto have wheel covers that advertise cell phone services. Gas stations play video ads on tiny screens at the pump. Advertising messages are painted on pool tables. There's even a company called Zoom Media that distributes advertising messages in the form of real postcards in bars and advertising posters on the backs of bathroom stalls.

Claude Lessard, CEO of Cossette Communications Group, Canada's largest marketing communications firm, believes that the shift from traditional mass media to non-traditional media, such as the Internet, event marketing, and public relations, is "a fundamental trend." It's a long term movement.

As network television costs soar and audiences shrink, many advertisers are looking for new ways to reach consumers. The move toward micromarketing strategies, focused more narrowly on specific consumer groups, has also fuelled the search for alternative media to replace or supplement network television. Advertisers are shifting larger portions of their budgets to media that cost less and target more effectively. As a result, ads are popping up in the most unlikely places. In their efforts to find less costly and more highly targeted ways to reach consumers, advertisers have discovered a dazzling collection of alternative media. As consumers, we're used to ads on television, in magazines and newspapers, on the radio, and along the roadways. But these days, no matter where you go or what you do, you'll probably run into some new form of advertising.

Tiny billboards attached to shopping carts, ads on shopping bags, and decals on supermarket floors urge you to buy Pampers. Signs atop parking meters hawk everything from Jeeps to Minolta cameras to Recipe dog food.

A city bus rolls by, fully wrapped in an ad for Yellow Pages. You escape to the ballpark, only to find billboard-size video screens running Labatt Blue ads while a blimp with an electronic message board circles lazily overhead. You pay to see a movie at your local theatre, but first you view a short film about the new BMW. Then the movie itself is full of not-so-subtle promotional plugs for Pepsi, MasterCard, Fritos, or Ray Ban sunglasses. At home, you watch a rerun of *Friends* in which an article of furniture from The Pottery Barn is prominently featured. You attend a play and notice that a character orders not a shot of tequila but a shot of Gran Centenario.

For many marketers, these media can save money and provide a way to hit selected consumers where they live, shop, work, and play. "We like to call it the captive pause," says an executive of an alternative media

firm, a pause in which consumers "really have nothing else to do but either look at the person in front of them or look at some engaging content as well as 15-second commercials." Of course, this may leave you wondering whether there are any commercial-free havens remaining for ad-weary consumers. The backseat of a taxi, perhaps, or public elevators, or stalls in a public restroom? Forget it! Each has already been invaded by innovative marketers.

Sources: See Cara Beardi, "From Elevators to Gas Stations, Ads Multiplying," *Advertising Age,* November 13, 2000, pp. 40–42; Charles Pappas, "Ad Nauseam," *Advertising Age,* July 10, 2000, pp. 16–18; Beardi, "Airport Powerhouses Make Connection," *Advertising Age,* October 2, 2000, p. 8; Wayne Friedman, "Eagle-Eye Marketers Find Right Spot," *Advertising Age,* January 22, 2001, pp. S2–S3; Chris Powell, "One-stop Media," *Marketing,* February 28, 2005, pp. 13–14; and Lisa Sanders, "Tequila Brand Placed in Broadway's 'Sweet Charity,'" *Advertising Age,* May 23, 2005.

Today, ads are popping up in the most unlikely places.

Media buyers evaluate the cost of the media vehicle not by looking at its absolute cost, but by comparing the cost per person reached. This cost, for broadcast, print, and online media, is expressed as the *cost per thousand exposures (CPM)*. Media sales representatives quote media prices to media buyers in terms of CPM, and present these prices on a *rate card* as part of the *media kit*. If you visit the website of any major media vehicle, such as *Maclean's* magazine or the *Globe and Mail*, you'll find a link (usually at the very bottom of the home page) to advertising rates and information. If you click on that link you'll be able to see the media kit, which contains information about the size and demographic characteristics of the audience. Rate cards, or specific prices, may not be available to the public through the media vehicle's site, as these prices are typically negotiated between the advertising sales representative and the media buyer.

The costs of a direct mail campaign, in contrast, are calculated in terms of the number of pieces to be sent: the cost to produce and mail each piece, and the cost per address if a mailing list is to be rented.

Deciding on Media Timing. The media planner must also decide exactly when each advertisement will be placed in each media vehicle. Newspaper may be the medium chosen, and the *Globe and Mail* may be the media vehicle selected, but should the ad be run every day, or only in the Saturday edition? If the Saturday edition, every Saturday, or every other Saturday, and for how many weeks? Is the ad also running on the *Globe and Mail's* website? If so, for how many days, weeks, or months should it appear?

The media planner also makes decisions about the pattern of scheduling. *Continuous scheduling* means the ad appears in every issue of the magazine, or on television at the same time every day; the timing of the placement is even, over a specific time. A pulsing schedule, on the other hand, means that ads are placed in bursts; for example, an ad for Labatt's latest beer brand may appear several times on CBC during *Hockey Night in Canada*, but not appear at all during the week. Mass media advertising is purchased in *flights*, or scheduled blocks of time. For example, Ford may purchase a one-month flight of advertising on the Canada.com site for January, April, September, and December.

Factors affecting media timing decisions include the timing of a product launch, the timing of a sales promotion, the stage of the product life cycle, the nature of the product (golf clubs and lawnmowers tend to be advertised in the summer, skates and oatmeal in the winter) and, of course, the advertising budget.

Evaluating Advertising

The simplest way for marketers to judge whether advertising has been successful is to review sales figures. If sales have increased, the advertising is deemed to have been a success. When sales decrease, advertising is often blamed.

The evaluation of an advertising program, however, should measure the effects of the campaign, and state the results in terms of whether or not they satisfied the original goals of the advertising. For example, if the goal of the campaign was to increase brand awareness, then brand awareness should be measured before the campaign begins and again after the campaign ends, and the results compared. If the goal of the campaign was to introduce a new product to the market and create initial awareness of its benefits, then a market survey should be conducted only after the end of the campaign and the percentage of people aware of the product measured (assuming that awareness at the beginning of the campaign is zero). If the goal of the campaign was to drive preference—this is often the goal of beer advertising, which is typically persuasive advertising—the campaign is evaluated by a change in market share.

Advertising can be evaluated even before it is delivered to an audience. Copy testing, for example, determines whether the ad is communicating well. Copy testing can be done before the ad is placed, by showing it to members of the target market, and asking how they like it and measuring recall or attitude changes resulting from it. After the ad is run, the advertiser can measure how the ad affected recall or product awareness, knowledge, and preference.

Online advertising is often evaluated simply by counting the number of visitors to a site, the number of times an online ad was displayed, or the number of permission-based email messages sent. One of the great advantages of the Internet as a medium for advertising is this ability to exactly count and measure responses. Online advertising can also be evaluated in terms of conversion rates; that is, by measuring the number of viewers who see an ad and dividing it by the number of people who take the desired action—for example, clicking on the ad to visit the advertiser's site, or interacting with the ad by filling out a form to enter a contest, or registering as a member on the advertiser's site.

International Advertising Decisions

When a product is available in international markets, it must be supported by advertising in those markets. Advertisers need to decide whether the advertising should be stan-

Standardized worldwide advertising: Gillette's ads for its Venus razors are almost identical worldwide, with only minor adjustments to suit the local market.

dardized—in other words, running the same ad in every market, in every country—or adapted to suit the unique characteristics of each country market.

Standardization has its benefits, primarily lower costs and a more consistent worldwide image. But it also has drawbacks. Standardizing international advertising ignores the fact that country markets differ greatly in their cultures, demographics, and economic conditions. So, in the new global economy, many marketers have adopted the "Think globally but act locally" philosophy. In other words, they develop global advertising *strategies* that make their worldwide advertising efforts more efficient and consistent. Then they adapt their advertising *programs* to make them more responsive to consumer needs and expectations within local markets.

Many car advertisers take this approach. They produce a set of television commercials showing the car in action, but adapt the voiceover, the music, or the graphic taglines to suit the local market. For example, recent advertising for Ford vehicles in the United States uses the tagline "Built Ford Tough," while in Canada the tagline is "Built for life in Canada." Ford, like many other car brands, also produces a website for each of its country markets, showcasing the vehicles available in that market and collecting sales leads for local dealers.

Coca-Cola has a pool of different commercials that can be used in or adapted to several different international markets. Some can be used with only minor changes—such as language—in several different countries. Local and regional managers decide which commercials work best for which markets. But recently, in a reverse of the usual order, a series of Coca-Cola commercials developed for the Russian market, using a talking bear and a man who transforms into a wolf, was shown in the United States. "This approach fits perfectly with the global nature of Coca-Cola," says the president of Coca-Cola's Nordic division. "[It] offers people a special look into a culture that's different from their own."[11]

International advertising presents many challenges. Media costs and availability differ vastly from country to country. Countries also differ in the extent to which they regulate advertising practices. Many countries have laws restricting how much a company can spend on advertising, what media may be used for advertising, the nature of advertising claims, and even the words that may—or may not—be used in an ad. Cigarette brands are not permitted to advertise in Canada. Alcohol cannot be advertised in Muslim countries. In Norway and Sweden, no TV ads may be directed at children under 12. Comparative ads, while acceptable and even common in the United States and Canada, are unaccept-

IN-CLASS NOTES

Advertising

- Reaches large masses of geographically dispersed buyers
- Allows for repetition and targeting of audience
- Builds awareness, image, positioning
- Provides wide artistic possibilities
- Can be expensive, impersonal, one-way
- Media fragmentation makes finding large audience difficult

able in Japan, and illegal in India and Brazil. China has restrictive censorship rules for TV and radio advertising; for example, the words *the best* are banned, as are ads that "violate social customs" or present women in "improper ways." Coca-Cola's Indian subsidiary was forced to end a promotion that offered prizes because it violated India's established trade practices by encouraging customers to buy in order to "gamble."[12]

Linking the Concepts

Think about an advertising campaign you've noticed recently.

- What forms of mass media advertising were used in the campaign? Which media vehicles (which particular magazine, or newspaper, or television program) were used? Why do you think the marketers made those particular choices?
- Visit the website of the marketer behind the product or service in the campaign. Is the site integrated with the offline forms of promotion? If so, how? If not, suggest how the site might have been used for the campaign.
- What is the message of the campaign? What is the message strategy and message execution?

SALES PROMOTION

If you've been in a grocery store lately, read a newspaper, opened your mailbox, or turned on your TV, chances are you came into contact with a *sales promotion*. Examples of sales promotions are found everywhere: a freestanding insert in *The Toronto Star* announces The Brick's "boxing week sale;" an email from Indigo offers you a $5 discount on your next purchase over $40; a display in Loblaws offers cases of Diet Coke at a special price; a code on the back of your Pepsi label gives you a chance to win an iPod; purchase a package of Energizer batteries and enter to win a trip to Mexico; buy a laptop today and get a free carrying case; shop today and pay no GST!

Sales promotions are short-term incentives designed by marketers for the purpose of encouraging the purchase of a product. More specifically, the marketing purpose of a sales promotion is to give the buyer an incentive to buy the product *now*.

Manufacturers also create sales promotions for their distributors and retailers in order to encourage them to sell a product. These types of sales promotions, directed at members of the marketing channel, are called *trade promotions*. As well, in a company with an internal sales force, promotions may be created by the marketing department for the purpose of encouraging the sales representatives to push a particular product. These are *sales force promotions*. B2B marketers design sales promotions for their business customers—business promotions. But the most common form of sales promotion is the kind that we as consumers see every day—*consumer promotions*.

In an effective integrated marketing communications campaign, sales promotions are planned and executed in conjunction with other elements of marketing communications, such as mass media advertising, personal selling at the point of sale, and public relations.

Sales Promotion Objectives

The overall objective of any sales promotion is to encourage sales, but depending on the type of promotion, the specific goals may vary. For example, marketers of consumer products often use a three-month sales promotion when launching a new product into

Perhaps the best known sales promotion in Canada is the annual Tim Hortons "Roll Up The Rim To Win" sweepstakes.

the market, especially when that product is only a new brand in an existing product category, such as toothpaste. A sales promotion is an excellent way to attract attention to the new product. Sales promotions are also used by marketers to boost sales in what would otherwise be a slow time of year. This is the reason for the annual Tim Hortons "Roll Up the Rim to Win" promotion, which begins in March—as the weather gets warmer, people tend to drink less coffee.

The objectives of trade promotions include getting retailers to carry new items and more inventory, getting them to promote the product in their stores, and encouraging them to give the product more or better shelf space. The objectives of a sales force promotion are typically to generate enthusiasm for a new product among the sales force, and to encourage them to focus their sales efforts on it.

Sales promotions are also used to encourage temporary brand switching during peak buying periods. Furniture and appliances are often promoted with price discounts and other special offers (Free DVD player with every mattress purchase!) just after the Christmas season ends, because January is peak buying time for these items. During hockey playoff season, and again during the summer, the major beer brands usually offer something "free" inside each case.

Sales promotions can also be used to clear out inventory. Every fall, major car manufacturers offer dealer incentives or cash-back rebates to help clear last year's automobile models off the lot before the new models arrive. In all these examples the marketing tactic is the same: A purchase must be made *now* in order to take advantage of the offer.

Though sales promotions are typically used to accomplish short-term goals, they can also help reinforce the product's position and build long-term *customer relationships*. Loyalty programs such as Air Canada's Aeroplan frequent flyer program, Shoppers Drug Mart's Optimum card, and Chapters/Indigo's iREWARDS program are all examples of sales promotions designed with long-term marketing goals in mind.

Major Sales Promotion Tools

Marketers may choose from many different sales promotion tools when designing consumer promotions, trade promotions, business promotions, and sales force promotions.

Consumer Promotion Tools The main *consumer promotion tools* include samples, coupons, rebates, price packs, premiums, advertising specialities, patronage rewards, point-of-purchase displays and demonstrations, and contests, sweepstakes, and games.

Samples are offers of a trial amount of a product. Sampling is a very effective, though very costly, way to introduce a new product. The sample might be delivered door to door, sent by mail, handed out in a store, attached to another product, attached to an ad in a magazine, or requested through a website.

When Procter & Gamble decided to relaunch Pert Plus shampoo, it extended its $30 million ad campaign by constructing a new website for the brand at www.pertplus.com. P&G had three objectives for the site: to create awareness for reformulated Pert Plus, to get consumers to try the product, and to gather data about Web users. The site invited visitors to place their heads against the computer screen in a mock attempt to measure the cleanliness of their hair. After "tabulating the results," the site told visitors that they "need immediate help." The solution: "How about a free sample of new Pert Plus?" Visitors obtain the sample by filling out a form and submitting it online. The site offered other interesting features as well. For example, clicking "get a friend in a lather" would allow the visitor to send an email to a friend with an invitation to visit the site and receive a free sample. Within two months of launching the site, 170 000 people visited and 83 000 requested samples. More surprising, given that the site consisted of only 10 web pages, the average person visited the site 1.9 times and spent a total of 7.5 minutes each visit.[13]

Coupons are certificates that, when redeemed, give buyers a price discount on a product. Coupons are found in newspapers and magazines, in direct mail packages, and, increasingly, on brand websites. When Procter & Gamble launched Mr. Clean AutoDry car wash in 2004, the company offered a $5.00 coupon for the purchase of the starter kit through a special site, www.mrcleanautodry.com. Now that the product is no longer new to the market, the site that had been created for the sales promotion redirects the visitor to one of P&G's year-round sites, HomeMadeSimple.com, and the coupons are no longer available.

Rebates are cash refunds are discounts given after the purchase occurs. The buyer sends a "proof of purchase" to the manufacturer, which then issues a cheque to the buyer. Nokia offers rebates to buyers of its cell phones through carriers such as Rogers and Telus. When the new phone is purchased, the buyer fills out a form and mails it off with the proof of purchase. The rebate appears in the form of a discount on the customer's invoice from the carrier.

Price packs take the form of single packages sold at a reduced price (such as two for the price of one), or two related products bundled together (such as a toothbrush and toothpaste). This type of sales promotion is also referred to as "gift with purchase."

Premiums are goods offered either free or at low price as an incentive to buy a product. If reusable, the package itself may serve as a premium—such as a decorative tin. Premiums are sometimes mailed to consumers who have sent in a proof of purchase, such as a box top. "Drink it. Get it" was the slogan for the Pepsi Stuff premium offer that one industry analyst called the "most successful promotion run in Canada in the last 40 years." Pepsi added value to a purchase of their product in a highly "youth-relevant" way by letting people redeem points of specially marked packages for "must-be-seen" merchandise from the Pepsi stuff catalogue. Eighty-one percent of soft-drink users were aware of the offer. The promotion increased Pepsi's market share by 7 percent. Although 53 percent of the gain came from people switching brands, the remainder came because heavy Pepsi drinkers consumed more product. Although the share gains are impressive, the program also improved consumer attitude and imagery measures of Pepsi.[14]

Advertising specialties are useful articles, such as pens, calendars, T-shirts, and coffee mugs, imprinted with an advertiser's name and given as gifts to customers. One study showed that 63 percent of consumers surveyed were either carrying or wearing an advertising specialty, and more than three-quarters of those who had an item could recall the advertiser's name or message before showing the item to the interviewer.[15]

Patronage rewards or *loyalty programs* take the form of "points" or merchandise awarded to regular, frequent, or loyal customers. Air Miles are just one example of the many rewards programs available to consumers today.

Point-of-purchase (POP) promotions include displays or demonstrations that take place at the point of purchase or sale. In Canada, in the weeks leading up to the Super Bowl, the Lays, Doritos, and Pepsi brands are typically promoted together (they're all owned by the same company) in Shoppers Drug Marts and Loblaws grocery stores. Life-sized sports figure cut-outs draw the shopper's attention to a display, where new products may be displayed, coupons offered, or sweepstakes entered.

Contests, sweepstakes, and *games* give consumers the chance to win something, such as cash, trips, or goods, by luck or through extra effort. A *contest* calls for consumers to

The Pepsi Stuff premium offer was called the "most successful promotion run in Canada in the last 40 years."

submit an entry—a jingle, a guess, a suggestion—to be judged by a panel that will select the best entries. A *sweepstakes* calls for consumers to submit their names for a drawing. A *game* presents consumers with something—bingo numbers, missing letters—every time they buy, which may or may not help them win a prize.

Trade Promotion Tools Manufacturers direct more sales promotion dollars toward retailers and wholesalers (68 percent) than to consumers (32 percent). Trade promotion can persuade resellers to carry a brand, give it shelf space, promote it in advertising, and push it to consumers. Shelf space is so scarce these days that manufacturers often have to offer price-offs allowances, volume rebates, buy-back guarantees, or free goods to retailers and wholesalers to get products on the shelf and, once there, to stay on it.

Many of the tools used for consumer promotions—contests, premiums, displays, can be also be used in trade promotions. Or the manufacturer might offer the retailer a straight *discount* off the list price on each product purchased during a stated period. This is also called a *price-off*, *off-invoice*, or *off-list* promotion. Manufacturers may also offer an *allowance* (usually so much off per item) in return for the retailer's agreement to feature the manufacturer's products in some way. An advertising allowance compensates retailers for advertising the product. A *display allowance* compensates them for using special displays.

As well, manufacturers may offer free goods, which are extra cases of merchandise, to resellers who buy a certain quantity or who feature a certain product.

Business Promotion Tools B2B companies spend millions of dollars each year on promotion to their customers. These business promotion tools are used to generate business leads, stimulate purchases, reward customers, and motivate salespeople. B2B marketers use many of the same tools used for consumer promotions. Here, we focus on two additional major business promotion tools: conventions and trade shows, and sales contests.

Many B2B marketers participate in *conventions and trade shows* to promote their products. Trade shows provide the marketer with the opportunity to find new sales leads, contact customers, introduce new products, meet new customers, sell more to present customers, and educate customers with publications and audiovisual materials. Trade shows also help companies reach many prospects not reached through their sales forces. About 90 percent of a trade show's visitors see a company's salespeople for the first time at the show. Business marketers may spend as much as 35 percent of their annual promotion budgets on trade shows.[16]

A *sales contest* is a contest for sales representatives or dealers to motivate them to increase their sales performance over a given period. Sales contests motivate and recognize good company performers, who may receive trips, cash prizes, or other gifts. Some companies, such as Pfizer, a drug manufacturer whose customers are pharmacies, doctors, and veterinarians, award points for performance, which the receiver can redeem for any of a variety of prizes. Sales contests work best when they are tied to measurable and achievable sales objectives (such as finding new accounts, reviving old accounts, or increasing account profitability).

Sales Promotion Decisions

The marketer must make several other decisions in designing the full sales promotion program. First, the marketer must decide on the *size of the incentive.* A certain minimum incentive is necessary if the promotion is to succeed; a larger incentive will produce more sales response. The marketer also must set *conditions for participation.* Incentives might be offered to everyone or only to select groups.

The marketer must then decide how to *promote and distribute the promotion* program itself. A 50-cents-off coupon could be given out in a package, at the store, by mail, or in an advertisement. Each distribution method involves a different level of reach and cost. Increasingly, marketers are blending several media into a total campaign concept. The *timing* and *length of the promotion* is also important. If the sales promotion period is too short, many prospects (who may not be buying during that time) will miss it. If the promotion runs too long, the deal will lose some of its "act now" force.

Evaluation is also very important. Yet many companies fail to evaluate their sales promotion programs, and others evaluate them only superficially. The most common evaluation method is to compare sales before, during, and after a promotion. Suppose a company has a 6 percent market share before the promotion, which jumps to 10 percent during the promotion, falls to 5 percent right after, and rises to 7 percent later on. The promotion seems to have attracted new buyers and more buying from current customers. After the promotion, sales fell as consumers used up their inventories. The long-run rise to 7 percent means that the company gained some new users. If the brand's share had returned to the old level, then the promotion would have changed only the *timing* of demand rather than the *total* demand.

Marketers must also educate themselves about the rules and regulations governing sales promotions. Contests and sweepstakes, for example, are regulated, and in Canada a marketer may not legally tie a "free" offer to a purchase. Though Tim Hortons offers everyone who buys a medium or large coffee the chance to "roll up the rim" and win a prize, legally they must provide a way for individuals to enter the contest *without* buying

IN-CLASS NOTES

Sales Promotion

- Coupons, contests, premiums, incentives
- Used to attract attention
- Provides incentive for trial or purchase
- Generates results now versus later
- Effectiveness easier to track than advertising

_____

_____

_____

_____

_____

_____

_____

Linking the Concepts

Think about a promotional campaign you've noticed recently. (It could be the same one you considered earlier in the chapter.)

- Was mass media advertising used in the promotion? Was a sales promotion part of the promotion? Do some research online, on television, in magazines, and in retail stores. What other forms of promotion or marketing can you find that are part of this same campaign?
- Do you think this campaign is a good example of an integrated marketing communications campaign? Explain why or why not.

a cup of coffee—and they do. If you visit the Tim Hortons website during the months of the promotion you'll find the sweepstakes rules and regulations, which explain how you can get the special cup without making a purchase.

PERSONAL SELLING

All businesses require salespeople—representatives whose job it is to demonstrate or explain the product to potential customers. But sales representatives are also found in many other kinds of organizations. For example, universities use recruiters to attract new students, churches use membership committees to attract new members, and hospitals and museums use fundraisers to contact donors and raise money. Even governments use sales forces. Canada Post, for instance, uses a sales force to sell direct-mail offerings, courier services, and other services to corporate customers.

Most salespeople are educated, trained professionals who work to build and maintain long-term customer relationships by listening to their customers, assessing customer needs, and organizing the company's efforts to solve customer problems. Consider Boeing, the aerospace giant competing in the rough-and-tumble worldwide commercial aircraft market. It takes more than a warm smile to sell expensive airplanes:

Selling high-tech aircraft at $70–$90 million or more a copy is complex and challenging. A single big sale can easily run into billions of dollars. Boeing salespeople head up an extensive team of company specialists—sales and service technicians, financial analysts, planners, engineers—all dedicated to finding ways to satisfy airline customer needs. The salespeople begin by becoming experts on the airlines, much like Wall Street analysts would. They find out where each airline wants to grow, when it wants to replace planes, and details of its financial situation. The team runs Boeing and competing planes through computer systems, simulating the airline's routes, cost per seat, and other factors to show that their planes are most efficient. Then the high-level negotiations begin. The selling process is nerve-rackingly slow—it can take two or three years from the first sales presentation to the day the sale is announced. Sometimes top executives from both the airline and Boeing are brought in to close the deal. After getting the order, salespeople then must stay in almost constant touch to keep track of the account's equipment needs and to make certain the customer stays satisfied. Success depends on building solid, long-term relationships with customers, based on performance and trust.[17]

Whereas most of the elements of marketing communications we have examined so far are one-way, impersonal forms of communication, personal selling involves two-way, personal communication between salespeople and individual customers—whether face to face, by telephone, through video or Web conferences, or by other means. Personal selling is typically used when the product being marketed is a complex one, for example a software system, mail processing equipment, or machinery for a car assembly plant. The job of the sales representative is more than just selling; it is building a relationship with the customer.

The role of personal selling varies from company to company. Some firms have no salespeople at all—for example, companies that sell only through mail-order catalogues or companies that sell through manufacturer's reps, sales agents, or brokers. In companies that sell business products and services, the company's sales representatives work directly with customers. In consumer product companies such as Procter & Gamble or Wilson Sporting Goods, the role of the sales representatives is to work with channel members such as retailers and wholesalers—not with consumers.

Organizing the Sales Force

A company can divide its sales responsibilities along any of several lines. In the **territorial sales force structure**, each salesperson is assigned to an exclusive geographic area and sells the company's full line of products or services to all customers in that territory. A company that sells only one product line to one industry, with customers in many locations, will typically choose this form of sales organization.

A company that adopts a **product sales force structure** organizes the sales representatives so that each salesperson specializes in selling only a portion of the company's products or lines. For example, Kodak uses different sales forces for its consumer film and camera products than for its industrial products such as film processing equipment.

Service companies often organize their sales representatives in a **customer sales force structure**, in which salespeople specialize in selling only to certain types of customers. Sprint Canada, for example, uses third-party telemarketers to sell to residential customers and its own trained sales representatives to sell telephone and Internet services to small businesses and larger businesses—two groups of customers that have very different needs.

A company may have an outside sales force (or *field sales force*), an inside sales force, or both. The members of the **outside sales force** work "in the field" and visit customers. The members of the **inside sales force** conduct business from their offices, usually via telephone and email, and rarely meet in person with customers. Inside salespeople may include technical support people, sales assistants, telemarketers, and customer service

Territorial sales force structure A sales force organization under which each salesperson is assigned to an exclusive geographic area and sells the company's full line of products or services to all customers in that territory.

Product sales force structure A sales force organization under which each salesperson specializes in selling only a portion of the company's products or lines.

Customer sales force structure A sales force organization under which salespeople specialize in selling only to certain types of customers.

Outside sales force Salespeople who work "in the field" and visit customers.

Inside sales force Salespeople who conduct business from their offices, usually via telephone and email, and rarely meet in person with customers.

people. The inside sales force frees outside salespeople to spend more time selling to major accounts and prospecting for new customers.

Many companies now use *team selling* to service large, complex customer accounts. Companies are finding that sales teams can unearth problems, solutions, and sales opportunities that no individual salesperson could. Such teams might include experts from any area or level of the selling firm: sales, marketing, technical and support services, R&D, engineering, operations, finance, and others.

Some companies, such as IBM, Xerox, and Procter & Gamble, have used teams for a long time. For example, Cutler-Hammer, which supplies circuit breakers, motor starters, and other electrical equipment to heavy industrial manufacturers such as Ford, employs "pods" of salespeople that focus on a specific geographical region, industry, or market. Each pod member contributes unique expertise and knowledge about a product or service that salespeople can leverage when selling to increasingly sophisticated buying teams.[18]

Many firms have adopted *sales force automation systems*, computerized sales force operations for more efficient order-entry transactions, improved customer service, and better salesperson decision-making support. Salespeople use laptops, handheld computing devices, and Web technologies, coupled with customer-contact software and customer relationship management (CRM) software, to profile customers and prospects, analyze and forecast sales, manage account relationships, schedule sales calls, make presentations, enter orders, check inventories and order status, prepare sales and expense reports, process correspondence, and carry out many other activities. Sales force automation not only lowers sales force costs and improves productivity, but also improves the quality of sales management decisions.

Finally, the Internet offers new ways and means for conducting sales operations. More and more companies are now using the Internet to support their personal selling efforts—not just for selling, but for everything from training salespeople to conducting sales meetings and servicing accounts (see Marketing at Work 12.3).

Marketing at Work 12.3

Welcome to the Web-Based Sales Force

There are few rules at Fisher Scientific International's sales training sessions. The chemical company's salespeople are allowed to show up for workshops in their pyjamas—because for the past year and a half, the company has been using the Internet to teach the majority of its salespeople in the privacy of their homes, cars, hotel rooms, or wherever else they bring their laptops. To get updates on pricing or refresh themselves on one of the company's highly technical products, all salespeople have to do is log on to the website and select from the menu. Welcome to the new world of the Web-based sales force.

Modern sales organizations have discovered they can save money and time by using a host of new Web-based applications and services to train reps, hold sales meetings, and even conduct live sales presentations. "Web-based technologies are becoming really hot in sales because they save salespeople's time," says technology consultant Tim Sloane.

Training is only one of the ways sales organizations are using the Internet. Many companies are using the Web to make sales presentations and service accounts. The sales representative can demonstrate a product online, in real time, highlighting and pointing out specific items—while the customers, who are also online, observe. The beauty of the whole process? It's so fast. "The use of [the Web] clearly helps shorten our sales cycle," says one sales manager.

Other companies are using Web-based sales presentations to find new prospects. Oracle Corporation conducts online, live product seminars for prospective clients. The seminars, which usually consist of a live lecture describing the product's applications followed by a question-and-answer session, average about 125 prospective clients apiece. Once a seminar is completed, prospects are directed to

(continued)

another part of Oracle's site, from which they can order products. "It costs our clients nothing but time," says Oracle's manager of Internet marketing programs, "and we're reaching a much wider audience than we would if we were doing in-person seminars."

Even sales meetings can be held online. Consider Cisco Systems, which provides networking solutions for the Internet. Sales meetings used to take an enormous bite out of Cisco's travel budget. Now the company saves about $1 million per month by conducting many of those sessions on the Web. "Our salespeople are actually meeting more online than they ever were face to face," says Mike Mitchell, Cisco's distance learning manager. "That's very empowering for the sales force, because they're able to make suggestions at every step of the way about where we're going with our sales and marketing strategies."

The Internet provides some wonderful advantages for salespeople, but "When push comes to shove, if you've

got an account worth closing, you're still going to get on that plane and see the client in person," says sales consultant Sloane. "Your client is going to want to look you in the eye before buying anything from you, and that's still one thing you just can't do online."

Sources: Adapted from Melinda Ligos, "Point, Click, and Sell," *Sales and Marketing Management,* May 1999, pp. 51–55. Also see Chad Kaydo, "You've Got Sales," *Sales and Marketing Management,* October 1999, pp. 29–39; Ginger Conlon, "Ride the Wave," *Sales & Marketing Management,* December 2000, pp. 67–74; and Tom Reilly, "Technology and the Salesperson," *Industrial Distribution,* January 2001, p. 88.

Sales organizations use the Internet to train sales representatives, hold sales meetings, and conduct customer presentations.

The Personal Selling Process

The **personal selling process** consists of several steps that the salesperson follows when selling, including prospecting and qualifying, preapproach, approach, presentation and demonstration, handling objections, closing, and follow-up (see Figure 12.3). These steps focus on the goal of getting new customers and obtaining orders from them. However, most salespeople spend much of their time maintaining existing accounts and building long-term *customer relationships.*

Personal selling process Several steps that the salesperson follows when selling, including prospecting and qualifying, preapproach, approach, presentation and demonstration, handling objections, closing, and follow-up.

Figure 12.3   Steps in the Personal Selling Process

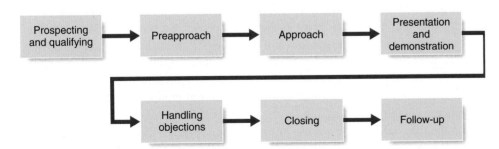

The first step in the selling process is *prospecting*—identifying qualified potential customers. Approaching the right potential customers is crucial to selling success. The salesperson must often approach many prospects to get just a few sales. Although the company supplies some leads, salespeople need skill in finding their own. They can ask current customers for referrals. They can cultivate referral sources, such as suppliers, dealers, noncompeting salespeople, and bankers. They can search for prospects in directories or on the Web. Or they can drop in or telephone a company, unannounced (a practice known as "cold calling").

The next step is to *qualify* those leads—that is, to identify the good ones and screen out the poor ones. Prospects can be qualified by looking at their financial ability, volume of business, special needs, location, and possibilities for growth.

Before calling on a prospect, the salesperson should learn as much as possible about the organization (what it needs, who is involved in the buying) and its buyers (their characteristics and buying styles). This step is known as the *preapproach*. The salesperson can consult standard industry and online sources, acquaintances, and others to learn about the company.

During the *approach* step, the salesperson should know how to meet and greet the buyer and get the relationship off to a good start. The opening lines should be positive to build goodwill from the beginning of the relationship. This opening might be followed by some key questions to learn more about the customer's needs or by showing a display or sample to attract the buyer's attention and curiosity. As in all stages of the selling process, listening to the customer is crucial.

The *needs analysis* step is the root of needs-based selling. A needs analysis is a diagnosis of a buyer's needs accomplished through skillful questioning, listening, and observing. This precedes the recommendation or a demonstration of a seller's product or service. Questioning in this case focuses on customer benefits or results rather than on features of the product or service. This *need-satisfaction approach* calls for good listening and problem-solving skills. "I think of myself more as a . . . well, psychologist," notes one experienced salesperson. "I listen to customers. I listen to their wishes and needs and problems, and I try to figure out a solution. If you're not a good listener, you're not going to get the order." Another salesperson suggests, "It's no longer enough to have a good relationship with a client. You have to understand their problems. You have to feel their pain."[19]

During the *presentation* step of the selling process, the salesperson tells the product "story" to the buyer, presenting customer benefits and showing how the product meets the customers' needs that were identified in the needs analysis process. The problem-solver salesperson fits better with today's marketing concept than does a hard-sell salesperson or the glad-handing extrovert. Buyers today want solutions, not smiles; results, not razzle-dazzle. They want salespeople who listen to their concerns, understand their needs, and respond with the right products and services.

Customers usually have objections during the presentation or when asked to place an order. The problem can be either logical or psychological, and objections are often unspoken. In *handling objections*, the salesperson should use a positive approach, seek out hidden objections, ask the buyer to clarify any objections, take objections as opportunities to provide more information, and turn the objections into reasons for buying. Every salesperson needs training in the skills of handling objections.

After handling the prospect's objections, the salesperson now tries to close the sale. Some salespeople do not get around to *closing* or do not handle it well. They may lack confidence, feel guilty about asking for the order, or fail to recognize the right moment to close the sale. Salespeople should know how to recognize closing signals from the buyer, including physical actions, comments, and questions. Salespeople can use one of several closing techniques. They can ask for the order, review points of agreement, offer to help write up the order, ask whether the buyer wants this model or that one, or note that the buyer will lose out if the order is not placed now.

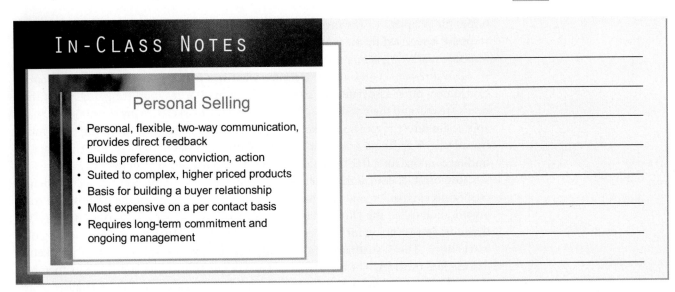

The last step in the selling process—*follow-up*—is necessary if the salesperson wants to ensure customer satisfaction and repeat business. Right after closing, the salesperson should complete any details on delivery time, purchase terms, and other matters. The salesperson should then schedule a follow-up call when the initial order is received to make sure there is proper installation, instruction, and servicing. This visit would reveal any problems, assure the buyer of the salesperson's interest, and reduce any buyer concerns that might have arisen since the sale.

Relationship Marketing

The principles of personal selling just described are *transaction oriented*—their aim is to help salespeople close a specific sale with a customer. But in many cases the company is not seeking simply a sale: It has targeted a major customer that it would like to win and keep. The company would like to show that it has the capabilities to serve the customer over the long haul in a mutually profitable *relationship*. **Relationship marketing** is the process of creating, maintaining, and enhancing strong, value-laden relationships with customers and other stakeholders. This is accomplished by creating superior customer value and satisfaction.

Today's large customers favour suppliers who can sell and deliver a coordinated set of products and services to many locations and who can work closely with customer teams to improve products and processes. For these customers, the first sale is only the beginning of the relationship. Wise marketers recognize that winning and keeping accounts requires more than making good products and directing the sales force to close lots of sales; it requires a carefully coordinated whole-company effort to create value-laden, satisfying relationships with important customers.

Relationship marketing The process of creating, maintaining, and enhancing strong, value-laden relationships with customers and other stakeholders.

DIRECT RESPONSE MARKETING

Direct response marketing combines the use of mass media to communicate with a large audience with the personal touch of communicating one-to-one with the customer. Although a mass media communications vehicle—television, print, the telephone, email, or the postal service—is used to deliver the message, at the same time the marketer also delivers a *personalized* message to the target audience. These messages typically include a strong *call to action*; in other words, it is clear what action the marketer hopes the recipient of the message will take. If and when the recipient responds, that response is received by the marketer and can be measured and counted. In short, direct response marketing is *interactive*.

Direct response is the newer term for what was previously called *direct marketing*. Consumers often associate the latter with junk mail or telemarketing. But when their needs are met and their preferences catered to by the marketer, many consumers actually appreciate direct response marketing—for example, when buying a computer online from Dell, or getting a great deal on The Shopping Channel's daily Show Stopper, or finding coupons for a free breakfast sandwich from McDonald's in their mailbox.

Responsible, ethical marketers that use direct response marketing, such as banks, credit card companies, and telephone companies, are members of the professional trade organization called the Direct Marketing Association. The DMA describes itself as "the largest trade association for businesses interested in direct, database, and interactive global marketing." The Canadian arm of this organization is the Canadian Marketing Association, or CMA. The approximately 800 organizations that constitute its membership include major financial institutions, insurance companies, publishers, retailers, charitable organizations, agencies, and e-businesses, and feature such companies as Reader's Digest, The Shopping Channel, The Bank of Montreal, Bell Canada, and Microsoft Canada. Direct response marketing is big business in Canada, with CMA member companies accounting for 480 000 jobs and generating more than $50 billion in annual sales.[20]

Direct Response and Database Marketing

Database A collection of data about existing or prospective customers, organized into records.

Direct response marketing requires a *database*. A **database** is a collection of data about existing or prospective customers, organized into records. Each record contains such information as the customer's name, address, telephone number, and email address. For B2B customers the record contains the company name and the name and title of the contact person; and for existing customers the record shows products they have purchased, the price paid, and date of purchase. Direct response marketers sort and organize these databases before each DR campaign in order to create a target audience for the communications.

For example, CIBC, which has an existing partnership with Visa, might wish to target basic Visa cardholders with a direct mail offer to upgrade to the CIBC Aerogold Visa. CIBC and Visa would work together to create a mailing list consisting of existing Visa cardholders who do not have an Aerogold Visa and who are also CIBC clients in good standing.

Direct response marketing is used not only to solicit new customers but to maintain strong relationships with existing customers. For example, once an individual has responded to the offer to apply for a CIBC Aerogold Visa and received the card, he or she becomes a member of the Air Canada Aeroplan loyalty program. This program allows members to collect points that can be exchanged for airplane tickets, hotel stays, car rentals, and other travel-related services. Aeroplan members receive newsletters in the mail every three months that contain special members-only offers such as discounts on vacation packages and double points on certain purchases. These newsletters are a form of direct response marketing managed by Aeroplan. Aeroplan members can also register on the Air Canada website to receive special offers via email, such as the "Air Canada Websaver" announcement, a weekly email listing seat sales for the upcoming weekend.

A database can also contain information about customers' preferences. For example, Ritz-Carlton's database holds more than 500 000 individual customer preferences. Pizza Hut's database lets it track the purchases of more than 50 million customers. And Wal-Mart's database contains more than 100 terabytes of data—that's 100 trillion bytes, equivalent to 16 000 bytes for every one of the world's 6 billion people.[21]

Armed with the information in their databases, these companies can identify small groups of customers to receive fine-tuned marketing offers and communications. Kraft Foods has amassed a list of more than 30 million users of its products who have responded to coupons or other Kraft promotions. Based on their interests, the company sends these customers tips on issues such as nutrition and exercise, as well as recipes and coupons for specific Kraft brands. FedEx uses its sophisticated database to create 100 highly targeted, customized direct-mail and telemarketing campaigns each year to its nearly 5 million customers shipping to 212 countries. By analyzing customers carefully and reaching the right customers at the right time with the right promotions, FedEx achieves response rates of 20 to 25 percent and earns an 8-to-1 return on its direct-marketing dollars.[22]

Databases allow marketers to design direct response campaigns to deepen customer loyalty. For example, customers of Amazon.com have the option of giving their birthday as part of their registration information. The data is optional; the customer need not give it, but those who do receive a pleasant surprise via email three weeks before their birthday: an Amazon.com coupon.

Forms of Direct Response Marketing **Telemarketing**, or using the telephone to sell directly to consumers or businesses, can be very effective, especially when the calls focus on existing customers who have a relationship with the company. Most of us have received a friendly "customer service call" from our bank or telephone company, ostensibly just to check whether we're happy with their service but subtly trying to sell us additional services. Telemarketing comprises *inbound* telemarketing and *outbound* telemarketing. Inbound telemarketers answer calls from customers, usually made to a toll-free number. Outbound telemarketing may be used by companies to solicit new customers or to sell new products to existing customers. For example, Bell Canada's local service customers who use third-party long-distance providers receive regular calls from Bell with offers to switch to Bell's own long distance program.

Direct mail involves sending an offer, announcement, reminder, or other item to an individual or a company at a particular address. Direct mail is well suited to one-to-one

Telemarketing Using the telephone to sell directly to consumers or businesses.

Direct mail Sending an offer, announcement, reminder, or other item to an individual or a company at a particular address.

Figure 12.4   Forms of Direct Response Marketing

communication. It permits high target-market selectivity, can be personalized, is flexible, and allows easy measurement of results. Although the cost per thousand people reached is higher than with mass media such as television or magazines, the people who are reached are much better prospects. Direct mail has proven successful in promoting all kinds of products, from books, magazine subscriptions, and insurance to gift items, clothing, gourmet foods, and industrial products. Direct mail is also used heavily by charities to raise billions of dollars each year.

Advances in technology, along with the move toward personalized, one-to-one marketing, have resulted in exciting changes in **catalogue marketing**—direct marketing through print, video, or electronic catalogues that are mailed to select customers, made available in stores, or presented online. *Catalog Age* magazine used to define a *catalogue* as "a printed, bound piece of at least eight pages, selling multiple products, and offering a direct ordering mechanism." Today, this definition is out of date. Most companies that formerly offered only print catalogues to their customers have either switched to online catalogues, available through their websites, or have added online offers to their print ones. Victoria's Secret, Tilley, Eddie Bauer, Ikea, The Shopping Channel, and Canadian Tire all offer both print and online catalogues. Specialty department stores, such as Holt Renfrew, Ashley China, and Neiman Marcus, also use catalogues to cultivate upper-middle-class markets for high-priced, often exotic merchandise. And Walt Disney Company mails out more than 6 million catalogues each year featuring videos, stuffed animals, and other Disney items.

Many forms of online communications can be used by direct response marketers. Web-based versions of catalogues allow customers to purchase merchandise directly from the seller; however, they present new challenges to marketers. "Attracting new customers is much more difficult to do with a Web catalogue," says an industry consultant. "You have to use advertising, linkage, and other means to drive traffic to it." Kevin Bartus, president of Blue*Spark, a Toronto-based Web development firm, says, "Retailers are learning an online business is not, in most cases, big enough to support a complete business offering. Retailers are turning to a tri-channel: bricks and mortar, catalogue, and Web."[23] Take the case of La Senza, the Montreal-based lingerie retailer. It first launched a website featuring a separate line of merchandise to avoid cannibalizing store sales, but finally had to relaunch the site as an arm of its existing business. Today, its traditional catalogue, site, and retail stores are so well integrated that customers can return items purchased on the La Senza site to their local store.

Other forms of direct marketing online include direct-to-consumer sales through e-commerce websites. Dell Canada, for example, sells computers to consumers and businesses *only* via the telephone and through its website. Cake Beauty, on the other hand, sells its products directly to consumers through its site, but also makes its product available through retailers.

Direct response marketers also use email to send regular messages to customers who have registered on their website and actively requested this form of communications. Responsible direct marketers send only such permission-based email; they never purchase lists or send unsolicited messages. Air Canada, for example, sends information about seat sales to its customers via email.

Kraft Canada sends a monthly email titled "What's Cooking—from Kraft Kitchens" containing recipes, coupons, and other special product-related offers to customers who have registered on their website. These reputable marketers use sophisticated email marketing management software programs to personalize, deliver, track responses, and manage subscriptions for their email campaigns.

Direct-response television involves television spots that persuasively describe a product and give customers a toll-free number for ordering. There are two forms of direct response television. The first is the *infomercial*, a form of paid programming, often as long as 30 minutes, that persuasively describes and demonstrates a product and

Catalogue marketing Direct marketing through print, video, or electronic catalogues that are mailed to select customers, made available in stores, or presented online.

Direct-response television Television spots that persuasively describe a product and give customers a toll-free number for ordering.

gives customers a toll-free number for ordering. Infomercials are typically associated with somewhat questionable pitches for juicers and other kitchen gadgets, get-rich-quick schemes, and nifty ways to stay in shape without working very hard at it. In the last few years, however, major advertisers have begun to include DR-TV in their marketing plans. The Ford Motor Company of Canada took a bold new step in the way it markets cars and trucks by airing Canada's first long-format "reality infomercial" for its new F-150 pickup, a highly anticipated new product in the automotive segment and Ford's number-one-selling vehicle in Canada. The infomercial took the form of a Fear Factor–like reality show but featured the truck, rather than the people, being challenged to perform such feats as driving up the side of a gravel pit.[24]

The other form of direct response television is the *home shopping channel*, where an entire television channel is dedicated to selling goods and services, broadcasting 24 hours a day. So far, Canada has only one such form of direct response television, The Shopping Channel.

Some companies place information and ordering machines, called *kiosks*, in stores, airports, and other locations. The Liquor Control Board of Ontario installed interactive kiosks to run advertisements for featured products and to enhance customer service, and IKEA allows UNICEF to set up fundraising kiosks in its stores.[25]

Public Policy and Ethical Issues in Direct Response Marketing

Direct marketers and their customers usually enjoy mutually rewarding relationships. Occasionally, however, a darker side emerges. The aggressive and sometimes shady tactics of a few direct marketers can bother or harm consumers, giving the entire industry a bad reputation. Abuses range from simple excesses that irritate consumers to instances of unfair practices or even outright deception and fraud. The direct marketing industry has also faced growing concerns about invasion of privacy issues.

Sometimes direct mail copy is designed to mislead buyers. Even well-known direct marketers have been accused of deceiving consumers. Sweepstakes promoter Publishers Clearing House, for example, paid $52 million to settle accusations that its high-pressure mailings confused or misled consumers, especially the elderly, into believing that they had won prizes or would win if they bought the company's magazines.[26]

Other direct marketers pretend to be conducting research surveys when they are actually asking leading questions to screen or persuade consumers. Fraudulent schemes, such as investment scams or phony collections for charity, have also multiplied in recent years. Crooked direct marketers can be hard to catch: Customers often respond quickly, do not interact personally with the seller, and usually expect to wait for delivery. By the time buyers realize that they have been bilked, the thieves are usually somewhere else plotting new schemes.

Invasion of privacy is perhaps the toughest public policy issue now confronting the direct marketing industry. Every time consumers enter a sweepstakes, apply for a credit card, take out a magazine subscription, or order products by mail, telephone, or the Internet, their names are entered into some company's database. Direct marketers then use these databases to target their selling efforts. Consumers often benefit from such marketing, since they receive more offers that are closely matched to their interests. However, many critics worry that marketers may know too much about consumers' lives, and that they may use this knowledge to take unfair advantage of consumers. At some point, they claim, the extensive use of databases intrudes on consumer privacy.

For example, they ask, should Bell or Telus or SaskTel be allowed to sell marketers the names of customers who frequently call the 800 numbers of catalogue companies? Should a company such as American Express be allowed to make data on cardholders available to merchants who accept AmEx cards? Is it right for credit bureaus to compile

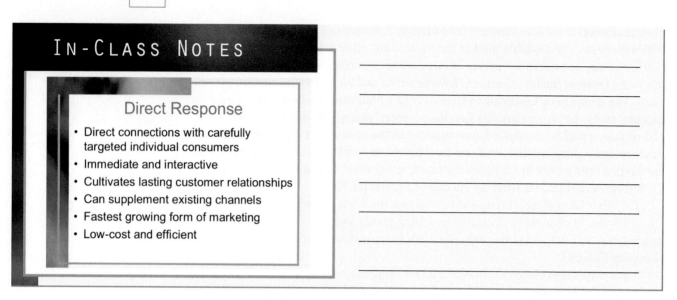

IN-CLASS NOTES

Direct Response

- Direct connections with carefully targeted individual consumers
- Immediate and interactive
- Cultivates lasting customer relationships
- Can supplement existing channels
- Fastest growing form of marketing
- Low-cost and efficient

and sell lists of people who have recently applied for credit cards—people who are considered prime direct-marketing targets because of their spending behaviour? Is it right for provinces to sell the names and addresses of driver's licence holders?

In one survey of consumers, 79 percent said they were concerned about threats to their personal privacy. In their drives to build databases, companies sometimes do get carried away. For example, when it was first introduced, Intel's Pentium III chip contained an embedded serial number that allowed the company to trace users' equipment. When privacy advocates screamed, Intel disabled the feature. Similarly, Microsoft caused substantial privacy concerns when it introduced its Windows 95 software. It used a "Registration Wizard" that allowed users to register their new software online. However, when users went online to register, without their knowledge, Microsoft "read" the configurations of their PCs to learn about the major software products running on each customer's system. When users learned of this invasion, they protested loudly and Microsoft abandoned the practice. Such actions have spawned a quiet but determined "privacy revolt" among consumers and public policymakers.[27]

Privacy is a hot issue in many countries in the world right now. Canadians are protected by two federal privacy laws, the *Privacy Act* and the *Personal Information Protection and Electronic Documents Act*. The *Privacy Act* took effect on July 1, 1983. This Act imposes obligations on some 150 federal government departments and agencies to respect the privacy rights of Canadians by placing limits on the collection, use, and disclosure of personal information. It also gives Canadians the right to access and correct personal information about them held by these federal government organizations.

On January 1, 2001, the *Personal Information Protection and Electronic Documents Act* (formerly Bill C6) came into effect. The Act governs all federally regulated industries and businesses that operate interprovincially, and, since 2004, within provinces. It uses several guiding principles to protect consumers and control how firms gather and use their personal information (see Chapter 13 for a list of these principles).[28] And, since the enactment of this legislation, all major Canadian organizations have prepared privacy policies and published them on their websites where customers and prospective customers can easily access them.[29]

Another hot-button issue in recent years is the proposed "do not call" registry in Canada and the United States, which would allow consumers to register their name, address, and telephone number along with a request that they not receive any direct response marketing communications via mail or the telephone. In fact, the Direct Marketing Association and the Canadian Marketing Association have always offered do-not-call registration to consumers—but only members of these organizations honour the request.[30]

The DMA and the CMA are also concerned with issues of ethics in direct response marketing. Members of the CMA must agree to abide by the association's Code of Ethics and Standards of Practice[31] which states that "All persons involved in the information-based marketing industry in Canada shall be cognizant of and conduct themselves according to the laws of Canada." The Code outlines, in detail, the rules that ethical direct response marketers must follow. One of the first rules is this: "Offers must be clear and truthful and shall not misrepresent a product, service, solicitation or program and shall not mislead by statement, or technique of demonstration or comparison."

Public Relations

Public relations is a very important form of marketing communications, but it differs from advertising, sales promotion, personal selling, and direct marketing in that its purpose is not to communicate to the market about the company's products but rather to communicate to the company's *publics* about the company.

Recall from Chapter 4 that publics are any group of people, large or small, who have an interest in what the company does. There are internal publics, such as employees, vendors and other business partners, and customers; and external publics, such as shareholders, the media, government departments or agencies, the local community, and the general public. Whereas employees and shareholders are stakeholders in the company and have a vested interest in what it does, the general public—people who have no vested interest in the company and may never have purchased one of its products—may still be interested in news about it. For example, during the lengthy legal troubles of Martha Stewart, news about Martha Stewart Living Omnimedia Inc. regularly appeared in national newspapers and business magazines. Many of the people reading those articles had no vested interest in the company or its products, and yet formed an opinion about the company.

Public relations functions may be handled within the company—large, publicly traded firms typically have a director of corporate communications—or by agencies. Edelman is one of the largest public relations firms in the world, and handles PR functions for clients such as Microsoft, Johnson & Johnson, Samsung, and Kraft. Currently, Edelman is helping the Motion Picture Association and the Recording Academy shape public awareness campaigns against digital piracy.[32] Smaller companies, such as Cake Beauty, typically handle their own public relations and press relations.

Public relations is used to promote products, people, places, ideas, activities, organizations, and even nations. Trade associations have used public relations to rebuild interest in declining commodities such as eggs, apples, milk, and potatoes. Nations have used public relations to attract more tourists, foreign investment, and international support.

Public relations can have a strong impact on public awareness at a much lower cost than advertising can. The company does not pay for the space or time in the media. Rather, it pays a staff to develop and circulate information and to manage events. If the company develops an interesting story, it could be picked up by several different media, having the same or even greater effect as advertising that would cost millions of dollars. To the reading and viewing public, an article in a reputable newspaper or a segment on the CTV news has much more credibility than any advertisement could ever have. Articles about Cake Beauty products have appeared in *Canadian Living*, *Elle*, *InStyle*, *Chatelaine*, *Teen People*, *People*, *Us*, *Flare*, and *Girl's Life* magazines. *Cosmopolitan* magazine wrote, "Cake has to be the most delicious smelling range out there right now."

Public relations results can sometimes be spectacular. Something as simple as the launch of a new book can be turned into a major international event, all on a very small budget, as demonstrated by the release of the most recent Harry Potter book:

J.K. Rowling read from her new book, *Harry Potter and the Half-Blood Prince*, at Edinburgh Castle on the stroke of midnight. Before midnight on Friday evening, J.K. Rowling arrived at the Esplanade outside Edinburgh Castle to be greeted by 2,000 Edinburgh schoolchildren and their families. Street performers, torch bearers, jugglers and entertainers completed the carnival atmosphere outside the dramatic backdrop of Edinburgh Castle's medieval facade. Onto the castle was projected a giant image of the *Harry Potter and the Half-Blood Prince* book jacket. . . .

. . . [J.K. Rowling's] audience was 70 children, including four Canadians, who travelled to the Edinburgh Castle Esplanade by horse-drawn carriages and had exclusive access inside Edinburgh Castle. These aspiring cub reporters (aged 8–16) won media competitions to attend the Harry Potter Children's Press Conference Weekend on behalf of selected English-language newspapers and broadcasters from around the world. [33]

Major Functions of Public Relations

The job of public relations management includes the following functions:[34]

☐ *Press relations:* Preparing written press releases and organizing press conferences in an attempt to encourage the news media to cover the company's story. Organizations can make their press releases available to the news media through a national service called Canada Newswire. It is important to keep in mind that PR managers cannot offer to pay or otherwise directly influence the press, but can only present their stories to them in the best possible light and answer any questions the press might have.

☐ *Product publicity:* Publicizing new products, perhaps by organizing public demonstrations or by sending samples to reviewers of that product category at appropriate magazines.

American Standard issued a press release on January 18, 2005, with the headline "Survey Says: Michigan Town Goes Plunger-Free with In-Home Toilet Consumer Satisfaction Test." The press release went on to describe the results of a clever public relations initiative in which the company installed, free of charge, its new Champion brand toilet in the homes of nearly every resident of tiny Champion, Michigan (population 294). After "test driving" the new toilets

Public relations results can sometimes be spectacular, as demonstrated at the launch of the sixth installment of the Harry Potter series.

for a month, the residents reported their opinions of the new product to American Standard, and the company chose the best of these quotes to include in its press release: "It flushes everything the first time," says Jackie Adair, a Champion resident and mother of three young boys. "We haven't had to pull the plunger out of the closet since getting our Champion."[35]

☐ *Public affairs:* Building and maintaining national or local community relations. Businesses whose activities may affect residents living in the vicinity typically retain public relations firms to manage public affairs communications. Such businesses include pulp and paper producers, steel companies, nuclear power plants, and waste disposal facilities. The Canadian Nuclear Association, for example, manages a website for the purpose of communicating information about nuclear energy. In the public affairs section of its site, visitors can learn about the deregulation of electricity and how climate changes affect our need for nuclear power.[36]

☐ *Lobbying:* Building and maintaining relations with legislators and government officials to influence legislation and regulation.

☐ *Investor relations:* Maintaining relationships with shareholders and others in the financial community. All publicly traded firms have an investor relations department, and most have a section on their corporate websites with that same heading.

☐ *Development:* Public relations activities directed at donors or members of nonprofit organizations for the purpose of gaining financial or volunteer support. For nonprofit organizations, having a useful, functional website that reaches a national audience is an important part of their public relations activities. On the Canadian Cancer Society's site, for example, members of the public can learn how to become a volunteer, find out about fundraising and other public activities, and even make a donation online.[37]

☐ *Crisis management:* When a company finds itself in the media spotlight because of a problem with its products, its employees, or its organization, it is the job of public relations to react to the situation and manage communications demanded by the publics.

> Whistler Mountain Resort Association faced a crisis when its Quicksilver chairlift failed, detaching several chairs from the cable, injuring several skiers and killing one. Whistler marketing director David Perry's first priority was to manage information flow and keep panic under control. He quickly informed parents waiting at the bottom of the hill that their kids were safe. Perry also opened up a media centre from which reporters could work. He recruited senior managers to call all the skiers who had been on the lift that day and arranged for counselling for employees affected by the stress of the accident. Whistler ran ads thanking the community for its support during the crisis and conducted technical investigations to prevent such a failure from occurring in the future. It also adjusted its PR policies based on this experience to ensure that they were even more effective.[38]

Though most modern marketing organizations understand and respect the role of public relations, marketing managers and public relations practitioners do not always speak the same language. Many public relations practitioners see their job as simply communicating. In contrast, marketing managers tend to be much more interested in how advertising and public relations affect sales and profits. This situation is changing, however. Many companies now want their public relations departments to manage all their activities with a view toward marketing the company and improving the bottom line. They know that good public relations can be a powerful brand-building tool.

Two well-known marketing consultants even went so far as to conclude that advertising doesn't build brands, PR does. In their book *The Fall of Advertising and the Rise of PR*, the consultants proclaim that the era of advertising is over, and that public relations is quietly becoming the most powerful marketing communications tool:[39]

> The birth of a brand is usually accomplished with [public relations], not advertising. Our general rule is [PR] first, advertising second. [Public relations] is the nail, advertising the hammer. [PR] creates the credentials that provide the credibility for advertising. . . . Anita Roddick built the Body Shop into a major brand with no advertising at all. Instead, she traveled the world on a relentless quest for publicity. . . . Until recently Starbucks Coffee Co. didn't spend a hill of beans on advertising, either. In 10 years, the company spent less than $10 million on advertising, a trivial amount for a brand that delivers annual sales of $1.3 billion. Wal-Mart Stores became the world's largest retailer . . . with very little advertising. . . . On the Internet, Amazon.com became a powerhouse brand with virtually no advertising.[40]

Although the book created much controversy, and most advertisers wouldn't agree about the "fall of advertising" part of the title, the point is a good one. Advertising and public relations should work hand in hand to build and maintain brands.

The Tools of Public Relations

Since press relations is one of the major tasks of public relations, the PR professional must communicate regularly with the press. When noteworthy events occur at the company—for example, the hiring of a new CEO, the newest release of a popular product, or the reporting of financial results—the PR department attempts to get favourable press in reputable newspapers and trade magazines. The PR professional presents this information to journalists in the form of *press releases*. A press release contains all the details of the event or happening, including the names of all the people involved, and, frequently, quotes from senior managers or independent commentators or analysts. In the days before the Internet, press releases were put "on the wire" and sent to newspapers, magazines, and television stations around the country. Today, companies pay online service providers such as Canada Newswire, Business Wire, and PR Newswire to distribute their press releases via the Web and email. Of course, every company today has a website, and most companies publish their press releases there as well. Cake Beauty, for example, posted press releases announcing "Cake Beauty at Sundance Film Festival 2005" and "Cake Beauty Is 'Going' to the 77th Annual Academy Awards."

When a company does something particularly newsworthy a *press conference* may be organized, in which members of the press are invited to meet and question a company spokesperson.

Speeches can also create product and company publicity. Company executives or spokespersons may give talks at trade association meetings, sales meetings, conventions, and trade shows. Some company spokespeople, such a Bill Gates, the chairman of Microsoft, and Jeff Bezos, the founder of Amazon.com, have become highly sought after as public speakers, and do wonders for the company as public relations ambassadors.

Special events such as grand openings, sports challenges, charitable events, and product launches are typically managed by an organization's public relations team. The annual CIBC Run for the Cure, for example, is a joint effort organized by the public relations professionals at CIBC and the Canadian Breast Cancer Foundation.

Corporate communications, such as annual reports, financial statements, and shareholder communications, are also handled by public relations professionals, usually working inside the company.

Beyond simply communicating news about the company to the press, organizations today use their websites to communicate directly to the general public. Consider all the organizations and companies all over the world that posted notices and helpful links on their home pages in the wake of the December 2004 tsunami in Southeast Asia that claimed more than 300 000 lives. Many companies placed small, eye-catching graphics reading "Tsunami Relief" on their home pages and encouraged employees and cus-

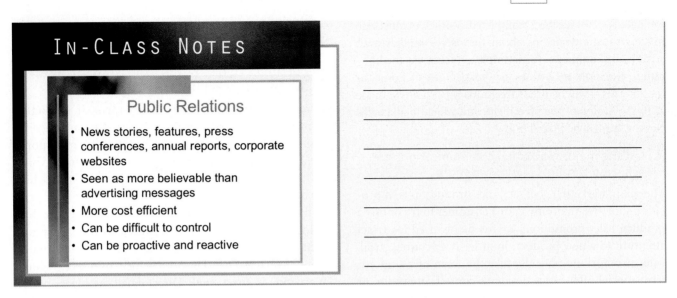

IN-CLASS NOTES

Public Relations

- News stories, features, press conferences, annual reports, corporate websites
- Seen as more believable than advertising messages
- More cost efficient
- Can be difficult to control
- Can be proactive and reactive

tomers to donate. Notes one analyst, "Today, public relations is reshaping the Internet and the Internet, in turn, is redefining the practice of public relations." Says another, "People look to the Net for information, not salesmanship, and that's the real opportunity for public relations."[41]

LOOKING BACK

In this chapter, you've been introduced to the concept of integrated marketing communications (IMC), learned about the five major elements of marketing communications, and read examples of how many different companies put those elements to work in an integrated campaign.

Modern marketing calls for more than just developing a good product, pricing it, and making it available to the market. Marketers, whether they market a product to consumers or a service to businesses or an idea to the general public, must communicate effectively with their existing customers, prospective customers, employees, suppliers, and other publics.

REVIEWING THE CONCEPTS

1. Explain why it is important for organizations to integrate their marketing communications.

Recent shifts toward targeted or one-to-one marketing, coupled with advances in information technology, have had a dramatic impact on marketing communications. As marketing communicators adopt richer but more frag-

mented media and promotion mixes to reach their diverse markets, they risk creating a communications hodgepodge for consumers. To prevent this, more companies are adopting the concept of *integrated marketing communications (IMC)*. Guided by an overall IMC strategy, the company works out the roles that the various promotional tools will play and the extent to which each will be used. It carefully coordinates the promotional activities and the timing of major campaigns. To oversee and guide its integrated marketing strategy, the company appoints a marketing communications director who has overall responsibility for the company's communications efforts.

2. Describe and discuss the major decisions involved in developing an advertising program.

Advertising is the use of paid media by a marketer to inform, persuade, or remind the market about its products or organization. In developing an advertising campaign the marketer must work within the marketing communications budget and make decisions about the objective of the advertising program, the message, message strategy, message execution, as well as how the campaign will be evaluated after it has been completed. Marketers must also make strategic decisions about the use of media in an advertising campaign, for example, which mass media—radio, television, magazines, newspaper, out-of-home, or the Internet—will be used? Decisions must then be made as to the timing of the placement, and which media vehicles the ads will be placed in.

3. List the major marketing communications goals achieved through sales promotions.

The main marketing goal of a sales promotion is to provide a short-term incentive for a customer to try or buy a product. Sales promotions are frequently used to attract attention to a new product, in order to encourage trial. Sales promotions typically take the form of a limited-term special offer, price discount, contest, premium, or other bonus that encourages the customer to act now rather than wait until later—because if they wait, it might be too late. Sales promotions may be aimed at consumers (consumer promotions) or at channel members (trade promotions) or at sales representatives (sales force promotions), but all three types of sales promotion have the same goal, that is, to stimulate sales in the short term. Loyalty programs, a form of sales promotion, have a longer-term goal as well as the short-term goal. Though a loyalty program may offer a special bonus to encourage the customer to sign up, the long-term goal is to cultivate a lasting relationship with the customer.

4. List and describe the steps in the personal selling process.

The art of selling involves a seven-step process. The first step is prospecting, in which potential new customers are identified and qualified. Next, the sales representative investigates the potential customer. This is called the preapproach. The best prospects are then approached directly in a sales call, either in person or on the telephone. If the customer is interested, the sales representative talks at length with the customer to understand their needs for the product. This is called the needs analysis. Next, a presentation or demonstration is prepared, to show the customer how the product serves their needs. If the customer has any objections, the sales representative must deal with them. Perhaps the most difficult part of the sales process is the closing. This is when the sales representative must ask for the business and sign the deal. But that's not the final step in the process. Even after the

sale is closed, a good sales representative follows up and builds a long-term relationship with the customer.

5. Identify and discuss the major forms of direct response marketing.

Direct response marketing is any form of marketing communication that asks the receiver of the message for a specific response. The main forms of direct response marketing are *telemarketing*, which includes both inbound and outbound sales calls; *direct mail*, in which an offer is sent via postal mail; *catalogues*, both in print and online; *direct response television*, or DR-TV, such as infomercials and The Shopping Channel; *kiosks*; and *direct-to-customer retail* (whether over the telephone or online) such as Dell. The newest form of direct response marketing is *direct email*. Direct email messages are sent by reputable, responsible marketers only by request to customers who have given permission to receive such offers and messages via email. Most reputable companies that engage in direct response marketing are members of the Canadian Marketing Association and abide by its code of ethics.

6. Explain how companies use public relations to communicate with their publics.

Public relations is the task of communicating to the company's *publics* about the company. Every company and organization has publics—groups of people, large or small, who have an interest in what the company does. *Press relations* is one of the major tasks of public relations. It requires the PR professional to communicate regularly with members of the press, typically by preparing written press releases. The media, or members of the press, are examples of the organization's publics, but the general public, those who read the newspapers or watch the news on TV, and see or hear about an item mentioning the company, are also publics. A *press conference* is another method of communicating with the media. *Corporate communications*, communicating with the company's shareholders and investors, falls under the umbrella of public relations. *Speeches* given by company executives or high-ranking officials in a charity or other nonprofit organization are also a form of public relations, in which the organization communicates with the general public. *Special events* are a form of public relations that may be designed to communicate with employees, customers, or other internal or external publics.

KEY TERMS

STUDY GUIDE

After completing this self-test, check your answers against the Answer Key
at the back of the book.

MULTIPLE CHOICE

1. Molson's highly successful "I Am Canadian" campaign
    was consistently used across a number of media, from
    TV and print advertising to the website, in-store dis-
    plays, and packaging. This type of campaign illustrates
    the power of
    a.   Integrated marketing communications
    b.   Large advertising budgets
    c.   Canadian advertising agencies
    d.   Product name branding
    e.   Sales promotions

2. New vehicles for advertising and marketing communica-
    tions are popping up everywhere. From televisions in the
    1940s to the Web in 1990s, marketers are looking for new
    ways to get their message out. One of the latest forms is
    product placement, typically a technique that
    a.   Actually puts the product into consumers' hands
         in non-traditional locations like buses, cinemas,
         airports, and so on
    b.   Showcases products and their brand names in
         movies, TV shows, or other entertainment
         productions
    c.   Places product on store shelves so that all the labels
         and brand names attractively line up
    d.   Compares products against competing products
         based on scientifically controlled experiments
    e.   Allows companies to write articles about their
         product and then have those articles placed in
         magazines and journals as though they were writ-
         ten by objective reporters

3. The type of advertising that a company would choose
    to use for a particular product is partly driven by where
    the product is in its life cycle. For example, Toyota
    would likely have chosen to use _____ when
    it first introduced the Prius into the North American
    market.
    a.   Informative advertising
    b.   Selective advertising
    c.   Introductory advertising
    d.   On-point advertising
    e.   Persuasive advertising

4. Viagra's award-winning commercial showed nothing
    more than a happy man dancing along the sidewalk
    while someone sang "Good morning, good morning."
    Nothing was said of the product at all, except the brand
    name, which appeared just as the happy man stepped
    into the elevator. The Viagra ad is an excellent example
    of what type of message execution?
    a.   Musical
    b.   Slice of life
    c.   Distinctive
    d.   Mood or image
    e.   Compelling

5. Radio stations use a wide range of marketing communication techniques, from personal selling to win advertisers to out-of-home advertising on buses and billboards. Another technique is the use of on-air contests and giveaways. These consumer-oriented activities, designed to increase listenership, are part of what major marketing communication element?
   a. Sales promotion
   b. Discounts
   c. Sweepstakes
   d. Listener incentives
   e. Loyalty programs

6. Many marketers within certain types of industries or structures view personal selling as the most important part of the promotion mix in building and maintaining long-term customer value. Which of the marketing situations would be especially suited to concentrating on personal selling in the marketing communications mix?
   a. Body Shop selling gift packaging through its personalized online shopping website
   b. Bombardier selling electric streetcars to the city of Montreal
   c. Bombardier selling snowmobiles to Montrealers
   d. Future Shop selling computer systems to University of British Columbia students
   e. All of the above

7. Hybrid retail and business-to-business distribution channels often combine such methods as catalogues, online Web stores, physical stores, and telemarketing. The marketing communication element that these hybrid operations are leveraging to build flexible distribution mixes is
   a. Direct response marketing
   b. Open marketing systems
   c. Personal selling
   d. Indirect marketing
   e. Relationship marketing

8. New, emerging companies in the technology sector tend to avoid advertising and rely instead on public relations as the key tool in building awareness and brand. Why would these companies select public relations over advertising in their quest for customers?
   a. Because public relations stresses the value of the message rather than the glitz and gloss used to relay it
   b. Because hard-nosed business buyers of new technologies will believe an objective article in a computer magazine before they will believe paid-for advertising
   c. Because public relations campaigns are usually much less expensive than advertising campaigns
   d. Because the nature of public relations complements personal selling better than does advertising
   e. All of the above

9. Some years ago Johnson & Johnson faced potential disaster for its Tylenol brand. Some bottles of the product were found to contain poisonous substances, and several people died as a result. Johnson & Johnson averted disaster, not only saving the Tylenol brand but building up J&J's reputation for socially responsible marketing through masterly execution of what public relations function?
   a. Sense-of-mission marketing
   b. Press conferences
   c. Public apology
   d. Crisis management
   e. Consumer advocacy

10. Loyalty programs help build databases of customer information, which in turn supports database marketing initiatives. Unlike other forms of the integrated marketing communications mix, database marketing is particularly open to what ethic abuse?
    a. Excessive telemarketing
    b. Pinpoint messaging
    c. Dynamic pricing
    d. Neighbourhood targeting
    e. Privacy invasion and violation

TRUE/FALSE

T F 1. Nike's approach to marketing communications is a pull strategy while New Balance shoes employs a push strategy.

T F 2. Setting an advertising budget based on competitive parity presumes that the competitive leader has established the correct spending levels to maximize sales return for each promotion dollar spent.

T F 3. Advertising is never used in successful consumer sales promotions.

T F 4. Direct marketing is used only when traditional advertising is failing to meet objectives.

T F 5. Public relations is a particularly attractive marketing communications tool for not-for-profit organizations.

CONCEPT CHECK

1. A company's marketing communications mix consists of a blend of _____, _____, _____, _____, and _____.

2. _____ is any paid form of nonpersonal presentation and promotion of ideas, goods, or services by an identified sponsor.

3. _____ builds strong brand identity in the marketplace by tying together and reinforcing all your images and messages.

4. Using a _____ strategy, the producer directs its marketing activities toward consumers to induce them to buy the product.

5. Advertising objectives can be classified by primary purpose—whether the aim is to _____, _____, or _____.

6. There are four common methods used to set the marketing communications budget: the affordable method, the _____ method, the _____ method, and the _____ method.

7. _____ consists of short-term incentives to encourage the immediate purchase of a product or service.

8. The selling process consists of the following steps: _____ and qualifying, _____, approach, needs analysis, presentation and demonstration, _____, _____, and follow-up.

9. The biggest concern consumers have about direct marketing is _____. Consumers who feel that a marketer has violated their privacy may direct their complaints to an official government office called the _____.

10. Effective public relations is significantly less expensive than _____ yet can lead to spectacular results.

STUDENT MATERIALS

Visit our website at www.pearsoned.ca/armstrong for online quizzes, Internet exercises, and more!

NOTES

DISCUSSING THE ISSUES

1. The shift from mass marketing to targeted marketing, and the corresponding use of a richer mix of marketing communications tools, pose challenges for many marketers. Draft a marketing communications plan for either your university or college, McDonald's, or Cake Beauty, with the goal of more effectively integrating the organization's marketing communications.

2. The chapter lists nine different styles of advertising message execution. With reference to current mass media advertising, which of these styles appears to be most commonly used? Explain why you believe this is the case, using examples. Consider the target market for each of these examples. Are they similar? Does that explain the reason for the preference for this type of advertising, or can you think of some other reason?

3. Which of the sales promotion tools described in the chapter would be best for stimulating sales of the following products or services: (a) a dry cleaner wanting to emphasize low prices on washed and pressed dress shirts, (b) Gummy Bears new black cherry flavour, (c) Procter & Gamble's efforts to bundle laundry detergent and fabric softer together in a combined marketing effort, (d) a company that wants its customers to aid in developing a new jingle.

4. Which of the eight steps in the personal selling process do you think is the most difficult for the average salesperson? Which step is the most critical to successful selling? Which step do you think is usually done most correctly?

5. Identify products that would be appropriate for each of the types of direct response marketing presented in this chapter. What is it about the products that make them appropriate for these forms?

6. Compare and contrast the public relations functions of press relations, product publicity, public affairs, lobbying, investor relations, and development.

MARKETING APPLICATIONS

In Germany, it's "Ich liebe es"; in France, "C'est tout ce que j'aime." In China, it translates into "I like it," because one doesn't say "love" lightly in that culture. In September 2003 the McDonald's "I'm lovin' it" campaign was launched simultaneously in more than 100 countries.

The campaign was unprecedented in McDonald's history, because it was the first time an international campaign was consistent in flavour and brand message in every country McDonald's serves. "It's much more than just a new tagline or commercials—it's a new way of thinking about and expressing our worldwide brand appeal to the consumer," said Larry Light, McDonald's executive vice president and global chief marketing officer, and the man behind the campaign.

The McDonald's website at mcdonalds.com features an international welcome page with a drop-down selection for each country's site. Here the online marketing is localized, the campaign adapted, the words translated, but even while capturing the spirit, music, and flavour of each country the brand message remains consistent.

THINKING LIKE A MARKETING MANAGER

1. Find the McDonald's corporate website. List all the publics and audiences this site communicates with.

2. Go to the McDonald's site, choose a country, and explore that country's site. How is the "I'm lovin' it" message translated and adapted? What are the signs that local culture, language, and customs have been incorporated into the campaign?

3. In response to public pressure and claims that fast food makes children obese, in the spring of 2005 McDonald's geared up a major public relations campaign on the theme "It's what I eat and what I do . . . I'm lovin' it." Describe how this new public relations initiative could be integrated with each of the other four major elements of marketing communications for McDonald's.

VIDEO CASE

Go to Pearson Canada's Video Central site (www.pearsoned.ca/highered/videocentral) to view the video and accompanying case for this chapter.

CASE 12 LOVING YOUR BATHROOM

You probably haven't thought much about your bathroom—it's not something that most of us get very inspired about. But you probably have a relationship with your bathroom unlike that with any other room in your house. It's where you start and end your day, primp and preen and admire yourself, escape from the rigours of everyday life, and do some of your best thinking. The marketers at American Standard, the plumbing fixtures giant, understand this often-overlooked but special little room. And that understanding led to the creation of a successful integrated marketing communications strategy.

Working with its ad agency, Carmichael Lynch, American Standard created a wonderfully warm and highly effective marketing campaign called "We want you to love your bathroom." The communications targeted men and women aged 25 to 54 from households planning to remodel bathrooms or replace fixtures. The campaign employed a carefully integrated mix of brand-image and direct-response media ads, direct mailings, and personal contacts to create a customer database, generate sales leads, gently coax customers into its retail showrooms, and build sales and market share.

The campaign began with a series of humorous, soft-sell brand-image ads in magazines such as *Home*, *House Beautiful*, and *Country Living*, which are typically read by homeowners who are considering undertaking remodelling projects. Featuring simple but artistic shots of ordinary bathroom fixtures and scenes, the ads positioned American Standard as a company that understands the special relationships we have with our bathrooms. For example, one ad showed a white toilet and a partially unwound roll of toilet paper, artfully arranged in a corner against plain blue-grey walls. "We're not in this business for the glory," proclaimed the headline. "Designing a toilet or sink may not be as glamorous as, say, designing a Maserati. But to us, it's every bit as important. After all, more people will be sitting on our seats than theirs."

Another ad showed the feet of a man standing on a white tile bathroom floor wearing his goofy-looking floppy-eared dog slippers. "The rest of the world thinks you're a genius," noted the ad. But "after a long day of being brilliant, witty, and charming, it's nice just to be comfortable. The right bathroom understands. And accepts you unconditionally." Each simple but engaging ad included a toll-free phone number and urged readers to call for a free guidebook "overflowing with products, ideas, and inspiration."

The communications goal of these brand-image ads was to position American Standard and its products, but when it came to generating responses, the company turned to couponlike direct-response ads that ran in the same magazines. One such ad noted, "You will spend seven years of your life in the bathroom. You will need a good book." Readers could obtain the free guidebook by mailing in the coupon or calling the toll-free number listed in the ad—and, of course, American Standard could measure the response.

Consumers who responded found that they'd taken the first step in a carefully orchestrated relationship-building venture. First, they received the entertaining, highly informative, picture-filled 30-page guidebook *We Want You to Love Your Bathroom*, along with a folksy letter thanking them for their interest and noting the locations of nearby American Standard dealers. The guidebook's purpose was straightforward: "Walk into your bathroom, turn the knob and suddenly, for a moment or an hour, the world stops turning. You should love the place. If you don't, well, American Standard wants to further your relationship. Thumb through this book. In the bathroom, perhaps. . . ." The guidebook was full of helpful tips on bathroom design, starting with answers to some simple questions: What kind of lavatory—what colour? The bathtub—how big? big enough for two? The toilet—sleek one-piece or familiar two-piece? The faucet? "You'll fumble for it every morning, so be particular about how it operates." To spice things up, the guidebook also contained loads of entertaining facts and trivia. An example: Did you know that "you will spend seven years in your bathroom . . . here's hoping your spouse doesn't sneak in first!" Another example: "During the Middle Ages, Christianity preached that to uncover your skin, even to bathe it, was an invitation to sin. Thank heavens for perfume. These days, we average about 4 baths or 7.5 showers a week." And, of course, the booklet contained plenty of information on American Standard products, along with a tear-out card that prospective customers could return to obtain more detailed guides and product catalogues.

Other marketing communications sent to the consumer, by request, from American Standard included a series of "Bathroom Reading" bulletins, each containing information on specific bathroom design issues. For example, one issue contained information and tips on how to make a bathroom safer; another offered "10 neat ways to save water."

The "call to action" in all these integrated marketing communications elements was either to telephone a toll-free number to request more information, or else to return a coupon or fill in a form to request more information. Every time a prospective customer requested more information from American Standard, their contact details went into American Standard's customer database. This data was then sorted and organized into "leads"—lists of interested customers—which were given to American Standard's sales representatives, their distributors, and kitchen and bath dealers, to follow up on.

The key was to get customers who'd made inquiries to come into the showroom. Not long after making their inquiries, prospective customers would receive either a postcard in the mail, or a phone call, from a local dealer's showroom consultant, who extended a personal invitation to visit, see American Standard products firsthand, and discuss bathroom designs. Thus, the integrated marketing communications program built relationships not just with buyers but with dealers as well.

American Standard's "We want you to love your bathroom" campaign also did wonders for the company's positioning and performance. After the campaign began, American Standard's plumbing division experienced steady increases in sales and earnings. The campaign generated tens of thousands of qualified leads for local showrooms. Market research conducted by the company after the campaign showed that consumer perceptions of American Standard and its products shifted from "boring and institutional" to well designed and loaded with "personal spirit." According to Bob Srenaski, group vice president of marketing at American Standard, the campaign "totally repositioned our company and established a momentum and winning spirit that is extraordinary." Says Joe Summary, an account manager at Carmichael Lynch, "the campaign was incredible. It gave American Standard and its products a more personal face, one that's helped us to build closer relationships with customers and dealers. From the first ad to the last contact with our dealers, the campaign was designed to help customers create bathrooms they'd love."

Questions

1. Which method of setting the marketing communications budget do you think American Standard used? Explain why you think so.

2. How would you describe the style of the American Standard ads? Do you think this style is appropriate for the target market? Explain why or why not.

3. If you were American Standard's media planner, which media vehicles would you chose for the print advertising? Explain your choices.

4. Which forms of direct response marketing were used in this campaign? What was the desired response, and how would American Standard measure it? What information would American Standard have in their database as a result of this campaign?

After studying this chapter, you should be able to

After studying this chapter, you should be able to

1. define the three areas of e-commerce and explain the benefits of e-commerce

2. describe the different ways a company can use its website to support its marketing communications programs

3. differentiate between Web publishers and Web advertisers and define the major forms of online advertising

4. outline how email can be used for marketing and list the rules of email etiquette for online marketers

5. describe the new forms of Internet marketing

6. outline the legal and ethical issues involved in Internet marketing

Marketing and the Internet

13

Looking Ahead   Marketing, as we have seen in previous chapters, is more than just advertising and promotion. Marketing starts with a business strategy, a view to the market and the needs and wants of the customer. A marketing plan is then developed, including plans for new product development. When those new products are developed they must be priced, placed (i.e., distributed through marketing channels), and promoted. Marketers must also work closely with sales, and with after-sales support of the customer.

Marketing on the Internet, just like marketing itself, is not one simple task or function. Marketing on the Internet does not mean simply creating a website for a product or an organization. The Internet can be used for marketing communications, direct sales, and customer service. In this chapter, we look at all the ways the Internet can be used to support an organization's marketing efforts.

First, we'll examine how a well-established Canadian retailer, Canadian Tire, expanded its business and its marketing efforts online. Canadian Tire's e-commerce website was launched in 2000. Since then, the retailer has expanded beyond online sales to integrate its website into its marketing efforts.

C anadian Tire's familiar red and white signs have been part of the Canadian landscape since 1922. In 2000, this traditional retailer expanded its marketing channels by launching an e-commerce website, where consumers anywhere in Canada—even those in remote locations, far from a Canadian Tire store—could order Canadian Tire products online, pay for them online, and have them delivered to their doorsteps.

But Canadian Tire didn't stop there; during its first five years its website has been constantly evolving. After all, a website must be part of a business's ongoing marketing strategy, and smart marketers like Canadian Tire know not to rest on their laurels. They continually strive to improve their website to better serve their customer.

Front and centre on the Canadian Tire website you'll see a button labelled "e-flyer weekly specials"—integrating the website with the print version of the ubiquitous

Canadian Tire flyer. When you click on the button, you are asked to enter your postal code so that you can view the in-store specials available in your area. This section of the site is continually updated with messages such as "Hurry, sale ends May 14!" And most items available in Canadian Tire stores can be purchased online—even the barbeques. The online version of the flyer performs the same marketing communications function as the print flyer; that is, it brings your attention to limited-time specials. And if you act on this information by either ordering the product online or getting into your car and going to the nearest Canadian Tire store, the marketer's goals have been achieved.

The Canadian Tire home page advertises current and seasonal promotions available either online, in its stores, or both. For example, during May 2005, advertised promotions included free shipping on selected items when bought online; 10 percent off auto accessories (both in store and online) until May 31; and the "5X" promotion, which offered opportunities to earn five times the normal amount of Canadian Tire money on selected purchases. A promotion with partner Bel Air Travel also offered a chance to win a trip to the Mayan Riviera simply by subscribing online to receive the Canadian Tire e-flyer via email.

Every page on the Canadian Tire website clearly displays the "Shop by phone 1-866-746-7287" message. The marketers are aware that some visitors to the website may not feel comfortable providing their credit card information over the Internet, and therefore will not be willing to shop online. Some of these same people may not have a car, or may live in a remote area far from a Canadian Tire store, so shopping by phone would be their most convenient option. The marketers strive to make shopping at Canadian Tire accessible for everyone. This is truly a company that is following the marketing concept.

Pricing online is no easy task. Decisions must be made as part of the marketer's overall pricing strategy. For example, while traditional brick-and-mortar retail stores may offer different prices for the same item in different geographic regions, a retailer's website reaches everyone in the country. If the price of a product on the website is different from the price in the store, consumers will be annoyed and feel that they are being treated unfairly.

Canadian retailer Chapters/Indigo has this problem. Customers are able to use in-store computer kiosks to search for specific titles. If the book is not in stock at that specific store, the customer can order it. The problem is that the price shown on the kiosk is often higher than the price for the same book on the Indigo website. Canadian Tire has overcome this problem by asking visitors to its website to enter their postal code. The price displayed for an item is the same online as it is in that consumer's local Canadian Tire store.

And there's more to marketing on the Canadian Tire website than simple e-commerce: It features a gift registry similar to those for brides and grooms at retailers such as The Bay. The engaged couple can set up a registry online, and wedding guests can search for the couple by name, see what gifts they'd like, purchase them online, and have them sent directly to the couple.

Another function of the Canadian Tire website is its store locator, which allows you to search for a Canadian Tire store, a Canadian Tire gas bar, a Canadian Tire Pit Stop (convenience store), or a Canadian Tire car wash. You select the type of retail outlet you're looking for, enter your postal code, province, and city, and a list is displayed of all the Canadian Tire retail outlets along with their street addresses, phone numbers, and a link for more detail about each location's hours of operation, major cross streets, and available services—for example, skate sharpening.

Canadian Tire also uses its website for corporate communications. The site includes a section with information about the organization, including a history of the company, career opportunities, investor information, public relations contacts for the media, and information about Canadian Tire's community activities, for example its JumpStart program, which helps children from less privileged families participate in organized sports and such recreational activities as hockey, soccer, and swimming.

All the functions of the Canadian Tire website are available in both English and French, and that's no easy task. Not many online retailers bother to make their sites fully bilingual, since to do so is equivalent to building and maintaining two websites. As Canadians, we should be proud that companies like Canadian Tire have put us on the forefront of global e-commerce.

TEST YOURSELF

Answers to these questions can be found on our website at www.pearsoned.ca/armstrong.

1. Why does Canadian Tire use so many different methods for customers to place orders and shop?
   a) To be able to service customers with different ordering requirements
   b) Because Canadian Tire is unsure of the segments it should be targeting
   c) Because Canadian Tire store owners are unwilling to lose any customers
   d) Because Canadian Tire is mandated by law to service every Canadian regardless of geography or Internet/phone access
   e) Because it will allow Canadian Tire to more easily move into the United States market later

2. Why would Canadian Tire use a dynamic pricing strategy on its website instead of just having a flat price for each product in its online catalogue?
   a) Because Canadian Tire wants to experiment with different pricing levels
   b) Because Canadian Tire's suppliers recommend pricing based on geography
   c) Because Canadian Tire can adjust the price upward if inventory levels fall
   d) Because stores in different parts of the country have different pricing and every ordering mechanism must reflect that difference
   e) Because Canadian Tire can match or better the price of Home Depot instantly on the website

3. If Canadian Tire already has a successful e-commerce site, why would it also undergo the expense and trouble of maintaining a company website?
   a) Because Canadian Tire also needs to communicate with all stakeholders besides consumers
   b) Because Canadian Tire wants to communicate its sense of strong social responsibility
   c) Because Canadian Tire is a public company and must communicate with its shareholders
   d) Because people looking for jobs will want to look online for available work at Canadian Tire
   e) All of the above

4. By building such features as product tips, registries, and store locators into its e-commerce website, Canadian Tire is also offering what in addition to products?
   a) The ability to charge higher prices
   b) Online customer service
   c) Customization capabilities
   d) Public relations information
   e) Competitive advantage

5. Canadian Tire makes sure that the website works in tandem with its other marketing initiatives. For example, the website features the ability to view a store's print flyer online, and most products available in the store or print catalogue can also be bought online or through a toll-free number. What is the main reason why Canadian Tire takes this approach?
   a) So that customers don't get confused by different offers
   b) Because Canadian Tire can run the online operation less expensively as part of the main Canadian Tire company
   c) An integrated approach ensures a consistent message and a stronger brand
   d) Because Canadian Tire can price according to the promotion vehicle
   e) Because Canadian Tire does not need to hire as many marketing people if everything is the same

It seems inevitable that marketers will quickly discover any new form of mass media communications. Marketing, after all, is tasked with communicating information about an organization and its products and services to the organization's publics and to the market. The Internet, as a relatively new vehicle for communications, has provided marketers with some powerful new marketing tools.

The major forms of Internet marketing are, of course, the website, online advertising, and email. New forms are evolving as well. In this chapter we'll look more closely at each of these forms of Internet marketing.

INTRODUCTION TO INTERNET MARKETING

Integrated marketing communications, as we have already seen, is the strategy of using multiple forms and tactics of marketing communications, all working together to communicate the same message about the brand, the company, or the product. Today, marketers are using *Internet marketing* to integrate their online communications with their traditional marketing communications. **Internet marketing** consists of company efforts to communicate about, promote, and sell products and services over the Internet.

For example, not-for-profit agencies with public relations or corporate communications departments use their website as a new place to publish press releases and to communicate with investors and other stakeholders. After the devastating tsunami in Southeast Asia in December 2004, the Red Cross used its website to communicate with the public about its relief efforts, and anyone with a credit card was able to make a donation online. And Unilever Canada, the marketer behind such popular brands as Lipton, Dove, Knorr, Sunlight, and Q-tips, integrates its Homebasics website—which features food and entertainment, health and nutrition, and a home and garden section—with a monthly print magazine, also called *Homebasics*. The glossy magazine is mailed monthly to consumers who have registered on the Homebasics website and asked to receive it.

Today, marketers are changing their products and services to meet the needs of increasingly time-challenged and value-conscious consumers, and the marketing communications that support those products and services must adapt to these changing needs as well. Advertising campaigns that are designed to be shown on television and in print can easily be adapted to include an online element such as a banner or interstitial ad, or a feature on the company's website.

E-Business and E-Commerce

E-business is a very broad term that refers to any business activity carried out using electronic technology. Bank transactions carried out by electronic transfers between

Internet marketing Company efforts to communicate about, promote, and sell products and services over the Internet.

E-business Any business activity carried out using electronic technology.

branches, for example, are a form of e-business. So is any form of information processing, either within a company or between a company and its suppliers or customers. E-business, then, existed long before the Internet and the World Wide Web were in popular use.[1] In contrast, **e-commerce** is more specific than e-business. It involves buying and selling processes supported by electronic means, primarily the Internet.

There are three main types of e-commerce, which are discussed below. They include B2B (business to business), B2C (business to consumer), and C2C (consumer to consumer). According to the *Globe and Mail,* online sales in Canada totalled $28.3 billion in 2004.[2]

Business-to-business (B2B) e-commerce refers to electronic transactions that take place between businesses. An automobile manufacturer, for example, must purchase thousands of parts from parts manufacturers. The ordering and payment transactions for these types of purchases are done electronically, using private Internet networks. Most business purchasing today is carried out with B2B e-commerce.

Business-to-consumer (B2C) e-commerce refers to electronic transactions that take place between businesses and consumers (as opposed to businesses and their business customers, such as in the auto manufacturer example). This is the form of e-commerce that we, as consumers, are familiar with. If you buy body lotion from Cake Beauty's website, place an order for a lawnmower on Canadian Tire's website, purchase an airline ticket at Air Canada's website or a concert ticket from Ticketmaster.ca, pay your bills online at Canada Post's epost, or bank online, you are a consumer taking part in B2C e-commerce.

The years 1999 and 2000 were the first to see significant online shopping in Canada. According to 2003 Household Internet Use Survey (HIUS) conducted by Statistics Canada, approximately 7.9 million (64 percent) of the 12.3 million Canadian households had at least one member who used the Internet regularly in 2003. This represents a 5 percent increase from 2002, but well below the annual gains of 19 and 24 percent observed in 2000 and 2001. And collectively, these users spent $3.0 billion shopping online—a 25 percent increase from $2.4 billion spent online in 2002. The use of Canadian websites for online shopping is also growing: For every $10 spent by households on Internet purchases in 2003, $6.90 was spent on Canadian websites.[3]

We bank online, we make airline reservations online, we buy books from Indigo, computers from Dell, and camping equipment from MEC. The top categories for online consumer research or transactions in Canada are, in order: banking services, downloaded computer software, clothing, automobiles, music, books, air travel, and consumer electronics.

All in all, Canadian consumers are leading the development of e-commerce worldwide, perhaps as a result of enjoying the lowest fees for residential Internet services in the world, or because Canadian companies have been at the forefront of e-commerce (a Canadian bank was the first online bank and a Canadian airline was the first to offer online transactions to consumers). Whatever the reasons, there is no doubt that Canadian consumers are leaders in online shopping, and Canadian marketers are leaders in e-commerce. To learn more about the characteristics of online consumers, see Marketing at Work 13.1.

Consumer-to-consumer (C2C) e-commerce refers to electronic transactions taking place online between consumers. Online auction sites such as eBay serve as a virtual meeting place for consumers who have items to sell and consumers who wish to make purchases. EBay functions much like a giant international classified ads section of the newspaper. EBay's business is to provide the technology that allows for these C2C transactions to take place, and their revenue comes from the small fees they charge the consumer who is selling the item. The consumer who buys an item can pay for it online using a credit card, and that payment is transmitted electronically to the seller's PayPal account. PayPal is a subsidiary of eBay that manages the funds transfers between consumers.

E-commerce Buying and selling processes supported by electronic means, primarily the Internet.

Business-to-business (B2B) e-commerce Electronic transactions that take place between businesses.

Business-to-consumer (B2C) e-commerce Electronic transactions that take place between businesses and consumers.

Consumer-to-consumer (C2C) e-commerce Electronic transactions taking place online between consumers.

Marketing at Work   13.1

Today's Online Consumers

The Internet presents a multitude of different kinds of people seeking different types of online experiences. While online consumers do tend to be younger, more affluent, and better educated than the general population, the Internet population is becoming increasingly representative of the Canadian population as a whole. The age group with the highest proportion of Internet users is the 18-to-24-year-old demographic. Jupiter Research, an American organization that tracks online marketing trends, reported in August 2005 that consumers between the ages of 25 and 34 spend more time online (14 hours per week) than watching television (10 hours per week). Consumers in the 35–44 age group behave similarly, spending 14 hours a week online and 12 hours watching television. Fifty-six percent of people aged 50 to 64 are online, but only 17 percent of people over 65 use the Internet. Men still make up a slightly larger portion of Internet users, but the percentages are evening out. More and more children are using the Internet, and are drawn to sites such as TVO Kids and CBC Kids that are both entertaining and educational.

As with other things Canadian, regional differences also exist with regard to Internet usage and spending patterns. Ontario still accounts for almost one-half of the national Internet usage and spending, followed by Alberta and British Columbia. There are also marked differences between Canadian and American Internet users.

While more Americans shop online (77 percent compared with 68 percent in Canada), more Canadians bank online (61 percent compared with 29 percent in the U.S.), and more have high-speed connections.

Of course, spending more time on the Web doesn't necessarily mean spending more money there. A kind of e-haviioural divide is emerging in how different kinds of people use the Internet. Affluent, time-pressed consumers tend to view the Web as a transactional arena—a place to gather information or buy big-ticket items. They visit news, travel, and financial sites, such as americanexpress.com. To them, the Internet is just one more tool to help them get information or buy things.

By contrast, people at the lower end of the socioeconomic ladder are more likely to view the Internet as a kind of home entertainment centre for fun and games. They are attracted to portal sites like Yahoo! Canada for its games section with popular card and board games, and Sympatico/MSN, which offers crosswords and other entertainment activities. They are more likely to view a variety of entertainment and sweepstakes sites, including icq.com, youwinit.com, and gamesville.com, and they are more likely to view the Internet as a replacement for television.

Along with the socioeconomic differences, many researchers report a growing gender gap on the Internet. Although men and women engage in

many activities at roughly equal rates—such as banking and downloading music—the sexes then part company. Men are more likely to go online to buy stocks, get news, compare and buy products, bid at auctions, and visit government websites. Women are more likely to send email, play games, score coupons, and get information on health, jobs, and religion.

Internet researchers differ in their predictions on how long it will take for the Internet audience to mirror the Canadian population. However, they're in remarkable agreement on one point: The latest generation of connected Canadians looks a lot more like the folks who cruise your local mall.

Sources: "Top 10 Web Properties: Week of September 2, 2001, Canada," *Nielsen//NetRatings,* http://reports.metratings.com/ca/web/NRpublicreports.toppropertiesweekly, accessed April 29, 2002; "Average Web Usage, Month of March 2002, Canada," *Nielsen//NetRatings,* http://reports.metratings.com/ca/web/NRpublicreports.usagemonthly, accessed April 29, 2002; "The Internet: Who's Connected—Who's Shopping?" *Focus on Culture,* Statistics Canada Catalogue no. 87-004, pp. 10–12; Mark W. Vigoroso, "Report: Canada Closes E-Biz Gap with U.S.," *E-Commerce Times,* March 25, 2002, www.ecommercetimes.com/5perl/story/16928.html; Statistics Canada, "E-commerce: Household Shopping on the Internet 2000," *The Daily,* October 23, 2001, www.statcan.ca/Daily/English/011023/d011023b.htm; Michael J. Weiss, "Online America," *American Demographics,* March 2001, pp. 53–60; "A Nation Online: How Americans Are Expanding Their Use of the Internet," Department of Commerce, February 2002; and Robyn Greenspan, "The Web as a Way of Life," May 21, 2002, accessed online at http://cyberatlas.internet.com; Online Media Daily (publications.mediapost.com), August 9, 2005.

E-commerce and the Internet bring many benefits to both buyers and sellers. Let's review some of these major benefits.

Benefits to Buyers

Internet buying benefits both consumers and business buyers in many ways. It can be *convenient:* Customers don't have to battle traffic, find parking spaces, and trek through stores and aisles to find and examine products. They can do comparative shopping by

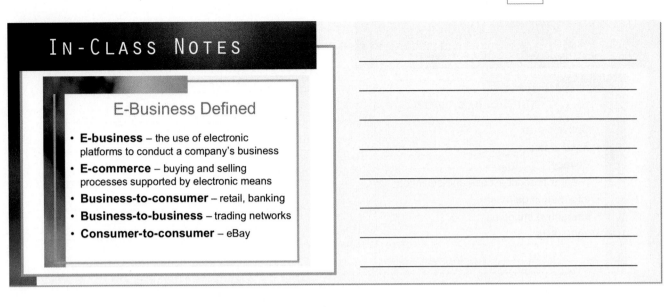

IN-CLASS NOTES

E-Business Defined

- **E-business** – the use of electronic platforms to conduct a company's business
- **E-commerce** – buying and selling processes supported by electronic means
- **Business-to-consumer** – retail, banking
- **Business-to-business** – trading networks
- **Consumer-to-consumer** – eBay

browsing through mail catalogues or surfing websites. Online retailers never close their doors. Buying is *easy* and *private:* Customers encounter fewer buying hassles and don't have to face salespeople or open themselves up to persuasion and emotional pitches. Business buyers can learn about and buy products and services without waiting for and tying up time with salespeople.

In addition, the Internet often provides buyers with greater *product access and selection.* Unrestrained by physical boundaries, online sellers can offer an almost unlimited selection. Compare the incredible selections offered by Web merchants such as Chapters/Indigo to the more meagre assortments of their counterparts in the brick-and-mortar world. For example, while approximately 3 million book titles are available in print, most physical bookstores hold only about 125 000 titles. By selling books online, Indigo can make all 3 million titles available to its customers.

Beyond a broader selection of sellers and products, e-commerce channels also give buyers access to a wealth of comparative *information* about companies, products, and competitors. Good sites often provide more information in more useful forms than even the most solicitous salesperson. For example, HMV.com offers music and movie bestseller lists, extensive product descriptions, and expert and customer reviews. It even lets you listen to clips of songs so that you can try before you buy. Today, almost no one enters a car

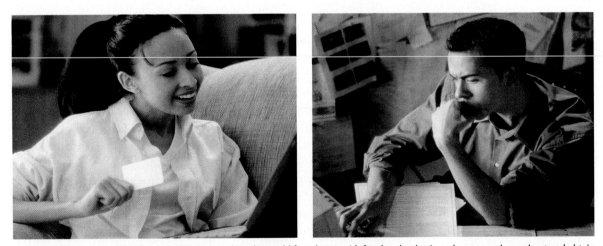

Internet buying is easy and private: Consumers can shop the world from home with few hassles; business buyers can learn about and obtain products and information without tying up time with salespeople.

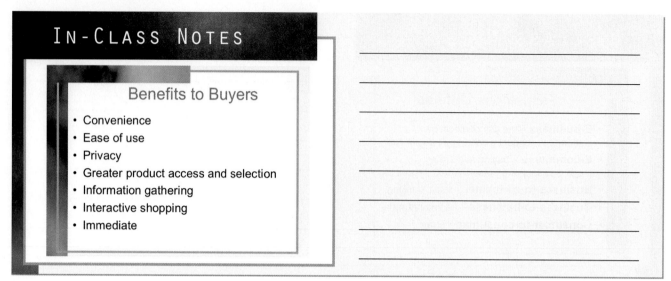

IN-CLASS NOTES

Benefits to Buyers

- Convenience
- Ease of use
- Privacy
- Greater product access and selection
- Information gathering
- Interactive shopping
- Immediate

dealership before they've researched prices and features of various car models online. According to Industry Canada, the Internet has changed the way cars are purchased.[4] A survey of 1000 Canadian consumers in 2003 revealed that almost two-thirds had searched for new or used vehicle prices, or searched for information about car features, online. Such free and readily available information empowers consumers today like never before.

Finally, online buying is *interactive* and *immediate*. Buyers can often interact with the seller's site to create exactly the configuration of information, products, or services they desire, then order or download them on the spot.

Benefits to Sellers

E-commerce also offers many benefits to sellers. First, the seller is able to reach a wider audience—an international one, in fact—with its products. The next benefit is that the seller can utilize direct distribution and may actually eliminate intermediaries, thereby reducing costs, increasing profits, and getting the product into the hands of the consumer faster. The Internet is also a powerful tool for *customer relationship building* because of its one-to-one, interactive nature. Such online interaction allows the firm to learn more about specific needs and wants of its customers. Moreover, online customers can ask questions and volunteer feedback.

In fact, the number one reason why a person visits any website, whether for personal or business reasons, is to find information. This is a big bonus for marketers who normally have to push information about their products and services onto consumers. In the online world, they have the opportunity to present detailed information about their firms, products, and services to a willing and receptive audience. Furthermore, consumers will often "reward" the company that provides them with the best, or most comprehensive, or most useful, information—by buying their products instead of those of their competitors. Based on this ongoing interaction, companies can increase customer value and satisfaction through product and service refinements.

The Internet and other electronic channels yield additional advantages, such as *reducing costs* and *increasing speed and efficiency*. Internet marketers who sell their products only online avoid the expense of maintaining stores and the related costs of rent, insurance, and utilities. Furthermore, they benefit from positive cash flow, because credit card payments from customers are posted almost immediately to the company's accounts; however, suppliers may not have to be paid until 30 to 60 days later.

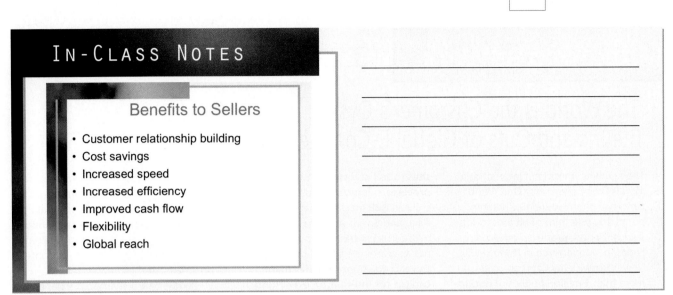

By using the Internet to link directly to suppliers, factories, distributors, and customers, businesses such as Dell Computer and General Electric are cutting costs and passing savings on to customers. Because customers deal directly with sellers, online direct sales often result in lower costs and improved efficiencies for channel and logistics functions such as order processing, inventory handling, delivery, and trade promotion. Finally, online communication between buyers and sellers is nearly instantaneous—much faster, more efficient, and cheaper than communicating via telephone, fax, or mail.

Selling online also offers greater *flexibility,* allowing the marketer to make ongoing adjustments to its offers and programs. For example, once a print catalogue is mailed to customers, the products, prices, and other catalogue features are fixed until the next catalogue is sent. However, an online catalogue like Canadian Tire's can be adjusted daily or even hourly, adapting product assortments, prices, and promotions to match changing market conditions.

Finally, the Internet is a truly *global* medium that allows buyers and sellers to click from one country to another in seconds. GE's GXS network provides business buyers with immediate access to suppliers in 58 countries, ranging from the United States and the United Kingdom to Hong Kong and the Philippines. A customer in Paris or Istanbul can access an online Tilley Endurables catalogue as easily as someone living in Toronto, the company's hometown. Thus, even small Internet marketers find that they have ready access to global markets (see Marketing at Work 13.2).

MARKETING AND THE WEBSITE

Though the Internet as a communications technology has existed since the 1960s, it was only with the development in 1994 of the first Web browser, an easy-to-use graphical interface for navigating websites, that non-technical consumers were able to view information published on the World Wide Web. It didn't take long before businesses and other organizations began setting up their websites. Early corporate sites were, for the most part "brochureware"; that is, the company would simply post static pictures and information about their products. These early websites were nothing like the flashy, colourful, animated sites that we see today on the Web. Rather, they were black text on a white background, maybe with a few pictures, and had very limited functionality—often nothing more complicated than email links or forms through which visitors could contact the organization.

Marketing at Work 13.2

The World Is the Customer's Oyster: The Ins and Outs of Global E-Commerce

The headline on McCain International Inc.'s website says it all: "One World. One Fry." It may sound like bragging, but nearly one-third of all the world's french fries are produced by McCain Foods, headquartered in Florenceville, New Brunswick. McCain can produce more than 1 million pounds of potato products every hour in its 30 potato processing plants around the world. And it uses the Web to reach both consumers and vendors, using websites tailored specifically to the needs of certain country-markets, including the United States, the Netherlands, Poland, Scandinavia, the United Kingdom, and Germany.

Like McCain, companies large and small are discovering that the Internet reduces time and space restrictions, allowing marketers access to a truly global, 24-hour marketplace. E-commerce can take many forms, from car makers General Motors and Ford ordering parts through private B2B exchanges, to online retailers such as Dell and Indigo selling products directly to consumers, to newspaper and magazine publishers taking subscription payments online and selling archived stories to researchers.

Marketers are using the Internet to reach new customers outside their home countries, support existing customers who live abroad, request and receive quotes from international suppliers, and build global brand awareness. Most international companies have adapted their websites to provide country-specific content and services to their best potential international markets, often in the local language. Go to www.nike.com and Nike's home page first asks which site you want: North America, Europe, Asia Pacific, or Latin America. The European option lists five language choices: English, Deutsch, Français, Español, and Italiano. Similarly, Texas Instruments uses tailored "TI & Me"

sites to sell and support its signal processors, logic devices, and other chips in B2B markets across Europe, Asia, and South America.

Internet marketers must be careful not to overstate global opportunities. Developed countries offer many choices for Internet access—Hong Kong alone has more than 240 registered Internet service providers (ISPs). However, less-developed countries in Central and South America or Africa have fewer or none at all, forcing users to make international calls to go online. As of 2000, only 6 percent of the world's population had Internet access. Even with adequate phone lines and PC penetration, high connection costs sharply restrict Internet use. In Asia, ISP subscriptions can run up to $60 a month, more than triple the average rate in Canada.

In addition, global marketers may run up against governmental or cultural restrictions. France, for instance, has laws against providing encrypted content. In Germany, a vendor can't accept payment via credit card until two weeks after an order has been

sent. German law also prevents companies from using certain marketing techniques, such as unconditional lifetime guarantees. This affects companies such as Lands' End, which prominently features its lifetime guarantee on its website.

Today, nearly every business, no matter how large or small, is using the Internet in one way or another, whether it's selling products online, providing customer service, or offering detailed product information for consumers researching their purchases before going into a store. Internet marketing in its many forms is turning the world into one great big oyster for consumers to enjoy.

Sources: www.mccain.com/McCainWorldWide/McCainOperatingCompanies, accessed November 2003; Brandon Mitchener, "E-Commerce: Border Crossings," *Wall Street Journal,* November 22, 1999; Janet Purdy Levaux, "Adapting Products and Services for Global E-Commerce," *World Trade,* January 2001, pp. 52–54; "Nielsen/NetRatings Find China Has the World's Second Largest At-Home Internet Population," April 22, 2002, www.nielsen-netratings.com; "Internet Penetration in Europe Plateaus," www.europemedia.net, accessed July 2002.

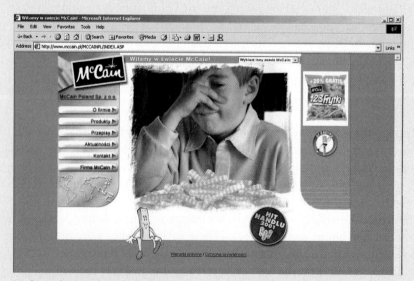

Marketers large and small are taking advantage of the Internet's global reach. McCain uses the World Wide Web to market its products worldwide.

Today, almost every business and every organization has its own website. And the modern website can be used to perform a wide variety of marketing functions.

The 7 Cs of Effective Website Design

Whatever marketing purpose a website serves, it must be designed, managed, and regularly updated. In the 10 years since commercial organizations first began including websites as part of their marketing strategy, certain principles of effective website design have emerged. These are referred to as the "7 Cs of effective design."[5]

- ☐ *Context:* The site's layout and design; the surrounding environment of the content
- ☐ *Content:* All the text, images, and sound on the site
- ☐ *Community:* Functionality that allows visitors or registered members of a site to communicate with each other, for example, eBay's feedback ratings system
- ☐ *Customization:* Functionality that allows a registered member or customer of the site to select preferences that present a personal online experience, for example, Amazon's "My Store" feature
- ☐ *Communication:* How the site presents methods for the visitor or customer to communicate directly with the organization, or to subscribe to receive communications from the organization
- ☐ *Connection:* The degree to which the site is connected to the Web, measured by the number of incoming and outgoing links
- ☐ *Commerce:* The site's ability to enable commercial transactions

Overall, the website should be easy to navigate, pleasing to the eye, and should load quickly. The website must be interesting, and must serve the purpose it is intended to serve. For example, an online gaming site or an entertainment site such as Disney.com must be entertaining. On the other hand, a news website or an automobile shopping comparison site must be informative. Ultimately, it is the value of the site's content that attracts visitors, encourages them to stay, and results in them returning again and again.

Clinique's Canadian website offers content, communication, and customization, in addition to commerce.

IN-CLASS NOTES

7 Cs of Effective Design

- **Context:** layout and design elements
- **Content:** text, pictures, sound, and video
- **Community:** user-to-user communication
- **Customization:** personalized for each user
- **Communication:** two-way communication
- **Connection:** links to other relevant sites
- **Commerce:** commercial transactions

_____

_____

_____

_____

_____

_____

_____

_____

Effective websites contain deep and useful information, interactive tools that help buyers find and evaluate products of interest, links to related sites, engaging promotional offers, and entertaining features. Cosmetics manufacturer Clinique, for example, has a comprehensive, international website, serving the U.S., Canada, France, Germany, Korea, Japan, China, Spain, the U.K., and Ireland. The Canadian Clinique site is available in both English and French. Registered members can join Club Clinique and receive personal product recommendations (*customization*), information about new products (*content*), and email notifications of when Clinique's Bonus Time will be taking place at their nearest retailer (*communication*). And the Canadian Clinique website offers e-commerce functionality in partnership with Sears Canada, allowing site visitors to buy Clinique products directly through the site (*commerce*).

Online marketers must understand that a website is not something you design once, publish, then leave alone. An effective website must be constantly evolving in response to customer needs. For example, Otis Elevator Company, whose website serves 20 000 registered customers around the world, among them architects, general contractors, and building managers, asks these experts for advice by regularly surveying them. Such customer satisfaction tracking has resulted in many site improvements. For example, Otis found that customers in other countries were having trouble linking to the page that would let them buy an elevator online. Now, the link is easier to find. Some customers were finding it hard to locate a local Otis office, so the company added an office locator feature.[6]

Functions of a Website

The website is a key element in marketing on the Internet and can be used for a number of marketing functions. A company's website can serve as an e-commerce site where consumers can buy the company's products online. The website can also support sales of a product by acting as a vehicle for marketing communications or customer service. Alternatively, a website may be the product itself, providing information or services to the consumer.

The Website as a Sales Channel Websites can be used as a sales channel, providing a virtual place where a consumer may purchase a product or service, either direct from the manufacturer, from an agent, or from a retailer.

Dell, for example, has always been a direct marketer. Since the company was founded in 1984, it has sold computers directly to consumers. Before the Internet, its direct channel consisted of telephone and catalogue orders. With the advent of the World Wide Web, Dell placed its catalogue online, built a functional e-commerce website, and offered consumers the ability to purchase computers directly, online. Dell claims that it was the first company to record online sales of $1 million a day. It hit this target in 1997, three years after taking its direct-order business to the Web. By 2005 the company reported receiving more than 15 000 orders and information requests every minute from its 81 country websites. According to Michael Lombardo, general manager of home and small business for Dell Canada, more than half of its $49.2 billion in annual sales are enabled by the Web.[7]

Though Dell was one of the earliest Internet marketers, other traditional catalogue marketers have followed suit, and today function online in much the same manner as the old Sears and Eaton's catalogues did. Victoria's Secret, Veseys (a PEI-based plant supplier), Eddie Bauer, and Tilley are just a few examples of long-established catalogue marketers that now make their products available to a worldwide market through their websites. Traditional retailers such as Canadian Tire, Indigo, and HMV similarly make their products available for consumers to buy on the Internet.

Small retailers and wholesalers also sell their products online. For example, Clearwater Seafood Company of Bedford, Nova Scotia, sells live lobsters through its website and ships them anywhere in North America. Retail products frequently purchased over the telephone, such as concert tickets and flowers, can now be purchased just as easily, if not more easily, online.

For some manufacturers and retailers, such as Dell and Amazon, the website is the *only* sales channel, but for many marketers, such as Cake Beauty, it is only one part of their marketing channel strategy. Cake Beauty sells its products directly to consumers through its website but also distributes its products through retailers such as Caban in Vancouver, Roxy Tonic in Saskatoon, and Blossom Bath & Body in Unionville. The Cake Beauty website displays a link called "Where to get a piece of cake," which connects to a page listing all the retailers in Canada, the United States, Australia, Europe, and Hong Kong that carry Cake Beauty products.

Services can also be sold online. Air Canada was one of the first airlines in the world to provide consumer services online through its website. The Air Canada website was launched in 1995, and in its early days had very limited functionality. In 1997 the site

Clearwater Seafood Company of Bedford, NS, sells live lobsters through its website.

began to offer flight schedules and launched its Websaver email. By the end of 1997, the website offered customers the ability to purchase tickets online.[8] Today, Air Canada offers its Aeroplan members the ability to manage their accounts online and to book reward tickets online. And Air Canada recently changed the way it presents visitors with flight options, allowing those who are flexible with their travel dates to see a variety of flights from which they may choose. You can even select your seat and print your boarding pass online. Other service providers such as travel agents aggregate services from a variety of suppliers such as airlines, car rental companies, and hotels, and present options to consumers through sites such as Hotels.com and Travelocity.

The Website as a Marketing Communications Vehicle All websites are a form of marketing communications, whatever their functionality. For companies that sell their products and services online, the website is used not only as a sales channel but also to communicate information about those products to consumers. But how can companies that do not, or cannot, sell their products and services online still make good marketing use of their websites?

One strategy, used by automobile marketers, is to use the website to bring the customer as close to the sale as possible. Visit the website of your favourite car brand today and you'll find detailed information and photographs of the latest models. You'll be able to build your own virtual car, choosing the interior and exterior colours and options, then price your choice and find the dealer nearest you who can help you complete your purchase.

In Canada, wine, beer, and alcohol cannot be sold directly to consumers online, yet retailers such as the LCBO and The Beer Store have marketing websites. On the LCBO's website, consumers can learn about new products, find gift suggestions, and look up the address and the store hours of the LCBO nearest them. The LCBO also offers courses in wine appreciation and cooking, with details about these courses promoted on the website.

Pharmaceutical giant Pfizer manufactures prescription drugs, veterinary products, and consumer products such as Listerine, Rolaids, and Visine. Pfizer's customers are retailers such as grocery stores and drug stores which, in turn, sell Pfizer's products to consumers. Pfizer does not sell directly to consumers. Prescription drugs must be purchased from a pharmacy, and no consumer would find it worthwhile to buy a product like mouthwash directly from the manufacturer, online or not. Pfizer uses its website to support its marketing efforts in several ways. Consumers who visit the site can read

Pharmaceutical giant Pfizer markets its products to veterinarians in part through a website tailored to their customer needs.

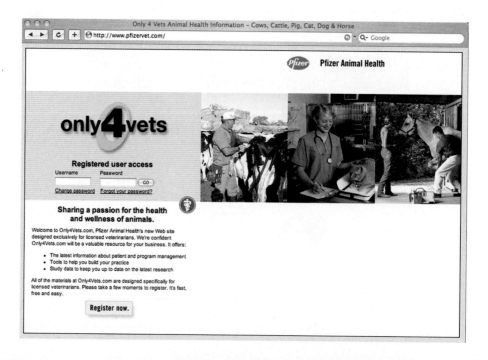

detailed information about all the prescription drugs the company markets. One section of the site is devoted to veterinarians. And, since Pfizer is a publicly traded company, there's a section for investor information.

For large businesses and not-for-profit agencies with public relations or corporate communications departments, the website is a place to publish press releases and to communicate with investors and other stakeholders. Websites can also be used for such time-honoured forms of sales promotion as coupons, sweepstakes, and contests. The Internet provides a simple, inexpensive distribution method for coupons and other special offers. Most contests and sweepstakes today allow online entry, which gives the marketer a database of interested potential customers to further market to.[9]

Marketers have found that all of these forms of marketing communications must be simplified in order to attract the attention of today's busy consumers. A sales promotion must be easy for the consumer to participate in, and must provide significant value in order to be successful. For example, Cake Beauty ran a promotion on its website allowing visitors to enter to win a year's supply of "sinfully smoothing scrubs." Another promotion offered an exclusive introductory price plus a free nail file when consumers bought both Milk Maid Hand Buffer and Milk Maid Hand Creme.

The Website as a Customer Service Channel Most corporate websites provide some customer service information. FedEx was one of the first Internet marketers to take advantage of the interactivity of the Web and use it to communicate with its customers. Launched in 1995, the FedEx website allowed the user to enter the waybill number of the package he or she was expecting, and be presented with up-to-date information about its delivery status. Within the first few weeks of the launch of the website, FedEx reported that it was saving approximately $1 million per day—*per day*—in customer service costs, because customers could now serve themselves.

The gift registry is another type of customer service that has been made much easier and more efficient by placing it online. Before the Web, an engaged couple would visit a department store and be assigned a customer service representative who would walk through the store with them, holding a clipboard and writing down the couple's choice of wedding gifts. Friends and relatives would have to visit that store in person, ask for the list, make their purchase, and deliver it themselves to the couple. Today, there are some registries where the couple can create their gift registry online, without any assistance, and friends and relatives with Internet access need only sit at their own computer, look up the registry, and order and pay for their choice online.

Canada Post is in the business of delivering the mail, a service that for obvious reasons cannot be performed online. So how does this business use its website to communicate with and serve its customers? Canada Post may not be able to deliver your packages via the Internet, but it can, and does, allow consumers and businesses to look up a postal code for any address in Canada; fill out and submit a change of address form; and calculate the postage costs to send an envelope or a package anywhere in the world. The Canada Post website also features a service called epost, which allows you to receive and pay bills from Rogers, BMO Mosaik MasterCard, HBC, and Canadian Tire online.

The Website as Content Content websites are those provided by Web publishers such as Yahoo!, Sympatico/MSN, Canada.com, and *The Globe and Mail*. Much like newspapers and magazines, content sites provide information in the form of text and graphics, and consumers visit these sites to read about news, sports, entertainment, and the weather—in much the same way as they read the daily newspaper.

There are two main types of content sites: portal websites and websites of traditional publishers. A **portal website** is a large, comprehensive, general interest, public website. Portal sites typically offer news, sports, and weather information, much as the nightly TV news and your daily newspaper do. The information published on these sites is free to the public, and because large numbers of consumers visit these portal sites daily, the site

portal website A large, comprehensive, general interest, public website.

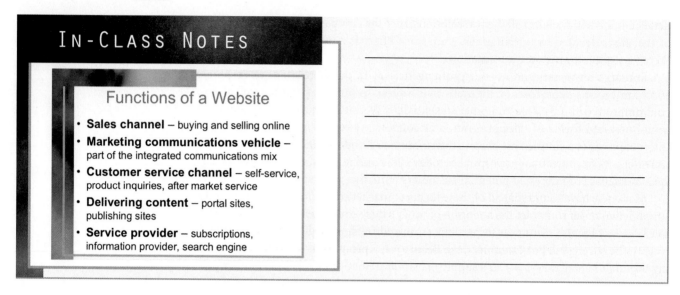

IN-CLASS NOTES

Functions of a Website

- **Sales channel** – buying and selling online
- **Marketing communications vehicle** – part of the integrated communications mix
- **Customer service channel** – self-service, product inquiries, after market service
- **Delivering content** – portal sites, publishing sites
- **Service provider** – subscriptions, information provider, search engine

publisher is able to run a profitable business by selling advertising space. Canada.com, Sympatico/MSN, Yahoo! Canada, and Canoe are all examples of portal websites.

Traditional newspaper and magazine publishers, such as *The Globe and Mail*, *National Post*, *Chatelaine*, and *Maclean's*, have long been in the business of selling advertising space in their print publications. Since the advent of the Internet most traditional publishers have built comprehensive websites, and, just like as they do with their print publications, they generate revenue by selling space to advertisers.

The Website as a Service   Some websites, rather than functioning as a marketing channel for the organization, are services in and of themselves. For example, a **search engine** is a free, public website that allows users to search for information available anywhere on the Web simply by typing keywords into a field and clicking a button to execute the search. Yahoo! and Google are both search engines. They do not operate any retail stores or manufacturing operations; their websites are their business.

Workopolis, Canada's largest job site, is also a service-in-itself website. While job seekers can post their résumés and search for jobs on the site free of charge, employers pay to have their job listings posted. More than 30 000 jobs are typically posted on the site on any given day, generating revenue for this Bell Globemedia organization.

search engine A free, public website that allows users to search for information available anywhere on the Web simply by typing keywords into a field and clicking a button to execute the search.

ONLINE ADVERTISING

Advertising, as we saw in Chapter 12, is the paid placement of a marketer's message in the mass media. Television, radio, newspapers, magazines, and billboards are traditional media used by advertisers. The World Wide Web can be used by advertisers in much the same way as traditional forms.

A website that generates revenue by selling advertising space to advertisers is called a **Web publisher.** Most major content websites, such as those operated by traditional newspaper and magazine publishers, sell advertising space. Just as a particular newspaper, such as the *National Post*, is a media vehicle for print advertising, so are particular websites media vehicles for online advertising.

We've seen how companies can use their own websites to provide services, sell products, and communicate with their customers. But a company's own website is not advertising. A company that publishes a website pays for the maintenance of that site and can use the site for a variety of purposes; however, just as advertising in traditional media means paying the owner of the medium (the television station or network, or the publisher of the magazine) for the placement of the advertising message, online advertising

Web publisher A website that generates revenue by selling advertising space to advertisers.

means the marketer pays the owner of the medium—the website—for placement of the advertising message.

Worldwide online advertising revenues were US$9.6 billion in 2004. In the same year in Canada, online spending reached $300 million. Paula Gignac, executive director of the Interactive Advertising Bureau of Canada, points out that "Revenue numbers have grown as marketers have become more familiar with the medium, but also as research has shown the benefits of re-distributing ad dollars within campaigns to include online."[10]

Online advertising offers many benefits that are simply not available to advertisers who choose traditional media. The main benefit is a direct result of Internet technology. Online ads are "served" onto a webpage using programmable software. Therefore, every single time an ad appears on a webpage it can be counted. Advertisers who buy online media can view real-time reports of how many times their ad has been viewed, exactly the time of day it was viewed, and whether or not the ad was clicked on. But it doesn't stop there. Let's say a banner ad advertises a contest. The advertiser who pays for the banner ad is able to know not only how many times the ad was viewed and clicked on, but how many visitors linked to the contest entry form and how many filled it out. Response rates can then be easily calculated.

By comparison, the number of people who view a television ad can only be estimated, and even then, services such as Nielsen that measure television audience size are estimating the number of people who watched the television program, not the number who viewed the ad—a figure that simply cannot be known with any degree of accuracy. The number of people who see a newspaper or magazine ad cannot be known, either. Advertisers who choose print media base their decision on the circulation numbers for the publication, but they have no way of knowing how many of the publication's readers actually saw, noticed, or read their ad.

In 2004 Canadian Tire added an online advertising component to its Father's Day advertising campaign, and reported a 6 percent increase in ad awareness as a result. Says media integration manager Terry Yakimchick, "Canadian Tire strives to be a leader in the area of cross media campaigns. We strongly believe in the integration of consistent themes and branding through all of our communications as well as our in-store customer experience. We have seen recent increases in the amount of dollars we are investing in online media and believe that online plays an important role in our overall media mix."[11]

Even with these benefits, online media purchase typically accounts for less than 5 percent of an advertiser's total media budget. By comparison, television accounts for approximately 35 percent.[12] Jupiter Research notes that in 2005 online advertising accounted for just 5.6 percent of all advertising spending, and predicts that this figure will rise to only 7 percent by 2010.

Critics point to the relatively low investment in online spending, and many marketers are still hesitant to buy online media, preferring traditional forms of marketing communications with which they are familiar. Still, the Jupiter survey, conducted in June 2005, revealed that consumers are responding to Web ads. Almost one-third of consumers surveyed, 31 percent, reported having made an online purchase as a result of viewing an online ad, while 22 percent stated that online ads had influenced an offline purchase.

Forms of Online Advertising

The particular form an online advertisement takes depends on the site that is selling the advertising space as well as the marketer's requirements for effective delivery of its advertising (see Marketing at Work 13.3). The most commonly used forms include the following.

Banner Ads Banner ads are graphic ads that are rectangular or square in shape, can be of any size, and may be placed anywhere on the publisher's webpage. The Interactive Advertising Bureau of Canada, whose members are companies and organizations that

Banner ads Graphic online ads that are rectangular or square in shape, can be of any size, and may be placed anywhere on the publisher's webpage.

Marketing at Work 13.3

Online Advertising Isn't Just for High-Tech Products

Everyone expects high-tech companies like Dell, Nokia, and RIM to use the Internet to advertise their products—after all, it's a high-tech communications medium. But what about an old-fashioned product like hardware? Or a service, like Weight Watchers? The companies that market these types of products are new to the world of Internet marketing and advertising, and Canadian portal sites like Sympatico/MSN, which sell online advertising space, must work closely with these advertisers to help them develop an online media strategy that will realize their goals.

RONA, a national Canadian hardware retailer, had some very specific marketing communications goals in mind when it decided to advertise on Sympatico/MSN. The company already had an e-commerce website, and offered registered customers a free email newsletter. One of RONA's goals was to increase the number of subscribers to its English-language monthly email newsletter, particularly in western Canada and Ontario, where it had recently opened new stores. The retailer hoped to sign up 20 000 new members over the course of the campaign.

RONA's marketing team, its marketing communications agency, Carat Interactive, and the advertising specialists at Sympatico/MSN worked together to come up with an online strategy. They decided to run a contest to attract consumer attention and drive newsletter subscriptions.

Once the strategy was in place it was time for the Web designers at Sympatico/MSN to get to work. Banner ads promoting the contest were created and placed in appropriate locations on the portal, such as the Home & Family section. Advertisements and editorial mentions were placed in the Sympatico/MSN monthly newsletter, which is distributed to 1.2 million Canadians via email. A microsite was created for consumers to enter the contest, and the entry form prompted them to opt in to receive the English-language newsletter. Viral marketing was also used—the entry form offered another chance at winning with every invitation sent to a friend. Sympatico/MSN drove traffic directly to the RONA website, where consumers could find the answers to the questions on the contest entry form.

The results were better than expected—and ultimately measurable. The RONA campaign on Sympatico/MSN attracted 42 000 people who entered the contest. Of those, 60 percent opted to receive the newsletter, far surpassing RONA's goal of 20 000 new subscribers. The viral marketing aspect of the campaign was also a success. More than 40 000 people were sent invitations from their friends and of those, 11 000 accepted and returned to the site to enter the contest themselves.

Weight Watchers, the leading international weight loss program, also approached Sympatico/MSN for help in generating awareness of WeightWatchers.ca and in driving Canadian subscribers to Weight Watchers Online and Weight Watchers eTools. The online advertising strategy that was developed involved integrating the advertising with the editorial content in appropriate spots on the Sympatico/MSN site. A sponsorship program was created in which Weight Watchers was the exclusive weight-loss content provider for the Health & Fitness channel on the Sympatico/MSN site. There was also a link to sign up for the Weight Watchers free online newsletter. Since the campaign began in September 2004, Weight Watchers has reported consistently meeting or exceeding its marketing communications goals.

An online contest to promote a hardware store, advertising integrated with content for a weight loss program—these types of approaches make it clear that high-tech advertising isn't just for high-tech products any more.

Source: Information about these and other case studies are available on Sympatico/MSN at advertise.sympatico.msn.ca.

Weight Watchers is a sponsor of Sympatico/MSN's Health & Fitness channel. Though other companies may purchase advertising in this space, Weight Watchers is the exclusive weight loss provider on the channel.

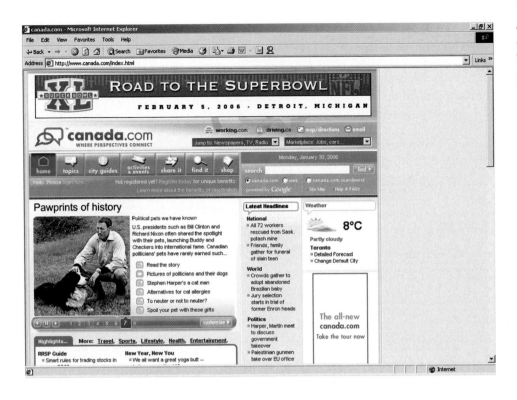

Advertisers may place their banner ad in a particular section of a portal website or purchase run-of-site advertising, which means their banner appears all over the site.

buy and sell online advertising, suggests several standard sizes for banner ads. Following these standards is a convenience for both the advertiser and the publisher: For the advertiser, it allows the same ad to be placed on multiple sites, and for the publisher, ads from different companies can be placed in the same spot.

When purchasing ad space on a website, advertisers can choose to have their ads displayed in a particular section of the site or they can purchase general "run of site" advertising. An advertiser may place its banner ad in a particular section of a website or purchase run-of-site advertising, which means its banner appears all over the site.

Text Links According to Lesley Wheldrake, marketing manager for MSN Canada, a typical Canadian conducts an average of 40 online searches a month.[13] With that kind of traffic, search sites like MSN, Google, and Yahoo! are finding that advertisers are increasingly interested in buying advertising space.

Online advertising on search engines usually takes the form of **text links** rather than graphics and banner ads. The advertiser purchases certain words or phrases, called keywords, and pays the search engine company to have its ad displayed whenever a visitor to the site searches for that keyword.

For example, a search on Google Canada for "new cars," where the user has specified that only results from Canada should be shown, would display a text link for GM Canada at the top of the list of search results and text links for Acura, Car Buying Tips, BMW Canada, and Mitsubishi on the right-hand side of the results window. Both of these sections of the page are identified as "sponsored links." In other words, they are identified as paid placement on the search engine, and differentiated from the regular, non-sponsored search engine listings that appear in the centre of the page.

Search engine marketing expert Dan Wiest, of Wiest & Associates Inc. in Georgetown, Ontario, notes that "We've been talking [as marketers] for decades about the right offer, at the right time, to the right person. [Search engine marketing] has got the added dimension of that very moment when that prospect happens to be wanting what it is you're offering."[14]

Text links A form of online advertising where an advertiser purchases words or phrases, called keywords, and pays the search engine company to have its ad displayed whenever a visitor to the site searches for that keyword.

Sponsored text links on Google.ca appear at the top of the list of search results and on the right-hand side of the window.

Sponsorships A form of Internet promotion where companies gain name exposure on the Internet by sponsoring special content on a website.

Interstitial A large, animated online advertisement that pops up onto the screen for several seconds.

Microsite A small website consisting of a few pages of detailed information about the marketer's goods or services.

Media kit A set of documents describing the advantages of advertising on a particular website, the number of site visitors and registered users, and the demographic, geographic, and psychographic characteristics of the site's audience.

Rate card The price list for advertising on a particular website.

Sponsorships **Sponsorships** are another form of Internet promotion where companies gain name exposure on the Internet by sponsoring special content on a website. For example, L'Oréal Paris sponsors the television show *Canadian Idol*, and its sponsorship includes placement on the *Canadian Idol* website. No other cosmetics marketer can advertise on the site during the time of the negotiated sponsorship.

Interstitials An **interstitial** is a large, animated ad that covers the user's screen for several seconds before "allowing" them to see the website content. In other words, an interstitial is similar to a television commercial. They may be placed anywhere on a website, though they typically interrupt the visitor briefly on the site's home page.

Microsites A **microsite** is a small website consisting of a few pages of detailed information about the marketer's goods or services. A microsite is built for a specific marketing purpose, and may be available for only a limited time. For example, when Mr. Clean Autodry was launched as a new product in 2004, its marketers created a microsite called "Save the Chammy" as a branding and promotional vehicle. The site told the story of the mythical chammy, a creature made from a soft fabric. The site indicated that the chammy was endangered because car owners were using them to polish their cars. Therefore the site implored consumers to save the chammy—by buying Mr. Clean Autodry.

Purchasing Online Advertising

Online advertising is bought and sold according to the specifications outlined in the media property's *media kit* and *rate card*. A **media kit** is a set of documents describing the advantages of advertising on a particular website, the number of site visitors and registered users, and the demographic, geographic, and psychographic characteristics of the site's audience. Advertisers consider this information when deciding which website to purchase advertising on. The **rate card** is the price list for that advertising.

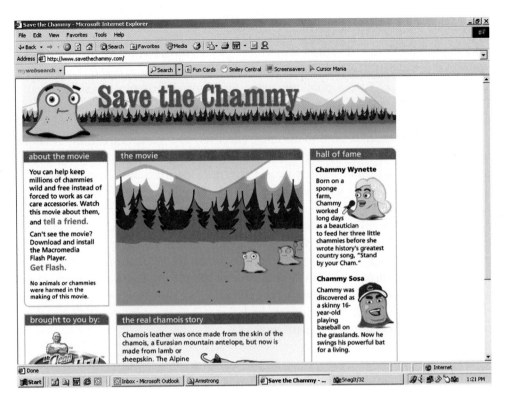

Procter & Gamble created a microsite called "Save the Chammy" for the launch of their new product, Mr. Clean Autodry.

There are three pricing models for selling online advertising:

CPM is a rate paid per thousand impressions of an online advertisement. Every time the advertisement is downloaded to a webpage, it is counted as one impression. Advertisers pay not per impression, but per thousand impressions. CPM rates range from $5 to $100, depending upon the value of the website's audience.

Cost-per-click is a pricing model in which the advertiser pays only when the advertisement is clicked on. Search engine advertising is usually purchased in this manner.

Sponsorships are sold on a per time, rather than a per impression, basis, and can take a variety of forms, from a simple icon on a webpage to site-wide coverage, such as what L'Oréal Paris has with *Canadian Idol*.

Linking the Concepts

Take a moment to think about your responses as a consumer to the various marketing functions a website can perform. Choose three websites that you visit regularly and visit them, but this time with an eye to the goals of the marketers behind them.

■ Do these sites sell online advertising to third parties, or do they use their site only to promote their own organization?

■ Is there content on the site that is of interest to you as a consumer?

■ How does the organization attempt to collect information from you as a site visitor, and what benefits does it offer in exchange for that information?

EMAIL MARKETING

Spam Email sent by unscrupulous individuals and organizations to a computer-generated list of email addresses.

Ethical, professional Internet marketers know that consumers who use email get a lot of spam messages. **Spam** is email sent by unscrupulous individuals and organizations to a computer-generated list of email addresses. Spam usually attempts to sell the naive consumer pornography, prescription medications, get-rich-quick-schemes, or phony university degrees.

As Internet marketers learn to use email effectively as a marketing communications tool, consumers are learning that there are benefits to receiving email messages from organizations—when they request it, and give the organization their permission to receive it. Email messages sent by marketers with the permission of the recipient are referred to as **permission marketing**, and it's a growing trend among marketers. According to an Ipsos-Reid report on Internet trends, in 2004 Canadians received an average of 177 email messages per week, 49 percent of which were spam. Though this percentage seems high, it dropped from 2003, when 68 percent of email messages received by the average Canadian consumer were spam.[15] As consumers increasingly give their permission to receive email, the gulf between legitimate email marketing and spam is becoming larger, and marketers look forward to the day when unscrupulous spammers no longer clutter the email landscape.

Permission marketing Email messages sent by marketers with the permission of the recipient.

Using Email Marketing

When used properly, e-mail can be the ultimate direct marketing medium. Blue-chip marketers such as Amazon.com, Schwab, Dell, L.L. Bean, and Office Depot use it regularly, and with great success. E-mail lets these marketers send highly-targeted, tightly personalized, relationship-building messages to consumers who actually *want* to receive them, at a cost of only a few cents per contact. E-mail ads really can command attention and get customers to act. ITM Strategies, a sales and marketing research firm, estimates that well-designed email campaigns typically achieve 10 to 15 percent click-through rates. That's pretty good when compared with the 0.5 to 2 percent average response rates for traditional direct mail.

There are many ways to use email to communicate to consumers about special offers or sales promotions. Cake Beauty customers who have signed up to be on the online mailing list receive email notices about new Cake products and special events. Customers of Amazon.com who have opted to receive special offers via email are sent a $5.00 coupon a few weeks before their birthday.

One company that uses email very effectively for promoting upcoming events is Ticketmaster, the ticket sales organization that sells tickets for local concerts and sporting events. Ticketmaster customers who purchase tickets online are given the option to sign up to receive email notifications of upcoming events in their city. Not only do these customers hear about events as soon as they are announced, but they receive special offers such as advance "best seats" ticket purchase, discount coupons, two-for-one offers, and similar preferred customer promotions.

It's not only consumer products marketers who use email marketing. Quarry Integrated Communications, of Waterloo, provides website design, advertising planning and execution, public relations, database and direct marketing, and other communications services to its business customers. One of these services is search engine optimization for small businesses. Search engine optimization is a consulting service that helps small businesses get their websites "found" on search engines, by carefully placing appropriate keywords into the body of their site's pages. Visitors to Quarry's website can request a free search engine optimization analysis, customized for their business.

The report is delivered to the customer in two stages. First, a thank-you email from Quarry's senior partner is sent. Attached to this email is a white paper—a general document describing the topic—on search engine optimization. The second email is delivered three business days later, and contains the customized report, describing what exactly the customer can do to its website to improve its search engine rankings.

Some organizations circulate a regular email *newsletter*—an email version of the familiar print newsletter. It may contain news items and articles as well as graphics and links. Registered users of *Chatelaine* magazine's website, for example, can sign up to receive a monthly email newsletter that briefly outlines what's new on the site and in the magazine that month.

"Kraft Kitchens" is the title of a regular email sent to registered users of the Kraft Canada website. It contains recipes and food preparation tips, and is sent every two weeks. The content of the email message is prepared by the marketing team at Kraft, and is carefully designed and structured so as to look professional, to represent the Kraft brand favourably, and, above all, to not be mistaken as spam. The email message is always identified as being from "Kraft Kitchens" and the subject line always begins with the words "What's Cooking," so that the person receiving the email knows who it's from and why they are receiving it. Most importantly, the bottom of every message includes an unsubscribe link which, if clicked, will automatically unsubscribe the recipient from the newsletter.

There are also a number of online services that automatically download customized information to recipients' computers. The *Globe and Mail*, for example, offers morning news headlines delivered to your email box each morning. It also offers a host of other online subscriptions—daily, weekly, and monthly news about politics, sports, or whatever you are interested in. And when the email message is delivered to you, it will identify the sender, encourage you to sign up for other services, and explain to you how to unsubscribe. It will also undoubtedly contain sponsorships or advertising.

Email lends itself quite easily to **viral marketing**, the Internet version of word-of-mouth marketing. Viral marketing involves creating an email message or other marketing event that's so infectious customers will want to pass it along to their friends. Because customers do the work, viral marketing can be very inexpensive. And when the information comes from a friend, the recipient is much more likely to open and read it. "The idea is to get your customers to do your marketing for you," notes a viral marketing expert.

For example, when seeking ways to get teenage girls to check out its Clean and Clear skin-care products, Johnson & Johnson created a microsite from which teens could send a "talking postcard" to their friends. The teens could design an email greeting card using graphics and easy-to-use design tools provided on the site. They could even call a phone number and dictate a short voice message that would be included with the greeting. Friends receiving the email message heard the recording through their computer's speakers, and when they played the message they were invited to click on a button called "Skin analyzer" that would link them to Clean and Clear's main website.[16]

Viral marketing can also work well for B2B marketers:

> To improve customer relationships, Hewlett-Packard sent tailored email newsletters to customers who registered online. The newsletters contained information about optimizing the performance of HP products and services. The newsletters also featured a button that let customers forward the newsletters to friends or colleagues. New recipients were then asked if they'd like to receive future HP newsletters themselves. In this textbook case of viral marketing, Hewlett-

Viral marketing The Internet version of word-of-mouth marketing—email messages or other marketing events that are so infectious that customers will want to pass them along to friends.

Packard inexpensively met its goal of driving customers to its website and ultimately increasing sales. "For those on our original email list, the click-through rate was 10 to 15 percent," says an HP executive. "For those who received it from a friend or colleague, it was between 25 and 40 percent."[17]

Rules of Email Marketing

When Internet marketers use email to deliver legitimate marketing messages, they must take great care to follow the rules of etiquette for email marketing so that their messages are not perceived as spam by the recipient or their Internet service provider's email filters.

Legitimate email marketing is sent only to those consumers who have asked to receive it. Most businesses offer some form of user registration on their websites, and ask permission of those who register to send them email. For example, consumers who purchase tickets online from Ticketmaster have the option of signing up to receive notices of future events that might interest them. And when these email offers are delivered there is often a discount or special deal, which is offered only to those customers who have subscribed. Air Canada offers its weekly sell-off seats only to those customers who have subscribed through its website to receive its Websaver email.

Seth Godin, author of the groundbreaking book *Permission Marketing*, believes that the worse the clutter in our email inboxes gets, the more profitable email marketing can be, if done correctly—that is, if sent only to those recipients who have asked to receive it.[18]

The Canadian Marketing Association (CMA), a professional trade association for companies that engage in direct marketing, has 800 corporate members. Members of the CMA are prohibited from sending "unsolicited commercial e-mail or spam to acquire new customers."[19]

The CMA strives to differentiate legitimate email marketing from spam, and says, "If you asked for it, it's not spam." They go on to say, "If you've signed up for a newsletter and no longer wish to receive it, just unsubscribe. Any legitimate organization will provide an easy way for you to be taken off their subscription list. However, be cautious when unsubscribing to a newsletter from an unknown organization. Some spammers masquerade as newsletters with 'unsubscribe information' that can serve to confirm that your e-mail is valid and cause you to receive even more spam."[20]

Professional Internet marketers must follow the rules of etiquette when it comes to email marketing, so as to be sure to differentiate their subscription-based, permission-based email messages from those sent by disreputable spammers.

Here are the rules:[21]

☐ *Send email only by permission.* The ethical email marketer never buys a list of email addresses. The ethical email marketer sends email messages only to those consumers who have subscribed to receive it.

☐ *Clearly identify the sender.* The name of the company must appear on the "from" line when the subscriber receives the email message.

☐ *Remind the recipient why they're receiving the message.* Every marketing message sent via email should include a brief note to remind the customer where and how they subscribed to receive it.

☐ *Provide an easy way to unsubscribe.* Ethical email marketers use complex software systems to manage the delivery and tracking of email campaigns sent to subscribers. Thousands, if not tens or hundreds of thousands of messages are sent simultaneously by the email management system. These systems also manage the subscribe/unsubscribe function automatically.

☐ *The default is always opt-in, never opt-out.* Subscribing to receive email offers typically involves checking a box on a Web form. If the box is pre-checked, and the user is forced to uncheck it in order to *not* receive email, that is called opting out. The smart Internet marketer knows that it's better to have the conscious permission of 100 consumers than to have tricked 1000 consumers; therefore, ethical email marketers always leave the box unchecked and allow consumers to opt in to receive email.

New Forms of Internet Marketing

It's only been a little longer than 10 years since marketers first began experimenting with the Internet as a marketing communications tool. The Web, email, and all the forms of e-commerce have provided new opportunities for sales, advertising, public relations, entertainment, information distribution, and customer transactions. New forms of Internet marketing and advertising are popping up nearly every day.

Online Movies

In 2001, BMW's advertising agency, Fallon Minneapolis, proposed a radical idea to its client. Instead of spending millions of dollars producing and airing television commercials, it decided to spend it producing short films featuring its client's products. Five well-known feature film directors, including Guy Ritchie and Ang Lee, were each commissioned to produce a seven-minute movie. They were given a budget but were free to hire any actors and create any storyline they wished. The only requirement was that a BMW car be, in some way, part of the story. British actor Clive Owen plays a character known only as The Driver in each film. The series of films is known collectively as The Hire.

The BMW Films website explains, "*The Hire* debuted in 2001, marking a new era in short films. Executive-produced by David Fincher and starring Clive Owen, this revolutionary series of short films brought the power and quality of feature-length movies to a format designed for the Internet."

Once produced, the movies were not aired on television as commercials, but rather were made available, for free, on a special website created by BMW. The movies themselves were unapologetically advertisements for BMW, but they were also entertaining. And rather than paying to see them in a theatre, people could simply visit the website and watch them online.

The success of BMW's online movies led other companies to experiment with this new form of Internet marketing. American Express produced a short, entertaining film called "Seinfeld and Superman," starring comedian Jerry Seinfeld interacting with a cartoon Superman. In the story, the two are friends. They eat at a diner, then go shopping for a DVD player for Jerry. As they are exiting the store a thief steals the box and runs off with it. Superman flies off to the rescue, chasing the thief, but when he catches him, the thief drops the box, breaking the DVD player. Jerry arrives on the scene and says it's a good thing he paid for it using his American Express card, because new purchases are insured. At the end of the "movie" visitors to the website are presented with links and encouraged to find out more about the benefits of an American Express card, and, if they wish, to fill out an application online.

Not to be outdone, in the fall of 2004 Amazon produced a series of short films known collectively as Amazon Theatre, and made a new one available on their home page once a week for six weeks. In one film titled "Tooth Fairy," actor Chris Noth plays a father who forgets to be the tooth fairy for his little girl. To teach him a lesson the daughter leaves a note under her pillow the next night, sending her father on an all-night scavenger hunt to find her tooth. She leaves clues such as "It's under something blue." After examining all the blue items in the house—a serving tray, coffee cups, picture frames—the father finally finds, under the dog's blue water dish, the next clue. At the end of the story the father collapses in bed, exhausted, only to have the clock alarm sound a moment later. During the escapade the father goes in and out of every room in the house, picking up items, sitting at his kids' drum set, even looking under the barbeque hood. As the credits roll we see not only the actors being credited, but all the items we saw in the film. Cookware: Calphalon Tri-Ply Stainless Cookware; Drum Set: Pulse Pro 5-Piece Drum Set; Barbeque: Weber Genesis Gold C Grill. And, of course, all the items are available for sale on Amazon.com.

Wireless and Podcasting

Internet communications allows the delivery of information via wired networks but also via wireless. Content publishers and advertisers are closely watching technology developments so that they may understand how to effectively send content and advertising to wireless devices such as telephones, PDAs, cameras, and personal music devices.

Google, currently the most popular Internet search engine and a major seller of advertising space, is building an international wireless network that will allow it to deliver content (search results) and advertisements to users through its wireless devices. Advertisers are especially interested in this technology because of the possibility of pinpointing the user's geographic location at the time the ad is sent.[22]

Podcasting Sending information to a consumer's iPod or other portable entertainment device.

The newest form of information and entertainment delivery via the Internet is **podcasting**. The word evolved from the combination of broadcasting and iPod, and refers to information sent to a consumer's iPod or other portable entertainment device. Described as "the aural equivalent of blogging, podcasting enables users of iPods and other portable listening devices to download shows and listen at their convenience."[23]

Podcasting is similar to broadcasting, in that entertainment providers, such as television and radio stations, create the content that will be "podcast." The CBC has made podcasts of some of its radio programs, and Toronto's CHUM-FM is podcasting its morning show, *Roger Rick & Marilyn*.

The technology and format of podcasting are in their very early stages, and yet marketers are already experimenting with ways to use it to promote their messages. Some possibilities are sponsored podcast content and branded podcast content. Marketers can also use the medium directly to produce their own podcasts. GM recently introduced a podcast called "Fastlane Radio," and Heineken podcast an interview with Italian DJ and personality Daniele Davoli, which included several subtle mentions of the beer brand.

Blogs

Blog A website that consists of regular date-stamped compositions written by an individual or a group of individuals and published online for the public to read.

The term *blog* is an abbreviation of web log. A **blog** is a website that consists of regular date-stamped compositions written by an individual or a group of individuals and published online for the public to read. Blogs are part journalism, part creative writing, part opinion commentary. They tend to be topical, focusing on technology, music, or culture. Many are simply personal diaries used by individuals to communicate with their friends and family.

Most importantly, a blog is a conversation between individuals or between groups. Blog readers post comments on entries, and bloggers respond to one another in their own blogs. Marketers who aspire to use the blog format to support their marketing communications must learn how to take part in this conversation.

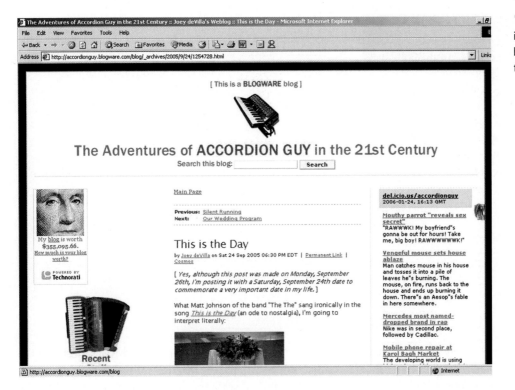

"The Adventures of Accordion Guy in the 21st Century" is a personal blog published online for the public to read.

In Canada, David Akin, a journalist for *CTV News* and *The Globe and Mail*, writes a blog called "David Akin's on the Hill: Working notes by a Canadian politics reporter." Canadian software company Tucows publishes a blog called "The Farm" for the community of programmers and developers who use its software. This blog serves the marketing communications function of communicating with customers and allowing customers to communicate with each other. Writing and updating The Farm is the full-time job of Joey DeVilla, who also writes a popular personal blog called "The Adventures of Accordion Guy in the 21st Century."

Dr. David Weinberger, co-author of *The Cluetrain Manifesto* and author of *Small Pieces Loosely Joined*, has this to say about the potential for blogs as marketing communications vehicles:

> Companies traditionally communicated with their markets by selectively releasing information about the company's products or services because the companies were the only source available to customers. Once the Web came along, customers quickly learned to find one another, and talk about products honestly, humorously and sometimes savagely. Blogs further that conversation and present a real marketing opportunity . . . but not for old-style, one-way messages. Businesses need to learn how to enter the conversation that's already going on, with a human and passionate voice. But it has to be real and not overly controlled. Otherwise this opportunity to build long-term relationships with customers will backfire.[24]

LEGAL AND ETHICAL ISSUES

From a broader societal viewpoint, Internet marketing practices have raised a number of ethical and legal questions. In previous sections, we've touched on some of the negatives associated with the Internet, such as email spam. Here we examine concerns about consumer online privacy and security and other legal and ethical issues.

IN-CLASS NOTES

Online Promotion Methods

- **Online advertising:** banners, text links, sponsorships, interstitials, microsites
- **Email direct response:** permission-based
- **Viral marketing:** word-of-mouth based
- **Online movies:** mini-movies as ads
- **Podcasting:** sending information to wireless devices
- **Blogging:** two-way dialogue

Online Privacy and Security

Online privacy is perhaps the number-one e-commerce concern. Most Internet marketers have become skilled at collecting and analyzing detailed information from online customers, visitors to their website, and subscribers to their permission marketing emails. Many consumers who participate in online activities provide extensive personal information to the websites with which they do business. Some consumers fear that this leaves them open to information abuse if companies make unauthorized use of that information. Many consumers and policymakers worry that marketers have stepped over the line and are violating consumers' right to privacy.[25] A recent survey found that seven out of ten consumers are concerned about online privacy. In response to these concerns, the Canadian government passed the *Personal Information Protection and Electronic Documents Act* in 2001. The act is based on four key principles:

☐ *Consumer knowledge and consent.* Consumers must know that information about them is being gathered and they must provide consent before firms can collect, use, or disclose consumers' personal information.

☐ *Limitations.* Firms can only collect and use information appropriate to the transaction being undertaken. For example, if a firm needs to mail you something, it can ask for your home address, but it may not request additional information unrelated to this task.

☐ *Accuracy.* Firms must be sure that the information they gather is recorded accurately. Firms must appoint a privacy officer to be responsible for this task.

☐ *Right to access.* Finally, individuals have the right to know what information is being held about them. They can also demand that errors in their personal information be corrected, and they may request that their personal information be withdrawn from a firm's database.

Ethical Internet marketers understand these consumer concerns, and guard the information they collect just as they guard any other confidential company data. Ethical—not to mention smart—marketers would never sell their consumer data because, as we learned in Chapter 5, customer information is extremely valuable. In fact, in 2005 former AOL employee Jason Smathers was first fired by the company, then sentenced to 15 months in prison for selling customers' email addresses to an unscrupulous individual who wanted to use them to send unsolicited spam promoting an online casino. The buyer of the customer data paid Smathers US$28 000 for the information. As part of his sentence, Smathers was ordered to pay $84 000 in restitution to his former employer.[26]

Many consumers also worry about *online security*. They fear that by engaging in online transactions they put their personal computer at risk of acquiring a virus, or worm, or other invasive software program. In turn, companies doing business online fear that hackers will invade their computer systems for the purposes of commercial espionage or even sabotage. There appears to be an ongoing competition between the technology of Internet security systems and the sophistication of those seeking to break them.

Today, most organizations have responded to consumer privacy and security concerns with actions of their own. Online customer registration forms, contest entry forms, and email subscription forms typically include links to the organization's privacy policy.

> RBC Financial has developed a progressive privacy policy to differentiate itself from competitors. For the past two years, the company has used some 15 different programs to show consumers that it strives to exceed government-mandated privacy regulations. For instance, the company is preparing to give away so-called personal firewall software to its online banking customers. RBC also delayed the rollout of wireless banking until it found a Nokia phone with a chip that allowed customers to encrypt passwords and other information. RBC has tried to quantify the effects of its privacy policies, relying on research suggesting that 7 percent of a customer's buying decision relates to privacy issues. Using that and other assumptions, RBC's privacy policies were responsible for $700 million worth of consumer banking business.[27]

Other Legal and Ethical Issues

Beyond issues of online privacy and security, consumers are also concerned about *Internet fraud*, including identity theft, investment fraud, and financial scams. There are also concerns about *segmentation and discrimination* on the Internet. Some social critics and policymakers worry about the so-called *digital divide*—the gap between those who have access to the latest Internet and information technologies and those who don't. They are concerned that in this information age, not having equal access to information can be an economic and social handicap. The Internet currently serves upscale consumers well. However, poorer consumers still have less access to the Internet, leaving them increasingly less informed about products, services, and prices.

It's not only online consumers who have concerns, or are vulnerable to unscrupulous online activities. An online retailer that accepts an order for a product, then ships the product only to find that the credit card used had been stolen, is out the value of the product, which will never be recovered. When the owner of the stolen credit card discovers the unauthorized charge the credit card company will reverse it, but no one reimburses the retailer that sold the goods.

Marketers of adult-oriented materials have found it difficult to restrict access by minors, and fall under criticism for "allowing" children to view inappropriate content. Online auction site eBay recently found itself the victim of a 13-year-old boy who had bid on and purchased more than $3 million worth of high-priced antiques and rare artworks on the site. eBay has a strict policy against bidding by anyone under age 18, but it works largely on the honour system. Unfortunately, this honour system did little to prevent the teenager from taking a cyberspace joyride.[28]

Despite these challenges, companies large and small are increasingly integrating the technology of the Internet into their marketing strategies and programs. As it continues to grow, online marketing will prove to be a powerful tool for building customer relationships, improving sales, communicating company and product information, and delivering products and services more efficiently and effectively.

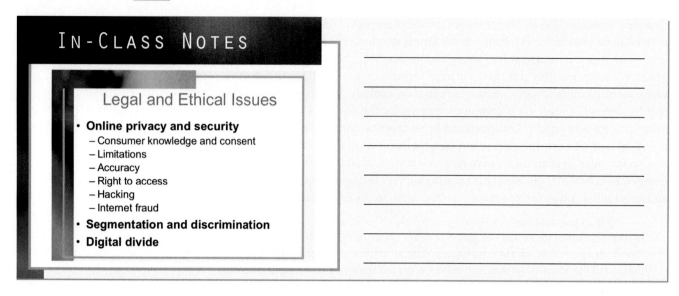

In-Class Notes

Legal and Ethical Issues

- **Online privacy and security**
  - Consumer knowledge and consent
  - Limitations
  - Accuracy
  - Right to access
  - Hacking
  - Internet fraud
- **Segmentation and discrimination**
- **Digital divide**

LOOKING BACK

In this chapter we saw how marketing on the Internet, just like marketing itself, is not one simple task or function, but rather is a set of strategies and plans that starts with a view to the market and the needs and wants of the customer. The Internet—the Web, email, e-commerce—provides the marketer with a high-tech set of tools with which to support the organization's marketing efforts.

REVIEWING THE CONCEPTS

1. Define the three areas of e-commerce and explain the benefits of e-commerce.

E-commerce includes all buying and selling processes supported by electronic means, primarily the Internet. Online banking, online retail, and online corporate purchasing or procurement are all forms of e-commerce. The three main types of e-commerce are B2B, which refers to electronic transactions that take place between businesses; B2C, which refers to electronic transactions that take place between businesses and consumers, such as when an individual buys cosmetics from Cake Beauty's website; and C2C, which refers to electronic transactions between consumers, such as on eBay's auction site.

E-commerce benefits both buyers and sellers. For buyers, e-commerce makes buying convenient and private, provides greater product access and selection, and makes available a wealth of product and buying information. It is interactive and immediate, and gives the consumer a greater measure of control over the buying process. For sellers, e-commerce is a powerful tool for building customer relationships. It also increases the sellers' speed and efficiency, helping to reduce selling costs. E-commerce also offers great flexibility and better access to global markets.

2. Describe the different ways a company can use its website to support its marketing communications programs.

The website is a key element in marketing on the Internet and can be used for a number of marketing functions. If a website includes e-commerce capabilities it serves as a *sales channel* where consumers or other businesses can buy the company's products or services online. For companies that sell their products and services online, the website is used not only as a sales channel but also to communicate information about those products to consumers. All websites are, in one way or another, performing some *marketing communications* function. For organizations that cannot sell their products online, one marketing communications strategy is to use the website to bring the customer as close to the sale as possible. The website can also be used for *public relations* and *sales promotions*. Most corporate websites provide some contact information for customers, but for some marketers the focus of the website is *customer service*. Web communities take advantage of the C2C properties of the Internet. Such sites allow members to congregate online and exchange views on issues of common interest. *Content websites* are those provided by Web publishers such as Yahoo!, Sympatico/MSN, and Canada.com. Much like newspapers and magazines, content sites provide information in the form of text and graphics, and consumers visit these sites to read about news, sports, entertainment, and the weather. Finally, some websites are *services* in and of themselves. They do not operate any retail stores or manufacturing operations; their websites *are* their business.

3. Differentiate between Web publishers and Web advertisers, and define the major forms of online advertising.

A Web publisher is a content website whose main purpose is to provide information, such as news, sports, and entertainment, to the public—as opposed to focusing on selling or promoting products. Yahoo!, Sympatico/MSN, CNN.com, and GlobeAndMail.com are all Web publishers. Web publishers typically sell online advertising to Web advertisers such as Nissan, Weight Watchers, La Senza, and RONA. The most common forms of online advertising are *banner ads*, small graphical ads that are embedded into the content of a webpage, much like a display ad in a newspaper; text links, which are typically the form of advertising sold by search engine companies; *sponsorships*, which can take many different forms and are negotiated between a major advertiser and the Web publisher; *interstitials*, which are animated ads that appear on the screen in a manner similar to a television commercial; and *microsites*, which are small, temporary marketing websites built for the purpose of a sales promotion or new product launch.

4. Outline how email can be used for marketing and list the rules of email etiquette for online marketers.

E-mail allows marketers to send highly targeted, tightly personalized, relationship-building messages to consumers who actually *want* to receive them, at a cost of only a few cents per contact. Email can be used to communicate to consumers about special offers, sales promotions, or upcoming events. Some organizations circu-

late a regular email *newsletter*—an email version of the familiar print newsletter. It may contain news items, articles, as well as graphics and links. There are also a number of online services that automatically download customized information to recipients' PCs. Email also lends itself quite easily to viral marketing, the Internet version of word-of-mouth marketing.

Professional Internet marketers must follow the rules of etiquette for email marketing so that their permission-based email messages are not mistaken for spam by the recipients. The most important rule of email marketing is to send mail only by permission to those individuals who have actively requested it. Permission is typically sought on the marketer's website. The sign-up form must always allow the subscriber to opt in rather than trying to trick them into opting out. When an email message is sent to the list of subscribers, the sender's identity must be clearly stated on the "from" line. Email etiquette for marketers suggests that reminding the recipient why they're receiving the message will help to differentiate it from spam. Finally, ethical email marketers always include unsubscribe instructions with every message.

5. Describe the new forms of Internet marketing.

Internet marketers are constantly experimenting with new forms of online promotion and advertising that will capture the attention of the market. Online movies such as BMW Films combine the format of a television commercial with the longer, story-based form of a movie, and also combine entertainment with advertising. Internet marketers are also closely watching technology developments so that they may understand how to effectively send content and advertising to wireless devices such as telephones, PDAs, cameras, and personal music devices. Podcasting refers to information sent to a consumer's iPod or other portable entertainment device. Content publishers who create and deliver these podcasts may also sell advertising on this media. Finally, blogs are a new form of online communication that are part journalism, part creative writing, part opinion commentary. Marketers are struggling to understand how to use the blog format to support their marketing communications.

6. Outline the legal and ethical issues involved in Internet marketing.

Internet marketing practices have raised a number of ethical and legal questions. Because marketers can easily track website visitors, and many consumers who participate in website activities provide extensive personal information, online privacy is perhaps the number-one e-commerce concern. In response to privacy concerns, the Canadian government passed the *Personal Information Protection and Electronic Documents Act* in 2001.

Many consumers also worry about *online security*. They fear that unscrupulous snoopers will eavesdrop on their online transactions or intercept their credit card numbers and make unauthorized purchases. Companies doing business online fear that others will use the Internet to invade their computer systems for the purposes of commercial espionage or even sabotage. Consumers are also concerned about *Internet fraud*, including identity theft, investment fraud, and financial scams. There are also concerns about *segmentation and discrimination* on the Internet. Some social critics and policy makers worry about the so-called digital divide—the gap between those who have access to the latest Internet and information technologies and those who don't. A final Internet marketing concern is that of *access by vulnerable or unauthorized groups*.

KEY TERMS

business-to-business (B2B)
  e-commerce   *519*
business-to-consumer (B2C)
  e-commerce   *519*
banner ads   *531*
blog   *540*
consumer-to-consumer (C2C)
  e-commerce   *519*

e-business   *518*
e-commerce   *519*
Internet marketing   *518*
interstitial   *534*
media kit   *534*
microsite   *534*
permission marketing   *536*
podcasting   *540*

portal website   *529*
rate card   *534*
search engine   *530*
spam   *536*
sponsorships   *534*
text links   *533*
viral marketing   *537*
Web publisher   *530*

STUDY GUIDE

After completing this self-test, check your answers against the Answer Key at the back of the book.

MULTIPLE CHOICE

1. One of the key benefits that tempts manufacturers to disintermediate traditional channels by selling directly online is that e-commerce can
    a. Allow manufacturers to reduce inventory levels
    b. Eliminate middleman margins, allowing either an increase in profits or a reduction in the selling price
    c. Adjust pricing levels quickly up or down
    d. Guard against disloyal retailers
    e. Build brand awareness directly with consumers

2. Which traditional direct-response promotion method has made the transition to the online world best?
    a. Telemarketing
    b. Banner advertising
    c. Cataloguing
    d. Personal selling
    e. Virtual testing

3. Many manufacturers and retailers choose not to sell online for a number of reasons. One of the main reasons is to
    a. Avoid the higher pricing usually found in online selling
    b. Avoid the cost of maintaining a customer database
    c. Avoid alienating the channel partners that often own the customer relationships
    d. Avoid gaining a reputation for sending annoying spam and pop-ups
    e. Avoid the high costs of maintaining an e-commerce capability

4. Companies like DeWalt, a maker of professional-grade power tools are careful not to sell online. However, DeWalt does help both itself and Home Depot sell more product by
   a. Keeping retail prices as low as possible
   b. Maintaining competition between Home Depot and other hardware retailers
   c. Using online advertising heavily to drive customers to Home Depot
   d. Providing a marketing website loaded with product information
   e. None of the above

5. The Body Shop provides a wide array of pre-created gift sets. Were the Body Shop to add a feature that allowed the customer to choose the basket itself and then load it from a selection of available products, the Body Shop would have added _____ to its e-commerce offerings.
   a. Customization
   b. Individuality
   c. Collaborative filtering
   d. Cookie settings
   e. Virtual promotion

6. A company purchases several keywords on Google and provides a small ad when a Google user searches on one of the keywords. When the Google user clicks on the ad, he is taken to a special website containing a few pages with in-depth product information. This company has used _____ and _____ as part of their Internet marketing plan.
   a. Banner ads and marketing sites
   b. Subscriptions and micro sites
   c. Interstitials and marketing sites
   d. Text links and interstitials
   e. Text links and microsites

7. Blogs offer a major opportunity for marketers to establish deeper customer relationships. However, leveraging blogs correctly may be difficult for most traditional marketers because
   a. Blogging is technology unstable
   b. Blogging is effective only if it's controlled by customers
   c. Blogging tends to be too politically charged
   d. Blogging is particularly vulnerable to privacy abuses
   e. Customers continue to value online anonymity

8. Phishing is a new Internet abuse whereby criminals trick people into providing online ID numbers and passwords. Phishing is an example of _____,

a growing problem as the popularity of e-commerce increases.
   a. Digital dividing
   b. Right to access
   c. Internet fraud
   d. Spamming
   e. Webcasting

9. What is the actual value to a company when it goes to the trouble of publishing an extensive privacy policy on its website?
   a. It protects the company from certain legal liabilities
   b. It sends a clear message to employees about the importance of protecting customer information
   c. It informs customers about how their personal information will be used and protected
   d. It helps establish the company's attitudes toward social responsibility and ethical behaviours
   e. All of the above

10. The meteoric rise in the purchase of _____ is a clear signal that many online advertisers need to rethink their approaches.
    a. Spam, banner, and pop-up blockers
    b. Anti-virus software
    c. Blogging tools
    d. Cookie traps
    e. Dynamic HTML

True/False

T   F   1. Peer-to-peer computing, which allows Internet users to share files such as music files, is an example of consumer-to-consumer e-business.

T   F   2. Due to the mass communications aspect of the Internet, e-commerce does not lend itself well to building stronger customer relationships.

T   F   3. The Internet is an effective business leveller, allowing smaller companies to appear larger and compete more successfully online with larger companies.

T   F   4. For greatest effect, a company's Internet-based marketing strategy should be planned and executed separately from the rest of the company's marketing mix.

T   F   5. To be successful, any website must incorporate each of the 7 Cs of effective website design.

CONCEPT CHECK

1. The three forms of e-commerce are _____, _____, and _____. Cake Beauty's website is an example of _____ e-commerce.

2. Internet buying benefits both final buyers and sellers in many ways. It is _____; buying is _____ and _____; buyers have greater _____ and _____; channels give comparative information; and online buying is interactive and immediate.

3. A website's ability to tailor itself to different users or to allow users to personalize the site is called _____.

4. When an organization publishes press releases on its website, this is an example of _____, which is a form of traditional marketing communications.

5. A _____ is a large, comprehensive, general interest, public website that typically offers news, sports, and weather information.

6. Frequently used forms of online advertising are _____, _____, _____, _____, and _____.

7. Online advertising on search engines usually takes the form of _____, rather than graphics and banner ads.

8. A _____ is a form of email marketing sent on a regular basis to registered members of a website who have subscribed to it.

9. The Internet version of word-of-mouth marketing, usually sent via email, is referred to as _____.

10. A _____ is a popular new form of personal, Internet-based communication that is part journalism, part creative writing, and part opinion commentary.

STUDENT MATERIALS

Visit our website at www.pearsoned.ca/armstrong for online quizzes, Internet exercises, and more!

NOTES

_____

_____

_____

_____

_____

_____

_____

_____

_____

_____

_____

_____

_____

_____

_____

_____

_____

_____

_____

_____

_____

_____

_____

DISCUSSING THE ISSUES

1. Visit the Cake Beauty website (www.cakebeauty.com). How many of the 7 Cs of effective Web design are evident on the site? Explain how each "C" is used. If there are any Cs that have not been used, can you think of a way for them to be incorporated?

2. Choose your favourite portal website and explore its various sections. What forms of online advertising are sold on the site? Choose three ads from three different advertisers on the site, and explain why each company chose to advertise on that part of the portal.

3. Describe the differences in e-commerce sites between a B2B marketer such as Cisco Systems and a B2C marketer such as La Senza. Dell is a company that markets its products both to businesses and consumers. How does its e-commerce website serve these two separate markets?

4. Write a short email marketing message for RONA Hardware. Be sure to follow the rules of email marketing etiquette. If you were the online marketing manager at RONA, to whom would you send this message?

MARKETING APPLICATIONS

Maestro is an upscale seafood restaurant and oyster bar on trendy St. Lawrence Street in Montreal. The clientele of the restaurant is mainly tourists, especially during the summer season, but there are also many regular customers who return again and again because they enjoy the food and the atmosphere, and because they have an oyster shell with their name on it installed on the oyster wall of fame.

The chef is famous for his unique and flavourful seafood sauces, and customers often ask whether they can purchase these sauces to take home. Responding to market demand, the owner has recently begun packaging and retailing a line of Maestro sauces, such as Havane sauce for tuna, and Porto & Raspberry sauce, which is excellent with mussels.

Maestro has only one location, and, so far, has sold its sauces only from within the restaurant. The business has never had a website, but lately the owner has been wondering whether some form of Internet marketing might help grow her business.

THINKING LIKE A MARKETING MANAGER

1. Taking into consideration the 7 Cs of effective Web design, outline a proposal for a website for Maestro. Would you recommend that the owner include e-commerce capabilities on the site? Explain why or why not.

2. Maestro has never done any mass media advertising, but the owner has been informed that some forms of Internet advertising are within the price range of a small business. Investigate possible websites on which Maestro could run an online ad. Find the website's media kit and rate card to determine whether the price of advertising on this site would be feasible for Maestro.

3. Describe how Maestro could use email marketing to promote and grow its business.

VIDEO CASE

Go to Pearson Canada's Video Central site (www.pearsoned.ca/highered/videocentral) to view the video and accompanying case for this chapter.

CASE 13 CARS DIRECT: SHAKING UP THE COMPETITION

Not long ago, buying a car was an onerous task. When consumers visited a dealership, they were at a disadvantage. Not only did they have little information, they also couldn't negotiate. Because consumers buy cars infrequently, few develop strong negotiation skills and most forget what they learned the last time.

Even consumers who took the time and effort to gather information and who were skillful negotiators found the process long and tedious. They visited the car lot, haggled with the salesperson, and then haggled more with the business manager over financing. The process could take hours, even days. At the end, many consumers believed that they had been taken advantage of by the dealer, who had all the power.

Then along came the Internet, which let consumer-oriented organizations distribute information freely and easily. Consumer Reports at www.consumerreports. org, AutoSite at www.autosite.com, Car and Driver at www.caranddriver.com, Kelley Blue Book at www.kbb.com, and Edmund's at www.edmunds.com quickly set up websites offering performance, pricing, and dealer information to people in the market for a new car. Carforums.com even offered model-specific chat rooms so that people could talk with one another about their cars and car problems.

Although helping consumers get more information was fine, savvy e-commerce entrepreneurs saw that the Internet offered a way to begin to change the car-buying process itself. Autobytel at www.autobytel.ca was one of the first companies to offer car-buying assistance. Other companies, such as Cost Finder Canada at www. costfindercanada.com, AutoConnect at www.autoconnect.com, AutoWeb at www. autoweb.com, and AutoVantage at www.autovantage.com quickly followed. In fact, analysts estimated that more than 100 automotive websites were offering some type of car-shopping help. Autobytel and similar services signed up dealers who agreed to participate and pay fees for referrals. The sites helped consumers identify dealers in their areas who had the cars they were seeking. The services would either notify the dealer about an interested consumer or simply let the consumer know where to find the dealer. Some sites allowed consumers to submit electronic, no-haggle bids to dealers. The consumer still had to visit the dealer to conclude the negotiations and take possession of the car, however.

It was only a matter of time before some bold entrepreneur took the next logical step. As a result of having gone through the traditional car-buying process himself, Internet entrepreneur Bill Gross realized there had to be a better way. Gross had previously founded the Pasadena, California–based Internet incubator Idealab!, which had already spawned such companies as eToys, GoTo.com, and Free-PC. Gross and other investors, including Michael Dell of Dell Computer, established CarsDirect. com at www.carsdirect.com.

Rather than just serving as an electronic intermediary, CarsDirect actually closes the sale and delivers the car to the consumer. A consumer visiting the CarsDirect website finds a simple, three-step process to follow. First, the site guides the consumer through the process of selecting the vehicle. Using information and guidance that the site provides, consumers can choose from a complete selection of production vehicles available in the United States. Consumers who want a specialty vehicle, such as a Ferrari, or who don't find the vehicle they are seeking, can e-mail the company directly. A service advisor contacts them within 24 hours.

Once a consumer selects a car, CarsDirect negotiates with the 1700 dealers in its network to find it. CarsDirect tries to set a price for the consumer that is in the bottom 10 percent of the market price range for the particular vehicle. Its substantial buying power allows CarsDirect to get the vehicle from the dealer at an even lower price, then make a profit on the difference between what it pays the dealer and what it charges the consumer. One dealer reported selling 53 cars to CarsDirect in three months. Selling to CarsDirect lowers the dealer's costs because the dealer doesn't have to pay the sales commission it would normally pay to salespeople.

Having found a car and set a price, CarsDirect offers the car to the consumer. Consumers can lock in the price by making a fully refundable $50 deposit. They can pay cash; use their own financing, such as through a local bank; or select a lease or loan package that CarsDirect.com offers. Consumers who want to use a CarsDirect financing package can fill out an application online.

Finally, the consumer decides how to take delivery. The company offers consumers the option of going to a local CarsDirect Priority Dealer to pick up the vehicle. Or, depending on where they live and the vehicle purchased, CarsDirect will deliver the vehicle to a consumer's home or office. (In Los Angeles, CarsDirect delivery trucks display the slogan "Cars Delivered Fresh Daily.") No matter which option consumers select, they will be able to inspect their vehicles, find out about service options, and ask questions.

CarsDirect was the first company to offer the consumer the opportunity to purchase a vehicle, finance the purchase, and take delivery without ever leaving home. Based on the initial success of the concept, CarSmart.com opened up a used channel in late 2001 to sell high-quality used vehicles through a selective dealer network.

In mid-2002 CarSmart.com was identified by *Time* magazine as one of their 50 Best Web Sites, and *Forbes Magazine* recognized CarSmart.com as Forbes' Favorite for online car buying. Notwithstanding the accolades, as in many industries, consolidation has become a survival strategy—and the online car business is not immune to the pressures of the e-commerce marketplace. CarsDirect.com is now a unit of Autobytel Inc., the organization that now owns and operates the major automobile sales sites on the Internet, namely, Autobytel.com, Autoweb.cam, CarSmart.com, and A.I.C (Automotive Information Centre), a provider of automotive marketing data and technology for manufacturers and dealerships. Combined, these sites are responsible for $17 billion in sales (approximately 4 percent of total North American new car sales), represent 8900 dealers, and attract 3.5 million unique visitors.

We could surmise then that in the short term, the online concept is working. But where are the manufacturers in this? Although Ford and DaimlerChrysler allow you to custom build and price your new car, the websites continue to refer buyers to dealers.

However, several companies are experimenting with e-commerce car-buying strategies in foreign markets. GM is testing strategies in Taiwan, where it already sells 10 percent of its vehicles via the Internet. It began building cars to order in 2000. Ford has set up a seamless e-commerce system in the Philippines that links consumers, dealers, Ford, and its suppliers. Meanwhile, Autobytel has moved into Europe. There, European Union laws enable manufacturers to restrict new car sales to captive dealers. Such laws have led to inflated prices in many markets, as much as 25 percent higher on average than in the United States. When this exemption expires in 2002, Autobytel hopes to be able to offer direct sales over the Internet.

Where will this lead? No one's sure. An analyst for one company argues that, "All [CarsDirect has] is motivated salespeople in a call centre" who try to get dealers to sell cars for less than CarsDirect's customer is paying. Other analysts note that online advertising impressions grew 136 percent from May 2001 to May 2002 and that 94 percent of consumers who started looking for a car in March 2002 went online for price quotes, dealer locations, and model information. However, CarsDirect and other online vehicle retailers face restrictive state franchise laws, some of which ban Internet sales. They also face political and legal actions by some of the 20 000 established dealers and complicated ordering systems by which automakers require dealers to take unwanted cars to get hot-selling models.

Finally, CarsDirect has proven that some consumers will make a five-figure purchase over the Internet without having seen the car. However, some analysts still wonder: Are there enough such consumers out there for CarsDirect to become profitable?

Questions

1. How do customers and CarsDirect each benefit from online marketing?

2. Outline CarsDirect's marketing strategy. What problems do you see with its strategy?

3. What marketing recommendations would you make to CarsDirect? Specifically, how can CarsDirect get more people to visit its site and purchase cars using its service?

4. What advantages or disadvantages will CarsDirect and its competitors face in foreign markets? How are Canadian auto dealers preparing for the entry of firms like CarsDirect?

5. What ethical issues does CarsDirect face? How should it deal with those issues?

Sources: www.carsdirect.com; Edward Harris, "Web Car-Shopping Puts Buyers in Driver's Seat," *The Wall Street Journal,* April 15, 1999, p. B10; Daniel Taub, "Firm Proves People Are Ready to Buy Cars on the Web," *Los Angeles Business Journal,* August 23, 1999, p. 5; John Couretas, "CarsDirect Tops Online Buying List from Gomez," *Automotive News,* September 20, 1999, p. 10; Fara Warner, "Internet Auto Retailer CarOrder.com Receives Funds to Acquire Dealerships," *The Wall Street Journal,* September 29, 1999, p. B2; Tim Burt, "Autobytel to Push Online Car Sales in Europe," *Financial Times,* October 8, 1999, p. 30; Fara Warner, "New Tactics Shake up Online Auto Retailing," *The Wall Street Journal,* October 18, 1999, p. B1; and Fara Warner, "GM Tests E-Commerce Plans in Emerging Markets," *The Wall Street Journal,* October 25, 1999, p. B6, *eMarketer Daily,* Issue 110, 2002.

COMPREHENSIVE CASE

Canadian marketing features many David and Goliath stories, but one that's emerging as a true battle of the small and nimble against the international established giants is the story of Cake Beauty. Toronto-based Heather Reier developed the company and its products literally from scratch, whipping up trial versions of products in her kitchen. After the company's launch in 2001, the newborn firm racked up amazing sales that increased 42 percent over the first year of operations. Today, the products are sold in trendy boutiques, beauty bars, spas, and department stores across Canada and the U.S. and in selected outlets in Australia, the U.K., Europe, and Hong Kong. The products can also be purchased from numerous e-commerce sites, as well as from the company's own website (www.cakebeauty.com).

THE BIRTH AND HISTORY OF CAKE

Cake evolved from Reier's passion for beauty products and her astute observations of the beauty market. As a consumer of many of the best-known brands and products, she observed that a hole existed in the market. If you were a knowledgeable, informed consumer, you had two choices: very expensive apothecary-style products or mass-produced lines that were well-packaged but full of cheap filler ingredients. There were absolutely no sassy, fun, affordable products with decadent ingredients and sophisticated packaging.

Reier believed that many women would appreciate high-quality, luxurious products with a sense of fun. And so, drawing on her background operations in retail at Roots, she decided to create the products herself and test the market for her idea. She devoted the majority of her spare time to researching ingredients that would deliver both physical and emotional benefits and to developing products with incredible textures and delicious scents. Her original plant was her kitchen, and her original equipment often consisted of only her blender. Her first product was a winner—a whipped, fluffy concoction called Supreme Body Mousse that is today a hallmark of Cake Beauty.

After many test batches, Reier soon had a sampling of what she felt was a superior line. Her next task was to study the competition, particularly their pricing and distribution. Armed with unique products, a vision, some guerrilla marketing strategies, and boundless enthusiasm, Cake was launched simultaneously in Canada and the United States in August 2001.

DESIGNING A CUSTOMER-DRIVEN MARKETING STRATEGY

Reier's first step in developing a customer-driven marketing strategy was to define the market segment to be served. But instead of embarking on expensive and time-consuming consumer research for developing a target market framework, she used her feel for the market, product knowledge, and experience. And as her products continue to gain acceptance, Reier personally researches users and retailers alike to determine shifts in consumer profiles and tastes.

Cake's target market includes professional working women aged 18 to 34 who demonstrate mid-range spending habits on beauty products ($18 to $38 per product). Cake customers demand quality and keep up with trends, but they're smart with their money. They may own one Louis Vuitton bag, but they shop at Winners. These women can be classified as beauty junkies and social butterflies, but they're also intelligent, health-conscious, and informed.

Cake sets itself apart from the competition by positioning itself as indulgent, trendy, and fun. Another important point of difference is that Cake uses nourishing key ingredients throughout the entire collection. It doesn't try to compete directly with the industry giants like Olay and L'Oréal—in fact, Cake's limited distribution in carefully chosen outlets adds to its trendy, exclusive image.

The Marketing Program

In order to establish Cake as a must-have brand, Reier had to create an outstanding product. She did this by using such premium ingredients as mango and shea butters, marshmallow, turbinado sugar, jojoba and coconut oils, and whole milk. Cake started small, with a product line of 12 items, including Milk Made Velveteen Hand Creme, Cake Walk Triplemint Foot Creme, Citrus Squeeze Sinfully Smooth Brown Sugar Scrub, and Desserted Island Body Mousse. As the brand became more well known, new products were added to the line. Reier recognized that future growth would be contingent on a stream of appealing new products focused on the same target markets. As a result, research and development was increased substantially with the objective of creating numerous innovative new products.

In the interest of maintaining the high quality that is the essence of the brand, production has been expanded to include multiple manufacturers. In this way, each stock-keeping unit (sku) is produced by a different manufacturer with a demonstrated expertise in that specific product. The strategy also insulated the new company from potential competition. No single manufacturer would be able to re-create the entire product line and become a rival to Cake.

Also important was the branding of the company and its products. The company name itself, Cake, was chosen to capture the self-indulgence and decadence of the products. Furthermore, each item in the product line was cleverly named to "reflect the scent, texture, and overall experience that women would encounter when they used the product."

Packaging innovations have also been used to promote the brand. In 2004, Cake realized that the original packaging did not reflect the high-quality ingredients and luxurious textures of the products, nor did the original logo showcase the name of the brand. As a result, the entire Cake collection was repackaged, rebranded, and then relaunched. The new packaging complemented the brand's prestige, with silkscreen printing on bottles, bows and hang tags, and boxes for selected products. The new logo and packaging created a product line with a better merchandising presence at the store level and a more memorable appeal for consumers. As well, late 2004 saw the launch of boxed sets containing multiple products and suitable for gift giving.

Cake's pricing strategy reflects the status and quality of the brand. Its prices are considerably higher than those of drugstore brands, but competitive with other trendy brands such as Jaqua and Philosophy.

Much of Cake's success is a result of its clever promotional strategies. Reier's first marketing package, which she sent to 100 Canadian and U.S. retailers, built on the Cake name in a unique, innovative, but cost-effective way—each package included a birthday candle. And knowing that she couldn't build the company on her own, Reier hired publicists in Toronto and New York who generated news stories about the company and its products in trendy magazines.

In 2002 Cake received some major recognition from one of Hollywood's hottest stars. Kate Hudson tried the products and subsequently had her assistant order a multitude of them to send out as Christmas presents for her friends. This generated an incredible amount of publicity, with magazines such as *InStyle* and *Cosmopolitan* featuring Hudson's favourite Cake products. That same year, Cake was featured on *Oprah* during a show titled "Destressing Your Life" in which noted life coach Martha Beck appeared as a guest. Later in 2002 Cake was invited to be part of a VH1 "Save the Music Foundation" event in Las Vegas featuring such superstar divas as Cher, Mary J. Blige, The Dixie Chicks, and Céline Dion.

Providing products for the gift bags handed out to headliners at such events gets Cake products into the hands of more celebrities, leading to opportunities for further promotion. In the past few years, Cake has earned public praise from such stars as Debra Messing of *Will & Grace* and Rachel Bilson of *The O.C.* This priceless publicity, combined with ongoing, timely product and promotion announcements through the press, continues to provide reinforcement for the brand's positioning while supporting Cake's retail partners.

In the initial launch stages, Reier concentrated on executing an exclusive distribution strategy targeted at niche beauty boutiques with a cult following. This focus on retail industry innovators was instrumental in establishing Cake as a must-have brand. The goal was to create a positive image with these retailers and their trendy customers and create a positioning for Cake synonymous with quality, fashion, and flair.

By the beginning of 2003, with 2002 year-end sales showing an increase of 150 percent over the previous year, the original distribution and positioning objectives had been achieved and the next stage of Cake's expansion was implemented. The overriding distribution strategy remained exclusive, but was expanded from smaller boutiques to include larger retailers such as Caban and Holt Renfrew.

The final stage in Cake's aggressive growth strategy was international expansion—and so in 2004 it was launched in Australia and Hong Kong. In 2005 Cake introduced its products in Europe. Eventually, it also intends to expand into China, Japan, Singapore, Thailand, and the Philippines.

BUILDING RELATIONSHIPS

Reier values her relationships with Cake customers. The staff at Cake "nurture all of [their] relationships and believe that this personal touch and attention to detail is what sets [them] apart." Hand-written notes are attached to products, special cake boxes are available for gifts, and if a customer decides she doesn't like the flavour of her Cake product, it can be returned. And with the launch of the online shopping boutique on the Cake website in 2003, Cake was able to provide customers with direct access to their favourite products.

Cake has also built relationships with numerous marketing partners. It holds promotions in the retail outlets where its products are sold—sometimes with Reier making an appearance. Cake has also partnered with Rethink Breast Cancer, a Toronto-based, forward-thinking organization with a trendy and fashionable approach to fighting the battle against breast cancer. As well, Cake nurtures its relationships with the media: When the brand was repackaged and relaunched in 2004, Reier, along with key marketing personnel, met with editors and writers from 40 fashion, beauty, and lifestyle magazines in Canada and the United States for desk-side briefings. This allowed Cake to establish personal relationships with members of the media and resulted in more than 15 editorial pieces on Cake Beauty.

MOVING FORWARD

Heather Reier and Cake have demonstrated the ability to succeed in the face of heavy competition, an aging demographic, and a shifting retail environment. The formula for this success is built on unique products for a well-defined target market, a well-conceived distribution strategy, and a necessary ingredient in many successful enterprises—luck.

Can the success continue? Cake's primary promotional thrust is through marketing and public relations, whereas the industry giants are some of Canada's largest advertisers. For example, Procter & Gamble, perennially listed among the top five advertisers in Canada, heavily advertises its Olay brand. Another rival is L'Oréal, an international giant named Canadian Marketer of the Year in 2003 by *Marketing* magazine. Although Cake only indirectly competes with product offerings from these companies, they remain a force in the industry.

Reier wants to continue to grow the company, but her options seem somewhat limited. Based on available data, she believes that major volume gains, at least in North America, are available only by expanding distribution. However, if she moves the products into department stores and retail drug stores, she'll face intense competition and risk losing the sense of exclusivity associated with her products.

Smaller organizations like Cake that operate in a global environment also run the risk of spreading their resources too thinly. Growth takes a lot of resources, and cash flow can be an issue. Cake's recent expansion into Asian and Australian markets may put additional pressure on this entrepreneurial organization. In addition, Reier has to wonder if new product research and development targeted at North American consumers will be applicable to consumer needs in international markets. She isn't sure she can afford the extra market research or product development efforts required to tailor products specifically to foreign markets.

Cake's responses to these challenges are detailed in the marketing plan that follows.

QUESTIONS

1. Go to Cake's website (**www.cakebeauty.com**) and review the information available on the company, including product lines, products, and availability. Compare and contrast this information with the site of an industry giant such as Olay (**www.olay.com/en_ca/docs/homepage/olay.htm**) or L'Oréal (**www.lorealparis.ca/en/skincare/index_frame.asp**). In this context, what can you define as Cake's competitive advantage? Support your answer.

2. Based on the previous analysis, go to the websites of Dessert (**www.dessertbeauty.com**), Philosophy (**www.philosophy.com**), Jaqua Girls (**www.jaquabeauty.com**), and Bliss (**www.blissworld.com**). Compare and contrast the product offerings and brand promises of these Cake competitors. Are their products directly competitive? If so, what competitive advantage does Cake have over these brands? If not directly competitive, are there any product lines that match up with those of Cake? Does Cake have a competitive advantage in these lines?

3. Analyze Cake's distribution strategy to this point in its history. Did it make sense to expand internationally before its Canadian and overall North American distribution strategy was fully executed? Support your answer.

4. In analyzing these various websites and possibly doing some in-store research on retailers carrying these products, can you define a precise target market for these

products? Justify your answer using such demographic criteria as age, income level, and occupation.

5. We know that Cake has done well with minimal advertising support. If it's been so successful using public relations and marketing to create a loyal following of consumers, why don't the large organizations significantly reduce their advertising spending and use the same tactics?

6. Based on your previous analyses, what would you recommend as the next new product or product line to be launched by Cake? Support your answer.

Sources: L. Zilke, "From A to Zilke, Cosmetics," Canada.com News, September 24, 2004; D. Kucharsky, "Because You're Worth It, L'Oréal," *Marketing*, February 9, 2004; Kristen Vinakmens, "Beauty Junkies Get Their Fix," *Strategy*, August 25, 2003, p. 5; H. Shaw, "Smell of Cosmetics Battle in the Air: Things Could Get Ugly with New Retail Players Entering the Beauty Market," *National Post*, November 16, 2004, accessed March 6, 7, 2005; B. Hitchcock, "Thank Heaven for Little Girls," *Marketing*, January 1, 2001, p. 14; "Beauty Business Booms," *The Futurist*, September–October 2004, pp. 8, 9; S. Thompson, Revlon Looks for New Image—Again," *Advertising Age*, November 11, 2004, p. 3; P. Gogoi, "An Ugly Truth About Cosmetics," Business Week Online, November 30, 2004, accessed March 9, 2005; Waheeda Harris, "Piece of Cake," *Style Magazine*, www.style.ca/Features/Features2.jsp; www.euromonitor.com.innopac.lib.bcit.ca/gmid/scripts, accessed March 5, 2005; www.cakebeauty.com; www.jaquabeauty.com; www.philosophy.com; www.blissworld.com.

APPENDIX 2

SAMPLE MARKETING PLAN FOR cake

This section takes you inside a sample marketing plan for Cake Beauty. The annotations explain more about what each section of the plan should contain—and why.

EXECUTIVE SUMMARY

Executive summary This section summarizes the main goals, recommendations, and points as an overview for senior managers who must read and approve the marketing plan. Generally a table of contents follows this section, for management convenience.

Cake Beauty has grown dramatically since its launch in 2001. Initial growth resulted from the founder's ability to recognize an unserved segment of the Canadian market that demanded a trendy, fashionable, yet edgy line of health and beauty products. Cake's ability to create a unique line of bath and shower products; hand, body, and foot lotions; and innovative products such as a moisturizing body glaze, hair and body refresher, and flavoured whipped body creme fostered ongoing growth. And since the company was able to leverage public relations and celebrity endorsements, the cost of its promotions budget was kept low compared to that of other cosmetics firms.

Through the use of its innovative website, the firm was able to expand internationally and has continued to experience rapid growth. For the 2005 plan year, the primary objectives are to increase sales by 150 percent and to increase brand awareness by 100 percent. This strategy of rapid growth will be challenging. The marketplace is becoming more competitive and some new entrants are replicating the strategy of celebrity endorsement. The company must generate enough sales in its core markets to fund ongoing growth and must manage its inventory carefully to keep costs low.

A number of tactics will be undertaken to achieve the plan's objectives:

☐ Pricing and promotional strategies for existing (more mature) products will be reviewed. Marginal products will be dropped. Promotions for remaining products will be assessed and re-designed as needed.

☐ New products will be developed and launched.

☐ New agreements will be signed with retailers in Canada and the U.S.

☐ Expansion into the European, Australian, and Hong Kong marketplaces will be undertaken.

☐ Programs to generate new publicity will be developed.

CURRENT MARKETING SITUATION

Current marketing situation In this section, marketing managers discuss the overall market, identify the market segments they will target, and provide information about the company's current situation.

Cake Beauty has established itself among the clientele of beauty boutiques and specialty stores as a brand synonymous with quality, fashion, and style. The estimated size of the Canadian market for bath and shower products in 2005 is $662.6 million, with 2.3 percent growth expected by 2008. The estimated size of the Canadian market for skin care products in 2005 is $697.8 million, with 11.4 percent growth expected by 2008. To increase its sales, Cake Beauty must introduce a greater variety of products and increase the number of distribution outlets without compromising the trendiness of the brand.

Market Description

Cake Beauty's target market consists of young, professional women, affluent stay-at-home moms, and female post-secondary students who lead busy lives and enjoy taking time out to indulge themselves with high-quality, trendy beauty products. Exhibit 1 shows how Cake products address the needs of the targeted market segment.

EXHIBIT 1   Needs and Corresponding Features/Benefits of Cake Beauty Products

Targeted Segment	Customer Need	Corresponding Feature/Benefit
Young, professional women	• Find a balance between good value and high-quality, natural products	• High-quality products for a competitive price
Affluent stay-at-home moms	• Relax and take time out for pampering	• Luxurious scent and feel of products
Female students	• Keep up with trends	• Featured in magazines; used by celebrities • Sold in trendy stores

Product Review

Cake Beauty's product line is a collection of stylish, sophisticated, decadent products including sugar scrubs, bath and shower froths, and body mousses and cremes. Exhibit 2 profiles Cake's products. Each product features:

- ☐ High-quality, natural ingredients
- ☐ Delicious scent
- ☐ Luxurious texture
- ☐ Clever, cute name
- ☐ Distinctive packaging

EXHIBIT 2   Product Size and Price

Product Name	Size	Price
Citrus Squeeze Sinfully Smoothing Brown Sugar Scrub	625 g	$32
Sweet Cheeks Sinfully Smoothing Brown Sugar Scrub	625 g	$32
Desserted Island Supremely Rich Bath & Shower Froth	250 mL	$24
It's A Slice Supremely Rich Bath & Shower Froth	250 mL	$24
Creme de la Creme Supremely Rich Bath & Shower Froth	250 mL	$24
Desserted Island Supremely Rich Body Mousse	250 mL	$26
It's A Slice Supremely Rich Body Mousse	250 mL	$26
Creme de la Creme Supremely Rich Body Mousse	250 mL	$26
Dessert's on Me Whipped Body Spread	266 mL	$32
Dolce Super-lux Body Crème	250 mL	$30
Milk Made Velveteen Hand Creme	100 mL	$22
Cake Walk Triplemint Foot Creme	100 mL	$20
Desserted Island Moisturizing Body Glaze	118 mL	$24
Cake Kiss Silky Smooth Lip Butter	10 mL	$14
Desserted Island Piece of Cake Gift Set	2 x 250 mL	$45
It's A Slice Piece of Cake Gift Set	2 x 250 mL	$45
Creme de la Creme Piece of Cake Gift Set	2 x 250 mL	$45

Competitive Review

The product categories in which Cake competes are dominated by large multinational firms such as L'Oréal Paris, Procter & Gamble, and Estée Lauder. However, these large firms tend to offer products that are either low-cost, utilitarian products (e.g., Olay Body Wash) or high-cost, problem-solving products (e.g., Biotherm Hydraflex Reshaping Body Moisturizer). Thus, Cake competes only indirectly with the industry giants. Cake's key direct competitors include

☐ *Dessert Beauty.* Dessert Beauty is a collection of fragrance, makeup, and bath and body products created by Clean Perfume Fragrance founder Randi Shinder and superstar Jessica Simpson. "Dessert girls make it their mission to always be sexy and smoochable." The line is presented as very sexy and provocative. Simpson's current popularity is an asset to the brand at the moment, but could become a liability if her appeal starts to fade. The line includes sugar scrubs and body creams, but also branches out into products such as body shimmer and blush. The prices of the bath and body products range from $24 to $59.

☐ *Philosophy.* Philosophy founder Cristina Carlino has over 20 years of experience as a product researcher and skin care specialist. Before launching Philosophy, she was the CEO of BioMedic, a highly acclaimed medical company. As a recognized leader in pioneering and identifying medically based skin care technologies, she has a lot of credibility in the industry. "Philosophy products are a way of life for the thinking mind and feeling heart in search of simplicity and balance." The Philosophy brand centres on a Zen-like minimalist concept. The product line is extensive, with a wide range of products, including bath and body products, skin care, hair products, makeup, and fragrances. Prices for bath and body products range from $23 to $48.

☐ *Bliss.* Described as "beauty online from New York's hottest spa," Bliss's product line has been growing. Known for "professional strength pampering products," Bliss emphasizes solving problems (fat, breakouts, bunions, wrinkles, etc.) more than indulging oneself. Product descriptions focus on results rather than the scent and texture of the products. The product line is made up of skin care and body care products, priced between $26 and $51.

☐ *Jaqua.* Founded by two sisters whose favourite childhood game was beauty parlour, this California-based team works with top specialists in the beauty and skin care industry to create products they describe as fragrant and fun to use as well as great for the skin. Their friends are often their first test market and their slogan could well be "Get the girls together for pampering, bonding, and fun." Thus, Jaqua has a strong focus on kits (containing various body care products) to encourage home spa parties. Their first kit, "Beauty Parlor Night Kit," debuted in Nordstrom's department store in 1997. The look of the brand has changed a number of times, so the brand can be difficult to identify. Jaqua's products are priced from $24 to $35.

Despite this strong competition, with careful attention to creating new products that fit into the concept of the brand, choosing distribution outlets that reinforce the brand's image and make the products available to a greater number of consumers, and continuing to create opportunities to promote the brand, Cake Beauty can continue to grow.

Distribution Review

Cake Beauty products will be distributed through a network of select store and nonstore retailers in Canada, the United States, Australia, Europe, and Hong Kong. Among the most important channel partners are

☐ *Trendy, fashionable boutiques.* Boutiques such as Lola and Emily in Montreal, Gilded Lily in Winnipeg, and Here Toronto in Toronto will carry Cake Beauty products in their stores.

☐ *Beauty bars.* Bars such as Lux in Calgary, Delineation in Toronto, and Gloss in Victoria will carry Cake Beauty products.

☐ *Spas.* Spas such as Stillwater Spa in Toronto and Spirit Spa in Halifax will carry Cake Beauty products.

☐ *Lifestyle stores.* Caban stores across Canada will carry Cake Beauty products and participate in promotional events.

☐ *Mid- to high-end department stores.* Stores such as Caban in Canada, Nordstrom in the United States, and David Jones in Australia will carry Cake Beauty products.

☐ *Online retailers.* Cake Beauty products will be available on the Cake website and the websites of other online niche beauty product retailers.

Cake also plans to expand in Europe (specifically in the United Kingdom, France, and Italy), Australia, and Hong Kong in 2005.

STRENGTHS, WEAKNESSES, OPPORTUNITIES, AND THREAT ANALYSIS

Cake Beauty has several powerful strengths on which to build, but its major weakness is the small scale of the company. The major opportunity is to capitalize on the increasing demand for spa products and experiences. Cake faces threats from increased competition and the current strength of the Canadian dollar.

EXHIBIT 3	Cake Beauty's Strengths, Weaknesses, Opportunities, and Threats		
Strengths	**Weaknesses**	**Opportunities**	**Threats**
• Strong awareness of brand among target market.	• Small scale of internal staff	• Increasing demand for spa products and experiences	• Increasing competition
• Strategic use of marketing and public relations.	• Product line not as extensive as other brands	• Continuing fascination with celebrities	• Strength of Canadian dollar
• Team of dedicated, loyal staff members and reputable manufacturers and chemists.	• Absence of Cake display fixtures	• Growth of 13–24 age group	

Strengths

Cake Beauty can build on three important strengths:

1. ***Strong brand awareness.*** Cake Beauty has achieved a high level of brand recognition within the target market. Cake is known for its use of high-quality, natural ingredients, a consistent concept, distinctive packaging, and personal touches.

2. ***Public relations.*** Cake's strategic use of public relations has allowed the brand to achieve a high level of brand awareness without spending money on expensive advertisements. Cake's efforts to have its products used by celebrities and featured in magazines and newspapers have reinforced the trendy image of the brand.

Strengths Strengths are internal capabilities that can help the company reach its objectives.

3. *People.* Cake is composed of loyal staff members who are willing to do whatever it takes to make the brand successful. Cake also works closely with a number of reputable manufacturers and chemists, each specializing in a particular type of product.

Weaknesses

Cake Beauty has the following three main weaknesses:

1. *Small scale.* Although the internal staff at Cake is very loyal and dedicated, their limited numbers mean that there is only so much they can do. Cake must be wary of expanding so fast that the staff is unable to keep up with demand.

2. *Limited product line.* A small number of products limits the revenue that can be brought in. Also, there is a danger of losing customers to other brands if they can't find exactly what they are looking for at Cake.

3. *Absence of display fixtures.* Since Cake does not have its own display fixtures to provide to retailers, Cake must depend on retailers to display its products prominently.

Opportunities

Cake Beauty can take advantage of three major market opportunities:

1. *Increasing demand for spa products and experiences.* The past few years have witnessed the emergence of a new "spa culture." More people are visiting spas on a regular basis and they want to bring the spa home with them, as evidenced by the increase in renovating bathrooms into spa-like oases.

2. *Continuing fascination with celebrities.* Celebrities seem to have more influence than ever. Rather than simply dreaming about owning and using the same products as celebrities, consumers are actually buying the same products themselves. Therefore, endorsements by the right celebrities are very valuable.

3. *Growth of 13–24 age group.* This age group is growing up within the new spa culture. Although these young women are not yet a part of Cake's target market, they present a large opportunity for future growth, as they are accustomed to being pampered and will seek out trendy, luxurious products as they move into their twenties.

Threats

Cake Beauty faces the following two threats:

1. *Increasing competition.* Retailers are introducing their own private lines of competing products, which may drive prices down and limit the number of retailers who will enter into partnerships with Cake. Large international companies are launching new lines to compete with products like those from Cake.

2. *Strength of Canadian dollar.* The current strength of the Canadian dollar makes Canadian products less attractive to foreign retailers and may hinder Cake's international growth.

OBJECTIVES AND ISSUES

Cake has set aggressive but achievable objectives for 2005.

Objectives

☐ Increase sales by 150 percent by year end 2005.

☐ Increase overall brand awareness by 100 percent.

☐ Negotiate partnerships with additional major retailers in Canada, the U.S., Australia, Europe, and Hong Kong.

Issues

☐ How will Cake increase sales without compromising the status of the brand?

☐ How will Cake increase brand awareness without a large increase in spending on advertising and promotion?

☐ Will Cake products appeal to consumers in Europe, Australia, and Hong Kong?

MARKETING STRATEGY

Cake Beauty's marketing strategy is based on a positioning of product differentiation. The primary target consists of educated, professional, health-conscious 18- to 34-year-old females who live and work primarily in urban centres and seek leading edge health and beauty products with a promise of luxury and indulgence. This select target market shuns mainstream products, preferring to shop at trendy, exclusive retailers and spas for these types of products.

Each of the four marketing-mix strategies conveys Cake Beauty's differentiation to the target market segment identified above.

Positioning

Using product differentiation, Cake Beauty is positioning its products as fun yet luxurious high-quality goods that provide a feeling of self-indulgence and well-being.

Product Strategy

Cake will introduce 13 new products in 2005. Some of these products are innovative, cutting edge, and unlike anything else on the market. Others are part of Cake's brand extension. Cake listens to and values customer input and has considered this with the creation of several of the new products. Cake will add to the existing line in all of the flavours to give consumers more of what they love. This is a strategic move that will help expand the line and pull it together. As with all Cake products, the new products must appeal to health-conscious women while emphasizing the positive personal experience of usage (the indulgence factor). The products must appeal to a market segment who makes purchases based on the cachet of the brand, but must also live up to the consumers' expectations, as repeat purchase will not ensue if the brand promise is not kept.

> **Positioning** A positioning built on meaningful differences, supported by appropriate strategy and implementation, can help the company build competitive advantage.
>
> **Marketing mix** These sections summarize the broad logic that will guide decisions made about the marketing mix in the period covered by the plan.

Pricing Strategy

Cake products will continue to be priced competitively against their direct competitors. A pricing review will be conducted during the plan year since the more mature products are facing increasing price competition. Decisions will be made about whether to adjust prices or drop marginal products based on this review.

Distribution Strategy

Retail outlets for Cake products must be chosen carefully, in order to ensure that they enhance the image of the brand. Cake will continue to grow by creating new partnerships with mid to high-end specialty or department stores in Canada and the U.S., and expanding its distribution in the European, Australian and Hong Kong markets. In support of its channel partners, Cake will organize in-store promotions in selected retail outlets and arrange special terms when appropriate.

Marketing Communications Strategy

Given that the target market for Cake products keeps up with what is trendy and hot by reading the lifestyle and fashion sections in the newspaper, celebrity magazines such as *US Weekly* and *People*, and fashion magazines such as *InStyle*, it is important to continue to generate publicity about Cake in these places. To do this, Cake will continue to provide samples to celebrities at special events and circulate press releases about new products and special offers that are targeted to key cities in Canada and the United States. This will help get coverage not only for the Cake brand but also for the retailers—by getting them press and encouraging consumers to go into their stores and buy Cake there as well. To attract, retain, and motivate channel partners, Cake will use trade promotion incentives such as off-invoice and display allowances and sales incentives for employees.

Marketing Research

Marketing research Management should explain in this section how marketing research will be used to support development, implementation, and evaluation of strategies and action programs.

Using research, Cake Beauty is identifying the specific features and benefits that the target market segment values. This research will be used to inform future decisions on product development, branding, pricing, distribution, and promotion. Cake will also conduct research into the needs and values of Asian and European women to determine what adjustments need to be made to the marketing program in order to be successful in those markets.

Marketing Organization

Marketing organization The marketing department may be organized by function, as in this sample, by geography, by product, or by customer (or some combination).

Cake Beauty marketing and communications manager Lauren Baswick holds overall responsibility for marketing strategy and direction.

ACTION PROGRAM

Action programs Action programs should be coordinated with the resources and activities of other departments, including production, finance, purchasing, etc.

Cake recognizes that in order to grow, it must continue to attract new celebrity fans, increase awareness of the brand, develop new products, enact new partnerships, and motivate existing partners. Following are summaries of the action programs to be used throughout 2005.

January

Sundance Film Festival 2005. Cake will partner with Seven for All Mankind jeans and Swarovski to host a suite where celebrities can relax with champagne and cupcakes and pick out their favourite Cake products and Seven jeans. Celebrities who are not able to make it to the suite will be sent a gift bag containing Sweet Cheeks Sinfully Smooth Brown Sugar Scrub, Cake Kiss Silky Smooth Lip Butter, a Desserted Island Gift Set, a pair of Seven jeans, a Swarovski crystal necklace, and a bottle of Moët Special Edition Perrier Jouët champagne.

February

Academy Awards. Cake will provide Sweet Cheeks Sinfully Smooth Brown Sugar Scrub, Cake Kiss Silky Smooth Lip Butter, and Desserted Island Gift Sets to be included in the Ultimate Nominee gift bag at the Academy Awards.

Rethink Breast Cancer Red & White Ball. Cake will donate a gift basket in support of this event and will also have a Cake Girl at the event sampling the guests.

March

Bridget Jones: The Edge of Reason DVD. Cake will partner with Universal Canada for the Canadian DVD release of *Bridget Jones: The Edge of Reason.* Cake will provide an on-pack coupon and gift with purchase offer. This is an online initiative only and consumers will receive a free Cake Kiss Lip Butter with the purchase of Dessert's On Me Whipped Body Spread. The Cake logo will be included on all of Universal's advertisements, appearing in magazines such as *Flare, Fashion,* and on ad space in washrooms, as well as on the coupon that will appear on 250 000 copies of the DVD—creating brand awareness and coverage across Canada. The logo will also be included on a separate website linking to Cake's website. This promotion will be ongoing throughout the spring and summer.

April

New Product Launch for Satin Sugar. Cake will send out a release about the first new product of 2005, Satin Sugar Hair and Body Refreshing Powder. Fashion and beauty editors and writers will be invited to a media launch event to introduce the new product. The whole concept and campaign surrounding the event will be 'What would you do if you had more time?' The launch and campaign will be supported by a feature on Cake's home page, a mass email to the mailing list, and an email to Cake's retailers.

What a Girl Wants Event with Caban. Cake will be one of the title sponsors for Caban's national event. On April 27, 2005, simultaneously in Vancouver, Montreal, and Toronto, Caban stores will host an event geared toward Cake's target demographic. Caban will be offering a sales discount and Cake will be providing mini-manicures using Cake product. Cake will give local spas that carry Cake the opportunity to be part of the event through providing the spa services. Cake's logo will appear on the invitation and in-store signage.

Put a Spring in Your Step Campaign. Cake will launch a campaign focused on Cake Walk Triplemint Foot Creme, supported by a feature on Cake's home page, a mass email to the mailing list, and an email to Cake's retailers.

Caban Sampling Program. On selected Saturdays throughout the spring and summer, a Cake Girl will be present at Caban's flagship store to sample the customers. This promotion will support Caban as an important marketing partner and provide an opportunity for new customers to try the products.

Bridget Jones DVD promotion is ongoing.

May

New Product Launch for Milk Made Smoothing Hand and Cuticle Buffer. This new product will be a complement to the popular Milk Made Velveteen Hand Creme. The launch will be supported by a feature on Cake's home page, a mass email to the mailing list, and an email to Cake's retailers. A press release will also be sent out and a media relations campaign will ensue.

Mother's Day Promotion. Cake will send out a mass email about special gifts to give for Mother's Day. A feature on Cake's home page will also be included.

Bridget Jones DVD promotion is ongoing.

Put a Spring in Your Step Campaign is ongoing.

Caban Sampling Program is ongoing.

June

Rethink Breast Cancer Event. Cake will participate in Rethink Breast Cancer's big event of the year. Cake will provide products for VIPs and will have a Cake Girl available to sample the guests.

Bridget Jones DVD promotion is ongoing.
Caban Sampling Program is ongoing.

July

Bridget Jones DVD promotion is ongoing.
Caban Sampling Program is ongoing.

August

Launch of the Cake Kiss Collection. This launch will introduce a new fruity vanilla flavour of Cake Kiss Silky Smooth Lip Butter and a Lip Exfoliator in the same buttery caramel flavour as the original Lip Butter. The launch will be supported by a feature on Cake's home page, a mass email to the mailing list, and an email to Cake's retailers. A press release will also be sent out and a media relations campaign will ensue.

Bridget Jones DVD promotion is ongoing.
Caban Sampling Program is ongoing.

September

Toronto International Film Festival. Cake, along with other buzz-worthy brands, will participate in a celebrity gift lounge that is designed to get products into the hands of celebrities. Instead of getting the traditional gift bag, the celebrities will be invited to come to the private suite, have a drink, and get whatever they like. This will be an opportunity for Cake to gain further recognition from celebrities and establish key relationships. Interviews with celebs will be broadcast from the lounge.

Launch of the Dream Puff Night Time Collection. This collection will include a Pillow Spray, Night Time Body Lotion, and a Candle, all featuring the Dream Puff scent of sweet cherry pie with a hint of lavender. The launch will be supported by a feature on Cake's home page, a mass email to the mailing list, and an email to Cake's retailers. A press release will also be sent out and a media relations campaign will ensue.

Bridget Jones DVD promotion is ongoing.

October

Breast Cancer month. Cake will support Breast Cancer month by donating a percentage of all online sales of Milk Made Velveteen Hand Creme to Rethink Breast Cancer. Aside from supporting a good cause, this promotion will attract a great deal of media attention and will draw consumers to Cake's website. Cake will hold events with Caban and Nordstrom to promote the product, the cause, and strengthen the partnership with retail partners.

November

Caban Holiday Promotion. Cake will begin its holiday promotion at Caban, providing free hand massages using Cake products to customers on selected Saturdays in Montreal, Toronto, and Vancouver. This promotion will support Caban as an important marketing partner, provide an opportunity for new customers to try the products, and promote Cake products as great holiday gifts.

Holiday sets. Three holiday sets will be designed to include Cake's top selling skus. The theme will be "Icing on the Cake." The packaging will be fashion savvy and thematic.

December

The Caban promotion is ongoing throughout the holiday season.

BUDGETS

Revenue	2004	2005
Number of units sold	XXXX	XXXX
Average net price	XXXX	XXXX
Expenses		
Production costs	XXXX	XXXX
Distribution costs	XXXX	XXXX
Marketing costs	XXXX	XXXX
Profit	XXXX	XXXX

Budgets Budgets serve two main purposes: to project profitability and to help managers plan for expenditures, scheduling, and operations related to each action program.

CONTROLS

Cake is planning tight control measures to closely monitor quality and customer service satisfaction. This will enable us to react very quickly in correcting any problems that may occur. Other early warning signals that will be monitored for signs of deviation from the plan include monthly sales (by segment and channel) and monthly expenses.

Controls Controls help management measure results after the plan is implemented and identify any problems or performance variations that need corrective action.

MARKETING PLAN TOOLS

Pearson offers two valuable resources to assist you in developing a marketing plan:

☐ *The Marketing Plan: A Handbook* by Marian Burk Wood explains the process of creating a marketing plan, complete with checklists, real-world examples, and a listing of marketing-related websites.

☐ *Marketing Plan Pro* software is an award-winning package that includes sample marketing plans, step-by-step guides, help wizards, and customizable charts for documenting a marketing plan.

APPENDIX 3

MARKETING ARITHMETIC

One aspect of marketing not discussed within the text is marketing arithmetic. The calculation of sales, costs, and certain ratios is important for many marketing decisions. This appendix describes three major areas of marketing arithmetic: the *operating statement, analytic ratios,* and *markups, margins, and markdowns.*

OPERATING STATEMENT

The operating statement and the balance sheet are the two main financial statements used by companies. The **balance sheet** shows the assets, liabilities, and net worth of a company at a given time. The **operating statement** (also called **profit-and-loss statement** or **income statement**) is the more important of the two for marketing information. It shows company sales, cost of goods sold, and expenses during a specified period. By comparing the operating statement from one time period to the next, the firm can spot favourable or unfavourable trends and take appropriate action.

Table AII-1 shows the 2003 operating statement for Dale Parsons Men's Wear, a specialty store in the Prairies. This statement is for a retailer; the operating statement for a manufacturer would be different. Specifically, the section on purchases within the "cost of goods sold" area would be replaced by "cost of goods manufactured."

The outline of the operating statement follows a logical series of steps to arrive at the firm's $25 000 net profit figure:

Net sales	$300 000
Cost of goods sold	−175 000
Gross margin	$125 000
Expenses	−100 000
Net profit	$25 000

The first part details the amount that Parsons received for the goods sold during the year. The sales figures consist of three items: *gross sales, returns and allowances,* and *net sales.* **Gross sales** is the total amount charged to customers during the year for merchandise purchased in Parsons's store. As expected, some customers returned merchandise because of damage or a change of mind. If the customer gets a full refund or full credit on another purchase, we call this a *return.* Or the customer may decide to keep the item if Parsons will reduce the price. This is called an *allowance.* By subtracting returns and allowances from gross sales, we arrive at net sales—what Parsons earned in revenue from a year of selling merchandise:

Gross sales	$325 000
Returns and allowances	−25 000
Net sales	$300 000

The second major part of the operating statement calculates the amount of sales revenue Dale Parsons retains after paying the costs of the merchandise. We start with the inventory in the store at the beginning of the year. During the year, Parsons bought $165 000 worth of suits, slacks, shirts, ties, jeans, and other goods. Suppliers gave the store discounts totaling $15 000, so that net purchases were $150 000. Because the store is located away from regular shipping routes, Parsons had to pay an additional $10 000 to get the products delivered, giving the firm a net cost of $160 000. Adding the beginning inventory, the cost of goods available for sale amounted to $220 000. The $45 000 ending inventory of clothes in the store on 31 December is then subtracted to come up with the $175 000 **cost of goods sold.** Here again we have followed a logical series of steps to figure out the cost of goods sold:

Amount Parsons started with (beginning inventory)	$ 60 000
Net amount purchased	1150 000
Any added costs to obtain these purchases	110 000
Total cost of goods Parsons had available for sale during year	$220 000
Amount Parsons had left over (ending inventory)	245 000
Cost of goods actually sold	$175 000

The difference between what Parsons paid for the merchandise ($175 000) and what he sold it for ($300 000) is called the **gross margin** ($125 000).

To show the profit Parsons "cleared" at the end of the year, we must subtract from the gross margin the *expenses* incurred while doing business. *Selling expenses* included two sales employees, local newspaper and radio advertising, and the cost of delivering merchandise to customers after alterations. Selling expenses totalled $50 000 for the year. *Administrative expenses* included the salary for an office manager, office supplies

TABLE ALL-1   Operating Statement: Dale Parsons Men's Wear Year ending 31 December, 2003

Gross Sales			$325 000
Less: Sales returns and allowances			25 000
Net sales			$300 000
Cost of goods sold			
Beginning inventory, January 1, at cost		$ 60 000	
Gross purchases	$165 000		
Less: Purchase discounts	15 000		
Net Purchases	$150 000		
Plus: Freight-in	10 000		
Net cost of delivered purchases		$160 000	
Cost of goods available for sale		$220 000	
Less: Ending inventory, December 31, at cost		$ 45 000	
Cost of goods sold			$175 000
Gross margin			$125 000
Expenses			
Selling expenses			
Sales, salaries, and commissions	$ 40 000		
Advertising	5 000		
Delivery	5 000		
Total selling expenses		$ 50 000	
Administrative expenses			
Office salaries	$ 20 000		
Office supplies	5 000		
Miscellaneous (outside consultant)	5 000		
Total administrative expenses		$ 30 000	
General expenses			
Rent	$ 10 000		
Heat, light, telephone	5 000		
Miscellaneous (insurance, depreciation)	5 000		
Total general expenses		$ 20 000	
Total expenses			$100 000
Net profit			$ 25 000

such as stationery and business cards, and miscellaneous expenses including an administrative audit conducted by an outside consultant. Administrative expenses totalled $30 000 in 2003. Finally, the general expenses of rent, utilities, insurance, and depreciation came to $20 000. Total expenses were therefore $100 000 for the year. By subtracting expenses ($100 000) from the gross margin ($125 000), we arrive at the net profit of $25 000 for Parsons during 2003.

ANALYTIC RATIOS

The operating statement provides the figures needed to compute some crucial ratios. Typically these ratios are called **operating ratios**—the ratio of selected operating statement items to net sales. They let marketers compare the firm's performance in one year to that in previous years (or with industry standards and competitors in the same year). The most commonly used operating ratios are the *gross margin percentage,* the *net profit percentage,* the *operating expense percentage,* and the *returns and allowances percentage.*

Another useful ratio is the *stockturn rate* (also called *inventory turnover rate*). The stockturn rate is the number of times an inventory turns over or is sold during a specified period (often one year). It may be computed on a cost, selling price, or units basis. Thus, the formula can be

$$\text{Stockturn rate} = \frac{\text{cost of goods sold}}{\text{average inventory at cost}}$$

or

$$\text{Stockturn rate} = \frac{\text{selling price of goods sold}}{\text{average selling price of inventory}}$$

or

$$\text{Stockturn rate} = \frac{\text{sales in units}}{\text{average inventory in units}}$$

We will use the first formula to calculate the stockturn rate for Dale Parsons Men's Wear:

$$\frac{\$175\ 000}{(\$60\ 000\ +\ \$45\ 000)/2} = \frac{\$175\ 000}{\$52\ 500} = 3.3$$

Ratio	Formula	Computation from Table AII-1
Gross margin percentage	$= \dfrac{\text{gross margin}}{\text{net sales}}$	$= \dfrac{\$125\ 000}{\$300\ 000} = 42\%$
Net profit percentage	$= \dfrac{\text{net profit}}{\text{net sales}}$	$= \dfrac{\$25\ 000}{\$300\ 000} = 8\%$

Ratio	Formula	Computation from Table AII-1
Operating expense percentage	$= \dfrac{\text{total expenses}}{\text{net sales}}$	$= \dfrac{\$100\ 000}{\$300\ 000} = 33\%$
Returns and allowances percentage	$= \dfrac{\text{returns and allowances}}{\text{net sales}}$	$= \dfrac{\$25\ 000}{\$300\ 000} = 8\%$

That is, Parsons's inventory turned over 3.3 times in 2003. Normally, the higher the stockturn rate, the higher the management efficiency and company profitability.

Return on investment (ROI) is frequently used to measure managerial effectiveness. It uses figures from the firm's operating statement and balance sheet. A commonly used formula for computing ROI is

$$ROI = \frac{net\ profit}{sales} \times \frac{sales}{investment}$$

You may have two questions about this formula: Why use a two-step process when ROI could be computed simply as net profit divided by investment? And what exactly is "investment"?

To answer these questions, let's look at how each component of the formula can affect the ROI. Suppose Dale Parsons Men's Wear has a total investment of $150 000. Then ROI can be computed as follows:

$$ROI = \frac{\$25\ 000(net\ profit)}{\$300\ 000(sales)} \times \frac{\$300\ 000(sales)}{\$150\ 000(investment)}$$

$$= 8.3\% \times 2 = 16.6\%$$

Now suppose that Parsons had worked to increase his share of market. He could have had the same ROI if his sales had doubled while dollar profit and investment stayed the same (accepting a lower profit ratio to get higher turnover and market share):

$$ROI = \frac{\$25\ 000(net\ profit)}{\$600\ 000(sales)} \times \frac{\$600\ 000(sales)}{\$150\ 000(investment)}$$

$$= 4.16\% \times 4 = 16.6\%$$

Parsons might have increased its ROI by increasing net profit through more cost cutting and more efficient marketing:

$$ROI = \frac{\$50\ 000(net\ profit)}{\$300\ 000(sales)} \times \frac{\$300\ 000(sales)}{\$150\ 000(investment)}$$

$$= 16.6\% \times 2 = 33.2\%$$

Another way to increase ROI is to find some way to get the same levels of sales and profits while decreasing investment (perhaps by cutting the size of Parsons's average inventory):

$$ROI = \frac{\$25\ 000(net\ profit)}{\$300\ 000(sales)} \times \frac{\$300\ 000(sales)}{\$75\ 000(investment)}$$

$$= 8.3\% \times 4 = 33.2\%$$

What is "investment" in the ROI formula? *Investment* is often defined as the total assets of the firm. But many analysts now use other measures of return to assess performance. These measures include *return on net assets (RONA)*, *return on stockholders' equity (ROE)*, or *return on assets managed (ROAM)*. Because investment is measured at a point in time, we usually compute ROI as the average investment between two time periods (say, January 1 and December 31 of the same year). We can also compute ROI as an "internal rate of return" by using discounted cash flow analysis (see any finance textbook for more on this technique). The objective in using any of these measures is to determine how well the company has been using its resources. As inflation, competitive pressures, and cost of capital increase, such measures become increasingly important indicators of marketing and company performance.

Markups, Margin, and Markdowns

Retailers and wholesalers must understand the concepts of **markups, margins** and **markdowns.** They must make a profit to stay in business, and the markup percentage affects profits. Markups and markdowns are expressed as percentages.

There are two different ways to compute markups—on *cost* or on *selling price:*

$$\text{Markup} = \frac{\text{dollar markup}}{\text{cost}}$$

$$\text{Margin} = \frac{\text{dollar markup}}{\text{selling price}}$$

Dale Parsons must decide which formula to use. If Parsons bought shirts for $15 and wanted to mark them up $10 to a price of $25, his markup percentage on cost would be $10/$15 = 67.7%. If Parsons wanted to calculate margin, the percentage would be $10/$25 = 40%.

Suppose Parsons knew his cost ($12) and desired markup on price (25%) for a man's tie, and wanted to compute the selling price. The formula is

$$\text{Selling price} = \frac{\text{cost}}{1 - \text{markup}}$$

$$\text{Selling price} = \frac{\$12}{0.75} = \$16$$

As a product moves through the channel of distribution, each channel member adds a markup before selling the product to the next member. This "markup chain" is shown for a suit purchased by a Parsons customer for $200:

		$ Amount	% of Selling Price
Manufacturer	Cost	$108	90%
	Markup	12	10
	Selling price	120	100
Wholesaler	Cost	120	80
	Markup	30	20
	Selling price	150	100
Retailer	Cost	150	75
	Markup	50	25
	Selling price	200	100

The retailer whose markup is 25 percent does not necessarily enjoy more profit than a manufacturer whose markup is 10 percent. Profit also depends on how many items with that profit margin can be sold (stockturn rate) and on operating efficiency (expenses).

Sometimes a retailer wants to convert margins to markups, and vice versa. The formulas are:

$$\text{Margin} = \frac{\text{markup}}{100\% + \text{markup}}$$

$$\text{Markup} = \frac{\text{margin}}{100\% - \text{margin}}$$

Suppose Parsons found that his competitor was using a markup of 30 percent based on cost and wanted to know what this would be as a percentage of selling price. The calculation would be:

$$\frac{30\%}{100\% + 30\%} = \frac{30\%}{130\%} = 23\%$$

Because Parsons was using a 25 percent markup on suits, he felt that his markup was suitable compared with that of the competitor.

Near the end of the summer Parsons still had an inventory of summer slacks in stock. Therefore, he decided to use a *markdown,* a reduction from the original selling price. Before the summer he had purchased 20 pairs at $10 each, and he had since sold 10 pairs at $20 each. He marked down the other pairs to $15 and sold 5 pairs. We compute his *markdown ratio* as follows:

$$\text{Markdown percentage} = \frac{\text{dollar markdown}}{\text{total net sales in dollars}}$$

The dollar markdown is $25 (5 pairs at $5 each) and total net sales are $275 (10 pairs at $20 + 5 pairs at $15). The ratio, then, is $25/$275 = 9%.

Larger retailers usually compute markdown ratios for each department rather than for individual items. The ratios provide a measure of relative marketing performance for each department and can be calculated and compared over time. Markdown ratios can also be used to compare the performance of different buyers and salespeople in a store's various departments.

Key Terms

Balance Sheet
Cost of goods sold
Gross margin
Gross sales
Margin
Markdown
Operating ratios
Operating statement (for profit-and-loss
  statement or income statement)
Return on investment (ROI)

Chapter 1

Multiple Choice

1. a
2. c
3. d
4. a
5. e
6. b
7. a
8. d
9. c
10. a

True/False

1. F
2. F
3. T
4. F
5. T

Concept Check

1. Marketing; 2. satisfying customer needs; 3. product; product; 4. Customer value; 5. delight; 6. relationship marketing; 7. market; 8. production; product; selling; marketing; societal marketing; 9. marketing; 10. technology.

Chapter 2

Multiple Choice

1. c
2. e
3. e
4. a
5. d
6. c
7. a
8. b
9. d
10. a

True/False

1. F
2. T
3. F
4. T
5. F

Concept Check

1. Strategic planning; 2. mission statement; 3. realistic, specific, market environment, motivating; 4. best fits the company's strengths and weaknesses to opportunities in the environment; 5. cash cows; 6. build, hold, harvest, divest; 7. market penetration; 8. value chain; 9. Market segmentation; 10. product, price, place, promotion; 11. analysis, planning, implementation, control; 12. marketing strategy.

Chapter 3

Multiple Choice

1. b
2. a
3. c
4. e
5. a

6. c
7. d
8. a
9. b
10. c

True/False

1. F
2. T
3. F
4. F
5. T

Concept Check

1. high-pressure selling, shoddy or unsafe products, planned obsolescence; 2. high costs of distribution, high advertising and promotion costs, excessive markups; 3. Canadian Environmental Assessment; 4. planned obsolescence; 5. false wants and too much materialism, too few social goods, cultural pollution; 6. Consumerism; 7. the product to be safe; the product to perform as claimed; 8. Environmentalism; 9. pollution prevention, sustainability vision, product stewardship; 10. innovative marketing, value marketing, sense-of-mission marketing; 11. sense-of-mission.

Chapter 4

Multiple Choice

1. a
2. b
3. c
4. e
5. c
6. a
7. b
8. d
9. e
10. e

True/False

1. F
2. T
3. T
4. F
5. F

Concept Check

1. marketing environment; 2. microenvironment; 3. Marketing intermediaries; 4. local; 5. Engel's; 6. growing shortages of raw materials, increased pollution, and increased government intervention in natural resource management; 7. companies from each other, consumers from unfair business practices, the interests of society against unrestrained business behaviour; 8. we; 9. environmental management perspective.

Chapter 5

Multiple Choice

1. c
2. a
3. e
4. b
5. d

6. c
7. a
8. b
9. d
10. e

True/False

1. F
2. T
3. F
4. F
5. T

Concept Check

1. Marketing information system (MIS); 2. internal data, marketing intelligence, marketing research; 3. Marketing intelligence; 4. Marketing research; 5. defining the problem and the research objectives, developing the research plan, implementing the research plan, and interpreting and reporting the findings; 6. exploratory; 7. Primary; 8. ethnographic; 9. Survey; 10. online; 11. convenience; 12. Customer relationship management (CRM).

Chapter 6

Multiple Choice

1. e
2. a
3. d
4. c
5. b
6. d
7. a
8. c
9. b
10. a

True/False

1. F
2. T
3. F
4. F
5. T

Concept Check

1. Consumer buyer behaviour; 2. Culture; 3. Social classes; 4. opinion leaders; 5. activities, interests, and opinions; 6. physiological needs, safety needs, social needs, esteem needs, and self-actualization needs; 7. need recognition, information search, evaluation of alternatives, purchase decision, and postpurchase behaviour; 8. awareness, interest, evaluation, trial, and adoption; 9. relative advantage; 10. straight rebuy, modified rebuy, and new task; 11. buying centre; 12. suppliers search, proposal solicitation, supplier selection, and order-routine specification.

Chapter 7

Multiple Choice

1. d
2. c
3. a
4. e
5. b

6. a
7. d
8. b
9. e
10. a

True/False
1. T
2. T
3. F
4. T
5. F

Concept Check
1. market segmentation; 2. market targeting, and market positioning; 3. mass marketing, segment marketing, niche marketing, and micromarketing; 4. geographic, demographic, psychographic, and behavioural; 5. Demographic; 6. gender; 7. measurable, accessible, substantial, differentiable, actionable; 8. target market; 9. differentiated; 10. under, over, confused; 11. superior, communicable, preemptive, affordable; 12. value proposition.

Chapter 8

Multiple Choice
1. a
2. c
3. e
4. b
5. c
6. a
7. c
8. e
9. b
10. c

True/False
1. T
2. F
3. F
4. T
5. F

Concept Check
1. product; 2. Services; 3. core benefit, actual, augmented; 4. materials, capital items, supplies; 5. brand; 6. benefits and qualities; pronounce, recognize, remember; distinctive; extendible; 7. Line extensions; 8. width; 9. intangibility, inseparability, variability, perishability; 10. satisfied and productive service employees; greater service value; satisfied and loyal customers.

Chapter 9

Multiple Choice
1. a
2. d
3. b
4. e
5. a
6. d
7. b
8. d
9. a
10. d

True/False
1. T
2. F
3. F
4. F
5. T

Concept Check
1. new products; 2. idea screening, marketing strategy, product development, commercialization; 3. product concept; 4. the planned long-run sales, profit goals, and marketing mix strategy; 5. Test marketing; 6. introduction, growth, maturity, decline; 7. maturity; 8. product concept testing; 9. fad; 10 growth.

Chapter 10

Multiple Choice
1. b
2. b
3. d
4. e
5. b
6. a
7. d
8. e
9. b
10. c

True/False
1. T
2. F
3. T
4. F
5. T

Concept Check
1. dynamic; 2. current profit maximization, market share leadership, product quality leadership; 3. pure competition, monopolistic competition, oligopolistic competition, and pure monopoly; 4. elastic; 5. cost-plus pricing; 6. Value-based; 7. Competition; 8 market-penetration; 9. captive-product; 10. cash; 11. psychological; 12. f.o.b origin.

Chapter 11

Multiple Choice
1. e
2. c
3. b
4. d
5. b
6. a
7. c
8. c
9. e
10. a

True/False
1. F
2. T
3. T
4. F
5. T

Concept Check
1. distribution channel; 2. information, promotion, contact, matching, negotiation; 3. direct; 4. retailing 5. wholesaling; 6. vertical; 7. disintermediation; 8. intensive; 9. wheel of retailing; 10. marketing logistics; 11. supply chain; 12. order processing, warehousing, inventory management, transportation.

Chapter 12

Multiple Choice
1. a
2. b
3. a
4. d
5. a
6. b
7. a
8. e
9. d
10. e

True/False
1. T
2. F
3. F
4. F
5. T

Concept Check
1. advertising, sales promotion, personal selling, direct response marketing and public relations; 2. Advertising; 3. Integrated marketing communications (IMC); 4. pull; 5. inform, persuade, or remind; 6. percentage-of-sales, competitive-parity, objective-and-task; 7. Sales promotion; 8. Prospecting, preapproach, handling objections, closing; 9. invasion of privacy, Office of the Privacy Commissioner of Canada; 10. advertising.

Chapter 13

Multiple Choice
1. b
2. c
3. c
4. d
5. a
6. e
7. b
8. c
9. e
10. a

True/False
1. T
2. F
3. T
4. F
5. F

Concept Check
1. business-to-business (B2B), business-to-consumer (B2C), consumer-to-consumer (C2C), business-to-consumer (B2C); 2. convenient, easy, private, product access, selection; 3. customization; 4. public relations; 5. portal website; 6. banner ads, text links, sponsorships, interstitials, microsites; 7. text links; 8. newsletter; 9. viral marketing; 10. blog

NOTES

Chapter 1

1. See Stewart Alsop, "I'm Betting on Amazon," *Fortune*, April 30, 2001, p. 48; Kathleen Doler, "Interview: Jeff Bezos, Founder and CEO of Amazon.com Inc.," *Upside*, September 1998, pp. 76–80; Susan Stellin, Geoffrey Colvin, "Shaking Hands on the Web," *Fortune*, May 14, 2001, p. 54; Fred Vogelstein, "Amazon's Second Act," September 2, 2002, pp. 186–188; Jonathon Krim and Dina ElBoghdady, "On Balance, Amazon.ca Is Likely a Good Thing," *The Globe and Mail*, June 26, 2002, p. B12; Hollie Shaw, "Amazon.ca Takes Direct Aim at Indigo," *The Financial Post*, June 25, 2002, p. FP1, Elizabeth Church, "Amazon.ca Set to Go Today," June 25, 2002, p. B6; "About Amazon.com," www.amazon.com, accessed July 2002; "Amazon Posts Profit for 2nd Time; Firm May Prove to Be a Rare E-Commerce Site with Staying Power," *The Washington Post*, January 24, 2003; Nick Wingfield, "Amazon Narrows Loss as Revenue Increases by 28%," *Wall Street Journal*, April 25, 2003, p. B8; Fred Vogelstein, "Mighty Amazon," *Fortune*, May 26, 2003, pp. 60–74; annual reports and other information at www.amazon.com, www.amazon.ca/exec/obidos/subst/marketplace/sell-your-stuff.html, accessed October 24, 2004.

2. The American Marketing Association offers this definition: "*Marketing* is the process of planning and executing the conception, pricing, promotion, and distributing of ideas, goods, and services to create exchanges that satisfy individual and organizational objectives." See www.marketingpower.com/live/content.php?Item_ID54620, July 2003.

3. For an interesting discussion of creating customer value and extracting value in return, see Natalie Mizik and Robert Jacobson, "Trading Off Between Value Creation and Value Appropriation: The Financial Implications of Shifts in Strategic Emphasis," *Journal of Marketing*, January 2003, pp. 63–76.

4. Jack Neff, "Humble Try," *Advertising Age*, February 18, 2002, pp. 3, 12; and Mark Ritson, "The Best Research Comes from Living the Life of Your Customer," *Marketing*, July 18, 2002, p. 16.

5. Industry Canada, "Gross Domestic Product (GDP) by Industry by Services-Producing Sectors of the Canadian Economy 1997–2003," Industry Canada, http://strategis.ic.gc.ca/sc_ecnmy/sio/cis41–91gdpe.htm, accessed June 14, 2004.

6. See Theodore Levitt's classic article, "Marketing Myopia," *Harvard Business Review*, July–August 1960, pp. 45–56. For more recent discussions, see Colin Grant, "Theodore Levitt's Marketing Myopia," *Journal of Business Ethics*, February 1999, pp. 397–406; Jeffrey M. O'Brien, "Drums in the Jungle," *MC Technology Marketing Intelligence*, March 1999, pp. 22–30; Hershell Sarbin, "Overcoming Marketing Myopia," *Folio*, May 2000, pp. 55–56; and James R. Stock, "Marketing Myopia Revisited: Lessons for Logistics," *International Journal of Physical Distribution Logistics Management*, vol. 2, issue 1/2, 2002, pp. 12–21.

7. Erika Rasmusson, "Marketing More Than a Product," *Sales Marketing Management*, February 2000, p. 99. Also see B. Joseph Pine II and James Gilmore, "Welcome to the Experience Economy," *Harvard Business Review*, July–August 1998, p. 99;

Stephen E. DeLong, "The Experience Economy," *Upside*, November 2001, p. 28; and Pat Esgate, "Pine and Gilmore Stage a Fourth Think About Experience," *Strategy Leadership*, vol. 30, issue 3, 2002, pp. 47–48.

8. For more information visit the BC Hydro website at www.bchydro.com.

9. Ralph Waldo Emerson offered this advice: "If a man makes a better mousetrap the world will beat a path to his door." Several companies, however, have built better mousetraps yet failed. One was a laser mousetrap costing $1500. Contrary to popular assumptions, people do not automatically learn about new products, believe product claims, or willingly pay higher prices.

10. See James Bandler, "Kodak Advances in Marketing Share of Digital Cameras," *Wall Street Journal*, December 21, 2001, p. B2; and Bandler, "Leading the News: Kodak Posts Disappointing Net, Plans New Layoffs," January 23, 2003, p. A3.

11. See John Goodman and Steve Newman, "Understand Customer Behavior and Complaints," *Quality Progress*, January 2003, pp. 51–55.

12. Kotler, *Marketing Management: Analysis, Planning, Implementation, and Control*, 11th ed., p. 19. Also see Kotler, *Marketing Insights from A to Z* (Hoboken, NJ: Wiley, 2003), pp. 32–34.

13. See Gary Hamel and C. K. Prahalad, "Seeing the Future First," *Fortune*, September 5, 1994, pp. 64–70; Philip Kotler, *Kotler on Marketing* (New York: Free Press, 1999), pp. 20–24; and Anthony W. Ulwick, "Turn Customer Input Into Innovation," *Harvard Business Review*, January 2002, pp. 91–97.

14. See Sonia Reyes, "Fighting the Fat Backlash," *Brandweek*, May 5, 2003, pp. 24–30; and Nat Ives, "Fast-Food Chains Are Adding Premium Salads to Their Menus After Success of Rival," *New York Times*, May 5, 2003, p. C10.

15. See "Leaders of the Most Admired," *Fortune*, January 29, 1990, pp. 40–54; Thomas A. Stewart, "America's Most Admired Companies," *Fortune*, March 2, 1998, pp. 70–82; and www.jnj.com/our_company/credo_heading.htm, September 2003.

16. Siri Agrell, "Farewell to Full Serve," *National Post*, October 23, 2004, pp. RB1, 4.

17. See Erika Rasmusson, "Complaints Can Build Relationships," *Sales Marketing Management*, September 1999, p. 89; "King Customer," *Selling Power*, October 2000, pp. 124–125; Renee Houston Zemansky and Jeff Weiner, "Just Hang On to What You Got," *Selling Power*, March 2002, pp. 60–64; and Marc R. Okrant, "How to Convert '3's and '4's into '5's," *Marketing News*, October 14, 2002, pp. 14, 17.

18. www.purolator.com/media/corporate/corporate_history.html, accessed October 23, 2004; www.purolator.com/media/corporate/faq.html, accessed January 31, 2006.

19. For more on customer satisfaction, see Regina Fazio Marcuna, "Mapping the World of Customer Satisfaction, *Harvard Business Review*, May–June 2000, p. 30; David M. Szymanski, "Customer

Satisfaction: A Meta-Analysis of the Empirical Evidence," *Academy of Marketing Science Journal*, Winter 2001, pp. 16–35; Vikas Mittal and Wagner Kamakura, "Satisfaction, Repurchase Intent, and Repurchase Behavior: Investigating the Moderating Effect of Customer Characteristics," *Journal of Marketing Research*, February 2001, pp. 131–142; and Robert C. Blattberg, Gary Getz, Jacquelyn S. Thomas, *Customer Equity* (Boston, MA: Harvard Business School Press, 2001, pp. 75; and Marc R. Okrant, "How to Convert '3's and '4's into '5's," *Marketing News*, October 14, 2002, pp. 14, 17.

20. For more on this measure and for recent customer satisfaction scores, see Eugene W. Anderson and Claes Fornell, "Foundations of the American Customer Satisfaction Index," *Total Quality Management*, September 2000, pp. S869–S882; and Fornell, "The Science of Satisfaction," *Harvard Business Review*, March 2001, pp. 120–121. Cited facts from www.theacsi.org, accessed September 2003.

21. Leonard L. Berry and A. Parasuraman, *Marketing Services: Competing Through Quality* (New York: Free Press, 1991), pp. 136–142. Also see Richard Cross and Janet Smith, *Customer Bonding: Pathways to Lasting Customer Loyalty* (Lincolnwood, IL: NTC Business Books, 1995); and Michelle L. Roehm, Ellen Bolman Pullins, and Harpeer A. Roehm, "Building Loyalty-Building Programs for Packaged Goods Brands," *Journal of Marketing Research*, May 2002, pp. 202–213.

22. See Mary M. Long and Leon G. Schiffman, "Consumption Values and Relationships: Segmenting the Market for Frequency Programs," *The Journal of Consumer Marketing*, 2000, pp. 214+; and Patrick LePointe, "Loyalty Marketing's Newest Challenges," *Marketing News*, October 14, 2002, pp. 16–17. Examples based on information at www.hog.com and www.swatch.com, accessed September 2003.

23. Kotler, *Kotler on Marketing*, p. 20.

24. Thor Valdmanis, "Alliances Gain Favor over Risky Mergers," *USA Today*, February 4, 1999, p. 3B. Also see Gabor Gari, "Leveraging the Rewards of Strategic Alliances," *Journal of Business Strategy*, April 1999, pp. 40–43; Rosabeth Moss Kanter, "Why Collaborate?" *Executive Excellence*, April 1999, p. 8; Matthew Schifrin, "Partner or Perish," *Forbes*, May 21, 2001, pp. 26–28; and Kim T. Gordan, "Strong Partnerships Build Marketing Muscle," *CRN*, February 10, 2003, p. 14A.

25. See Thomas O. Jones and W. Earl Sasser Jr. "Why Satisfied Customers Defect," *Harvard Business Review*, November–December 1995, pp. 88–99, Thomas A. Stewart, "A Satisfied Customer Isn't Enough," *Fortune*, July 21, 1997, pp. 112–113; and Philip Kotler, *Marketing Insights from A to Z* (Hoboken, NJ: Wiley, 2003), pp. 36–40.

26. www.stew-leonards.com, accessed August 2002.

27. See Libby Estell, "This Call Center Accelerates Sales," *Sales Marketing Management*, February 1999, p. 72; Mark McMaster, "A Lifetime of Sales," *Sales Marketing Management*, September 2001, p. 55; and Lauren Keller Johnson, "The Real Value of Customer Loyalty," *MIT Sloan Management Review*, Winter 2002, pp. 14–17.

28. Erin Stout, "Keep Them Coming Back for More," *Sales and Marketing Management*, February 2002, pp. 51–52.

29. See Roland T. Rust, Valerie A. Zeithaml, and Katherine A. Lemon, *Driving Customer Equity* (New York Free Press 2000); Rust, Lemon, and Zeithaml, "Where Should the Next Marketing Dollar Go?" *Marketing Management*, September–October 2001, pp. 24–28; Robert C. Blattberg, Gary Getz, Jacquelyn S. Thomas, *Customer Equity* (Boston, MA: Harvard Business School Press, 2001); and John E. Hogan, Katherine N. Lemon, and Roland T. Rust, "Customer Equity Management: Charting New Directions for the Future of Marketing," *Journal of Service Research*, August 2002, pp. 4–12.

30. This example is adapted from Rust, Lemon, and Zeithaml, "Where Should the Next Marketing Dollar Go?" *Marketing Management*, p. 25. For in-depth discussions of how to measure customer equity, see Blattberg, Getz, and Thomas, *Customer Equity*.

31. Ravi Dhar and Rashi Glazer, "Hedging Customers," *Harvard Business Review*, May 2003, pp. 86–92.

32. Werner Reinartz and V. Kumar, "The Mismanagement of Customer Loyalty," *Harvard Business Review*, July 2002, pp. 86–94. For more on customer equity management, see Kotler, *Marketing Insights from A to Z*, pp. 38–40; Blattberg, Getz, and Thomas, *Customer Equity*, chapters 3–6; Sunil Gupta and Donald R. Lehman, "Customers as Assets," *Journal of Interactive Marketing*, Winter 2003, pp. 9–24; and Reinartz and Kumar, "The Impact of Customer Relationship Characteristics on Profitable Lifetime Duration," *Journal of Marketing*, January 2003, pp. 77–79.

33. www.statcan.ca/Daily/English/040708/d040708a.htm, accessed October 23, 2004.

34. Bruce Little, "Who Exports Canada's Goods to the World?" *The Globe and Mail*, January 29, 2001, p. B10; Press Release No. 172, "Pettigrew Announces Finalists for 2000 Canada Export Awards," Department of Foreign Affairs and International Trade, July 4, 2000; Press Release, "International Trade Minister Pettigrew—Talking Trade," Department of Foreign Affairs and International Trade, www.dfait-maeci.gc.ca/trade/canadexport/docs/active, accessed November 14, 2002; John Alden, "What in the World Drives UPS?" *International Business*, April 1998, pp. 6–7; Karen Pennar, "Two Steps Forward, One Step Back," *Business Week*, August 31, 1998, p. 116; Michelle Wirth Fellman, "A New World for Marketers," *Marketing News*, May 10, 1999, p. 13.

35. www.vancity.com/documents/2731_sovac.pdf, accessed October 23, 2004.

36. www.ccp.ca/Files/pressrelease/English_Release_NSNVO, accessed October 24, 2004. For other examples, and for a good review of nonprofit marketing, see Philip Kotler and Alan R. Andreasen, *Strategic Marketing for Nonprofit Organizations*, 6th ed. (Upper Saddle River, NJ: Prentice Hall, 2003); Philip Kotler and Karen Fox, *Strategic Marketing for Educational Institutions* (Upper Saddle River, NJ: Prentice Hall, 1995); Norman Shawchuck, Philip Kotler, Bruce Wren, and Gustave Rath, *Marketing for Congregations: Choosing to Serve People More Effectively* (Nashville, TN: Abingdon Press, 1993); and Philip Kotler, John Bowen, and James Makens, *Marketing for Hospitality and Tourism*, 3d ed. (Upper Saddle River, NJ: Prentice Hall, 2003).

Chapter 2

1. Airlines in Canada, Industry Profile, Data Monitor, Ref. Code 0070-0756, November 2004, pp. 7–17; J. Chidley, "Up in the Air," *Canadian Business*, September 27, 2004, p. 6; www.flyjazz.ca/english/aboutUs/history.asp, accessed December 2004; John Gray, "Treasure or Trash?," *Canadian Business*, June 7, 2004, p. 1; A.

Gollner, "On a Wing and a Joke," *Maclean's,* August 23, 2004, p. 52; www.highbeam.com/library, accessed December 2004.

2. See Philip Kotler, *Kotler on Marketing,* New York: Free Press, 1999, pp. 165–166.

3. For a more detailed discussion of corporate- and business-level strategic planning as they apply to marketing, see Philip Kotler, *Marketing Management,* 11th ed. (Upper Saddle River, NJ: Prentice Hall, 2003), chapter 4.

4. For more on mission statements, see Barbara Bartkus, Myron Glassman, and R. Bruce McAfee, "Mission Statements: Are They Smoke and Mirrors?" *Business Horizons,* November–December 2000, pp. 23–28; George S. Day, "Define Your Business," *Executive Excellence,* February 2001, p. 12; and Forest R. David and Fred R. David, "It's Time to Redraft Your Mission Statement," *The Journal of Business Strategy,* January–February 2003, pp. 11–14.

5. www.family-business-experts.com/sample-mission-statements. html, accessed December 12, 2004.

6. www.bce.ca/en/company/ourstrategy/index.php

7. Digby Anderson, "Is This the Perfect Mission Statement?" *Across the Board,* May–June 2001, p. 16.

8. www.celestialseasonings.com/whowear/corporatehistory/ mission.html, accessed June 2003.

9. www.girlguides.ca

10. www.hummingbird.com/about/index.html, accessed December 12, 2004.

11. www.telusmobility.com/about/company_background_telus. shtm, accessed September 12, 2004.

12. For more on strategic planning, see John A. Byrne, "Strategic Planning," *Business Week,* August 26, 1996, pp. 46–51; Pete Bogda, "Fifteen Years Later, the Return of Strategy," *Brandweek,* February 1997, p. 18; Ian Wilson, "Strategic Planning for the Millennium: Resolving the Dilemma," *Long Range Planning,* August 1998, pp. 507–513; Tom Devane, "Ten Cardinal Sins of Strategic Planning," *Executive Excellence,* October 2000, p. 15; Dave Lefkowith, "Effective Strategic Planning," *Management Quarterly,* Spring 2001, pp. 7–11; and Stan Abraham, "The Association of Strategic Planning: Strategy Is Still Management's Core Challenge," *Strategy Leadership,* 2002, pp. 38–42.

13. H. Igor Ansoff, "Strategies for Diversification," *Harvard Business Review,* September–October 1957, pp. 113–124. Also see Philip Kotler, *Kotler on Marketing* (New York: Free Press, 1999), pp. 46–48; and Kevin Lane Keller, *Strategic Brand Management,* 2nd ed. (Upper Saddle River, NJ: Prentice Hall, 2003), pp. 576–578.

14. John Gray, *Canadian Business,* June 7, 2004, pp. 45–46.

15. See "Crest, Colgate Bare Teeth in Competition for China," *Advertising Age International,* November 1996, p. I3; Mark L. Clifford, "How You Can Win in China," *Business Week,* May 26, 1997, pp. 66–68; and Ben Davies, "The Biggest Market Retains Its Luster," *Asia Money,* January 1998, pp. 47–49.

16. Michael E. Porter, *Competitive Advantage: Creating and Sustaining Superior Performance,* New York: Free Press, 1985; and Michel E. Porter, "What Is Strategy?" *Harvard Business Review,* November–December 1996, pp. 61–78. Also see Jim Webb and

Chas Gile, "Reversing the Value Chain," *Journal of Business Strategy,* March–April 2001, pp. 13–17.

17. Omar El Akkad and Tim Lai, "Cellphone Companies Reach Out to Tween Market," *The Globe and Mail,* July 7, 2005, p.; Tyler Hamilton and Robert Cribb, "Kids at Risk?" *Toronto Star,* July 9, 2005.

18. The four Ps classification was first suggested by E. Jerome McCarthy, *Basic Marketing: A Managerial Approach* (Homewood, IL: Irwin, 1960). For more discussion of this classification scheme, see Walter van Waterschoot and Christophe Van den Bulte, "The 4P Classification of the Marketing Mix Revisited," *Journal of Marketing,* October 1992, pp. 83–93; Michael G. Harvey, Robert F. Lusch, and Branko Cavarkapo, "A Marketing Mix for the Twenty-First Century," *Journal of Marketing Theory and Practice,* Fall 1996, pp. 1–15; and Don E. Schultz, "Marketers: Bid Farewell to Strategy Based on Old 4 Ps," *Marketing News,* February 12, 2001, p. 7.

19. Robert Lauterborn, "New Marketing Litany: 4Ps Passé; C-Words Take Over," *Advertising Age,* October 1, 1990, p. 26. Also see Kotler, *Marketing Management,* Chapter 1.

20. For a good discussion of gaining advantage through implementation effectiveness versus strategic differentiation, see Michael E. Porter, "What Is Strategy," *Harvard Business Review,* November–December 1996, pp. 61–78. Also see Charles H. Noble and Michael P. Mokwa, "Implementing Marketing Strategies: Developing and Testing a Managerial Theory," *Journal of Marketing,* October 1999, pp. 57–73; and Thomas W. Porter and Stephen C. Harper, "Tactical Implementation," *Business Horizons,* January–February 2003, pp. 53–60.

21. Brian Dumaine, "Why Great Companies Last," *Business Week,* January 16, 1995, p. 129. See James C. Collins and Jerry I. Porras, *Built to Last: Successful Habits of Visionary Companies* (New York: HarperBusiness, 1995); Rob Goffee and Gareth Jones, *The Character of a Corporation: How Your Company's Culture Can Make or Break Your Business* (New York: HarperBusiness, 1998); Thomas A. Atchison, "What Is Corporate Culture?" *Trustee,* April 2002, p. 11; and Jeff Rosenthal and Mary Ann Masarech, "High-Performance Cultures: How Values Can Drive Vision," *Journal of Organizational Excellence,* Spring 2003, pp. 3–18.

22. Joseph Winski, "One Brand, One Manager, *Advertising Age,* August 20, 1987, p. 86; see also Jack Neff, "The New Brand Management," *Advertising Age,* November 8, 1999, pp. S2, SA18.

23. See Roland T. Rust, Valerie A. Zeithaml, and Katherine N. Lemon, *Driving Customer Equity: How Lifetime Customer Value Is Reshaping Corporate Strategy* (New York: Free Press, 2000); and Rust, Lemon, and Zeithaml, "Where Should the Next Marketing Dollar Go?" *Marketing Management,* September–October 2001, pp. 24–28; Robert C. Blattberg, Gary Getz, and Jacquelyn S. Thomas, *Customer Equity* (Boston, MA: Harvard Business School Press, 2001); and John E. Hogan, Katherine N. Lemon, and Roland T. Rust, "Customer Equity Management: Charting New Directions for the Future of Marketing," *Journal of Service Research,* August 2002, pp. 4–12.

Chapter 3

1. www.ethicalbean.com.

2. "HP Presses for Corporate Responsibility," GlobeandMail.com, April 21, 2005.

3. www.suncor.com, accessed July 15, 2003.

4. Sara Minogue, "Sustainable PR," *Strategy*, November 4, 2002, p. 17.

5. Kerry Gillespie, "Consumer Rights Beefed Up," *Toronto Star*, July 21, 2005.

6. Competition Bureau News Releases, "Sears Deceptive Tire Marketing Case," Ottawa, April 1, 2005; "Competition Bureau Reaches Settlement with Goodlife Fitness Clubs in Advertising Case," Ottawa, February 9, 2005, www.competitionbureau.gc.ca/internet/index.

7. www.phonebusters.com/english/fraudprevention_backgrounder.html, accessed August 18, 2005.

8. John Gustavson, "The New Fraud Busters," *Marketing*, August 16, 1999, www.marketingmag.ca.

9. "Arthritis Drug Vioxx Recalled," *CBC News*, September 30, 2004; "Vioxx Widow Awarded $250 Million by Texas Jury," *CBC News*, August 19, 2005; "Merck Shares Plunge on Vioxx Recall," *CBC News*, October 1, 2004.

10. Cliff Edwards, "Where Have All the Edsels Gone?" *Greensboro News Record*, May 24, 1999, p. B6. For a short, thought-provoking case involving planned obsolescence, see James A. Heely and Roy L. Nersesian, "The Case of Planned Obsolescence," *Management Accounting*, February 1994, p. 67. Also see Joel Dryfuss, "Planned Obsolescence Is Alive and Well," *Fortune*, February 15, 1999, p. 192; and Atsuo Utaka, "Planned Obsolescence and Marketing Strategy," *Managerial and Decision Economics*, December 2000, pp. 339–344.

11. Adapted from John Markoff, "Is Planned Obsolescence Obsolete?" *New York Times*, February 17, 2002, pp. 4, 6.

12. Marcia Stepanek, "Weblining: Companies Are Using Your Personal Data to Limit Your Choices—and Force You to Pay More for Products," *Business Week*, April 3, 2000.

13. Richard W. Pollay, "The Distorted Mirror: Reflections on the Unintended Consequences of Advertising," *Journal of Marketing*, April 1986, pp. 18–36.

14. Carolyn Setlow, "Profiting from America's New Materialism," *Discount Store News*, April 17, 2000, p. 16. For interesting discussions on materialism and consumption, see Mark Rotella, Sarah F. Gould, Lynn Andriani, and Michael Scharf, "The High Price of Materialism," *Publishers Weekly*, July 1, 2002, p. 67; Lin Chiat Chang and Robert M. Arkin, "Materialism as an Attempt to Cope with Uncertainty," *Psychology & Marketing*, May 2002, pp. 389–406; John De Graaf, "The Overspent American/Luxury Fever," *Amicus Journal*, Summer 1999, pp. 41–43; and Professional Marketing Research Society, "Not Your Average Beer Drinking, Igloo-Dwelling, Hockey-Playing, 'Eh'-Sayers. Now Are We?" (press release), June 2002, www.pmrs-aprm.com/specialpr/release11.html.

15. From an advertisement for *Fact* magazine—which does not carry advertisements.

16. Michael Janiga, "Permanent Holding Pattern for Canadian Air Travellers," *Straight Goods*, undated, www.straightgoods.com/item410.asp, accessed July 17, 2003.

17. Paul Skippen and Geoff Wallace, "Both Protests and the Summit Process Depart from Genoa's Trends," *G8 Bulletin*, Volume 5, Issue 6, June 27–30, 2002, www.g7.utoronto.ca/g8bulletin/2002/bulletin6.htm. For more on the evolution of consumerism, see Paul N. Bloom and Stephen A. Greyser, "The Maturing of Consumerism," *Harvard Business Review*, November–December 1981, pp. 130–139; Robert J. Samualson, "The Aging of Ralph Nader," *Newsweek*, December 16, 1985, p. 57; Douglas A. Harbrecht, "The Second Coming of Ralph Nader," *Business Week*, March 6, 1989, p. 28; George S. Day and David A. Aaker, "A Guide to Consumerism," *Marketing Management*, Spring 1997, pp. 44–48; Benet Middleton, "Consumerism: A Pragmatic Ideology," *Consumer Policy Review*, November/December, 1998, pp. 213–217; and Penelope Green, "Consumerism and Its Malcontents," *New York Times*, December 17, 2000, p. 9.

18. See Consumers' Association of Canada, "Educational Publications: Be a Wise Consumer—We'll Show You How," www.consumer.ca/educationalprograms-showyouhow.htm.

19. Government of Canada news release, "Canada Shows Continued Leadership on Protecting the Ozone Layer," December 18, 2000, www.ec.gc.ca/press/001219_n_e.htm.

20. Ken MacQueen, "Ministers Declare War on Excess Packaging," *Kingston Whig-Standard*, March 22, 1990, p. 11.

21. Stuart L. Hart, "Beyond Greening: Strategies for a Sustainable World," *Harvard Business Review*, January–February 1997, pp. 66–76. Also see James L. Kolar, "Environmental Sustainability: Balancing Pollution Control with Economic Growth," *Environmental Quality Management*, Spring 1999, pp. 1–10; and Trevor Price and Doug Probert, "The Need for Environmentally Sustainable Developments," *International Need for Environmentally-Sustainable Developments*, 2002, pp. 1–22.

22. Peter M. Senge, Goran Carstedt, and Patrick L. Porter, "Innovating Our Way to the Next Industrial Revolution," *MIT Sloan Management Review*, Winter 2001, pp. 24–38.

23. Based on information from "BP Launches World's Greenest Service Station" (BP press release), www.bp.com/centres/press/media_resources/press_release/index.asp, accessed April 25, 2002; and www.bp.com/centres/press/hornchurch/index.asp, accessed September 2002.

24. See John Audley, *Green Politics and Global Trade: NAFTA and the Future of Environmental Politics* (Georgetown: Georgetown University Press, 1997); Lars K. Hallstrom, "Industry Versus Ecology: Environment in the New Europe," *Futures*, February 1999, pp. 25–38; Joe McKinney, "NAFTA: Four Years Down the Road," *Baylor Business Review*, Spring 1999, pp. 22–23; Andreas Diekmann and Axel Franzen, "The Wealth of Nations and Environmental Concern," *Environment and Behavior*, July 1999, pp. 540–549.

25. Linda Sutherland, "Brothers Find Focus in Waste," *Globe and Mail*, January 6, 1997, p. B8.

26. Michelle Wirth Fellman, "New Product Marketer of 1997," *Marketing News*, March 30, 1998, pp. E2, E12; Mercedes M. Cardona, "Colgate Boosts Budget to Further 5-Year Plan," *Advertising Age*, May 15, 2000, p. 6; Emily Nelson, "Colgate's Net Rose 10 Percent in Period, New Products Helped Boost Sales," *Wall Street Journal*, February 2, 2001, p. B6; and Lesley Young, "Colgate Adds Motion to Brush Market," *Marketing*, April 8, 2002, www.marketingmag.ca.

27. Mountain Equipment Co-op, "Mission and Values," undated, www.mec.ca, accessed July 17, 2003.

28. Tim Kavander, "The Creative Eye: Canadian Hockey Association," *Marketing*, January 27, 2003, p. 16; Roy MacGregor, "Boors Under Heavy Fire in Hockey Parent Ads," *The Globe and Mail*, November 28, 2003, p. A2.

29. www.HermanMiller.com, accessed October 2001. See also Jacquelyn A. Ottman, "Green Marketing: Wake Up to the Truth About Green Consuming," *In Business*, May–June 2002, p. 31.

30. Dan R. Dalton and Richard A. Cosier, "The Four Faces of Social Responsibility," *Business Horizons*, May–June 1982, pp. 19–27.

31. Joseph Webber, "3M's Big Cleanup," *Business Week*, June 5, 2000, pp. 96–98. Also see Kara Sissell, "3M Defends Timing of Scotchgard Phaseout," *Chemical Week*, April 11, 2001, p. 33; and Peck Hwee Sim, "Ausimont Targets Former Scotchgard Markets,"*Chemical Week*, August 7, 2002, p. 32.

32. Barbara Crossette, "Russia and China Top Business Bribers," *New York Times*, May 17, 2002, p. A10.

33. John F. Magee and P. Ranganath Nayak, "Leaders' Perspectives on Business Ethics," *Prizm*, Arthur D. Little, Inc., Cambridge, Mass., First Quarter, 1994, pp. 65–77. Also see Turgut Guvenli and Rajib Sanyal, "Ethical Concerns in International Business: Are Some Issues More Important than Others?" *Business and Society Review*, Summer 2002, pp. 195–206.

34. See Samuel A. DiPiazza, "Ethics in Action," *Executive Excellence*, January 2002, pp. 15–16.

Chapter 4

1. Jack Neff, "In Dove Ads, Normal Is the New Beautiful," *Advertising Age*, September 27, 2004; Sarah Dobson, "Interactive Outdoor," *Marketing*, May 16, 2005, p. 15; Michelle Halpern, "Dove Boosts Girls' Self-Image," *Marketing*, February 14, 2005, p. 3; David Menzies, "Fat, Fab, or Fantasy," *Marketing*, January 31, 2005, p. 10; Molly Prior, "Dove Ad Campaign Aims to Redefine Beauty," *Women's Wear Daily*, October 8, 2004; campaignforrealbeauty.ca.

2. Statistics Canada, *Population and Dwelling Counts, for Canada, Provinces and Territories, 2001 and 1996 Censuses*, www12.statcan.ca/english/census01/products/standard/popdwell/Table-PR.cfm, accessed October 2004

3. World POP Clock, U.S Census Bureau, www.census.gov, accessed August 2003. This site provides continually updated population projections for the U.S and world populations.

4. Elizabeth Church, "Birth Bulge Breeds Its Own Industry," *The Globe and Mail*, September 24, 1996, p. B12.

5. Jane Gadd, "Commitment to Healthy Diet Declines," *The Globe and Mail*, November 11, 1997, p. A10.

6. www.statcan.ca/english/Pgdb/demo31j.htm, accessed November 2004.

7. See Thomas Exter, "And Baby Makes 20 Million," *American Demographics*, July 1991, p. 55; Joseph Spiers, "The Baby Boomlet Is for Real," *Fortune*, February 10, 1992, pp. 101–104; Joe Schwartz, "Is the Baby Boomlet Ending?" *American Demographics*, May 1992, p. 9; and Christopher Farrell, "The Baby Boomlet May Kick in a Little Growth," *Business Week*, January 10, 1994, p. 66.

8. See Diane Crispell and William H. Frey, "American Maturity," *American Demographics*, March 1993, pp. 31–42; Charles F. Longino, "Myths of an Aging America," *American Demographics*, August 1994, pp. 36–43; Melissa Campanelli, "Selling to Seniors: A Waiting Game," *Sales & Marketing Management*, June 1994, p. 69.

9. www.statcan.ca/english/Pgdb/famil40a.htm, modified September 2004.

10. Human Resources Development Canada, Section 5.2 "Women," http://info.load-otea.hrdc-drhc.gc.ca/workplace_equity/leep/annual/2002/2002annualrep08.shtml, accessed May 5, 2003.

11. "Canada's Population," *The Daily*, September 29, 2004. www.statcan.ca/Daily/English/040929/d040929d.htm, accessed November 2004.

12. GDSourcing, "Who Works from Home," *The Business Researcher Newsletter Archives*, Vol. 5 (3), March 22, 2002.

13. Statistics Canada, "Visible Minority Population, Provinces and Territories," 2001 Census Release, April 23, 2003, www.statcan.ca/english/Pgdb/demo40a.htm.

14. For these and other examples, see "Marketing to Americans with Disabilities," *Packaged Facts*, New York, 1997; Dan Frost, "The Fun Factor: Marketing Recreation to the Disabled," *American Demographics*, February 1998, pp. 53–58; Michelle Wirth Fellman, "Selling IT Goods to Disabled End-Users," *Marketing News*, March 15, 1999, pp. 1, 17; Alison Stein Wellner, "The Internet's Nest Niche," *American Demographics*, September 2000, pp. 18–19; Alan Hughes, "Taking the 'Dis' Out of Disability," *Black Enterprise*, March 2002, p. 102; and Volkswagen's website, www.vw.com, accessed August 2002.

15. Alison Stein Wellner, "The Next 25 Years," *American Demographics*, April 2003, pp. 23–27.

16. James W. Hughes, "Understanding the Squeezed Consumer," *American Demographics*, July 1991, pp. 44–50. For more on consumer spending trends, see Cheryl Russell, "The New Consumer Paradigm," *American Demographics*, April 1999, pp. 50–58.

17. Department of Finance Canada, "The Economy in Brief: March 2003," March 20, 2003, www.fin.gc.ca/purl/econbr-e.html.

18. Statistics Canada, "Average Household Expenditures, Provinces and Territories," Canadian Statistics, www.statcan.ca/english/Pgdb/famil16a.htm, accessed November 2004.

19. For more discussion, see the "Environmentalism" section in Chapter 4. Also see Patrick Carson and Julia Moulden, *Green Is Gold* (Toronto: Harper Business Press, 1991); Michael E. Porter and Claas van der Linde, "Green and Competitive: Ending the Stalemate," *Harvard Business Review*, September–October 1995, pp. 120–134; Stuart L. Hart, "Beyond Greening: Strategies for a Sustainable World," *Harvard Business Review*, January–February 1997, pp. 67–76; Forest L. Reinhardt, "Bringing the Environment Down to Earth," *Harvard Business Review*, July–August 1999, pp. 149–157; "Earth in the Balance," *American Demographics*, January 2001, p. 24; and Subhabrata Bobby Banerjee, "Corporate Environmentalism: The Construct and Its Measurement," *Journal of Business Research*, March 2002, pp. 177–191.

20. For more on Yankelovich Monitor, see http://secure.yankelovich.com/solutions/monitor/ y-monitor.asp.

21. See Cyndee Miller, "Trendspotters: 'Dark Ages' Ending; So Is Cocooning," *Marketing News*, February 3, 1997, pp. 1, 16.

22. Michael Adams, *Better Happy Than Rich: Canadians, Money, and the Meaning of Life* (Toronto: Viking, 2000), p. 85.

23. Agriculture and Agri Food Canada, "Organics Industry" (fact sheet), 2002, http://atn-riae.agr.ca/supply/e3313.htm.

24. Michael Valpy, "Religious Observance Continues to Decline," *Globe and Mail*, March 19, 2003, p. A18; and Clifford Krauss, "In God We Trust . . . Canadians Aren't So Sure," *New York Times*, www.nytimes.com, March 26, 2003.

25. "The Unique Japanese," *Fortune*, November 24, 1986, p. 8. For more on nontariff and other barriers, see Warren J. Keegan and Mark C. Green, *Principles of Global Marketing*, Upper Saddle River, NJ: Prentice Hall, 1997, pp. 200–203.

26. Tom McFeat, "NAFTA—10 Years Later," *CBC News Online*, www.cbc.ca/news/background/summitofamericas/nafta.html, accessed January 7, 2004; Rob Portman, "Washington Speaks: Good Neighbours Must Talk," *The Globe and Mail*, September 3, 2005, p. A23; Norman Spector, "Old Fights, New Rounds, Same Politicization," *The Globe and Mail*, September 5, 2005, p. A15.

27. Philip Kotler, *Kotler on Marketing* (New York: Free Press, 1999), p. 3.

28. See Carl P. Zeithaml and Valerie A. Zeithaml, "Environmental Management: Revising the Marketing Perspective," *Journal of Marketing*, Spring 1984, pp. 46–53.

Chapter 5

1. "Loyalty Cards: Getting to Know You," *Marketplace*, broadcast on CBC, October 24, 2004.

2. See Philip Kotler, *Kotler on Marketing* (New York: Free Press, 1999), p. 73.

3. Christina Le Beau, "Mountains to Mine," *American Demographics*, August 2000, pp. 40–44. Also see Joseph M. Winski, "Gentle Rain Turns into Torrent," *Advertising Age*, June 3, 1991, p. 34; David Shenk, *Data Smog: Surviving the Information Glut* (San Francisco: HarperSanFrancisco, 1997); Diane Trommer, "Information Overload—Study Finds Intranet Users Overwhelmed with Data," *Electronic Buyers' News*, April 20, 1998, p. 98; and Stewart Deck, "Data Storm Ahead," *CIO*, April 15, 2001, p. 97.

4. Alice LaPlante, "Still Drowning!" *Computer World*, March 10, 1997, pp. 69–70; and Jennifer Jones, "Looking Inside," *InfoWorld*, January 7, 2002, pp. 22–26.

5. Philip Kotler, Gary Armstrong, and Peggy H. Cunningham, *Principles of Marketing*, 5th Cdn ed. (Toronto: Pearson Education, 2002).

6. For these and other examples, see Stan Crock, "They Snoop to Conquer," *Business Week*, October 28, 1996, p. 172; and James Curtis, "Behind Enemy Lines," *Marketing*, May 24, 2001, pp. 28–29.

7. See Suzie Amer, "Masters of Intelligence," *Forbes*, April 5, 1999, p. 18.

8. Adapted from information in Ellen Neuborne, "Know Thy Enemy," *Sales Marketing Management*, January 2003, pp.29–33.

9. For more on marketing and competitive intelligence, see David B. Montgomery and Charles Weinberg, "Toward Strategic Intelligence Systems," *Marketing Management*, Winter 1998, pp. 44–52; Morris C. Attaway Sr., "A Review of Issues Related to Gathering and Assessing Competitive Intelligence," *American Business Review*, January 1998, pp. 25–35; and Conor Vibert, "Secrets of Online Sleuthing," *Journal of Business Strategy*, May–June 2001, pp. 39–42.

10. For more on research firms that supply marketing information, see Jack Honomichl, "Honomichl 50," special section, *Marketing News*, June 10, 2002, pp. H1–H43.

11. Example adapted from Douglas McGray, "Babes in R&D Toyland," *Fast Company*, December 2002, p. 46.

12. Adapted from Rebecca Piirto Heather, "Future Focus Groups," *American Demographics*, January 1994, p. 6. For more on focus groups, see Holly Edmunds, *The Focus Group Research Handbook* (Lincolnwood, Ill.: NTC Business Books, 1999); and R. Kenneth Wade, "Focus Groups' Research Role Is Shifting," *Marketing News*, March 4, 2002, p. 47.

13. Adapted from examples in Gary H. Anthes, "Smile, You're on Candid Computer," *Computerworld*, December 3, 2001, p. 50.

14. Marc L. Songini, "FedEx Expects CRM System to Deliver," *Computerworld*, November 6, 2000, p. 10.

15. Darrell K. Rigby, "Avoid the Four Perils of CRM," *Harvard Business Review*, February 2002, pp. 101–109.

16. Michael Krauss, "At Many Firms, Technology Obscures CRM," *Marketing News*, March 18, 2002, p. 5.

17. Ravi Kalakota and Marcia Robinson, *E-Business: Roadmap for Success* (Reading, Mass: Addison-Wesley, 1999).

18. For some good advice on conducting market research in a small business, see "Marketing Research Basics 101," www.onlinewbc.gov/docs/market/mkt_res_basics.html, accessed June 2003.

19. Many of the examples in this section, along with others, are found in Subhash C. Jain, *International Marketing Management*, 3rd ed. (Boston: PWS-Kent, 1990), pp. 334–339. Ken Gofton, "Going Global with Research," *Marketing*, April 15, 1999, p. 35; Naresh K. Malhotra, *Marketing Research*, 3d ed. (Upper Saddle River, N.J.: Prentice Hall, 1999), Chapter 23; and Tim R. V. Davis and Robert B. Young, "International Marketing Research," *Business Horizons*, March–April 2002, pp. 31–38.

20. Subhash C. Jain, *International Marketing Management*, p. 338. See also Alvin C. Burns and Ronald F. Bush, Marketing Research, 3rd ed. (Upper Saddle River, NJ, Prentice Hall 2000), pp. 317–318.

21. Professional Marketing Research Society, "Market Research Uncovers the Canadian Identity" (press release), June 2002, www.csrc.ca/CSRC/news/news200206.php; and Canadian Survey Research Council, "Canadian Attitudes Towards Survey Research and Issues of Privacy," October 2001, www.csrc.ca/CSRC/news/2001CSRC.pdf.

22. Canadian Survey Research Council, "Prison Call Centres Terminated" (press release), March 28, 2003, www.csrc.ca/CSRC/news/news20030328.php.

23. Canadian Survey Research Council, "Canadian Attitudes Towards Survey Research and Issues of Privacy," October 2001, www.csrc.ca/CSRC/news/2001CSRC.pdf.

24. David Eggleston, "Canadians Condemn Doubleclick Profiling Plans," *Strategy,* March 13, 2000, p. 2.

25. Susan Vogt, "Online Privacy Laws All Over the Map," *Strategy,* September 11, 2000, p. 12.

26. Cynthia Crossen, "Studies Galore Support Products and Positions, but Are They Reliable?" *Wall Street Journal,* November 14, 1991, pp. A1, A9. Also see Allan J. Kimmel, "Deception in Marketing Research and Practice: An Introduction," *Psychology and Marketing,* July 2001, pp. 657–661.

Chapter 6

1. Greg Schneider, "Toyota's Prius Proving to Be the Hotter Ride in Hybrids," *The Washington Post,* August 23, 2004; "Is Toyota Prius the Most Important 2004 Model?" *Motor Trend,* November 11, 2003; "Toyota Boosts 2004 Prius Output," *Motor Trend,* December 9, 2003.

2. www.macleans.ca/topstories/polls/article.jsp?content= 20031218_150312_2984, accessed November, December 2004.

3. Ministry of Supply and Services Canada, "Shared Values: The Canadian Identity," 1991, p. 1; Craig McKie and Keith Thompson, *Canadian Social Trends* (Toronto: Thompson Educational Publishing Inc.).

4. www.statcan.ca/english/Pgdb/demo39b.htm, accessed November, December 2004.

5. Sinclair Stewart, "Multicultural Marketing: A Long and Winding Road," *Strategy,* August 17, 1998, p. 20.

6. Race Relations Advisory Council on Advertising, "The Color of Your Money," (video), 1995.

7. See Darla Dernovsek, "Marketing to Women," *Credit Union Magazine,* October 2000, pp. 90–96; Sharon Goldman Edry, "No Longer Just Fun and Games," *American Demographics,* May 2001, pp. 36–38; Joanne Thomas Yaccato, *Reaching the Real World of Women: The 80 Per Cent Minority* (Toronto: Viking Canada, 2003); and Dana Flavelle, "'Gender Intelligence' Is Her Message," *Toronto Star,* April 9, 2003, www.torontostar.com.

8. David Leonhardt, "Hey Kids, Buy This," *Business Week,* June 30, 1997, pp. 62–67; and Jean Halliday, "Automakers Agree, Winning Youth Early Key to Future," *Advertising Age,* April 1, 2002, p. S16.

9. Tobi Elkin, "Sony Marketing Aims at Lifestyle Segments," *Advertising Age,* March 18, 2002, pp. 3, 72.

10. Paul C. Judge, "Are Tech Buyers Different?" *Business Week,* January 26, 1998, pp. 64–65, 68; Josh Bernoff, Shelley Morrisette, and Kenneth Clemmer, "The Forrester Report," Forrester Research, Inc., 1998; www.forrester.com, accessed July 2001.

11. Jennifer Aaker, "Dimensions of Measuring Brand Personality," *Journal of Marketing Research,* August 1997, pp. 347–356. Also see Aaker, "The Malleable Self: The Role of Self-Expression in Persuasion," *Journal of Marketing Research,* May 1999, pp. 45–57; and Swee Hoon Ang, "Personality Influences on Consumption: Insights from the Asian Economic Crisis," *Journal of International Consumer Marketing,* 2001, pp. 5–20.

12. Myron Magnet, "Let's Go for Growth," *Fortune,* 7 March 1994, p. 70.

13. Charles Pappas, "Ad Nauseam," *Advertising Age,* July 10, 2000, pp. 16–18.

14. David Todd, "Quebec Milk Producers Play on Emotional Ties," *Strategy,* March 1, 1999, p. 31; and Stephanie Whittaker, "Milk Grows Up," *Marketing,* August 9, 1999, www.marketingmag.ca.

15. See Leon Festinger, *A Theory of Cognitive Dissonance* (Stanford, Calif.: Stanford University Press, 1957); Leon G. Schiffman and Leslie L. Kanuk, *Consumer Behavior,* 6th ed. (Upper Saddle River, N.J.: Prentice Hall, 1997), pp. 219–220; Jeff Stone, "A Radical New Look at Cognitive Dissonance," *American Journal of Psychology,* Summer 1998, pp. 319–326; Thomas R. Schultz, Elene Leveille, and Mark R. Lepper, "Free Choice and Cognitive Dissonance Revisited: Choosing 'Lesser Evils' Versus 'Greater Goods,'" *Personality and Social Psychology Bulletin,* January 1999, pp. 40–48; Jillian C. Sweeney, Douglas Hausknecht, and Geoffrey N. Soutar, "Cognitive Dissonance After Purchase: A Multidimensional Scale," *Psychology & Marketing,* May 2000, pp. 369–385; and Patti Williams and Jennifer L. Aaker, "Can Mixed Emotions Peacefully Coexist?" March 2002, pp. 636–649.

16. The following discussion draws heavily from Everett M. Rogers, *Diffusion of Innovations,* 3rd ed. (New York: Free Press, 1983). Also see Hubert Gatignon and Thomas S. Robertson, "A Propositional Inventory for New Diffusion Research," *Journal of Consumer Research,* March 1985, pp. 849–867; Marnik G. Dekiple, Philip M. Parker, and Milos Sarvary, "Global Diffusion of Technological Innovations: A Coupled-Hazard Approach," *Journal of Marketing Research,* February 2000, pp. 47–59; Peter J. Danaher, Bruce G.S. Hardie, and William P. Putsis, "Marketing-Mix Variables and the Diffusion of Successive Generations of a Technological Innovation," *Journal of Marketing Research,* November 2001, pp. 501–514; and Eun-Ju Lee, Jinkook Lee, and David W. Schumann, "The Influence of Communication Source and Mode on Consumer Adoption of Technological Innovations," *Journal of Consumer Affairs,* Summer 2002, pp. 1–27.

17. Sarah Lorge, "Purchasing Power," *Sales & Marketing Management,* June 1998, pp. 43–46.

18. Patrick J. Robinson, Charles W. Faris, and Yoram Wind, *Industrial Buying Behavior and Creative Marketing* (Boston: Allyn & Bacon, 1967). Also see Erin Anderson, Weyien Chu, and Barton Weitz, "Industrial Purchasing: An Empirical Exploration of the Buyclass Framework," *Journal of Marketing,* July 1987, pp. 71–86; and Michael D. Hutt and Thomas W. Speh, *Business Marketing Management,* 7th ed. (Upper Saddle River, N.J.: Prentice Hall, 2001), pp. 56–66.

19. Frederick E. Webster Jr. and Yoram Wind, *Organizational Buying Behavior* (Upper Saddle River, N.J.: Prentice Hall, 1972), pp. 78–80. Also see James C. Anderson and James A. Narus, *Business Market Management: Understanding, Creating and Delivering Value* (Upper Saddle River, N.J.: Prentice Hall, 1998), Chapter 3; and Michael D. Hutt and Thomas W. Speh, *Business Marketing Management,* 7th ed. (Upper Saddle River, N.J.: Prentice Hall, 2001), pp. 73–77.

20. Thomas V. Bonoma, "Major Sales: Who Really Does the Buying," *Harvard Business Review,* May–June 1982, p. 114. Also see Ajay Kohli, "Determinants of Influence in Organizational

Buying: A Contingency Approach," *Journal of Marketing,* July 1989, pp. 50–65; and Jeffrey E. Lewin, "The Effects of Downsizing on Organizational Buying Behavior: An Empirical Investigation," *Academy of Marketing Science,* Spring 2001, pp. 151–164.

21. Robinson, Faris, and Wind, *Industrial Buying Behavior,* p. 14.

22. Bernadette Johnson, "Business Depot targets SOHO sector," *Strategy,* June 19, 2000, p. D1.

23. "E-Procurement: Certain Value in Changing Times," *Fortune,* April 30, 2001, pp. S2–S3; and "Benchmark Survey: E-Procurement Adoptions Progress Slowly and Steadily," *Purchasing,* June 20, 2002, p. S8.

24. See Verespej, "E-Procurement Explosion," pp. 25–28; Andy Reinhardt, "Extranets: Log On, Link Up, Save Big," *Business Week,* June 22, 1998, p. 134; "To Byte the Hand That Feeds," *The Economist,* January 17, 1998, pp. 61–62; Ken Brack, "Source of the Future," *Industrial Distribution,* October 1998, pp. 76–80; James Carbone, "Internet Buying on the Rise," *Purchasing,* March 25, 1999, pp. 51–56.

Chapter 7

1. Steve Jarvis, "P&G's Challenge," *Marketing News,* August 28, 2000, pp. 1, 13; Robert Berner, "Can P&G Clean Up Its Act?" *Business Week,* March 12, 2001, pp. 80–83; www.pg.com; www.tide.com.

2. "Absolut East," *Marketing,* September 18, 1995, p. 2.

3. www.freehotelsearch.com/ca/Alberta-Four_Points_Hotels_By_Sheraton-chain.html.

4. Bruce Hager, "Podunk Is Beckoning," *Business Week,* December 2, 1991, p. 76; David Greisling, "The Boonies Are Booming," *Business Week,* October 9, 1995, pp. 104–110; Mike Duff, "Home Depot Drops Villager's Hareware for New Concept," *DSN Retailing Today,* April 22, 2002, pp. 5, 28; and Stephanie Thompson, "Wal-Mart Tops List for New Food Lines, *Advertising Age,* April 29, 2002, pp. 4, 61.

5. www.olay.com, accessed July 2002.

6. Pat Sloan and Jack Neff, "With Aging Baby Boomers in Mind, P&G, Den-Mat Plan Launches," *Advertising Age,* April 13, 1998, pp. 3, 38.

7. See Hillary Chura, "Marketing Messages for Women Fall Short," *Advertising Age,* September 23, 2002, pp. 1, 14–15; Alice Z. Cuneo, "Advertisers Target Women, but Market Remains Elusive," *Advertising Age,* November 10, 1997, pp. 1, 24; and Bruce Upbin, "Merchant Princes," *Forbes,* January 20, 2003, pp. 52–56.

8. "Grocery Gateway to Deliver for Home Depot," *The Globe and Mail,* November 26, 2002, www.globeandmail.com.

9. Michelle Orecklin, "What Women Watch," *Time,* May 13, 2002, pp. 65–66; www.oxygen.com, accessed July 2002; www.wnetwork.com, accessed July 2003.

10. Amanda Beeler, "Heady Rewards for Loyalty," *Advertising Age,* August 14, 2000, p. S8; www.neimanmarcus.com/store/sitelets/incircle/index.jhtml, accessed July 2002.

11. Marina Strauss, "The Best Bet for Your Bottom Dollar," *The Globe and Mail,* August 2, 2003, pp. B1, B5.

12. "Lifestyle Marketing," *Progressive Grocer,* August 1997, pp. 107–110; Philip Kotler and Peggy Cunningham, *Marketing Management: Analysis, Planning, Implementation, and Control,* Canadian 11th ed. (Toronto: Pearson Education Canada, 2004), pp. 296–298.

13. Laurie Freeman and Cleveland Horton, "Spree: Honda's Scooters Ride the Cutting Edge," *Advertising Age,* September 5, 1985, pp. 3, 35; "Scooter Wars," *Cycle World,* February 1998, p. 26; Jonathon Welsh, "Transport: The Summer of the Scooter: Boomers Get a New Retro Toy," *Wall Street Journal,* April 13, 2001, p. W1; www.hondamotorcycle.com/scooter, accessed July 2002.

14. "RadioShack Giving E-Gifts This Holiday Season," *Adnews On-Line Daily,* November 13, 2000, www.adnews.com.

15. www.kodak.com, August 2003.

16. British Columbia Ministry of Health, "The Need for Blood Donors" (news release), May 29, 2003, www2.news.gov.bc.ca/nrm_news_releases/2003HSER0028–000531.htm, accessed August 18, 2003; Will Stos, "A Bloody Mess: When the Gift of Life Is Refused," *Centretown News,* February 7, 2003, www.carleton.ca/ctown/archiv/ feb0703/insite1.htm.

17. See Jennifer Ordonez, "Cash Cows: Hamburger Joints Call Them 'Heavy Users,' " *Wall Street Journal,* January 12, 2000, p. A1; and Brian Wonsink and Sea Bum Park, "Methods and Measures That Profile Heavy Users," *Journal of Advertising Research,* July–August 2000, pp. 61–72.

18. Kendra Parker, "How Do You Like Your Beef?" *American Demographics,* January 2000, pp. 35–37.

19. Daniel S. Levine, "Justice Served," *Sales & Marketing Management,* May 1995, pp. 53–61.

20. For more on segmenting business markets, see John Berrigan and Carl Finkbeiner, *Segmentation Marketing: New Methods for Capturing Business* (New York: HarperBusiness, 1992); Rodney L. Griffith and Louis G. Pol, "Segmenting Industrial Markets," *Industrial Marketing Management,* no. 23, 1994, pp. 39–46; Stavros P. Kalafatis and Vicki Cheston, "Normative Models and Practical Applications of Segmentation in Business Markets," *Industrial Marketing Management,* November 1997, pp. 519–530; James C. Anderson and James A. Narus, *Business Market Management* (Upper Saddle River, N.J.: Prentice Hall, 1999), pp. 44–47; and Andy Dexter, "Egotists, Idealists, and Corporate Animals—Segmenting Business Markets, *International Journal of Marketing Research,* First Quarter 2002, pp. 31–51.

21. See Warren J. Keegan, *Global Marketing Management* (Upper Saddle River, NJ, 2002), p. 194; Arundhati Parmar, "Global Youth United," *Marketing News,* October 28, 2002, pp. 1, 49; www.mtv.com/mtvinternational; "MTV: Music Television: The Facts," www.viacom.com/prodbyunit1.tin?ixBusUnit519, accessed July 2003.

22. See Michael Porter, *Competitive Advantage* (New York: Free Press, 1985), pp. 4–8, 234–236. For more recent discussions, see Leyland Pitt, "Total E-clipse: Five New Forces for Strategy in the Digital Age," *Journal of General Management,* Summer 2001, pp. 1–15; and Stanley Slater and Eric Olson, "A Fresh Look at Industry and Market Analysis," *Business Horizons,* January–February 2002, p. 15–22.

23. Peter Burrows, "How to Milk an Apple," *Business Week,* February 3, 2003, p. 44.

24. Paul Davidson, "Entrepreneurs Reap Riches from Net Niches," *USA Today,* April 20, 1998, p. B3; and Ostriches On Line website, www.ostrichesonline.com, accessed July 2002.

25. Quoted in Philip Kotler, Gary Armstrong, and Peggy Cunningham, *Principles of Marketing,* 5th Cdn. ed., Toronto: Pearson Education Canada, 2002.

26. See Philip Kotler, *Kotler on Marketing* (New York: Free Press, 1999), pp. 149–150; and Faith Keenan, "A Mass Market of One," *Business Week,* December 2, 2002, pp. 68–72.

27. See Jerry Wind and Arvid Rangaswamy, "Customerization: The Next Revolution in Mass Customization," *Journal of Interactive Marketing,* Winter 2001, pp. 13–32; and Yoram Wind and Vijay Mahajan, "Convergence Marketing," *Journal of Interactive Marketing,* Spring 2002, pp. 64–69.

28. Sony A. Grier, "The Federal Trade Commission's Report on the Marketing of Violent Entertainment to Youths: Developing Policy-Tuned Research," *Journal of Public Policy and Marketing,* Spring 2001, pp. 123–132; and Greg Winter, "Tobacco Company Reneged on Youth Ads, Judge Rules," *New York Times,* June 7, 2002, p. A18. Also see Deborah L. Vence, "Marketing to Minors Still under Careful Watch," *Marketing News,* March 31, 2003, pp. 5–6.

29. Joseph Turow, "Breaking Up America: The Dark Side of Target Marketing," *American Demographics,* November 1997, pp. 51–54; and Bette Ann Stead and Jackie Gilbert, "Ethical Issues in Electronic Commerce," *Journal of Business Ethics,* November 2001, pp. 75–85.

30. Adapted from a positioning map prepared by students Brian May, Josh Payne, Meredith Schakel, and Bryana Sterns, University of North Carolina, April 2003. SUV sales data furnished by WardAuto.com, June 2003. Price data from www.edmunds.com, June 2003.

31. See Philip Kotler, *Kotler on Marketing* (New York: Free Press, 1999), pp. 59–63.

32. See Bobby J. Calder and Steven J. Reagan, "Brand Design," in Dawn Iacobucci, ed., *Kellogg on Marketing* (New York: John Wiley, 2001) p. 61.

33. The Palm Pilot and Mountain Dew examples are from Alice M. Tybout and Brian Sternthal, "Brand Positioning," in Dawn Iacobucci, ed., *Kellogg on Marketing* (New York: John Wiley, 2001), p. 54.

Chapter 8

1. Excerpt adapted from Penelope Green, "Spiritual Cosmetics. No Kidding," *New York Times,* January 10, 1999, p. 1. Also see Elizabeth Wellington, "The Success of Smell," *The News Observer,* June 11, 2001, p. E1; Mary Tannen, "Cult Cosmetics," *New York Times Magazine,* Spring 2001, p. 96; Sandra Yin, "The Nose Knows," *American Demographics,* February 2002, pp. 14–15; and "Pots of Promise—The Beauty Business," *The Economist,* May 24, 2003, pp. 69–71.

2. Joel Parent, "Top Three Contests," *Strategy,* August 2005, p. 9.

3. For more on experience marketing, see B. Joseph Pine and James H. Gilmore, *The Experience Economy* (New York: Free Press,

1999); Jane E. Zarem, "Experience Marketing," *Folio: The Magazine for Magazine Management,* Fall 2000, pp. 28–32; Scott Mac Stravic, "Make Impressions Last: Focus on Value," *Marketing News,* October 23, 2000, pp. 44–45; and Stephen E. DeLong, "The Experience Economy," *Upside,* November 2001, p. 28.

4. See Philip Kotler, Irving J. Rein, and Donald Haider, *Marketing Places: Attracting Investment, Industry, and Tourism to Cities, States, and Nations* (New York: Free Press, 1993), pp. 202, 273. Additional information at www.ireland.travel.ie and www.ida.ie, accessed August 2003.

5. www.social-marketing.org/aboutus.html, accessed August 2003.

6. See Alan R. Andreasen, Rob Gould, and Karen Gutierrez, "Social Marketing Has a New Champion," *Marketing News,* February 7, 2000, p. 38. Also see Philip Kotler, Ned Roberto, and Nancy Lee, *Social Marketing: Improving the Quality of Life,* 2nd ed. (Thousand Oaks, CA: Sage Publications, 2002); and www.social-marketing.org, August 2003.

7. Quotes and definitions from Philip Kotler, *Kotler on Marketing* (New York: Free Press, 1999), p. 17; and www.asq.org, August 2003.

8. See Roland T. Rust, Anthony J. Zahorik, and Timothy L. Keiningham, "Return on Quality (ROQ): Making Service Quality Financially Accountable," *Journal of Marketing,* April 1995, pp. 58–70; and Roland T. Rust, Christine Moorman, and Peter R. Dickson, "Getting Return on Quality: Revenue Expansion, Cost Reduction, or Both?" *Journal of Marketing,* October 2002, pp. 7–24.

9. Quote from Mike Musgrove, "Think Discontinued: Apple Retires Its Original iMac Line," *The Washington Post,* March 19, 2003, p. E2. Also see "Hot R.I.P.: The Floppy Disk," *Rolling Stone,* August 20, 1998, p. 86; Robert Dwek, "Apple Pushes Design to Core of Marketing," *Marketing Week,* January 24, 2002, p. 20; "John Markoff, "Apple Computer Beats Earnings Estimates in Second Quarter," *New York Times,* April 18, 2002, p. C7; and Chee Pearlman, "Designer of iMac Wins Designer of the Year Award," *New York Times,* June 5, 2003, p. 3.

10. See Kate Fitzgerald, "Packaging Is the Capper," *Advertising Age,* May 5, 2003, p. 22.

11. Adapted from examples found in Julie Dunn, "Pouring Paint, Minus a Mess," *New York Times,* October 27, 2002, p. 3.2; "Look Ma, No Drip," *Business Week,* December 16, 2002, p. 74; and Seth Godin, "In Praise of the Purple Cow," *Fast Company,* February 2003, pp. 74–85.

12. Robert M. McMath, "Chock Full of (Pea)nuts," *American Demographics,* April 1997, p. 60. For more on packaging, see Robert L. Underwood, "The Communicative Power of Product Packaging: Creating Brand Identity via Lived and Mediate Experience," *Journal of Marketing Theory and Proactice,* Winter 2003, p. 62.

13. Health Canada, "Health Canada Announces New Mandatory Nutrition Labelling to Help Canadians Make Informed Choices for Healthy Eating" (news release), January 2, 2003, www.hc-sc.gc.ca/english/media/releases/2003/2003_01.htm.

14. Bro Uttal, "Companies That Serve You Best," *Fortune,* December 7, 1987, p. 116; and American Customer Satisfaction Index ratings at www.theasci.org, accessed July 2003.

15. See "On Mother's Day, Advice Goes a Long Way," *PR Newswire,* Ziff Communications, May 2, 1995; Mike Campbell,

"Floral Web Site Ends Online Stress," *Bank Marketing,* April 1999, p. 8; David L. Margulius, "Smarter Call Centers: At Your Service?" *New York Times,* March 14, 2002, p. G1, and information found at www.1800flowers. com, July 2003.

16. www.marriott.com, accessed August 2003.

17. www.pg.com and www.crest.com, accessed August 2003. For more on product line strategy, see Robert Bordley, "Determining the Appropriate Depth and Breadth of a Firm's Product Portfolio," *Journal of Marketing Research,* February 2003, pp. 39–53.

18. See "McAtlas Shrugged," *Foreign Policy,* May–June 2001, pp. 26–37; and Philip Kotler, *Marketing Management,* 11th ed. (Upper Saddle River, NJ: Prentice Hall, 2003), p. 423.

19. Douglas Holt, "What Becomes an Icon Most?" *Harvard Business Review,* March 2003, pp. 43–49.

20. John Gray, "What's Your Brand Worth?," *Canadian Business,* November 22, 2004.

21. David C. Bello and Morris B. Holbrook, "Does an Absence of Brand Equity Generalize Across Product Classes?" *Journal of Business Research,* October 1995, p. 125; and Scott Davis, *Brand Asset Management: Driving Profitable Growth through Your Brands* (San Francisco: Jossey-Bass, 2000). Also see Kevin Lane Keller, *Building, Measuring, and Managing Brand Equity,* 2nd ed. (Upper Saddle River, NJ: Prentice Hall, 2003), Chapter 2.

22. "Brands in an Age of Anti-Americanism," *Business Week,* August 4, 2003, pp. 69–78.

23. See Roland T. Rust, Valerie A. Zeithaml, and Katherine A. Lemon, *Driving Customer Equity* (New York Free Press, 2000); Rust, Lemon, and Zeithaml, "Where Should the Next Marketing Dollar Go?" *Marketing Management,* September–October 2001, pp. 24–28; Robert C. Blattberg, Gary Getz, and Jacquelyn S. Thomas, *Customer Equity* (Boston: Harvard Business School Press, 2001); and John E. Hogan, Katherine N. Lemon, and Roland T. Rust, "Customer Equity Management: Charting New Directions for the Future of Marketing," *Journal of Service Research,* August 2002, pp. 4–12.

24. See Davis, *Brand Asset Management*; and Kotler, *Marketing Management,* pp. 419–420.

25. Marc Gobe, *Emotional Branding* (New York: Allworth Press, 2001).

26. Carole Pearson, "Grocery Slotting Fees Deprive Consumers and Manufacturers of Shelf-Respect," *The Straight Goods,* March 19, 2001, www.straightgoods.com/item428.asp. See also Paul N. Bloom, Gregory T. Gundlach, and Joseph P. Cannon, "Slotting Allowances and Fees: School of Thought and the Views of Practicing Managers," *Journal of Marketing,* April 2000, pp. 92–108; and Julie Forster, "The Hidden Cost of Shelf Space," *Business Week,* April 15, 2002, p. 103.

27. Warren Thayer, "Loblaws Exec Predicts: Private Labels to Surge," *Frozen Food Age,* May 1996, p. 1; "President's Choice Continues Brisk Pace," *Frozen Food Age,* March 1998, pp. 17–18; David Dunne and Chakravarthi Narasimhan, "The New Appeal of Private Labels," *Harvard Business Review,* May–June 1999, pp. 41–52; "New Private Label Alternatives Bring Changes to Supercenters, Clubs," *DSN Retailing Today,* February 5, 2001, p. 66;

and "The President's Choice Story," www.presidentschoice.ca/products/pc_story.aspx, accessed July 2003.

28. Peter Berlinski, "Retailers Push Premium PL," *Private Label Magazine,* May/June 2003, www.privatelabelmag.com/pdf/may2003/canada.cfm. For more reading on store brands, see David Dunne and Chakravarthi Narasimham, "The New Appeal of Private Labels," *Harvard Business Review,* May–June 1999, pp. 41–52; Kusum L. Ailawadi, Scott Neslin, and Karen Gedenk, "Pursuing the Value-Conscious Consumer: Store Brands Versus National Promotions," *Journal of Marketing,* January 2001, pp. 71–89; and Pradeep K. Chintagunta, "Investigating Category Pricing Behavior at a Retail Chain," *Journal of Marketing Research,* May 2002, pp. 141–151.

29. See Doug Desjardins, "Popularized Entertainment Icons Continue to Dominate Licensing," *DSN Retailing Today,* July 9, 2001, p. 4; Patricia Winters Lauro, "Licensing Deals Are Putting Big Brand Name into New Categories at the Supermarket," *New York Times,* June 18, 2002, p. C14; Derek Manson, "Spidy Cents," *Money,* July 2002, p. 40; Tobi Elkin, "Mopping Up the Licensing Buck," *Advertising Age,* March 24, 2003, p. S4; and David D. Kirkpatrick, "A New Sign on Harry's Forehead: For Sale," *New York Times,* June 16, 2003, p. 1.

30. See Terry Lefton, "Warner Brothers' Not Very Looney Path to Licensing Gold," *Brandweek,* February 14, 1994, pp. 36–37; Robert Scally, "Warner Builds Brand Presence, Strengthens 'Tunes' Franchise," *Discount Store News,* April 6, 1998, p. 33; "Looney Tunes Launched on East Coast," *Dairy Foods,* April 2001, p. 9; "Looney Tunes Entering 696 Publix Super Markets," *Dairy Foods,* April 2002, p. 11; and Tobi Elkin, "Struggling Toy Industry Looks to Licensing," *Advertising Age,* February 17, 2003, pp. 4, 36.

31. See Laura Petrecca, "'Corporate Brands' Put Licensing in the Spotlight," *Advertising Age,* June 14, 1999, p. 1; and Bob Vavra, "The Game of the Name," *Supermarket Business,* March 15, 2001, pp. 45–46.

32. Phil Carpenter, "Some Cobranding Caveats to Obey," *Marketing News,* November 7, 1994, p. 4; Gabrielle Solomon, "Co-Branding Alliances: Arranged Marriages Made by Marketers," *Fortune,* October 12, 1998, p. 188; "Kmart Licensing Will Continue," *New York Times,* March 21, 2002, p. C5; and Michael Barbaro, "Indictment Tests Shoppers' Loyalty," *The Washington Post,* June 5, 2003, p. E1.

33. For more on the use of line and brand extensions and consumer attitudes toward them, see Deborah Roedder John, Barbara Loken, and Christopher Joiner, "The Negative Impact of Extensions: Can Flagship Brands Be Eroded?" *Journal of Marketing,* January 1998, pp. 19–32; Zeynep Gurrhan-Canli and Durairaj Maheswaran, "The Effects of Extensions on Brand Name Dilution and Enhancement," *Journal of Marketing,* November 1998, pp. 464–473; Vanitha Swaminathan, Richard J. Fox, and Srinivas K. Reddy, "The Impact of Brand Extension Introduction on Choice," *Journal of Marketing,* October 2001, pp. 1–15; Kalpesh Kaushik Desai and Kevin Lane Keller, "The Effect of Ingredient Branding Strategies on Host Brand Extendibility," *Journal of Marketing,* January 2002, pp. 73–93; and Subramanian Balachander and Sanjoy Ghose, "Reciprocal Spillover Effects: A Strategic Benefit of Brand Extensions," *Journal of Marketing,* January 2003, pp. 4–13.

34. "Top 200 Megabrands," www.adage.com, accessed June 2003.

35. See Kevin Lane Keller, "The Brand Report Card," *Harvard Business Review*, January 2000, pp. 147–157; and Keller, *Strategic Brand Management*, pp. 766–767.

36. Steve Jarvis, "Refocus, Rebuild, Reeducate, Refine, Rebrand," *Marketing News*, March 26, 2001, pp. 1, 11; and "Top 10 Wireless Phone Brands," *Advertising Age*, June 24, 2002, p. S–18.

37. Statistics Canada, "Gross Domestic Product at Basic Prices, Primary Industries," www.statcan.ca/english/Pgdb/prim03.htm, accessed June 14, 2004.

38. Adapted from information in Leonard Berry and Neeli Bendapudi, "Clueing in Customers," *Harvard Business Review*, February 2003, pp. 100–106.

39. See James L. Heskett, Thomas O. Jones, Gary W. Loveman, W. Earl Sasser Jr., and Leonard A. Schlesinger, "Putting the Service-Profit Chain to Work," *Harvard Business Review*, March–April, 1994, pp. 164–174; James L. Heskett, W. Earl Sasser Jr., and Leonard A. Schlesinger, *The Service Profit Chain: How Leading Companies Link Profit and Growth to Loyalty, Satisfaction, and Value* (New York: Free Press, 1997); and Heskett, Sasser, and Schlesinger, *The Value Profit Chain: Treat Employees Like Customers and Customers Like Employees* (New York: Free Press, 2003).

40. C.I.P.A. 2004 Award Winners, ING Direct Canada, www.cipa.com/award_winners/winners_04/INGDirectCnd.html, accessed March 11, 2005; Keith McArthur, "Are Americans Ready to Save Their Money?," *The Globe and Mail*, February 22, 2005, p. B1.

41. For discussions of service quality, see A. Parasuraman, Valerie A. Zeithaml, and Leonard L. Berry, "A Conceptual Model of Service Quality and Its Implications for Future Research," *Journal of Marketing*, Fall 1985, pp. 41–50; Zeithaml, Berry, and Parasuraman, "The Behavioral Consequences of Service Quality," *Journal of Marketing*, April 1996, pp. 31–46; Thomas J. Page Jr., "Difference Scores Versus Direct Effects in Service Quality Measurement," *Journal of Service Research*, February 2002, pp. 184–192; Richard A. Spreng; James J. Jiang, Gary Klein, and Christopher L. Carr, "Measuring Information System Service Quality: SERVQUAL from the Other Side," *MIS Quarterly*, June 2002, pp. 145–166; and Y. H. Hung, M. L. Huang, and K. S. Chen, "Service Quality Evaluation by Service Quality Performance Matrix," *Total Quality Management Business Excellence*, January 2003, pp. 79–89.

42. See James L. Heskett, W. Earl Sasser Jr., and Christopher W. L. Hart, *Service Breakthroughs* (New York: Free Press, 1990).

43. Laura Bogomolny, "Canada Post Goes Wireless for Marketers," *Canadian Business*, June 6, 2005.

44. See the *Hazardous Products Act* at http://laws.justice.gc.ca/en/H–3/index.html and the *Food and Drugs Act* at http://laws.justice.gc.ca/en/F–27/index.html.

45. Toby Herscovitch Tips from the Top: Winners of the Canada Export Awards, Export Development Canada, Spring 2004, www.edc.ca/corpinfo/pubs/exportwise/spring04/p32_e.htm, accessed August 21, 2005.

46. For these and other examples, see Andrew Kupfer, "How to Be a Global Manager," *Fortune*, March 14, 1988, pp. 52–58; Maria Shao, "For Levi's: A Flattering Fit Overseas," *Business Week*, November 5, 1990, pp. 76–77; Joseph Weber, "Campbell: Now It's M-M-Global," *Business Week*, March 15, 1993, pp. 52–53; Zachary Schiller, "Make It Simple," *Business Week*, September 9, 1996, p. 102; Chester Dawson, "Gerber Feeding Booming Japanese Baby Food Market," *Durham Herald-Sun*, February 21, 1998, p. C10; and Jack Neff, "Test It in Paris, France, Launch It in Paris, Texas," *Advertising Age*, May 31, 1999, p. 28.

47. See Philip Cateora, *International Marketing*, 8th ed. (Homewood, IL: Irwin, 1993), p. 270; David Fairlamb, "One Currency—But 15 Economies," *Business Week*, December 31, 2001, p. 59; and www. walkabouttravelgear.com, July 2003.

48. J. S. Perry Hobson, "Feng Shui: Its Impacts on the Asian Hospitality Industry," *International Journal of Contemporary Hospitality Management* 6(6), 1994, pp. 21–26; Bernd H. Schmitt and Yigang Pan, "In Asia, the Supernatural Means Sales," *New York Times*, 19 February 1995, pp. 3, 11; Sally Taylor, "Tackling the Curse of Bad Feng Shui," *Publishers Weekly*, April 27, 1998, p. 24.

49. www.deutsche-bank.com, accessed August 2003.

50. www.cossette.com, accessed August 2003.

Chapter 9

1. Rebecca Harris, "People's Choice," *Marketing*, March 7, 2005, pp. 10–13; Coca-Cola Ltd. press release, January 31, 2005, "Orange Juice Lovers See the Light: Half the Sugar and Calories"; "Minute Maid Tests an Integrated Online/Offline Product Launch Campaign," March 28, 2002, e-consultancy.com; SimplyOrangeJuice.com.

2. "Bright Ideas," *Royal Bank Reporter*, Fall 1992, pp. 6–15; www.jollyjumper.com/History.aspx, accessed February 27, 2005; www.inventivewomen.com/library/library_wendy_murphy_on.shtml, accessed February 27, 2005.

3. Lesley Young, "New and Approved," *Marketing*, April 5, 2004.

4. See Philip Kotler, *Kotler on Marketing*, New York: Free Press, 1999, p. 51; Martha Wirth Fellman, "Number of New Products Keeps Rising," *Marketing News*, March 29, 1999, p. 3; Sarah Theodore, "Heads or Tails?" *Beverage Industry*, September 2000, p. NP4; and Eric Berggreb and Thomas Nacher, "Why Good Ideas Go Bust," *Management Review*, February 2000, pp. 32–36.

5. Gary Hamel, "Innovation's New Math," *Fortune*, July 9, 2001, pp. 130–131.

6. See Tim Stevens, "Idea Dollars," *Industry Week*, February 16, 1998, pp. 47–49; and William E. Coyne, "How 3M Innovates for Long-Term Growth," *Research Technology Management*, March–April 2001, pp. 21–24.

7. Paul Lukas, "Marketing: The Color of Money and Ketchup," *Fortune*, September 18, 2000, p. 38.

8. Pam Weisz, "Avon's Skin-So-Soft Bugs Out," *Brandweek*, June 6, 1994, p. 4; www.avon.com, accessed August 2001.

9. Kotler, *Kotler on Marketing*, pp. 43–44. For more on developing new product ideas, see Andrew Hargadon and Robert I. Sutton, "Building an Innovation Factory," *Harvard Business Review*, May–June 2000, pp. 157–166.

10. "The Fascinating World of Research Vehicles . . . From the NECAR to the F-Cell," www.daimlerchrysler.com, accessed February 27, 2005.

11. See Faye Rice, "Secrets of Product Testing," *Fortune*, November 28, 1994, pp. 172–174.

12. Ibid.

13. Judann Pollack, "Baked Lays," *Advertising Age*, June 24, 1996, p. S2; and Jack Neff and Suzanne Bidlake, "P&G, Unilever Aim to Take Consumers to the Cleaners," *Advertising Age*, February 12, 2001, pp. 1, 2.

14. "Nokia's N-Gage Shakes Up the Gaming Market," *Electronic Business*, April 1, 2003, p. 28 and "Hands-on: Nokia's N-Gage" in *The Register* (UK), September 12, 2003; Nokia press release, "Nokia Ships One Million N-Gage Game Decks," September 1, 2004.

15. See Robert McMath, "To Test or Not to Test," *Advertising Age*, June 1998, p. 64.

16. Jim McElgunn, "The Ultimate Test Market," *Marketing*, February 10, 2003, www.marketingmag.ca/magazine/current/editorial/article.jsp?content=20030210_24163.

17. Emily Nelson, "Colgate's Net Rose 10% in Period, New Products Helped Boost Sales," *Wall Street Journal*, February 2, 2001, p. B6.

18. For a good review of research on new-product development, see Rajesh Sethi, "New Product Quality and Product Development Teams," *Journal of Marketing*, April 2000, pp. 1–14; Shikhar Sarin and Vijay Mahajan, "The Effect of Reward Structures on the Performance of Cross-Functional Product Development Teams," *Journal of Marketing*, April 2001, pp. 35–54; Joseph M. Bonner, Robert W. Ruekert, and Orville C. Walker Jr., "Upper Management Control of New Product Development Projects and Project Performance," *Journal of Product Innovation Management*, May 2002, pp. 233–245; Avan R. Jassawalla and Hemant C. Sashittal, "Building Collaborative New Product Processes," *S.A.M. Advanced Management Journal*, Winter 2003, pp. 27–36; and Sandra Valle and Lucia Avella, "Cross-Functionality and Leadership of the New Product Development Teams," *European Journal of Innovation Management*, 2003, pp. 32–47.

19. Laurie Freeman, "Study: Leading Brands Aren't Always Enduring," *Advertising Age*, February 28, 2000, p. 26.

20. www.wd40.com, accessed February 2005.

21. www.apple.com, accessed February, 27, 2005.

22. Michael Hartnett, "Cracker Jack: Chris Neugent," *Advertising Age*, June 26, 2000, p. S22.

23. "Low Carb—Low Margins," *Marketing Magazine*, September 6, 2004.

Chapter 10

1. Thomas T. Nagle and Reed K. Holden, *The Strategy and Tactics of Pricing*, 3d ed. (Upper Saddle River, NJ: Prentice Hall, 2002), Chapter 1.

2. About Wal-Mart—Company Overview, www.walmartcanada.ca/Canada-About_Walmart.html, accessed May 2005; "Provincial and Territorial Economic Accounts Review: Preliminary Estimates, 2004," Statistics Canada, www.statcan.ca/english/freepub/13–016-XIE/13–016-XIE2005001.pdf; www.statcan.ca/english/edu/clock/population.htm; www.walmart.ca; Charles Fishman, Patrick E. Murphy and Gene R. Laczniak, "The Wal-Mart You Don't Know: Why Low Prices Have a High Cost," *Marketing Ethics Cases and Readings* (Pearson, 2006); David Brodie, "Wal-Mart Store Closing Chills Union Drive in 25 Canada Outlets," April 29, 2005, Bloomberg.com, www.bloomberg.com/apps/news?pid=10000082&sid=alpljhOyZjW4&refer=canada; "Hudson Bay Company Fined $600,000," news release, May 4, 1998, Competition Bureau of Canada, www.competitionbureau.gc.ca/internet/index.cfm?itemID=627&lg=e; www.brandchannel.com/view_comments.asp?dc_id=46; Rita Trichur, "U.S. Investor Says Nostalgia Will Lure Canadians to HBC; Analysts Dubious," Canadian Press, February 26, 2005, http://money.canoe.ca/News/Other/2005/02/26/943586-cp.html.

3. Dean Foust, "Raising Prices Won't Fly," *Business Week*, June 3, 2002, p. 34; Stephanie N. Mehta, "How to Thrive When Prices Fall," *Fortune*, May 12, 2003, pp. 131–134.

4. Philip Kotler, *Marketing Management*, 11th ed. (Upper Saddle River, NJ: Prentice Hall, 2003), p. 470.

5. See Michael Vizard, Ed Scannell, and Dan Neel, "Suppliers Toy with Dynamic Pricing," *InfoWorld*, May 14, 2001, p. 28; and Faith Keenan, "The Price Is Really Right," *Business Week*, March 31, 2003, pp. 60–68.

6. For an excellent discussion of factors affecting pricing decisions, see Nagle and Holden, *The Strategy and Tactics of Pricing*, Chapter 1.

7. See Robert Berner, "Why PG's Smile Is So Bright," *Business Week*, August 12, 2002, pp. 58–60; and Jack Neff, "Power Brushes a Hit at Every Level," *Advertising Age*, May 26, 2003, p. 10.

8. Joshua Rosenbaum, "Guitar Maker Looks for a New Key," *Wall Street Journal*, February 11, 1998, p. B1; www.gibson.com, accessed July 2003.

9. See Nagle and Holden, *The Strategy and Tactics of Pricing*, Chapter 4.

10. For a comprehensive discussion of pricing strategies, see Nagle and Holden, *The Strategy and Dynamics of Pricing*. Also see Robert J. Dolan and Hermann Simon, *Power Pricing: How Managing Price Transforms the Bottom Line* (New York: The Free Press, 1997).

11. Kotler, *Marketing Management*, p. 474; Kara Swisher, "Electronics 2001: The Essential Guide," *Wall Street Journal*, January 5, 2001; Cliff Edwards, "HDTV: High-Anxiety Television," *Business Week*, June 10, 2002, pp. 142–146; and Eric Taub, "HDTV's Acceptance Picks Up Pace as Prices Drop and Networks Sign On," *New York Times*, March 31, 2003, p. C1.

12. See Nagle and Holden, *The Strategy and Tactics of Pricing*, pp. 244–247; and Stefan Stremersch and Gerard J. Tellis, "Strategic Bundling of Products and Prices: A New Synthesis for Marketing," *Journal of Marketing Research*, January 2002, pp. 55–72.

13. Seanna Browder, "Nintendo: At the Top of Its Game," *Business Week*, June 9, 1997, pp. 72–73; "Console Competition Lowers Opening Price Points," *DSN Retailing Today*, March 25, 2002, p. 18; and Ken Belson, "Sony Profits Climb 96% in Quarter," *New York Times*, January 30, 2003, p. W1.

14. E.M. Phillips, "Capitalizing on Your Wood By-Products," *FDM*, March 2002, pp. 48–51; www. woodworkingsite.com, accessed July 2003.

15. Example adapted from Greco, "Are Your Prices Right?" p. 88.

16. For more reading on reference prices and psychological pricing, see Robert M. Schindler and Patrick N. Kirby, "Patterns of Right-Most Digits Used in Advertised Prices: Implications for Nine-Ending Effects," *Journal of Consumer Research,* September 1997, pp. 192–201; Dhruv Grewal, Kent B. Monroe, Chris Janiszewski, and Donald R. Lichtenstein, "A Range Theory of Price Perception," *Journal of Consumer Research,* March 1999, pp. 353–368; Tridib Mazumdar and Purushottam Papatla, "An Investigation of Reference Price Segments," *Journal of Marketing Research,* May 2000, pp. 246–258; Indrajit Sinha and Michael Smith, "Consumers' Perceptions of Promotional Framing of Price," *Psychology Marketing,* March 2000, pp. 257–271; Tulin Erdem, Glenn Mayhew, and Baohong Sun, "Understanding Reference-Price Shoppers: A Within- and Across-Category Analysis," *Journal of Marketing Research,* November 2001, pp. 445–457; and Nagle and Holden, *The Strategy and Tactics of Pricing,* pp. 83–90.

17. Tim Ambler, "Kicking Price Promotion Habit Is Like Getting Off Heroin—Hard," *Marketing,* May 27, 1999, p. 24. Also see Robert Gray, "Driving Sales at Any Price?" *Marketing,* April 11, 2002, p. 24; and Lauren Kellere Johnson, "Dueling Pricing Strategies," *MIT Sloan Management Review,* Spring 2003, pp. 10–11.

18. Philip R. Cateora, *International Marketing,* 7th ed. (Homewood, IL: Irwin, 1990), p. 540. Also see S. Tamer Cavusgil, "Pricing for Global Markets," *Columbia Journal of World Business,* Winter 1996, pp. 66–78; Barbara Stottinger, "Strategic Export Pricing: A Long and Winding Road," *Journal of International Marketing,* 2001, pp. 40–63; and Warren J. Keegan, *Global Marketing Management* (Upper Saddle River, NJ: Prentice Hall, 2002), Chapter 12.

19. See Michael Oneal, "Harley-Davidson: Ready to Hit the Road Again," *Business Week,* July 21, 1986, p. 70; and "EU Proposes Dumping Change," *East European Markets,* February 14, 1997, pp. 2–3.

20. Ram Charan, "The Rules Have Changed," *Fortune,* March 16, 1998, pp. 159–162.

21. See John Greenwald, "Cereal Showdown," *Time,* April 29, 1996, p. 60; "Cereal Thriller," *The Economist,* June 15, 1996, p. 59; Terril Yue Jones, "Outside the Box," *Forbes,* June 14, 1999, pp. 52–53; "Kellogg Concedes Top Spot to General Mills," *New York Times,* February 22, 2001, p. C4; and "Kellogg Company," *Hoover's Company Profiles,* Austin, June 15, 2003.

22. See the *Competition Act,* Sections 34–38, http://laws.justice.gc.ca/en/C–34/.

23. For an excellent discussion of these issues, see Dhruv Grewel and Larry D. Compeau, "Pricing and Public Policy: A Research Agenda and Overview of Special Issue," *Journal of Marketing and Public Policy,* Spring 1999, pp. 3–10.

Chapter 11

1. Anne T. Coughlin, Erin Anderson, Louis W. Stern, and Adel El-Ansary, *Marketing Channels,* 6th ed., Upper Saddle River, NJ: Prentice Hall, 2001, p. 116.

2. Pat Curry, "Channel Changes," *Industry Week,* April 2, 2001, pp. 45–48; "Reinventing Partnership: Kevin Gilroy Answers Questions from the Channel," http://partner.americas.HP.com/partner/harddeck.pdf, accessed July 2003; Craig Zarley, "Making the Call," *CRN,* February 11, 2002, pp. 14–17; Joseph F. Kovar, "Channel Champions 2002: HP Software Decisive," *CRN,* March 18, 2002, p. 52; Jennifer Hagendorf Follett, "Channel Champions 2002: HP's Hard Deck Is Aces," *CRN,* March 18, 2002, p. 66; Mike Cruz, "Channel Champions 2002: HP Takes All in Printers," *CRN,* March 18, 2002, p. 84; Jeff O'Heir, "HP's Fiorina: Know the Value You Add," *CRN,* April 14, 2003, pp. 6, 16; John Longwell, "Solution Provider Poll Looks at All the Variables in the Partner Satisfaction Equation," www.crn.com, accessed July 2003; http://partner.americas.HP.com/partner/harddesk. pdf, accessed July 2003.

3. For definitions and a complete discussion of distribution channel topics, see Anne T. Coughlin, Erin Anderson, Louis W. Stern, and Adel El-Ansary, *Marketing Channels,* 6th ed., Upper Saddle River, NJ: Prentice Hall, 2001, pp. 2–3.

4. See Malcolm P. McNair and Eleanor G. May, "The Next Revolution of the Retailing Wheel," *Harvard Business Review,* September–October 1978, pp. 81–91; Stephen Brown, "The Wheel of Retailing: Past and Future," *Journal of Retailing,* Summer 1990, pp. 143–147; Stephen Brown, "Variations on a Marketing Enigma: The Wheel of Retailing Theory," *Journal of Marketing Management,* 7, no. 2, 1991, pp. 131–155; Stanley C. Hollander, "The Wheel of Retailing," reprinted in *Marketing Management,* Summer 1996, pp. 63–66; and Jennifer Negley, "Retrenching, Reinventing and Remaining Relevant," *Discount Store News,* April 5, 1999.

5. Ian Jack, "Dealers Declare War on Ford Canada," *Financial Post,* March 31, 2000, pp. C1, C5; Greg Keenan, "Ford Targets Bigger Stake in Dealerships," *The Globe and Mail,* November 18, 1998, pp. B1, B16.

6. Anne T. Coughlin, Erin Anderson, Louis W. Stern, and Adel El-Ansary, *Marketing Channels,* 6th ed., Upper Saddle River, NJ: Prentice Hall, 2001, p. 241.

7. Ibid, p. 259.

8. See Richard C. Hoffman and John F. Preble, "Franchising into the Twenty-First Century," *Business Horizons,* November–December 1993, pp. 35–43; "Canada's Largest Franchise-Only Show Returns," advertising supplement, *The Globe and Mail,* September 24, 1997, p. 1; strategis.ic.gc.ca/SSG/ dm01179e.html.

9. Peter Fitzpatrick, "Airlines of the World—Unite," *Financial Post,* November 22, 1997, p. 8.

10. http://exportsource.ca/gol/exportsource/site.nsf/en/ es02153.html#index2.

11. Subhash C. Jain, *International Marketing Management,* 3rd ed., Boston: PWS-Kent Publishing, 1990, pp. 489–491. Also see Emily Thronton, "Revolution in Japanese Retailing," *Fortune,* February 7, 1994, pp. 143–147.

12. For examples, see Philip Cateora, *International Marketing,* 7th ed., Homewood, IL: Irwin, 1990, pp. 570–571; Dexter Roberts, "Blazing Away at Foreign Brands," *Business Week,* May 12, 1997, p. 58; and "Taking on Distribution," *Business China,* June 5, 2000, p. 2.

13. Jennifer Wells, "We Can Get It for You Wholesale," *Report on Business*, March 1995, pp. 52–62.

14. For more on channel relationships, see James A. Narus and James C. Anderson, "Rethinking Distribution," *Harvard Business Review*, July–August 1996, pp. 112–120; James C. Anderson and James A. Narus, *Business Market Management*, Upper Saddle River, NJ: Prentice Hall, 1999, pp. 276–288; and Jonathon D. Hibbard, Nirmalya Kumar, and Louis W. Stern, "Examining the Impact of Destructive Acts in Marketing Channel Relationships," *Journal of Marketing Research*, February 2001, pp. 45–61.

15. For a full discussion of laws affecting marketing channels, see Anne T. Coughlin, Erin Anderson, Louis W. Stern, and Adel El-Ansary, *Marketing Channels*, 6th ed., Upper Saddle River, NJ: Prentice Hall, 2001, Chapter 12.

16. See Robert E. Danielson, "CPFR: Improving Your Business without Being Limited by Technology," *Apparel Industry Magazine*, February 2000, pp. 56–57; and Ben A. Chaouch, "Stock Levels and Delivery Rates in Vendor-Managed Inventory Programs," *Production and Operations Management*, Spring 2001, pp. 31–44.

17. Mike Troy, "Wal-Mart: Behind the Scenes Efficiency Keeps Growth Curve on Course," *DSN Retailing Today*, June 4, 2001, pp. 80, 91.

18. J. William Gurley, "Why Dell's War Isn't Dumb," *Fortune*, July 9, 2001, pp. 134–136.

19. See Lara L. Sowinski, "Supply Chain Management and Logistics Software," *World Trade*, February 2001, pp. 34–36; Keith Schultz, "Supply Chain Management Tools," *Internetweek*, June 25, 2001, pp. PG25–PG34; and Karen Lundegaard, "E-Commerce (A Special Report)—Bumpy Ride: Supply-Chain Management Sounds Beautiful in Theory; In Real Life, It's a Daunting Task," *The Wall Street Journal*, May 21, 2001, p. R21.

20. Anne T. Coughlin, Erin Anderson, Louis W. Stern, and Adel El-Ansary, *Marketing Channels*, 6th ed., Upper Saddle River, NJ: Prentice Hall, 2001, p. 336.

Chapter 12

1. www.cassies.ca/caselibrary/winners/NB.pdf.

2. The first four of these definitions are adapted from Peter D. Bennett, *Dictionary of Marketing Terms*, Chicago: American Marketing Association, 1995.

3. "Advertising Industry in Canada," Industry Canada, http://strategis.ic.gc.ca/epic/internet/inimr-ri.nsf/en/gr117002e.html.

4. See Don E. Schultz, Stanley I. Tannenbaum, and Robert F. Lauterborn, *Integrated Marketing Communication*, Chicago, IL: NTC, 1992, Chapters 3 and 4. Also see James R. Ogdan, *Developing a Creative and Innovative Integrated Marketing Communications Plan*, Upper Saddle River, NJ: Prentice Hall, 1998; and David Picton and Amanda Broderick, *Integrated Marketing Communications*, New York: Financial Times Management, 1999.

5. P. Griffith Lindell, "You Need Integrated Attitude to Develop IMC," *Marketing News*, May 26, 1997, p. 6. For more discussion of integrated marketing communications, see J. P. Cornelissen and Andrew L. Lock, "Theoretical Concept of Management Fashion: Examining the Significance of IMC," *Journal of Advertising Research*, September–October 2000, pp. 7–15; Stephen J. Gould, "The State of IMC Research and Applications," *Journal of Advertising Research*, September–October 2000, pp. 22–23; and Kim Bartel Sheehan and Caitlin Doherty, "Re-Weaving the Web: Integrating Print and Online Communications," *Journal of Interactive Marketing*, Spring 2001, pp. 47–59.

6. For more on advertising budgets, see Andrew Ehrenberg, Neil Barnard, and John Scriven, "Justifying Our Advertising Budgets," *Marketing and Research Today*, February 1997, pp. 38–44; Dana W. Hayman and Don E. Schultz, "How Much Should You Spend on Advertising?" *Advertising Age*, April 26, 1999, p. 32; and Laura Q. Hughes, "Measuring Up," *Advertising Age*, February 5, 2001, pp. 1, 34.

7. Stuart Elliott, "Fewer Viewers, More Commercials," *New York Times*, June 8, 1999, p. 1; Bill Carter, "After Super Bowl, 'Survivor' Is the Season's Top Hit on TV," *New York Times*, January 30, 2001, p. C8; and Joe Flint, "Oscar Ratings Fall, but the Program Finishes on Time," *The Wall Street Journal*, March 27, 2001, p. B8.

8. Stan Sutter, "5 Big Trends," *Marketing*, April 4, 2005, p. 11; Danny Kucharsky, "CTV's Idol Helped Drive L'Oreal sales," *Marketing*, January 26, 2004, p. 4; Danny Kucharsky, "Because You're Worth It, L'Oréal," *Marketing*, February 9, 2004, p. 9.

9. Larry Armstrong, "Smart TV Get Even Smarter," *Business Week*, April 16, 2001, pp. 132–134; and Jeff Howe, "Total Control," *American Demographics*, July 2001, pp. 28–32.

10. Edward A. Robinson, "Frogs, Bears, and Orgasms: Think Zany if You Want to Reach Today's Consumers," *Fortune*, June 9, 1997, pp. 153–156. Also see Chuck Ross, "MBC Blasts Beyond the 15-Minute Barrier," *Advertising Age*, August 7, 2000, p. 3.

11. Patti Bond, "Today's Topic: From Russia with Fizz, Coke Imports Ads," *Atlanta Journal and Constitution*, April 4, 1998, p. E2.

12. See "U.K. Tobacco Ad Ban Will Include Sports Sponsorship," *AdAgeInternational.com*, May 1997; "Coca-Cola Rapped for Running Competition in India," *AdAgeInternational.com*, February 1997; Naveen Donthu, "A Cross Country Investigation of Recall of and Attitude Toward Comparative Advertising," *Journal of Advertising*, June 22, 1998, p. 111; and John Shannon, "Comparative Ads Call for Prudence," *Marketing Week*, May 6, 1999, p. 32.

13. Debra Aho Williamson, "P&G's Reformulated Pert Plus Builds Consumer Relationships," *Advertising Age*, June 28, 1999, p. 52.

14. Jeff Lobb, "Stuff-ing It to Coke," *Marketing Magazine*, January 27, 1997, p. 15.

15. See "Power to the Key Ring and T-Shirt," *Sales and Marketing Management*, December 1989, p. 14; and Chad Kaydo, "Your Logo Here," *Sales and Marketing Management*, April 1998, pp. 65–70.

16. See Richard Szathmary, "Trade Shows," *Sales and Marketing Management*, May 1992, pp. 83–84; Srinath Gopalakrishna, Gary L. Lilien, Jerome D. Williams, and Ian Sequeira, "Do Trade Shows Pay Off?" *Journal of Marketing*, July 1995, pp. 75–83; Peter Jenkins, "Making the Most of Trade Shows," *Nation's Business*, June 1999, p. 8; and Ben Chapman, "The Trade Show Must Go On," *Sales and Marketing Management*, June 2001, p. 22.

17. See Don E. Schultz, Stanley I. Tannenbaum, and Robert F. Lauterborn, *Integrated Marketing Communication,* Chicago, IL: NTC, 1992, Chapters 3 and 4. Also see James R. Ogdan, *Developing a Creative and Innovative Integrated Marketing Communications Plan,* Upper Saddle River, NJ: Prentice Hall, 1998; and David Picton and Amanda Broderick, *Integrated Marketing Communications,* New York: Financial Times Management, 1999.

18. Rosalind Stefanac, "Corporate Ads in Rainbow Colours: Big Mainstream Marketers Are Crafting Innovative Advertising Strategies in a Bid to Get Closer to Gay and Lesbian Consumers," *Marketing On-Line,* May 1, 2000; Gary Levin, "'Meddling' in Creative More Welcome," *Advertising Age,* April 9, 1990, pp. S4, S8; Eleftheria Parpis, "TBWA: Absolut," *Adweek,* November 9, 1998, p. 172; Sarah Theodore, "Absolut Secrets," *Beverage Industry,* July 2000, p. 50; and the Q & A section of the Absolut website, www.absolut.com, accessed July 2001.

19. NCH Promotional Services Ltd., www.wattsgroup.com/nch/ SR102.htm.

20. For more information about direct response marketing and the Direct Marketing Association, see their website at www.the-dma.org. For information about the Canadian Marketing Association, see their website at www.the-cma.org.

21. Carol Krol, "Pizza Hut's Database Makes Its Couponing More Efficient," *Advertising Age,* November 30, 1998, p. 27; and Dana Blakenhorn, "Marketers Hone Targeting," *Advertising Age,* June 18, 2001, p. T16.

22. For these and other examples, see Jonathan Berry, "A Potent New Tool for Selling: Database Marketing," *Business Week,* September 4, 1994, pp. 56–62; Weld F. Royal, "Do Databases Really Work?" *Sales and Marketing Management,* October 1995, pp. 66–74; Daniel Hill, "Love My Brand," *Brandweek,* January 19, 1998, pp. 26–29; "FedEx Taps into Data Warehousing," *Advertising Age's Business Marketing,* January 1999, p. 25; and Harriet Marsh, "Dig Deeper into the Database Goldmine," *Marketing,* January 11, 2001, pp. 29–30.

23. Andrea Zoe Aster, "Deciphering the New E-Retail," *Marketing On-Line,* November 20, 2000.

24. Lynda Rinkenbach, "Ford Meets Fear Factor," *Marketing,* June 21, 2004, p. 32.

25. David Chilton, "LCBO Installs Interactive Kiosks," *Strategy,* January 24, 1997, p. 13; "For the Record: UNICEF Kiosks at IKEA," *Strategy,* November 24, 1997, p. 15.

26. "Sweepstakes Groups Settles with States," *New York Times,* June 27, 2001, p. A14; and "PCH Reaches $34 Million Sweepstakes Settlement with 26 States," *Direct Marketing,* September 2001, p. 6.

27. John Hagel III and Jeffrey F. Rayport, "The Coming Battle for Customer Information," *Harvard Business Review,* January–February 1997, pp. 53–65; Bruce Horovitz, "AmEx Kills Database Deal After Privacy Outrage," *USA Today,* July 15, 1998, p. B1; and Carol Krol, "Consumers Reach the Boiling Point," *Advertising Age,* March 29, 1999, p. 22.

28. Office of the Privacy Commissioner of Canada, www.privcom. gc.ca/index_e.asp.

29. For example, see the Royal Bank's privacy policy at www. rbcroyalbank.com/privacy/info_we_col.html.

30. Canadian consumers may register on the CMA's do-not-contact list at www.cmaconsumersense.org/marketing_lists.cfm.

31. See www.the-cma.org/consumer/ethics.cfm.

32. www.edelman.com/expertise/industries/technology, accessed March 3, 2005.

33. Raincoast Wizarding News, www.raincoast.com/harrypotter/ wizarding-news.html.

34. Adapted from Scott Cutlip, Allen Center, and Glen Broom, *Effective Public Relations,* 8th ed., Upper Saddle River, NJ: Prentice Hall, 1999, Chapter 1.

35. American Standard's press releases are available on their website at www.americanstandard.com.

36. Canadian Nuclear Association, www.cna.ca/english/policy.asp, accessed March 3, 2005.

37. Canadian Cancer Society, www.cancer.ca.

38. Gail Chiasson, "PR in Action: When the Media Come Calling," *Marketing,* February 12, 1996, p. 23.

39. See Al Ries and Laura Ries, *The Fall of Advertising and the Rise of PR* (New York: HarperBusiness, 2002). For counterpoints, see O. Burtch Drake, "'Fall' of Advertising? I Differ," *Advertising Age,* January 13, 2003, p. 23.

40. Al Ries and Laura Ries, "First Do Some Publicity," *Advertising Age,* February 8, 1999, p. 42. Also see Ries and Ries, *The Fall of Advertising and the Rise of PR.* For counterpoints, see Drake, "'Fall' of Advertising? I Differ."

41. See Mark Gleason, "Edelman Sees Niche in Web Public Relations," *Advertising Age,* January 20, 1997, p. 30; Michael Krauss, "Good PR Critical to Growth on the Net," *Marketing News,* January 18, 1999, p. 8; Steve Jarvis, "How the Internet Is Changing Fundamentals of Publicity," *Marketing News,* July 17, 2000, p. 6; and Don Middleberg, *Winning PR in the Wired World: Powerful Communications Strategies or the Noisy Digital Space,* New York: McGraw-Hill Professional Publishing, 2000.

Chapter 13

1. Trites, Boritz, and Pugsley, *E-Business: A Canadian Perspective for a Networked World,* 2nd ed., Pearson Education, 2006.

2. Simon Avery, "Internet: E-Commerce Anniversary: From Early Web Visions, They Spun Gold," *Globe and Mail,* August 1, 2005, p. B4.

3. "Internet Use in Canada," Statistics Canada, www.statcan.ca/ english/freepub/56F0003XIE, accessed September 6, 2005; "E-commerce: Household Shopping on the Internet," *The Daily,* Statistics Canada, www.statcan.ca/Daily/English/040923/ d040923a.htm, accessed September 6, 2005.

4. Industry Canada's website at http://strategis.ic.gc.ca offers consumer and business information.

5. Adapted from Jeffrey F. Rayport and Bernard J. Jaworski, *e-Commerce* (New York: McGraw-Hill, 2001), p. 116.

6. Lisa Bertagnoli, "Getting Satisfaction," *Marketing News,* May 7, 2001, p. 11.

7. "Internet Use in Canada," Statistics Canada, www.statcan.ca/english/freepub/56F0003XIE, accessed September 6, 2005; "E-commerce: Household Shopping on the Internet," *The Daily,* Statistics Canada, www.statcan.ca/Daily/English/040923/d040923a.htm, accessed September 6, 2005.

8. Fawzia Sheikh, "The Sky's the Limit: Canada's Lucrative Online Travel Industry Is Fuelled Up and Ready to Take Off," *Digital Marketing,* Sept 2000, Vol 1, p. 16.

9. Wayne Mouland, "Coupon Convenience," *Marketing,* May 9, 2005, p. 16.

10. *Marketing,* May 9, 2005, p. 5; also Interactive Advertising Bureau of Canada press release, November 2, 2004.

11. "Fourth CMOST Study Demonstrates Online's Ability to Influence Behavior in Short Period of Time," Interactive Advertising Bureau of Canada, press release, March 16, 2005.

12. Industry Canada, http://strategis.ic.gc.ca.

13. Chris Daniels, "Dot-gone," *Marketing,* March 21/28, 2005, pp. 19–20.

14. Michelle Halpern, "Word Hunters," *Marketing,* May 2, 2005, p. 16.

15. Rebecca Harris, "Less Spam Means More Trust In E-mail," *Marketing,* March 21/28, 2005, p. 9.

16. For these and other examples, see William M. Bulkeley, "E-Commerce (A Special Report): Cover Story—Pass It On: Advertisers Discover They Have a Friend in 'Viral' Marketing," *Wall Street Journal,* January 14, 2002, p. R6.

17. Eilene Zimmerman, "Catch the Bug," *Sales & Marketing Management,* February 2001, pp. 78–82. Also see Ellen Neuborne, "Viral Marketing Alert," *Business Week,* March 19, 2001, p. EB8.

18. Seth Godin, *Permission Marketing,* New York: Simon & Shuster, 1999.

19. Canadian Marketing Association, www.cmaconsumersense.org/dealing_spam.cfm, accessed May 9, 2005.

20. www.cmaconsumersense.org/dealing_spam.cfm.

21. Adapted from the CMA's guidelines for Internet marketing, and the principles expressed in Seth Godin's *Permission Marketing.*

22. Om Malik, "Free Wi-Fi? Get Ready for GoogleNet." *Business 2.0,* August 12, 2005.

23. Chris Powell, "On the Pod," *Marketing,* April 11, 2005, p. 8.

24. Personal email communication with Dr. Weinberger.

25. See Peter Han and Angus Maclaurin, "Do Consumers Really Care About Online Privacy?" *Marketing Management,* January–February 2002, pp. 35–38.

26. "AOL Worker Who Stole E-Mail List Sentenced," by Larry Neumeister, Associated Press, August 17, 2005.

27. Bob Tedeschi, "Everybody Talks About Online Privacy, but Few Do Anything About It," *New York Times,* June 3, 2002, p. C6.

28. "13-Year-Old Bids over $3M for Items in eBay Auctions," *USA Today,* April, 1999, p. 10B.

GLOSSARY

Adapted marketing mix An international marketing strategy for adjusting the marketing mix elements to each international target market, bearing more costs but hoping for a larger market share and return. *270*

Adoption process The mental process through which an individual passes from first hearing about an innovation to final adoption. *223*

Advertising objective A specific communication task to be accomplished with a specific target audience during a specific time. *476*

Advertising Any paid form of nonpersonal presentation and promotion of ideas, goods, or services by an identified sponsor. *468*

Affordable method Setting the budget at the level management thinks the company can afford. *475*

Age and life-cycle segmentation Dividing a market into different age and life-cycle groups. *252*

Agent A wholesaler who represents buyers or sellers on a relatively permanent basis, performs only a few functions, and does not take title to goods. *424*

Allowance Promotional money paid by manufacturers to retailers in return for an agreement to feature the manufacturer's products in some way. *395*

Attitude A person's relatively consistent evaluations, feelings, and tendencies toward an object or idea. *218*

Baby boom The major increase in the annual birth rate following World War II and lasting until the early 1960s. The baby boomers, now moving into middle age, are a prime target for marketers. *133*

Banner ads Graphic online ads that are rectangular or square in shape, can be of any size, and may be placed anywhere on the publisher's webpage. *531*

Behavioural segmentation Dividing a market into groups based on consumer knowledge, attitude, use, or response to a product. *255*

Belief A descriptive thought that a person holds about something. *218*

Benefit segmentation Dividing the market into groups according to the different benefits that consumers seek from the product. *256*

Blog A website that consists of regular date-stamped compositions written by an individual, or a group of individuals, and published online for the public to read. *540*

Brand equity The usually positive but sometimes negative differential effect that knowing the brand name has on customer response to the product. *311*

Brand extension Using a successful brand name to launch a new or modified product in a new category. *317*

Brand A name, term, sign, symbol, or design, or a combination of these intended to identify the goods or services of one seller or group of sellers, and to differentiate them from those of competitors. *303*

Break-even pricing (target profit pricing) Setting price to break even on the costs of making and marketing a product; or setting price to make a target profit. *386*

Broker A wholesaler who does not take title to goods and whose function is to bring buyers and sellers together and assist in negotiation. *424*

Business-to-business (B2B) e-commerce Electronic transactions that take place between businesses. *519*

Business-to-consumer (B2C) e-commerce Electronic transactions that take place between businesses and consumers. *519*

Business analysis A review of the sales, cost, and profit projections for a new product to determine whether the company's objectives will be met. *350*

Business buyer behaviour The buying behaviour of organizations that buy goods and services for use in the production of other products and services that are sold, rented, or supplied to others. *227*

Business portfolio The collection of businesses and products that compose the company. *55*

Buying centre All the individuals and units that participate in the business buying-decision process. *230*

Byproduct pricing Setting a price for byproducts in order to make the main product's price more competitive. *394*

Captive-product pricing Setting a price for products that must be used along with a main product, such as blades for a razor and film for a camera. *393*

Catalogue marketing Direct marketing through print, video, or electronic catalogues that are mailed to select customers, made available in stores, or presented online. *498*

Category killer Giant specialty store that carries a very deep assortment of a particular line and is staffed by knowledgeable employees. *429*

Causal research Marketing research to test hypotheses about cause-and-effect relationships. *170*

Chain stores Two or more outlets that are owned and controlled in common, have central buying and merchandising, and sell similar lines of merchandise. *430*

Channel Captain A leader, whether formally chosen or rising to the role by virtue of demonstrated skills, who helps the channel deal with conflict. *435*

Channel conflict Disagreement among channel members on goals and roles—who should do what and for what rewards. *435*

Channel level A layer of intermediaries that performs some work in bringing the product and its ownership closer to the final buyer. *422*

Co-branding The practice of using the established brand names of two different companies on the same product. *315*

Cognitive dissonance Buyer discomfort caused by postpurchase conflict. *222*

Collaborative filtering The method of making automatic predictions about the interests of an individual user by collecting taste information from many users. *266*

Commercialization The full-scale introduction of the new product into the market. *354*

Competition-based pricing Setting prices based on the prices that competitors charge for similar products. *389*

Competitive advantage An advantage over competitors gained by offering greater value, either through lower prices or by providing more benefits that justify higher prices. *273*

Competitive parity method Setting the budget to match competitors' outlays. *475*

Concentrated (niche) marketing A market-coverage strategy in which a firm goes after a large share of one or a few segments, or niches. *264*

Concept development and testing Developing the new product idea into various alternative forms and testing the concepts with a group of potential customers. *347*

Consumer-to-consumer (C2C) e-commerce Electronic transactions taking place online between consumers. *519*

Consumer buyer behaviour The buying behaviour of consumers—individuals who buy goods and services for their own use or consumption. *204*

Consumer market All individuals in a particular geographic region, who are old enough to have their own money and to choose how to spend it. *204*

Consumer product Product bought by individuals for personal consumption. *297*

Consumerism An organized movement of citizens and government agencies to improve the rights and power of buyers in relation to sellers. *98*

Contract manufacturing A joint venture in which a company contracts with manufacturers in a foreign market to produce the product. *446*

Convenience product Consumer product that the individual usually buys frequently, immediately, and with a minimum of comparison and buying effort. *297*

Convenience store A small store located near a residential area that is open long hours seven days a week and carries a limited line of high-turnover convenience goods. *429*

Conventional distribution channel A channel consisting of one or more independent producers, wholesalers, and retailers, each a separate business seeking to maximize its own profits even at the expense of profits for the system as a whole. *436*

Cost-plus pricing Adding a standard markup to the cost of the product. *386*

Cultural environment Institutions and other forces that affect society's basic values, perceptions, preferences, and behaviours. *147*

Culture The set of basic values, perceptions, wants, and behaviours learned by a member of society from family and other important institutions. *205*

Customer-oriented marketing A philosophy of enlightened marketing that holds that the company should view and organize its marketing activities from the customer's point of view. *104*

Customer equity The total combined customer lifetime values of all of the company's customers. *26*

Customer lifetime value The value of the entire stream of purchases that the customer would make over a lifetime of patronage. *25*

Customer perceived value The customer's evaluation of the difference between all the benefits and all the costs of a marketing offer relative to those of competing offers. *20*

Customer relationship management (CRM) Any corporate software system that collects and organizes customer data and provides marketing managers, customer service representatives, and sales representatives with powerful information tools. *184*

Customer relationship management The overall process of building and maintaining profitable customer relationships by delivering superior customer value and satisfaction. *19*

Customer sales force structure A sales force organization under which salespeople specialize in selling only to certain types of customers. *491*

Customer satisfaction The extent to which a product's perceived performance matches a buyer's expectations. *20*

Database A collection of data about existing or prospective customers, organized into records. *496*

Decline stage The product life cycle stage in which a product's sales begin to decrease. *361*

Demand curve A curve that shows the number of units the market will buy in a given time period at different prices that might be charged. *382*

Demands Human wants that are backed by buying power. *8*

Demarketing Marketing to reduce demand temporarily or permanently; the aim is not to destroy demand but only to reduce or shift it. *13*

Demographic segmentation Dividing the market into groups based on demographic variables such as age, gender, family size, family life cycle, income, occupation, education, religion, race, generation, and nationality. *251*

Demography The study of human populations in terms of size, density, location, age, gender, race, occupation, and other statistics. *132*

Department store A retail organization that carries a wide variety of product lines—typically clothing, home furnishings, and household goods; each line is operated as a separate department managed by specialist buyers or merchandisers. *428*

Derived demand Business demand that ultimately comes from (derives from) the demand for consumer goods. *228*

Descriptive research Marketing research to better describe marketing problems, situations, or markets, such as the market potential for a product or the demographics and attitudes of consumers who buy the product. *170*

Differentiated (segmented) marketing A market-coverage strategy in which a firm decides to target several market segments and designs separate offers for each. *264*

Direct-response television marketing Television spots that persuasively describe a product and give customers a toll-free number for ordering. *498*

Direct distribution channel A marketing channel that has no intermediary levels. *422*

Direct investment Entering a foreign market by developing foreign-based assembly or manufacturing facilities. *446*

Direct mail Sending an offer, announcement, reminder, or other item to an individual or a company at a particular address. *497*

Direct response marketing Direct communications with carefully targeted customers to obtain an immediate response. *468*

Discount store A retail institution that sells standard merchandise at lower prices by accepting lower margins and selling at higher volume. *429*

Discount A straight reduction in price on purchases during a stated period of time. *395*

Disintermediation The displacement of traditional resellers from a distribution channel by radical new types of intermediaries or by product and service producers going directly to final buyers. *438*

Distribution centre A large, highly automated warehouse designed to receive goods from various plants and suppliers, take orders, fill them efficiently, and deliver goods to customers as quickly as possible. *453*

Distribution channel A set of interdependent organizations involved in the process of making a product or service available for use or consumption by the consumer or business user. *421*

Diversification A strategy for company growth by starting up or acquiring businesses outside the company's current products and markets. *59*

Downsizing Reducing the business portfolio by eliminating products or businesses that are not profitable or that no longer fit the company's overall strategy. *59*

Dynamic pricing Charging different prices depending on individual customers and situations. *377*

E-business Any business activity carried out using electronic technology. *518*

E-commerce Buying and selling processes supported by electronic means, primarily the Internet. *519*

Economic community A group of nations organized to work toward common goals in the regulation of international trade. *151*

Economic environment Factors that affect consumer purchasing power and spending patterns. *141*

Embargo A ban on the import of certain goods. *151*

Engel's laws Differences noted over a century ago by Ernst Engel in how people shift their spending across food, housing, transportation, health care, and other goods and services categories as family income rises. *142*

Enlightened marketing A marketing philosophy holding that a company's marketing should support the best long-run performance of the marketing system. *103*

Environmental management perspective A management perspective in which the firm takes aggressive actions to affect the publics and forces in its marketing environment rather than simply watching and reacting to them. *153*

Environmental sustainability A management approach that involves developing strategies that both sustain the environment and produce profits for the company. *100*

Environmentalism An organized movement of concerned citizens, businesses, and government agencies working to protect and improve the natural environment. *100*

Everyday low pricing (EDLP) Charging a constant, everyday low price with few or no temporary discounts. *388*

Exchange controls Government limits on the amount of its foreign exchange with other countries and on its exchange rate against other currencies. *151*

Exchange The act of obtaining a desired object from someone by offering something in return. *10*

Exclusive distribution Giving a limited number of dealers the exclusive right to distribute the company's products in their territories. *443*

Experimental research The gathering of primary data by selecting matched groups of subjects, giving them different treatments, controlling unrelated factors, and checking for differences in group responses. *176*

Exploratory research Marketing research to gather preliminary information that will help define problems and suggest hypotheses. *170*

Exporting Entering a foreign market by sending products and selling them through international marketing intermediaries (indirect exporting) or through the company's own department, branch, or sales representatives or agents (direct exporting). *444*

Factory outlet Off-price retailing operation that is owned and operated by a manufacturer and that normally carries the manufacturer's surplus, discontinued, or irregular goods. *430*

Fad A fashion that enters quickly, is adopted with great zeal, peaks early, and declines very quickly. *363*

Fashion A currently accepted or popular style in a given field. *363*

Fixed costs Costs that do not vary with production or sales level. *380*

Focus group A moderated, small-group discussion, typically conducted by marketers during the new product development process. *177*

Franchise A contractual association between a manufacturer, wholesaler, or service organization (a franchiser) and independent businesspeople (franchisees) who buy the right to own and operate one or more units in the franchise system. *431*

Gender segmentation Dividing a market into different groups based on gender. *253*

Geographic segmentation Dividing a market into different geographical units such as nations, regions, provinces, counties, cities, or neighbourhoods. *251*

Global firm A firm that, by operating in more than one country, gains R&D, production, marketing, and financial advantages that are not available to purely domestic competitors. *32*

Global industry An industry in which the strategic positions of competitors in given geographic or national markets are affected by their overall global positions. *32*

Group Two or more people who interact to accomplish individual or mutual goals. *209*

Growth-share matrix A portfolio-planning method that evaluates a company's SBUs in terms of their market growth rate and relative market share. SBUs are classified as stars, cash cows, question marks, or dogs. *56*

Growth stage The product life cycle stage in which a product's sales start climbing quickly. *358*

Harvest (a product) To reduce various costs in hopes that sales hold up. *362*

Horizontal marketing system A channel arrangement in which two or more companies at one level join together to follow a new marketing opportunity. *436*

Hybrid marketing system Multichannel distribution system in which a single firm sets up two or more channels to reach one or more customer segments. *437*

Idea generation The systematic search for new product ideas. *345*

Idea screening Sorting through new product ideas to identify good ideas, and separate them from the not-so-good ideas. *347*

Income segmentation Dividing a market into different income groups. *253*

Independent off-price retailer Off-price retailer that is either owned and run by entrepreneurs or is a division of a larger retail corporation. *430*

Indirect distribution channel Channel containing one or more intermediary levels. *422*

Individual marketing Tailoring products and marketing programs to the needs and preferences of individual customers—also labelled "markets-of-one marketing," "customized marketing," and "one-to-one marketing." *266*

Industrial product Product bought by individuals and organizations for further processing or for use in conducting a business. *298*

Innovative marketing A principle of enlightened marketing that requires a company to continuously seek real product and marketing improvements. *104*

Inside sales force Salespeople who conduct business from their offices, usually via telephone and email, and rarely meet in person with customers. *491*

Integrated marketing communications (IMC) The approach under which a company carefully integrates and coordinates its many communications channels to deliver a clear, consistent, and compelling message about the organization and its products. *470*

Integrated supply chain management The logistics concept that emphasizes teamwork, both inside the company and among all the channel organizations, to maximize the performance of the entire distribution system. *454*

Intensive distribution Stocking the product in as many outlets as possible. *442*

Interactive marketing Marketing by a service firm that recognizes that perceived service quality depends heavily on the quality of buyer–seller interaction. *324*

Intermarket segmentation Forming segments of consumers who have similar needs and buying behaviour even though they are located in different countries. *261*

Intermodal transportation Combining two or more modes of transportation. *454*

Internal databases Electronic collections of data obtained from sources within the company. *167*

Internal marketing Marketing by a service firm to train and effectively motivate its customer-contact employees and all the supporting service people to work as a team to provide customer satisfaction. *322*

Internet marketing Company efforts to communicate about, promote, and sell products and services over the Internet. *518*

Interstitial A large, animated online advertisement that pops up onto the screen for several seconds. *534*

Introduction stage The product life cycle stage in which the new product is first launched into the market. *357*

Joint ownership A joint venture in which a company joins investors in a foreign market to create a local business in which the company shares joint ownership and control. *446*

Joint venturing Entering foreign markets by joining with foreign companies to produce or market a product or service. *445*

Learning Changes in an individual's behaviour arising from experience. *218*

Licensing A method of entering a foreign market in which the company enters into an agreement with a licensee in the foreign market, offering the right to use a manufacturing process, trademark, patent, trade secret, or other item of value for a fee or royalty. *445*

Lifestyle A person's pattern of living as expressed in his or her activities, interests, and opinions. *212*

Line extension Using a successful brand name to introduce additional items in a given product category under the same brand name, such as new flavours, forms, colours, added ingredients, or package sizes. *316*

Local marketing Tailoring brands and promotions to the needs and wants of local customer groups—cities, neighbourhoods, and even specific stores. *266*

Loss leaders Products priced below their cost to attract customers to the store in the hope that they will buy other items at normal markups. *397*

Macroenvironment The larger societal forces that affect the organization's marketing activities—demographic, economic, natural, technological, political, and cultural forces. *128*

Management contracting A joint venture in which the domestic firm supplies the management expertise to a foreign company that supplies the capital; the domestic firm exports management services rather than products. *446*

Manufacturers' sales branches and offices Wholesaling by sellers or buyers themselves rather than through independent wholesalers. *424*

Market-penetration pricing Setting a low price for a new product in order to attract a large number of buyers and a large market share. *391*

Market-skimming pricing Setting a high price for a new product to skim maximum revenues layer by layer from the segments willing to pay the high price; the company makes fewer but more profitable sales. *391*

Market development A strategy for company growth by identifying and developing new market segments for current company products. *58*

Market penetration A strategy for entering the market with a new product, then focusing efforts on increasing the sales of that product in order to capture market share. *58*

Market positioning Arranging for a product to occupy a clear, distinctive, and desirable place relative to competing products in the minds of target consumers. *250*

Market segment A group of potential customers who respond in a similar way to a given set of marketing efforts. *65*

Market segmentation Dividing a market into distinct groups with distinct needs, characteristics, or behaviour that might need separate products or marketing mixes. *65, 250*

Market The set of all actual and potential buyers of a product or service. *10*

Marketing audit A comprehensive, systematic, independent, and periodic examination of a company's environment, objectives, strategies, and activities to determine problem areas and opportunities and to recommend a plan of action to improve the company's marketing performance. *74*

Marketing communications mix (promotion mix) The specific blend of advertising, sales promotion, public relations, personal selling, and direct marketing tools a company uses to pursue its advertising and marketing objectives. *468*

Marketing concept The marketing management philosophy that holds that achieving organizational goals depends on knowing the needs and wants of target markets and delivering the desired satisfactions better than competitors do. *15*

Marketing control The process of measuring and evaluating the results of marketing strategies and plans and taking corrective action to ensure that objectives are achieved. *73*

Marketing environment The forces outside marketing that affect marketing management's ability to build and maintain successful relationships with target customers. *128*

Marketing implementation The process that turns marketing plans into marketing actions to accomplish strategic marketing objectives. *71*

Marketing information system The people, equipment, and procedures to gather, sort, analyze, evaluate, and distribute needed, timely, and accurate information to marketing decision makers. *165*

Marketing intelligence A systematic collection and analysis of publicly available information about competitors and developments in the marketing environment. *168*

Marketing intermediaries Firms that help the company to promote, sell, and distribute its goods to its customers. *130*

Marketing logistics (physical distribution) The tasks involved in planning, implementing, and controlling the physical flow of materials, final goods, and related information from points of origin to points of consumption to meet customer requirements at a profit. *451*

Marketing management The art and science of choosing target markets, presenting a marketing offer to them, acquiring customers, and building profitable relationships with them. *13*

Marketing mix The set of controllable tactical marketing tools—product, price, place, and promotion—that the firm blends to produce the response it wants in the target market. *67*

Marketing offer Some combination of goods, services, information, or experiences offered to a market to satisfy a need or want. *9*

Marketing plan A detailed plan for a business, product, or brand that assesses the current marketing situation and outlines marketing objectives, a marketing strategy, action programs, budgets, and controls. *69*

Marketing research The systematic design, collection, analysis, and reporting of data relevant to a specific marketing situation facing an organization. *169*

Marketing strategy development Designing an initial marketing strategy for a new product based on the product concept. *349*

Marketing strategy The marketing logic by which the company hopes to achieve strong and profitable customer relationships. *64*

Marketing A social and managerial process by which individuals and groups obtain what they need and want through creating and exchanging value with others. *7*

Maturity stage The stage in the product life cycle in which sales growth slows, then levels off. *358*

Media kit A set of documents describing the advantages of advertising on a particular website, the number of site visitors and registered users, and the demographic, geographic, and psychographic characteristics of the site's audience. *534*

Merchandising conglomerates A free-form corporation that combines several diversified retailers under central ownership. *431*

Merchant wholesaler Independently owned business that takes title to the merchandise it handles. *424*

Microenvironment The forces close to the company that affect its ability to serve its customers—the company, suppliers, marketing intermediaries, customer markets, competitors, and publics. *128*

Micromarketing The practice of tailoring products and marketing programs to the needs and wants of specific individuals and local customer groups—includes local marketing and individual marketing. *266*

Microsite A small website consisting of a few pages of detailed information about the marketer's goods or services. *534*

Mission statement A statement of the organization's purpose—what it wants to accomplish in the larger environment. *51*

Modified rebuy A business buying situation in which the buyer wants to modify product specifications, prices, terms, or suppliers. *230*

Motive (drive) A need that is sufficiently pressing to direct the person to seek satisfaction of the need. *215*

Natural environment Natural resources that are needed as inputs by marketers or that are affected by marketing activities. *142*

Needs States of felt deprivation. *8*

New product development The development of original products, new brands, and product improvements and modifications, through the firm's own research and development (R&D) efforts. *343*

New product A good, service, or idea that is perceived by some potential customers as new. *223*

New task A business buying situation in which the buyer purchases a product or service for the first time. *230*

Nontariff trade barriers Nonmonetary barriers to foreign products, such as biases against a foreign company's bids or product standards that go against a foreign company's product features. *151*

Objective-and-task method Setting the budget by (1) defining specific objectives, (2) determining the tasks that must be performed to achieve these objectives, and (3) estimating the costs of performing these tasks. *475*

Observational research The gathering of primary data by observing relevant people, actions, and situations. *174*

Occasion segmentation Dividing the market into groups according to occasions when buyers get the idea to buy, actually make their purchase, or use the purchased item. *255*

Off-price retailer Retailer that buys at below wholesale prices and sells at less than retail. Examples are factory outlets, independents, and warehouse clubs. *430*

Online databases Computerized collections of data available online, either from closed, subscriber-only services, or via the public Internet. *172*

Opinion leader A person within a reference group who, because of special skills, knowledge, personality, or other characteristics, exerts influence on others. *209*

Optional-product pricing The pricing of optional or accessory products along with a main product. *393*

Outside sales force Salespeople who work "in the field" and visit customers. *491*

Packaging The activities of designing and producing the container or wrapper for a product. *304*

Partner relationship management Working closely with partners in other company departments and outside the company to jointly bring greater value to customers. *24*

Percentage-of-sales method Setting the budget at a certain percentage of current or forecast sales or as a percentage of the unit sales price. *475*

Perception The process by which people select, organize, and interpret information to form a meaningful picture of the world. *217*

Permission marketing Email messages sent by marketers with the permission of the recipient. *536*

Personal selling process Several steps that the salesperson follows when selling, including prospecting and qualifying, preapproach, approach, presentation and demonstration, handling objections, closing, and follow-up. *493*

Personal selling Personal presentation by the firm's sales representatives for the purpose of making sales and building customer relationships. *468*

Podcasting Sending information to a consumer's iPod or other portable entertainment device. *540*

Political environment Laws, government agencies, and pressure groups that influence and limit various organizations and individuals in a given society. *145*

Portal website A large, comprehensive, general interest, public website. *529*

Portfolio analysis A tool management uses to identify and evaluate the businesses that compose the company. *55*

Positioning statement A statement that summarizes company or brand positioning—it takes this form: To (target segment and need) our (brand) is (concept) that (point-of-difference). *279*

Predatory pricing Selling a product at a loss to drive competitors out of the market. *405*

Price elasticity A measure of the sensitivity of demand to changes in price. *383*

Price The amount of money charged for a product or service, or the sum of the values that buyers exchange for the benefits of having or using the product or service. *376*

Primary data Information collected for the specific purpose at hand. *171*

Private (or store) brand A brand created and owned by a reseller of a product. *313*

Product adaptation Adapting a product to meet local conditions or wants in foreign markets. *327*

Product bundle pricing Combining several products and offering the bundle at a reduced price. *393*

Product concept A detailed version of the new product idea that can be shown to potential customers. *347*

Product concept The idea that buyers will favour products that offer the most in quality, performance, and innovative features. *15*

Product development and testing Developing the product concept into a real working version of the product and subjecting it to a variety of tests. *351*

Product development A strategy for company growth by offering modified or new products to current market segments. *58*

Product invention Creating new products for foreign markets. *328*

Product life cycle (PLC) The lifespan of a new product, from its development to its eventual decline. *356*

Product line pricing Setting the price steps between various products in a product line based on cost differences between the products, customer evaluations of different features, and competitors' prices. *392*

Product line A group of products that are closely related because they function in a similar manner, are sold to the same customer groups, are marketed through the same types of outlets, or fall within given price ranges. *307*

Product mix (or product assortment) The set of all product lines and items that a particular seller offers for sale. *309*

Product position The way the product is defined by consumers on important attributes—the place the product occupies in consumers' minds relative to competing products. *271*

Product quality The ability of a product to perform its functions; it includes the product's overall durability, reliability, precision, ease of operation and repair, and other valued attributes. *301*

Product sales force structure A sales force organization under which each salesperson specializes in selling only a portion of the company's products or lines. *491*

Product–market expansion grid A portfolio-planning tool for identifying company growth opportunities through market penetration, market development, product development, or diversification. *58*

Product Anything that can be offered to a market for attention, acquisition, use, or consumption that might satisfy a want or need. *294*

Production concept The idea that buyers will favour products that are widely available and highly affordable. *14*

Promotional pricing Temporarily pricing products below the list price, and sometimes even below cost, to increase short-run sales. *397*

Psychographic segmentation Dividing a market into different groups based on social class, lifestyle, or personality characteristics. *254*

Psychological pricing A pricing approach that considers the psychology of prices and not simply the economics; the price is used to say something about the product. *396*

Public relations Building good relations with the company's various publics by obtaining favourable publicity, building a good corporate image, and handling or heading off unfavourable rumours, stories, and events. *468*

Public Any group that has an actual or potential interest in or impact on an organization's ability to achieve its objectives. *131*

Pull strategy A promotion strategy that calls for using advertising and consumer promotion to build consumer demand. *474*

Push strategy A promotion strategy that calls for using the sales force and trade promotion to push the product through channels. *474*

Quota A limit on the amount of goods that an importing country will accept in certain product categories to conserve on foreign exchange and to protect local industry and employment. *151*

Rate card The price list for advertising on a particular website. *534*

Reference prices Prices that buyers carry in their minds and refer to when they look at a given product. *397*

Relationship marketing The process of creating, maintaining, and enhancing strong, value-laden relationships with customers and other stakeholders. *495*

Retailer cooperative Independent retailers banded together for central buying and promotion. *430*

Retailer A business whose sales come primarily from retailing. *427*

Retailing All activities involved in selling goods and services directly to consumers for their personal, nonbusiness use. *427*

Sales promotion Short-term incentives designed to encourage the purchase of a product or service. *468*

Sample A segment of the population selected to represent the population as a whole. *178*

Search engine A free, public website that allows users to search for information available anywhere on the Web simply by typing keywords into a field and clicking a button to execute the search. *530*

Secondary data Information that already exists somewhere, having been collected for another purpose. *171*

Segmented pricing Selling a product or service at two or more prices, where the difference in prices is not based on differences in costs. *395*

Selective distribution The use of more than one, but fewer than all, of the intermediaries who are willing to carry the company's products. *443*

Selling concept The idea that the market will not buy enough of the firm's products unless it undertakes a large-scale selling effort. *15*

Sense-of-mission marketing A principle of enlightened marketing that holds that a company should define its mission in broad social terms rather than narrow product terms. *105*

Sequential product development A new product development approach in which one company department works to complete its stage of the process before passing the new product along to the next department and stage. *355*

Service-profit chain The chain that links service firm profits with employee and customer satisfaction. *322*

Service inseparability A major characteristic of services—they are produced and consumed at the same time and cannot be separated from their providers, whether the providers are people or machines. *321*

Service intangibility A major characteristic of services—they cannot be seen, tasted, felt, heard, or smelled before they are bought. *320*

Service perishability A major characteristic of services—they cannot be stored for later sale or use. *321*

Service retailers Retailers that sell services rather than goods. *429*

Service variability A major characteristic of services—their quality may vary greatly, depending on who provides them and when, where, and how. *321*

Service Any activity or benefit that one party can offer to another that is essentially intangible and does not result in the ownership of anything. *294*

Share of customer The portion of the customer's purchasing in its product categories that a company gets. *25*

Shopping product Consumer product that people, in the process of selection and purchase, characteristically compare on bases such as suitability, quality, price, and style. *297*

Simultaneous product development A new product development approach in which various company departments work closely together, overlapping the steps in the product-development process to save time and increase effectiveness. *355*

Single-source data systems Systems that combine surveys of huge consumer panels and electronic monitoring of respondents' purchases and exposure to various marketing activities in an effort to better understand the link among consumer characteristics, attitudes, and purchase behaviour. *175*

Social classes Relatively permanent and ordered divisions of a society into groups whose members share similar values, interests, and behaviours *207*

Social marketing The design, implementation, and control of programs seeking to increase the acceptability of a social idea, cause, or practice among a target group. *301*

Societal marketing concept A principle of enlightened marketing that holds that marketing strategy should deliver value to the organization's customers in a way that maintains or improves the well-being of society. *17*

Societal marketing A principle of enlightened marketing that holds that a company should make marketing decisions by considering consumers' wants, the company's requirements, and society's long-run interests. *105*

Spam Email sent by unscrupulous individuals and organizations to a computer-generated list of email addresses. *536*

Specialty product Consumer product with unique characteristics or brand identification for which a significant group of buyers is willing to make a special purchase effort. *298*

Specialty store A retail store that carries a narrow product line with a deep assortment within that line. *428*

Sponsorships A form of Internet promotion where companies gain name exposure on the Internet by sponsoring special content on a website. *534*

Standardized marketing mix An international marketing strategy for using basically the same product, advertising, distribution channels, and other elements of the marketing mix in all of the company's international markets. *269*

Straight product extension Marketing a product in a foreign market without any change. *326*

Straight rebuy A business buying situation in which the buyer reorders something without any modifications. *230*

Strategic business unit (SBU) A unit of the company that has its own mission and objectives and that can be planned independently from other company businesses. *55*

Strategic planning The process of developing and maintaining a strategic fit between the organization's goals and capabilities and its changing marketing opportunities. *51*

Style A basic and distinctive mode of expression. *363*

Subculture A group of people with shared value systems based on common life experiences and situations. *206*

Supermarket Large, low-cost, low-margin, high-volume, self-service store that carries a wide variety of food, laundry, and household products. *429*

Superstore A store much larger than a regular supermarket that carries a large assortment of routinely purchased food and non-food items and offers services such as dry cleaning, post offices, photo finishing, cheque cashing, bill paying, lunch counters, car care, and pet care. *429*

Supply chain management Managing value-added flows of materials, final goods, and related information between suppliers, the company, resellers, and final users. *452*

Supply chain A collection of organizations that in a collaborative manner handles production, marketing, and logistics for a product. *421*

Survey research The gathering of primary data by asking people questions about their knowledge, attitudes, preferences, and buying behaviour. *175*

Systems selling Buying a packaged solution to a problem from a single seller, thus avoiding all the separate decisions involved in a complex buying situation. *230*

Target costing Pricing that starts with an ideal selling price, then targets costs that will ensure the price is met. *379*

Target market A set of buyers sharing common needs or characteristics that the company decides to serve. *263*

Target marketing The process of evaluating each market segment's attractiveness and selecting the most appropriate ones to enter. *65, 250*

Tariff A tax levied by a government against certain imported goods to either raise revenue or protect domestic firms. *150*

Technological environment Forces that create new technologies, creating new product and market opportunities. *143*

Telemarketing Using the telephone to sell directly to consumers or businesses. *497*

Territorial sales force structure A sales force organization under which each salesperson is assigned to an exclusive geographic area and sells the company's full line of products or services to all customers in that territory. *491*

Test marketing Testing the product and marketing program in real, but limited, market conditions. *351*

Text links A form of online advertising where an advertiser purchases words or phrases, called keywords, and pays the search engine company to have its ad displayed whenever a visitor to the site searches for that keyword. *533*

Third-party logistics (3PL) provider An independent logistics provider that performs any or all of the functions required to get its clients' product to market. *454*

Total costs The sum of the fixed and variable costs for any given level of production. *380*

Transaction A trade of values between two parties. *10*

Undifferentiated (mass) marketing A market-coverage strategy in which a firm decides to ignore market segment differences and go after the whole market with one offer. *264*

Unsought product Consumer product that the consumer either does not know about or knows about but does not normally think of buying. *298*

Value-based pricing Setting price based on buyers' perceptions of value rather than on the seller's cost. *387*

Value analysis An approach to cost reduction in which components are studied carefully to determine whether they can be redesigned, standardized, or made by less costly methods of production. *234*

Value chain The series of departments that carry out value-creating activities to design, produce, market, deliver, and support a firm's products. *62*

Value delivery network The network made up of the company, suppliers, distributors, and ultimately customers who partner with one another to improve the performance of the entire system. *63*

Value marketing A principle of enlightened marketing that holds that a company should put most of its resources into value-building marketing investments. *104*

Value pricing Offering just the right combination of quality and good service at a fair price. *388*

Value proposition The full positioning of a brand—the full mix of benefits on which it is positioned. *276*

Variable costs Costs that vary directly with the level of production. *380*

Vertical marketing system (VMS) A distribution channel structure in which producers, wholesalers, and retailers act as a unified system. One channel member owns the others, has contracts with them, or has so much power that they all cooperate. *436*

Viral marketing The Internet version of word-of-mouth marketing—email messages or other marketing events that are so infectious that customers will want to pass them along to friends. *537*

Voluntary chain A wholesale-sponsored group of independent retailers that engages in group buying and common merchandising. *430*

Wants The form human needs take as shaped by culture and individual personality. *8*

Warehouse club Off-price retailer that sells a limited selection of brand-name grocery items, appliances, clothing, and a hodgepodge of other goods at deep discounts to members who pay annual membership fees. *430*

Web publisher A website that generates revenue by selling advertising space to advertisers. *530*

Whole-channel view Designing international channels that take into account all the necessary links in distributing the seller's products to final buyers, including the seller's headquarters organization, channels between nations, and channels within nations. *446*

Wholesaler A firm engaged *primarily* in wholesaling activity. *423*

Wholesaling All activities involved in selling goods and services to those buying for resale or business use. *423*

INDEX

Author Index

Company Index

Subject Index

CREDITS

Chapter 1

2 Ben Margot/CP Photo Archive; **9** © Queen's Printer for Ontario, 2005. Reproduced with permission; **11** (both) Nigel Kinrade/Nigel Kinrade Photography; **13** Used with permission of BC Hydro; **17** John Grees/Reuters/Landov; **15** Used with permission of Johnson & Johnson; **21** Courtesy of Purolator; **22** Frank LaBua/Pearson Education/PH College; **23** Courtesy of Steve Niedorf, photographer; Harley Davidson and Carmichael Lynch. All rights reserved; **29** George B. Diebold/Corbis/Stock Market; **31** Coca-Cola, BMP, Fanta, NaturaAqua, Bitter Mare Rosso, and accompanying trade dress are trademarks of the Coca-Cola Company. Sprite Ice is a trademark of Coca-Cola Ltd.

Chapter 2

46 Richard Lam/CP Photo Archive; **52** Courtesy of Norco.com; **53** 3m. All rights reserved. Reprinted with permission; **59** © Alene McNeill; **62** PhotoCornett; **66** 2003 General Motors Corporation. Used with permission of HUMMER and General Motors; **69** Jeff Zaruba/CORBIS.

Chapter 3

82 Courtesy of Ethical Bean Coffee Company; **88** Frank Gunn/CP Photo Archive; **90** Courtesy of PhoneBusters; **95** Lester Lefkowitz/CORBIS; **99** Courtesy of Campbell Soup Company, Ltd.; **102** BP p.l.c.; **106** Copyright 2003 General Motors Corp. Used with permission of GM Media Archives; **107** Used with permission of Herman Miller, Inc.; **115** Reprinted with permission of PricewaterhouseCoopers LLP. Copyright 2003 PWC. All rights reserved.

Chapter 4

124 Reprinted with permission of Unilever Canada; **134** Courtesy of Index Stock Imagery, Inc.; **136** Courtesy of Wildseed Ltd.; **137** © Index Stock Imagery, Inc.; **139** Courtesy of Air Canada; **140** Used with permission of Volkswagen of America, Inc. All rights reserved; **142** David Vandenheede; **145** Joseph Van Os/Getty Images, Inc.—Image Bank.

Chapter 5

160 Courtesy of Shoppers Drug Mart; **164** Tom and Deeann McCarthy, Corbis/Stock Market; **174** © The Dialog Corporation. Used with permission; **175** © 2003 Mattel Inc. All rights reserved; **179** © Greenfield Online, 2001. Used with permission; **182** (both) Courtesy Douglas A. Fidaleo and Integrated Media Systems Center, University of Southern California, Los Angeles and Teradata, a division of NCR; **184** © 2003, SAS Institute Inc., Cary, NC, USA. All rights reserved. Reproduced with permission

of SAS Institute Inc., Cary, NC, USA.; **188** Source: Industry Canada. Reproduced with the permission of the Minister of Public Works and Government Services, 2005.; **189** © 2003 by Roper ASW, Inc. All rights reserved.

Chapter 6

200 Richard Buchan/CP Photo Archive; **210** © Warner Bros. Courtesy of Chevrolet and Warner Bros.; **213** Bachman/PhotoEdit; **216** Image copyright the DaimlerChrysler Corporation; **219** Photographer: Dominique Malaterre (Ad agency: PNMD); **221** Bell Sports; **228** Courtesy of Intel Corporation; **231** © Volvo Trucks North America, Inc.; **235** Used with permission of the Wal-Mart Stores.

Chapter 7

246 Frank LaBua/Pearson Education/PH College; **251** Courtesy of Seagram Canada; **255** Courtesy of neimanmarcus.com; **256** (both) Reprinted with permission of Callard & Bowser-Suchard, Inc.; **261** (left) Jeff Baker/Getty Images Inc.–Hulton Archive Photos; **261** (right) SW Productions/ Getty Images Inc.–Photo Disc; **265** Courtesy of Apple Computer, Inc., and Sophia Chang. Photographer: Matthew Welch; **270** Courtesy of Nacara Cosmetiques; **274** Suave® used courtesy of Unilever; **277** Courtesy of Pillsbury Europe; **278** Deddeda Stemler/CP Photo Archive.

Chapter 8

290 Used with permission of Philosophy, Inc.; **296** Courtesy of Sony Electronics Inc.; **300** Produced pro bono by TAXI Toronto; **303** Apple Computer Inc.; **305** Used with permission of the Sherwin-Williams Co. Courtesy of Robert Falls & Co., **306** Courtesy of Gary Armstrong; **308** Courtesy of Marriott International, Inc.; **311** Courtesy of Aaron Goodman; **314** Courtesy of Loblaw Brands Limited; **317** © Simon and Schuster; **323** © 1992 The Ritz Carlton Hotel Company. All rights reserved. Reprinted with the permission of The Ritz Carlton Hotel Company, L.L.C.; **328** Courtesy of Munshi Ahmed Photography.

Chapter 9

338 © Valerie Simmons/Masterfile.com; **342** Courtesy of Research in Motion; **346** © Avon Corporation; **348** Courtesy of Daimler/Chrysler Corporation; **351** Shaw Industries, Inc.; **352** Courtesy of Nokia; **353** Photo courtesy of Elumens Corporation © 2005; **355** Courtesy of Rockwell Automation Control Systems; **359** Frank Siteman/Stock Boston; **361** Reprinted by permission of Frito-Lay, Inc.

Chapter 10

372 Courtesy of Brian Coates Photography. © 1999 Brian Coates; **379** Courtesy of Four Seasons Hotels; **382** Used with permission of Robin Hood Multifoods Corporation; **383** Used with permission of Gibson Guitar. All rights reserved; **388** Courtesy of Steinway & Sons; **389** Reprinted courtesy of Caterpillar Inc.; **393** Daniel Acker/Bloomberg News/Landov; **396** Dick Hemingway; **398** (top left and bottom right) AP/Wide World Photos; **398** (bottom left) Dennis MacDonald/PhotoEdit; **398** (top right) Tim Boyle/Getty Images Inc.–Hulton Archive Photos.

Chapter 11

416 © 1994-2000 Hewlett-Packard Company. Reproduced with permission; **437** Dick Hemingway; **442** (left) Lee Lockwood/Black Star, (right) © Michael Rizza/Stock Boston; **443** Courtesy of Medicrome—The Stock Shop, Inc.; **448** Charles Gupton/Stock Boston; **449** Courtesy of GE Consumer Products; **454** Courtesy of Roadway Express.

Chapter 12

464 Courtesy of Tourism New Brunswick and lg2. Photo by Luc Robitaille; **471** Photo courtesy of Molson Canada; **473** Courtesy of BMW of North America, LLC; **481** Tobin Grimshaw/Toronto Star; **483** Used with permission of Gillette. All rights reserved; **486** Don Denton/CP Photo Archive; **488** By permission of Pepsi-Cola Canada Ltd.; **493** Jon Feingersh/CORBIS/Corbis/Bettmann; **502** Trent Keegan/EPA/Landov.

Chapter 13

514 Norm Betts/Bloomberg News/Landov; **521** © Jose Luis Pelaez Inc./Corbis/Stock Market; **524** Courtesy of McCains Poland; **523** Courtesy of Clinique; **527** Clearwater Seafoods Limited Partnership; **528** Reprinted by permission of Pfizer Inc.; **532** Getty Images News; **533** Material reprinted with the express permission of "CANWEST NEWS SERVICE", a CanWest Partnership; **534** Reprinted by permission of Google; **535** Reprinted by permission of Procter & Gamble; **541** Courtesy of Joey deVilla.

Appendix

553 By permission of Cake Beauty; **555** By permission of Cake Beauty.